Travel Discount

⌂ W9-ATL-206

This coupon entitles you to special discounts when you book your trip through the

🌺 *TRAVEL NETWORK* ®
RESERVATION SERVICE

Hotels ♦ Airlines ♦ Car Rentals ♦ Cruises
All Your Travel Needs

Here's what you get: *

♦ A discount of $50 USD on a booking of $1,000** or more for two or more people!

♦ A discount of $25 USD on a booking of $500** or more for one person!

♦ Free membership for three years, and 1,000 free miles on enrollment in the unique Travel Network Miles-to-Go® frequent-traveler program. Earn one mile for every dollar spent through the program. Redeem miles for free hotel stays starting at 5,000 miles. Earn free roundtrip airline tickets starting at 25,000 miles.

♦ Personal help in planning your own, customized trip.

♦ Fast, confirmed reservations at any property recommended in this guide, subject to availability.***

♦ Special discounts on bookings in the U.S. and around the world.

♦ Low-cost visa and passport service.

♦ Reduced-rate cruise packages and special car rental programs worldwide.

> Visit our website at http://www.travelnetwork.com/Frommer or call us globally at 201-567-8500, ext. 55. In the U.S., call toll-free at 1-888-940-5000, or fax 201-567-1838. In Canada, call at 1-905-707-7222, or fax 905-707-8108. In Asia, call 60-3-7191044, or fax 60-3-7185415.

* To qualify for these travel discounts, at least a portion of your trip must include destinations covered in this guide. No more than one coupon discount may be used in any 12-month period, for destinations covered in this guide. Cannot be combined with any other discount or promotion.

**These are U.S. dollars spent on commissionable bookings.

***A $10 USD fee, plus fax and/or phone charges, will be added to the cost of bookings at each hotel not linked to the reservation service. Customers must approve these fees in advance. If only hotels of this kind are booked, the traveler(s) must also purchase roundtrip air tickets from Travel Network for the trip.

Valid until December 31, 1999. Terms and conditions of the Miles-to-Go® program are available on request by calling 201-567-8500, ext 55.

AL234

"Amazingly easy to use. Very portable, very complete."

◆

"The only mainstream guide to list specific prices. The Walter Cronkite of guidebooks—with all that implies."

◆

"Complete, concise, and filled with useful information."

◆

"Hotel information is close to encyclopedic."

Frommer's®

5th
Edition

Alaska

by Charles P. Wohlforth
with Peter Oliver
on Wilderness Adventures

Macmillan • USA

ABOUT THE AUTHORS

Charles P. Wohlforth is a lifelong Alaskan who has been a writer and journalist since 1986. After graduating from Princeton University, he worked as a newpaper reporter in the small town of Homer, Alaska, and then for the *Anchorage Daily News,* where he covered the *Exxon Valdez* oil spill. In 1992, Wohlforth went on his own as a freelance writer for various regional and national magazines and as the author of books such as this one. He has won more than 20 awards for his writing and is currently researching a new book for Frommer's on family travel to the national parks. Wohlforth lives in Anchorage with his wife Barbara, son Robin, and daughter Julia. He was elected to the Anchorage Municipal Assembly in 1993; his second term ends in 1999.

Peter Oliver writes about sports and the outdoors for a number of publications, including *Backpacker,* the *New York Times, Skiing, Summit,* and *USA Today.* He was awarded the 1995 Lowell Thomas Award for ski journalism. His most recent book is Bicycling: Touring and Mountain Biking Basics (W. W. Norton). He lives in Warren, Vermont.

Cruise coverage was compiled by Frommer's cruise editor **Matt Hannafin,** with additional reviews from **Matthew Poole, Melissa Rivers,** and *Travel Weekly's* **Fran Golden.** Special thanks go out to Dolores Stallings, Darwin Porter, Danforth Prince, and Ben Arnold for info, help, and commentary.

MACMILLAN TRAVEL

A Simon & Schuster Macmillan Company
1633 Broadway
New York, NY 10019

Find us online at **www.frommers.com** or on America Online at Keyword: **Frommers**

ISBN 0-02-861640-5
ISSN 1042-8283

Editor: Matt Hannafin
Production Editor: Carol Sheehan
Design by Michele Laseau
Digital Cartography by Peter Bogaty and Ortelius Design

SPECIAL SALES

Bulk purchases (10+ copies) of Frommer's and selected Macmillan travel guides are available to corporations, organizations, mail-order catalogs, institutions, and charities at special discounts, and can be customized to suit individual needs. For more information write to special Sales, Macmillan General Reference, 1633 Broadway, New York, NY 10019.

Manufactured in the United States of America

Contents

List of Maps

ACKNOWLEDGMENTS

Friends all over Alaska keep me updated on the latest restaurants and B&Bs in their towns, and show me around when I drop in for one of my visits as a "professional tourist." But a few people in particular did much more. My wife, Barbara, was almost a coauthor, visiting sights and hotels and keeping our family in order and happy as we traveled together. My young son, Robin, and even younger daughter, Julia, provided lots of unique perspectives for "our travel book," and made the discoveries of travel a joy, as only children can. I had several assistants, both paid and volunteer, whose contributions are found all through this book, including Kathryn Gerlek, Wendy Feuer, Lynn Englishbee, Eric and Caroline Wohlforth, Eric Troyer, Mark Handley, Catherine Reardon, Tom Begich, Dean Mitchell, and Laura Mathews. Many other friends offered help and advice, and I'm grateful to all of them.

—Charles P. Wohlforth

AN INVITATION TO THE READER

In researching this book, we discovered many wonderful places—hotels, restaurants, shops, and more. We're sure you'll find others. Please tell us about them, so we can share the information with your fellow travelers in upcoming editions. If you were disappointed with a recommendation, we'd love to know that, too. Please write to:

Frommer's Alaska, 5th Edition
Macmillan Travel
1633 Broadway
New York, NY 10019

AN ADDITIONAL NOTE

Please be advised that travel information is subject to change at any time—and this is especially true of prices. We therefore suggest that you write or call ahead for confirmation when making your travel plans. The authors, editors, and publisher cannot be held responsible for the experiences of readers while traveling. Your safety is important to us, however, so we encourage you to stay alert and be aware of your surroundings. Keep a close eye on cameras, purses, and wallets, all favorite targets of thieves and pickpockets.

WHAT THE SYMBOLS MEAN

✪ Frommer's Favorites

Our favorite places and experiences—outstanding for quality, value, or both.

The following abbreviations are used for credit cards:

AE	American Express	EU	Eurocard
CB	Carte Blanche	JCB	Japan Credit Bank
DC	Diners Club	MC	MasterCard
DISC	Discover	V	Visa
ER	enRoute		

FIND FROMMER'S ONLINE

Arthur Frommer's Outspoken Encyclopedia of Travel (www.frommers.com) offers more than 6,000 pages of up-to-the-minute travel information—including the latest bargains and candid, personal articles updated daily by Arthur Frommer himself. No other website offers such comprehensive and timely coverage of the world of travel.

The Best of Alaska

As a child, when my family traveled outside Alaska for vacations, I often met other children who asked, "Wow, you live in Alaska? What's it like?" I never did well with that question. To me, the place I was visiting was far simpler and easier to describe than the one I was from. The Lower 48 seemed a fairly homogenous land of freeways and fast food, a well-mapped network of established places. Alaska, on the other hand, wasn't—and isn't—even completely explored. Natural forces of vast scale and subtlety still were shaping the land in their own way, inscribing a different story on each of an infinite number of unexpected places. Each region, whether populated or not, was unique far beyond my ability to explain. Unlike the built environment where human endeavor held sway, Alaska was so large and new, unconquered and exquisitely real, as to defy summation.

In contrast to many places you might choose to visit, it's Alaska's unformed newness that makes it so interesting and fun. For the best efforts of tour planners and the like, the most memorable parts of a visit are unpredictable and often unexpected: a humpback whale leaping clear of the water, the face of a glacier releasing huge ice chunks, a bear feasting on salmon in a river, a huge salmon chomping onto your own line. You can look at totem poles and see Alaska Native cultural demonstrations, and you can also get to know living indigenous people who still know and live by many of the traditional ways. And sometimes grand, quiet moments endure most deeply.

As the writer of this guidebook, I aim to help you get to places where you may encounter what's new, real, and unexpected. Opening yourself to those experiences is your job, but it's an effort that's likely to pay off. Although I have lived here all my life, I often envy the stories visitors tell me about the Alaskan places they have gone to and what happened there. No one owns Alaska, and most of us are newcomers here. In all this immensity, a visitor fresh off the boat is as likely to see or do something amazing as a lifelong resident is.

The structure of the book is intended to make it a useful tool in your exploration. This first chapter gives broad-brush ideas about some of the best Alaska has to offer (the entries aren't in any particular order). Chapter 2 provides an overview of the people, social history, and natural history of the state. Chapters 3 and 4 have practical information for planning a trip. Chapter 5, by Frommer's cruise experts, is a guide to voyaging to Alaska by cruise ship. Chapter 6, by Peter Oliver, serves the same function for joining guided outdoor adventures. Chapters 7 through 11 cover each of the state's regions in detail, broken into subregions or towns.

1 The Best Views

You can find your own best views almost anywhere in Alaska. But here are some of the sorts of visions you may have:

- **From the Chugach Mountains Over Anchorage, at Sunset:** The city sparkles below, on the edge of an orange-reflecting Cook Inlet, far below the mountainside where you stand. Beyond the pink and purple silhouettes of mountains on the other side of the Inlet, the sun is spraying warm, dying light into puffs of clouds. It's midnight. (See chapter 8.)
- **Polychrome Pass, Denali National Park:** Riding in a bus rising up the narrow park road on a cliff face, you're too nervous to notice the horizon. And then, there it is—a great valley of green tundra, mountain peaks receding in every direction, and, on either side of the valley, mountains of colored rock standing like gates. (See chapter 9.)
- **Punchbowl Cove, Misty Fjords National Monument:** A sheer granite cliff rises smooth and implacable 3,150 feet straight up from the water. A pair of bald eagles wheel and soar across its face, providing the only sense of scale. They look the size of gnats. (See chapter 7.)
- **The Northern Lights, Alaska's Interior or Southcentral Region:** Blue, purple, green, and red lines spin from the center of the sky, draping long tendrils of slow-moving light. Flashing, bright, sky-covering waves wash across the dome of stars like ripples driven by a gust of wind on a pond. Looking around, your companions' faces are rosy in a silver, snowy night, all gazing straight up with their mouths open. (See chapter 10.)
- **A First Sight of Alaska:** Flying north from Seattle, you're in clouds, so you concentrate on a book. When you look up, the light from the window has changed. Down below, the clouds are gone, and under the wing, where you're used to seeing roads, cities, and farms on most flights, instead you see only high, snowy mountain peaks, without the slightest mark of human presence, stretching as far as the horizon. Welcome to Alaska.

2 The Best of Cruising Alaska

Whether you're looking for the pampered luxury of a big ship or the you-and-the-sea immediacy of a small ship, the cruise lines that serve the Alaskan coast will provide. Here's a few of the better choices and a couple of the better sights you'll see from on deck. See chapter 5 for details.

- **The Best Luxury Liners:** For luxury travel on the high seas, Crystal and its *Crystal Harmony* have the Alaskan market cornered. The gourmet cuisine is incredible, as are the cabins, the casino, the entertainment, the ship facilities, and the level of service.
- **The Best of the Mainstream Ships:** A step lower than Crystal in price but still providing a high comfy-quotient are Celebrity Cruises' twins *Galaxy* and *Mercury,* the latter making its Alaska debut in 1998. Both ships feature beautiful design inside and out, plus great food, service, and amenities. **Holland America's** ships lead the pack when it comes to onboard activities, and our top

choice for families with kids or active travelers who appreciate plenty of sports amenities would be Norwegian Cruise Line's *Norwegian Wind.*

- **The Best of the Small Ships:** Alaska Sightseeing / Cruise West's *Spirit of '98* gets the nod in the small ship sweepstakes. Its turn-of-the-century decor, cozy lounges, comfortable cabins, and ability to squeeze into the narrowest of Alaskan waterways provide passengers with the best combination of comfort and authentic natural experiences, all in a dress-down, casual atmosphere.

- **The Best Cruising Itinerary:** There's no contest. The best Alaskan itinerary is the 14-day trip aboard World Explorer Cruises' *Universe Explorer,* which includes eight ports of call (Wrangell, Juneau, Skagway, Seward, Valdez, Sitka, Ketchikan, and Victoria) plus days cruising Yakutat Bay/Hubbard Glacier, Glacier Bay, the Gulf of Alaska, and the Inside Passage—all for about the same cost as the standard week-long itinerary on other lines.

- **The Best Ports of Call:** Let's pick two. **Juneau,** Alaska's state capitol, gets the nod for the most tasteful shopping, the best coffee bars, good sightseeing and entertainment options, and an all-around congenial atmophere—not too touristy yet not too limited, either. **Skagway,** on the other hand, is tourism personified, but it's the very frankness with which it entertains that gives it its charm. You'll find great entertainment, excursion, and outdoors options, enthusiastic cast members (er, I mean residents), and some decent and not too pricey shopping.

- **The Best Natural Sights from On Board:** When it comes to glaciers, Prince William Sound's **College Fjord** wins out: The number and variety of glaciers there far outrank Glacier Bay. On the other hand, when it comes to the sheer scenic beauty of Alaska, the thickly forested peaks, mist-shrouded crags, tremendously quiet inlets, lichen-encrusted cliffs, and shimmering waterfalls of **Misty Fjords National Monument** are hard to beat (even though you won't find a glacier there).

3 The Best Glaciers

More than 100 times more of Alaska is covered by glacier ice than is settled by human beings. There are plenty of glaciers, and after a couple weeks, you may become a glacier connoisseur. Here are some favorites.

- **Grand Pacific Glacier, Glacier Bay National Park:** Two vast glaciers of deep blue meet at the top of an utterly barren fjord. They rubbed and creased the gray rock for thousands of years before just recently releasing it to the air again. Boats that pull close to the glaciers seem surrounded by the intimidating walls of ice on three sides. (See chapters 5 and 7.)

- **Childs Glacier, Cordova:** Out the Copper River Highway from Cordova, this is a participatory glacier-viewing experience. The glacier is cut by the Copper River, a quarter mile broad; standing on the opposite shore (unless you're up in the viewing tower), you have to be ready to run like hell when the creaking, popping ice gives way and a huge berg falls into the river. Waves created by the falling ice have thrown boulders and people around the picnic area and left salmon high up in the tree branches. (See chapter 8.)

- **Exit Glacier, Seward:** This is a family glacier—not so large, not so dramatic, but you can drive near it and walk the rest of the way on a gravel path. Then it towers above like a huge blue sculpture, the spires of broken ice close enough to breathe a freezer-door chill down on watchers. (See chapter 8.)

- **College Fjords, Prince William Sound:** In this area of western Prince William Sound, you can see a couple of dozen glaciers in a day. Some of these are the amazing tidewater glaciers that dump huge, office-building-sized spires of ice into the ocean, each setting off a terrific splash and outward radiating sea wave. (See chapters 5 and 8.)

4 The Most Beautiful Drives & Train Rides

There aren't many highways in Alaska, but all are worth exploring. You'll find a description of each in chapters 8 through 10. Here are some highlights:

- **White Pass and Yukon Route Railway, Skagway to Summit:** The narrow-gauge excursion train, sometimes pulled by vintage steam engines, climbs the steep grade chiseled into the granite mountains by stampeders to the Klondike gold rush. The train is a sort of mechanical mountain goat, balancing on trestles and steep rock walls far above deep gorges. (See chapter 7.)
- **Seward Highway, Turnagain Arm:** Just south of Anchorage, the highway has been chipped into the side of the Chugach Mountains over the surging gray water of Turnagain Arm. Above, Dall sheep pick their way along the cliffs, within easy sight. Below, white beluga whales chase salmon through the turbid water. (See chapter 8.)
- **Alaska Railroad, Anchorage to Seward:** The line follows the same stretch of Turnagain Arm as the Seward Highway, then splits off as it rises into the mountains of the Kenai Peninsula, rumbling close along the face of a glacier and clinging to the edge of a vertically walled gorge with a roaring river at bottom. When it descends, the line follows a series of sparkling alpine lakes into a spruce forest and finally emerges at tidewater in Seward. (See chapter 8.)
- **Denali Highway:** Leading east-west through the Alaska Range, the Denali Highway crosses terrain that could be another Denali National Park, full of wildlife and with views so huge and grand, they seem impossible. (See chapter 9 and 10.)
- **Richardson Highway:** Just out of Valdez heading north, the Richardson Highway rises quickly from sea level to more than 2,600 feet, switching back and forth on the side of a mountain. With each turn, the drop down the impassable slope becomes more amazing. North of Glennallen, the highway rises again, through a low boreal forest of black spruce, past small lakes and roaring rivers, and suddenly bursts through the tree line between a series of mountains. Then for miles it traces the edge of long, alpine lakes, before descending, parallel with the silver skein of the Alaska Pipeline, to Delta Junction. (See chapter 10.)
- **Top of the World and Taylor Highways:** Leading over the top of rounded, tundra-clothed mountains from Dawson City, Yukon Territory, to the Alaska Highway near Tok, this gravel route floats on a waving sea of terrain, with mountains receding to the infinite horizon in every direction, then traces steep canyons in uninhabited territory. (See chapter 10.)
- **The Roads Around Nome:** You can't drive to Nome, but 250 miles of gravel roads radiate from the Arctic community into tundra populated only by musk oxen, bears, reindeer, birds, and other wildlife. (See chapter 11.)

5 The Best Fishing

- **Sheenjek River, Arctic National Wildlife Refuge:** The grayling aren't big—they never are—but they're abundant. (See chapter 6.)
- **Copper River Valley, Cordova:** The Copper itself is silty with glacial run-off, but feeder streams and rivers are rich with trout, Dolly Varden, and salmon. (See chapters 6 and 8.)

- **Gustavus:** Charter boats from Gustavus get big halibut without long trips in the area of Icy Strait, and see humpback whales feeding on the same afternoon, off Point Adolphus. (See chapter 7.)
- **Prince of Wales Island:** Fly-in trips or roadside fishing yield some of the most prolific salmon fishing anywhere. (See chapter 7.)
- **The Kenai River:** The biggest king salmon—up to 98 pounds—come from the swift Kenai River. Big fish are so common in the second run of kings that there's a special, higher standard for what makes a trophy from this river. Silvers and reds add to a mad, summer-long fishing frenzy. (See chapter 8.)
- **Homer:** One of the state's largest charter fishing fleets goes for halibut ranging into the hundreds of pounds, accessible on the road network. (See chapter 8.)
- **Kodiak Island:** The bears are so big because they live on an island that's crammed with spawning salmon in the summer. Kodiak has the best roadside salmon fishing in Alaska, and the remote fishing, at lodges or fly-in stream banks, is legendary. (See chapter 11.)

6 The Best Tips for Cooking Salmon

Now that you've caught a Pacific salmon, you need to know how to cook it—or order it in a restaurant—to avoid spoiling the rich flavor.

- **Freeze as Little as Possible:** It's a sad fact that salmon loses some of its richness and gets more "fishy" as soon as it's frozen. Eat as much as you can fresh, because it'll never be better. Most fishing towns also have sportfish processors who will smoke or flash freeze the rest.
- **Choose the Best Fish:** The finest restaurants advertise where their salmon comes from on the menu—in early summer, Copper River kings and reds are the richest in flavor; later in the summer, Yukon River salmon are best. King, red, and silver are the only species you should find in a restaurant. The oil in the salmon gives it the rich, meaty flavor; the fish from the Copper and Yukon are high in oil.
- **Keep It Simple:** When ordering salmon or halibut in a restaurant, avoid anything with cheese, heavy sauces, or brown sugar. When salmon is fresh, it's best with light seasoning, perhaps just a little lemon, dill weed, and pepper and salt—or without anything on it, grilled over alder coals.
- **Don't Overcook It:** Salmon should be cooked just until the moment the meat changes color through to the bone. A few minutes more, and some of the texture and flavor are lost. That's why those huge barbecue salmon bakes often are not as good as they should be—it's too hard to cook hundreds of pieces of fish just right and serve them all hot.
- **Filets, not Steaks:** Salmon is cut two ways in Alaska—lengthwise filets or crosswise steaks. The filet is cut with the grain of the flesh, keeping the oil and moisture in the fish.

7 The Best Guided Wilderness Adventures

Here are a few of the guided wilderness trips available. More choices, and details on these, are in chapter 6.

- **Chitistone Canyon Backpacking, Wrangell—St. Elias National Park:** This is a rigorous, rewarding backpack of 7 to 12 days, through deep canyons and heavily glaciated country. (St. Elias Alpine Guides, ☎ and fax **907/277-6867**)

- **Prince William Sound Sea Kayaking, Southcentral Alaska:** The Sound is recovering from the notorious 1989 oil spill. Its islands and coves still offer some of the best kayaking in Alaska. (Alaska Wilderness Sailing Safaris, ☎ **907/835-5175;** fax 907/835-5679)
- **Kongakut River Rafting, Arctic National Wildlife Refuge:** One of the wildest of 26 wild and scenic rivers in Alaska, the Kongakut cuts a wide path through the Brooks Range. (Alaska Discovery, ☎ **800/586-1911** or 907/780-6226, fax 907/780-4220)
- **Tatshenshini River Rafting, Southeastern Alaska and the Yukon Territory:** This is one of the most renowned white-water-rafting trips in the world, through the heavily glaciated mountains of Southeast Alaska. (Mountain Travel • Sobek, ☎ **800/227-2384**)
- **Wild River Valley Dog Mushing, the Brooks Range:** For anyone interested in experiencing the Alaskan wilderness to its fullest, dog mushing in the Brooks Range is about as full as it gets. (Sourdough Outfitters, ☎ **907/692-5252**)

8 The Best Sea Kayaking

Sea kayaking is like backpacking on the water, and comparing it to riding in an average boat is like comparing hiking to driving a car. Here are some areas for trips you'll find more fully described in chapter 6 and in the individual regional chapters:

- **Glacier Bay National Park:** Cruise ships frequent the main bay, but to escape the crowds, explore the smaller inlets: Muir Inlet, Johns Hopkins Inlet, and Tarr Inlet—a kayak is the way to go.
- **Kodiak Island:** The coast is pocked with coves and inlets and is abundant with bird life. Fly south to the bays of Kodiak National Wildlife Refuge, famous for excellent fishing and bears.
- **Misty Fjords National Monument:** Coves, inlets, and canals framed by high granite walls are the principal features of Misty Fjords. There's also lots of rain, but you can stay relatively dry by reserving public-use cabins for overnight stays.
- **Prince William Sound:** Whittier is probably the best place to start for exploring the fjords and glaciers that feed the Sound.
- **Shuyak Island, Kodiak Archipelago:** Whether exploring the protected bays or rugged coastline of this island north of Kodiak, Shuyak kayakers are assured of seeing plenty of birds and sea life.

9 The Best Bear Viewing

There are lots of places to see bears in Alaska, but if your goal is to make *sure* you see a bear—and potentially lots of bears—these are the best places:

- **Katmai National Park:** During the July and September salmon runs, bears congregate around Brooks Camp, where, from wooden platforms a few yards away, you can watch them going about their business. Flight services from King Salmon and Kodiak also bring guests to bears in lesser-used areas of the park. (See chapters 6 and 11.)
- **Anan Bear Observatory:** Accessed from Wrangell or Petersburg by float plane, at Anan you see bears feeding in a salmon stream from close at hand when the fish are running. (See chapter 7.)
- **Pack Creek, Admiralty Island:** The bears of the island, which is more thickly populated with bears than anywhere else on earth, have learned to ignore the daily

visitors who stand on the platforms at Pack Creek. Access is by air from Juneau. (See chapter 7.)

- **Denali National Park:** The park is the best and least expensive wildlife-viewing safari in the state. The buses that drive the park road as far as the Eielson Visitor Center usually see at least some grizzlies. (See chapter 9.)
- **Kodiak, Homer:** Air-taxi operators take passengers to streams and beaches where bears congregate, offering a virtual guarantee of seeing one. If you're lucky enough to win a permit for the McNeil River State Game Sanctuary, you can live for a while among dozens of feeding bears (See chapters 8 and 11.)

10 The Best Marine Mammal Viewing

You've got a good chance of seeing marine mammals almost anywhere you go boating in Alaska, but in some places, it's almost guaranteed.

- **Frederick Sound, Petersburg:** A humpback gave Steve Berry's whale-watching trips the ultimate recommendation in 1995, when it jumped right into his boat. Petersburg boats also see otters and baby seals sitting on icebergs floating in front of LeConte Glacier. (See chapter 7.)
- **Point Adolphus, Gustavus:** Humpback whales show up almost on schedule off the point in Icy Strait, just a few miles from little Gustavus, a town of luxurious country inns. (See chapter 7.)
- **Sitka Sound:** Lots of otters—and, in late fall, lots of whales—show up on wildlife cruises in the island-dotted waters around Sitka. (See chapter 7.)
- **Kenai Fjords National Park, Seward:** You don't have to go all the way into the park—you're pretty well assured of sea otters and sea lions in Resurrection Bay, near Seward, and humpbacks often show up, too. (See chapter 8.)
- **Prince William Sound:** Otters, seals, and sea lions are easy—you'll see them on most trips out of Valdez, Whittier, or Cordova—but you also have a good chance of seeing both humpback and killer whales in the Sound. (See chapter 8.)

11 The Best Encounters with Native Culture

Alaska's Native people live all over the state, and you can learn about their cultures just by meeting them. Here are some of the best, organized ways to encounter Native culture:

- **Chilkat Dancers, Haines:** The Tlingit dances of Haines are authentically loose—children learn their new parts by being thrown into the dance and picking it up. The totem-carving studio is wonderfully casual, standing open for visitors to wander in and meet the artists. (See chapter 7.)
- **Saxman Totem Park:** Just south of Ketchikan, a Tlingit Native corporation owns a major totem pole collection and clan house, and provides tours and cultural demonstrations for visitors. The informal part of the experience is the best part, because in the workshop you can meet the carvers. (See chapter 7.)
- **Dig Afognak, Kodiak Archipelago:** The Koniag people's attempt to reclaim their culture from more than 200 years of suppression has turned to the work of archeology, which visitors are invited to join in, on 6-day expeditions. (See chapter 11.)
- **NANA Museum of the Arctic, Kotzebue:** Eskimos of this still-traditional city/village proudly show off their Inupiat way of life with a combination of high-tech and age-old entertainment. (See chapter 11.)

12 The Best Museums & Historic Sites

- **Anchorage Museum of History and Art:** Alaska's largest museum has the room and expertise to tell the story of Native and white history in Alaska, and to showcase contemporary Alaskan art and culture. (See chapter 8.)
- **Pratt Museum, Homer:** The Pratt explains the life of the ocean in an intimate and clear way you'll find nowhere else in Alaska. (See chapter 8.)
- **Sitka National Historical Park:** The site of the 1804 battle between the Tlingits and Russians, in a totem pole park and seaside stand of old-growth forest, allows you to really appreciate what the Native people were fighting for. Inside the visitor center, Native craftspeople carry on their traditional work and talk with visitors. (See chapter 7.)
- **The State Museum, Juneau:** The museum is far too small for its purpose of representing the natural history of Alaska and the culture and history of each of its regions, yet it succeeds in offering discoveries all through the galleries. (See chapter 7.)
- **University of Alaska Museum, Fairbanks:** The wealth of the university's study of Alaska, in all its forms, is put on display in galleries and daily shows, from equipment to study the aurora borealis to the petrified bison that stands above everything. (See chapter 10.)

13 The Best Places for the Gold Rush Centennial

- **Dawson City, Yukon Territory:** A group of prospectors made the Klondike gold strike in 1896, returned to tell of it in 1897, and tens of thousands of greedy gold seekers arrived after an arduous stampede in 1898. Dawson City is ground zero, and the town is dedicated to preserving and sharing the history of the gold-rush phenomenon. (See chapter 10.)
- **Skagway:** The little town at the top of Lynn Canal was where most of the gold-rush stampeders got off the boat to head over the mountains to the Klondike. Spared of fire, flood, or even much significant economic development other than tourism, Skagway contains a large collection of gold rush–era buildings protected by the National Park Service. (See chapter 7.)
- **Eagle:** Unlike the other tourist-thronged gold-rush towns, Eagle is a forgotten backwater where the gold rush was the last significant thing to happen. It's real and unspoiled, with lots to see but few other people to see it with. (See chapter 10.)
- **Nome:** The great Nome gold rush came next after the Klondike. Although few buildings remain from the gold-rush period, the spirit and industry of that time remain authentically alive in Nome. (See chapter 11.)
- **Fairbanks:** The gold rush in Fairbanks, just after the turn of the century, is not entirely done yet—there's a big, new mine north of town. The city is large enough to provide lots of interesting and fun activities that exploit gold-rush history. (See chapter 10.)

14 The Best Winter Destinations

- **Sitka:** Much of historic Sitka is just as good in winter as at any other time of year, but with fewer crowds and lower prices, and the humpback whale watching is exceptional in the late fall and early winter, as the whales stop off on their migration. (See chapter 7.)

- **Alyeska Resort, Girdwood:** Alaska's premier downhill skiing area has lots of snow over a long season, fantastic views, new lifts, and a luxurious hotel (see "The Best Hotels," below). (See chapter 8.)
- **Anchorage:** The Fur Rendezvous and Iditarod sled-dog races keep a winter-carnival atmosphere going through much of February and March. But those who enjoy participatory winter sports will enjoy Anchorage most, with some of the best Nordic and telemark skiing anywhere, close access to three downhill skiing areas, dog mushing, and lake skating. (See chapter 8.)
- **Chena Hot Springs Resort:** A 90-minute ride from Fairbanks, and you're out in the country, where the northern lights are clear on a starry winter afternoon and night. The resort has lots of activities to get you out into the snowy countryside, or you can just relax in the hot mineral springs. (See chapter 10.)

15 The Best Unspoiled Small Towns

- **Gustavus:** It's a lovely little town near Glacier Bay National Park, except it isn't really a town. There's no local government or town center, just a collection of luxurious country inns and lodges in a setting of great scenic beauty, close to some of the best fishing, whale watching, and sea kayaking in Alaska. (See chapter 7.)
- **Petersburg:** The town is so easy to get to, right on the Inside Passage ferry route, it's incredible it has kept its quaint, small-town identity as perfectly as it has. Part of the formula is a conspicuous lack of catering to tourists, but there is a wonderfully diverse choice of outdoor activities. (See chapter 7.)
- **Cordova:** This fishing town off the beaten track is a forgotten treasure, caught at some mythical point in the past when Norman Rockwell's paintings were relevant. That atmosphere combines with the best bird watching, fishing, scenic grandeur, and other outdoor activities to make Cordova one of Alaska's most charming and attractive destinations. (See chapter 8.)
- **Halibut Cove:** Halibut Cove has no roads, only the calm green water in an ocean channel between docks and floats and houses on boardwalks. There are three art galleries, but the main activities are slowing down, paddling around, and walking in the woods. (See chapter 8.)
- **Kodiak:** This hub for an area with the biggest bears, most plentiful salmon, richest wilderness sea kayaking waters, and much other natural beauty is virtually untouched by visitors. In town there are narrow, winding streets, Russian and Native historic sites, and wonderfully hospitable people. (See chapter 11.)

16 The Most Bizarre Community Events

- **Cordova Ice Worm Festival:** The truth is, ice worms do exist. Really. This winter carnival celebrates them in February. The highlight is the traditional annual march of the ice worm (a costume with dozens of feet sticking out) down the main street. (See chapter 8.)
- **Snow Man Festival, Valdez:** A community that counts its winter snowfall by the yard makes the most of it in March, with a winter carnival that includes ice bowling, snowman building, and a drive-in movie projected on a snow bank. (See chapter 8.)
- **Midnight Sun Baseball Game, Fairbanks:** The semipro baseball game, without lights, doesn't begin until 10:30pm on the longest day of the year.(See chapter 10.)
- **Bering Sea Ice Golf Classic, Nome:** The greens are Astroturf, as the sea ice won't support a decent lawn in mid-March. Hook a drive, and you could end up

spending hours wandering among the pressure ridges, but you must play the ball as it lies. (See chapter 11.)

- **Nome Polar Bear Swim / Bathtub Race:** Nome has so *many* strange community events. Memorial Day is marked by the polar bear swim, sea ice permitting. Labor Day is celebrated by a bathtub race down Front Street, with water and a bather in each tub. (See chapter 11.)
- **Pillar Mountain Golf Classic, Kodiak:** The course is one hole, par is 70, and elevation gain is 1,400 feet. Having a spotter in the deep snow of late March is helpful, but use of two-way radios and dogs is prohibited. Also, no cutting down power poles, and cursing tournament officials carries a $25 fine. (See chapter 11.)

17 The Best Hotels

- **Westmark Cape Fox Lodge, Ketchikan (☎ 907/225-8001):** Standing in its own little forest atop a rocky promontory that dominates downtown Ketchikan, this cleanly luxurious hotel has the feel of a mountain lodge or resort. A funicular tram carries visitors to the Creek Street boardwalks, or you can take the wooded, cliffside path. Exceptional views of the city and Tongass Narrows through the trees decorate rooms and common areas accented with masterpieces of Tlingit art. For its setting and perfect execution of an understated theme, this hotel is the most attractive in Alaska. (See chapter 7.)
- **Alyeska Prince Hotel, Girdwood (☎ 800/880-3880):** The first sight of this new ski resort hotel—designed in a château style and standing in an undeveloped mountain valley—is enough to make you catch your breath. Wait till you get inside and see the starscape and polar bear diorama in the lobby atrium, or the large swimming pool, with its high-beamed ceiling and wall of windows looking out on the mountain. The cozy rooms are full of cherry wood. A tram carries skiers and diners to the top of the mountain. (See chapter 8.)
- **Hotel Captain Cook, Anchorage (☎ 907/276-6000):** This is the grand old hotel of downtown Anchorage, with a heavy nautical theme, teak paneling, and furniture that carries through to the smallest detail in the rooms. It also remains the state's standard of service and luxury. (See chapter 8.)
- **Kenai Princess Lodge, Cooper Landing (☎ 907/595-1425):** The Princess Cruise Line has built four good hotels in Alaska, but this one is like no other. Perched on a mountainside above the Kenai River, each room has the feel of a wilderness cabin, with a wood stove stocked with firewood, a balcony overlooking the valley, and a pervasive forest scent emanating from the cedar walls. But, of course, it's not a wilderness cabin—it has all the comforts of a top hotel. A wonderfully romantic retreat. (See chapter 8.)
- **Land's End, Homer (☎ 907/235-2500):** The hotel itself has some nice touches, but it wouldn't be in a class with the others on this list if not for the location. The low, wood buildings lie like a string of driftwood beached on the tip of Homer Spit, out in the middle of Kachemak Bay. Nothing stands between the rooms or restaurant and the ocean, across the beach. Sometimes whales and otters swim along the shore, just outside the windows. (See chapter 8.)
- **The Grand Aleutian Hotel, Unalaska/Dutch Harbor (☎ 800/891-1194):** Not long ago, it wasn't much of a distinction to be the best hotel in the Alaska Bush. Then the UniSea fish company built this large, lodge-style, luxury hotel, which is competitive with the best in the state. Offering this level of service in this remote Aleutian archipelago setting is quite an accomplishment, and creates a unique opportunity for those who want to stay in a fine hotel and see

the Bush, with the best unexploited fishing and wildlife and bird watching. (See chapter 11.)

18 The Best Moderately Priced Lodgings

- **All Seasons Inn, Fairbanks** (☎ **907/451-6649**): This is a small country inn on a quiet street a couple of blocks from the downtown center. The rooms are comfortable and the common areas elegant and inviting. (See chapter 10.)
- **Colony Inn, Palmer** (☎ **907/745-3330**): A perfect country inn in a historic building with luxurious features and, at this writing, an amazing bargain price. (See chapter 8.)
- **Harborview Bed and Breakfast / Seaview Apartments, Seward** (☎ **907/224-3217**): When the friendly hosts showed me their large, very clean, bright, attractively decorated rooms, and the beachfront apartments they rent for a great bargain price, I kept waiting for the other shoe to drop. It never did—they simply take pride in offering much better for much less than others. (See chapter 8.)
- **The Perch, South of Denali National Park** (☎ and fax **907/683-2523**): In an area dominated by hotels with so-so rooms renting for sky-high rates, these reasonably priced cabins next to rushing Carlo Creek are cute and comfortable and feel like they're out in the wilderness, although they're just off the Parks Highway. (See chapter 9.)
- **The New York Hotel, Ketchikan** (☎ **907/225-0246**): An old building right on the water has been lovingly restored into just a few charming rooms, decorated with antiques and with views out on the town's most attractive, historic district. (See chapter 7.)
- **The Northern Lights Inn, Cordova** (☎ **907/424-5356**): Located in a historic hillside house with just a few rooms, the inn is operated by an old Cordova family with lots of energy and hospitality. The upstairs rooms have every amenity and are furnished with antiques, but rent for very low rates. (See chapter 8.)

19 The Best Bed & Breakfasts

- **Alaska Ocean View Bed and Breakfast, Sitka** (☎ **907/747-8310**): Here a family has set out to turn their home into perfect accommodations. Among other details, the elaborate decor in each room matches a unique packet of souvenir wildflower seeds given to each guest. (See chapter 7.)
- **Captain's Quarters Bed & Breakfast, Ketchikan** (☎ **907/225-4912**): On a hill where some of the streets are staircases, the ocean-facing rooms have unbelievable views of Tongass Narrows. The decor matches—a nautical theme, all in oak, lovingly crafted by the hands of the meticulous proprietor. (See chapter 7.)
- **Pearson's Pond Luxury Inn and Garden Spa, Juneau** (☎ **907/789-3772**): Diane Pearson takes the prize for the most obsessive attention to detail at any B&B in Alaska. Not only are the bathrooms stocked with condoms, but the private pond, with a fountain spraying, is stocked with fish. (See chapter 7.)
- **Skagway Inn Bed and Breakfast** (☎ **907/983-2289**): The place has the genteel feeling of an English country inn, and the region's best restaurant serves meals in the evening in the breakfast room. (See chapter 7.)
- **Aurora Winds B&B Resort, Anchorage** (☎ **907/346-2533**): An enormous house on the hillside above Anchorage has rooms so completely and theatrically decorated you'll feel as if you're sleeping in a movie set. Details like an

"environmental chamber" off one room make this the most excessively luxurious B&B in Alaska. (See chapter 8.)

- **Cliff House Bed and Breakfast, Valdez** (☎ 907/835-5244): With a spectacular location atop a wooded rock outcropping right on the ocean, but with downtown right at hand beyond the thick screen of trees, the house is an architectural masterpiece for the way it fits its surroundings. The rooms are luxurious. (See chapter 8.)

- **Forget-Me-Not Lodge and the Aurora Express Bed & Breakfast, Fairbanks** (☎ 907/474-0949): This family bought an old-fashioned railroad train, hauled it up the side of a mountain above Fairbanks, and remodeled the cars in luxurious, theme decor as a bed-and-breakfast. The story of why they did it is as improbable as Hollywood's worst scripts (see the write-up in chapter 10), but the sight of the rail cars in this incongruous location and their extraordinary interiors will enable you to believe anything. (See chapter 10.)

20 The Best Wilderness Lodges

- **Riversong Lodge, Northwest of Anchorage** (☎ 907/274-2710): Fishing and wilderness treks to Lake Clark National Park are the outdoor attractions of this lodge, but the food is what makes it famous. Kirsten Dixon is hailed as one of the best chefs in Alaska, drawing people out to the wilderness just for the meals. (See chapter 6.)

- **Ultima Thule Lodge, Wrangell–St. Elias National Park** (☎ 907/258-0636): The rugged surroundings in the park and the enthusiasm of the proprietors provide a seemingly limitless range of outdoor activities on mountains, glaciers, rivers, ocean, horseback—you get the idea. Once back in the lodge, your stay is in comfort, with a skylight over your bed to watch the midnight sun or, in winter, the northern lights. (See chapter 6.)

- **Gustavus Inn at Glacier Bay** (☎ 907/697-2254): Gustavus has several exceptional country inns, all similar to wilderness lodges, and this is the best of that superb collection. The rooms are charming, the grounds lovely, the meals incomparable, and the hospitality warm and welcoming. (See chapter 7.)

- **Kachemak Bay Wilderness Lodge, Near Homer** (☎ 907/235-8910): This is the state's original ecotourism lodge, and still one of the best. The lodgings are completely comfortable while also fitting in with their rich maritime wilderness surroundings, the food is famous, and the hosts are expert at sharing their deep knowledge of the area and its natural history. (See chapter 8.)

- **Camp Denali, Kantishna, Denali National Park** (☎ 907/683-2290): This lodge, on private land at the end of the national park road, is more than a place to relax and get into the wilderness—it also has a highly regarded program of natural-history education. (See chapter 9.)

Alaska: Experiment in Magnificence

An old photo album opens, breathing a scent of dust and dried glue. Inside, pale images speak wanly of shrunken mountains and glaciers, a huge blue sky, water and trees, a moose standing way off in the background. No family photographer can resist the drive to capture Alaska's vastness in the little box of a camera, and none, it seems, has ever managed it. Then, turning the page, there it is—not in another picture of the landscape, but reflected in a small face at the bottom of the frame: my own face, as a child. For anyone who hasn't experienced that moment, the expression is merely enigmatic—slightly dazed, happy but abstracted, as if hearing a far-off tone. But if you've been to Alaska, that photograph captures something familiar: It's an image of discovery. I've seen it on the fresh, pale faces in photographs stamped with the dates of my family's first explorations of Alaska more than 30 years ago. And then, researching this book, I got to see it once again, on my own young son's face. And I knew that, like me, he had discovered something important.

So what am I talking about? Like anything worth experiencing, it's not simple to explain. But I'll try. And, with luck, you'll know much better after you've been to Alaska.

Tour guides try to get it across with statistics. Not much hope of that, although some of the numbers do give you a general idea of scale. Once you've driven across the continental United States and know how big that is, seeing a map of Alaska placed on top of the area you crossed, just about spanning it, provides some notion of size. Alaskans always like to threaten that we'll split in half and make Texas the third-largest state. Alaska has about 600,000 residents. If you placed each of them an equal distance apart, no one would be within a mile of anyone else. Of course, that couldn't happen. No one has ever been to some parts of Alaska.

But none of that expresses what really matters. It's not just a matter of how big Alaska is or how few people it contains. It's not an intellectual conception at all. None of that crosses your mind when you see a chunk of ice the size of a building fall from a glacier and send up a huge splash and wave surging outward. Or when you hike for a couple of days to stand on top of a mountain, and from there see more mountaintops, layered off as far as the horizon, in unnamed, seemingly infinite multiplicity. A realization of what Alaska means can come in a simple little moment. It can come at the end of a long day driving an Interior Alaska highway, as your car

Alaska

MILEAGE CHART
Approximate driving distances in miles between cities.

	Anchorage	Circle	Eagle	Fairbanks	Haines	Homer	Prudhoe Bay	Seward	Skagway	Tok	Valdez
Anchorage		520	501	358	775	226	847	126	832	328	304
Circle	520		541	162	815	746	1972	646	872	368	526
Eagle	501	541		379	620	727	868	627	579	173	427
Fairbanks	358	162	379		653	584	489	484	710	206	364
Haines	775	815	620	653		1001	1142	901	359	447	701
Homer	226	746	727	584	1001		1073	173	1058	554	530
Prudhoe Bay	847	1972	868	489	1142	1073		973	1199	695	853
Seward	126	646	627	484	901	173	973		958	454	430
Skagway	832	872	579	710	359	1058	1199	958		504	758
Tok	328	368	173	206	447	554	695	454	504		254
Valdez	304	526	427	364	701	530	853	430	758	254	

Chukchi Sea

RUSSIA

Little Diomede Island

Nome

Norton Sound

St. Lawrence Island

Yukon Delta National Wildlife Refuge

St. Matthew Island

Bethel

Yukon Delta National Wildlife Refuge

Bering Sea

Nunivak Island

Attu Island

Pribilof Islands

Bristol Bay

Cape St. Stephen

Rat Islands

Alaska Peninsula

Unimak Cold Island Bay

Dutch Harbor

Adak

Atka Island

Atka

Fort Glen

Unimak

Adak Island

Unalaska

Aleutian Islands

PACIFIC

1-0001

200 mi
322 km

Arctic Ocean

Barrow

Prudhoe Bay

Deadhorse

Beaufort Sea

Cape Krusenstern National Monument

Brooks Range

Anaktuvuk Pass

Noatak National Preserve

Arctic National Wildlife Refuge

Kobuk Valley National Park

Gates of the Arctic National Park and Preserve

Brooks Range

Dalton Hwy.

Kotzebue

Bettles

Bering Land Bridge National Preserve

Fort Yukon

Yukon Flats National Wildlife Refuge

Arctic Circle

Dempster Hwy.

⑧

⑤

Galena

Chena Hot Springs

Circle

Yukon-Charley Rivers National Preserve

CANADA

United States / Canada

Unalakleet

Manley Hot Springs

②

⑥

Fairbanks

North Pole

Eagle

YUKON

Nenana

⑤

Delta Junction

Dawson City, Yukon

Yukon River

McGrath

Denali National Park

Mt. McKinley

Alaska   Range

③

⑧

④

Tok

⑨

United States / Canada

⑥

Kuskokwim River

Talkeetna

①

Willow

Glennallen

④

Dawson City, Yukon

Wasilla

Palmer

①

Wrangell Mts.

⑩

McCarthy

②

Whitehorse, Yukon

④

ANCHORAGE

Valdez

Wrangell-St. Elias National Park and Preserve

①

①

Lake Clark National Park and Preserve

Kenai

Soldotna

Whittier

Cordova

⑦

Skagway

BRITISH COLUMBIA

Dillingham

Homer

Seward

Prince William Sound

①

Halibut Cove

King Salmon

Seldovia

Kenai Fjords National Park

Yakutat

Haines

Juneau

Katmai National Park and Preserve

Alaska Marine Highway

Glacier Bay National Park and Preserve

Gustavus

Admiralty Island National Monument

Gulf of Alaska

Chichagof Island

Kodiak

Admiralty Island

Petersburg

Kodiak Island

Baranof Island

Sitka

Wrangell

Aniakchak National Monument and Preserve

Prince of Wales Island

Craig

Ketchikan

Misty Fjords National Monument

Prince Rupert B.C.

To Seattle ↘

OCEAN

Legend
— Paved Road
—①— State or Provincial Route
— Dirt Road

15

climbs into yet another mountain range, the sun still hanging high in what should be night, storm systems arranged before you across the landscape, when you realize that you haven't seen another car in an hour. Or standing on an Arctic Ocean beach, it could happen when you look around at the sea of empty tundra behind you, the sea of green water before you, and your own place on what seems to be the edge of the world. Or you might simply be sitting on the sun-warmed rocks of a beach in Southeast or Southcentral Alaska when you discover that you're occupying only one of many worlds—a world of intermediate size, lying in magnitude between the tiny tide-pool universes of life all around you and the larger world seen by an eagle gliding through the air high above.

What's the soul alchemy of such a moment? I suppose it's different for each person, but for me it has something to do with realizing my actual size in the world, how I fit in, what it means to be just another medium-sized mammal, unarmed with the illusions supplied by civilization. On returning to the city from the wilderness, there's a re-entry process, like walking from a vivid movie to the mundane, gray street outside—it's the movie that seems more real. For a while, it's hard to take human institutions seriously after you've been deep into Alaska.

Some people never do step back across that boundary. They live their lives out in the wilderness, away from people. Others compromise, living in Alaskan cities and walking out into the mountains when they can, the rest of the time just maintaining a prickly notion of their own independence. But anyone can make the same discovery, if he or she has the courage to come to Alaska and the time to let the place sink in. You don't have to be an outdoor enthusiast or a young person. You only have to be open to wonder and able to slow down long enough to see it. Then, in a quiet moment when you least expect it, things may suddenly seem very clear and all that you left behind oddly irrelevant.

How you find your way back to where you started is your affair.

1 The Regions in Brief

SOUTHEAST ALASKA   The Southeast Panhandle is the relatively narrow strip of mountains and islands that lies between Canada and the Gulf of Alaska. To Alaskans, it's the Southeast, but to the rest of the country, it's more like the northernmost extension of the lush Pacific Northwest. It's a land of huge rain-forest trees, glacier-garbed mountains, and countless islands ranging in size from the nation's third largest to tiny, one-tree islets strewn like confetti along the channels and fjords. The water is the highway of Southeast Alaska, as the land is generally too steep and rugged to build roads, but there are lots of towns and villages reachable by the ferry system or cruise ships. Southeast contains Juneau, Alaska's capital and third-largest city, and Ketchikan, next in size to Juneau. Southeast's towns are as quaint and historic as any in Alaska, especially Sitka, which preserves the story of Russian America and its conflict with the indigenous Native people. Nowhere in Alaska is Native culture—here, Tlingit and Haida—richer or closer to hand. Nor is any region much richer in opportunities for boating or seeing marine wildlife. The weather is wet and temperate.

SOUTHCENTRAL ALASKA   As a region, Southcentral is something of a catch-all, weaker in identity than other parts of the state. The area is roughly defined by the arc of the Gulf of Alaska from the straight portion of the Canadian border, on the east, to Cook Inlet and the end of the road network, to the west. It's a microcosm of the state, containing Prince William Sound, which is similar to the wooded island habitat of Southeast; the Kenai Peninsula, a roaded fishing, boating, and outdoor Mecca; Anchorage, the state's modern, major city; the Matanuska and Susitna valleys, an agricultural and suburban region of broad flatlands between steep mountains; and the Copper River country, a rugged and sparsely populated region along the border with Canada, with much in common with the Interior. Southcentral dominates Alaska, with most of the state's population and a more highly developed transportation system than elsewhere, including a network of highways and the Alaska Railroad. Southcentral's weather is influenced by the ocean, keeping it from being very hot or very cold. The coastal areas are wet, while just behind the coastal mountains the weather is drier.

THE INTERIOR   The vast central part of the state is crossed by highways and by rivers that act as highways. There are huge, generally flat areas lying between the Alaska Range, which contains Mount McKinley, North America's tallest peak, and the Brooks Range, a continental divide between the Interior's great rivers and the Arctic. The region's dominant city is Fairbanks, Alaska's second largest, which lies on the Chena River in the middle of the state. The natural environment is drier and less abundant than Southeast or Southcentral. Consequently, the Athabascans, the Interior's first people, are less numerous and traditionally lacked the rich natural endowments of Southeast's Native peoples. Summers can be hot and winters very cold in the Interior, because of the distance from the ocean.

THE BUSH   Bush Alaska is linked by lifestyle rather than by geography. One good definition would be that the Bush is that part of the state that's closer to the wilderness than to civilization. It's also the only part of the state where Native people outnumber whites and other relative newcomers. In many Bush villages, readily accessible to the outside world only by small plane, people still live according to age-old subsistence hunting-and-gathering traditions. The Bush region includes the majority of Alaska outside the road network, ranging from the north end of the Canadian border all the way around the coast, out the Aleutians, and the Alaska Peninsula and Kodiak Island, at the border of the Southcentral region. But some towns in each of the other regions also could be called "Bush villages." The Bush contains many regions, including the Arctic, Northwest, and Southwest Alaska.

2 Natural History: Rough Drafts & Erasures

THE SURGING ICE   In 1986, Hubbard Glacier, north of Yakutat, suddenly decided to surge forward, cutting off Russell Fjord from the rest of the Pacific Ocean. A group of warm-hearted but ill-advised wildlife lovers set out to save the marine mammals that had been trapped behind the glacier. Catching a dolphin from an inflatable boat isn't that easy—they didn't accomplish much, but they provided a lot of entertainment for the locals. Then the water burst through the dam of ice and the lake became a fjord again, releasing the animals anyway.

Bering Glacier can't decide which way to go. Apparently surging and retreating on a 20-year cycle, it recently reversed course after bulldozing a wetland migratory bird stopover and speedily contracted back up toward the mountains. Meares Glacier has plowed through old-growth forest. On the other hand, some glaciers are so stable they gather a layer of dirt where trees and brush grow to maturity. When Malspina Glacier retreated, the trees on its back toppled. And on a larger scale, all the land of Glacier Bay—mountains, forests, sea floor—is rising $1\,{}^{1}/_{2}$ inches a year as it rebounds from the weight of melted glaciers that 100 years ago were a mile thick and 65 miles longer.

Yet these new and erased lands are just small corrections around the margins compared to what the earth has done before in setting down, wiping out, and rewriting the natural history of Alaska. In the last Ice Age, 15,000 years ago, much of what is Alaska today was one huge glacier. At the tops of granite mountains in Southeast Alaska, especially in the northern Lynn Canal, it's possible to see a sort of high-water mark—the highest point the glaciers came in the Ice Age. Even looking from the deck of a boat, thousands of feet below, you can see where mountain shoulders, rounded by the passage of ice, are much smoother than the sharp, craggy peaks just above, which stuck above that incredible sheet of ice.

Some 7-year-old children worry about the bogeyman or being caught in a house fire. When I was that age, living with my family in Juneau—and I learned how Gastineau Channel was formed, and we went to see Mendenhall Glacier, and I was told how it was really a river of ice, advancing and retreating—I developed a deeper fear: ice. I was afraid that while I slept, another Ice Age would come and grind away the city of Juneau.

It's possible that a glacier *could* get Juneau—the city fronts on the huge Juneau Ice Field—but there would be at least a few centuries' warning before it hit. Glaciers are essentially just snow that doesn't get a chance to melt. It accumulates at higher altitudes until it gets deep enough to compress into ice and starts oozing down the side of the mountain. When the ice reaches the ocean, or before, the melt and calving of icebergs at the leading edge reaches a point of equilibrium with the snow that's still being added at the top. The glacier stops advancing, becoming a true river of ice, moving a snow flake from the top of the mountain to the bottom in a few hundred years. When conditions change—more snow or colder long-term weather, for example—the glacier gets bigger; that's called advancing, and the opposite is retreating. Sometimes, something strange will happen under the glacier—in the case of Bering Glacier, it started to float on a cushion of water—and it will surge forward, several feet or even dozens of feet a day in extreme cases. But most of the time, the advance or retreat is measured in inches or feet a year. Today, Alaska's 100,000 glaciers cover about 5% of its land mass.

THE TREMBLING EARTH   Despite my early glacier phobia, I never had a similar fear of earthquakes. Living in Anchorage, I'd been through enough of them that, as early as I can remember, I generally didn't bother to get out of bed when they hit.

It's all part of living in a place that isn't quite done yet. Any part of Alaska could have an earthquake, but the Pacific Rim from Southcentral Alaska to the Aleutians is the shakiest. That's because this is where Alaska is still under construction. The very rocks that make up the state are something of an ad hoc conglomeration, still in the process of being assembled. They've been gathered from all over the Pacific and slammed together to make a single land mass—a thrift-store grab bag of land from tropical waters and beyond, carried north by a terrestrial conveyor belt called the Pacific tectonic plate.

Here's how it works. The center of the Pacific plate is expanding, with underwater volcanoes and cracks that constantly ooze new rock. That forces the existing sea floor to spread, at perhaps an inch a year. At the other side of the Pacific plate, there's not enough room for the sea floor that's being created, and the crust bends and cracks as it's forced downward into the planet's great, molten recycling mill of magma. Land masses that are along for the ride smash into the continent that's already there. When one hits—the so-called Yakutat block is still in the process of docking—a mountain range gets shoved up. Earthquakes and volcanoes are a byproduct.

Living in such an unsettled land is a matter of more than abstract interest. The Mount Spurr volcano, which erupted most recently in 1992, turned day to night in Anchorage, dropping a blanket of ash all over the region, choking lungs and machines. A Boeing 747 full of passengers flew into the plume and lost power in all its engines, falling in darkness for several minutes before pilots were able to restart the clogged jets. After that incident, the airport was closed until aviation authorities could find a way to keep volcanic plumes and planes apart. More than 80 volcanoes have been active in Alaska in the last 200 years. Earthquakes over 7 on the Richter scale—larger than the 1994 Los Angeles quake—have occurred every 15 months, on average, over the last century.

The worst of the quakes, on March 27, 1964, was the strongest ever to hit North America. It ranked 9.2 on the Richter scale, lowering an entire region of the state some 10 feet and moving it even farther laterally. No other earthquake has ever moved so much land.

There are lots of tales about what people did when the quake hit—it lasted a good 10 minutes, long enough for a lot to happen. My wife, Barbara, a 1-year-old at the time, is said to have found it hilariously funny while everyone else ran around in panic. A family friend rushed out into the street from bathing, stark naked; a neighbor who had been doing laundry when the earth started shaking met him there and handed him a pair of socks she had happened to carry with her.

The earthquake destroyed much of Anchorage and several smaller towns, and killed more than 131 people, mostly in sea waves created by underwater landslides. In Valdez, the waterfront was swept clean of people. In the Prince William Sound village of Chenega, built on a hill along the water, people started running for higher ground when the wave came. About half made it. Families were divided by just yards between those who ran fast enough and those who were caught by the water and disappeared. But the earthquake could have been much worse—it occurred in the early evening, on Good Friday, when most public buildings were empty. An elementary school in Anchorage that broke in half and fell into a hole didn't have anyone inside at the time.

THE FROZEN TUNDRA   The Interior and Arctic parts of the state are less susceptible to earthquakes and, since they receive little precipitation, they don't have glaciers, either. But there's still a sense of living on a land that's not quite sure of itself, as most of northern Alaska is solid only by virtue of being frozen. When it thaws, it turns to mush. The phenomenon is caused by permafrost, a layer of earth a little below the surface that never thaws—or at least, you'd better hope it doesn't. Buildings erected on permafrost without some mechanism for dispersing their own heat—pilings, or even refrigerator coils—thaw the ground below and sink into a self-made quicksand. You occasionally run across such structures. There's one in Dawson City, Yukon Territory, still left from the gold rush, that leans at an alarming angle with thresholds and lower tiers of siding disappearing into the ground.

Building sewer and water systems in such conditions is a challenge still unmet in much of Alaska's Bush, where village toilets are often "honey buckets" and the septic systems are sewage lagoons on the edge of town where the buckets are dumped. Disease caused by the unsanitary conditions sweeps the villages as if rural Alaska were a Third World country, but the government has been slow to provide the funds required to solve the problem.

The Arctic and much of the Interior are a sort of swampy desert. Most of the time, the tundra is frozen in white; snow blows around, but not much falls. That snow melts in the summer and stands on the surface, on top of the permafrost, creating ponds—Alaska is a land of 10 million lakes, with 3 million larger than 20 acres. Migratory birds arrive to feed and paddle around those shallow circles of deep green and sky blue. Flying over the Arctic in a small plane is disorienting, for no pattern maintains in the flat green tundra, and irregularly shaped patches of water stretch as far as the eye can see. Pilots find their way by following landmarks like tractor tracks etched into the tundra. Although few and far between, the tracks remain clearly delineated for decades after they're made, appearing as a pair of narrow, parallel ponds reaching from one horizon to the other.

The permafrost also preserves much older things. The meat of prehistoric mastodons, still intact, has been unearthed from the frozen ground. On the Arctic Coast, the sea eroded ground near Barrow that contained ancient ancestors of the Eskimos who still inhabit the same neighborhood. In 1982, they found a family that apparently was crushed by sea ice up to 500 years ago. Two of the bodies were well preserved, sitting in the home they had occupied and wearing the clothes they had worn the day of the disaster, perhaps around the same time Columbus was sailing to America.

Sea ice is the frozen ocean that extends from northern Alaska to the other side of the world. At the very top of the world it never thaws, but the water opens for a few months of summer along the shore. Then, in September, when the ocean water falls below 29°F, ice forms along the beach and expands from the North Pole's permanent ice pack until the two sides meet. The clash of huge ice floes creates towering pressure ridges, small mountains of steep ice that are difficult to cross. The Eskimo blanket toss—the game of placing a person in the center of a walrus-skin blanket and bouncing him or her high in the air—traditionally got hunters high enough to see over the pressure ridges so they could spot game. At its extreme, in March, the ice extends solidly all the way to the Pribilof Islands, and it's possible to drive a dog team across the Bering Sea to Siberia. The National Weather Service keeps track of the ice pack and issues predictions, as crabbing boats like to tempt its south-moving edge in the fall. Ice even interferes with shipping in Cook Inlet, around Anchorage, although the floes never form a solid pack. Walking on the downtown coastal trail, you can hear their eerie crunch and squeal as they tumble together in the fast tidal currents.

The Arctic and Interior are relatively barren biologically compared to the southern coastal areas of the state. Polar bears wander the Arctic ice pack, but they, like the Eskimos, feed more on marine mammals than on anything found on the shore. A 1,200-pound adult polar bear can make a meal of a walrus, and they're expert at hunting seal. In the summer, huge herds of caribou come north to their eastern Arctic calving grounds, but they migrate south when the cold, dark winter falls unremittingly on the region. In Barrow, the sun doesn't rise for more than 80 days in the winter. In February, the average daily high temperature is −12°F, and the average low is −24°F.

THE VIRGIN WOOD   By comparison, southern coastal Alaska is warm and biologically rich. Temperate rain forest ranges up the coast from Southeast Alaska into Prince William Sound. Bears, deer, moose, wolves, and even big cats live among the massive western hemlock, Sitka spruce, and cedar. This old-growth forest, too wet to burn in forest fires, is the last vestige of the virgin, primeval woods that seemed so limitless to the first white settlers who arrived on the east coast of the continent in the 17th century. The trees grow on and on, sometimes rising more than 200 feet high, with diameters of 10 feet, and falling only after hundreds of years. The trunks rot on the damp moss of the forest floor and return to soil to feed more trees.

Standing among these giants, one feels dwarfed by their age and size, living things of so much greater life span and magnitude than any person. Part of the mystery and grandeur also comes from the knowledge that, here at least, Alaska *does* seem permanent. That sense helps explain why cutting the rain forest is so controversial. Just one of these trees contains thousands of dollars worth of wood, a prize that drives logging as voraciously as the federal government, which owns most of the coastal forest, may choose to allow.

The rivers of the great coastal forests bring home runs of big salmon, clogging in spawning season like a busy sidewalk at rush hour. The fish spawn only once, returning by a precisely tuned sense of smell to the streams where they were hatched as many as 7 years before. When the fertilized eggs have been left in the stream gravel, the fish often conveniently die on the beach, making themselves a smorgasbord for bears. The huge Kodiak brown bear, topping 1,000 pounds, owes everything to the millions of salmon that return to the island each summer. By comparison, the brown bears of the Interior—living on berries or an occasional ground squirrel—are mere midgets, their weight counted in the hundreds of pounds. Forest-dwelling black bears grow to only a few hundred pounds.

TAIGA & FIRE   But rain forest covers only a small fraction of Alaska. In fact, only a third of Alaska is forested at all, and most of this is the boreal forest that covers the central part of the state, behind the rain-shadow of coastal mountains that intercept moist clouds off the oceans. Ranging from the Kenai Peninsula, south of Anchorage, to the Brooks Range, where the Arctic begins, this is a taiga of smaller, slower-growing, hardier trees. In well-drained areas, on hillsides and southern land less susceptible to permafrost, the boreal forest is a lovely, broadly spaced combination of straight, proud white spruce and pale, spectral paper birch. Along the rivers, poplar and cottonwood grow, with deep-grained bark and branches that spread in an oaklike matrix—if they could speak, it would be as wise old men. Where it's wet and swampy—over more and more land as you go north—all that will grow is the glum black spruce, which struggles to become a gnarled stick a mere three inches thick in 100 years, if it doesn't burn first. As the elevation grows, the spruce shrink, turning into weirdly bent, ancient shrubs just before the tree line and the open alpine tundra.

Forest fires tear through as much as several million acres of Alaska's boreal forest each summer. In most cases, forest managers do no more than note the occurrence on a map. Unlike the rain forest, there's little commercially valuable timber in these thin stands, and, anyway, it isn't possible to halt the process of nature's self-immolation over the broad expanse of Alaska. The boreal forest regenerates through fire—it was made to burn. The wildlife that lives in and eats it needs new growth from the burns as well as the shelter of older trees. When the forest is healthiest and most productive, the dark green of the spruce is broken by streaks and patches of light-green brush in an ever-changing succession.

MOOSE & MAN   This is the land of the moose. They're as big as a large horse, with a long, bulbous nose and big eyes that seem to know, somehow, just how ugly they are. Their flanks look like a worn-out shag carpet draped over a sawhorse. But moose are survivors. They thrive in land that no one else wants. In the summer, they wade out into the swampy tundra ponds to eat green muck. In the winter, they like nothing better than an old burn, where summer lightning has peeled back the forest and allowed a tangle of willows to grow—a moose's all-time favorite food. Eaten by wolves, hunted and run over by man, stranded in the snows of a hard winter, the moose always come back, as if just to show that same self-pitying expression on their faces.

Or so you can imagine, until you get up close. Then you can smell the beast's foul scent and see, if the moose is under stress, the ears turn back and the whites of the eyes showing, and you know that this huge animal is no teddy bear—it could easily kill you. During a hard winter, moose starve in the deep snow, show up dead in people's driveways, even, in one case I know, die on their feet and rot that way. When they wander into the city in search of food and the easy walking on roads and railroad tracks, they're under stress and dangerous. In Anchorage's snowy winter of 1994 to 1995, a man who tried to walk around a starving moose on a public sidewalk was knocked down and trampled to death.

MAN & NATURE Anthropomorphizing wild animals—thinking of them in human terms—is a way of making nature seem more predictable and friendly. Whether you're afraid of bears, moose, earthquakes, or even glaciers, the evolving natural history of Alaska can make for an unsettling home. Thinking of wild animals as furry people is a useful, if dangerous, crutch—dangerous because the best protection from wild animals is to take them seriously and to keep your distance.

It's not that nature is malicious; it's just brutally indifferent. In a land where environmental forces seem as willing to erase as to create, any animal, human beings included, is far from indelible. Our species has only begun to scratch the edges of Alaska—we're still barely guests. Only 160,000 acres of Alaska today show any sign of human habitation. More than 100 times that much land is covered by glacier ice. Who knows, in another 15,000 years, the whole thing may be erased by another Ice Age—rain forests, salmon streams, mountains, and cities ground to oblivion under a mile-thick sheet of ice, as it was 15,000 years ago.

3 Politics & History: Living a Frontier Myth

Alaska Timeline

- Perhaps up to 30,000 years ago First human explorers arrive in Alaska from Asia.
- 1741 Vitus Bering, on a mission originally chartered by Peter the Great, finds Alaska; ship's surgeon and naturalist Georg Steller goes ashore for a few hours, the first white to set foot in Alaska.
- 1743 Enslaving the Aleuts, Russian fur traders enter the Aleutian Islands; Aleuts are massacred when they try to revolt—their cultural traditions are eliminated, and they are relocated as far south as California for their hunting skills.
- 1772 Unalaska, in the Aleutian Islands, becomes a permanent Russian settlement.
- 1776–79 British Captain James Cook makes voyages of exploration to Alaska, seeking the Northwest Passage from the Pacific to the Atlantic, and draws charts of the coast.

continues

The occupations of prospector, trapper, and homesteader—rugged individualists relying only on themselves in a limitless land—would dominate Alaska's economy if the state's image of itself were accurate. Alaskans talk a lot about the Alaskan spirit of independence, yearn for freedom from government, and declare that people from "Outside" just don't understand us when they insist on locking up Alaska's lands in parks and wilderness status. The bumper sticker says, simply, WE DON'T GIVE A DAMN HOW THEY DO IT OUTSIDE. A state full of self-reliant frontiersmen can't be tied down and deterred from their manifest destiny by a bunch of Washington bureaucrats. At the extreme, there has even been a movement to declare independence as a separate nation so Alaskans could extend the frontier, extracting its natural resources unfettered by bunny-hugging easterners.

But just because you wear a cowboy hat doesn't mean you know how to ride a horse. In Las Vegas you find a lot more hats than horsemen, and Alaska is full of self-reliant frontier pioneers who spend rush hour in traffic jams and worry more about urban drug dealing and air pollution than where to catch their next meal or dig the mother lode. As for self-reliance and independence from government, Alaska has the highest per capita state spending of any state in the nation, with no state income or sales taxes and an annual payment of more than $1,200 a year to every man, woman, and child just for living here. The state government provides such socialistic benefits as retirement homes and automatic income for the aged; it owns various businesses, including a dairy, a railroad, and a subsidized mortgage lender; it has built schools in the smallest communities, operates a state ferry system and a radio and television network, and owns nearly a third of the land mass of Alaska. And although the oil money that funds state government has been in decline in recent years, forcing the legislature to dig into savings to balance its books, the independent, self-reliant citizens have successfully resisted having to pay any taxes.

That conflict between perception and reality grows out of the story of a century of development of Alaska. The state is a great storehouse of minerals, oil, timber, and fish. A lot of wealth has been extracted, and many people have gotten rich. But it has always been because the federal government let them do it. Every acre of Alaska belonged to the U.S. government from the day Secretary of State William Seward bought Alaska from Russia in 1867. Since then, the frontier has never been broader than Uncle Sam made it.

But today, amid deep conflicts about whether areas should remain natural or be exploited for natural resources, federal control stands out far more clearly than it did 100 years ago, when the gold rush was on, and the government offered the land and its wealth to anyone with strength enough to take it. Alaskans who want to keep receiving the good things that government brings today equate the frontier spirit of the past with their own financial well-being, whether that means working at a mining claim or at a desk in a glass office tower. But other Americans feel they own Alaska, too, and they don't necessarily believe in giving it away anymore. They may want the frontier to stay alive in another sense—unconquered and still wild.

White colonization of the territory came in boom and bust waves of migrants arriving with the goal of making a quick buck and then clearing out—without worrying about the people who already lived there. Although the gold-rush pioneers are celebrated today, the Klondike rush of 1898 that opened up and populated the territory was motivated by greed and was a mass importer of crime, inhumanity, and, for the Native people, massive epidemics of new diseases that killed off whole villages. Like the Russians 150 years before, who had made slaves of the Natives, the new white population considered the indigenous people less than human. Segregation was overcome only after World War II. Native land

- **1784** Russians build settlement at Kodiak.
- **1799** Russians establish settlement at present-day Sitka, which later becomes their capital; Tlingits attack fort and destroy it but are later driven off in a counterattack; the Russian-America Company receives a 20-year exclusive franchise to govern and exploit Alaska.
- **1821** Russian naval officers are placed in control of Russian-America Company, which begins to decline in profitability.
- **1824** Boundaries roughly matching Alaska's current borders are set by treaty between Russia, Britain, and the United States.
- **1839** The British Hudson's Bay Company, surpassing Russia in trade, begins leasing parts of Southeast Alaska and subsequently extends trading outposts into the Interior.
- **1843** First overtures are made by American officials interested in buying Alaska from the Russians, so U.S. instead of British power could expand there.
- **1867** In need of money and fearful that Russia couldn't hold onto Alaska anyway, Tsar Alexander II sells Alaska to the U.S.; Secretary of State William Seward negotiates the deal for a price of $7.2 million, roughly 2¢ an acre; the American flag is raised in Sitka, and the U.S. military assumes government of Alaska.
- **1870** The Alaska Commercial Company receives a monopoly on harvesting seals in the Pribilof Islands and soon expands across the territory (the company

continues

remains a presence in the
Alaska Bush today).

- 1879 Naturalist and writer
John Muir explores Southeast
Alaska by canoe, discovering
Glacier Bay with Native
guides.
- 1880 Joe Juneau and Richard
Harris, guided by local
Natives, find gold on
Gastineau Channel, founding
city of Juneau; gold strikes
begin to come every few years
across the state.
- 1884 Military rule ends in
Alaska, but residents still
have no right to elect a
legislature, governor, or
congressional representative,
or to make laws.
- 1885 Christian missionaries
meet to divide up the
territory, parceling out each
region to a different religion;
they begin to fan out across
Alaska to convert Native
peoples, largely suppressing
their traditional ways.
- 1897 After prospectors arrive
in Seattle with a ton of gold,
the Klondike gold rush
begins; gold rushes in Nome
and Fairbanks follow within a
few years; Americans begin to
populate Alaska.
- 1906 Alaska's first
(nonvoting) delegate in
Congress takes office;
the capital moves from
Sitka to Juneau.
- 1908 The Iditarod Trail,
a sled-dog mail route, is
completed, linking trails
continuously from Seward
to Nome.
- 1913 The first territorial
legislature convenes, although
it has few powers; the first
automobile drives route of
Richardson Highway, from
Valdez to Fairbanks.
- 1914 Federal construction of
the Alaska Railroad begins;
the first tents go up in the

continues

was taken and their culture suppressed by missionaries who forbade Native peoples telling the old stories or even speaking in their own languages. Meanwhile, the salmon that fed the people of the territory were overfished by a powerful, Outside-owned canning industry with friends in Washington and Juneau.

It was only with World War II, and the Japanese invasion of the Aleutian Islands, that Alaska developed an industry not based on exploitation of natural resources: the military industry. It was another boom. To this day, the federal government remains a key industry whose removal would deal the economy a grievous blow.

The fight for Alaska statehood also came after the war. Alaskans argued that they needed local, independent control of natural resources, pointing to the example of overfishing in the federally managed salmon industry. Opponents said that Alaska would never be able to support itself, always requiring large subsidies from the federal government, and therefore should not be a state. The discovery of oil on the Swanson River, on the Kenai Peninsula, in 1957 helped tip the balance, and in 1959, Alaska finally joined the union as the 49th state. To aid the new state in becoming self-sufficient, Alaska was given the right to select 104 million acres of land for state ownership from the total 365 million acres of land mass, virtually all of which still remained in federal hands. But to this day, the federal government still spends a lot more in Alaska than it receives from the residents in taxes.

From the beginning, the new state government relied on oil revenues to support itself and to start extending services to the vast, undeveloped expanse of Alaska. Anchorage boomed in the 1960s in a period of buoyant optimism. Leaders believed that the age-old problems of the wide-open frontier—poverty, lack of basic services, impenetrable remoteness—would succumb to the new government and new money, while the land still remained wide open. Then the pace of change redoubled with the discovery of the largest oil field in North America at Prudhoe Bay in 1968—land that had been a wise state selection in the federal land-grant entitlement. The state government received as much money in a single oil lease sale auction as it had spent in total for the previous 6 years. This was going to be the boom of all booms.

The oil bonanza on the North Slope would change Alaska more than any other event since the gold rush—change that came in many unexpected ways. Once, opening the frontier had only meant letting a few prospectors scratch the dirt in search of a poke of gold—nothing to make a federal case over. But getting the oil to market, from one of the most remote spots on the globe, would require allowing the world's largest companies to build across Alaska a pipeline that, when completed, could credibly claim to be the largest privately financed construction project in world history. With the stakes suddenly so much higher, it came time to figure out exactly who owned which parts of Alaska. That wouldn't be easy—much of the state had never even been mapped, much less surveyed, and there were some outstanding claims that had to be settled.

Alaska Natives, who had lost land, culture, and health in two centuries of white invasion, finally saw their luck start to turn. It wouldn't be possible to resolve the land issues surrounding the pipeline until their claims to land and compensation were answered. Native leaders cannily used that leverage to assure that they got what they wanted. In the early 1970s, America had a new awareness of the way its first people had been treated in the settlement of the West. When white frontiers expanded, Native traditional homelands were stolen. In Alaska, with the powerful lure of all that oil providing the impetus, Native people were able to insist on a fairer resolution. In 1971, with the support of white Alaskans, Congress passed the Alaska Native Claims Settlement Act, called ANCSA, which transferred 44 million acres of land and $962.5 million to corporations whose shareholders were all the Native peoples of Alaska. Those corporations would be able to exploit their own land for their shareholders' profit. Some Natives complained that they'd received only an eighth of the land they had owned before white contact, but it was still the richest settlement any of the world's indigenous people had received.

It was a political deal on a grand scale. It's unlikely that Natives would have gotten their land at all but for the desire of whites to get at the oil, and their need of Native support. Nor could the pipeline have overcome environmental challenges without the Natives' dropping their objections. Even with Native support in place, legislation authorizing the pipeline passed the U.S. Senate by only one vote, cast by Vice President Spiro Agnew.

But there were other side effects of the deal that white Alaskans didn't like so well. After the Native settlement passed, the state—which still hadn't

river bottom that will be Anchorage, along the rail line.

- **1917** Mount McKinley National Park is established.
- **1920** The first flights connect Alaska to the rest of the U.S. by air; aviation quickly becomes the most important means of transportation in the territory.
- **1923** President Warren Harding drives final spike on the Alaskan Railroad at Nenana, then dies on the way home, purportedly from eating bad Alaskan seafood.
- **1925** Leonhard Seppala and other dog mushers relay diphtheria serum on the Iditarod Trail to fight an epidemic in Nome; Seppala and his lead dog, Balto, become national heroes.
- **1934** Federal policy of forced assimilation of Native cultures is officially discarded, and New Deal efforts to preserve Native cultures begin.
- **1935** New Deal "colonists," broke farmers from all over the U.S., settle in the Matanuska Valley north of Anchorage.
- **1940** A military buildup begins in Alaska; bases built in Anchorage accelerate city's growth into major population center.
- **1942** Japanese invade Aleutians, taking Attu and Kiska islands and bombing Unalaska/Dutch Harbor (a U.S. counterattack the next year drives out the Japanese); Alaska Highway links Alaska to the rest of the country overland for the first time but is open to civilians only after the war.
- **1957** Oil is found on Kenai Peninsula's Swanson River.
- **1959** Alaska becomes a state.

continues

- **1964** The largest earthquake ever to strike North America shakes Southcentral Alaska, killing 131 people, primarily in tsunami waves.
- **1968** Oil is found at Prudhoe Bay, on Alaska's North Slope.
- **1970** Environmental lawsuits tie up work to build the Alaska pipeline, which is needed to link the North Slope oil field to markets.
- **1971** Congress acknowledges and pays the federal government's debt to Alaska's indigenous people with the Alaska Native Claims Settlement Act, which transfers 44 million acres of land and almost $1 billion to new Native-owned corporations.
- **1973** The first Iditarod Trail Sled Dog Race runs more than 1,000 miles from Anchorage to Nome.
- **1974** Congress clears away legal barriers to construction of the trans-Alaska pipeline; Vice President Spiro Agnew casts the deciding vote in the U.S. Senate.
- **1977** The trans-Alaska pipeline is completed and begins providing up to 25% of the U.S. domestic supply of oil.
- **1980** Congress sets aside almost a third of Alaska in new parks and other land-conservation units; awash in new oil wealth, the state legislature abolishes all taxes paid by individuals to state government.
- **1982** Alaskans receive their first Alaska Permanent Fund dividends, interest paid on an oil-wealth savings account.
- **1985** Declining oil prices send the Alaska economy into a tailspin; tens of

continues

received much of its land entitlement—and the Native corporations both had a right to select the land they wanted. But that didn't mean the issue was resolved. There still remained the question of who would get what—and of the wild lands that Congress, influenced by a strong new environmental movement, wanted to maintain as national parks and wilderness and not give away. That issue wasn't settled until 1980, when the Alaska National Interest Lands Conservation Act passed, setting aside an additional 106 million acres—nearly a third of the state—for conservation. Alaska's frontier-minded population screamed bloody murder over the "lock-up of Alaska," but the act was only the last, tangible step in a process started by the coming of big oil and the need its arrival created to draw lines on the map, tying up the frontier.

When construction of the $8 billion pipeline finally got underway in 1974, a huge influx of new people chasing the high-paying jobs put any previous gold rush to shame. The newcomers were from a different part of the country than previously, too. Alaska had been a predominately Democratic state, but oil workers from Texas, Oklahoma, and other Bible-belt states helped shift the balance of Alaska's politics, and now it's solidly Republican. In its frontier days, Alaska had a strong Libertarian streak—on both the liberal and the conservative side—but now it became more influenced by fundamentalist Christian conservatism. A hippie-infested legislature of the early 1970s legalized marijuana for home use. Conservatives at the time, who thought the government shouldn't butt into its citizens' private lives, went along with them. After the pipeline, times changed, and Alaska developed tough anti-drug laws.

Growth also brought urban problems, just as it has anywhere else. As the pipeline construction boom waned with completion in 1977, a boomtown atmosphere of gambling and street prostitution went with it, but other big-city problems remained. No longer could residents of Anchorage and Fairbanks go to bed without locking their doors. Both cities were declared "nonattainment" areas by the Environmental Protection Agency because of air pollution near the ground in cold winter weather, when people leave their cars running during the day to keep them from freezing. We got live television but also serial murderers.

But the pipeline seemed to provide limitless wealth to solve the problems. For fear that too much money would be wasted, the voters altered the state constitution to bank a large portion of the new riches; the politicians in Juneau could spend only half the Permanent Fund's earnings, after paying out half the annual income as dividends to every citizen of the state. The fund now contains over $21 billion in savings and has become one of the largest sectors of the economy simply by virtue of paying out more than $600 million a year in dividends to everyone who lives at least a year in the state. All major state taxes on individuals were canceled, and people got used to receiving everything free from the government.

Then, in 1985, oil prices dropped, deflating the overextended economy like a pin in a balloon. Housing prices crashed, and thousands of people simply walked away from their mortgages. All but a few of the banks in the state went broke. Condo-

- thousands leave the state and most of the banks collapse.
- **1989** The tanker *Exxon Valdez* hits Bligh Reef in Prince William Sound, spilling 11 million gallons of North Slope crude in the worst oil spill ever in North America.
- **1994** A federal jury in Anchorage awards $5 billion to 10,000 fishermen, Natives, and others hurt by the Exxon oil spill; Exxon appeals.
- **1996** Wildfire rips through the Big Lake area, north of Anchorage, destroying 400 buildings.

miniums that had sold for $100,000 sold for $20,000 or less a year later. It was the bust that always goes with the boom; but even after so many previous examples, it still came as a shock to many. The spending associated with the *Exxon Valdez* oil spill in 1989 restarted the economy, and it generally has been on an even keel ever since; but the wealth of the earlier oil years never returned.

Meanwhile, the oil from Prudhoe Bay started running out. Oil revenues, an irreplaceable 85% of the state budget, started an irrevocably downward trend in the early 1990s. The oil companies downsized. Without another boom on the horizon, the question became how to avoid, or at least soften, the next bust. That question remains unanswered.

Culture moves slower than politics or events, and Alaskans still see themselves as those gold-rush prospectors or wildcat oil drillers, adventuring in an open land and striking it rich by their own devices. But today the state's future is as little in its own hands as it has ever been. There may be more oil in protected wilderness areas on the North Slope, and there certainly is plenty of natural gas that could be exploited. But whether or not to explore those avenues will be decided in corporate board rooms around the world and in Congress, not in Alaska. Ultimately, an economy based on exploiting natural resources is anything but independent.

Haggling over one plot of land or another will always continue, but the basic lines have been drawn on the map. The frontier has been carved up and regulated— today it's mostly just a state of mind. Or a myth we like to believe about ourselves.

4 The People: Three Ways to Win an Argument in Alaska

#1: WAIT FOR SPRING

A small town in Alaska in March. Each time it snows, you have to throw shovels of it farther over your head to dig out. The air in the house is stale, and out the window all you see is black, white, and gray. Everyone's ready to go nuts with winter. It's time for a good political ruckus. No one can predict exactly what will set it off—it could just be an ill-considered letter to the editor in the local newspaper, or it could be something juicier, like a controversial development proposal. At some point, when the cabin fever gets bad enough, it almost doesn't matter what sparks the inferno. Alaskans can generate outrage about almost anything, with a ritual of charges and countercharges, conspiracy theories and impassioned public testimony.

It's particularly amusing when some outsider is involved, thinking he's at the town council meeting in a normal political process to get some project approved, only to wind up on the receiving end of a public hearing from hell. I'll never forget a sorry businessman who was trying to lease some land from the town of Homer. He endured hours of angry public testimony one night. He was sweating, the only person in the packed city hall meeting room wearing a tie, surrounded by flannel shirts, blue jeans, and angry faces. Finally, he stood up at his chair and, in a plaintive tone of frustration and near tears, declared, "You're not very professional as a community!" For once, no one could disagree.

He gave up. He didn't know that if he had only waited a couple of months, the opposition would dry up as soon as the salmon started running. Then most of the city council meetings would be canceled, and those that weren't would be brief and sparsely attended. If anything really important came up, the council would be smart enough to postpone it till fall. In the summer, Alaskans have more important things to attend to than government.

The sun shines deep into the night, so you can catch fish and tourists, not sit inside. It's the season when the money is made. The streets are full of new people, like a bird rookery refreshed by migrants. Everyone stays awake late pounding nails, playing softball, and fly casting for reds. Office workers in Anchorage depart straight from work for a three-hour drive down to the Kenai Peninsula, fish through the night, catch a quick nap in the car in the wee hours, and make it to work on time the next morning, with fish stories to share at the coffee machine. Sleep is expendable—you don't seem to need it that much when the sky is light all night.

In the Native villages of the Bush, everyone has gone to fish camp. Families load everything in an aluminum river boat and leave town, headed upriver and back to a time of purer cultural traditions. On the banks and beaches, they set up wall tents and spruce-log fish-drying racks, maybe a basketball hoop and campfire, too. The huge extended families work as a unit. Men gather in the salmon, and the women gut them with a few lightning strokes of a knife and hang them to dry on the racks. Children run around in a countryside paradise, watched by whatever adults are handiest.

Suddenly, August comes. For the first time in months, you can see the stars. It comes as a shock the first time you have to use your car headlights. The mood gets even more frantic. There's never enough time in the summer to do everything that needs to get done. Construction crews can count the days now till snow and cold will shut them down. Anything that's not done now won't be done until next May. Labor Day approaches as fast as 5pm on a busy business day.

As September turns to October, everything had better be done. The last tourists are gone, and T-shirt shops are closed for the season. The commercial fishing boats are tied up back in the harbor, and the fishermen prepare for vacation. Deckhands and cannery workers are already back at college. For the first time in months, people can slow down long enough to look at each other and remember where they left off in the spring. It's time to catch up on sleep, think longer thoughts, make big decisions. The hills of birch turn bright yellow, the tundra goes brick red, and the sky turns gray— there's the smell of wood smoke in the air—and then, one day, it starts to snow.

It's not the velvet darkness of midwinter that gets you. December is bearable, even if the sun rises after the kids get to school, barely cruises along the horizon, and sinks before they start for home. Nowhere is Christmas more real than Alaska, singing carols with cheeks tingling from the cold. January isn't so hard. You're still excited about the skiing. The phone rings in the middle of the night—it's a friend telling you to put on your boots and go outside to see the northern lights. February is a bit harder to take, but most towns have a winter carnival to divert your attention from the cold.

March is when bizarre things start to happen. People are just holding on for the end of winter, and you never know what will set them off. That's when you'd better hunker down and lay low, watch what you say, bite your tongue when your spouse lets hang a comment you'd like to jump on like a coho hitting fresh bait. Hold on—just until the icicles start to melt, the mud shows around the snowbanks, and the cycle starts fresh.

#2: BE HERE FIRST

There's a simple and effective way to win an argument in Alaska—state how long you've lived here. If it's longer than your adversary, he'll find it difficult to put up a fight. This is why, when speaking in public, people will often begin their remarks by stating how many years they've been in Alaska. It's a badge of authenticity and status in a place with a young, transient population that's grown fast. No one cares where you came from, or who you were back there, and there's no such thing as class in Alaska—anyone who tries to act superior will quickly find that no one else notices. But if you haven't made it through a few winters, you probably don't know what you're talking about.

It's also traditional—although, sadly, a fading tradition—to treat strangers as friends until they prove otherwise. The smaller the town you visit, the more strongly you'll find that hospitality still alive. Visitors can find it pleasantly disorienting to arrive in a small town and have everyone in the street greet them with a smile. These traditions of hospitality and respect for experience run deepest in Alaska's Native people. (Alaskans use the word "Native" to mean all the indigenous peoples of Alaska.) But instead of beginning a conversation by stating how long they've lived here, Natives—who've always been here—try to find a relation with a new person by talking about where their families are from.

The first people to come to the Americas arrived in the area between Nome and Kotzebue, probably first crossing a land bridge from Asia through the dry Bering Sea, 20,000 to 30,000 years ago, in pursuit of migrating game. Several waves of immigrants came, the last of which probably arrived about 6,000 years ago. Those who kept going south from Alaska were the ancestors of the Incas in South America, the Cherokee in North America, and all the other indigenous people of the hemisphere. Those who stayed in Alaska became the Eskimos—the Inupiat of the Arctic, the Yup'ik of the west, the Aleuts of the Aleutian Islands, and the Chugach, Koniag, and Eyak of Southcentral. They also became the Athabascans of the Interior, and the Tlingit, Haida, and Tsimshian of Southeast Alaska, who are known as Indians rather than Eskimos.

The Native groups of Alaska have a lot in common culturally, but before the white invasion, they had well-defined boundaries and didn't mix much. They didn't farm, and the only animal they domesticated was the dog—dog teams and boats were the primary means of transportation and commerce. But they generally were not nomadic, and no one lived in igloos. Where there was no wood, houses were built of sod. Typically, a family-connected tribal group would have a winter village and a summer fish camp for gathering and laying up food. Elders guided the community in important decisions. A gifted shaman led the people in religious matters, relating to the spirits of ancestors, animals, trees, and even the ice that populated their world. Stories passed on through generations explained the universe.

Those oral traditions kept Native cultures alive. Twenty distinct Native languages were spoken—some elders still speak only their Native language yet today.

An Alaska Glossary

If Alaska feels like a different country from the rest of the United States, one reason may be the odd local usage that makes English slightly different here—different enough, in fact, that the Associated Press publishes a separate style-book dictionary just for Alaska. Here are some Alaskan words you may run into:

break up   When God set up the seasons in Alaska, He forgot one—spring. While the rest of the United States enjoys new flowers and baseball, Alaskans are looking at melting snowbanks and mud. Then, in May, summer miraculously arrives. Break up officially occurs when the ice goes out in the Interior's rivers, but it stands for the time period of winter's demise and summer's initiation.

bunny boots   If you see people wearing huge, bulbous white rubber boots in Alaska's winter, it's not necessarily because they have enormous feet. Those are bunny boots, super-insulated footwear originally designed for Arctic air force operations—they're the warmest things in the world.

cheechako   A newcomer or greenhorn. Not used much anymore, because almost everyone is one.

dry or damp   Many towns and villages have invoked a state law that allows them to outlaw alcohol completely—to go dry—or to outlaw sale but not possession—to go damp.

Lower 48   The contiguous United States.

Native   When capitalized, the word refers to Alaska's indigenous people. "American Indian" isn't used much in Alaska, "Alaska Native" being the preferred term.

Native corporation   In 1971, Congress settled land claims from Alaska's Natives by turning over land and money; corporations were set up, with Natives as shareholders, to receive the property. Most of the corporations still thrive.

The languages break into three major groups: Eskimo-Aleut, Athabascan, and Tlingit. The Eskimo-Aleut language group includes languages spoken by coastal people from the Arctic Ocean to the Gulf of Alaska, including Inupiaq, in the Arctic; Yup'ik, in the Yukon–Kuskokwim Delta area of the southwest; Aleut, in the Aleutian Islands; and Sugpiaq, in Southcentral Alaska. There are 12 Athabascan and Eyak languages in the central part of the state. In Southeast Alaska, Tlingit was spoken across most of the Panhandle. Haida was spoken on southern Prince of Wales Island and southward into what's now British Columbia.

The first arrival of whites was often violent and destructive, spanning a 100-year period that started in the 1740s with the coming of the Russian fur traders, who enslaved and massacred the Aleuts, and continued to the 1840s, when whalers and other mariners met the Inupiat of the Arctic. There were many battles, but nonviolent destruction of oral traditions was more influential. Christian missionaries, with the support of government assimilation policy, drove the old stories and even Native languages underground. Lela Kiana Oman, who has published traditional Inupiat stories to preserve them, told me of her memories of her father secretly telling the ancient tales at night to his children. She was forbidden to speak Inupiaq in school and did not see her first traditional Native dance until age 18.

Oman's work is part of today's Native cultural renaissance. It's not a moment too soon. In some villages, children know more about the geography of Beverly

oosik   The huge penile bone of a walrus. Knowing this word could save you from being the butt of any of a number of practical jokes people like to play on cheechakos.

Outside   Anywhere that isn't Alaska. This is a widely used term in print, and is capitalized, like any other proper noun.

PFD   No, not personal floatation device; it stands for Permanent Fund Dividend. When Alaska's oil riches started flowing in the late 1970s, the voters set up a savings account called the Permanent Fund. Half the interest is paid annually to every man, woman, and child in the state. With more than $21 billion in investments, the fund now yields more than $1,200 in dividends to each Alaskan annually—and as a consequence, the fund has never been raided by the politicians.

pioneer   A white settler of Alaska who has been here longer than most other people can remember—25 or 30 years usually does it.

salmon   There are five species of Pacific salmon, each with two names. The king or Chinook is the largest, growing up to 90 pounds in some areas; the silver or coho is next in size, a feisty sport fish; the red or sockeye has rich red flesh; the pink or humpy and the chum or dog are smallish and not as tasty, mostly ending up in cans and dog lots.

Southeast   Most people don't bother to say "Southeast Alaska." The region may be to the northwest of everyone else in the country, but it's southeast of most Alaskans, and that's all we care about.

tsunami   Earthquake-caused sea waves are often called tidal waves, but it's a bit of a misnomer. The most destructive waves of the 1964 Alaska earthquake were tsunami waves caused by underwater upheavals like landslides.

village   A small, Alaska Native settlement in the Bush, usually tightly bound by family and cultural tradition.

Hills, which they see on television, than about their own culture. Some don't share a language with their own grandparents. But schools in many areas have begun requiring Native language classes. For the Aleut, whose cultural traditions were almost completely wiped out, the process of renewal involves a certain amount of invention. On the other hand, some villages remain, especially deep in the country of the Yukon–Kuskokwim Delta, where Yup'ik is still the dominant language and most of the food comes from traditional subsistence hunting and gathering, altered only by the use of modern materials and guns.

Alaska Natives also are fighting destruction fueled by alcohol and other substance-abuse problems, which have created an epidemic of suicide, accidents, and domestic violence in the Bush. Statistically, virtually every Alaska Native in prison is there because of alcohol. A sobriety movement is attacking the problem one person at a time. One of its goals is to use traditional Native culture to fill a void of rural despair where alcohol now flows in. Politically, a "local option" law provides individual communities the choice of partial or total alcohol prohibition; it has been used in many villages and towns but remains a divisive battle in others, where Native residents tend to support going dry but whites more often vote against.

There are social and political tensions between Natives and whites on many levels and over many issues. Some urban white hunters and sport fishermen, for example, feel they should have the same rights to fish and game as the Natives.

Rural Natives, who have so far won the day, maintain that subsistence hunting and fishing are an integral part of their cultural heritage, far more important than sport, and should take priority. Darker conflicts exist, too, and it's impossible to discount the charges of racism that Native Alaskans raise.

Alaska Natives have become a minority in their own land. In 1880, Alaska contained 33,000 Natives and 430 whites. By 1900, with the gold rush, the numbers were roughly equal. Since then, whites have generally outnumbered Natives in ever greater numbers. Today there are about 94,000 Alaska Natives—22,000 of whom live in the cities of Anchorage and Fairbanks—out of a total state population of about 600,000 people of all races. Consequently, Alaska Natives learn to walk in two worlds. The North Slope's Inupiat, who hunt the bowhead whale from open boats as their forefathers did, must also know how to negotiate for their take in international diplomatic meetings. And they have to use the levers of government to protect the whale's environment from potential damage by the oil industry. The 1971 Alaska Native Claims Settlement Act, which ceded 44 million acres of land and almost $1 billion to Alaska Natives, created a new class, the corporate Native, responsible for representing rural needs but also obliged to function as an executive for large, far-reaching business concerns. Outnumbered by white voters, Bush politicians in the legislature must be especially skilled, sticking together, crossing political boundaries, and forming coalitions to protect their constituencies.

Non-Natives traveling to the Bush also walk in two worlds, but they may not even know it. In a Native village, a newly met friend will ask you in for a cup of coffee; it can be rude not to accept. Looking a person in the eye in conversation also can be rude—that's how Native elders look at younger people who owe them respect. If a Native person looks down, speaks slowly, and seems to mumble, that's not disrespect, but the reverse. Fast-talking non-Natives have to make a conscious effort to slow down and leave pauses in conversation, because Natives usually don't jump in or interrupt—they listen, consider, and then respond. Of course, most Native people won't take offense at your bad manners—they're used to spanning cultures, and they know whites may not know how to act in a village. When I was in a village recently, I looked in confusion at a clock that didn't seem right. "That's Indian time," my Athabascan companion said. Then, pointing to a clock that was working, "White man time is over there."

Urban visitors who miss cultural nuances rarely overlook the apparent poverty of many villages. Out on a remote landscape of windswept tundra, swampy in summer and frozen in winter, they may secretly wonder why Natives stay there, enduring the hardships of rural Alaskan life when even the most remote villager can see on cable television how easy it is in southern California. Save your pity. As Yup'ik leader Harold Napoleon has said, "We're poor, all right, but we've got more than most people. Our most important asset is our land and our culture, and we want to protect it come hell or high water."

Alaska's Natives may be outnumbered, but they've been here a lot longer than anyone else. My money is on them.

#3: BE A REAL ALASKAN

Alaska's history books are full of the stories of economic booms, the people who came, what kind of wealth they were after, and how they populated and developed the land. In a largely empty place, you can make it into history just by showing up. But every wave is followed by a trough—the bust that comes after the boom—when those who came just for the money go back where they came from. Those are the times when the real Alaskans—those who live here for the love of the place, not only the money—are divided from the rest. The real Alaskans stay; the others leave. It's the perfect way to settle an argument.

Other people have other definitions of what it takes to be a real Alaskan. One definition, which I once read on a place mat in a diner in Soldotna, holds that to be a real Alaskan, you have to know how to fix a tractor. Similar definitions require various feats in the outdoors—hunting, fishing, or shooting—and even acts in the bar room or the bedroom. They all assume that a real Alaskan is a big, tough, white, male bulldozer-driving type of guy. But those can be the first to leave when the economy goes down the tubes.

The first group to leave were the Russians sent by the tsar and the Russian-America Company. On October 18, 1867, their flag came down over Castle Hill in Sitka in a solemn ceremony, got stuck, and had to be untangled by a soldier sent up the pole. The territory was virtually empty of Russians before the check was even signed, as Congress didn't much like the idea of the purchase and took a while to pay. The gold-rush stampeders were the next to leave. The population of Nome went from 12,500 to 852 after the stampede was over. The oil years have seen the same phenomenon, as people who can't find work in the bust years pack up and leave.

But each time the boom has gone bust, enough have stayed so that Alaska ended up with more people than it had before. Over the long term, the population has kept growing dramatically. It doubled from 1890 to 1900 (the gold rush); doubled again by 1950 because of World War II and the Cold War; doubled again by 1964, with statehood and the early oil years; and doubled again by 1983, because of the trans-Alaska pipeline and the arrival of big oil. Since then, it has grown another 20%.

Each set of migrants has been similar—young, coming mostly from the West, but from other parts of the United States, too. Most people who have come to Alaska have been white—minority populations are smaller than in the nation as a whole—but there are strong minority communities in Anchorage, and in Kodiak, the canneries are run by a tight Filipino community started by just a few pioneer immigrants. Today the population of Alaska as a whole is young and relatively well paid and educated. Six times as many babies are born as people die.

Historically, old people often moved somewhere warmer when they retired. Some migrate annually, spending only the summer in Alaska—they are called snowbirds. Over the years, the state government set out to keep more old people in the state, to help build the continuity and memory a community needs. Special retirement homes were built, local property-tax breaks were granted to the elderly, and the legislature created a "Longevity Bonus" entitlement whereby elders who'd been in the state at least 25 years were automatically paid $250 a month for life. When a court ruled that the state couldn't impose a residency requirement of more than 1 year for the program, Alaska began to import thousands of new elderly people who were coming north to take advantage of the handouts. Now the bonus is being phased out.

It wasn't the first time Alaska has tried to reward real Alaskans just for staying. When the Permanent Fund Dividend program started in the 1970s, to distribute some of the state's new oil riches to the citizens, it was designed to provide more money for each year of residency. A 1-year greenhorn would get $50 and a 20-year pioneer $1,000. The Supreme Court threw out the plan—apparently being a "real Alaskan" isn't a special category of citizen in the U.S. Constitution.

Alaskans have always been well paid. Until recently, the popular explanation always held that prices are higher because of shipping costs, so salaries needed to match. That's still true in rural Alaska and for some purchases in the large cities. But generally, fierce competition in the retail trade has driven prices down. Large national chains moved in all at once in 1994. Today the cost of living in Anchorage,

Fairbanks, and Juneau compares to most parts of the country. Wages have gone down a little, largely because all those new retail jobs lowered average pay, but the federal government still pays a premium to its Alaskan employees, and oil workers, fishermen, and other skilled workers make a very good living.

Prices for hotel rooms and restaurant meals also remain quite high. The best explanation is the seasonal nature of the economy—tourism operators need to make their full income in the summer season. The other explanation is that they'll charge what the market can bear, and empty hotel rooms are in high demand in summer.

The non-Native part of Alaska, 100 years old with the anniversary of the gold rush, hasn't had time to develop a culture of its own, much less an Alaskan accent. It's a melting pot of the melting pot, with a population made up of odds and ends from all over the United States. People tend to judge each other on the basis of their actions, not on who they are or where they came from. New arrivals to Alaska have been able to reinvent themselves since the days when Soapy Smith, a small-time con man, took over Skagway with a criminal gang and had the territorial governor offer to make him the town marshal—all in the period of a year. Everyone arrives with a clean slate and a chance to prove himself or herself, but on occasion, that ability to start from scratch has created some embarrassing discoveries, when the past does become relevant. There have been a series of political scandals uncovered by reporters who checked the résumés of well-known politicians, only to find out they had concocted their previous lives out of thin air. One leading legislative candidate's husband found out about his wife's real background from such a news story.

If an Alaskan culture hasn't had time to develop, Alaska does have traditions, or at least accepted ways of thinking—among them tolerance and equality, hospitality, independence, and a propensity for violence. Several years ago, in Homer, there was a gunfight over a horse that left a man lying dead on a dirt road. In the newspaper the next week, the editorial called for people not to settle their differences with guns. A couple of letters to the editor shot back, on the theme, "Don't you tell *us* how to settle our differences." Guns are necessary tools in Alaska. They're also a religion. I have friends who exchanged handguns instead of rings when they got married.

The tradition of tolerance of newcomers has made Alaska a destination for oddballs, religious cults, hippies, and people who just can't make it in the mainstream. Perhaps the most interesting of the religious groups that formed its own community is the Old Believers, who in recent decades have built villages of brightly painted, gingerbreadlike houses around Kachemak Bay, near Homer. Their resistance to convention dates back to Peter the Great's reforms to Russian Orthodoxy in the 18th century, which they reject. After centuries of persecution, in Alaska they've found a place where they can live without interference—in fact, they've thrived as fishermen and boat builders. You see them around town, in their 18th-century Russian peasant dress. Even the girls' high-school basketball team wears long dresses, with their numbers stitched to the bodice.

Nikolaevsk was the first of the Russian Old Believer villages. In the public school there, they don't teach about dinosaurs or men landing on the moon—that's considered heresy. Yet other Old Believers rebelled, convinced that Nikolaevsk was making too many compromises and was bound to lose the next generation to decadent American ways. They broke off and formed another village, farther up the bay, unreachable except by all-terrain vehicle, and adhered to stricter rules. They, in turn, suffered another schism and another village was formed, farther up the bay, virtually inaccessible and with even stricter rules. The process continues. The fight against assimilation may be hopeless, as children will ultimately do as they please, but it's the Old Believers' own struggle. No one in Homer pushes them to change. No one pays any attention at all, except to buy their fish and their top-quality boats.

After several decades, it looks as if the Old Believers are here to stay. Whether they speak English or not, I'd say they're real Alaskans.

5 Recommended Books

Coming into the Country, by John McPhee (Farrar, Straus and Giroux, 1976), is the classic portrait of Alaska, telling the stories of people in the Yukon region, around Eagle. Covering much of the same territory, *Tisha*, by Richard Specht (Bantam, 1976), is among the most popular novels of Alaska. Based closely on a true story, it's the tale of a young white schoolteacher in Chicken in the 1920s and 1930s who courageously insisted on treating the Natives as equals. Of course, no one has surpassed Jack London's 1904 *Call of the Wild* and his short stories as classic adventure yarns; he based his work on a winter prospecting on the Klondike.

The best firsthand accounts of early Alaska are still fresh. John Muir chronicled his voyage of discovery in Southeast in *Travels in Alaska*. Libby Bearman's journals and letters about living on the Pribilof Islands in 1879 and 1880, recently reprinted by Oak Council Books, are strongly authentic and reveal a powerful personality.

For deeper insight into Native culture, *Fifty Years Below Zero*, a memoir by Charles Brower (University of Alaska Press reprint, 1994), is a standard. Brower came to the Arctic as a whaler in 1884 and stayed 60 years. *The Wake of the Unseen Object*, by Tom Kizzia (Henry Holt, 1991), is a more recent journey into the Bush.

Several writers have recorded Native stories and legends in their own words. *Two Old Women*, by Velma Wallis (Harper Perennial, 1994), is one of the most popular; it's based on Athabascan legend, telling a suspenseful story of survival and renewal. *The Epic of Qayaq; The Longest Story Ever Told by My People*, by Lela Kiana Oman (Carlton University Press, 1995), is an Inupiat story originally told over many nights, like Homer's *Odyssey*.

Many practical books are recommended in the text. A full catalogue of field guides and other nonfiction works on Alaska is available from **Alaska Northwest Books**, P.O. Box 10306, Portland, OR 97210 (☎ **800/452-3032**).

3 Planning a Trip to Alaska

Planning a trip to Alaska can be a bit more complicated than traveling in the rest of the United States. Besides the vast distances and range of climatic conditions, Alaska travel in the high summer season usually requires long advance preparations and reservations. This chapter provides the general information you'll need to get started.

1 Visitor Information & Money

VISITOR INFORMATION

The **Alaska Division of Tourism,** P.O. Box 110801, Juneau, AK 99811-0801 (☎ **907/465-2010;** website http://www.state.ak.us/ tourism), provides an *Official State Guide and Vacation Planner* with information on traveling to all parts of Alaska, including advertising from many tourism-related businesses. The booklet is sent free to domestic addresses and costs $10 to be sent internationally, payable by Visa or MasterCard, check or money order.

The Alaska Department of Transportation provides an updated recording with **weather and road information** for various regions of the state (☎ **800/478-7675**).

For outdoor recreation, the **Alaska Public Lands Information Centers** are centralized sources of information on all government lands—which takes in more than 85% of the state. The centers are operated cooperatively by seven land agencies. The Anchorage center is at 605 W. Fourth Ave., Suite 105, Anchorage, AK 99501 (☎ **907/271-2737;** fax 907/271-2744; website http://www. nps.gov/aplic). See the Fairbanks and Tok listings in chapter 10 for the centers there. Information on a center in Ketchikan is in chapter 7.

ON THE NET The Internet has become a popular way to plan a vacation, and it makes a lot of sense. Sitting at a computer, you can call up information and pictures on destinations, attractions, lodgings, and activities, and make reservations or ask questions without the delays of the mail or worrying about time differences on the telephone. I've listed well over 100 websites in the text and many e-mail addresses. In addition, below are some of the best places to go to link to Alaska information. Of course, websites change even faster than other travel services, so by the time you read this, addresses may have changed.

The state **Division of Tourism (http://www.state.ak.us/tourism)** has links to every community that's on the Web, lots of other information, and a place to ask general questions. **The Alaska Information Cache (http://www.akcache.com/ akhome.html)** is an extensive commercial site with lots of well-organized links for travel, fishing, and other Alaska topics. The supercomputer at the University of Alaska–Fairbanks, **(http://www.arsc.edu/misc/AlaskaWebServers.html)** contains a general index leading to many Alaska websites. Finally, **The State of Alaska (http:// www.state.ak.us)** is fully linked to the Web, allowing you to connect with the Alaska Department of Fish and Game, the Alaska Marine Highway System, and any other agencies you may need to contact. Various towns and cities have sites, too, with perhaps the most comprehensive being the Municipality of Anchorage's website, **http:// www.ci.anchorage.ak.us/.**

The easiest way to find particular airlines, rental car companies, and other businesses is through **Yahoo!** at **http://www.yahoo.com/.** Two of the most useful addresses for Alaska travelers are **Alaska Airlines (http://www.alaskaair.com)** and the **Alaska Marine Highway ferry system (http://www.dot.state.ak.us/external/amhs/ home.html).**

Most government land agencies have websites, but they're generally not very good. The **National Park Service** is at **http://www.nps.gov.** The Alaska office of the Bureau of Land Management is at **http://wwwndo.ak.blm.gov/.** The Alaska Division of Parks is at **http://www.dnr.state.ak.us/parks/index.htm.** A great overall site for outdoor information nationally is the **Great Outdoor Recreation Pages, http:// www.gorp.com/.**

Finally, I welcome your e-mail to my own personal account, **wohlforth@ compuserve.com**. I'd appreciate your comments on your best or worst experiences in Alaska, and any errors or outdated material you find in the book. I'll answer questions to the extent that I have time, but I'm not in the trip-planning business, so please contact the many professional sources listed elsewhere in the book for that kind of advice.

MONEY

HOW MUCH MONEY YOU'LL NEED Alaska is an expensive place to get to, to get around, and to stay in. In popular spots, a good, standard motel double room is rarely available for less than $90 to $100. Airfare from Seattle to Anchorage fluctuates wildly with competition among the airlines, but a $300 round-trip, with advance purchase, is a fair deal. You can easily pay twice that to fly to an Alaska Bush community. Even the train is expensive, with a one-way fare from Anchorage to Fairbanks, a 350-mile trip, at $149 on the least luxurious of three choices of cars. A couple ordering a good salmon dinner, appetizers, and wine will likely pay $90 to $100 in a fine restaurant, including tip. One reason cruise ships have become so popular is that, for this quality level, they're comparable in price on a daily basis to independent travel; see chapter 5 for details on cruising.

To travel at a standard American comfort level, a couple should allow $100 per person, per day, for room and board. The cost of an activity such as flightseeing, wildlife cruises, or guided fishing typically is $75 to $175 per person. Also add ground transportation—you may need to rent a car, the best way to see much of the state, for around $55 a day (weekly rentals are less, and check for sales). You also will likely need train and ferry tickets. Two weeks for a couple, then, will cost in the neighborhood of $4,100, including airfare to Alaska, two $100-per-person activities, and $500 for ground transportation, but without going to the Bush. For high luxury, you can spend much more—as much, in fact, as you might be willing to spend.

Of course, you also can trim down your costs by cutting your demands. You'll learn more about the real Alaska staying in bed-and-breakfast accommodations than in a standard hotel room. Expect to pay $75 to $90 for a decent room with a shared bath, $80 to $95 for a private bath. The breakfast cuts your food costs, too. And there are plenty of family restaurants where you can eat a modest dinner for two for $30, with a tip and a glass of beer. Traveling in that style will bring the cost of room and board down to about $60 per person, per day, for a couple. Leaving the rest of the costs the same, with airfare, ground transportation, and activities, that couple would spend about $3,000 for two weeks.

Another way to save money is to travel in the shoulder season, before and after the peak summer season. Hotel and guided activity prices drop significantly, typically 25% or more. May and September are solidly in the shoulder season, and sometimes you get bargains as late as June 15 or as early as August 15. Traveling in the winter is a whole different experience, but certainly saves a lot of money—where hotels are open, rates are typically half of peak rates. For other considerations on off-season and shoulder-season travel, see "When to Go," later in this chapter.

You can save the most money by giving up a private room every night and cooking some of your own meals. Camping is a fun way to really see Alaska and costs only $8 to $10 a night in state and federal government campgrounds. Hostels are available in most towns, typically for around $12 a night. Thousands of young people come to Alaska each summer and spend almost nothing, replenishing their funds when necessary with stints working at a fish cannery or restaurant—low-wage, long-hour jobs are usually available in the summer (see "Tips for Students" under "Tips for Special Travelers," later in this chapter). People who own recreational vehicles travel for a cost little greater than staying at home, except for the fuel to navigate the beast down the road. A family can have the experience of a lifetime by driving the Alaska Highway or taking the family car up the Inside Passage on a state ferry, and camping at night. Unfortunately, most people don't have the time for these options. It adds up to a week to each end of your trip to drive to Alaska, and puts thousands of miles and heavy wear and tear on your vehicle. Depending on where you start from, I wouldn't attempt it with less than four to six weeks for the trip.

HOW TO CARRY YOUR MONEY   There are few special warnings to be given about money in Alaska other than the caution you'd use in any other part of the United States. Don't carry enough cash to tempt a criminal, or to ruin your trip if it's lost, but make sure you have enough before going to very small towns or villages or on rural highways. Only the smallest towns and outdoor destinations still lack automatic-teller machines (ATMs) and have businesses that don't take credit or charge cards. The "Fast Facts" section for each town in this book will tell you if there's an ATM and where to find it; few towns that are large enough to be in this volume lack an ATM. Alaska ATMs generally are all on the Cirrus and Plus networks and other major ATM networks. Alaska banks generally charge no or very low ATM use fees, but your own bank may. In larger towns, you'll find that every business you'd expect to take credit, charge, or debit cards at home will accept them here. Some bed-and-breakfasts and inexpensive restaurants don't take credit or charge cards, however, and few businesses of any kind will take an out-of-state personal check. Traveler's checks are good just about anywhere.

When I travel around Alaska, I carry at least $100 in cash, plus a couple of different kinds of credit/charge cards, and an ATM card. I use a credit or charge card (preferably earning frequent-flier miles) whenever I can, and stop at an ATM whenever my emergency cash falls under $100. If I'm going to a small village for a while,

I load up on cash first. I've rarely run into a problem with this system, and it saves the cost and inconvenience of using traveler's checks.

2 When to Go

CLIMATE & SEASONS

Nothing makes a bigger difference in the success of your vacation than the weather, and the weather in Alaska can be extreme and unpredictable. We're the first to get whatever Arctic Siberia or the void of the North Pacific have to throw at North America. The extremes of recorded temperatures are a high of 100°F and low of –80°F. A single spring day in the Southcentral or Southeast region can include snow flurries, sun, rain, and a combination of all three at once. Statistics give means and averages of the climate, but that doesn't mean your vacation couldn't be made perfect by weeks of unbroken sunny weather or marred by weeks of unbroken rain. All you can do is play the averages, hope for the best, and, if you do get bad weather, get out and have fun anyway—that's what Alaskans do. (My own subjective summary of the visitor season in various Alaska places is found below in the chart "Alaska by the Numbers."

JUNE, JULY & AUGUST   Summer in Alaska is a miraculous time, when the sun refuses to set and people are energized with limitless energy. The sun dips below the horizon in Anchorage for only about four hours on June 21, the longest day of the year, and the sky is light all night. The state fills with people coming to visit and to work in the seasonal fishing, timber, and construction industries. Weather gets warmer, although how warm depends on where you go (see the chart below). June is the driest of the three summer months, July the warmest, and August generally the rainiest month of the brief summer, but warmer than June. In most respects, June is the best summer month to make a visit, but it does have some drawbacks to consider: Vestiges of winter linger in some areas until mid-month; in the Arctic, snow doesn't all melt till mid-June; in Southcentral Alaska, trails at high elevation or in the shade may be too muddy or snowy; and not all activities or facilities at Denali National Park open until late June. It's also the worst time for mosquitoes. The salmon-fishing season depends on where you are. July is generally its height, followed by August and September, but there are salmon to be found somewhere all summer.

Summer also is the season of high prices. Most operators in the visitor industry have only these 90 days to make their year's income, and they charge whatever the market will bear. July is the absolute peak of the tourist season, when you must book well ahead and crowds are most prevalent. (Of course, crowding is relative. With a population density of roughly one person per square mile, Alaska is never really crowded.) Before June 15 and after August 15, the season begins to decline, providing occasional bargains and more elbow room. But the length and intensity of the visitor season varies widely in different areas, and in some places it stays very busy from Memorial Day to Labor Day.

MAY & SEPTEMBER   More and more visitors are coming to Alaska during these shoulder months to take advantage of the lower prices, absence of crowds, and special beauty.

May is the drier of the two months and can be as warm as summer, if you're lucky, but as you go farther north and earlier in the month, your chances increase of finding cold, mud, and even snow. In Alaska, we don't have spring—the melt of snow and resultant seas of mud are called *break up*. Many outdoor activities aren't possible during break up, which can extend well into May. Before May 15, most tourist-oriented activities and facilities are still closed, and a few don't open until Memorial Day or June 1. Where visitor facilities are open, they often have significantly lower prices. Also, the first visitors of the year always receive an especially warm welcome. The very earliest salmon runs start in May, but for a fishing-oriented trip it's better to come later.

Sometime from late August to mid-September, weather patterns change, bringing clouds, frequent rainstorms, and cooling weather, and signaling the trees and tundra to turn bright, vivid colors. For a week or two, the bright-yellow birches of the boreal forest and rich red of the heathery tundra make September the most lovely time of year. But the rain and the nip in the air, similar to late October or November in New England, mean you'll likely have to bundle up; and September is generally the wettest month of the year. Most tourist-oriented businesses stay open, with lower prices, till September 15, except in the Arctic. After September 15, it's pot luck. Some areas close up tight, but the silver salmon fishing hits prime time on the Kenai Peninsula, and the season stays active till the end of the month. A lucky visitor can come in September and hit a month of crisp, sunny, perfect weather, and have the state relatively to him- or herself. Or it can be cold and rain all month.

WINTER   One of the most spectacular trips I ever took was a train ride from Fairbanks to Anchorage in January. Outside the windows, Mount McKinley stood clear and so vivid in a vast, smooth landscape of pale blue and rich orange that I felt as if I could reach out and touch it. A young woman from South Africa was on the train. When I asked her why she came to Alaska in January, she only had to point out the window. She said, "Alaska is all about snow and ice."

She was right, but visitors and the people who serve them generally haven't figured that out yet. Some towns—such as Skagway and Dawson City—close down almost completely. In others—most places on the ocean, for example—nearly all activities and attractions are closed for the season, but services remain open for business travelers. Where facilities are open, hotel prices are often less than half of what you'd pay in the high season. Quite luxurious rooms sometimes go for the cost of a budget motel. Visitors who seek out places of interest can have an exceptional and memorable time, enjoying some of the best alpine, Nordic, and backcountry skiing, outdoor ice skating, dog mushing, and aurora and wildlife watching available anywhere, at any time. The best time to come is late winter, from mid-February through March, when the sun is up longer and winter carnivals and competitive dog mushing hit their peak.

WHAT TO WEAR

SUMMER   You're not going to the North Pole, and you don't need a down parka or winter boots weighing down your luggage. But you do need to be ready for a variety of weather, from sunny, 80° days to windy, rainy, 50° outings on the water. The way Alaskans prepare for such a range is with layers.

WINTER   Normal alpine and Nordic skiing garb are adequate for skiing in Southcentral Alaska. Cross-country skiing in the Interior may require you to dress more warmly than you're accustomed to. Snowmobiling or dog mushing in winter requires the warmest possible clothing—you'll need the stoutest Sorel or Air Force bunny boots, insulated snow pants, thermal underwear, a heavy down parka with a hood, thick mittens (not gloves), and a wool hat or face-covering mask. Expect to spend at least $500 on a full winter outfit adequate for backcountry winter travel. You can buy what you need in Anchorage or Fairbanks when you arrive. If you're not

ALASKA'S CLIMATE, BY MONTHS & REGIONS

	Jan	Feb	Mar	Apr	May	June	July	Aug	Sept	Oct	Nov	Dec
Anchorage: Southcentral Alaska												
Average high/low**	21/8	26/12	33/18	43/29	54/39	62/47	65/52	63/50	55/42	41/29	27/15	23/10
Hours of light*	6:30	9:15	12	15:30	17:45	19:30	18:15	15:30	12	9:30	7	5:30
Sunny days†	12	10	13	12	11	10	9	9	9	10	10	10
Rainy or snowy days	8	8	8	6	7	8	11	13	14	12	10	11
Precipitation‡	0.8	0.8	0.7	0.7	0.7	1.1	1.7	2.4	2.7	2	1.1	1.1
Barrow: Arctic Alaska												
Average high/low**	−7/−19	−12/−24	−9/−21	5/−9	24/14	38/30	45/34	42/33	34/27	18/9	3/−7	−5/−17
Hours of light*	0:00	6:00	12:00	20:00	24:00	24:00	24:00	20:00	13:00	7:30	0:00	0:00
Sunny days†	7	18	21	18	8	9	11	5	4	6	8	4
Rainy or snowy days	4	4	4	4	4	5	9	11	11	11	6	5
Precipitation‡	0.2	0.2	0.2	0.2	0.2	0.3	1	1	0.6	0.5	0.3	0.2
Cold Bay: Aleutian Archipelago												
Average high/low**	33/24	32/23	35/25	38/29	44/35	50/41	55/46	56/47	52/43	44/35	39/30	35/27
Hours of light*	8:00	10:00	12:00	14:30	16:30	17:30	16:30	14:00	12:30	9:00	8:00	7:00
Sunny days†	8	6	8	4	3	3	3	2	4	6	6	7
Rainy or snowy days	19	17	18	16	17	16	17	20	21	23	22	21
Precipitation‡	2.8	2.3	2.2	2	2.3	2.1	2.5	3.2	4.4	4.3	4.2	3.7
Fairbanks: Interior Alaska												
Average high/low**	−2/−18	7/−14	24/−2	41/20	59/38	70/50	72/53	66/47	55/36	32/18	11/−6	2/−15
Hours of light*	6:45	9:00	11:00	15:30	19:00	21:00	19:00	16:00	13:45	9:00	6:00	4:00
Sunny days†	15	14	17	14	16	13	12	10	10	9	12	12
Rainy or snowy days	8	7	6	5	7	11	12	12	10	11	11	9
Precipitation‡	0.5	0.4	0.4	0.3	0.6	1.4	1.9	2	0.9	0.9	0.8	0.8
Juneau: Southeast Alaska												
Average high/low**	29/19	34/23	39/27	47/32	55/39	61/45	64/48	63/47	56/43	47/37	37/27	32/23
Hours of light*	7:30	9:30	12:00	14:30	17:00	18:15	17:30	15:30	12:30	10:00	7:30	6:30
Sunny days†	8	7	7	8	8	8	8	9	6	4	6	5
Rainy or snowy days	18	17	18	17	17	15	17	17	20	24	20	21
Precipitation‡	4.5	3.7	3.3	2.8	3.4	3.1	4.2	5.3	6.7	7.8	4.9	4.4
Valdez: Prince William Sound												
Average high/low**	26/15	30/18	36/22	44/30	52/38	59/44	62/48	61/46	54/40	43/33	32/22	28/18
Hours of light*	6:30	9:15	12:00	15:15	17:45	19:30	18:00	15:15	12:30	9:45	7:00	5:45
Sunny days†	9	9	11	11	9	8	8	10	8	8	10	7
Rainy or snowy days	17	14	16	14	17	15	17	17	20	20	16	18
Precipitation‡	5.6	5.1	4.7	3.2	3.8	3.1	3.8	6	8.4	8	5.5	6.8

*Hours of light is an approximation of the possible daylight on the 20th day of each month.
**All temperatures are given in degrees Fahrenheit.
†Sunny days includes the average observed clear and partly cloudy days per month.
‡Precipitation is the average water equivalent of rain or snow.

planning anything so rugged, you can get by in a city with a normal great coat, gloves, and wool socks; if you're like most Alaskans, you'll just make a quick dash from car to heated building when really cold weather hits.

ALASKA CALENDAR OF EVENTS

Here are some of the biggest community events of the year in Alaska's cities and towns. You'll also find fishing derbies going on all summer almost anywhere you go in Alaska. The dates, in many cases, are estimates: Don't plan a vacation around them. Instead, call the organizers or visitor information centers listed in each of the towns for late details.

January

- **Russian Orthodox Christmas,** Kodiak and Sitka. Celebrated with solemn services and the starring ceremony, in which a star is carried through the streets from house to house, with song and prayer at each door. Call ☎ **907/486-4782** for information on Kodiak and ☎ **907/747-5940** for information on Sitka. January 7.

February

- **The Cordova Iceworm Festival,** a winter carnival in Cordova on Prince William Sound; the big iceworm—or, to be precise, ice centipede—marches in a parade. Call ☎ **907/424-6665** for information. First full weekend in the month.
- **The Yukon Quest International Sled Dog Race** starts or finishes in Fairbanks. (Fairbanks has the start in even-numbered years; Whitehorse, Yukon Territory, in odd years.) The challenge of the 1,000-mile race is equal to the Iditarod. Call ☎ **907/452-7954** for information. Mid-month.
- ✪ **The Anchorage Fur Rendezvous,** a huge, city-wide winter carnival, over 10 days. The main event is the **World Championship Sled Dog Race,** a three-day sprint event of about 25 miles per heat. Call ☎ **907/277-8615** for information. Second and third weekends of the month.
- **The Nenana Ice Classic** starts with a weekend celebration at the end of the month. The Classic is a sweepstakes on who can guess closest to the exact date and time ice will go out on the Tanana River. You can buy tickets all over Alaska. Call ☎ **907/832-5446** for information.

March

- ✪ **The Iditarod Trail Sled Dog Race.** The famous race starts the first Saturday in March with much fanfare from **Anchorage,** then the teams are loaded in trucks for the **Iditarod Restart,** in **Wasilla,** which is the real beginning of the race. Here the historic gold-rush trail becomes continuous for the dogs' 1,000-mile run to Nome. The event enlivens Wasilla at the end of a long winter. The finish in Nome is the biggest event of the year in the Arctic, drawing world media attention and turning Nome into a huge party for a few days. The race solicits volunteers to help, which is a much better way to experience it than just watching. Call ☎ **907/376-5155** for information.
- **The Bering Sea Ice Golf Classic** showcases Nome's well-developed sense of humor—six holes are set up on the sea ice. Various similar silly events take place all year—you can get a list from the visitors center. Call ☎ **907/443-5278** for information. Mid-month.
- **The North American Sled Dog Championships,** in Fairbanks, a sprint with two 20-mile heats and one 30-mile heat, begins and ends downtown. Call ☎ **907/479-8166** for information. Mid-month.

✪ **The Ice Art Competition,** also in Fairbanks, brings carvers from all over the world to create spectacular sculptures out of immense chunks cut from Fairbanks lakes. Call ☎ **907/452-8250** for information. Toward the end of the month.

• **The World Extreme Skiing Championships,** Valdez. Held at the end of March or early April on the vertical faces of mountains north of Valdez, this is a spectacular daredevil competition, with skiers literally risking their lives for the coolest run. Call ☎ **907/835-2108** for information.

April

• **The Alaska Folk Festival,** Juneau. A community-wide celebration drawing musicians, whether on the bill or not, from all over the state. Call ☎ **907/789-0292** for information. April 13 to April 19, 1998.

• **The Garnet Festival,** in Wrangell the third week of April, marks the arrival of the massive shorebird migration and bald eagle congregation on the Stikine River Delta, a chance to see a tornado of wildlife in the region's largest coastal marshes. Call ☎ **800/367-9745** or 907/874-3901 for information.

May

• **The Copper River Delta Shorebird Festival,** in Cordova, revolves around the arrival of swarms of shorebirds that use the delta, and the beaches near the town, as a migratory stopover. The whole community gets involved to host bird watchers and put on a full schedule of educational and outdoor activities. Call ☎ **907/424-7260** for information. Early May.

• **Kachemak Bay Shorebird Festival,** Homer. Includes guided bird watching, art activities, and other events for the migration. Call ☎ **907/235-7740** for information. Early May.

• **Little Norway Festival,** Petersburg, celebrating the May 17, 1814, declaration of independence of Norway from Sweden. The town goes wild, and lots of community events are planned. Call ☎ **907/772-4636** for information. May 14 to May 17, 1998.

✪ **The Crab Festival,** Kodiak. Includes a carnival, fleet parade, and various competitions, as well as a solemn service for lost fishermen, which occurs at the fishermen's memorial by the boat harbor. Call ☎ **907/486-4782** for information. Memorial Day weekend.

• **The Polar Bear Swim,** Nome, occurs in the Bering Sea on Memorial Day, ice permitting. Call ☎ **907/443-5535** for information.

June

• **Celebration,** Juneau. Modestly titled gathering of some 1,000 Native dancers at the Juneau Centennial Hall. Call ☎ **907/463-4844** for information. June 26 to June 28, 1998.

✪ **The Sitka Summer Music Festival,** a chamber music series that began in 1972, is one of Alaska's most important cultural events, drawing musicians from all over the world. Call ☎ **907/747-6774** for information. All month.

• **Dyea to Dawson Race,** Skagway and Dawson City. Pairs of racers commemorating the centennial of the Klondike Gold Rush will retrace the stampeders' 500-mile route from Dyea, near Skagway, to Dawson City, carrying with them the same gear the prospectors hauled. Call ☎ **907/983-2854** for information. Mid-June.

• **Midnight Sun Baseball Game,** Fairbanks. A summer-solstice event—the local semipro baseball team, the **Fairbanks Goldpanners,** plays a game under the midnight sun, beginning at 10:30pm. Call ☎ **907/451-0095** for information. June 20/21.

- **Solstice Gathering,** Eagle Summit. On the Steese Highway, 107 miles out of Fairbanks, an informal gathering occurs to celebrate the solstice at the 3,624-foot Eagle Summit highway pass. See chapter 10 for more information. June 21.
- **Midnight Sun Festival,** Nome. Celebrates the summer solstice, when Nome gets more than 22 hours of direct sunlight, with a parade, beauty pageant, and similar events. Call ☎ **907/443-5535** for information. June 21.

July

- **The Yukon Gold Panning Championships and Canada Day Celebrations,** Dawson City. The Canadian equivalent of the Fourth of July in the U.S. will be an especially big deal with the 1998 Gold Rush Centennial in Dawson. Call ☎ **867/993-7228** for information. July 1.
- ✪ **Independence Day.** Most of the small towns in Alaska make a big deal of the 4th of July. In 1998, it will mark the 100th anniversary of Soapy Smith's notorious ride in **Skagway's** parade, and a big event is planned. Seward always has a huge celebration, exploding with visitors, primarily from Anchorage. Besides the parade and many small town festivities, the main attraction is the **Mount Marathon Race,** from the middle of town straight up rocky Mount Marathon to its 3,022-foot peak and down again. **Seldovia, Kenai, Ketchikan,** and **Juneau** also have exceptional 4th of July events. See the individual town write-ups for more information.
- **The Fairbanks Summer Arts Festival.** Offerings in music, dance, theater, opera, ice skating, and the visual arts. Call ☎ **907/474-8869** for information. July 24 to August 9, 1998.

August

- ✪ **Southeast Alaska State Fair** and **Bald Eagle Music Festival,** Haines. The area's biggest summer event, it's a regional small-town get-together, with livestock, cooking, a logging show, a parade, music, and other entertainment. Call ☎ **907/766-2476** for information. Mid-August.
- **Concert on the Lawn,** Homer. Put on by KBBI radio (☎ **907/235-7721**), this is a day-long outdoor music festival that brings together the whole town for a day in mid-August.
- ✪ **Prince William Sound Community College Theater Conference,** Valdez. Brings famous playwrights and directors to the community for seminars and performances. Call ☎ **907/835-2678** for information. Mid-August.
- ✪ **Alaska State Fair,** Palmer. The biggest event of the year for the Matanuska Valley, and one of the biggest for Anchorage. It's a typical state fair, except for the huge vegetables. The good soil and long days in the Valley grow cabbages the size of a bean-bag chair. A mere beach-ball-sized cabbage wouldn't even make it into competition. Call ☎ **907/745-2880** for information. The 11 days before Labor Day.

October

- **Alaska Day Festival,** Sitka. Alaska Day, commemorating the Alaska purchase on October 18, 1867, is a big deal in this former Russian and U.S. territorial capital city. Call ☎ **907/747-5940** for information. October 14 to October 18, 1998.

November

- **Athabascan Fiddling Festival,** Fairbanks. Draws together musicians and dancers from the Interior region for performances and workshops. Call ☎ **907/452-1825** for information. Early in the month.
- **Alaska Bald Eagle Festival,** Haines. Seminars and special events to mark the annual eagle congregation in early November. Call ☎ **800/246-6268** for information.

- **Great Alaska Shootout Men's Basketball Tournament,** Anchorage. The University of Alaska Seawolves host a roster of the nation's top-ranked NCAA Division I teams at the Sullivan Arena. See chapter 8 for more information. Thanksgiving weekend.
- **Christmas Tree Lighting,** Anchorage. Takes place in town square, with Santa arriving behind a team of real reindeer. It's usually followed by a performance of *The Nutcracker* in the Alaska Center for the Performing Arts. Call ☎ **907/ 276-4118** for information. The Saturday after Thanksgiving.

December

- **Christmas,** Anchorage. A full schedule of community Christmas festivities, including crafts fairs and performances, takes place all month. Call ☎ **907/276-4118** for information. Similar events take place all over the state.

3 Health, Safety & Traveler's Insurance

HEALTH

You'll find modern, full-service hospitals in each of Alaska's larger cities, and even in some small towns that act as regional centers. There's some kind of clinic even in tiny villages. Travelers who don't plan to spend time in the outdoors need take no health precautions beyond what they'd do when traveling anywhere else in the U.S. If you'll be doing any hiking, boating, camping, or other outdoor activities, the tips below may be more relevant.

HYPOTHERMIA Sometimes known as exposure, hypothermia is a potentially fatal lowering of core body temperature. It can sneak up on you, and it's most dangerous when you don't realize how cold you are, on a damp mountain hike or wet boating trip. The weather doesn't have to be very cold if you're damp and not adequately dressed in a material (whether wool or synthetic) that keeps its warmth when wet. Among the symptoms are cold extremities, shivering, being uncommunicative, poor judgment or coordination, and sleepiness. The cure is to warm the victim up— getting indoors, forcing him or her to drink hot liquids, and, if shelter is unavailable, applying body heat from another person, skin on skin, in a sleeping bag.

INSECT BITES The good news is that Alaska has no poisonous snakes or spiders. The bad news is the mosquitoes and other biting insects. They're not dangerous, but they *can* ruin a trip. Insect repellent is a necessity, as is having a place where you can get away from them. Hikers in the Interior, where mosquitoes are worst, use head nets. Mosquitoes can bite through light fabric, which is why people in the Bush wear heavy Carharts even on the hottest days. Wasps, hornets, and other stinging insects are common in Alaska. If you're allergic, be ready with your serum.

PLANTS Two shrubs common in Alaska can cause skin irritation, but we've got nothing as bad as poison ivy or poison oak (and no snakes, either). Pushki, also called cow parsnip, is a large-leafed plant growing primarily in open areas, up to shoulder height by late summer, with white flowers. The celerylike stalks break easily, and the sap has the quality of intensifying the burning power of the sun on skin. Wash it off quickly. Devil's Club, a more obviously dangerous plant, grows on steep slopes and has ferocious spines that can pierce through clothing.

SHELLFISH Don't eat mussels or clams you pick or dig from the seashore unless the local office of the **Alaska Department of Fish and Game** (Cook Inlet, ☎ **907/ 267-2100;** Southeast ☎ **907/465-4270;** Kodiak **907/486-1840;** Prince William Sound **907/459-7207**) indicates that the area is safe. Most of Alaska's remote beaches are not tested and so are not safe. The risk is paralytic shellfish poisoning, a fatal malady caused by a naturally occurring toxin. It causes total paralysis, including breathing. A victim may be kept alive with mouth-to-mouth respiration until medical help is obtained.

SWIMMING Ask about lake water before swimming in it. In recent years, some lakes have been infested with a bug that causes an itchy rash.

WATER Authorities advise against drinking unpurified river or lake water. Hand-held filtration devices and iodine kits are available from sporting-goods stores, but boiling is the best precaution. The danger is giardia, a bug that causes diarrhea. It may not show up until a couple of weeks after exposure and could last up to 6 weeks. If you get symptoms on getting home, tell your doctor you were exposed so you can get tested and cured.

SAFETY

I've listed a few important safety tips for traveling in Alaska, but the most important safety advice is to be cautious and use common sense. People who are hurt while visiting Alaska often are doing stupid things they wouldn't think of doing at home—like the otherwise intelligent woman from Australia a few years ago who climbed into the polar bear cage at the Alaska Zoo to get a better picture.

BEARS Being eaten by a bear is probably the least likely way for your vacation to end. Deaths from dog bites are much more common, for example. But bears are one of those deep-seated fears, and if you're spending any time in the outdoors, you should be prepared. Use common sense: If you see a bear from a car, don't get out, and if you're near the car, get in. The first rule of defense is equally simple: Don't attract bears. All food must be kept in airtight containers when you're camping (when car camping, the trunk of the vehicle will do), and be careful when you're cooking and cleaning up not to spread food odors. Never keep food in your tent. When walking through brush or thick trees, make lots of noise to avoid surprising a bear or moose—singing, loud conversation, and bells all work. Never intentionally approach a bear. At all costs, avoid coming between a bear and its cubs or a bear and food. If you see a bear, stop, wave your arms, make noise, and (if you're with others) group together so you look larger to the bear. Stand your ground to avoid enticing the bear to chase; depart only by slowly backing away, at an angle. If the bear follows, stop. Almost every time, if you stand still, the bear will turn and walk off. Once in a great while, the bear may bluff a charge; even less often, it may attack. Fall and play dead, rolling into a ball face down with your hands behind your neck. The bear should lose interest, but you have to stay still till it's gone. In rare instances, a bear may not lose interest, because it's planning to make a meal of you. Black bears are most likely to make this unlikely choice. If this happens, fight back for all you're worth. Many Alaskans carry a gun for protection in bear country, while some carry pepper spray that's available in sporting-goods stores. In either case, you have to hold back the weapon as a last resort, when the bear is quite close and in the process of an attack. If you take a gun, it had better be a big one. Even a .45-caliber handgun won't stop a bear in time if you don't get off a precise shot. A .300-Magnum rifle or 12-gauge shotgun loaded with rifled slugs is the weapon of choice.

BOATING Going out on the water is more hazardous in Alaska than in most other places, and you should only go with an experienced, licensed operator unless you really know what you're doing. The weather can be severe and unpredictable, and there's no margin for error if you fall into the water or capsize—you have only minutes to get out and get warm before hypothermia and death. A life jacket will keep you afloat, but it won't keep you alive in 40°F water.

CRIME Sadly, crime rates are not low in Alaska's major cities, although muggings are rare. Take the normal precautions you'd take at home. You're safe in daylight hours anywhere tourists commonly go, less so late at night leaving a bar. Women need to be especially careful on their own, as Alaska has a disproportionately high rate of rape. Most women I know avoid walking by themselves at night in Alaskan towns and cities, especially in wooded or out-of-the-way areas. The late-night sunlight can be deceiving—just because it's light doesn't mean it's safe. Assaults occur in big towns and small. Women should never hitchhike alone.

SUMMER DRIVING Keep your headlights on for safety on the highway. Drivers are required to pull over at the next pull-out whenever five or more cars are trailing on a two-lane highway, regardless of how fast they're going. This saves the lives of people who otherwise will try to pass. When passing a truck going the other way on a gravel highway, slow down or stop and pull as far as possible to the opposite side of the road to avoid losing your windshield to a flying rock. Always think about the path of rocks you're kicking up toward others' vehicles. Make sure you've got a good spare and jack, especially if driving a gravel highway. For remote driving, take a first-aid kit, emergency food, a tow rope, and jumper cables.

WINTER DRIVING Drivers on Alaska's highways in winter should be prepared for cold-weather emergencies far from help. Take all the items listed for rural summer driving, plus a flashlight, matches and materials to light a fire, chains, a shovel, and an ice scraper. A camp stove to make hot beverages also is a good idea. If you're driving a remote highway such as the Alaska Highway between November and April, take along gear adequate to keep you safe from the cold even if you have to wait 24 hours with a dead car at –40°F—parkas, boots, hats, mittens, blankets, and sleeping bags. Never drive a road marked "Closed" or "Unmaintained in Winter." Even on maintained rural roads, other vehicles come by rarely. All Alaska roads are icy all winter. Studded tires are a necessity—nonstudded snowtires or so-called "all-weather" tires aren't adequate. Also, never leave your car's engine stopped for more than 4 hours in extreme cold (–10°F or colder). Alaskans generally have electrical head-bolt heaters installed to keep the engine warm overnight; you'll find electrical outlets everywhere on rural highways.

TRAVELER'S INSURANCE

Travel insurance falls into three categories: (1) health and accident, (2) lost luggage, and (3) trip cancellation.

ACCIDENT Review your present policies—you may already have adequate coverage between them and what's offered by credit/charge-card companies. Many card companies insure their users in case of a travel accident, providing the transit ticket was purchased with their card. Make sure your policy provides advances in cash or transfers of funds so you won't have to dip into your precious travel funds to settle medical bills. Also, to submit a claim, you'll likely need a statement from a medical authority itemizing your costs.

LUGGAGE Many homeowner's insurance policies cover theft of luggage during travel and loss of documents—your airline ticket, for instance. Coverage is usually limited to about $500. You'll need police reports substantiating your claim.

CANCELLATION Charter flights and some accommodations and guided activities impose a fee even if a sudden cancellation was caused by delays or an unforeseen crisis. Insurance against this kind of loss may be the kind you are most likely to need when traveling in Alaska. Some travel agencies provide this coverage, and often flight insurance against a canceled trip is written into tickets paid for with credit or charge cards. Many tour operators or insurance agents provide this type of insurance.

The following companies offer various policies. Make sure to read the fine print and understand what you're buying.

Access America, 6600 W. Broad St., Richmond, VA 23230 (☎ **800/284-8300** or 804/285-3300), offers comprehensive travel insurance and assistance packages, which can include trip cancellation or interruption, emergency medical or dental care or medical transportation, baggage insurance, and missed connections. Their 24-hour hotline connects you to multilingual coordinators who can offer advice on medical, legal, and travel problems. Packages begin at $34.

Travel Guard International, 1145 Clark St., Stevens Point, WI 54481 (☎ **800/ 826-1300;** website http://www.travel-guard.com), sells packages covering trip cancellation or interruption, medical problems and transportation, and lost baggage. If you buy the policy within 7 days of booking the trip, pre-existing medical conditions are waived and children under 16 are covered free. Prices depend on coverage; a package for a trip that costs $1,500 is $82.

4 Tips for Travelers with Special Needs

FOR TRAVELERS WITH DISABILITIES   The Americans with Disabilities Act along with economic competition have sped the process of retrofitting hotels and even bed-and-breakfasts to be accessible for people with disabilities. They're often the best rooms in the house. Hotels without such facilities now are the exception; however, check when making reservations.

There are several Alaska agencies for people with disabilities. **Challenge Alaska,** P.O. Box 110065, Anchorage, AK 99511 (☎ **907/344-7399**), is a nonprofit organization dedicated to providing accessible outdoor activities. They have a skiing center on Mount Alyeska (☎ **907/783-2925**), in Girdwood, and also offer summer camping, sea kayaking, fishing, and other trips. **Access Alaska,** 3710 Woodland Dr., Suite 900, Anchorage, AK 99517 (☎ **907/248-4777** or 800/770-4488 in Alaska only; TTY/TDD 907/248-8799; fax 907/248-0639), advocates for people with disabilities and offers referrals and tour information packets. **Alaska Welcomes You! Inc.,** 7321 Branche Dr., P.O. Box 91333, Anchorage, AK 99509-1333 (☎ or TTY **800/ 349-6301** or 907/349-6301; fax 907/344-3259; website http://alaskan.com/vendors/ welcome.html), offers a variety of accessible tours in Southcentral Alaska, extended travel packages to Denali National Park and the Kenai Peninsula, and trip planning for independent travelers with special needs. Trips include rafting, boating, flightseeing, and fishing. A 4-day Denali tour is $849 per person, double occupancy. **Alaska Snail Trails,** P.O. Box 210894, Anchorage, AK 99521-0894 (☎ or TTY **800/348-4543** or 907/337-7517), operates tours to Fairbanks, Denali National Park, and Seward for people with disabilities and anyone who is interested in a slower pace of guided travel. A 10-day trip is $2,530 per person, double occupancy.

FOR SENIORS   People over age 65 get reduced admission prices to most Alaska attractions, and many accommodations have special senior rates. National parks offer free admission and special camping rates for people over 62 with a Golden Age Passport, which you can obtain at any of the parks for $10. Most towns have a senior citizens center where you'll find activities and help with any special needs. The

Native Art—Finding the Real Thing

In a gift shop in Southeast Alaska, a woman who said she was an artist's assistant was sanding a Tlingit-style carving. When I asked who made the carving, the artist said, "It's my work." At the time, that seemed like an odd way of putting it. Only later did I learn from one of the artist's former assistants that his "work" involved ordering the carvings from Southeast Asia and shipping them to Alaska, where he hired locals to pretend to be working on them in the shop. A journalist friend of mine met a boy in the alley behind a gift store in Ketchikan removing "Made in Taiwan" stickers from merchandise with a razor blade. The Federal Trade Commission recently fined an art dealer for peddling fake Native art. He was able to go on selling carvings signed by a person with a made-up, Native-sounding name along with the name of an Alaskan village. The artist was Cambodian and had spent only a few months in the village.

You may not care if the gifts and souvenirs you buy in Alaska really come from Alaska. But if you do, especially if you plan to spend a lot of money on authentic Alaska Native art, you need to take some care.

The most serious kind of counterfeit is fake Alaska Native fine art. Pieces sell for $500 or more, and the scam both defrauds the buyer and takes food off the tables of Alaska's village artists, who can't compete in price with Indonesian carvers. In 1995, *Anchorage Daily News* reporter Bruce Melzer documented that copying original Native art is a widespread practice. He found villages in Bali where hundreds of workers were turning out Eskimo masks and moose, otter, and sheep carvings from fossilized walrus ivory, whalebone, and other Alaskan materials, using designs taken from books sent from Alaska. (I am indebted to Melzer for much of the information in this essay.)

Ask some questions before you buy. Any reputable art dealer will provide you with a biography of the artist who created an expensive work. Ask specifically if that artist actually carved the piece: Some Native artists have sold their names and designs to wholesalers who produce knock-offs. Price is another tip-off: An elaborate mask is more likely to cost $3,000 than $300. Another indicator is the choice of materials: Most soapstone carvings are not made in Alaska.

A state program validates Native art and crafts with a "silver hand" label, which assures you it is a 100% Alaska Native product. But the program isn't universally used, so the absence of the label doesn't mean the work definitely isn't authentic. Other labels aren't worth much—an item could say "Alaska Made" even if only insignificant assembly work happened here. Of course, in Bush Alaska, and in some urban shops, you can buy authentic work directly from craftspeople.

For gifts that don't claim to be made by Natives but do at least purport to originate in the state, a symbol of two bears that says "Made in Alaska" validates that the item was at least substantially made here. Non-Natives produce Alaskan crafts of ceramics, wood, or fabric, but not plastic—if it's plastic, it probably was not made in Alaska. Again, price is an indicator: Like anywhere else in the U.S., the cheapest products come from Asia.

Mostly, finding something real is up to you. When Melzer interviewed dealers selling fake Alaska Native art and crafts, they said they tell customers where the work comes from if asked. But most people don't ask.

Anchorage Seniors Center (☎ 907/258-7823) offers guidance for visitors, as well as free RV parking and use of the restaurant, showers, gift shop, and fitness room; a big band plays Friday nights for dancing. **Elderhostel,** 75 Federal St., Boston, MA 02110-1941 (☎ 617/426-8056; fax 617/426-8351; website http://www.elderhostel.org), operates week-long learning vacations for groups of people 55 and older.

FOR GAY & LESBIAN TRAVELERS Anchorage and Juneau have active gay and lesbian communities. In Anchorage, **Identity Inc.** (☎ 907/258-4777) offers referrals, publishes a newsletter called *NorthView*, sponsors pot-luck dinners, and holds a gay pride picnic the last Sunday in June on the Delaney Park Strip. The **S.E. Alaska Gay/Lesbian Alliance** (☎ 907/586-4297) is a similar organization in Juneau. **Apollo Travel Agency,** 1207 W. 47th Ave., Anchorage, AK 99503 (☎ 907/561-0661), is a member of the International Gay Travel Agencies Association and can guide you to businesses, such as bed-and-breakfast accommodations and tours, that cater specifically to gays and lesbians. **Equinox Wilderness Expeditions,** 618 W. 14th Ave., Anchorage, AK 99501 (☎ 907/274-9087), offers wilderness trips ranging from 3 days to 3 weeks by canoe, kayak, rafting, or hiking, directed by noted outdoorswoman and writer Karen Jettmar. The extensive catalog of trips includes many for women or men only. A 7-day trip for lesbians to Denali National Park is $1,650 per person.

FOR STUDENTS Most museums offer free or greatly reduced admission for students and anyone under 18, although sometimes you have to ask. Make sure to bring a student identification card. There are hostels in most major towns in Alaska, mostly open in the summer only. You'll find them listed in the text for each town, and most are listed in the directory published by **Hostelling International–American Youth Hostels,** 733 15th St. NW, Suite 840, Washington, DC 20005 (☎ 202/783-6161). Membership costs $25 for adults, $10 for youths 17 and under, and $15 for those 55 and older.

Many students travel to Alaska for summer work. It's usually possible to get a job in a fish cannery in most coastal towns. Work on the slime line is hard and unpleasant, and the pay is low; but if the season is good, you can work long hours and earn considerably more than at a normal summer job. If you camp and keep your expenses low—most canneries have tent cities of summer workers nearby—you can take home decent money for your summer's work. Stay onshore, however, as offshore fish-processing ships are a truly miserable and dangerous place to work; and if the ship doesn't get any fish, you don't make any money. Don't come north expecting to make fabulous wages. The stories of college students making huge crew shares on fishing boats are legends—there are lots of experienced fishermen to take those jobs before boats hire raw hands they have to train.

Jobs are often available in the tourism industry, too. The **Alaska Department of Labor Job Service** posts job openings and advice on its website, **http://www.state.ak.us/local/akpages/LABOR/jobseek/jobseek.htm**, but does not respond to telephone inquiries.

FOR FAMILIES I researched most of this book while traveling with my wife, Barbara, 5-year-old boy, Robin, and 2-year-old girl, Julia. They made many of the best discoveries, and I've tried to include my advice for families throughout the text. I've left out places that were hostile to kids.

Alaska is a great place to take a family. The magnificent scenery is something even young children can understand and appreciate. Also, an Alaska vacation is largely spent outdoors, which is where kids like to be. Robin hadn't had enough ferry riding after we'd been doing it for weeks, and both children enjoyed camping immensely. We started camping with Julia at six months and never had a serious problem. When she realized everyone was going to sleep in the tent with her, on her level, her face lit up. The children taught the adults to slow down and find joy in new discoveries.

There are drawbacks to Alaska as a family destination. The primary one is the expense. Airlines offer insignificant discounts for children these days. Activities like flightseeing and tour-boat cruises tend to have less-than-generous children's discounts and cost too much for most families. Often bed-and-breakfasts have rooms too small for a family. Hotel rooms are expensive in Alaska. Restaurants that aren't too fancy to take the kids may be too smoky (any listed in this volume should be okay unless noted). Car camping solves many of those problems, with stops in a hotel every few days to get everyone cleaned up. But the highways in Alaska are long, and children will require a gradual approach to covering ground. You know your own family's limits. We have a family rule of never spending more than 5 hours a day in the car, which makes some Interior Alaska road trips quite long, but forces you to stop and enjoy the country.

You must be careful in choosing your itinerary and activities with children. There are the obvious things, like allowing time to play, to explore, and to rest, but also remember that children often don't enjoy activities like wildlife watching. It takes a long time to find the animals, and when you do, they're usually off in the distance—kids often don't have the visual skills to pick out the animals from the landscape. Don't overtax children with walks and hiking trips; it'll just make everyone miserable. We keep track of the longest hike we've managed without excessive whining, then try to extend that record just a little each time out. Short sea-kayaking excursions, on the other hand, are great for children who are old enough, riding in the front of a double-seat boat with a parent in back. Age limits depend on the outfitter and your child's responsibility level and ability to endure bad weather without complaining too much.

If you're flawed mortals like us, after the end of a few weeks on the road, you'll be getting on each other's nerves. We found success by leaving time for low-key kid activities, like beachcombing and playing in the park, while one grown-up would split off for a museum or special, more expensive activity. Of course, if you want to save your marriage, you'll have to be scrupulously fair about who gets to go flightseeing and who has to stay behind and change diapers, as you won't have my all-purpose excuse—research.

If you're interested in a package tour with your family, most of the companies listed below will take children. Some wilderness outfitters offer special trips for families, too (full addresses are listed below, under "Outdoor Packages"). **Alaska Wildland Adventures** (☎ 800/334-8730), listed in chapter 6, has eight trips for kids as young as 12, including a relatively inexpensive van-based camping trip. They even have a "Family Safari" for families with children ages 6 through 11 that strings together day trips in various places, including a float trip on the Kenai River and a look at an Iditarod champion's racing kennel, and finishes with 2 nights in Denali National Park. The 7-day trip costs $2,595 for adults and $2,295 for kids, exclusive of air travel to Anchorage. **Alaska Discovery** (☎ 800/586-1911), listed in chapter 6 and in the Juneau section in chapter 7, takes children as young as 10 on some of its extended Southeast Alaska sea kayaking trips, which start at $495 for 3 days and 2 nights.

5 Package Tour or Do-It-Yourself?

Hundreds of thousands of visitors come to Alaska each year on package tours, leaving virtually all their travel arrangements in the hands of a single company that takes responsibility for ushering them through the state for a single, lump-sum fee. But more and more visitors are cutting the apron strings and exploring Alaska on their own, and finding a more relaxed, spontaneous experience. There are advantages and disadvantages to each approach, and which way you choose to visit depends on how you value those pros and cons. Unfortunately, some people make the choice based on expectations that aren't valid, so it's important to know what you're getting into.

A package provides security. You'll know in advance how much everything will cost, you don't have to worry about making hotel and ground transportation reservations, you're guaranteed to see the highlights of each town you visit, and you'll have someone telling you what you're looking at. If there are weather delays or other travel problems, it's the tour company's problem, not yours. Everything happens on schedule, and you never have to touch your baggage other than to unpack when it magically shows up in your room. If you sometimes feel like you're a member of a herd on a package tour, you'll also meet new people, a big advantage if you're traveling on your own. Most passengers on these trips are retired, over age 65.

If you're short on time, packages make the most of it, often traveling at an exhausting pace. Passengers get up early and cover a lot of ground, with sights and activities scheduled solidly through the day. Stops last only long enough to get a taste of what the sight is about, not to dig in and learn about a place you're especially interested in. On a package, you'll meet few if any Alaska residents, since most tour companies hire college students from Outside to fill summer jobs. For visiting wilderness, such as Denali National Park, the quick and superficial approach can, in my opinion, spoil the whole point of going to a destination that's about an experience, not just seeing a particular object or place.

Studies by Alaska tourism experts have found that many people choose packages to avoid risks that don't really exist. Alaska still has the reputation of being an untamed frontier land—and in some sense it is, but that doesn't mean it's a dangerous or uncomfortable place to travel. Visitors who sign up for a tour to avoid having to spend the night in an igloo or use an outhouse may wish they'd been a bit more adventurous when they arrive and find that Alaska has the same facilities found in any other state. Except for tiny Bush villages that you're unlikely to visit anyway, you can find the standard American hotel room anywhere you go. The tourism infrastructure is well developed even in small towns—you're never far from help unless you want to be.

It's also possible for an independent traveler to obtain some of the predictability a package tour provides. You can reserve accommodations and activities and control your expenses by using a good travel agent experienced in Alaska travel. Some even offer fixed-price itineraries you do on your own (see "Custom Tours & Alaskan Travel Agencies" at the end of this section). But independent travelers never have the complete security of those on package tours. Once you're on the road, you'll be on your own to take care of the details, and weather delays and other cancellations confound the best-laid plans. If you can't relax and enjoy a trip knowing that could happen, then a package tour is the way to go.

LARGE TOUR COMPANIES

Three major tour and cruise ship companies dominate the Alaska package-tour market with "vertically integrated" operations that allow them to take care of everything you do while in Alaska with tight quality control. Each also offers tours as short as a couple of hours to independent travelers who want to combine their own exploring with a more structured experience. All can be booked through any travel agent.

Holland America Westours / Gray Line of Alaska. 300 Elliot Ave. West, Seattle, WA 98119. ☎ 800/628-2449.

The Holland America cruise line became the giant of Alaska tourism by buying local companies. It acquired the Gray Line and Westours tour companies to carry visitors in buses, trains, and boats, and the Westmark hotel chain to put them up for the night. Most clients arrive in the state on one of the company's ships (see chapter 5), but even within Alaska, chances are any tour you sign up for other than Princess or Alaska Sightseeing (see below) will put you on a Gray Line coach and exclusively in Westmark hotels. Descriptions of Westmark hotels are in each of the towns where they're found. The quality is not consistent—the Westmark Cape Fox in Ketchikan is among the best hotels in the state while the hotel in Skagway is below usually accepted standards. Most are adequate properties with standard American rooms. On a package, you don't spend much time in the room, as schedules generally are tightly planned and daily departures early. You'll find a description of the company's rail cars on the Anchorage–Denali–Fairbanks run in chapter 9. Gray Line coaches are first rate, especially several super-luxurious, extra-long vehicles that bend in the middle. And the company goes more places than any other. Some of its boat and tour excursions—on the Yukon River from Dawson City, or to St. Lawrence Island, for example—are entirely unique. Prices depend on a variety of factors, but in general a tour of a week to 10 days is $1,600 to $2,800 per person.

✪ **Princess Cruises and Tours.** 2815 Second Ave., Suite 400, Seattle, WA 98121-1299. ☎ **800/835-8907.**

The Princess cruise line has built its land-tour operation from the ground up instead of buying it, as Holland America did, and the result is a smaller but consistently top-quality collection of properties. The four Princess hotels—two near Denali National Park, and one each in Fairbanks and Cooper Landing, on the Kenai Peninsula—all are exceptionally good. Princess operates its own coaches and has the best rail cars on the Alaska Railroad route to Denali. Descriptions of each hostelry can be found in the appropriate chapter. Most people on the tours come to Alaska on a cruise ship, but tours are for sale separately, too. The company's network of tours is less extensive than Holland America's but covers much of the state.

Alaska Sightseeing / Cruise West. Fourth and Battery Bldg., Suite 700, Seattle, WA 98121. ☎ **800/426-7702.**

This relatively small company, started by Alaska-based tourism pioneers, offers a more intimate experience compared to the Princess and Holland America giants. The land tours are marketed primarily as add-ons to small-vessel cruises. The buses are less luxurious than the major competition. The company doesn't own its own hotels and uses the Alaska Railroad's cars on the train ride to Denali National Park.

SMALL & SPECIALTY TOURS

There seems to be an infinite number of small tour operators in Alaska. Contact the Alaska Division of Tourism, listed above, or a travel agent, for more ideas. In addition, see "Tips for Travelers with Special Needs," above.

FOR CAMPERS   Traveling in a van with only 12 adults and camping at night, **Camp Alaska Tours,** P.O. Box 872247, Wasilla, AK 99687 (☎ **800/376-9438** or 907/376-9438), offers trips lasting 6 to 22 days, with hiking, rafting, kayaking, and an opportunity to see the outdoors with a new group of outdoors-oriented friends. Prices are around $100 per day, and trips are available for families with children as young as age 10.

FOR CYCLISTS   Tours of Alaska and the Yukon Territory, with train and boat trips included, and Cannondale bikes, are offered by Anchorage-based **Alaska Bicycle**

Adventures, 2734 Iliamna Ave., Anchorage, AK 99517-1216 (☎ **800/770-7242** or 907/243-2329; fax 907/243-4985; website http://www.alaskabike.com).

FOR PHOTOGRAPHERS   In Talkeetna, **Alaska Photo Tours,** P.O. Box 141, Talkeetna, AK 99676-0141 (☎ **800/799-3051** or 907/733-3051; fax 907/ 733-3052), offers guided trips for small groups of photography enthusiasts ranging from 6 to 17 days. Everything is arranged to provide the best chance of capturing wildlife and scenery on film.

FOR RV OWNERS   Several companies offer caravans to Alaska each summer, with activities planned along the way. One long-time operator is **Point South RV Tours,** 11313 Edmonson Ave., Moreno Valley, CA 92555 (☎ **800/421-1394;** fax 909/924-3838).

FOR WOMEN   The nonprofit **Women of the Wilderness,** P.O. Box 773556, Eagle River, AK 99577 (☎ **907/688-2226,** 800/770-2226 within Alaska; fax 907/ 688-2285; e-mail akwow@alaska.net), teaches backcountry skills, empowerment, and New Age spirituality to women and girls through year-round treks and programs, including backpacking, sea kayaking, glacier travel, dog mushing, and rock climbing. A small Anchorage company, **Sourdough Sidekicks,** 4316 Upper Kegru Dr., Eagle River, AK 99577 (☎ **907/694-9694;** fax 907/694-9694), offers week-long van tours for up to eight women, designed around the interests of the participants. Trips are August through October only.

CUSTOM TOURS & ALASKAN TRAVEL AGENCIES

Any travel agency can book a trip to Alaska. Here are some good Alaska-based firms that specialize in setting up trips around the state for independent travelers and groups and creating special packages.

- **Alaska Rainforest Tours,** 369 S. Franklin St., Suite 200, Juneau, AK 99801 (☎ **907/463-3466;** fax 907/463-4453; e-mail artour@alaska.net).
- **Alaska Up Close,** P.O. Box 32666, Juneau, AK 99803 (☎ **907/789-9544;** fax 907/789-3205; website http://www. wetpage.com/upclose).
- **All Ways Travel,** 302 G St., Anchorage, AK 99501 (☎ **800/676-2946** or 907/ 276-3644; fax 907/258-2211; e-mail allways@alaska.net).
- **Eagle Custom Tours of Alaska,** 329 F St., Suite 206, Anchorage, AK 99501 (☎ **907/277-6228;** fax 907/272-7766; website http://www.arctic.net/~eagle/).
- **Viking Travel,** P.O. Box 787, Petersburg, AK 99833 (☎ **800/327-2571** or 907/772-3818; fax 907/772-3940; website http://alaska-ala-carte.com).
- **World Express Tours,** 200 W. 34th Ave., Suite 412, Anchorage, AK 99503-3969 (☎ **800/544-2235;** fax 425/828-4712; website http://worldexpresstour. com).

6 Planning Your Own Itinerary

Many visitors to Alaska feel compelled to cover the whole state, traveling to each region, and plan everything around seeing certain famous wilderness parks. By doing so, they spend a lot more time and money covering ground than is necessary. Each of Alaska's regions, by itself, has most of what you're coming to Alaska for—wildlife, mountains, glaciers, historic sites, cute little towns—and you can have a better trip touring one or two regions than spending precious time going from region to region.

The other mistake some people make is pursuing only the largest and most famous destinations. I think half the joy of traveling independently is discovering places off the beaten track where most tourists don't go. If you follow a set itinerary of places you're "supposed" to go see, you don't get that pleasure. I offer suggested itineraries here and at the beginning of regional chapters only to spark ideas. Get out and explore on your own.

In the interest of showing as much as I can about how to link the towns, these itineraries are fast paced. I recommend reducing stops and lengthening the visit to each town that especially interests you rather than trying to do any more.

If You Have 1 Week

If you have only a week, you need to choose an Alaska region to explore. If you try to cover the whole state, you'll just be moving around without doing anything.

In Southeast Alaska, try flying to Sitka, spending a day looking at the historic sights and a day on the water, meeting the sea otters, then catch the ferry on the third day for Juneau. There, take a look at the sights in town and Mendenhall Glacier, or take a 1-day hike. The next day, fly to Gustavus, spending the night at one of the charming inns there, and the following day take in Glacier Bay National Park on a boat tour, or go whale watching or sea kayaking off Point Adolphus. Another night in Gustavus, and it's time to fly home.

In Southcentral and Interior Alaska, you can fly to Anchorage and spend a day taking in the city, with a visit to the museum or zoo or a bike ride on the coastal trail. Next day, take the train to Seward and take a boat ride into Kenai Fjords National Park. Spend the night in Seward and enjoy the town and Exit Glacier the next day, perhaps taking a hike or a sea-kayak paddle, returning to Anchorage on the train that evening. Next morning, fly to Fairbanks and rent a car, spending the first day exploring the city and the next driving out into the country to soak at Chena Hot Springs Resort. The next day, go horseback riding, hiking, or rafting at the resort. The next day, it's time to drive back to Fairbanks and catch a plane home.

If You Have 2 Weeks

Starting in Southeast Alaska, take the ferry from Bellingham or Prince Rupert or fly to Ketchikan, spend at least a full day exploring there, and another day to get out on the water, fishing or visiting Misty Fjords National Monument. Go north on the ferry, stopping over for a day in Juneau, Wrangell, or Petersburg on the way to Skagway. Take a full day to see the gold-rush history, perhaps riding the Yukon and White Pass Route railway or going for a hike, then rent a car and retrace the route of the Klondike gold rush for the 435 miles to Dawson City. Depending on your interest, you may want 2 full days there before continuing west to the little-visited but historic little town of Eagle. The following day, continue toward Haines, a 2-day drive. You'll want to spend at least 1 full day in Haines to see the eagles and the quaint town, and maybe take a flightseeing trip to Glacier Bay National Park. Then return the car in Haines or take it back on the ferry to Skagway, then fly home.

Starting in Southcentral Alaska, fly to Anchorage, spend 2 days exploring the city, perhaps taking a hike in the Chugach Mountains or a flightseeing trip to Denali National Park on a classic DC-3. Then rent a car and drive down the Kenai Peninsula, stopping in Cooper Landing or Soldotna for king salmon fishing for a day, or continuing all the way to Homer, a 235-mile drive from Anchorage. In Homer, spend the next day visiting galleries and then take the boat to the waterside community of Halibut Cove to have dinner and spend the night. The next day, go sea kayaking or wildlife watching on the water, or take a hike in Kachemak Bay State Park. The following day, return to Homer and spend another day there, going for a halibut-fishing trip, or drive back up the highway and stop in Girdwood or Anchorage for the night. Next day, take the train to Whittier, and take a tour-boat cruise from there to see the glaciers of Prince William Sound, returning that evening to Anchorage. A day of rest or activities in Anchorage is in order. The next day, take the train to Denali National Park, spending the afternoon with a rafting excursion or other activities at the park entrance. Next day, get up early for a bus trip into the park to see wildlife and go for a walk on the tundra. The next day, catch the train to Fairbanks and spend the following day sightseeing. Then fly back to Anchorage and fly home.

If You Have 3 Weeks

Use the 2-week itinerary for **Southeast Alaska** but add 2 days in Petersburg, 2 days in Juneau, and 3 days in Glacier Bay National Park and Gustavus.

Use the 2-week itinerary for **Southcentral Alaska** and add the 1-week Southeast itinerary. Or amend the 2-week itinerary by driving to Denali, then spend an additional 2 days exploring the Interior Highways around Fairbanks or relaxing at Chena Hot Springs Resort. Then drive the Richardson Highway to Valdez, spend the night there, and take the ferry to Cordova, visiting the Copper River Delta and Childs Glacier before flying back to Valdez, driving to Anchorage, and catching the flight home the next day.

Or, in either case, you can add a 2- or 3-day excursion to the Bush, flying to Kotzebue, taking the Native culture tour there, then flying to Nome and exploring the tundra roads and gold-rush historic sights, and returning to Anchorage on the third or fourth day.

If You Have 6 Weeks

You have time to drive to Alaska or to ride up on the ferry, exploring each little Southeast Alaska town, then seeing each of the other regions in depth.

A WINTER ITINERARY   Arrive in Anchorage in February, during the Fur Rendezvous sled-dog races, or in March, to see the start of the Iditarod. If you're a Nordic skier, enjoy Kincaid Park. After checking on avalanche conditions, rent a car and make a day trip into Chugach State Park or to Turnagain Pass, south of Anchorage, or ski into one of many public cabins in Chugach National Forest. Alpine or Nordic skiers will want to spend at least a few days in Girdwood at the Alyeska Resort. Besides exceptional skiing, this is a good place for a sled-dog ride, and there are others at each stop on the itinerary. After Girdwood, catch the train from Anchorage to Fairbanks, spending the night in Fairbanks and catching the sled-dog races or ice-carving festivals in February or March. The following day, take the van out to the Chena Hot Springs Resort, for outdoor explorations, swimming, and aurora watching, returning and flying out of Fairbanks when your trip is over.

7 Getting There & Getting Around

BY PLANE   Anchorage is the main entry hub for Alaska. It's served by several major carriers to the rest of the United States, primarily through Seattle, including **United Airlines** (☎ **800/241-6522**), **Northwest Airlines** (☎ 800/225-2525), **Delta Air Lines** (☎ 800/221-1212), and **Alaska Airlines** (☎ 800/426-0333; TDD 800/682-2221). There usually is a charter or seat wholesaler in operation with below-market deals on economy seats. Use a travel agent to get the best price, as the route is highly competitive and prices are volatile. Most airlines also continue to Fairbanks. **Alaska Airlines** is the only jet carrier to Southeast Alaska and most of Alaska's small towns, and connects Anchorage to the Russian Far East. Alaska

Alaska by the Numbers

This chart shows some comparative indicators for 17 of Alaska's most popular destinations. The first column is the name of the destination; next is population. The third column is the season when there's enough going on and weather is suitable for a good visit (including for winter sports). The "Transportation" column shows ways of getting to each destination. The fifth column is average annual precipitation, in water equivalent (in inches), and the final column is average annual snowfall (in inches).

Place	Population	Season	Transportation	Precip.	Snow
Anchorage	240,258	May–Sept/ Feb–Mar	Road, air, rail	15.4	69
Barrow	3,986	June–Aug	Air	4.7	28
Denali National Park	35	June–Sept	Road, rail	15.0	54.8
Fairbanks	33,281	May–Sept/ Feb–Mar	Road, air, rail	10.4	68
Glacier Bay National Park	258	May–Sept	Air	53.9	70.2
Homer	4,349	May–Sept	Road, air, ferry	24.9	58
Juneau	29,078	May–Sept	Air, ferry	52.9	100
Kenai	6,535	May–Oct	Road, air	18.9	59.3
Ketchikan	8,478	May–Sept	Air, ferry	155.2	37
Kodiak	7,229	May–Sept	Air, ferry	74.3	80
Kotzebue	3,004	June–Aug	Air	9.0	47.6
Nome	4,184	June–Aug/ March	Air	15.6	56
Petersburg	3,419	May–Sept	Air, ferry	105.8	102
Seward	2,732	May–Sept	Road, rail, ferry, air	67.7	79.9
Sitka	9,052	May–Sept/ Nov	Air, ferry	86.8	40.7
Skagway	751	May–Sept	Road, ferry, air	23.0	35.7
Valdez	4,713	May–Sept/ Mar	Road, air, ferry	61.5	320

Airlines also has arrangements with commuter lines that fan out from its network to smaller communities.

To fly to the smallest villages, or to fly between some small towns without returning to a hub, you take a **Bush plane.** The legendary Alaska Bush pilot is alive and well, connecting Alaska's villages by small plane and flying air-taxi routes to fishing sites, lodges, remote cabins, or just about anywhere else you might want to go.

An authentic Alaskan adventure is to be had from many small towns by taking a **Bush mail plane** round-trip to a village and back. The ticket price is generally a fraction of the cost of a flightseeing trip, and you'll have at least a brief chance to look around a Native village. Cordova, Kodiak, Nome, Kotzebue, Barrow, and Fairbanks are places from which you can do this.

BY SHIP   The most popular way to get to Alaska is on a **cruise ship.** Chapter 5, "Cruising Alaska's Coast," provides an in-depth look at coming to the state that way.

The **Alaska Marine Highway System,** P.O. Box 25535, Juneau, AK 99802-5535 (☎ **800/642-0066;** TDD 800/764-3779; fax 907/277-4829; website http:// www.dot.state.ak.us/external/amhs/home.html), is the lowest-cost way to get to Alaska. The big blue, white, and gold ferries ply the Inside Passage from Bellingham, Washington, and Prince Rupert, B.C., to the towns of Southeast Alaska, with road links to the rest of the state at Haines and Skagway. For a complete discussion of using the ferries in Southeast, see chapter 7, "Southeast Alaska." Smaller ferries also connect towns in Prince William Sound and the Kenai Peninsula, in Southcentral Alaska, to Kodiak Island and the Aleutian Archipelago. I've described that service in the sections on individual towns served.

BY RAIL   You can't get to Alaska by train, but you can get close. **Amtrak** (☎ **800/ 872-7245**) runs daily from Seattle to Vancouver, B.C., with stops in Bellingham, Washington, where you can catch the Alaska ferry north at a dock a short walk from the depot. Or you can get to the ferry dock in Prince Rupert, B.C., which has more frequent sailings, with connections on **Via Rail Canada** (☎ **800/561-3949**) and **B.C. Rail** (☎ **800/663-8238**). Within Alaska, you can travel the **Alaska Railroad** (☎ **800/544-0552**) from Seward, on Resurrection Bay in Southcentral Alaska, north to Anchorage, in summer only; and from Anchorage north to Denali National Park and Fairbanks year-round. For a full description of the Alaska Railroad's service, see chapter 9, "Denali National Park: Wilderness by Bus," and the section on Seward in chapter 8, "Southcentral Alaska."

BY CAR OR RV   Driving to Alaska is a great adventure, but it requires thousands of miles on the road, and you have to be ready to spend plenty of time. Anchorage is almost 2,500 miles from Seattle by car, 3,700 miles from Los Angeles, and 4,650 miles from New York City. Some of the **Alaska Highway** is dull, but there are spectacular sections of the 1,400-mile route, too, and few experiences give you a better feel for the size and personality of Alaska. Putting your car on the ferry cuts the length of the trip considerably but raises the cost. Details on the Alaska section of the Alaska Highway, and other highways, are contained in chapter 10, "The Alaskan Interior." *The Milepost,* published by **Vernon Publications,** 300 Northrup Way, Suite 200, Bellevue, WA 98009 (☎ **800/726-4707**), contains mile-by-mile logs of all Alaska highways and approaches, but its commercial listings are sold as advertisements and thus are not objective. Inexpensive road maps also are widely available.

Renting a car in Alaska is the easiest way to see the Interior and Southcentral part of the state. All major car-rental companies are represented in Anchorage (see listing under "Automobile Rentals" in the "Fast Facts" section, below). In smaller cities and towns, you can usually rent from one of the majors or from a smaller company—individual town listings provide details on which firms are in each town. Base rates for major rental companies are in the range of $55 a day for a midsize car. You can save money by using a travel agent, reserving far in advance, renting by the week, or using a down-market franchise or independent company that rents older cars. One-way rentals between Alaska towns are an attractive way to travel, but you generally pay steep drop-off charges, so a more popular plan is to fly into and out of

Anchorage and use it as a base to pick up and return the car. There are two popular circle routes from Anchorage: to Fairbanks on the Parks Highway and back on the Richardson and Glenn Highways, or to Valdez by ferry from Whittier and back on another part of the Richardson Highway and the Glenn Highway.

Families will enjoy traveling by rented motorhome RV. Rentals don't really save much money over traveling with a rental car and renting hotel rooms, as a week's rental in the high season runs around $130–$200 a day, plus a lot of gas. But if you don't mind driving that huge beast, it's a great way to see the country while saving you from reserving everything far in advance and schlepping in and out of hotels or setting up tents. I've listed two major rental agencies in the Anchorage section of chapter 8.

FAST FACTS: Alaska

American Express   There are five American Express offices in Alaska: at 5011 Jewel Lake Rd., Suite 104, Anchorage, AK 99502 (☎ **907/266-6600**); 11409 Business Blvd., Suite 4, Eagle River, AK 99577 (☎ **907/694-2169**); 202 Center St., Suite 103, Kodiak, AK 99615 (☎ **907/486-6084**); 8745 Glacier Hwy., Suite 328, Juneau, AK 99801 (☎ **907/789-0999**); and at Front Street and Federal Way (P.O. Box 1769), Nome, AK 99762 (☎ **907/443-2211**).

Area Code   All of Alaska is in area code **907.** In the Yukon Territory, the area code is **867.** When placing a toll call within the state, you must dial 1, the area code, and the number. See "Telephone," below, for important tips.

Automobile Rentals   All the major car rental companies operate in Alaska. For reservations and information, call **Alamo** (☎ **800/327-9633**), **Avis** (☎ **800/831-2847**), **Budget** (☎ **800/527-0700**), **Dollar Rent a Car** (☎ **800/800-4000**), **Hertz** (☎ **800/654-3131**), and **National** (☎ **800/227-7368**). In smaller towns not serviced by one of the majors, cars may be rented from smaller operators. See individual town listings for information.

Banks & ATM Networks   Bank of America and Key Bank have branches in Alaska. There are Alaska-based banks in most towns, as noted in the listings for each. Automatic-teller machines are widely available, except in tiny towns. They generally are connected to the Plus and Cirrus networks, as well as other networks.

Business Hours   In the larger cities, major grocery stores are open 24 hours a day and carry a wide range of products in addition to food. At a minimum, **stores** are open Monday through Friday from 10am to 6pm, on Saturday afternoon, and often are closed on Sunday, but many are open much longer hours, especially in summer. **Banks** may close an hour earlier and, if open on Saturday, usually are open only in the morning. Under state law, **bars** don't have to close until 5am, but many communities have an earlier closing, generally around 2am.

Cellular Phone Coverage   Most towns have cellular coverage, including in some remote areas where it is used for backcountry safety. Your cell phone provider should be able to give you a "Roaming Guide" detailing coverage and charges.

Emergencies   Generally, you can call **911** for medical, police, or fire emergencies. On remote highways, there sometimes are gaps in 911 coverage. A widely available brochure called **"Help Along the Way"** provides emergency phone numbers on most highways and the location of emergency phone boxes. It contains a lot of other useful information for motorists, too. You can write for a free copy from the state Section of Community Health and Emergency Medical Services,

P.O. Box 110616, Juneau, AK 99811-0616. Dialing 0 will generally get an operator, who can connect you to emergency services. CB channels 9 and 11 are monitored for emergencies on most highways, as are channels 14 and 19 in some areas.

Internet Connection   Major networks have nodes in Anchorage and Fairbanks, and most smaller towns are connected by **Alaskanet,** operated by AT&T Alascom (☎ **800/252-7266**). Access numbers are listed in local phone books. I've found the service unreliable.

Liquor Laws   The minimum drinking age in Alaska is 21. Some rural communities have laws prohibiting the importation and possession of alcohol (this is known as being "dry") or only the sale but not possession of alcohol (known as being "damp"). Generally, these are Bush communities off the road network. (Urban areas are all "wet.") Check the listings for the towns you'll visit for details. If in doubt, ask, as bootlegging is a serious crime.

Maps   For driving maps, see "Getting There & Getting Around," earlier in this chapter. The **Alaska Public Lands Information Centers** have maps with outdoor information; for campers, their free map showing all the public campgrounds in the state is invaluable. For outdoor trips, the best trail maps are published by **Trails Illustrated,** P.O. Box 4357, Evergreen, CO 80437-4357 (☎ **800/962-1643** or 303/670-3457; fax 303/670-3644; website http://www.colorado.com/trails). They're sold in park visitor centers, too. The maps are printed on plastic, so they don't get spoiled by rain; however, they don't cover the whole state. **Official topographic maps** from the U.S. Geological Survey are sold at the public lands centers or directly from USGS-ESIC, 4230 University Dr., Anchorage, AK 99508 (☎ **907/786-7011**). *The Alaska Atlas and Gazetteer,* published by DeLorme Mapping, 2 DeLorme Dr., Yarmouth, ME 04096 (☎ **207/846-7000**), contains topographical maps of the entire state, most at 1:300,000 scale. It's widely available in Alaska.

Newspapers & Magazines   The state's dominant newspaper is the *Anchorage Daily News;* it's available everywhere but not easy to find in Southeast Alaska. Seattle newspapers and *USA Today* are often available, and in Anchorage you can get virtually any newspaper. *Alaska* magazine is the largest monthly; it's a general-interest popular magazine with features on the state and the outdoors.

Taxes   There is no state sales tax, but most local governments have a sales tax and a bed tax on accommodations. The tax rates are listed in each town section under "Fast Facts" and "Where to Stay."

Telephone   Making toll calls can be a headache for visitors. Before you leave for Alaska, contact your long-distance company for instructions on how to use your phone card and charges. AT&T calling cards should work, but you may not be able to use some other carriers. One solution is to bring one of the privately issued, by-the-minute cards. You may find a better deal if you buy before you leave home. (For further information, see "Fast Facts: For the Foreign Traveler" in chapter 4.)

Time Zone   Although the state naturally spans five time zones, in the 1980s, Alaska's central time zone was stretched so almost the entire state would lie all in one zone, known as Alaska time. It's one hour earlier than the U.S. West Coast's Pacific time. Crossing over the border from Alaska to Canada adds an hour. As with almost everywhere else in the U.S., daylight saving time is in effect from 1am on the first Sunday in April (turn your clocks ahead one hour) until 2am on the last Sunday in October (turn 'em back again).

For Foreign Visitors 4

This chapter provides some specifics about getting to the United States as economically and effortlessly as possible, and also gives some helpful information about how things are done in Alaska—from receiving mail to making a local or long-distance telephone call.

1 Preparing for Your Trip

ENTRY REQUIREMENTS

DOCUMENT REGULATIONS   Canadian citizens may enter the U.S. without visas, but they must carry proof of Canadian residence.

As of September 1, 1996, the following countries are included in the U.S. Visa Waiver Pilot Program: Andorra, Argentina, Australia, Austria, Belgium, Brunei, Denmark, Finland, France, Germany, Iceland, Ireland, Italy, Japan, Liechtenstein, Luxembourg, Monaco, the Netherlands, New Zealand, Norway, San Marino, Spain, Sweden, Switzerland, and the United Kingdom. Citizens of these countries, traveling with valid passports, may not need a visa for fewer than 90 days of holiday or business travel to the United States, provided that they hold a round-trip or return ticket and enter on an airline or cruise line participating in the visa-waiver program. (Note that citizens of these visa-exempt countries who first enter the United States may then visit Mexico, Canada, Bermuda, and/or the Caribbean Islands and then reenter the United States, by any mode of transportation, without needing a visa. Further information is available from any U.S. embassy or consulate.)

Citizens of countries other than those stipulated above must have a valid passport, with an expiration date at least 6 months later than the scheduled end of the visit to the United States, and a tourist visa, available without charge from the nearest U.S. consulate. Applicants for visitor visas must submit a completed application form (either in person or by mail) and a 1¹/₂-inch-square photo. The provisions of the Immigration and Nationality Act operate under the assumption that every visa applicant intends to stay in the U.S. *forever,* so you may be asked to show that: (1) you're entering the U.S. for business, pleasure, or medical treatment; (2) you plan to remain for a specific, limited period; and (3) you have a residence outside the U.S., as well as other "binding ties" (social, family, economic, or professional) that will insure your return abroad at the end of your visit. Round-trip airline tickets, hotel reservations, and other similar documentation should cover most of it.

It all sounds more complicated than it is. Usually you can obtain a visa at once or within 24 hours, but it may take longer during the summer rush from June to August. If you cannot go in person, contact the nearest U.S. embassy or consulate for directions on applying by mail. Your travel agent or airline office may also be able to provide you with visa applications and instructions. The U.S. consulate or embassy that issues your visa will determine whether you will be issued a multiple- or single-entry visa, and any restrictions regarding the length of your stay.

MEDICAL REQUIREMENTS   No inoculations are needed to enter the United States unless you're coming from, or have stopped over in, areas known to be suffering from epidemics, especially cholera or yellow fever.

If you have a disease requiring treatment with medications containing narcotics or drugs requiring a syringe, carry a valid signed prescription from your physician to allay any suspicions that you're smuggling drugs.

CUSTOMS REQUIREMENTS   Every adult visitor may bring in free of duty: 1 liter of wine or hard liquor; 200 cigarettes *or* 100 cigars (but no cigars from Cuba) *or* 3 pounds of tobacco; and $100 worth of gifts. These exemptions are offered to travelers who spend at least 72 hours in the United States and who have not claimed them within the preceding 6 months. Visitors are required to declare any meats, fruits, vegetables, plants, seeds, animals, and plant and animal products. You may bring in some fruits, vegetables, and plants without advance permission, provided they're declared, inspected, and found free of pests. Regulations prohibit you from bringing in fresh, dried, or canned meats and meat products from most foreign countries, though commercially canned meat is allowed if the inspector can determine that the meat was cooked in the can after it was sealed. (For more information, check the U.S. Department of Agriculture's Animal and Plant Health Inspection Service website at **http://www.aphis.usda.gov/oa/travel.html**.) Foreign tourists may bring in or take out up to $10,000 in U.S. or foreign currency with no formalities; larger sums must be declared to Customs on entering or leaving.

INSURANCE

There is no national health-care system in the United States. Because the cost of medical care is extremely high, I strongly advise every traveler to secure health insurance coverage before setting out. You may want to take out a comprehensive travel policy that covers (for a relatively low premium) sickness or injury costs (medical, surgical, and hospital); loss or theft of your baggage; trip-cancellation costs; guarantee of bail in case you are arrested; and costs associated with accidents, repatriation, or death. Such packages (for example, "Europe Assistance" in Europe) are sold by automobile clubs at attractive rates, as well as by insurance companies and travel agencies.

MONEY

CURRENCY & EXCHANGE   The U.S. monetary system has a decimal base: one American **dollar** ($1) = 100 **cents** (100¢).

Dollar bills commonly come in $1 ("a buck"), $5, $10, $20, $50, and $100 denominations (the last two are not welcome when paying for small purchases and are not accepted in taxis). There are also $2 bills (seldom encountered).

There are six denominations of coins: 1¢ (one cent, or a "penny"), 5¢ (five cents, or a "nickel"), 10¢ (ten cents, or a "dime"), 25¢ (twenty-five cents, or a "quarter"), 50¢ (fifty cents, or a "half dollar"), and the rare $1 piece.

Note: The "foreign-exchange bureaus" so common in Europe are rare even at airports in the United States and nonexistent outside major cities. Try to avoid having to change foreign money, or traveler's checks not denominated in U.S. dollars, at a small-town bank, or even a branch bank in a big city.

TRAVELER'S CHECKS   Traveler's checks denominated in U.S. dollars are readily accepted at most hotels, motels, restaurants, and large stores, but the best place to change traveler's checks is at a bank. Do not bring traveler's checks denominated in other currencies.

CREDIT CARDS   The method of payment most widely used is credit cards: Visa (BarclayCard in Britain), MasterCard (Eurocard in Europe, Access in Britain, Chargex in Canada), American Express, Diners Club, Discover, and Carte Blanche. You can save yourself trouble by using "plastic money" rather than cash or traveler's checks in most hotels, motels, restaurants, and retail stores (a growing number of food and liquor stores now accept credit cards). You must have a credit card to rent a car. It can also be used as proof of identity (it often carries more weight than a passport) or as a "cash card," enabling you to draw money from banks and automatic-teller machines (ATMs) that accept it.

SAFETY

GENERAL   While tourist areas are generally safe, U.S. urban areas tend to be less safe than those in Europe or Japan. Visitors should always stay alert. This is particularly true in large U.S. cities. It is wise to ask the city's or area's tourist office if you're in doubt about which neighborhoods are safe.

Remember that hotels are open to the public, and in a large hotel, security may not be able to screen everyone entering. Always lock your room door—don't assume that once inside your hotel, you are automatically safe and no longer need to be aware of your surroundings.

In Alaska, you still must be careful. Advice is provided in the section on safety in chapter 3. As a general rule, the smaller the town you are in, the safer you are.

DRIVING   Safety from crime while driving is particularly important on U.S. highways before you reach Alaska. Question your rental agency about personal safety or ask for a brochure of traveler safety tips when you pick up your car. Obtain from the agency written directions, or a map with the route marked in red, to show you how to get to your destination. If possible, arrive and depart during daylight hours.

Alaska, thankfully, lags behind the rest of the States in highway crime, and such incidents as carjackings are still rare enough in the state to make front-page news. On rural two-lane roads without many cars, there are unlikely to be many predators on the prowl for tourists to rob. Even if you have that fear, you will need help from another driver in case of a major breakdown, as the distances between settlements can be large. On the other hand, sexual assault is more prevalent in Alaska than in other parts of the country, and women traveling alone must use extra caution.

2 Getting To & Around the U.S.

Travelers from overseas can take advantage of the **APEX (advance-purchase excursion) fares** offered by the major U.S. and European carriers.

Some large airlines (for example, American Airlines, Delta, Northwest, TWA, and United) offer travelers on their transatlantic and transpacific flights special discount tickets under the name **Visit USA,** allowing travel between any U.S. destinations at minimum rates. They are not on sale in the U.S.; they must be purchased before you leave your foreign point of departure. This system is the best, easiest, and fastest way to see the United States at low cost. You should obtain information well in advance from your travel agent or the office of the airline concerned, since the conditions attached to these discount tickets can be changed without advance notice.

The visitor arriving by air, no matter what the port of entry, should cultivate patience and resignation before setting foot on U.S. soil. Getting through Immigration control may take as long as 2 hours on some days, especially summer weekends. Add the time it takes to clear Customs, and you'll see that you should make very generous allowance for delay in planning connections between international and domestic flights—an average of 2 to 3 hours at least.

In contrast, travelers arriving by car or by rail from Canada will find border-crossing formalities streamlined to the vanishing point. And air travelers from Canada, Bermuda, and some places in the Caribbean can sometimes go through Customs and Immigration at the point of departure, which is much quicker and less painful.

The United States is a nation of cars, and the most cost-effective, convenient, and comfortable way to travel through the country is by driving. The Interstate highway system connects cities and towns all over the country, and in addition to these high-speed, limited-access roadways, there's an extensive network of federal, state, and local highways and roads. Another convenience of traveling by car is the easy access to inexpensive motels at Interstate-highway off-ramps. Such motels are almost always less expensive than hotels and motels in downtown areas.

For further information about travel to and around Alaska, see "Getting There & Getting Around" in chapter 3.

FAST FACTS: For the Foreign Traveler

Accommodations   It's always a good idea to make hotel reservations as soon as you know your trip dates. Reservations usually require a deposit of 1 night's payment. In the Lower 48, major downtown hotels, which cater primarily to business travelers, commonly offer weekend discounts of as much as 50% to entice vacationers to fill up the empty hotel rooms. However, resorts and hotels near tourist attractions tend to have higher rates on weekends.

Throughout Alaska, hotels are particularly busy during the summer months and book up in advance, especially on holiday weekends. If you don't have a reservation, it's best to look for a room in midafternoon. If you wait until later in the evening, you run the risk that hotels will already be filled.

Automobile Organizations   Auto clubs will supply maps, suggested routes, guidebooks, accident and bail-bond insurance, and emergency road service. The major auto club in the United States, with 955 offices nationwide, is the **American Automobile Association (AAA).** Members of some foreign auto clubs have reciprocal arrangements with the AAA and enjoy its services at no charge. If you belong to an auto club in your home country, inquire about AAA reciprocity before you leave. The AAA can provide you with an **International Driving Permit** validating your foreign license. You may be able to join the AAA even if you aren't a member of a reciprocal club. To inquire, call ☎ **800/AAA-HELP.** In addition, some automobile-rental agencies now provide these services, so you should inquire about their availability when you rent your car.

Automobile Rentals   To rent a car, you need a major credit card and a valid driver's license. Sometimes a passport or an international driver's license is also required if your driver's license is in a language other than English. You usually need to be at least 25, although some companies do rent to younger people but may add a daily surcharge. Be sure to return your car with the same amount of gasoline you started out with, as rental companies charge excessive prices for gas. For phone numbers of the major rental companies, see "Automobile Rentals" in the "Fast Facts" section of chapter 3.

Business Hours   See "Fast Facts: Alaska" in chapter 3.

Electricity   The United States uses 110–120 volts, 60 cycles, compared to 220–240 volts, 50 cycles, as in most of Europe. In addition to a 110-volt transformer, small appliances of non-American manufacture, such as hairdryers or shavers, will require a plug adapter with two flat, parallel pins.

Emergencies   Call **911** to report a fire, to call the police, or to get an ambulance. This is a toll-free call (no coins are required at a public telephone).

Check the local directory to find an office of the **Traveler's Aid Society,** a nationwide nonprofit social-service organization geared to helping travelers in difficult straits. Their services might include reuniting families separated while traveling, providing food and/or shelter to people stranded without cash, or even providing emotional counseling. If you're in trouble, seek them out.

Mail   If you want to receive mail on your vacation and you aren't sure of your address, your mail can be sent to you, in your name, **c/o General Delivery** (Poste Restante) at the main post office of the city or region where you expect to be. The addressee must pick it up in person and produce proof of identity (driver's license, credit card, passport, and so on).

Domestic **postage rates** are 23¢ for a postcard and 32¢ for a letter. Check with any local post office for current international postage rates to your home country.

Generally found at intersections, **mailboxes** are blue with a red-and-white stripe and carry the inscription U.S. MAIL. If your mail is addressed to a U.S. destination, don't forget to add the five-figure **postal code,** or ZIP (Zone Improvement Plan) code, after the two-letter abbreviation of the state to which the mail is addressed (AK for Alaska, CA for California, and so on).

Taxes   In the United States, there is no VAT (value-added tax) or other indirect tax at the national level. Every state, and each city in it, is allowed to levy its own local tax on all purchases (including hotel and restaurant checks and airline tickets) and services. Taxes are already included in the price of certain services, such as public transportation, cab fares, telephone calls, and gasoline.

There is no state sales tax in Alaska, but many communities have imposed their own sales and bed taxes.

Telephone, Telegraph & Fax   The telephone system in the United States is run by private corporations, so rates, especially for long-distance service and operator-assisted calls, can vary widely—even on calls made from public telephones. Local calls usually cost 25¢.

Generally, hotel surcharges on long-distance and local calls are astronomical. You're usually better off using a **public pay telephone.** Outside metropolitan areas, public telephones are hard to find. Stores and gas stations are your best bet.

Most **long-distance and international calls** can be dialed directly from any phone. **For calls to Canada and other parts of the United States,** dial 1 followed by the area code and the seven-digit number. **For international calls,** dial the international access code (011) followed by the country code (Australia, 61; Republic of Ireland, 353; New Zealand, 64; United Kingdom, 44; codes for other counties can usually be found in the "White Pages" of the telephone directory), city code, and the telephone number of the person you wish to call. **To call the U.S. from another country,** dial the international access code of that country, then the country code (**1**), then the three-digit area code and seven-digit phone number.

Note that all calls to area code 800 are toll free. However, calls to numbers in area codes 700 and 900 (chat lines, bulletin boards, dating services, and so on) can be very expensive—usually a charge of 95¢ to $3 or more per minute, and they sometimes have minimum charges that can run as high as $15 or more.

For **reversed-charge (collect) calls** and for **person-to-person calls,** dial 0 (zero, not the letter "O") followed by the area code and number you want; an operator will then come on the line, and you should specify what you want. If your operator-assisted call is international, ask for the overseas operator.

For **local directory assistance** ("information"), dial 411; for **long-distance information,** dial 1, then the area code for the state you want to call, then 555-1212.

Like the telephone system, **telegraph** services are provided by private corporations like ITT, MCI, and, above all, Western Union. You can bring your telegram in to the nearest Western Union office (there are hundreds across the country) or dictate it over the phone (☎ **800/325-6000**). You can also telegraph money, or have it telegraphed to you, very quickly over the Western Union system. (Note, however, that this service can be very expensive—the service charge can run as high as 15% to 25% of the amount sent.)

If you need to send a fax, most shops that make photocopies offer **fax** service too.

Time   The United States is divided into six time zones. From east to west these are eastern standard time (EST), central standard time (CST), mountain standard time (MST), Pacific standard time (PST), **Alaska standard time (AST),** and Hawaii standard time (HST). Always keep changing time zones in your mind if you are traveling (or even telephoning) long distances in the U.S. For example, noon in Anchorage (AST) is 1pm in Seattle (PST), 2pm in Phoenix (MST), 3pm in Chicago (CST), 4pm in New York City (EST), and 11am in Honolulu (HST). **Daylight saving time** is in effect from 1am on the first Sunday in April until 2am on the last Sunday in October, except in Arizona, Hawaii, part of Indiana, and Puerto Rico.

Tipping   This is part of the American way of life, on the principle that you must expect to pay for any service you get (many service personnel receive little direct salary and must depend on tips for their income). Here are some rules of thumb:

In **hotels,** tip bellhops $1 per piece of luggage and tip the chamber staff $1 per day. Tip the doorman or concierge only if he or she has provided you with some specific service (for example, calling a cab or obtaining hard-to-get theater tickets).

In **restaurants, bars, and nightclubs,** tip the service staff 15% of the check, tip bartenders 10% to 15%, tip checkroom attendants $1 per garment, and tip valet-parking attendants $1 per vehicle. Tip the doorman only if he has provided you with some specific service (such as calling a cab for you). Tipping is not expected in cafeterias and fast-food restaurants.

Tip **cab drivers** 15% of the fare.

As for **other service personnel,** tip redcaps at airports or railroad stations $1 per piece of luggage and tip hairdressers and barbers 15% to 20%.

Tipping gas-station attendants and ushers in cinemas, movies, and theaters is not expected.

Toilets   Foreign visitors often complain that public toilets (or "rest rooms") are hard to find in most U.S. cities. True, there are none on the streets, but visitors can usually find one in a bar, restaurant, hotel, museum, department store, or service station—and it will probably be clean (although service-station rest rooms sometimes leave much to be desired). Note, however, that a growing number of restaurants and bars display a notice saying that rest rooms are for the use of patrons only. You can ignore this sign or, better yet, avoid arguments by paying for a cup of coffee or a soft drink, which will qualify you as a patron. The cleanliness and safety of toilets at public transportation depots is open to question. Some public places are equipped with pay toilets, which require you to insert one or more coins into a slot on the door before it will open. In rest rooms with attendants, leaving at least a 25¢ tip is customary.

Cruising Alaska's Coast 5

Sometime in the early 1930s, while on steamship passage from Seattle to Yokohama, Algonquin Round-Tabler and well-known rotund wit Alexander Woollcott was discussing the problems of world travel with his dining room steward, who brought to his attention the international dateline and "the rather high-handed decision to have no Thursday at all that week." Woollcott sat and mused, mock-bereft at the loss, staring out his porthole at the string of islands passing by as his ship left North American waters. "Ah, well," he murmured, "ah, well, I still have my Aleutians."

And here we are in 1998. The cruise lines haven't as yet seen fit to schedule trips among those far-flung islands, but they have managed to make Alaska into the top cruise destination in North America, with half a million passengers cruising the state's waters annually. The reason for this popularity is fairly simple—Alaska, one of the nation's last great frontiers, retains much of its natural scenic beauty. Wildlife and wilderness abound along its breathtaking coastline and are readily witnessed from the comfort of a deck chair or observation lounge. Snowcapped peaks and immense glaciers, islands cloaked in emerald rain forest, fjords where eagles soar and bear feed at the waterline, milky-green waters strewn with icebergs, silver seas with whales breaching in the distance—these are among the awe-inspiring sights the state holds in store.

1 Selecting the Right Cruise

Cruising experiences vary widely depending on the type of ship selected. There are casual and elegant cruises; learning cruises where you attend lectures to learn about the art, culture, and wildlife of the region you're visiting; adventure-oriented cruises where hiking, birding, or exploring in remote areas is the order of the day; and luxury cruises where gourmet dining, gambling, and other entertainment compete with the landscape for attention.

When it comes time to choose a particular cruise, start by asking yourself and the cruise lines a few pertinent questions—such as those we've posed below—to help you narrow the field. Once you've got your short-list ready, you'll want to get in touch with a travel agent. (You could try booking direct with the lines, but I wouldn't recommend it, as an agent will be more attuned to any good deals that are available—plus, many discounts are available *only* through travel agents, and some lines won't book their cruises any other way.)

You may want to find an agent who is a member of the National Association of Cruise Only Agents (NACOA). Many NACOA members are also accredited by CLIA (Cruise Line International Association); CLIA's website (http://www. ten-io.com/clia/), has a feature that allows you to search for accredited experts in your area by zip code and telephone area code. Agents who specialize in cruises will usually advertise the fact, so you shouldn't have trouble finding one in the Yellow Pages, in your newspaper's travel section, or on the Worldwide Web.

Another option is to contact a **cruise broker or discounter.** These operations tap into unsold inventories of cruise-ship cabins and offer them at rates significantly lower than the lines' published rates. The downside is that discounters are generally not full travel agents, and will probably not be able to book your flight, provide the exact cabin category you want, or secure the dinner seating you prefer, as a travel agent can. Some reputable cruise brokers—those with impressive buying clout, who are known for expending a bit more effort to match potential passengers with a suitable cruise line—include **Cruises, Inc.,** 5000 Campuswood Dr. East, Syracuse, NY 13057 (☎ **800/854-0500** or 315/463-9695; fax 315/434-9175; website http:// www.cruisesinc.com); **Cruises of Distinction, Inc.,** 2750 South Woodward Ave., Bloomfield Hills, MI 48304 (☎ **800/634-3445** or 810/332-3030); **Cruise Fairs Of America,** Century Plaza Towers, 2029 Century Park East, Suite 950, Los Angeles, CA 90067 (☎ **800/456-4FUN** or 310/556-2925); **Cruise Headquarters,** P.O. Box 12288, La Jolla, CA 92039 (☎ **800/424-6111** or 619/453-1201); **The Cruise Line, Inc.,** 150 NW 168th St., North Miami Beach, FL 33169 (☎ **800/777-0707**); **Don Ton Cruise Tours,** 3151 Airway Ave., Costa Mesa, CA 92626 (☎ **800/ 318-1818** or 714/545-3737); and **Time To Travel,** 582 Market St., San Francisco, CA 94104 (☎ **800/524-3300** or 415/421-3333).

SOME QUESTIONS TO ASK

Choosing a cruise is like choosing a mate—pick the wrong one and you'll not only be miserable, but you'll be stuck together for a long time. So, save yourself the heartache of an ill-chosen cruise: Do your homework and ask some questions before you book. Here's a few pertinent ones:

How large is the ship? Aside from the obvious differences in the number of passengers and crew it can carry and the number of amenities, activities, and dining options it can offer, the size of a ship does much to determine the kind of Alaska experience you'll have. If your primary goal is to see Alaska's wilderness and wildlife up-close, then smaller, shallow-draft ships will suit you. These vessels offer an experience that focuses on the scenic beauty and abundant wildlife of the state; they're often accompanied by one or more naturalists and offer few, if any, diversions to pull you away from deckside observations. Their smaller size allows them to navigate narrow passages, nosing up to sheer cliff faces, bird rookeries, cascading waterfalls, and bobbing icebergs. Sea animals are not as intimidated by these ships, and tend to stay put and continue their activity rather than flee—you can watch porpoises playing in the bow wake or, if you're lucky, humpbacks feeding scant yards away. The deck is also closer to the waterline, giving passengers a more intimate view of whales, dolphins, otters, seals, sea lions, and shorebirds. Lastly, the small-ship cruise is generally a more casual experience; the 75 to 100 passengers on board seldom dress up for dinner, and the close quarters tend to encourage quick camaraderie.

If you're looking for the traditional cruise experience—to be entertained, stuffed with gourmet cuisine, and pampered in a nice setting—opt for one of the larger cruise ships. The primary drawback of large ships is that the size tends to keep Alaska's wilderness and wildlife at a distance. Marine creatures veer away from the louder engines, and even those that do range close must be viewed from decks several stories above the water. On the plus side, the more powerful engines are faster, making it easier to squeeze more port visits into your trip. On the minus side, the big ships' size means less maneuverability , and less maneuverability means the ships must stay farther away from intriguing glaciers and shorelines, and their deeper drafts and broader beams keep them out of many pristine fjords, inlets, and narrows. They also carry between 1,000 and 2,000 passengers, so debarkation in the various ports of call can be a lengthy process, and once you and your 2,000 fellow passengers descend on that little Alaska town, there's little hope of seeing the place as its residents do.

What's the itinerary and how much time is spent in the various ports?   Most ships sail from Vancouver, British Columbia, on 7-day trips that are either round-trip with stops in Ketchikan, Sitka, and Juneau, or north- or southbound between Vancouver and Seward (near Anchorage) with additional stops in smaller ports such as Haines, Skagway, or Valdez. More and more vessels are sailing to Alaska from San Francisco and Seattle, offering itineraries of 7 to 12 days.

Land tours are frequently sold in conjunction with the cruise, allowing inland visits to stunning destinations such as Denali National Park, Fairbanks, and Nome, making it easy to stretch the holiday out and see the interior of the state as well. (If a cruise line doesn't offer land tours, contact the tour operators listed in chapter 3, "Planning a Trip to Alaska.") It's better to schedule land trips to fall at the beginning of your vacation than at the end—they're fast-paced and can be extremely tiring. The cruise will give you a chance to catch your breath and relax. This makes southbound trips from Seward a good choice. However, on northbound trips, the beauty of the scenery grows exponentially the farther north you travel, so northbound itineraries are a favorite.

Be aware that not all Alaskan cruises visit Glacier Bay or the historic gold-rush town of Skagway, or head as far north as Seward. Check the reviews below to see which ports of call the different ships visit, and how much time they stay in port (anywhere from a few hours to a full day). If you're pretty sure the Native and Russian cultures of Sitka will thrill you, be sure you'll be in port long enough to satisfy your curiosity. If you'll get bored looking at glaciers for hours on end, don't select an itinerary that spends a full day in Glacier Bay.

How much time is spent on open waters?   Most of your time in Alaska will be spent cruising the calm, protected waterways of the Inside Passage. However, if the itinerary starts or ends in San Francisco or Seward/Anchorage, the ship will be traveling a larger portion of the time on the open ocean, which tends to be rougher and creates noticeable rolling even on the largest, most stable vessels. If you or a traveling companion is susceptible to motion sickness, choose an Inside Passage itinerary. If the thrill of the open ocean appeals to you, select one of the north- or southbound itineraries.

How much does it cost and what's not included?   First off, never believe the brochure prices. They're a lot like the price of a new car: The lines don't really expect to get them, and you shouldn't really expect to pay them. Innumerable deals are offered by the various lines to entice you onto their ships. Your travel agent will be able to find you the best rate.

However, a number of expenses are not covered in the typical cruise package, and you should factor these in when planning your vacation budget. Airfare to and from your port of embarkation and debarkation is often extra, as is any necessary lodging before or after the cruise and all gratuities and port taxes. Shore excursions are rarely included, and—if you opt for pricey ones like flightseeing—can easily add a thousand dollars or more to your total. Alcoholic beverages and soft drinks will typically be extra, as will such incidentals as laundry.

I'll be travelling alone. Will it cost more?   Yes, but there are steps you can take to keep the cost down. Check to see if the line you're interested in offers a cabin share program, in which you'll be paired with another single passenger of the same sex and smoking preference. This will allow you to cruise for the standard fare. Some lines also offer a single guarantee program, which works much like standby tickets at the theater: Your cabin is assigned at the line's discretion, based on what's left over after most cabins are booked. This service will typically cost you a few hundred dollars more, but will still be cheaper than if you book a specific cabin as a single. If you don't want to share a stateroom, however, and insist on the cabin of your choice, you'll pay through the nose: Cruise lines typically charge 150–175% of the per person, double occupancy rate for solo passengers. Some lines offer single cabins, but these will cost you more as well. (See individual ship listings below for guidelines on single fares.)

What facilities does the ship feature?   Would the lack of a hot tub, fitness center, spa, casino, cigar bar, or shopping arcade leave you feeling deprived? If so, pick one of the larger ships, which offer these and many other facilities. If a good book, an informative lecture, a pair of binoculars, and an unobstructed view from a deck chair is enough, you'll be happy on one of the small ships.

What activities and entertainment does the ship offer?   Activities on smaller ships are usually limited by the available public space but often include recent-release videos, group-oriented games (bingo, poker, etc.), and perhaps an evening dance or social hour. They typically offer a lecture series dealing with the flora, fauna, and geography of Alaska, usually conducted by a trained naturalist. These lectures are also becoming more popular on the larger ships, and are offered along with more common activities such as fitness, self-enrichment, personal finance, photography, or art classes, and planned activities such as Ping-Pong tournaments or singles or newlywed gatherings. Glitzy floor shows are almost de rigueur.

What are the meals like?   Meals are a big part of the cruise experience. The larger the ship, the more choice you'll find. Ask about the selection of restaurants and snack bars and the types of cuisine that will be available, how many meals are served each day, and whether or not you must dine at set times or can take meals at your leisure. If you have any special dietary requirements, be sure that the line is informed well in advance; almost every ship can easily meet your needs. When booking your cruise on a larger vessel, you'll be asked ahead of time to schedule your preferred dinner hour since most feature two seatings each evening.

What are the cabins like?   Cabins come in all sizes and configurations. Some come with minibars, broad-view windows, verandas, TVs and VCRs, sitting areas, big beds, and roomy bathrooms with bathtubs. Others offer just the basics—narrow bunks, postage-stamp bathrooms, a porthole, and limited storage space. Consider carefully what would make you comfortable during your time at sea, how much time you might actually spend in your cabin, and what amenities you require or might easily do without.

Is the cruise formal or casual?   If you don't care to get dressed up, select a less formal cruise typical of small ships. If, on the other hand, the chance to parade that new Armani tux or Helmut Lang dress is your idea of cruise fun, select one of the larger, more elegant ships.

How many passengers and crew does the ship carry?   A large number of passengers provides the chance to meet lots of different people and ensures a certain amount of anonymity, but keep in mind that you'll be disembarking with all those other passengers, which means you'll be waiting in line, and then crowding the port along with the thousands from other ships, which means massive crowding. Small ships' smaller

Glaciers 101

Glaciers are one of the big draws of Alaska cruising, and with good reason: They're awesome. Seeing one spread between the comparatively insignificant bulk of massive mountains is like seeing the hand of God made manifest—this ice carved the valleys and thrust the mountains into the air. This ice made our world look as it does.

Glaciers are constantly on the move, sculpting the landscape below, grinding the shale and other rock forms and pushing rubble and silt ahead and to the sides. This sediment is known as *morain*. Terminal morain is the accumulation of rubble at the front of a glacier; lateral morain lines the sides of glaciers. A dark area in a glacier's center—seen when two glaciers flow together, pushing their ice and crushed rubble together—is median morain. When seen from above, glaciers that have run together (known as *piedmont glaciers*) resemble a highway interchange, edged by road slush, with the median morain looking like lane dividers. *Hanging glaciers* are just that—hanging high above on rounded hillsides. *Tidewater glaciers* are the kind most often gracing the postcards; they hang at the water's edge, like Margerie in Glacier Bay. There are also *alpine* or *cirque glaciers* high in the mountains, and *valley glaciers* that don't reach the sea at any point.

Some glaciers may "gallop," surging either forward or backward as much as 10 to 150 feet a day, and some may recede or retreat—like the Mendenhall Glacier in Juneau, which is backing away (melting away, really) at the rate of about 30 feet a year. Hubbard Glacier became a galloping glacier for a brief time in 1986, moving forward rapidly to block in Yakutat Bay for a few months.

When large chunks break off the face of a tidewater glacier and splash into the water below, the phenomenon is known as *calving*. Icebergs of different sizes have different names: Very large chunks are icebergs, pieces of moderate size are known as "bergy bits," "growlers" are slightly smaller still, and "brash ice" is little chunks no more than two meters long.

Some of the most visited glaciers in the various cruise itineraries include **Glacier Bay National Park and Preserve** and its sixteen tidewater glaciers (see pages 197–200); **Mendenhall Glacier** outside Juneau (pages 186–187); and **North and South Sawyer Glaciers** in Tracy Arm (page 190).

passenger lists tend to lead to a congenial group atmosphere, engendering fast and firm friendships; however, smaller ships necessarily carry smaller crews, which means less personalized attention and pampering.

What are the other passengers usually like?   Each cruise attracts a fairly predictable type of passenger, and you'll be more comfortable if you find out ahead of time which attracts which. In general, don't buy into the stereotype and believe that everyone aboard will require the use of a walker: Though many of your fellow passengers will be American retirees, more and more ships are attracting a younger crowd, and more and more are catering to families. On small ships you'll find a more physically active bunch that are highly interested in nature, but you'll find few families or single travelers. Larger ships cater to a more diverse group—singles, newlyweds, families, and couples over 55. The more expensive the trip, the more seasoned the travelers will be; the less expensive the cruise, the more likely you are to find passengers complaining loudly that the budget cruise isn't just like the "Love Boat" they saw on television. Certain lines, such as Crystal, have a strong following among Europeans and Asians, so you'll find a broader international mix on their cruises.

Does the ship have a children's program? More parents are taking their kids along on cruises to Alaska, and more lines are adding youth counselors to keep the kids entertained while their parents relax. Some ships even provide a supervised nursery or guaranteed babysitting. Ask whether the program is dependent on the number of children booked on any given cruise, and if it is, whether or not it will be available for your children on the dates of your cruise.

Is shipboard life heavily scheduled? If you're aboard to relax and catch up on reading and sleep, you may be annoyed at having to wake up early to eat breakfast at a set time. The larger the vessel, the more options you'll have and the less likely you'll be required to stick to someone else's schedule.

How far in advance do I need to book? Many itineraries sell out six or more months in advance. Once you've selected the cruise that's right for you, check to be sure there will be space available when you're ready to purchase your cruise package. The addition of new ships and new lines in Alaska brings more variety, but don't count on the additional space remaining available up to the last minute; plan to book your cabin of choice well in advance, or be prepared to accept whatever cabin category remains available—if any are available at all. Also, you'll often find early-booking discounts of 10% to 25% if you book at least 120 days prior to sailing.

2 Cruise Practicalities

WHEN TO GO The Alaska cruise season generally stretches from mid-May through late September, though a few ships will be in the water as early as mid-April. The driest days fall in May and June and the warmest and longest days fall in July and August (considered peak season, so these are the most expensive months to cruise). The least expensive cruises are typically the first and last runs of the season, though these have their own charm—specifically, fewer fellow passengers clogging the ports and, consequently, locals who are just that much more relaxed.

TIPS ON PACKING See chapter 3, "Planning a Trip to Alaska," for general advice on packing for Alaska's variable weather. A swimsuit is a must for cruising on a ship equipped with a heated pool or hot tubs. You'll also need to bring along enough dressy clothing for the number of formal evenings (on the big ships, usually two on weeklong cruises and correspondingly more on longer trips); dark suits or tuxedos are the uniform for men, cocktail dresses or evening gowns for women. For less formal evenings, men will need sports jackets (and, on some lines, ties) and women will want dresses or pant suits. Anything but swimsuits, shorts, and in some cases jeans is suitable for casual evenings. If your trip includes a theme night—say, a 1950s, country-western, or pirate night—you might want to consider bringing along that poodle skirt, Stetson, or stuffed parrot you have packed away. Check ahead to see what sort of costume will be appropriate for the cruise you select.

Pack your binoculars! Remember, you've come all this way to see the sights; you don't want to be caught saying "What bear? Where?" (Note that some smaller vessels keep binoculars stocked on board for passenger use.) You'll probably also want a camera and plenty of film, sunglasses, and sunblock.

Travel documents, passports, traveler's checks, medications, jewelry, a change of clothing, and other valuables or oft-needed items should be packed in a carry-on bag since your luggage will be inaccessible during embarkation and debarkation. This carry-on can also serve as an overnight bag for short land excursions.

CUSTOMS & IDENTIFICATION DOCUMENTS When transiting through Vancouver, British Columbia, you'll have to clear Immigration and Customs. See chapter 3, "Planning a Trip to Alaska," for details.

THE POLITICS OF TIPPING The cruise industry pays its staff low wages, with the understanding that the bulk of their salaries will be won through tips. If you worry that you won't know how exactly to go about the business, don't fret: You'll never be left in the dark about the line's tipping policy. At some point in your trip, it'll be laid out as cleanly as sharp cheddar on a cutting board. Amounts vary with the line and its degree of luxury, but as a rule of thumb you can expect to tip between $8 and $15 per day, per person. I suggest tipping your waiter and your cabin steward each between $4 and $7 per person, per day. Give the busperson an additional bonus of $1.50 or $2. Wine stewards and bartenders have probably already been rewarded with a 15% surcharge on every bill, but if they've been particularly helpful you should probably reward them with something extra. Tips are not automatically added to room service bills, so you should tip accordingly. As for the maitre d', this is the optimal time to do your Cary Grant impersonation and suavely palm a bill into his or her hand as you're guided to your table. Some lines (Alaska Sightseeing, for instance) ask that you give one big tip that the whole staff divvies up after you're gone.

Tipping the captain or one of the captain's officers is gauche and embarrassing for all involved. These are professionals. Don't do it.

3 The Cruise Lines & Their Ships

The itineraries and cruise prices included in the reviews below are for 1998; dates and prices for 1999 were simply unavailable at press time. If you're planning a cruise for the summer of 1999, these reviews should give you a good start, and your travel agent or cruise broker can fill you in on any new info you'll need.

SMALL SHIPS

These are the casual, shallow-draft vessels that can get in and out of tight areas. They're usually under 200 feet in length and carry 100 or so passengers. In addition to the lines reviewed below, **Glacier Bay Tours and Cruises** (☎ **800/451-5952**) operates small-ship cruises in Alaska. (Glacier Bay's ships are briefly described in the Glacier Bay National Park section of chapter 7.)

ALASKA SIGHTSEEING / CRUISE WEST

4th and Battery Building, Suite 700, Seattle, WA 98121. ☎ **800/426-7702** or 206/441-8687. Fax 206/441-4757. Website http://www.smallship.com.

If your idea of cruising Alaska is sitting so close to the water that you can feel the spray, and if a comfortable dinner means showing up in jeans and choosing your own table, this might be the line for you. The operative words here are casual, relaxed, and friendly. It's more like visiting your cabin on the lake than booking a room at the Hilton.

The line strives for a family feeling, and toward this end employs young, energetic crews who simply radiate enthusiasm, and who cover all shipboard tasks from waiting table at breakfast to unloading baggage at journey's end. Passengers tend to find them adorable. A cheerful and knowledgable cruise coordinator accompanies each trip to answer passengers' questions about Alaska's flora, fauna, geology, and history, and Forest Service rangers, local fishermen, and Native Alaskans sometimes come aboard to teach about the culture and industry of the state. The line's itineraries, land-tour options, and shore excursions are imaginative and distinctive, and if you have your heart set on a port activity that they don't offer—say, salmon fishing in Sitka—the cruise coordinator will do his or her best to set something up for you.

Who sails aboard these ships? According to cruise coordinator Janet Mowry of the *Spirit of '98* and *Spirit of Columbia*, passengers tend to be older, financially stable, and well educated, and consider themselves adventuresome. When I sailed, there were a good number of current or retired physicians and teachers aboard, a smattering of farmers and ranchers, a pair of behavioral psychologists, and several computer specialists and other high-tech types. True to Ms. Mowry's estimation, the larger percentage of passengers fell into the 60–75 age group, though I heard not a peep of complaint from younger passengers on board (those in their mid-30s on up). The unifying factor, cutting across age group, was that passengers wanted two things from their cruise: (1) a genuine, up-close Alaska experience and (2) a relaxed, dress-down atmosphere. On both these counts, ASCW delivers. (Regarding usual shipboard dress, they say that one gentleman got a standing ovation on a recent trip when he showed up for dinner in a tuxedo. Translation: Leave the fancy duds at home.) What you won't get aboard these ships is luxury and white-glove service. One crew tells of recently being sent into crisis mode when the occupants of their ship's most deluxe suite went into spasms because they couldn't order room service. If you see yourself in that scenario, cruise elsewhere.

ASCW ships' best point is their small size and ability to navigate tight areas such as Misty Fjords and Desolation Sound, visit tiny ports such as Petersburg, and scoot up close to shore for wildlife watching—all things that large ships just physically cannot do. Open bow areas on each vessel are the best observation points, and guests tend to congregate there and on the more sheltered sundeck aft to watch for wildlife. In inclement weather—or just to sit and get warm—passengers usually plunk down in the window-ringed forward lounge, which has both a bar and a 24-hour coffee/tea/cocoa station. Binoculars are provided for guests' use, and wildlife sightings are announced over the shipwide intercom system during the day. (You can even arrange to have a crew member wake you during the night if you don't want to miss the northern lights, breaching whales, or shadowy bears on shore.) If you're the "star to steer by" type, you're welcomed to take advantage of ASCW's open-bridge policy, in which passengers are invited to spend time with the captain and crew as they navigate the ship. Spend as much time as you like. Ask questions. Just don't touch the controls. (*Note:* Bridges remain closed in rough or particularly difficult water.)

While at sea, you'll find no one pressuring you to join in activities you'd rather not, leaving you free to scan for wildlife, peruse the natural sights, or read a book—your own or one from the small Alaska reference library in the lounge. Similarly, PA announcements are kept to a tasteful minimum, announcing mealtimes, port arrivals and departures, and wildlife sightings. What onboard activities there are may include post-dinner discussions of the port or region to be visited the next day, afternoon talks by expert guests while at sea, and perhaps a tour of the engine room or galley. Videos are available from a small library for your in-cabin use, and organized entertainment, such as it is, is sometimes provided by the crew or by your fellow passengers, perhaps in a humbly titled "No-Talent Night" or in a game of Truth or Dare. There's nothing special for kids to do, so ASCW cruises are not really suitable for families with children unless the kids are real nature buffs. Similarly, there aren't many onboard fitness options, though each ship carries some minimal exercise equipment (such as an exercise bike or stairmaster) and some have a wraparound deck that could do in a pinch for walking.

Breakfast, lunch, and dinner are served at set times at one unassigned seating, so you're free to mingle with the other passengers. An early-riser's buffet is set out in the lounge before the set breakfast time, but if you're a late-riser you'll miss breakfast entirely, as no room service is available. The fare is primarily home-style American, utilizing fresh products purchased in ports along the way. Presentation is not overly fancy, but the cuisine is tasty and varied. The galley can accommodate special diets (i.e., vegetarian, kosher, low-salt, low-fat), but be sure to make special arrangements for this when you book your cruise. Service can sometimes be a little slow as each waitperson must cover several tables, though when I overslept coming into Skagway and thought I'd only have time for toast and coffee, my waiter assured me he could have scrambled eggs and hash browns out in thirty seconds—and by God, he did.

Note: In addition to the cruises profiled here, ASCW offers what it calls **"Daylight Yacht Cruise-Tours & Cruises"** of 5 to 15 days aboard the motor yacht *Sheltered Seas,* a cabinless craft that cruises Alaska's waterways by day and deposits you at a hotel for the night. Additional travel by rail or motorcoach allows visits to Fairbanks and Denali National Park, and the timing of your arrival in ports—generally in the early evening—means that you'll be hitting the town after the hordes from larger cruise ships have left. If you can't decide between cruising Alaska and seeing it by land, this is an option worth exploring. (Cruises start at $815 for the 5-day cruise, $1,245 for the 6-day, $2,085 for the 10-day, $2,385 for the 11-day, $3,175 for the 14-day, and $3,425 for the 15-day, and vary within a $100–$600 range depending how close to the height of tourist season you sail.) Also, **11-day north- and southbound cruises between Juneau and Seattle** are offered aboard all of the ships profiled below from early April to mid-May and during the month of September. Prices run from $2,195–$4,655.

⚙ **Spirit of '98.** *Passenger capacity:* 101. *Crew complement:* 23. *Cabins:* 49, all outside. *Ship facilities:* dining room, open-access bow area, sundeck, lounge (with full bar, small library, and audiovisual equipment), video library, exercise bike and stairmaster, gift shop. *Activities:* lectures and discussions on Alaska, board games, occasional theme nights and crew entertainment. **Itineraries:** 9-day north- and southbound cruises with options for ground/air add-ons totaling 14 and 18 days. **9-day cruise-only trips** sail between Juneau and Seattle, with visits to Skagway, Sitka, Ketchikan, Glacier Bay, and Desolation Sound; departures Fri southbound and Sat northbound, mid-Apr to early Sept; cruise only, $2,665–$5,465 per person, double occupancy ($3,965–$5,115 single). **14-day trips** include pre- or postcruise extensions to Fairbanks and Denali National Park. *Departures:* Sun southbound and Sat northbound, early May to late Aug; $4,195–$6,675 per person, double occupancy ($6,115–$7,015 single). **18-day trips** include pre- or postcruise extensions to Fairbanks, Denali National Park, Anchorage, and Whittier, where you board the *Spirit of Alaska* for two days of cruising in Prince William Sound. *Departures:* Wed southbound and Sat northbound, late May to mid-Aug; $5,515–$8,075 per person, double occupancy ($8,345–$9,275 single). Single prices are for single cabins; for other cabins, solo passengers pay 175% of the double occupancy rate. Prices include taxes, port charges, and fees. Early-booking and third- and fourth-passenger discounts are available.

Nowhere in large-ship cruising is there anything like standing on the stern of the *Spirit of '98,* on the Main Deck, separated from the water by only three feet and a rail, watching the landscape recede behind you, or standing on the bow at midnight, with the northern lights glimmering above you, prow cutting the waves toward your next port of call.

The *'98* is a time machine. Built as a replica 19th century steamship in 1984 and extensively refurbished in 1995, it carries its Victorian flavor so well that fully two thirds of the people I met on a recent sailing thought the ship had been a private yacht at the turn of the century. Pressed-tin ceilings (aluminum actually, but why be picky?), floral carpeting, balloon-back chairs, ruffled drapery, domed lights in the dining room, and plenty of polished woodwork and brass throughout establish the mood, and a player piano in the lounge and huge wooden ship's wheel on the bridge drive home the 19th century point.

Cabins are comfortable and of decent size, and continue the Victorian motif with ornamental woodwork, brass lamps and window fixtures, and dark, quilted satin bedspreads (as well as singularly non-Victorian TV/VCR combos). Cabins on the Lounge

Deck and Upper Deck are accessed via the open (though covered) decks and offer unobstructed sea views from their windows, which open to collect the breeze. Cabins on the Main Deck open onto an interior corridor, though you'll still get fine views as well as added privacy, as the windows let directly onto the sea. (Unfortunately, to comply with new Coast Guard regulations, non-opening windows were installed on this deck for 1998.) Two cabin categories feature two twin beds while the third and deluxe categories feature queen-size beds. Mattresses are among the best I've found—very firm and very comfortable. The deluxe cabins are in the bow, on both the Main and Upper decks, and have a refrigerator, a seating area, and a trundle bed to accommodate a third passenger. Deluxe cabins on the Main Deck are slightly larger, but those on the Upper Deck provide forward views. An owner's suite—the only accommodation on the topmost deck, right behind the bridge—provides a spacious living room with meeting area, a large bathroom with whirlpool tub, a king-size bed, stocked bar with refrigerator, TV/VCR, stereo, and enough windows to take in all of Alaska in one sitting. (*Note:* The owner's suite always books up early, so plan ahead.) Bathrooms in all categories except the owner's suite are . . . functional. Not large, but not constricting, and no Victorian frills in sight—that stops at the door. A warning about the showers, though: The curtain will poof in, you will shrink away from it, you will turn around, and you will nudge the temperature control and be blasted with cold water. It happened to me almost every morning. You've been warned.

As on all ASCW ships, the '98 has two main public areas: the Grand Salon Lounge and the Klondike Dining Room. Noise levels are usually minimal in the lounge, but conversation can be difficult in the dining room if the engines are running full out (though the line says they're trying to remedy this problem). For whatever acoustic reason, the booths running along both the starboard and port sides seem to get less noise than the round tables in the middle, so try to snag one of those if you can. A small bar called Soapy's Parlour sits just aft of the dining room, though there's only a bartender at mealtime and it otherwise gets little use—meaning it's a good spot to sneak off and read your book if you want privacy but don't want to stay in your cabin.

If you use a wheelchair or otherwise have mobility problems, note that the '98 is the only ASCW ship with an elevator. Cabin 309, located on the Upper Deck right next to the elevator, is fully wheelchair accessible.

If you want to get a look at this ship before you sail, rent Kevin Costner's *Wyatt Earp* at your local Blockbuster—one of the final scenes was filmed on board. Also, Sue Henry's 1997 mystery novel *Death Takes Passage* is set entirely aboard the '98, and provides detailed descriptions of the ship.

Spirit of Endeavor. *Passenger capacity:* 102. *Crew complement:* 25. *Cabins:* 51, all outside. *Facilities:* dining room, open-access bow area, sundeck, lounge (with full bar, small library, and audiovisual equipment), video library, exercise machines, gift shop. *Activities:* lectures and discussions on Alaska, board games, occasional theme nights and crew entertainment. **Itineraries:** For 1998, *Endeavor* sails the same itineraries as the *Spirit of '98*, above. **9-day cruise-only trips:** cruise only, $2,665–$4,385 per person, double occupancy. **14-day trips:** $4,295–$5,695 per person, double occupancy. **18-day trips:** $5,815–$6,985 per person, double occupancy. Solo passengers pay 175% of the double occupancy rate; there are no single cabins aboard. Prices include taxes, port charges, and fees. Early-booking and third- and fourth-passenger discounts are available.

It's hard to imagine a more serene way to spend your tour than sipping a cocktail on the shaded stern deck of this glimmering 217-foot, four-deck cruiser, the new flagship of the Alaska Sightseeing line. Stealthy and silent, the thrum of the engines are barely discernable (soothing, actually) as the U.S.–registered *Spirit of Endeavor* plies through the beautiful waters of the Inside Passage or Glacier Bay.

On the lower levels are the dining room—the largest room on the ship, lined with wide picture windows and a cadre of round dinner tables—and plush piano lounge, where passengers congregate for coffee, drinks, impromptu dancing and singing, and the chance to get warm after some on-deck whale-watching. The upper levels include a large sundeck and stern deck (both of beautiful teakwood) and a bow viewing area just below the bridge. On the lower three decks are 51 cabins of varying size and amenities. All have twin beds, TV/VCR, binoculars, and private bathrooms, though two luxury features that are available in some cabins and definitely worth the added expense are large view windows and twin beds that convert into one queen-size bed. Most beds, though comfortably firm, are small; tall passengers of means may want to book the deluxe rooms, which come with additional legroom as well as a refrigerator and writing desk. Four rooms have one pullman berth for triple accommodations, and several cabins may be adjoined.

Though the ship has been newly refurbished from bow to stern, the furnishings are more or less dull. Cabin color schemes run from green, gray, and brown to simply varying shades of brown. Bathrooms are spotless, though small; bathtubs aren't an option, and the diminutive showers suffer from weak water pressure. The staff's low-tech do-not-disturb system involves a small loop of rope that's attached to the outer door handle, and if you're a late sleeper you'll need one, as the staff pops in several times a day to straighten your room and deliver the next day's itinerary. As on all ASCW ships, there are no keys for your cabin, but I'd think of this as a chance to revel in human honor rather than get paranoid—the line says they've never had a theft on board.

Spirit of Discovery / Spirit of Columbia. *Passenger capacity:* 84/78. *Crew complement:* 21. *Cabins:* 43/48, all outside. *Ship facilities:* dining room, open-access bow area, sundeck, lounge (with full bar, small library, and audiovisual equipment), video library, exercise machines, gift shop. *Activities:* lectures and discussions on Alaska, board games, occasional theme nights and crew entertainment. **Itineraries:** 9-day north- and southbound "All Alaska" cruises with options for ground/air add-ons totaling 14 and 18 days. **9-day cruise-only trip** sails between Juneau and Ketchikan, with visits to Skagway, Haines, Sitka, Petersburg, Glacier Bay, and LeConte Bay. *Departures:* Wed southbound and Thurs northbound, late April to early Sept; cruise only $2,315–$4,325 per person, double occupancy; **14-day trips** include pre- or postcruise extensions to Fairbanks, Denali National Park, and Anchorage. *Departures:* Fri southbound and Thurs northbound, mid-May to late Aug; $3,475–$5,625 per person, double occupancy. **18-day trips** include pre- or postcruise extensions to Fairbanks, Denali National Park, Anchorage, and Whittier, where you board the *Spirit of Alaska* for two days of cruising in Prince William Sound. *Departures:* Mon southbound and Thurs northbound, late May to mid-Aug; $5,015–$6,775 per person, double occupancy. Two single cabins are available aboard the *Discovery* at prices that approximate the upper-end per-person double-occupancy rate. For other cabins (and aboard the *Columbia,* which has no single cabins), solo passengers pay 175% of the double occupancy rate. Prices include taxes, port charges, and fees. Early-booking and third- and fourth-passenger discounts are available.

Decor aboard the *Spirit of Discovery,* launched in 1976 and extensively refurbished in 1992, has a streamlined, modern appearance. Big picture windows in the lounge and dining room let in scads of light, which reflects off shiny brass and mirrored surfaces to give a spacious, airy feel (note that engine noise reverberates in the dining room, making normal conversation difficult during meals). Cabins are very snug (slightly smaller than those on the '98), but comfortable, and feature cheery pastel color schemes, picture windows that open to ocean breezes, a radio, individual heating and cooling, a tight head with shower and toilet (the sink is in the main room), and lower twin or double platform beds (though deluxe cabins have queen-size beds and Cabins 101 and 102, situated forward on the main deck, have bunks). Storage space is ample.

The *Columbia* is slightly smaller than the *Discovery*, though it has four decks instead of three and features seven suites (including an owner's suite with picture windows looking over the bow) in addition to deluxe cabins similar to those on the *Discovery*. Owing to its origins as the *New Shoreham II* of Luther Blount's American Canadian Caribbean Line, it's equipped with ACCL's patented bow ramp—a portion of the bow that actually swings down to shore, forming a gangplank for debarkation. Other amenities are of the same kind as available on all ASCW ships.

Spirit of Alaska / Spirit of Glacier Bay. *Passenger capacity:* 78/52. *Crew complement:* 21/16. *Cabins:* 39/27, all outside. *Ship facilities:* dining room, open-access bow area, sundeck, lounge (with full bar, small library, and audiovisual equipment), video library, exercise machines, gift shop. *Activities:* lectures and discussions on Alaska, board games, occasional theme nights and crew entertainment. **Itineraries:** 4- and 5-day round-trip Prince William Sound cruises with options for ground/air add-ons totaling 9 and 10 days. **4-day cruise-only trip** sails from Whittier, cruising College Fjord and Prince William Sound and visiting Valdez and Columbia Glacier. *Spirit of Alaska* departures Fri late May to late Aug, *Spirit of Glacier Bay* departures Thurs late May to early Sept; cruise only, $865–$1,695. **5-day cruise-only trip** sails from Whittier and visits Cordova, Valdez, Columbia Glacier, College Fjord, Barry Arm, and Esther Passage. *Spirit of Alaska* departures Mon early June to late Aug, *Spirit of Glacier Bay* departures Sun mid-May to early Sept; cruise only, $1,115–$2,045. **9-day trips** incorporate the 4-day cruise itinerary and include extra time in Anchorage and visits via motorcoach to Denali National Park and via the Alaska Railroad to Fairbanks. *Spirit of Alaska* departures Thurs late May to late Aug, *Spirit of Glacier Bay* departures Wed late May to early Sept; $2,065–$2,975. **10-day trips** incorporate the 5-day cruise itinerary and includes extra time in Anchorage and visits via motorcoach to Denali National Park and via the Alaska Railroad to Fairbanks. *Spirit of Alaska* departures Sun late May to late Aug, *Spirit of Glacier Bay* departures Sat mid-May to early Sept; $2,175–$3,335. Two single cabins are available aboard the *Spirit of Glacier Bay* at prices that approximate the upper-end per-person double-occupancy rate. For other cabins (and aboard the *Spirit of Alaska*, which has no single cabins), solo passengers pay 175% of the double occupancy rate. Prices include taxes, port charges, and fees. Early-booking and third- and fourth-passenger discounts are available.

Dissimilar in size but close (as are all the ASCW ships) in onboard facilities, ambience, and activities, the *Alaska* and the *Glacier Bay* are the line's designees for its 1998 Prince William Sound cruises. The *Alaska* is almost identical in size, passenger capacity, and number of cabins to the *Spirit of Columbia*, reviewed above (though it lacks the *Columbia's* suites), but the *Glacier Bay* is the baby of the line, carrying only 52 passengers and with cabin dimensions that are correspondingly smaller (Category A cabins, for instance, measure 8 × 9 feet aboard the *Glacier Bay* but 9 × 10½ feet aboard the *Alaska*.) Other than these differences—and the fact that the *Glacier Bay* has three decks and the *Alaska* four—there is no major departure here from ASCW's other modern ships. Dining rooms similarly accommodate all guests at a single open seating, and there's the same lounge area in the bow and same open-bow viewing area. Due to its larger size, the *Alaska* has a substantially larger sun deck and unobstructed walking circuit.

As it sails only short cruises, I wouldn't let the *Glacier Bay's* small size put you off. It's a comfortable, homey vessel that you certainly won't tire of in the few days you're aboard. Like the *Spirit of Columbia*, both of these ships were built by American Canadian Caribbean Line, and so are equipped with facilities for debarking right from the bow of the ship, though in these cases it's via a gangplank-like bow ladder rather than through the swing-down bow ramp.

CLIPPER CRUISE LINE

7711 Bonhomme Ave., St. Louis, MO 63105. ☎ **800/325-0010.** Fax 314/727-6576. Website http://www.clippercruise.com.

This company, honored by *Conde Nast Traveler* as one of the top ten cruise lines in the world, focuses on providing cruises led by professional naturalists. Clipper's operation is more sophisticated and service-oriented than most ships of this size, primarily to meet the demand of its passengers, who are generally over 55, educated and wealthy, with higher expectations when it comes to food, comfort, and overall experience. Clipper's cruises are designed for those with an interest in exploring new places, rather than on shipboard entertainment. There are no special facilities or activities for children as there are on larger vessels, so this is not the line for a family cruise.

✪ **Yorktown Clipper.** *Passenger capacity:* 120. *Crew complement:* 43. *Cabins:* 69, all outside. *Ship facilities:* dining room, open-access bow area, sundeck, lounge (with full bar, small library, and audiovisual equipment), video library, gift shop. *Activities:* lectures and videos on Alaska, nightly social hour. **Itineraries: 8-day cruises** sail between Ketchikan and Juneau, with visits to Misty Fjords, Petersburg, Sitka, Taylor Bay, Chatham Strait, and Tracy Arm. *Departures:* Sat late May to late Aug; cruise only, $2,200–$3,380 per person, double occupancy ($3,800 single). One **14-day British Columbia and Southeast Alaska cruise** is offered at the beginning of the cruise season and one **12-day cruise** is offered at the end; cruise only, $3,100–$5,550. Two **8-day British Columbia and Southeast Alaska cruises** are offered in early May only; cruise only, $1,880–$2,930 per person, double-occupancy ($3,200 single). Rates include port charges.

The 138-passenger *Yorktown Clipper* looks more like an expensive yacht than a small cruise ship, and is dominated by a large bridge (which is usually open to passengers) and big picture windows that ensure bright interior public spaces and allow comfortable areas for viewing passing scenery. Public areas, from the glass-walled Observation Lounge to the decks, are larger and more inviting than most ships of comparable size, but remain cozy enough to engender camaraderie among crew and passengers. Staterooms are modern and pleasantly decorated, with lower beds (no bunks, except for a third fold-down bed in the largest cabin category), individual thermostats, and fairly roomy bathrooms.

Meals, prepared by chefs trained at the Culinary Institute of America, are a real treat, a cut above the average fare served on other small-ship cruise lines. Fresh salmon, Alaska king crab, Chesapeake soft-shell and blue crabs, gumbo, fresh tropical fruits, and regional specialties are highlighted. Fresh chocolate chip cookies (affectionately referred to as Clipper Chippers) are available every afternoon and disappear amazingly fast. There are two dressy evenings on each cruise, but they don't require formal attire (only about half the passengers dress up).

Shipboard life is easy-going, with no crowds and a more casual pace than found on many larger ships. Crews are young, cheerful, highly motivated, and as quick to please as the naturalists and historians are to answer questions. Motorized landing craft, carried aboard the ship, ferry passengers to remote beaches, pristine forests, small villages, and wildlife refuges; naturalists and/or historians and other experts give lectures on board and walking tours ashore.

SPECIAL EXPEDITIONS

720 Fifth Ave., New York, NY 10019. ☎ **800/762-0003** or 212/765-7740. Fax 212/265-3770.

In 1984, Sven-Olof Lindblad, son of adventure-travel pioneer Lars-Eric Lindblad, followed in his father's footsteps by forming Special Expeditions, a company that specializes in environmentally sensitive, soft-adventure vacations to remote places in the world. The trips are explorative and informal in nature, designed to appeal to the intellectually curious traveler seeking a vacation that's educational as well as relaxing.

Trips aboard the *Sea Lion* and *Sea Bird* in Alaska are anything but the traditional cruise experience; you'll find no casino, no disco, no dance lounges, no massage or fitness rooms, no telephones or TVs, no room service or laundry room, no recent-release movies, and no late-night buffet here. Instead, your days aboard are spent learning about the Alaskan outdoors from high-caliber expedition leaders trained in botany, anthropology, biology, and geology, and observing the world around you either from the ship or on shore excursions, which are included in the cruise package. (*Tip:* bring your own binoculars.) Educational films and slide presentations aboard ship precede nature hikes and quick jaunts aboard Zodiacs (motorized inflatible rafts).

On-board presentations and meals feature hearty but basic American fare at single open seatings and fall at set times, which are posted in a daily program and announced over the shipwide intercom system. Other than that, the schedule remains loose enough to diverge a bit to search out whales or stop for a cookout in a quiet cove. Passengers tend to be younger and more physically active, but even so, the ships become very quiet not long after dinner; everyone crashes early to store up energy for the next day's adventures. It's a casual experience suited for an easygoing crowd bent on learning about Alaska. As there are no facilities for children, these ships are not really suitable for families.

Sea Bird / Sea Lion. *Passenger capacity:* 70. *Crew complement:* 22. *Cabins:* 37, all outside. *Ship facilities:* dining room, observation lounge with bar and library, open bow area, sundeck, gift shop. *Activities:* lectures, educational videos; wheelhouse open for tours; books, cards, and board games on loan from library. **Itineraries: 8-day cruises** sail from Juneau to Sitka, with visits to Tracy Arm, LeConte Bay, Haines, Glacier Bay, Point Adolphus, and other small fjords. *Departures:* Fri and Sat, mid-June to late Aug. Cruise only $3,070–$4,470 per person, double occupancy. **11-day Alaska/B.C. shoulder season cruises** beween Seattle and Juneau with visits to Sitka, Glacier Bay, LeConte Bay, Ketchikan, Alert Bay, Johnstone Straight, and Washington's San Juan Islands. *Departures:* late May and late Aug from $3,490–$4,980 per person, double occupancy. Solo passengers pay 150% of the per-person double-occupancy rate in the smallest cabins only. No cabins are set up for third or fourth passengers.

The *Sea Lion* and *Sea Bird,* shallow-draft ships that are more like cruising yachts than ocean-going vessels, are identical twins down to their decor schemes and furniture. Public and private areas are very compact and informal, with public space limited to the open sundeck and bow areas, the dining room, and an observation lounge that serves as the nerve center for activities. In the lounge you'll find a bar; a library of atlases and books on Alaska's culture, geology, history, plants, and wildlife; a gift shop tucked into a closet; and audiovisual aids for the many naturalists' presentations.

Postage-stamp cabins are tight and functional rather than fancy. No cabins are large enough to accommodate more than two, and each features twin or double beds, a closet (there are also drawers under the bed for extra storage), a speaker for shipwide announcements, and a sink and mirror in the main room. Behind a folding door lies a Lilliputian bathroom with a toilet opposite the shower nozzle. Large passengers will find it very difficult to negotiate these showers. All cabins are located outside and have picture windows that open to fresh breezes.

CRUISE SHIPS

From the relatively modest 740-passenger SS *Universe Explorer* to the gargantuan 2,000-passenger *Rhapsody of the Seas,* the fleet of ships cruising Alaska is as large and diverse as the 49th state itself. You want luxury? You want fun? You want seasons in the sun? There's a ship out there for you. In this section I'll profile your options, clue you in to the practical matters of itineraries and prices, and give you the lowdown on each vessel and a handle on the onboard ambience you can expect.

CARNIVAL

3655 NW 87th Avenue, Miami, FL 33178-2428. ☎ **800/438-6744** or 305/599-2600. Fax 305/471-4740. Website http://www.carnival.com.

Carnival is the brash behemoth of the cruise industry, eschewing tux-and-champagne marketing in favor of a brightly colored, high-energy, mass-market esthetic that draws passengers by the millions. Their bookings account for a full 25% of the cruisegoing market, and more than 25,000 passengers sometimes sail aboard the Carnival fleet in a single week, among them not only the fun-loving singles and young couples you'd expect aboard a line that promotes its vessels as "Fun Ships," but also an increasing number of families, who find the line's patented diversions work just as well for kids as adults.

The line's reputation has been made in warm-weather ports, where the phrase "fun in the sun" pretty much sums up the expectations of most visitors. Transplanting this experience to Alaskan shores raises a couple of questions: For instance, can ships that are explicitly meant to house 24-hour orgies of good times fit themselves into a market where natural wonders are (in theory, at least) the big draw? Would a passenger in a Hawaiian shirt and Oakley sunglasses, dancing the Macarena after his third particolored drink, really rush to the side to see a pod of whales? Would this passenger be in Alaska in the first place? And if he was, would he be in your way when *you* rushed to the side?

To be in a party mood or not to be, that is the question. If you find it nobler to sit on deck with a copy of *Angela's Ashes* in hand and binoculars around your neck, waiting for a humpback whale to breach or a bald eagle to circle overhead, you might be happier aboard one of the small-ship lines profiled above, or perhaps aboard one of Holland America's ships, where—large scale and many amenities notwithstanding—there's still some focus on the world beyond the hull. Then again, Holland America's passengers tend to be in a different age bracket than those aboard Carnival, which is the only major cruise line where the majority of passengers are under 50. Also, singles take note: Carnival officials estimate that their ships attract more of you than any other line.

Regardless of their age, passengers who sail Carnival tend to be young at heart and fond of an activities schedule that keeps them in a state of frolic around the clock. If Atlantic City and Las Vegas appeal to you, Carnival will, too. If quiet times on deck would bore you to tears, this is the line for you, 'cause there won't be any. What you'll get aboard a Fun Ship is *fun*—lots of it, professionally and insistently delivered and spangled with glitter. Slot machines begin whirring at 8am and cocktails inevitably begin to flow before lunch. Singles and newlywed parties are frequent. Learn to country line-dance or ballroom dance, toss water balloons, practice your golf swing by smashing balls into a net, or join in a beer-drinking contest if your belly's up to it. Plus, there's always the on-board staples of eating, sunbathing, and shopping, and the Alaska-specific naturalist lectures that are delivered daily. On-board entertainment is lavish and bright, with each ship carrying a performing crew that includes a dozen dancers, a 12-piece orchestra, comedians, jugglers, rock-and-roll bands, country-western bands, cocktail pianists, and a Dorsey- or Glenn Miller–style big band. Once in port, Carnival lives up to its "more is more" ethos by offering up to 30 optional shore excursions per port.

For kids, Carnival offers many on-board activities that can be enjoyed by the entire family; however, children can get away from their parents and play for all or part of a day in Camp Carnival facilities created especially for them. Families can take advantage of heavily discounted rates for third and fourth occupants of double cabins, and a fifth berth is sometimes available in the form of a cot that rolls away beneath another bed. The purser's office can even arrange for a crib to be set up in your cabin.

Jubilee. *Passenger capacity:* 1,486. *Crew complement:* 670. *Cabins:* 453 outside (10 with verandas) and 290 inside. *Ship facilities:* two dining rooms (plus food service on the Lido deck), two pools, two Jacuzzis, kids' pool, fitness center, spa, jogging/walking track, six bars/lounges (including wine bar and piano bar), casino, disco, theater, beauty shop, library, laundry. *Activities:* wine tastings, white elephant auctions, mens' nightgown and knobby-knee contests, electronic games and virtual reality, singles and newleywed parties, dance lessons, trivia contests, golf, bingo, Ping-Pong and shuffleboard, talent shows, cooking lessons, and more. **Itineraries: 7-day north- and southbound sailings** between Vancouver and Seward/Anchorage, with visits to Skagway, Juneau, Ketchikan, Prince William Sound, and the Lynn Canal (northbound cruises also include Sitka and Endicott Arm or Tracy Arm, while southbound cruises visit Valdez, Yakutat Bay, and Hubbard Glacier). *Departures:* Wed mid-May through late Sept; cruise only, $1,549–$2,899 per person, double occupancy. **10- and 11-night cruisetours** incorporate 7-night cruise with pre- or postcruise land extensions to Anchorage, Fairbanks, and Denali National Park; 10-night $2,399–$3,749, 11-night $2,559–$3,909. Rates include port charges; $3–$9.50 taxes not included. Early-booking discounts of up to $1,600 per stateroom are available. Third and fourth passengers sail for $649–$749. Solo passengers pay 200% of the per-person double-occupancy rate.

Carnival's sourdough ship for 1998 is the *Jubilee*, which moves into Alaskan waters to replace the much smaller *Tropical*. The *Jubilee* is newer and roomier than its predecessor, though it's still not as gargantuan as the megaships. Cabins are larger than many others that you'll find in the same price category, and are furnished with twin beds that can be converted to king-size. Two dining rooms and a bevy of other food service options—such as burgers, hot dogs, ice cream, pasta, and salad on the Lido deck—keep the gourmandistic side of your cruise personality happy and full, while the hundreds of on-board activities for which Carnival is famous keep you on the fast track to that famous and oft-mentioned fun. It's up to you to find time to stop and catch the scenery.

CELEBRITY

5201 Blue Lagoon Dr., Miami, Fl 33126. ☎ **800/437-3111** or 305/262-8322. Fax 800/437-5111. Website http://www.celebrity-cruises.com.

Celebrity has class. Celebrity has taste. Celebrity has old shipping roots, young, beautiful ships, and a recently cemented partnership with Royal Caribbean that should increase its profile measurably. And, for 1998, Celebrity has its two newest ships, the two-year-old *Galaxy* and the brand-new *Mercury*, in Alaskan waters. Both are designed with crisp attention to detail and real decorative panache, and offer just the right combination of elegance, artfulness, excitement, and fun.

Who sails Celebrity? The typical guest is one who prefers to pursue his or her R&R at a relatively relaxed pace, with a minimum of aggressively promoted group activities. The overall impression leans more toward sophistication and less to the kind of orgiastic technicolor whoopie that you'll find, say, aboard a Carnival ship. Celebrity passengers are the type who prefer wine with dinner. They're willing and able to kick up their heels, but will likely do it with a certain amount of style. Most give the impression of being prosperous but not obscenely rich, congenial but not obsessively proper, animated and fun but not wearing a lampshade for a hat.

The line offers a variety of different activities, although many passengers prefer to go it on their own, enjoying the passing landscape or the company of friends. A typical day might offer bridge, darts, a culinary art demonstration, a trapshooting competition, a fitness fashion show, an art auction, or a volleyball tournament. Lectures on the various ports of call, the Alaskan environment, glaciers, and Alaskan culture are given by resident experts, who also provide commentary from the bridge as your ship arrives in a port and are available for one-on-one discussions with passengers at other times. For children, Celebrity ships employ a group of full-time counselors who direct and supervise a camp-style children's program. Activities are geared toward different age groups.

Although entertainment is not generally cited as a reason to sail with Celebrity, the line's shows are none too shabby. You won't find any big-name entertainers, but neither will you find any obvious has-beens. What you will find is material that's long on pizzazz and a bit short on plot and characterization. (But then, who expects Ibsen on a cruise, anyway?) If you tire of the glitter you can always find a cozy lounge or piano bar to curl up in, and if you tire of that, the disco and casino stay open late.

On-board cuisine, under the direction of master chef Michel Roux (formerly of London's La Gavroche and the Waterside Inn on the Thames), is one place where Celebrity really shines. Unlike many cruise lines, where quantity is more important than quality, Celebrity actually gives some thought to the food served aboard its vessels. Alaska cruises offer an array of Pacific Northwest regional specialties, and vegetarian dishes are offered at both lunch and dinner. Dinner is served at two assigned seatings, and each seven-night cruise includes two formal evenings. If you have the muchies, Celebrity offers one of the most extensive 24-hour room-service menus in the industry, plus a late-night buffet on every oceangoing night.

Service aboard Celebrity ships spins about the way it should. We've noted some slow service in the bars and a sometimes lethargic feeling in the casinos, but these minor criticisms are more than offset by the polite, accurate, and cheerful service one receives in the dining rooms. In the cabins, service is efficient and so discreet and unobtrusive you might never see your steward except at the beginning and end of your cruise. Five-star service can be had at the on-board beauty parlor or barber shop, and massages can be scheduled at any hour of the day. Laundry, dry cleaning, and valet services are fast and accurate.

✪ **Galaxy.** *Passenger capacity:* 1,870. *Crew complement:* 909. *Cabins:* 639 outside (220 with veranda) and 296 inside. *Ship facilities:* Dining room, two cafes, three pools (one indoor) and two whirlpools, AquaSpa, four bars/lounges, night club, casino, shopping, theater, video game room, cinema, conference center, card room, champagne bar, library. *Activities:* Alaska lecture program and numerous daily activities (see above). **Itineraries: 7-night round-trip cruises from Vancouver,** with visits to Glacier Bay or Hubbard Glacier, Skagway, Juneau, Haines, and Ketchikan. *Departures:* mid-May to mid-Sept; cruise only, $2,145–$7,445 per person, double occupancy ($2,645–$2,895 single, as part of single guarantee plan). Children under 12 sharing a stateroom with parents pay $845–$895, children under 2 sail free; third and fourth adult passengers in a stateroom pay $945–$995. Rates include port charges. Early booking discounts of up to 50% are available.

Painted in Celebrity's signature colors of dazzling white and navy blue, the *Galaxy* manages to be simultaneously bulky and streamlined-looking, with a stepped, pagoda-like stern and a rakishly angled bow designed for speed and grace. Unlike some other modern ships (for instance, those of the Princess line), *Galaxy* boasts a lot of open deck space, providing access to the wide skies and the grand Alaskan vistas. It's interior is the product of a collaboration between a dozen internationally acclaimed firms, working together to create a stylistically diverse yet harmonious whole. Throughout the ship, elements of an impressive art collection sometimes greet you at an unexpected moment. Don't be surprised if you bump into works by Robert Rauschenberg, Jasper Johns, David Hockney, Pablo Picasso, Andy Warhol, or Helen Frankenthaler.

Inside cabins are about par for the industry standard, but outside cabins are larger than usual, and suites—which come in five different categories—are particularly spacious. Some, such as the Penthouse Suites, offer more living space than you find in many private homes, and the Sky Suites offer verandas that, with 179 square feet, are among the biggest aboard any ship. Cabins are usually accented with rosewood trim and outfitted with built-in vanities, mini-bars, hairdryers, radios, and safes. Closets and drawer space are roomy, and all standard cabins have twin beds convertible to doubles. Bathrooms are sizeable and stylish. Overall, there are no really bad cabins aboard the *Galaxy*.

The AquaSpa Health Club has motifs inspired by Japanese gardens and bathhouses and treatments that include hairdressing, pedicures, manicures, and massage, plus a range of distinctive health and beauty treatments. The generously sized gym is filled with high-tech workout equipment, a jogging track and a golf simulator are available, and a retractable "magrodome" covers one of the ship's swimming pools with a sliding glass cupola.

Breakfast is served from a vast buffet that manages to accommodate everyone's preferred waking hour, and lunch is presented in both formal and informal venues. Dinner is served in two seatings in the grand Orion Restaurant. For posh relaxation there's Michael's Club, decorated like the parlor of a London men's club and devoted to the pleasures of fine cigars and cognac. For those who don't find that ambience appealing, Tastings Coffee Bar offers a caffeinated alternative. There's a two-deck theater with unobstructed views from every seat if you want to take in the show, but if you prefer to spend the evening socializing with friends there are various bars tucked into nooks and crannies throughout the ship.

✪ **Mercury.** *Passenger capacity:* 1,870. *Crew complement:* 909. *Cabins:* 639 outside (220 with veranda) and 296 inside. *Ship facilities:* Dining room, two cafes, three pools (one indoor) and four whirlpools, AquaSpa, four bars/lounges, night club, casino, shopping, theater, video game room, cinema, conference center, card room, champagne bar, library. *Activities:* Alaska lecture program and numerous daily activities (see above). **Itineraries: 7-night north- and south-bound cruises** between Vancouver and Seward, with visits to Hubbard Glacier, Juneau, Skagway, and Ketchikan, with Valdez and College Fjord added on the northbound trips and Sitka or Glacier Bay added on the Southbound trips. *Departures:* late May to mid-Sept; cruise only, $2,195–$7,495 per person, double occupancy ($2,695–$2,945 single, as part of single guarantee program). **7-night round-trip cruises from Vancouver,** with visits to Juneau, Skagway, Hubbard Glacier or Glacier Bay, and Ketchikan. *Departures:* late May, early June, early Sept; cruise only, $2,145–$7,445 ($2,645–$2,895 single). Children under 12 sharing a stateroom with parents pay $845–$895, children under 2 sail free; third and fourth adult passengers in a stateroom pay $945–$995. Rates include port charges. Early booking discounts of up to 50% are available.

Seen from the outside, the *Mercury* is almost indistinguishable from the *Galaxy*— same streamlined hull, pagoda-like stern, and thrusting bow, same blue-and-white color scheme, same giant "X" on the funnel (it's the Greek for "ch," as in Chandris, the line's founding family). Inside, layout and design motifs tell you this ship is its own animal.

The *Mercury* is structured with so many windows letting onto so many panoramic views that it seems born to sail Alaska. The Navigator's Club, for instance, is set high on the Sky Deck and incorporates a piano bar, lounge, dance floor, and private function room, all artfully arranged between four-meter-high windows that circle the room and let the great outdoors in—albeit in high, high style, and, when the place is in disco mode, at high, high volume. At the opposite end of the ship and somewhat closer to the water, the Manhattan Restaurant is a grand two-story, wood-paneled affair with a design that's equal parts deco New York and classic ocean liner—you keep expecting Rogers and Astaire to waltz through. The full-height windows at the stern allow a romantic view of the passing landscape, and the open design soaks up enough sound so that you don't have to shout to be heard across your table.

The restaurant is tied to the adjacent atrium and lounge through a design motif of three circular partitioning drums. Look closely, and with an open mind, and you'll notice that they suggest the three funnels of a classic ocean liner. The atrium functions as a lounge and champagne bar and features an 18-foot commissioned mural by artist Sol LeWit; the place is small enough to be intimate and open and light enough so that people will notice that new suit you bought for the trip. If you're having a bad hair day and can't face these stylish spaces, head up to the Palm Springs Cafe, aft of the pool area. With seating for 400 and full views, it's a nice alternative dining spot for breakfast, lunch, dinner, and midnight buffets.

The popular Michael's Club, established aboard the *Galaxy* (and older sibling *Century*), is repeated here, though I wish it didn't wrap around the atrium and provide such a bright and obvious view of the shops below. (Still, you can't beat those leather armchairs.) The Pavilion Night Club provides for larger-format good times. If it's live entertainment you want, visit the 950-seat Celebrity Theater. There's a cinema in case your taste runs more to the moving image, and if the gaming bug's got you, visit Fortunes Casino, with a decorative theme that carries over from the nightclub— a little less glitzy than some other cruise ship casinos, a little warmer and more restrained yet dramatic, with black baize covering the gaming tables and wood and brass predominating in the furniture.

And then there's the AquaSpa, a den of sensual pleasure perched on the Resort Deck, facing the bow. Decorated in Moorish/Moroccan/Ottoman design motifs, the spa area provides a tactile complement to the exotic and rejuvenating spa treatments designed by Steiner of London. Step into the main hydrotherapy pool for a water-jet massage, or insinuate yourself into the stream room, decorated in blue-and-white Turkish-style ceramic and featuring an internal warming system that heats all surfaces to a uniform temperature. Four private water therapy rooms (with large windows for taking in the scenery) are available for guests to use before their main body treatments, and the attached fitness area has an exceptionally large cardiovascular floor and a full complement of exercise machines, including virtual-reality bikes on which you can ride through simulated water and make squishy sounds when you ride out again. Fun! An 18-member fitness staff is on hand to assist.

Cabins are available in the same number of configurations as aboard the *Galaxy,* ranging from the enormous Penthouse Suite (with my favorite feature: a whirlpool bath on the veranda) down to the standard inside stateroom, with two twin beds, TV, private safe, minibar, and hair dryer. All feature innovative design that allows for more storage space—always at a premium aboard ship—and all have extremely well-designed and efficient bathrooms (a shower this good I should have in my home). As on the *Galaxy,* there's no really bad cabin aboard the *Mercury.*

CRYSTAL CRUISES
2121 Ave. of the Stars, Suite 200, Los Angeles, CA 90067. ☎ **310/785-9300.** Fax 310/785-0011.

Established in 1988, Los Angeles–based Crystal Cruises may be a new kid on the block, but the company is already setting new standards in the cruise industry. Its goal was to redefine luxury cruising, and it has accomplished this with flying colors. The deep pockets of Japanese parent company NYK Line (the largest shipping line in the world) allowed American-managed Crystal to build two incredible sister vessels, the *Crystal Harmony* and *Crystal Symphony,* and furnish them with exacting attention to detail and the finest of everything to provide first-class service to a discerning clientele.

Cruises with Crystal aren't cheap (though they've been discounted for '98—see below), but for the price, passengers are treated to the ultimate in elegant service, luxurious accommodations, outstanding gourmet cuisine, the best casino afloat (the drinks are free for gamblers), and top-quality entertainment, from classical recitals to Broadway-worthy musical reviews. Both its ships are family friendly, though children that misbehave among the typically well-to-do international passengers will stand out like a sore thumb. Shipwide announcements are kept to a minimum for the comfort of guests.

In addition to being among the most technologically advanced ships afloat, Crystal's vessels feature an exceptionally large number of staterooms and penthouses with verandas, two specialty restaurants for alternative dining, true concierge service available to all passengers, a business center for vacationers who can't let go of the outside world, and a library stocked with books, audio tapes, and videos.

This line spares no expense, from sumptuous flower arrangements to the very best in linens, crystal, china, and silver service. Guests sleep on down pillows under soft European duvets, step off the bed onto linen mats, nap wrapped in mohair blankets, and wander about in thick terry robes. A cadre of European chefs produces incredible gourmet fare, always fresh, utilizing the best ingredients. You'll find no rotating menus here, and with around 25,000 bottles in the cellar, there's sure to be a wine to complement every meal.

Even Crystal's onboard activities are tonier, with golf and bridge clinics, art auctions, wine tastings, current hit movies, elaborate stage shows, and classes in needlepoint, calligraphy, aerobics, and ballroom dance. The enrichment lecture series is also a cut above, and has featured such notables as Wolfgang Puck, Jacques Pepin, Pierre Salinger, Judith Krantz, and Caspar Weinberger in addition to local lecturers (from teachers and librarians to historians and anthropologists) aboard to broaden your knowledge of Alaska. Crystal sees to it that gentlemen hosts are available to entertain single female passengers, and they provide a cruise consultant on every sailing to help guests select future Crystal itineraries (which are deeply discounted when booked aboard the ship).

Good news for 1998 is that—"to generate Alaska excitement early," according to marketing VP Adam Leavitt—Crystal has introduced "Perfect Harmony" fares, by which Alaska sailings can be had for as much as a 32% reduction off the brochure rates reproduced below. Be sure to ask your travel agent or cruise broker about these deals.

✪ **Crystal Harmony.** *Passenger capacity:* 960. *Crew complement:* 545. *Cabins:* 480 outside (260 with veranda) and 19 inside. *Ship facilities:* dining room, cafe, two specialty restaurants, pâtisserie, snack bar, ice-cream bar, four bars, two entertainment lounges, casino, disco, spa and salon, two pools (one with a retractable roof), two whirlpools, basketball/paddle-tennis court, enclosed golf driving net, men's and women's saunas and steam rooms, library, card room, movie theater, shore-excursion desk, duty-free and photo shops, complimentary laundry facilities, medical facility. *Activities:* enrichment lecture series, craft and dance classes, shuffleboard, Ping-Pong, and board games, among other activities. **Itineraries: 10-day southbound cruises** between Anchorage to Vancouver, with visits to Juneau, Skagway, Sitka, Ketchikan, Hubbard Glacier, and Tracy Arm/Endicott Arm. *Departures:* Wed early June to early Sept; cruise only $4,325–$13,160 per person, double occupancy. **11-day northbound cruises** between Vancouver and Anchorage, with stops in Victoria, Ketchikan, Juneau, Skagway, Glacier Bay, Sitka, Hubbard Glacier, and Valdez. *Departures:* Sat late May to late Aug; cruise only, $4,735–$14,435 per person, double occupancy. One **7-day round-trip cruise** departs May 16 from Vancouver, with stops in Ketchikan, Skagway, and Sitka; cruise only, $2,915–$8,700 per person, double occupancy. Rates do not include $100–$115 port charges. Some single cabins are available, and standard cabins are offered to solo passengers at 120%–150% of the per-person double-occupancy rate. Early-booking discounts of 10%–17 1/2% are available.

The *Harmony* and its sister ship *Symphony* (see below) were built to pamper affluent travelers with demanding tastes. The plush staterooms were obviously well thought-out and are equipped with safes, mini-refrigerators, telephones with voice mail, dressing tables, coffee/dining tables, plenty of drawer space, closets with automatic lighting, and TV/VCRs. Bathrooms are long and narrow, but extremely functional, outfitted with double sinks, a deep oval tub with an adjustable shower head, a built-in hairdryer, a makeup mirror, and, in the penthouse suites, a telephone.

The few inside cabins are only slightly smaller than the outside cabins. Most outside cabins have a veranda; those that don't have large picture windows. Penthouses on both ships are enormous (measuring between 360 and 982 square feet), pricey, and immensely popular, perhaps because they're equipped with Jacuzzi bathtubs, bidets, and other extras such as a white-gloved butler who sees to every detail. This is not to say that the other members of the European hotel and dining staff are not as attentive, because they are, making every passenger walk away feeling he or she received VIP treatment during the cruise.

Specialty Japanese and Italian restaurants are aboard on the *Harmony* (they're Chinese and Italian on the *Symphony*) in addition to an elegant tiered dining room, a cafe, a pâtisserie, a snack bar, and an ice-cream bar.

There's always a chance the *Harmony's* sister ship, the **Crystal Symphony,** will be put on the Alaska route in 1999, as the company tends to rotate its ships' itineraries. If this happens, don't sweat it: The two ships are virtual twins, with the primary difference being in the number of outside cabins—480 on the *Symphony* (342 with a veranda), with no inside cabins at all. Public areas are slightly different as well, with slightly more interior public space aboard the *Harmony* and more exterior deck space aboard the *Symphony*.

HOLLAND AMERICA LINE–WESTOURS

300 Elliott Ave. W., Seattle, WA 98119. ☎ **800/426-0327** or 206/281-3535. Fax 800/628-4855. Website http://www.hollandamerica.com.

Founded in 1873, Holland America Line now operates one of the largest cruise fleets in the world and continues to grow. One of the pioneers of Alaska cruising, Holland America offers an amazing number of sailings and has also developed the state's most extensive land-tour operation (Westours, Inc.), so you'll have plenty of choices of shore excursions and land-tour extensions.

HAL stands out from the crowd in many ways. Its ships offer more activities than any other line—so many, in fact, that the selection can be overwhelming. Naturalists accompany every cruise in Alaska, lecturing on the flora and fauna. In addition to bingo, fashion and talent shows, board and card games, dancing or cooking classes, an extensive fitness program, tours of the bridge, and art auctions, there are a variety of enrichment lectures to choose from, covering everything from photography to finance to nutrition.

The carefully trained Indonesian and Filipino crews are cheerful, friendly, and solicitous, so service consistently receives outstanding ratings from passengers. Plus, Holland America's ships are always immaculately clean. The mixed international cuisine, overseen by executive chef Reiner Greubel, is well prepared, diverse, and attractively presented. Room service is available at all hours, and you can get anything from the daily menu delivered to your cabin during lunch and dinner hours.

Holland America features some of the lowest cruise fares in Alaska, especially with its early-booking discount of 25% and discounts for third and forth passengers per cabin.

Nieuw Amsterdam / Noordam. *Passenger capacity:* 1,250. *Crew complement:* 530. *Cabins:* 411 outside and 194 inside. *Ship facilities:* dining room, cafe with ice-cream bar, five bars, entertainment lounge, casino, disco, spa and salon, exercise room, two pools, whirlpool, men's and women's saunas, library, card room, children's activity room with video arcade, deck sports (shuffleboard, Ping-Pong, volleyball, tennis), shops, coin laundries, medical facility. *Activities:* up to 250 per 7-day cruise. **Nieuw Amsterdam itineraries: 7-day round-trip cruises from**

Vancouver, with visits to Ketchikan, Juneau, Skagway, and Glacier Bay. *Departures:* Thurs early May to late Sept; cruise only, $1,198–$3,732 per person, double occupancy. ***Noordam* itineraries: 7-day north- and southbound cruises** between Vancouver and Seward, with visits to Valdez, Sitka, Juneau, Ketchikan, College Fjord, and Hubbard Glacier or Glacier Bay. *Departures:* Fri mid-May to late Sept; cruise only, $898–$3,532 per person, double occupancy. Rates include taxes and port charges. Early-booking discounts of 25% and discounts for third and fourth passengers are available. Solo passengers pay 140%–200% of the per-person double-occupancy rate.

Launched in 1983 and 1984 respectively, the *Nieuw Amsterdam* and the *Noordam* are identical aside from their collections of decorative art and antiques and the color schemes of their public rooms. The *Nieuw Amsterdam* follows a Dutch seafaring theme while the *Noordam* features an antique Oriental theme. Equipped with spacious public areas and gyms, windowed dining rooms located on high decks designed for sea views, forward-view lounges on the top deck, and large cafes with double buffet lines, these twins fall mid-range in the Holland America line in terms of price and style (they're not quite as fancy as the *Maasdam, Ryndam,* and *Statendam,* reviewed below). Seating configurations in their bilevel entertainment lounges could be better for viewing the fine productions staged there, but shows and lectures are also broadcast on stateroom TVs, eliminating the need to show up early for the best seat in the house. Photo displays set up at the entrance to the Lido cafe tend to clog traffic at mealtimes.

Both ships were refurbished in stages during 1994 and 1995. Cabins on the upper four decks feature rectangular view windows (though many on the Navigation Deck have obstructed views) and twin beds that can be pushed together. Cabins on lower decks have portholes and twin beds in a fixed "L" configuration; you may also notice engine vibrations more on these lower decks. My favorite cabins (100 to 103) are actually the four handicapped-accessible rooms overlooking the bow of the ship; they're very spacious, have picture windows framing the broadest views, and are available to anyone when not booked by handicapped passengers. All cabins are well laid-out and provide ample storage space, multichannel music, TVs, telephones, individual climate control, lockable drawers, and tiled bathrooms with deep tubs (cabins in the lower price categories have showers only).

✪ **Maasdam / Ryndam / Statendam.** *Passenger capacity:* 1,300. *Crew complement:* 586. *Cabins:* 485 outside (129 with veranda) and 148 inside. *Ship facilities:* dining room, cafe with ice-cream bar, six bars, entertainment lounge, casino, disco, spa and salon, aerobics room, gym, two pools (one with retractable roof), two whirlpools, men's and women's saunas and steam rooms, library, card room, children's activity center with video arcade, deck sports (shuffleboard, Ping-Pong, tennis), duty-free shops, photo service, coin laundries, medical facility. *Activities:* extensive onboard activities. ***Maasdam* itineraries: 7-day round-trip cruises from Vancouver,** with visits to Ketchikan, Juneau, Skagway, and Glacier Bay. *Departures:* Mon mid-May to late Sept; cruise only, $1,398–$5,799 per person, double occupancy. ***Ryndam* and *Statendam* itineraries: 7-day north- and southbound cruises** between Vancouver and Seward, with visits to Ketchikan, Juneau, Sitka, Valdez, College Fjord, and Hubbard Glacier or Glacier Bay. *Departures:* Sundays, north- or southbound; cruise only, $1,198–$5,732 per person, double occupancy. ***Statendam*** is also scheduled for two Inside Passage cruises round-trip from Vancouver, on May 10 and Sept 20; cruise only, $1,398–$5,065. Rates include taxes and port charges. Early booking discounts of 25% and discounts for third and fourth passengers are available. Solo passengers pay 140%–200% of the per-person double-occupancy rate.

Introduced in 1993 and 1994, these three ships are glitzier than their older siblings, especially in their soaring grand atriums and their view lounges. Copious use of glass, high ceilings, shining metal trim, and light colors brighten them and make them feel more open and modern than the *Noordam* and *Nieuw Amsterdam* (but then, as these ships are almost twice the tonnage of their siblings, their public areas are bound to feel much larger). They also feature bigger, better designs in their show lounges, more elegant two-story dining rooms with glass walls, and better traffic flow through their Lido buffets. The ships vary only slightly in their decor and sports facilities; the *Statendam* feels a bit more formal and has a cushioned jogging track in place of sports courts, while the *Maasdam* and *Ryndam* feel slightly homier and have practice tennis courts.

These lovely vessels also feature large penthouses and a number of plush suites and deluxe staterooms with verandas, minibars, refrigerators, VCRs, whirlpool baths, sitting areas, and floor-to-ceiling windows. Standard cabins are comparable in design and amenities to those on the *Nieuw Amsterdam* and the *Noordam,* but twin beds in every room can be pushed together to form one double bed (even in the smallest inside cabins, which manage not to feel too confining). Another plus is that every outside cabin is equipped with a bathtub (inside cabins have showers only).

Westerdam. *Passenger capacity:* 1,494. *Crew complement:* 642. *Cabins:* 495 outside, 252 inside. *Ship facilities:* dining room, cafe, seven bars, entertainment lounge, casino, disco, spa and salon, gym, two pools (one with retractable roof), two whirlpools, men's and women's saunas and steam rooms, unobstructed jogging/walking track, library, card room, children's activity center with video arcade, deck sports (shuffleboard, Ping-Pong, tennis), duty-free shops, photo service, coin laundries, medical facility. *Activities:* extensive onboard activities. **Itineraries: 7-day round-trip cruises from Vancouver** with visits to Juneau, Skagway, Glacier Bay, and Ketchikan. *Departures:* Sat mid-May to late Sept; cruise only, $1,198–$5,332 per person, double occupancy. Rates include taxes and port charges. Early booking discounts of 25% and discounts for third and fourth passengers are available. Solo passengers pay 140%–200% of the per-person double-occupancy rate.

After Holland America bought this ship in 1989, it sawed the boat apart and inserted a 140-foot midsection, an $84-million effort that added almost 14,000 tons and some 200 additional cabins to the ship. Experts say the enlargement is seamless, as do many passengers who search (unsuccessfully) for weld marks and disjointed traffic flows. Despite its enlargement, *Westerdam* weighs a bit less than the ships commissioned by the line since 1993, and contains fewer decks. Since most of the ship's rebuilding occurred before Holland America was bought by Carnival, the ship is completely and resolutely unglittery.

The size of a standard outside cabin is a roomy 200 square feet. Cabins come in 15 different price and space configurations, many with one twin bed and one fold-away bed that functions during the day as a sofa. The cabins are decorated in conservative colors and batik prints. Although compact, bathrooms are well-designed and well-lit. Except for a few lower-priced cabins, all have tubs as well as a shower.

The public areas are similar to those aboard the *Nieuw Amsterdam* and *Noordam.* Unfortunately, *Westerdam's* dining room is positioned below decks, depriving you of Alaskan panoramas while you dine.

NORWEGIAN CRUISE LINE

95 Merrick Way, Coral Gables, FL 33134. ☎ **800/327-9020** or 305/447-9660. Fax 305/448-7936. Website http://www.ncl.com.

Founded in 1968 as Norwegian Caribbean Line, NCL concentrates on appealing to families and young, active passengers. Here's where the line excels: First, in activities: If they offered any more, passengers would be exhausted. Second, in entertainment: Their Las Vegas–style shows are first-rate. Third, NCL excels in theme cruises and theme nights. Want more? Recreational and fitness programs are among the best and most comprehensive afloat, with an incentive program that rewards cruise passengers who join in the fun, whether they play volleyball or take an aerobics class. The line also offers an good selection of soft-adventure shore excursions (including hiking, biking, and kayaking) in addition to all the popular standards. Additionally, NCL is a market leader in promoting a smoke-free environment for those who want it. At least half the cabins on its ships are non-smoking, and on any ship with more than one dining room, one will be non-smoking. There are even blackjack tables in its casinos reserved for nonsmokers.

✪ **Norwegian Dynasty.** *Passenger capacity:* 800. *Crew complement:* 320. Cabins: 276 outside (10 with veranda) and 124 inside. *Ship facilities:* dining room, cafe, three bars, nightclub, lounge, casino, fitness center, spa, pool, sauna, shopping, salon, and photo gallery. *Activities:* Alaskan lecturer, wine tastings, art auctions, trap shooting, cooking demonstrations, craft and dance classes, incentive fitness program, daily quizzes, board games, lotto, and bingo, among other activities. **Itineraries: 7-day north- and southbound cruises** between Vancouver and Seward, with visits to Ketchikan or Wrangell, Juneau, Skagway, Cordova, and Hubbard Glacier. *Departures:* Tues May to early Sept; cruise only, $1,735–$3,635 per person, double-occupancy. Rates include port charges; government fee of $9.50 per person not included. Discounts of $399–$599 are available for third and fourth passengers. Solo passengers pay 150%–200% of the per-person double-occupancy rate.

A recent acquisition for NCL, the *Dynasty* has in the last few years been associated with Crown, Cunard, and Majesty Cruise Lines, and makes its first NCL Alaska sailings in 1998. Overall, the *Dynasty* is a stylish, showy, and dramatic ship that offers many of the amenities and diversions of a medium-sized vessel while retaining some of the coziness of a much smaller one—which means you'll feel less like you're lost in a shopping mall and more like you're among friends.

The decor is contemporary and airy, with touches of marble, teak, and artwork, and a lovely five-deck atrium is positioned on the ship's starboard side, rather than in the conventional center location. Ringed with glass, brass, and polished stone, it's offset on the port side by an almost uninterrupted wall of glass that floods the interiors with natural light and allows stunning views of the passing landscape. Lounges overlook the ship's side, rather than the bow or stern. Most of Deck Five is reserved for public areas, lounges, tuck-away bars, a library, and a half-moon-shaped show lounge. There's a small-scale jogging track above the outdoor pool, plus two whirlpools and a wading pool for children. The health club has weight machines, free weights, stationary bikes, aerobics classes, and saunas, and treatments are available in the floating beauty salon and spa.

Cabins are cozy and compact, trimmed in light-grained wood with touches of brass. Each contains a safe and adequate storage space for a week's worth of clothes, and the beds can be configured either as doubles or twins. There are nine categories of cabins, and cabins within a category are almost identical. Ten suites have private verandas. Families or groups traveling together can book interconnected cabins.

✪ **Norwegian Wind.** *Passenger capacity:* 1,726. *Crew complement:* 614. *Cabins:* 651 outside (74 with veranda) and 212 inside. *Ship facilities:* three main dining rooms, specialty bistro, sports bar and grill, casino, six bars/lounges, show lounge, observation lounge/disco, spa and health club, men's and women's saunas and steam rooms, two heated pools, two whirlpools, terraced sundeck, basketball/volleyball court, shuffleboard, Ping-Pong, golf driving cage, jogging track, library/card room, shore-excursion desk, duty-free and photo shops, tuxedo rentals, medical facility. *Activities:* Alaskan lecturer, wine tastings, art auctions, trap shooting, cooking demonstrations, craft and dance classes, incentive fitness program, daily quizzes, board games, lotto, and bingo, among other activities. **Itineraries: 7-day round-trip cruises from Vancouver,** with visits to Skagway, Haines, Juneau, Ketchikan, and Glacier Bay or Sawyer Glacier. *Departures:* Mon early May to early Sept; cruise only, $1,944–$4,244 per person, double occupancy. Rates include port charges; government fee of $9.50 per person not included. Discounts of $399–$599 are available for third and fourth passengers. Solo passengers pay 150%–200% of the per-person double-occupancy rate.

Cruise veterans will know this ship as the *Windward,* but that was the old and this is the new: the ship is slated for an early–1998 overhaul at the Lloyd Werft shipyards in Bremerhaven, Germany, during which a new 130-foot midsection will be grafted into its hull, increasing capacity by over 500 berths and allowing for the addition of a new casual restaurant, a sports bar and grill, an expanded health club, new meeting facilities, improved children's facilities, and new gift shops, lounges, and a cigar/cordial club. All these new facilities will be up and running in time for the summer Alaska season. The same operation is being performed on NCL's *Norwegian Dream* (formerly the *Dreamward*), which primarily offers European sailings. NCL's stated intention is to "maintain the beauty, character, and popularity of these two premium vessels," so we're not talking all-new, all-different ships here—just bigger ones.

The *Norwegian Wind* is a very family-friendly vessel: There's at least one full-time youth-activity coordinator, a kid's activity room, a television lounge with video games, the all-important ice-cream bar, and guaranteed babysitting aboard. It's also well equipped for the sports-minded and active vacationer—in addition to the new fitness center, there are two heated pools, an unobtructed rubberized jogging/walking track, a sports bar with walls of TV screens showing ESPN, and a good selection of sports facilities (listed above). Miles of glass bring the outside in on this ship, and there are plenty of view lounges for relaxation. Windscreens wrap around the sports deck, protecting it and the terraced pool deck, so these areas remain warm even when you're cruising next to glaciers.

Instead of one or two giant dining rooms, the *Wind* has three smaller, more intimate restaurants and a romantic specialty bistro. Request a table in The Terraces or the Sun Terrace for panoramic sea views. Dinners follow a theme (Viking, Northern Lights, Klondike, International, etc.) as do the extravagant late-night buffets (don't miss the unique "Galley Raid" for a chance to meet the chefs and watch ice carving and cooking demonstrations as you pass through the galley, piling your plate high). Room service is available around the clock.

Cabins are fairly standard in size and vary little other than in their style of windows. About 85% of the cabins are outside, and most have picture windows. Suites have floor-to-ceiling windows, and a number of them have private balconies. All are equipped with multichannel TVs, telephones, small dressing tables, soundproofed doors, individual climate control, and sitting areas that are actually big enough to stretch out in. Closet and drawer space is quite limited, so pack light. There's no guest laundry aboard, but valet laundry service is available.

PRINCESS CRUISES
10100 Santa Monica Blvd., Los Angeles, CA 90067-4189. ☎ **800/421-0522** or 310/553-1770. Fax 310/284-2857. Website http://www.princesscruises.com.

Let's play a word-association test: What do you think of when I say the names Captain Stubing, Gopher, Doc, Isaac, and Julie? *The Love Boat,* of course, where every entertainment personality who ever lived found amour on the high seas, aboard a Princess ship. While you probably won't catch Charo aboard today, there's no escaping the TV association and the romantic self-image of the line, which has grown from a one-ship entity in 1965 to be ranked among the largest cruise lines in the world. It's debuted three ships since 1995 and will add an additional two by the year 2000. Think investment. Think big investment.

Princess works hard to maintain its "Love Boat" reputation through all this growth, responding as well to passenger suggestions by banning smoking in the main dining and show areas, adding children's activities and youth counselors, putting terry-cloth robes and fruit baskets in every cabin, and even placing a heart-shaped chocolate on your pillow at night. These are highly popular, fun, mass-market cruises that present elaborate Broadway-style shows (one of its strongest points), hire top entertainers, showcase bountiful buffets, and provide quality Italian-influenced cuisine.

As one of the pioneers in Alaska, Princess has also built one the state's two largest land-tour operation and offers an array of shore excursions and land-cruise tours rivaled only by Holland America–Westours. Due to the size of Princess's ships (and the consequent distance they have to keep from land), these outstanding excursions are really the only way you'll see much Alaskan wildlife; the focus on board is really on the cruise experience. True, a naturalist does lecture on whales and such during the cruise, but the ships don't typically go in search of wildlife, so you'll be on your own—just remember to bring *powerful* binoculars to spot critters from the high decks.

✪ **Dawn Princess / Sun Princess.** *Passenger capacity:* 1,950. *Crew complement:* 900. *Cabins:* 603 outside (410 with veranda) and 376 inside. *Ship facilities:* two main dining rooms; pizzeria; wine, champagne, and caviar bar; 24-hour food court; two main show lounges; pâtisserie; deck grill; six swimming pools and five whirlpools; ice cream bar; 24-hour room service; disco; six bars/lounges; spa and gym; salon with men's and women's saunas and steam rooms; children's and teen's activity areas; children's pool; basketball, volleyball, badminton, and paddle tennis courts; casino; jogging track; library; card room; movie theater; duty-free and photo shops; coin laundries; medical facility. *Activities:* naturalist lectures, craft and dance classes, incentive fitness program, cooking demonstrations, passenger talent show, board games and bingo, etc. **Itineraries: 7-day north- and southbound cruises** between Vancouver and Anchorage, with visits to Ketchikan, Juneau, Skagway, Glacier Bay, and College Fjord. *Departures:* Sat mid-May to mid-Sept; cruise only, $1,429–$5,379 per person, double occupancy. Rates include port charges. Early-booking discounts and 50% discounts for third and fourth passengers are available. Solo passengers pay 160%–200% of the per-person double-occupancy rate.

The *Dawn Princess* and *Sun Princess* are identical in every way except decor and the naming of certain public areas, and for 1998 will follow the same itinerary, with both ships departing on Saturdays, alternating north- and southbound routes. Both ships weigh in at 77,000 tons, yet prove that big can be beautiful. Their size allows them to offer a wide variety of entertainment, dining, and activity options, and provides enough space that passengers will rarely, if ever, feel crowded. Yet they're so well designed that passengers can also find on their 14 decks the kind of intimate and interesting spaces that make smaller ships so appealing.

The decor of both ships includes a liberal use of wood and marble. The effect, enhanced by numerous live plants and the ships' large, multi-million-dollar collections of contemporary art, is upscale and appealing, contemporary yet not glitzy. Guest cabins are well equipped and larger than the norm, and 410 feature private verandas. The hub of social activity on board each ship is the four-story atrium, which serves as an information, entertainment, dining, and shopping venue and also as a unique, multi-level setting for the captain's cocktail party.

The Broadway-style Princess Theatre is the premier entertainment venue aboard each ship, and offers both elaborate stage shows and movies. Glass cases outside hold a collection of movie memorabilia (the one on the *Dawn Princess* includes pantaloons worn by Vivian Leigh in *Gone With The Wind*). The Vista Lounge offers floor-to-ceiling windows and a sternward view for those who like to look backwards, and the disco features a dark decor that highlights psychedelic light and video displays, and is a magnet for the late-night party crowd. For those seeking quiet venues, the Promenade Deck offers a third of a mile of open-air space, with teakwood flooring and traditional wooden deck chairs. The library offers comfy leather chairs, some with built-in CD players, and the adjacent card room offers board games and doubles as a meeting space.

The extensive spa (called Oasis on the *Dawn* and Riviera on the *Sun*) offers a large oceanview room with exercise equipment, a mirrored aerobics studio with a full range of energy and strength classes, and a massage and treatment area with an impressive menu of options. An open-air sports deck, uniquely located in the ship's funnel, features basketball, volleyball, badminton, and paddle tennis. And each ship also has a computerized golf center where passengers can simulate play at the world's top golf courses. For kids, each *Princess* offers The Fun Zone, a bright area with a popular bank of computers, climbing apparatus, and a mini-theater, as well as a separate area for teens. Add in the staffed nursery and you have a package that's better for families than Princess's older ships.

Treats for expensive adult tastes are offered at the wine, champagne, and caviar bar (called Magnums on the *Dawn* and Rendez-Vous on the *Sun*), but a more popular drinking venue is the Wheelhouse Bar, where leather and brass and a collection of ship memorabilia create a clubby ambience.

Each ship has two identical 550-seat windowed dining rooms located on separate decks, and windowside seats are in high demand at each of two seatings. Food is also offered 24-hours a day at the bright and airy Horizon Court—which, with its position at the front of the ship, the number of windows, and the easy access it provides to outside decks, becomes a crowded spot when good sights appear. (Comparisonwise, this area is far more inviting than the cavernous casino/observation/dancing lounge on Princess's *Crown* and *Regal*). While there is a diverse selection of food offered on the ship—also including a pizzeria and hamburger grill—it's just above average and not the ships' strongest attribute.

The friendly staff on board is a big plus and displays a good sense of humor without being overpowering. Such annoyances on other cruise lines as bar personnel constantly pushing drinks are, pleasantly, not found here. A naturalist is aboard for lectures on wildlife, and locals often come aboard for special presentations—a park ranger might give a presentation on Glacier Bay, for instance, or a local performer might entertain with songs and stories. Many of the special presenatations and lectures are repeated on the ship's in-house TV system.

Crown Princess / Regal Princess. *Passenger capacity:* 1,590. *Crew complement:* 696. *Cabins:* 618 outside (184 with veranda) and 177 inside. *Ship facilities:* dining room, cafe, pizzeria, pâtisserie, wine and caviar bar, disco, casino/observation lounge, six bars/lounges, showroom, movie theater, gym, salon with men's and women's saunas and steam rooms, two pools (one heated), four whirlpools, basketball/volleyball court, shuffleboard, Ping-Pong, jogging track, library, card room, duty-free and photo shops, coin laundries, medical facility. *Activities:* life-enhancement and naturalist lectures, language lessons, cooking demonstrations, galley and bridge tours, craft and dance classes, incentive fitness program, passenger talent show, daily quizzes, board games, and bingo, etc. **Crown Princess itineraries: 7-day north- and southbound cruises** between Seward and Vancouver, with visits to Ketchikan, Juneau, Skagway, College Fjord, and Glacier Bay or Hubbard Glacier. *Departures:* Mon mid-May to mid-Sept; cruise only $1,479–$5,079 per person, double occupancy. **Regal Princess itineraries: 7-day round-trip cruises from Vancouver,** with visits to Juneau, Skagway, Sitka, and Glacier Bay. *Departures:* Sun mid-May to mid-Sept; cruise only, $1,479–$5,079 per person, double occupancy. Rates include port charges. Early-booking discounts can bring fares down by $550–$1,200 per person, and third- and fourth-passenger discounts are 50%. Solo passengers pay 160%–200% of the per-person double-occupancy rate.

The *Crown Princess* and the *Regal Princess,* designed by Italian architect Renzo Piano (best known for his design of Paris's Centre Pompidou) and introduced in 1991 and 1992, respectively, present a dramatic, aqualinear, almost dolphinlike appearance, with sweeping exterior lines and graceful curves. They are essentially identical in personality and in their sleek, modern decor, though the *Crown* tends to feel somewhat more formal than the *Regal* because of its interior color schemes and art collection. Catering to the whims of up to 1,600 passengers a week, these ships are equipped with virtually every facility you can imagine. One of their best features is the large number of dining and entertainment areas, which ensures something to please virtually anyone's taste in cuisine and music. There's no formal children's area such as you'll find aboard other Princess vessels (see the *Dawn* and *Sun Princess* review above); to compensate, Princess runs a children's activities program when at least 15 children are on board.

Cabins are spacious (as cabins on megaliners go), well laid out, and attractively decorated; many feature glass doors that open onto narrow balconettes, and outside cabins that don't are outfitted with picture windows. All have multichannel color TVs, telephones, safes, mini-refrigerators, and twin beds that convert to a double. Four of the ships' 10 handicapped-accessible cabins (nos. 101, 102, 104, and 106) are situated near the disco, but triple doors in the hallway suffice to block the night noise.

Sky Princess. *Passenger capacity:* 1,200. *Crew complement:* 535. *Cabins:* 385 outside (10 with veranda) and 215 inside. *Ship facilities:* two dining rooms, buffet, ice cream bar, three pools and one Jacuzzi, fitness center with hot tub and sauna, spa, paddle tennis/volleyball court, unobstructed walking/jogging track, five lounges/bars, theater, showroom, disco, beauty/barbershop, casino, shopping, library, laundry. *Activities:* see reviews above. **Itineraries: 7-night north- and southbound cruises** between Vancouver and Seward, with visits to Ketchikan, Juneau, Skagway, Glacier Bay or Hubbard Glacier, and College Fjord. *Departures:* Mon mid-May to mid-Sept (the *Sky Princess* alternates north- and southbound sailings with the *Crown Princess,* reviewed above); cruise only, $1,449–$4,789 per person, double occupancy. Rates include port charges. Early-booking discounts can bring fares down by $550–$1,200 per person, and third- and fourth-passenger discounts are 50%. Solo passengers pay 160%–200% of the per-person double-occupancy rate.

Originally built in 1984 as the *Fairsky* for the now-defunct Sitmar line, the *Sky Princess* was the last large steam turbine passenger ship to be built. Old-fashioned, you think? That depends. While modern diesel engines are cheaper to operate, they just don't offer the smooth, quiet ride of a steam turbine.

In 1992, Princess poured a few million dollars into refurbishing the *Sky,* handing it over to Italian architect Giacomo Mortola, who had been responsible for the ship's original interior back when it was built. (Mortola also designed some of the lounges aboard the *Crown Princess* and *Regal Princess.*) The original design features of the ship were kept intact, but updated with a comfortable, contemporary feel. The Veranda Lounge in the stern allows easy access to the pool deck (where the Deck Buffet will tempt you with hamburgers, hot dogs, soups, and salads) and features floor-to-ceiling windows for Alaska sightseeing. At night, the lounge doubles as a nightclub. In the bow, the Horizon lounge has tall windows facing forward and banquette window seats for your panoramic viewing pleasure. The Sky Princess Showroom offers good visibility for its Broadway-style presentations, and the Starlight Room in the stern serves as a nightclub and disco.

Cabins are large and have a generous amount of closet space, though the windows (oblong portholes, really) are somewhat small for major sightseeing. All cabins are outfitted with phones, TVs, and safes. Most have twin beds, and some can accommodate third and fourth passengers. (Combine this with the youth and teen centers on board and you have a good bet for family cruising.)

Two dining rooms—the Regency and Savoy, both on the Aloha Deck and each offering two seatings—provide a relatively intimate dining experience. As with all Princess vessels, meals tend toward Continental and American cuisine. Service is gracious and relaxed.

All the Stars Weren't in the Sky

Passengers on a recent *Dawn Princess* sailing from Vancouver didn't know where to look. Should they be checking out the calving Mergerie Glacier or watching scantily clad *Baywatch* star Carmen Electra doing a sexy dance for the cameras on the ship's bow? Electra's do-si-do with an ice sculpture seemed to be winning out for many (let's just say the ice melted). After all, there were other glaciers to see en route, but how often do you get to see Hollywood in action?

Princess Cruises hopes the attention of TV viewers will be similarly diverted when "Baywatch: White Thunder at Glacier Bay"—the hit show's special two-hour, 200th anniversary special—airs in May '98. The episode was filmed almost entirely on the ship, and with syndicated *Baywatch* the most-watched TV show in the world, it could draw as many as one billion viewers.

The idea of filming on the *Dawn Princess* came from the cruise line itself, no stranger to TV fame after it's stint as *The Love Boat*. Executives of *Baywatch* liked the concept of a cruise ship setting, and agreed, in exchange for cabins for the 120+ *Baywatch* cast and crew, to give Princess promotional consideration. That's why the script includes such lines as Ms. Electra gushing "This ship is known for its gourmet cuisine" during a dinner sequence. (It took her several takes to get it right.) Passengers and crew were pulled in as extras, including maitre d' Mario Propato and cruise director Billy Hygate, who plays the ship's captain during the wedding of Hasselhoff's character, Mitch. In addition to the *Dawn Princess's* impressive four-story atrium, where the wedding scene takes place, the show features the ship's exterior, casino, Wheelhouse Bar, dining room, gift shop, a suite, and the pool deck. Princess officials said they hoped "Baywatch: White Thunder at Glacier Bay" would promote the line, Alaska, and the cruise experience itself to an international audience of *Baywatch* fans. And given the skimpy costumes and shipboard glamour portrayed in the plot, it seems certain to do just that.

—Fran Golden

Island Princess. *Passenger capacity:* 640. *Crew complement:* 350. *Cabins:* 238 outside (none with veranda) and 67 inside. *Ship facilities:* dining room, two pools (one with retractable roof), gym, casino, beauty salon, barber shop, showroom, disco, three bars/lounges, shops, library, laundry. *Activities:* see reviews above. **Itineraries: 10- and 11-night north- and south-bound cruises** between Vancouver and Anchorage, with visits to Ketchikan, Sitka, Skagway, Juneau, Seward, Kodiak, Homer, College Fjord, and Hubbard Glacier. Sun and Thurs late May to early Sept; cruise only, $2,869–$7,629 per person based on double occupancy. Rates include port charges. Early-booking discounts can bring fares down by up to $1,500 per person, and third- and fourth-passenger discounts are 50%. Solo passengers pay 160%–200% of the per-person double-occupancy rate.

This is the Love Boat—the *real* love boat; the one you saw on TV (or at least one of them, as filming was split between the *Island Princess* and the *Pacific Princess*). I have two suggestions: (1) revel in the romance of that fact, and (2) don't go looking for the palacial accommodations that Charo and company stayed in while aboard—'cause you won't find 'em. Built in the 1970s and the smallest ship in Princess's fleet, the *Island Princess* is a classic cruise ship with all the traditional lines and all the wood and brass you'd expect. An extensive renovation in 1993 introduced a bit of contemporary style into the cabins and public rooms, added state-of-the-art exercise equipment to the fitness center, beefed up the size of the casino and video arcades, added new air-conditioning, and brought the operational technology up to date, but it did nothing to blur the legend.

Most public rooms are located on the Riviera Deck, including the Princess Theatre, Carousel Lounge and Bar, casino, Bridge Lounge, and Carib/Pacific Lounge. Topside, on the Sun Deck, you'll find the fitness center, pool, and Starlight Lounge, which is a good spot for an after-dinner drink.

One drawback so common to older ships is that the dining room lies on the Coral Deck, way down low on the ship, and so does not offer the kind of views that are so integral to the design of most modern ships. Thankfully, breakfast and lunch are served at the Lido Buffet on the Sun Deck. Afternoon tea is available in the dining room.

Cabins are small though not uncomfortable, and were all refurbished in the 1993 renovation. All have TVs, phones, four-channel radios, and twin beds, of which one generally can be folded into the wall for more space during the day. No cabins have verandas, and windows, while not tiny, are far from the enormous picture windows so common today. Most bathrooms have showers only, save for those in the suites, which come with tubs.

ROYAL CARIBBEAN INTERNATIONAL

1050 Caribbean Way, Miami, FL 33132. ☎ **800/327-6700** or 305/379-4731. Website http://www.rccl.com.

A pioneer in modern cruise vacationing since its inception in 1969, Royal Caribbean has grown to become one of the largest cruise lines in the world, operating twelve ships (with another on the way) on routes covering the Americas, Europe, and the Far East. As if that weren't enough, RCI added to its corporate cache in 1997 by merging with Celebrity Cruises—a deal that will by the year 2000 see the line floating a combined fleet of twenty ships with 38,000 berths. Big. Very Big. Beyond sheer size, though, the line has set many standards for the industry as a whole. It was the first to build a ship designed specifically for warm-water cruising in the Caribbean, first to introduce air/sea inclusive packages, first to introduce view lounges perched on the highest deck, and first to institute an incentive-based fitness program. Most obviously, though, it was first to ask the question "And why *can't* our ships be the size of Cincinnati?" Thus, the megaship, which was what journalists dubbed the massive *Sovereign of the Seas* when it debuted in 1988, and which is what RCI has continued to build to this day, with the enormous *Legend of the Seas* and *Rhapsody of the Seas* being the line's choices for Alaska in 1998.

Royal Caribbean's most obvious asset is its consistency, with activities, daily programs, cuisine, bar service, and cabin service that are all well-rehearsed and professional. The shipboard tone is classy, fun, and generally sane. There's not a hint of slapstick, no cornpone, and no gratuitous whoopie like you'll find elsewhere (read: Carnival). Karaoke is about as out-of-control as activities aboard RCI gets. Dress is generally casual but neat during the day and informal most evenings, with two semi-formal or formal nights per seven-day cruise.

What are the drawbacks with RCI? Anonymity, mostly. Big ships are just more anonymous than small-scale cruisers, and RCI's ships are *very* big, so if you feel agoraphobic or confused on a large ship, or if you can never remember what deck your cabin is on, this may not be the line for you. If, on the other hand, you're the outgoing type and enjoy ships that offer plenty to do, RCI might be your pick—but you'll experience the inevitable lines for buffets, debarkation, and boarding of buses during shore excursions, and will sometimes have to wait a while for your drink when a bar or lounge is particularly crowded.

Forced to generalize about the average RCI passenger, I'd say couples (and, to a lesser extent, singles) aged 30 to 60, with a good number of families thrown in the mix as well. The majority of passengers are professional, sedate, white-collar types who are out to have fun while maintaining some semblance of dignity.

Food aboard is good and sometimes even very good. It's not gourmet, but dishes are flavorful and well-conceived, in a primarily continental vein with a strong Italian influence (plenty of pastas and tangy herb sauces). Fresh Alaskan products are a highlight. Cuisine is often themed, with table settings, menus, and waiters' costumes reflecting the evening's topic of choice. Dining rooms feature two seatings with assigned tables at breakfast, lunch, and dinner. Every menu contains selections designed for low-fat, low-cholesterol, low-salt dining, as well as vegetarian and children's dishes. Other than that, special diets are obtained only with difficulty (inquire when you book your cruise). In addition to the midnight buffet, sandwiches are served throughout the night in the public lounges, and a pretty routine menu is available from room service 24 hours a day. During normal dinner hours, however, a cabin steward can bring you anything being served that night.

Activity-wise, Royal Caribbean offers plenty of the standard cruise line fare, but if you want to take it easy and watch the world go by or scan for wildlife, no one will bother you or cajole you into joining an activity. Children's activities are some of the most extensive afloat, and include a teen disco and children's play areas. Entertainment-wise, the line doesn't stint, incorporating sprawling, high-tech cabaret stages into each of its ships, usually with as many as 50 video monitors to complement live performances. Entertainment begins before dinner and continues late, late into the night.

✪ **Legend of the Seas / Rhapsody of the Seas.** *Passenger capacity:* 1,804/2,000. *Crew complement:* 720/765. *Legend* has 575 outside cabins (231 with veranda) and 327 inside cabins; *Rhapsody* has 593 outside cabins (287 with veranda) and 407 inside cabins. *Facilities:* dining room, cafe, snack bar, espresso bar, six bars/lounges, champagne and caviar bar, showroom, disco, casino, conference center, spa and salon, fitness center with aerobics room and weight room, two pools (one with retractable roof), four whirlpools, men's and women's saunas and steam rooms, observatory, cushioned jogging track, putting course (on *Legend* only), shuffleboard, Ping-Pong, library, card room, children's activity room, video-games room, teen center/disco, duty-free shops, photo services, tuxedo rental, medical facility. *Activities:* wine & cheese tasting program; fitness program; dance and gaming classes; health, beauty, and cooking demonstrations; lecture series; art auctions; and organized games and sports, among other activities. **Itineraries: 7-day round-trip cruises from Vancouver** with visits to Skagway, Haines, Juneau, Ketchikan, and Hubbard Glacier or Glacier Bay (the *Legend* also cruises Misty Fjords). *Legend departures:* Sun late May to mid-Sept; cruise only, $1,699–$6,749 per person, double occupancy. *Rhapsody departures:* Sat mid-May to mid-Sept; cruise only $1,699–$6,749 per person, double occupancy. Rates include port charges. Early-booking discounts of up to 30% and third- and fourth-passenger discounts are available. Solo passengers have option of share program or single guarantee program, or can pay 150–200% of the per-person double-occupancy rate.

Launched in early 1995 and mid-1997, respectively, sister ships *Legend of the Seas* and *Rhapsody of the Seas* are elegant down to the last well-planned detail, from their multimillion dollar art collections to their wide range of onboard facilities. Plenty of nice touches—sumptuous, big-windowed health club/spas with lots of health and beauty treatments; loads of fine shopping, dining, and entertainment options; and luxurious appointments such as triple sheeting on every bed (all of which convert to a double-bed configuration in every cabin)—give both ships the feel of a top-flight shore resort.

Of almost identical size and passenger capacity (though the *Rhapsody* is slightly larger), both megaships soar 10 stories above the waterline and feature 7-story glass-walled atriums with glass elevators and winding brass-trimmed staircases. At the peak of each is the Viking Crown, RCI's signature lounge and the highest bar afloat, affording a 360° view of the passing scenery. You'll also appreciate the view through the glass walls of the bilevel dining room. Actually, other than in the windowless casino and show lounge, there are great views to be found virtually everywhere on these ships.

Glass windbreaks shelter an observatory (complete with stargazing equipment), a cushioned jogging/walking track, a pool bar, whirlpools, outdoor swimming pool, and—on the *Legend*—a fancy 18-hole miniature putting course. A crystal-roofed solarium, decked out as a luxurious Roman bath on the *Legend* and with an Egyptian theme on the *Rhapsody,* features statues and fountains around the heated pool and whirlpools and an extensive fitness center, salon, and spa. A teen disco, a playroom, and a video arcade provide plenty to keep the kids happily occupied while you relax, gamble, attend one of the many activities (there are around 200 to select from each week, including informative nature lectures), or dance the night away in one of numerous lounges and bars. Each ship employs four youth counselors to organize children's activities for 5-to-17-year-olds—so many activities, in fact, that the kids get their own daily program delivered to their cabin.

Meals are served in several dining areas, so there's loads of freedom as to when you dine and choice as to what you'll eat. Lighter fare is served in the solarium at breakfast, lunch, teatime, and dinner.

Cabins are well proportioned and extremely quiet (other than a few located forward on the *Legend's* Mariner Deck, above an entertainment lounge). They have sitting areas, ample storage space, well-lit and moderately sized bathrooms, and TVs with movie, news, and information channels (excursion and debarkation talks are rebroadcast in-room just in case you missed something). All outside cabins on both ships' Bridge and Commodore Decks (and a few aft on the *Legend's* Mariner Deck) have balconies and can sleep up to four quite comfortably. The *Rhapsody* has six family staterooms that can accommodate six passengers, albeit tightly.

WORLD EXPLORER CRUISES

555 Montgomery St., San Francisco, CA 94111-2544. ☎ **800/854-3835** or 415/393-1145. Fax 415/391-1145. Website http://www.wecruise. com.

If immersion in Alaska is what you're after, World Explorer Cruises is your answer. This line has created its own niche by focusing on educational and cultural cruises that stay out longer and visit more ports than any other line cruising in the state. It was the originator of the "eco-cruise" in Alaska, and now almost every line has followed its example by adding naturalists or Alaskan lectures to their staff rosters. World Explorer continues to stand apart from the crowd by hiring top educators from institutions all over the United States to lead seminars and provide entertaining and informative lectures on the culture, history, geology, glaciers, flora, and fauna of Southeast and Southcentral Alaska. It also hires talented performers from around the globe to provide classical and folk entertainment—a Chinese pianist or American violin virtuoso might be followed the next night by a Russian balalaika player, flamenco guitarist, or a Native Alaskan drummer. Even their shore excursions are soft-adventure-oriented and educational in nature.

✪ **Universe Explorer.** *Passenger capacity:* 739. *Crew complement:* 330. *Cabins:* 290 outside (none with veranda) and 78 inside. *Ship facilities:* dining room, grill, two bars, four lounges (including theater and entertainment lounge), fitness and sports court, pool and Jacuzzi, library/computer room, card room, youth activity center, gift shop, launderette, beauty salon, barbershop, masseuse, medical facility. *Activities:* extensive onboard lectures and activities. **Itineraries: 14-day round-trip cruises from Vancouver** with visits to Wrangell, Juneau, Skagway, Seward, Valdez, Sitka, Ketchikan, Victoria, Glacier Bay, Yakutat Bay, and Hubbard Glacier. *Departures:* every other Tuesday, late May to early September; cruise only, $1,895–$3,595 per person, double occupancy. One **7-day cruise** departing Vancouver in mid-August visits Wrangell, Sitka, Juneau, Tracy Arm, and Ketchikan; cruise only $1,050–$1,795. Early-booking discounts of 25% and discounts for third and fourth passengers are available. Solo passengers pay 130% of the per-person double-occupancy rate.

While excessive purists might bemoan the fact that World Explorer has retired the old *Universe*—the former freighter that served as its sole ship for so many years—and replaced it with a ship that was actually constructed with passengers in mind, I find it hard to complain. Built in 1957 and sailing most recently as the *Enchanted Seas* for Commodore Cruise Line (and before that as the *Argentina, Monarch Star, Bermuda Star,* and, in the 1970s, as the *Veendam* of Holland America Line), the *Universe Explorer* is the only really classic cruise ship sailing in Alaskan waters now that HAL has sold off the *Rotterdam V*. Does this mean that World Explorer has gone soft? Can we now expect Vegas-style floorshows and all-night casino gambling instead of the cultural seminars and classical entertainment we've come to know and love?

Not hardly. The venue may have changed, but the song remains the same. As a matter of fact, when the *Explorer* came to World Explorer from Commodore, its casino was promptly transformed into a library to house the 15,000 books (many on Alaskan topics) transferred from the old *Universe* and continually added to; plus, a computer room was added to make your trip all the more educational. Any other differences you'll notice from old to new are for the best. Cabins are no longer of the college-dorm variety; most all the categories on the *Explorer* are comfortable and spacious, save the rather cramped lower-end inside cabins. Also, over 75% of cabins are now outside, almost exactly opposite the case aboard the old *Universe*. (If a good view is important to you, make sure your travel agent knows it, as the views from many outside cabins on the Navigation Deck are blocked by lifeboats.) The Promenade Deck holds most of the public areas and runs the full length of the ship, from the library towards the fore to the pool at the stern. Side decks are teakwood, and spacious. Another plus: While it may not be fast by the standards of newly built cruise ships, the *Explorer* still kicks butt over the old *Universe*, allowing longer stays in the eight ports of call—time that was formerly spent just getting from place to place.

Service aboard is warm and informal while still being accommodating. Meals are unfancy and perhaps somewhat limited, though this shouldn't put off passengers who are otherwise interested in the line. Special diets can be accommodated, but be sure to arrange for this when you book.

4 The Ports of Call

Water, water everywhere, but you will pull into port sometimes—and sometimes you'll pull into port a lot. With that fact in mind I've put together a little primer on the more frequently visited towns in Southeast, listing some of their high points and some of the shore excursions typically offered there. For all the detailed information you'll need and all the background information you'll want, turn to the sections of chapters 7 and 8 we've cross-referenced under each port, then strap on your walking shoes and shake out your sea legs: It's time to hit the town.

A word about shore excursions: They can be expensive, but don't write them off just because of that. After all, there's more of Alaska than what you can see from the deck of a ship. You'll find that there's an excursion to suit almost any interest you might have, whether it's Native culture, wildlife, watersports, or maybe a little salmon fishing. You might opt for a flightseeing tour to get an eagle's-eye view of the 49th state, or maybe a helicopter tour, where you'll land on a glacier and go for a hike.

City tours, whether by bus, on foot, or by horse-cart or bicycle, are generally inexpensive and give a good overview of the history, culture, and sights of interest in the town you're visiting—and they're a good way to get your feet wet before setting out on your own to explore and shop. If you can do without historical background, head for the visitors center and pick up a walking tour map before heading out.

We've listed some of the more popular and interesting tours under each port town. Some kinds of trips—such as flightseeing, kayaking, and fishing—are available in most every port; others are more site-specific. Prices are approximate within a few dollars in either direction, and vary by ship. As with the cruise prices I've listed, these prices may be slightly higher in 1999 than in 1998. You can save up to 25% by booking the same excursions dockside when you come into port, but you run a couple of risks: You won't know if the vendor is reputable, and you won't know for sure that you'll be brought back to your ship in time. Whether to gamble or not is up to you.

HAINES

See pages 203–210 for complete sightseeing information.

Surrounded by towering snowcapped peaks and centered around the parade grounds of Fort Seward and a single, short main street, Haines is as close as you'll find to mythic Cicely of *Northern Exposure* fame. It's quiet. Real quiet. On a misty Sunday afternoon it can look almost deserted, and a moose wandering through town wouldn't really look out of place. Not many of the big ships dock here, so the town is rarely inundated by crowds. It's a place where everyone knows everyone and the place to catch up really is the local watering hole. There's no way you'll pass for a local here, but don't sweat it—you'll still be welcomed.

HAINES ON YOUR OWN   They might be soaked from sitting out in the rain, but you should still pick up a town map from the kiosk at the end of the Port Chilkoot dock. From the dock, you have two choices: head straight up Portage Street to Fort William Seward or walk to the right down Front St. to the Main St. area. Ft. Seward is where you'll find the **Alaska Indian Arts Center** and its totem carvers and silversmiths; the **Chilkat Center for the Arts** and its famous Chilkat Dancers; a replica **Tlingit clan house;** the **Sea Wolf Gallery** woodcarving studio and **Whale Rider Gallery** for paintings, prints, and woodcarvings; the old fort barracks; and some lovely old officers' quarters running along the hilltop. In the downtown area there's the **Sheldon Museum and Cultural Center** and its displays of both Native and white history, the **American Bald Eagle Foundation History Museum** and its oddly compelling woodland diorama, and a handful of shops and galleries.

EXCURSIONS & TOURS

✪ **Chilkat Dancers & Salmon Bake** (3¹/₂ hours, $55): Enter a replica of a Chilkat Native tribal house on the parade grounds of Fort Seward to be regaled with Native legends and dances, then feast on salmon and ribs cooked over an open fire. (*Note:* The dancers tour a lot, so this excursion may not be offered when you're in town.)

Chilkoot Lake Boat Tour (3 hours, $65–$70): Sail beautiful Chilkoot Lake aboard an open pontoon boat, scan for wildlife, and take in the surrounding mountain peaks and lush forests.

Chilkat Nature Hike (4 hours, $40): You'll get a narrative on Alaskan old-growth rain forests and perhaps spot a bald eagle or two. The 4.8-mile round-trip hike is moderately difficult.

Fort Seward / Chilkat River Bike Ride (2 hours, $45): This moderate 6-mile guided ride takes in the sights and history of Fort Seward before pedaling along the Chilkat River estuary to see wildflowers, eagles, and other wonders. There are some small hills to deal with, but this is the easiest bike trip in town.

Glacier Flightseeing (1¹/₂ hours, $125): Here's a chance to fly over the Juneau Icefield and Glacier Bay, and—if the weather's clear—see majestic Mount Fairweather.

Haines Cultural & City Tour (3 hours, $25–$40): This narrated drive introduces you to Fort Seward, the Alaska Indian Art Center, and the Sheldon Museum and Cultural Center. The tour varies from cruise line to cruise line, but may also include a dog-sled demonstration or stop at the American Bald Eagle Interpretive Center.

Horse-Drawn Carriage Tour (1 hour, $25): Local guides take you through Fort Seward, along the Lynn Canal, and on downtown. It's a leisurely tour for a leisurely town (and the clip-clop sounds entirely right around Ft. Seward, let me tell you).

JUNEAU

See pages 178–196 for complete sightseeing information.

Surrounded on three sides by the Juneau Icefield and on the fourth by water, Juneau is simulataneously the largest state capitol in the land (its area encompasses 3,108 square miles, most of which is wilderness) and the most remote, with no roads going in and the icefield making sure none ever will. Still, it's a bustling place, and, owing to the many government workers, the most cosmopolitan town you'll find between Vancouver and Anchorage.

JUNEAU ON YOUR OWN   About midway down the cruise ship wharf is a blue building housing the **visitor information center;** stop in to pick up a walking tour map and visitors guide before striking out to see the sights. While you're there, look down the dock a bit for the oversize bronze statue of **Patsy Ann,** a beady-eyed bull terrier who in the 1930s was dubbed "the official boat greeter of Juneau" because she never failed to greet all arriving boats. Consider yourself greeted.

From the dock, look up the mountain to your right and you'll see two things: the **Mount Roberts Tramway** and the ruins of the **Alaska-Juneau Mill,** the most visible reminder of Juneau's gold mining history. The tramway will take you up 2,000 feet to a mountaintop observatory/restaurant, from which a series of nature trails branches out. Go near sunset for some spectacular views over the whole central Juneau area, but remember to bring bug repellent—Alaska has 55 different kinds of mosquitos, and I think they all live here. (Tickets are $16.95, good all day for unlimited tramway rides.)

Some points of historical interest in town (and all part of the standard walking tour) include the **Alaska State Capitol;** the **Juneau-Douglas City Museum;** the **Evergreen Cemetary,** final resting place of town founders Joe Juneau and Richard Harris; the **Davis Log Cabin** at Third and Seward streets, which is also an information center and presents an informative video orientation on the city; the **Alaska State Museum;** and the **Governor's Mansion.** A full walking tour takes an hour if you rush but can be extended to several hours, depending on how much time you spend exploring the various sights.

If time allows, take in a performance of Native song, story, and dance at the **Naa Kahidi Theater** (☎907/463-4844), located right on the docks. Check performance times as soon as you get into port, though, as they're not consistent. (Tickets $15 for adults, $9 for children.) If you have less time, stop in for a pint of Alaskan Amber and a side of cookhouse fries at the **Red Dog Saloon,** located just above the dock as you head into town. The place is a funny mix of roughhouse legend and hard tourist reality—they've got one of Wyatt Earp's guns on the wall above the bar, but the last time I was there I was served by a clean-cut college grad from Boston. So much for the frontier. (Bring the kids along—they'll love it.)

EXCURSIONS & TOURS

Gold History Tour (1½ hours, $30–$35): Juneau's gold-rush history comes to life (especially for kids) as you pan for gold near the ruins of a mine while a guide in prospector garb recounts colorful tales of the gold rush.

✪ Glacier Helicopter Tour (2–3 hours, $160–$165): Here's your chance to walk on the face of a glacier. After transferring to the airport by bus, guests are outfitted with ice boots and board helicopters bound for Mendenhall or Norris Glacier. After about 20 minutes on the glacier, you'll soar over the jagged peaks carved by the massive Juneau Icefield before turning back for the airport and town.

Mendenhall Glacier & City Highlights Tour (2–3 hours, $30–$35): Twelve miles long and 1½ miles wide, Mendenhall is the most visited glacier in the world and the most popular sight in Juneau. This trip will take you to the U.S. Forest Service Observatory, from which you can walk up a trail to within ½ mile of the glacier or take one of the nature trails if time allows. After this, you'll visit the Gastineau Salmon Hatchery, the University of Alaska campus, and downtown's historic highlights.

Mendenhall Glacier Float Trip (3½ hours, $100): On the shore of Mendenhall Lake you'll board 10-person rafts and an experienced oarsman will guide you out past icebergs and into the Mendenhall River. You'll encounter moderate rapids and stunning views, and be treated to a snack of smoked salmon and reindeer sausage somewhere along the way.

Wilderness Lodge Flightseeing Adventure (3 hours, $175–$200): This trip combines flightseeing over glaciers and an icefield with a stop at the Taku Glacier Lodge for a traditional all-you-can-eat salmon bake. After a hearty lunch, you can hike the nature trails around the wilderness lodge before reboarding the floatplane for the flight back to Juneau.

KETCHIKAN
See pages 141–154 for complete sightseeing information.

Ketchikan is a city of odd superlatives. "Alaska's First City" is a good, solid one, and derives from the fact that it's the first Alaskan town encountered on the marine route north. "Salmon Capital of the World" is another, based on the number of canneries located here. Perhaps the most descriptive of all, though, is "Rain Capital of Southeast Alaska," because in Ketchikan, a day without sunshine is basically just like every other day—the town gets an average of 156 inches a year; its citizens are waterproof. Once known for its tough reputation and its notorious red-light district, Ketchikan is now known more for its profusion of touristy gift shops, where on a busy day you'd think it was Christmas Eve and your shopping time was running out *fast*. That said, it's still a fascinating, beautiful, and historic town out beyond the tourist epicenter. The local vibe is there; you just have to know where to find it. (See pages 141–154 for guideposts.)

KETCHIKAN ON YOUR OWN   Your first stop should be the **Ketchikan Visitor Information Center,** on the pier, to pick up a walking-tour map. Then head up Mill St. or Spruce Mill Way to the corner of Main and the **Southeast Alaska Visitors Center.** For the price of a $3 ticket you can see totem poles being carved and baskets woven by local craftspeople, and tour a wonderful and intricate series of dioramas detailing the local flora, fauna, and industry. Their shop stocks a great selection of books on Native culture and Alaska history. Next, head up Mill Street to the triangular **Whale Park** for a look at the totem poles. There are more poles on Stedman Street at the rear of the park. Look for the tall, almost bare, raven-topped pole in front of the Westmark Tramway: This is where the natural beachfront of Ketchikan was, 100 years ago. Up the hill on the left, native heritage and local history are showcased in the **Tongass Historical Museum.** On your left as you exit the museum is **Creek Street,** the former red-light district, built on pilings over the creek and with a sign proclaiming "Where the fish and fishermen go up the creek to spawn." One industry has replaced another, however, and now instead of favors the houses dispense souvenirs, espresso, and some pretty good artwork. Check out **Dolly's House Museum** for a look at the district's bawdy past.

Backtrack to the **Westmark Tramway,** which'll take you up to the Westmark Cape Fox Lodge and a great view of the town. Out back, there's a fascinating group of totem poles at the hotel's entrance. (Why are they so short, you ask? 'Cause they used to be the corner interior supports of a Native house, and weren't intended for outdoor display.) From here, take the **Married Men's Trail** off to the left. You guessed it—this was the preferred route married men would take down to the houses on Creek Street. The trail involves some rocky trails and substantial stairs, but it's not so bad since they're all downhill. While you're in the area, check the creek for salmon (they come in by the thousands) and then check the shops and galleries on Stedman Street. The **Soundings Public Radio Store & Gallery,** right in the center of it all, has T-shirts, gifts, and some beautiful yellow cedar potlatch bowls.

A couple other interesting sights in town—and both included on the standard walking tour, and described on pages 144–146—include the **Deer Mountain Tribal Hatchery,** where you can watch the salmon hatchlings swim around, and the **Totem Heritage Center,** where aging Tlingit and Haida totem poles are preserved and displayed. Ask attendants to show you the two educational videos for a better understanding of this powerful art form.

EXCURSIONS & TOURS

Misty Fjords Flightseeing (2 hours, $140–$175): Everyone gets a window seat aboard the floatplanes that run these quick flightseeing jaunts over Misty Fjords National Monument. No icefields and glaciers on this trip, but Misty Fjords has another kind of majesty: You'll see sparkling fjords, cascading waterfalls, thick forests, and rugged mountains dotted with wildlife, then come in for a landing on a serene wilderness lake.

Saxman Native Village Tour (2½ hours, $45): This modern-day Native village, situated 3 miles outside Ketchikan, is home to hundreds of Tlingit, Tsimshian, and Haida, and is a center for the revival of Native arts and culture. The tour includes either a Native legend or a performance by the Cape Fox dancers in the park theater and a guided walk through the grounds to see the totem poles and learn their stories. Craftsmen are sometimes on hand in the working sheds to demonstrate totem pole carving.

Sport Fishing (4–6 hours, $140–$170): If catching salmon is your goal, Ketchikan is a good spot to do it. Chartered fishing boats come with tackle, bait, fishing gear, and crew to help you strike king and coho around the end of June or pink, chum, and silver from July through mid-September. (*Note:* $10 fishing license and $10 king salmon tag are extra.)

Totem Bight Historical Park Tour (2–2½ hours, $25–$35): This tour takes you by bus through the Tongass National Forest to see the historic Native fish camp where a ceremonial clan house and totem poles sit amid the rain forest. There's a fair amount of walking involved, making the tour a poor choice for anyone with mobility problems.

PETERSBURG

See pages 162–168 for complete sightseeing information.

Across the channel on Mitkof Island is Petersburg, a hardworking community where proud descendants of the town's Norwegian founders work and thrive. The first thing you'll see is the town's canneries perched on pilings and ringed on the water side by fishing vessels and private boats. Above the harbor, boardwalks and wooden bridges lead to the main street in town, and houses on pilings hang over a slough. Can you guess what the main industry is here? Right: Fish. Can you guess what the main industry *isn't?* Right: Tourism. The harbor is too small for the big ships, so Petersburg has never been overrun—and the people there like it that way.

PETERSBURG ON YOUR OWN   We'll start with **Hammer Slough,** to the south of the pier area. Turn right at the end of the dock parking lot to walk along the boardwalk streets and see the old wood-frame houses that hang out over the slough. When you've snapped enough photos, backtrack to the dock and keep heading straight past it on the boardwalk. You'll pass the **Sons of Norway Hall** (check the performance schedule if you're interested in cutural dancing) and a working model of a Viking ship on your right as you make your way into town via **Singh Lee Alley,** which intersects Main Street (also known as Nordic Drive) downtown. Turn left on Main Street and make your way past the seafood-processing plants along the waterfront. After a few blocks, turn right on Fram Street and stop in at the **visitor information center** on the corner of Fram and First streets to pick up a map (though you probably won't need it to get your bearings in this tiny village). One more block up the hill is the **Clausen Memorial Museum,** which focuses on the town's Norwegian heritage and fishing traditions. Back down the hill to Main, to the left and past the canneries, you'll find **Eagle's Roost Park,** where you'll often find bald eagles perched in the trees or swooping down to scoop fish out of Wrangell Narrows. There's a grassy area and a few benches near the street, but the better spot to watch is down the winding wooden staircase on the rocky beach.

Petersburg is not Alaska's shopping capitol, but if you've got the bug you can try **Diamante,** at Main and Fram streets, or the **Trading Union,** at Main and Dolphin streets.

EXCURSIONS & TOURS

✪ **Commercial Trawling** (3 hours, $100): This adventure aboard Syd and Vara Wright's gillnetter is a rare up-close view of what commercial fishing in Alaska is all about. Syd directs you on methods of trawling for shrimp, crab, and sole, then Vara takes over, preparing the catch for a feast aboard the boat. There are few better storytellers than Syd, and he won't take much coaxing.

LeConte Glacier Flightseeing (45 minutes, $125): This quick trip by floatplane takes in the Stikine Icefield, the Coastal Mountains, and the ice-filled bay below the towering face of LeConte Glacier.

Little Norway Bus Tour (2 hours, $25): The Norwegian heritage of Petersburg is the focus of this excursion, which takes in a performance by the Leikarring Dancers at the Sons of Norway Hall and a bus tour through the port area, downtown, the residential section, and the bog at the back of the village.

Waterfront Walk (1 1/2 hours, $10): Guides stroll with you through Hammer Slough, Singh Lee Alley, the bustling port area (with a stop to see the workings of a seafood-processing plant), and downtown before ending at Eagle's Roost Park to watch the eagles feeding and soaring over Frederick Sound.

SEWARD

See pages 257–264 for complete sightseeing information.

Because sailing around the Kenai Peninsula and up Cook Inlet into Anchorage adds another full day to itineraries, Seward has become the northern terminus of choice for many cruise lines. Cruises that include Anchorage either start or end here, meaning you're in for a three-hour bus ride along Turnagain Arm and through the Chugach National Forest to get from one to the other. It's a pretty ride, but does cut the time you'll have to sightsee in either city unless you book a pre- or post-cruise extension (mostly available for Anchorage only).

SEWARD ON YOUR OWN   Your first stop should be the **visitor information booth** on the pier to pick up a map. From there it's about a half-mile walk into town, or you can hop a shuttle on the pier for a quick orientation trip before striking out on your own. The **small-boat harbor,** on the other side of the industrial tracks, is the first picturesque area of Seward you'll encounter. Boutiques and bistros line the waterfront street. The **Kenai Fjords National Park Headquarters** is also located here, on Fourth Avenue; stop in to see the informative films on the wildlife and geography of the park and the major earthquake that changed the face of Seward in 1964. Displays of historical interest are found at the **Resurrection Bay Historical Society Museum,** at Third Avenue and Jefferson Street, and at the **Seward Community Library,** at Fifth and Adams. Ongoing oceanographic and aquaculture studies are the subjects of interest at the **Institute of Marine Science,** at Third and Railway avenues. You'll find the **Iditarod Trailhead** in the small park nearby on Railroad Avenue.

EXCURSIONS & TOURS

Anchorage City Tour (3^1/$_2$–9 hours, $30–$70): A restroom-equipped motorcoach takes you on a three-hour drive through the Chugach National Forest and along Turnagain Arm between Seward and Anchorage. Once you hit Anchorage, the bus makes a circuit through the downtown area, pointing out sights of interest, better shops, and popular restaurants. You'll then be free for a few hours to shop, eat, or visit the Museum of History and Art. The tour is either an all-day round-trip affair from Seward or a half-day trip that ends in Anchorage (either downtown at Egan Center or at the Anchorage Airport).

Exit Glacier (3 hours, $35): This excursion includes a quick orientation trip through town before heading out the Resurrection River Valley to Exit Glacier. After a short hike along nature trails, you'll come to the glacier face. (*Note:* Chunks fall off the glacier regularly, so keep your distance—park rangers are on hand to see that you do.)

Mount McKinley Flightseeing (3 hours, $290): This tour is often canceled because of weather conditions, but if it isn't you'll board a private airplane at the Seward Airport and swoop over the dramatic valleys of the Kenai Peninsula to watch for wildlife before heading over Anchorage and up the Susitna Valley and Kahiltna River to towering Mount McKinley, the highest peak in North America. On the return flight you'll pass over Prince William Sound for a different perspective.

Portage Glacier (2–8 hours, $30–$80): This tour is typically done en route to Anchorage via motorcoach, but is also available as a day-long round-trip excursion from Seward. A stop is made in the Kenai Mountains to board the MV *Ptarmigan,* an enclosed cruiser, for an hour-long sojourn that sometimes brings you as close as 300 yards from the glacier.

Resurrection Bay Wildlife Cruise (4 hours, $65): Board a 90-foot touring vessel for a 50-mile narrated tour into Resurrection Bay and the Kenai Fjords area. The highlight of this one is wildlife watching; the region is teeming with birds and sea mammals, so chances are good that you'll see eagles, puffins, kittiwakes, cormorants, harbor seals, otters, sea lions, porpoises, and maybe even humpbacks.

SITKA

See pages 168–178 for complete sightseeing information.

Once the capital of Russian America—and the site of a historic battle between the Russian colonists and the proud Tlingit tribe—Sitka retains much of the influence of both its formative cultures. Bounded by the Alaska Marine Highway and towering mountain peaks, the town has no pier facility large enough for the big ships, so passengers on all but the smallest vessels must tender in to the small-boat harbor in the heart of town.

SITKA ON YOUR OWN　Pick up a map at the **Sitka Convention and Visitor Bureau,** located right by the dock in the **Centennial Building,** which also houses the **Isabel Miller Museum** and its displays on Sitka history, as well as an auditorium where the **New Archangel Dancers**—a traditional Russian troop that at last report employed no actual Russians—perform regularly. Up the road to your left you'll see **St. Michael's Cathedral,** a functioning Russian Orthodox church with a beautiful display of icons. Past there on Lincoln Street (the main shopping thoroughfare) you'll find the pathway/stairway to **Castle Hill,** where the Americans took Alaska off the Russians' hands. Back down to Lincoln Street, stop in at the **Chocolate Moose** to satisfy your sweet tooth. **Totem Square,** with its Russian double-headed eagle-crested totem, sits in front of the **Pioneers Home** across the way. Some other sights of interest are the old **Russian blockhouse and cemetery,** the **Russian Bishop's House** at Lincoln and Monastery streets, and the intriguing **Sheldon Jackson Museum** down Lincoln Street at College Drive. Housed within its octagonal structure is a priceless collection of Native artifacts—other than the Smithsonian's, no other collection can match this one.

A few more blocks down Lincoln Street (though you'll probably want to take a shuttle) is the ✪ **Sitka National Historical Park,** where the Tlingits and Russians battled for control of the island; there are hiking trails lined with a collection of incredible totem poles and a fine interpretive center featuring displays of Native artifacts, films on the history of Sitka, and workshops where you can see demonstrations of Native weaving, totem carving, and silver etching. On Sawmill Creek Boulevard, not far from the park, is the ✪ **Alaska Raptor Rehabilitation Center,** where bald eagles, owls, and other taloned beasties are brought to be treated after injuries—it's like a VA hospital for birds. Your $10 admission price is the center's main source of income, so you're more than welcome to come in for a tour and a talk, and to watch the birds as they mend.

EXCURSIONS & TOURS

✪ **Sea Otter & Wildlife Quest** (3 hours, $92–$100): Board a comfortable jet boat to make the 50-mile round-trip journey to Salisbury Sound. A naturalist accompanies you to point out the various animals you'll encounter and explain the delicate balance of the region's marine ecosystem. They're so sure you'll see a whale, bear, or otter that they offer a partial cash refund if you don't.

Silver Bay Nature Cruise (2 hours, $35): An excursion vessel takes you through beautiful Silver Bay to view wildlife, scenery, the ruins of the Liberty Prospect Gold Mine, and a salmon hatchery.

Sitka Historical Tour (3 hours, $30–$35): This bus excursion hits all the historic sights, including St. Michael's Cathedral, the Russian Cemetery, Castle Hill, and Sitka's National Historic Park with its totem poles and forest trails. *Note:* This tour

Where the Whales Are

What is it about whales that makes the heart skip a beat? Their size? Their grace? Their long and troubled relationship with man? Whichever it is, it's an undeniable fact: All it takes is the swish of a humpback's tail to send a shipfull of Alaska cruisers into spasms of rapture. And if you're really lucky, and see one breaching—hurling itself from the water like it was trying to scoop light from the sky—it's a thrill you'll never forget.

Of course, they can be elusive. Humpbacks, orcas, belugas, and minkes—just some of Alaska's cetacean residents—can seem to be both everywhere and nowhere at all. They'll pop up when you least expect them and hide out in the deep when you're looking the hardest. The captain or officer on watch on most cruise ships will make an announcement when they spot one, but the ship probably won't stop and linger. On a few lines, though (notably those running smaller ships), whales are a big part of the trip's focus, so their ships will visit areas favored by whales and spend time waiting there for an encounter, or will monitor marine-traffic radio broadcasts and deviate from course to go where whale sightings have been reported.

The top spot to see **orca** (otherwise known as killer whales, the distinctive black-and-white whales with upright dorsal fins) is Robson Bight, an area in **Johnstone Strait** (between Vancouver Island and mainland British Columbia), where they tend to cruise slowly near the shoreline, rubbing their bellies on the rounded stones of the sloping beach. Some ships pass through at night, but most will time their transit, when possible, to match the best viewing hours in the day. **Beluga** (the small white or milky-gray whales with rounded beaks) frequently follow salmon to feed in **Turnagain Arm** near Anchorage; if your cruise starts or ends in Seward, you'll most likely take a bus transfer between Anchorage and Seward, driving along this arm a good portion of the way. **Humpback** whales, those gentle giants with the long flippers, tend to congregate to feed on the rich supply of krill off Point Adolphus and other spots in and near **Glacier Bay** and farther south around the Brothers Islands in **Frederick Sound,** where on a recent trip I saw two dozen within three hours.

Most large cruise ships don't generally focus on whale watching, but do offer onboard lectures about whales and announce sightings made along the course. Others (including Alaska Sightseeing, Crystal, and Special Expeditions) intentionally build whale-watching time into their cruise itineraries.

is often combined with a perfromance by the New Archangel Dancers and/or a visit to the Alaska Raptor Rehabilitation Center. (Tours including the latter typically cost $10 more.)

Sport Fishing (4 hours, $135–$170): An experienced captain will guide your fully equipped boat to good spot for halibut and salmon; the rest is up to you. Your catch can be frozen or smoked and shipped to your home, if you wish. (*Note:* $10 fishing license and $10 king salmon tag are extra.)

SKAGWAY
See pages 210–218 for complete sightseeing information.

Skagway, a gold-rush boomtown that went bust and turned to tourism instead, is what the folks at Disney would've come up with if people had let them into Alaska. It's as if the whole town had gone to acting school and had Walter Brennan as their drama coach. Go with it. Get in the mood. 'Cause even though its squinty-eyed prospector self-image is as contrived as it comes, the place is still *fun*.

SKAGWAY ON YOUR OWN   This is an easy one. Broadway runs up the center of town. Walk up it—everything is either there or just off to one side. First stop is the **Klondike Gold Rush National Historic Park** visitors center, at the corner of Second Avenue. Free guided tours leave from here several times a day and visit the **White Pass & Yukon Railway Depot, Soapy's Parlor, Moore House,** and the **Mascot Saloon.**

One of the most popular sights in town is the **Trail of '98 Historical Museum,** housed in the driftwood-faced **Arctic Brotherhood Hall.** You can't miss it—it's the one everybody's taking pictures of. One block farther up on the left is the **Gold Bar Pub / Skagway Brewing Company,** a brewpub/restaurant with saloon piano music, period details, a congenial, family atmosphere, good grub, and fine homebrewed beer on tap. Wet your whistle with an Oosik Stout or Chilkoot Trail Ale—it's what the prospectors would've done.

Up Broadway to Fifth Street, turn left and stop into the **Skagway Convention and Visitors Bureau** for a historical **walking-tour map** that'll fill you in on every historic spot in town, and if you have time for entertainment, stop in at one of the local theaters. You can hear **pickup jazz sessions** at the Red Onion Saloon, catch the Eagle Hall's **Days of '98 Show** at Sixth Avenue, watch a Vaudeville-style Victorian melodrama at the **Gold Pan Theater** up at Seventh, or hear a reading of Robert Service poetry by local man **Buckwheat Donohue** at the Westmark Inn.

EXCURSIONS & TOURS

Chilkoot Pass & Glacier Flightseeing (1¹/₂ hours, $150–$165): If the prospectors had known you could take a helicopter over the Chilkoot Trail, maybe they would have just waited. But would there then be a trail to see? Ah, a philosophical quandary. In any case, the trip will overfly the trail, then take you to the Chilkat glacier system, where you'll get to view glaciers in their high mountain peaks, then land on one for an ice age thrill.

✪ **Glacier Flight & Bald Eagle Float** (5¹/₂ hours, $195–$215): Board your plane in Skagway for a scenic flight over peaks and glaciers, then hop a raft in Haines for a gentle float trip through the Chilkat Bald Eagle Preserve to see eagles, wolves, moose, and bears. You rejoin your ship in Haines.

✪ **Skagway by Streetcar** (2 hours, $35–$40): As much performance art as historical tour, guides in period costume relate tales of the boomtown days as you tour the sights aboard vintage 1937 Kenworth sightseeing limousines. In addition to seeing the Historic District, the Lookout, and the Goldrush Cemetery, guests watch a fascinating multimedia presentation on Skagway history and become honorary members of the Arctic Brotherhood.

White Pass & Yukon Route Railway (3 hours, $85): The sturdy engines and vintage parlor cars of this famous narrow-gauge railway take you from the dock past waterfalls and parts of the famous "Trail of '98" to White Pass Summit, the boundary between Canada and the United States. Don't take this trip on an overcast day—you won't see anything. If you're lucky and have a clear day, you'll be able to see all the way down to the harbor, and you might see the occasional hoary marmot fleeing from the train's racket.

VALDEZ

See pages 291–297 for complete sightseeing information.

The little town of Valdez is where the pipeline meets the shoreline, where the oil flowing from Prudhoe Bay in the north meets the tankers that'll carry it to the lower 48. The storage tanks on the opposite shore are hard to ignore, but try and shift your attention to the surrounding 5,000-foot peaks of the Chugach Mountains, which are a much better sight to see.

VALDEZ ON YOUR OWN   Valdez is tiny and there's really not much to see while you're there. A shuttle bus carries passengers between the pier and the **Tourist Information Center,** where you can pick up a free town map. Other than a few overpriced souvenir outlets, the **Valdez Museum,** at 217 Egan Ave., is pretty much the only sight of interest.

EXCURSIONS & TOURS

✪ **Canyon Rafting** (2^1/$_4$ hours, $65–$70): You can't beat the rafting in Keystone Canyon. There are a few hiccups along the way, but it's a mild run for the most part and the sheer canyon walls and waterfalls pounding into the Lowe River are stunning. Knowledgeable guides and all equipment are provided.

Helicopter Flightseeing (1^1/$_2$ hours, $180–$200): This quick helicopter adventure zips you over old Valdez (destroyed in the 1964 earthquake), the Trans-Alaska Pipeline, the crevasses of the Columbia Glacier, Prince William Sound, and Anderson Pass, then lands on the beach at the face of Shoup Glacier for a little ground-level gawking.

Thompson Pass & Worthington Glacier Bus Tour (2^1/$_2$–3 hours, $35): This tour takes you past the old town site (destroyed in the 1964 earthquake), through narrow Keystone Canyon, and up to Thompson Pass to get a look at where the Trans-Alaska Pipeline is buried before reaching the Worthington Glacier Recreation Site, a prime spot to snap some photos.

Trans-Alaska Pipeline Tour (2–2^1/$_2$ hours, $25): If the pipeline project and Alaska's "black gold" are of interest, sign up for the tour of the Alyeska Marine Terminal. You'll see the storage tanks and tanker berths, and maybe see the giant ships getting tanked up.

VANCOUVER, BRITISH COLUMBIA

Vancouver is generally a transit point at either the beginning or end of your cruise, and unless you're booked on a pre- or postcruise extension, you won't have much time for sightseeing. There are two piers used by the cruise ships: **Canada Place,** in the heart of downtown, within walking distance of several sights of interest, and **Ballantyne Pier,** in an industrial section over a mile east of downtown.

VANCOUVER ON YOUR OWN   Since you probably won't have much time before you have to catch the boat or plane, we'll just hit the highlights here. Expect to spend anywhere from one to three hours in each area, and keep transit time in mind when mapping out your plans.

The cobblestone streets and historic buildings of ✪ **Gastown** are just blocks east of the pier at Canada Place, and if you only have a few hours, this is the area I recommend visiting. Gastown is the birthplace of Vancouver, established by "Gassy" Jack Deighton, who built a saloon here in 1867 to serve the area's loggers and trappers. His statue stands in Maple Tree Square at the intersection of Water, Alexander, and Carrall streets. A steam-powered clock near the corner of Water and Cambie streets is another draw, and if you've got shopping in mind there's plenty of boutiques and galleries to explore.

Vancouver has the second-largest **Chinatown** in North America; it stretches between Carrall, East Hastings, East Pender, and Gore streets. In addition to photogenic Chinese gates, bright-red buildings, and open-air markets, you'll find the amazing 6-foot-wide **Sam Kee Building,** at 8 W. Pender St., and the lovely ✪ **Dr. Sun Yat-sen Garden,** at 578 Carrall St.

Within the confines of **Stanley Park,** 1,000 acres nestled in the heart of down-town Vancouver, are rose gardens, totem poles, a yacht club, a kids' water park, miles of wooded hiking trails, great vantage points for views of Lions Gate Bridge, and the outstanding ✪ **Vancouver Aquarium** (☎ **604/682-1118**).

Granville Island is Nirvana for shoppers. Fifteen minutes from downtown Vancouver across False Creek, it has a vibrant daily market and streets lined with fine-art studios. **Robson Street,** chock-a-block with boutiques, souvenir shops, coffeehouses, and bistros, is part of the **Pacific Centre Mall,** which fills the city blocks between Robson, Dunsmuir, Howe, and Granville streets.

EXCURSIONS & TOURS

City Tour (3 hours, $20–$30): Very few lines offer a tour in Vancouver, but those that do use a motorcoach to drive you around, pointing out such major sights as Gastown, Chinatown, Stanley Park, high-end residential areas, and Queen Elizabeth Park, where you'll stop to tour the Bloedell Conservatory. This tour generally ends at the Vancouver International Airport.

VICTORIA, BRITISH COLUMBIA

Cruises that start in Los Angeles, San Francisco, and Seattle typically stop first in Victoria on Vancouver Island on the way up to Alaska. High tea, flowering gardens, and Victorian architecture set the prim and proper tone. Most cruisers leave wishing they'd had a few days to explore.

VICTORIA ON YOUR OWN   Take the shuttle to the **Inner Harbor,** where flower baskets, milling crowds, and street performers liven the scene under the watchful eye of the grand ✪ **Empress Hotel,** famed setting for English-style high tea (call ☎ **250/384-8111** ahead of time for reservations and ask about the dress code), and the lovely **Parliament Buildings** (call ☎ **250/387-3046** for information on free tours). You can pick up a map of the city at the **Visitors Information Center,** on the waterfront at 812 Wharf St.

There are plenty of kitschy attractions on the harbor as well, but skip them in favor of the ✪ **Royal British Columbia Museum,** 675 Belleville St. Behind the museum is **Thunderbird Park,** with Native totem poles and a ceremonial house. **Helmcken House,** 10 Elliot St., next to the park, is one of the oldest houses in British Columbia; it was the home of a pioneer doctor, and there are lots of torturous-looking medical tools to shudder over.

You'll have to take a cab to see **Craigdarroch Castle,** 1050 Joan Crescent (☎ **250/592-5323**), the elaborate home of a millionaire coal-mining magnate. Another cab ride and several free hours will be required for a visit to world-famous ✪ **Butchart Gardens,** 800 Benvenuto Ave. in Brentwood Bay (☎ **250/652-5256**), 13 miles north of downtown Victoria, a 130-acre estate featuring English, Italian, Japanese, water, and rose gardens.

Government Street, running north from the Inner Harbour, is lined with boutiques, curio shops, galleries, coffeehouses, and restaurants. Try **Hill's Indian Crafts,** 1008 Government St. (☎ **250/385-3911**), for Native art; the **Irish Linen Store,** 1090 Government St. (☎ **250/383-6812**), for fine linens and china; **Murchie's,** 1110 Government St. (☎ **250/383-3112**), for packaged teas; and **Roger's Chocolates,** 913 Government St. (☎ **250/384-7021**), for sweets.

EXCURSIONS & TOURS

City Tour & Butchart Gardens (3¹/₂–4 hours, $30–$40): After an abbreviated tour of the sights in Victoria, the bus makes the 13-mile trip out the Saanich Peninsula to world-renowned Butchart Gardens in Brentwood Bay, where you'll have two hours or so to explore the 130-acre grounds.

City Tour with High Tea or Castle Visit (2¹/₂–3 hours, $20–$30): This guided excursion aboard a double-decker bus takes you by the major sights of the Inner Harbour, downtown, and residential areas; the variation comes with a stop for afternoon high tea or a visit to Craigdarroch Castle.

WRANGELL

See pages 156–162 for complete sightseeing information.

Much less visited than other Alaskan ports of call, this former mill town has kept its blue-collar burliness and its a small-town intimacy while simultaneously shifting its economy to tourism. It's small, it's homey, and it's yours to explore for a few hours.

WRANGELL ON YOUR OWN   You'll find the **Visitor Information Center** at the end of the Stikine Inn nearest the city dock, where cruise ships tie up. Pick up a map there and take a walk up Front Street. After a while it becomes Shakes Street, and before long you'll see a footbridge on the left to tiny ✪ **Chief Shakes Island,** home to many Tlingit totem poles and a re-created clan house (which should be open for a guided tour since your ship is in town).

Backtrack a few blocks and you'll find Episcopal Avenue, where you can see another collection of totems at **Kiksadi Totem Park.** Up at the corner of Case Avenue, turn left and walk past St. Michael's Ave.to see the **Wrangell Museum** with its portrayal of Wrangell's history and industry. Farther up Church (to where it changes to Evergreen Ave.) is **Our Collections Museum,** a private museum showcasing 60 years of family and town memorabilia. Farther north on Evergreen, about one mile from the dock, watch for the path on the left leading down to **Petroglyph Beach** and its ancient geometric and animal designs. Visitors used to take rubbings of the rocks, but the practice is now discouraged since it wears away the images.

EXCURSIONS & TOURS

City Tour (1¹/₂ hours, $20–$30): This quick bus tour is a fine introduction to this small island community. Your guide will stop at Petroglyph Beach to see the ancient rock carvings and on Chief Shakes Island to explore the tribal house and look at the totem poles before making a pass through downtown to drop you off at the museum or back at your ship.

LeConte Glacier Flightseeing (1¹/₂ hours, $130): Your plane will overfly the Coastal Moutains, the Stikine Icefield, and LeConte Glacier, the southernmost glacier on the continent. Weather permitting, you'll descend toward the glacier face for a closer view of the iridescent blue crevasses before returning over Frederick Sound to the airport.

Stikine River Jet Boat Trip (3–3¹/₂ hours, $135–$145): Following the route of fur traders and prospectors of long ago, participants traverse open water, back sloughs, and clear tributaries to reach Shakes Lake, where your nimble jet boat navigates amid icebergs that have fallen from Shakes Glacier at the head of the lake. Colorful alpine meadows, lichen-coated cliffs, and cascading waterfalls cry out to be photographed.

6 Outside in Alaska

by Peter Oliver

You hear stories, plenty of them. People get hold of pictures or maps of Alaska's boundless wildlands, and they become, as the British say, a bit touched. They get ideas. Then they go out and do things to make more domesticated humans shake their heads incredulously. That's the way the stories—some true, some imaginatively reinvented—are born.

There is the story, for example, of a robust California woman determined to travel the entire length (roughly 2,300 miles) of the Yukon River on cross-country skis. Two-thirds of the way through her journey, the spring break-up of the river ice began prematurely. Undeterred, she laid over in a Native community and enlisted the help of village elders in building a canoe by hand. When the ice break-up was complete a month or so later, she boarded her newly handcrafted canoe and finished the trip.

Less admirable but no less astonishing is the story of a fellow, reportedly pumped full of amphetamines, who tried to paraglide over the unclimbable, 3,000-foot icefall above the Root Glacier in Wrangell–St. Elias National Park. Competing in a multiday race through the roadless, virtually trail-less wilderness from Nabesna to McCarthy, he decided he could win by taking a shortcut. Instead, he crash-landed among the treacherous seracs of the icefall before eventually straggling into McCarthy. Upon arrival, he was immediately disqualified.

Fortunately, a person needn't go to such extremes to experience the Alaskan wilderness—unless, of course, for the sake of a good story. But it's instructive to know the possibilities. The limits of what you can do in the vast Alaskan backcountry are defined not strictly by the land itself but by time, imagination, hardiness, and, to some degree, sanity.

The wilderness stats are dizzying. Alaska is the land of North America's biggest mountain (20,320-foot Mount McKinley), its biggest glacier (the 2,250-square-mile Bering Glacier), its biggest national park (13,188,000-acre Wrangell–St. Elias), and its biggest state park (Wood-Tikchik, at 1.6 million acres). National wildlife refuges cover 76 million acres, roughly equal to the geographic area of New Mexico. There are more than 3,000 rivers in Alaska, 26 of which are officially protected as Wild and Scenic Rivers, adding up to a total water mileage many times greater than the state's meager highway mileage of about 5,000. Think of it this way: If you really want to go places in Alaska, you're better off in a canoe than in a car. Or better still, in a sea kayak, given a tidal shoreline estimated at over 47,000 miles. Talk about an abundance of wilderness opportunity!

It's an abundance that can be as intimidating and downright scary as it is inspiring. Yet it's also surprisingly accessible and, under proper guidance, surprisingly manageable. Accessibility comes about thanks to the hundreds of Bush planes that flock the Alaskan skies more regularly than eagles or migratory waterfowl. Manageability is the mandate of wilderness outfitters and lodge operators, many of whom can deliver a remarkably high level of luxury in the heart of a land that remains decidedly precivilized.

How far you choose to push the envelope of possibility is entirely your call. Wilderness lodges are the way to go for anyone insistent upon such creature comforts as meals with fresh ingredients, a warm bed at night, and a roof to keep out the rain. Yet, inevitably, lodges, to a greater or lesser degree, impinge in subtle ways upon the intimacy between adventurer and wilderness.

Extended trips, involving camping in various forms, intensify the wilderness experience. Not incidental in that process is a unique bonding that develops among participants. Shut off for days from the whir and dither of the civilized world, groups in the wilderness have a way of forming cohesive social units, from which lasting friendships often evolve. However, the physical demands, the ubiquitous grime, and wilderness inconveniences (not least of which is the awkwardness of going to the bathroom *alfresco*) limit the appeal of camping trips for many people.

Anyone intent on setting off into the Alaskan wilds must start with the daunting enterprise of choosing an activity. Fishing, hiking, and water sports—canoeing, kayaking, and rafting—draw the most comers, but there are plenty of other ways to go, some obvious, others improbable. Surely it goes without saying that mountaineering attracts many enthusiasts to a state with more 14,000-foot peaks than any other in the United States. But there are less likely ways to spend time in the Alaskan outdoors—scuba diving, for one. A growing number of Anchorage-area coldbloods these days are not only probing undersea Alaska but—hard to imagine—prefer to do so in *winter*, when the sea water (so they claim) is not much colder but considerably clearer than in summer.

Don't forget that it is wilderness that spends most of its time under the shroud of winter, which is not necessarily a bad thing. Ironically, winter makes the Alaskan wilderness even more accessible than in summer. Impassable bogs and thickets, wind-whipped lakes, and fast-running rivers become solidified and smoothed over by snow and ice in winter. Dog mushing, snowmobiling, snowshoeing, and skiing—both downhill and cross-country—all draw their share of winter outdoor activists to Alaska. Sure it's cold, and −50°F is not uncommon. But it isn't always cold everywhere; average February temperatures in Southeast, for example, are well above freezing. And it need not be a debilitating cold if you dress for it and if you don't do some oddball thing like go scuba diving in the frigid winter sea. What you get in return is a white-cloaked (and bug-free!) Alaska of raw, fearsome beauty and the northern lights at full intensity.

Settling on an activity gets you only halfway there; you must also choose a place. That's no easy matter either, given the abundance and variety of wild country. Still, it's imperative to wrench yourself from the notion that all of Alaska's wilderness can be experienced in one mad-dash, see-Alaska rush. A vulgar comparison would be going to a multiplex cinema and watching a few minutes of 12 different movies. That's no way to treat Alaska.

Be willing to commit yourself to a specific region. Choose the arid wilds of the Brooks Range or the North Slope; the mountains of the Interior; the fjords and inlets of that unfathomably long coastline; the glaciers of Southeast. Full immersion in one region, for several days or more, is the fast track to a deeper, more fulfilling understanding of what wild Alaska is all about. It makes economic sense, too. Roaming around the Alaskan outback does not come cheaply.

At one time, wild Alaska was pretty much the exclusive province of leather-tough wilderness jocks. That isn't so any more. You don't necessarily need to be young, fit, and athletic. You don't need he-man skills or backcountry know-how. A willingness to give the great Alaskan outdoors a go is the only real prerequisite. Ordinary people of all ages are capable of amazing stuff once they give themselves a chance. Snow-cat skiing guide Chris Nettles tells the story of a 4-year-old boy, skis locked in a snow-plow, who skied the pants off the adults in his group, racking up 20,000 vertical feet in a day. Mountain-bike guide Robert Kozler, a robust, athletic 30-year-old, recalls approaching near-total exhaustion trying to keep pace with a rider in his 70s.

There are, certainly, activities inappropriate for older people or children. In some cases, a lack of certain skills and/or a lack of physical fitness, regardless of your age, may get you into serious trouble or at least a state of inconsolable discomfort. Alaska can be a punishing, uncompromising beast toward those who embark on adventures that are surely out of their league. But with so much to choose from, heading off on an adventure for which you're ill suited is inexcusable. Select a trip that you know you can handle—or that a guide or outfitter is confident you can handle—and the Alaskan wilderness can be remarkably obliging.

Not every story that comes from the Alaskan outback is peopled with expeditionary adventurers engaged in Odyssean feats. More common is the story of two self-described "unfit inhabitants of a New York apartment" who wrote in thanks to dog musher Ruth Hirsiger. Expressing initial trepidation about taking on the Alaskan winter and driving their own dog teams, the New Yorkers completed a 4-day trip saying they "wished to turn around and do it all over again." More common than any heady rush of "man vs. wilderness" accomplishment is the resonant, lasting sentiment expressed by outdoor writer John Barsness, after a fishing trip to Kodiak. Wrote Barsness in an article in *Alaska* magazine: "Not all of me leaves Alaska; some part is always getting there. Some particle, perhaps a piece of my heart, floats through the sky, over glacial mountains and silver rivers. Another, the part that is cousin of fish, always swims upstream, past the bears and gravel bars, into an Alaska that never ends." In other words, any story about the Alaskan wilds is not so much a story about doing anything—about catching a fish, climbing a mountain, or running a river. It's about being there.

1 Preparing for the Alaskan Wilderness

Most of the information agencies you'll want to turn to when planning a wilderness adventure are listed under "Visitor Information" in chapter 3 or under the "Outside in . . . " sections near the beginning of each regional chapter.

Depending on where you're going, specific public lands agencies may be of help. These include **Alaska State Parks,** P.O. Box 107001, Anchorage, AK 99510 (☎ 907/762-2617); the federal **Bureau of Land Management (BLM),** 701 C St. (P.O. Box 13), Anchorage, AK 99513 (☎ **907/271-5076**); **Chugach National Forest,** 201 E. Ninth Ave., Suite 206, Anchorage, AK 99501 (☎ **907/271-2599**); **Tongass National Forest,** USDA Public Affairs Office, P.O. Box 21628, Juneau, AK 99802 (☎ **907/586-8806**); and the **U.S. Fish and Wildlife Service,**

1101 E. Tudor Rd., Anchorage, AK 99503 (☎ **907/786-3486**), which manages national wildlife refuges.

The **U.S. Geological Survey,** 4230 University Dr., Anchorage, AK 99508 (☎ **907/ 786-7011**), is the primary source for topographical maps. You can also find USGS maps at the public lands information centers. Another source is the *Alaska Atlas & Gazetteer,* available in many bookstores and shops in Alaska or by calling ☎ **800/ 225-5669;** it includes excellent, large-scale topographical maps of the entire state.

Choosing the best time to travel in the Alaskan wilderness depends on several variables, among them temperature, bugs, daylight, and the principal activity you plan to engage in during your trip. Most outfitters operate June through August and begin closing up shop (or severely curtailing activities) after Labor Day. By September, the hunting season (primarily for moose or Dall sheep) occupies the attention of many pilots, outfitters, and lodges that stay in business. See the "When to Go" section in chapter 3 for details.

Early summer may be preferable for river-based activities, as waters are swollen by snowmelt and rivers run faster. However, glacially fed rivers may actually surge later, as warming temperatures melt glacial ice. For land-based activities—like backpacking or mountain biking—later in the summer may be the best time, when the bugs diminish, fall colors begin to emerge, and trails are relatively dry. In most parts of Alaska, however, precipitation—possibly in the form of snow—tends to increase later in the summer.

Regardless of when you go, be sure to allow extra time in your schedule, especially toward the end of your travels. The Alaskan wilderness doesn't run on a fixed schedule. Most adventures require some kind of small-plane shuttling to and/or from remote locations. Small planes require relatively good weather to fly; if the weather socks in, you may well find your group waiting an extra day for a pickup. Reliable outfitters prepare for this possibility with extra food, and you, in building extra time into your schedule, should prepare for it, too.

WHERE TO GO

Picking the perfect trip from among so many choices might seem hopeless, but you can narrow things down relatively quickly by assessing four variables: the type of activity you're interested in, the geography, the climate, and how much you want to rough it.

In a state interlaced with thousands of rivers and streams, you can go almost anywhere for canoeing, kayaking, and rafting. However, rivers in the north, particularly in the Brooks Range and the Arctic National Wildlife Refuge, typically feature the longest stretches of unspoiled wilderness. Popular northern rivers, including the Alatna, the John, the Kobuk, the Noatak, the Kongakut, and the Sheenjek, are for the most part relatively gentle and are suitable for canoeing. White-water–hungry rafters and kayakers generally stick to rivers farther south—among them the Alsek and the Tatshenshini (which begin in the Yukon), the Copper, the Nenana, and the Talkeetna.

Hiking and backpacking opportunities are plentiful throughout the state, but they may not involve the sort of clearly marked trails hikers elsewhere in the United States are accustomed to. In the late 19th century, one traveler over the Chilkoot Pass in Southeast Alaska wrote the following: "A trail in Alaska should not be confused with the ordinary highway of settled states. When a trail is spoken of as existing between two points in Alaska it has no further meaning than that a man . . . may travel that way over the natural surface of the ground." In 100 years, things haven't changed much.

The most developed trail systems are in Chugach State Park and Tongass National Forest, and on the Kenai Peninsula. There are virtually no trails in the Far North, but the springy tundra of the foothills and mountains means that you can go more or less where you want to go without a trail to follow. (The swampy ground and slippery tussocks of the low Arctic tundra north of the Brooks Range, on the other hand, can be a nightmare to hike in in the summer; it's actually easier to traverse in the winter when it's frozen solid—but then, of course, you've got −40°F cold and blasting wind to contend with.) Stream crossings probably present the biggest challenge and hazard to safe travel. Snow-fed streams tend to be highest in spring and early summer, but some glacially fed streams may rise later in the summer, when warm temperatures melt glacial ice.

With the highest concentration of roads and trails radiating north and south from Anchorage, cyclists—mountain bikers and road riders—will want to concentrate their attention in that area. Sea kayakers can obviously go wherever there is sea, but the fjords of Southeast, Prince William Sound, the Katmai coast, and the Kodiak Archipelago rank at the top of the list.

Wherever you go in Alaska, the landscape has a way of astonishing you in one way or another. The mountain ranges of the North tend to be stark, arid, and more treeless the farther north you go, while glaciers and deep forests are more prevalent in the South. In large part, this reflects a difference in climate. If you have a deep aversion to rain, head north, where summer days are usually dry and often surprisingly mild. Rain is a given the farther south you go; if you're planning any outdoor activities in Southeast, industrial-strength rain gear is a must.

The difference in climate between north and south may go far in determining how you'll spend your nights in the outdoors. Cabins and fixed, floored tents are common accommodations offered by outfitters who operate in southern Alaska, where good dry tent sites can be hard to find. Not so in the North, where tenting is the norm, as it must be; cabins and lodges are few and far, far between. The most comfortable way to go, of course, is to base yourself in a wilderness lodge, most of which are concentrated in Southwest (tons of fishing lodges), the Interior (usually not far from Denali National Park), in Southeast, and in Southcentral.

It's fairly safe to say that no matter where you go in Alaska, you'll encounter wildlife. Moose, Dall sheep, bears, caribou, eagles, and waterfowl are the most likely sightings. If you're interested in large caribou herds, you must head north, while the biggest bears (though by no means the only bears) are in Southeast, the Kodiak Archipelago, and elsewhere where fish and berries—staples of the ursine diet—are more plentiful.

The really legendary fishing is nearest to the coastlines, but it's fairly safe to say that you'll find good fishing almost anywhere you go, save for rivers and lakes milky with glacial silt. Good fishing in Alaska is less a matter of location than it is a matter of the time of year. Salmon runs change with the season: King salmon, which get the prize for size, can run in June but the real monsters in the Kenai River, for example, run in July; sockeyes (reds) can run as early as May, the smaller species—cohos and the unloved chums—run later. Grayling are usually abundant near where feeder streams meet larger rivers, while rainbow trout are most common in lakes and streams of the Interior and the Kenai Peninsula. There's no shortage of guides or charter-boat operators who can take you to some fish-rich hot spot. For a list of fishing guides in a given area, see the regional chapters later in this book.

WHAT TO BRING

Obviously, your packing list will be determined by the activity and time of the year you choose. If you're signing on with an outfitter, the outfitter should supply a detailed list of the gear you'll need. Stick religiously to the list; forgetting something so simple as extra socks can bring on great misery should you accidentally step into an ice-cold river. It needs to be emphasized that this is no place to try to develop skill in planning and executing a wilderness trip—if you're going out without the help of professional outfitters and guides, you need to know exactly what to bring and exactly how to deal with the curves wilderness can throw you. Some of these, like hordes of mosquitoes, can be unpleasant; others, like bears, stream crossings, injuries, and sudden extreme cold, can easily be life threatening.

Proper clothing, enabling you to adapt to the changing moods of Alaskan weather, should be your primary concern. Essential clothing items include: heavy-duty rain gear, warm outer coat, wool cap, at least one pair of gloves, wool sweater or fleece pullover, one or more sets of long underwear, several pairs of wool socks and synthetic liners, sun hat, shorts, sturdy hiking boots, and more comfortable footwear—sturdy nylon-and-rubber waterproof sandals are great—for lounging around camp.

Other than clothing, items you'll want to have along include: sunglasses, insect repellent, sunscreen, a small knife, binoculars, a camera, and pepper spray or a gun if you're venturing into bear country (and most of Alaska is bear country). Depending on the trip you choose, it may be necessary to bring a sleeping bag and pad, tent, rubber boots (for river trips), and fishing gear. Fishing and/or camping equipment may be available for rent from outfitters or Alaska sporting-goods stores (see "Planning an Independent Wilderness Adventure," later in this chapter).

ALASKA'S WILDERNESS TRAVEL OUTFITTERS

Ralph Waldo Emerson, after venturing deep into the Adirondack woods of New York, praised the men who had guided him as "doctors of the wilderness." You'll find many reliable wilderness doctors in Alaska, too—people who know the Alaskan backcountry and can safely lead you through it. But there are many fly-by-nighters as well. It doesn't take much to print a color brochure, sign up for an 800 number, advertise in magazines, and call yourself a wilderness outfitter. Proceed with caution.

What should you look for in an outfitter? The top outfitters put together well-organized, air-tight trips, never leaving you wondering, for example, how to get from the airport to some rendezvous point. Experienced guides, reliable equipment (no leaky rafts, for example), and responsiveness to your needs (such as unusual diets) are other strong points. The best guides have not only backcountry skills but "people" skills as well—when in remote environments, perhaps waiting out a storm, a cheerful, helpful attitude can make a difference. An area of weakness for many outfitters, even the good ones, is naturalist training. A good boatman may get you down the river smoothly, and a good fishing guide may know all the hot spots, but when you have questions about a particularly intriguing flower, or animal, or geological curiosity, it's a decided bonus when a correct and satisfying answer is forthcoming.

QUESTIONS TO ASK A PROSPECTIVE TRIP ORGANIZER

What level of fitness and experience is required?   For extended wilderness trips, the top outfitters are likely to beat you to the punch, over the phone or through questionnaires: How fit are you, and how much experience do you have in the activity you're interested in? For many trips, you hardly have to be a hard-bodied outdoorsperson in order to participate. However, misjudging your fitness and ability can be a hazard not only to you but to your fellow participants as well. Be sensible and don't get your heart set on a specific trip. Discuss options—Alaska offers plenty—with prospective outfitters, trying to settle on a trip that's right for you. If you don't have outdoors experience, start with a trip no more than a few days long—you might not like it after all, and you could save yourself a lot of money and misery if you ease yourself into this kind of travel. This is a less critical issue if you're planning a lodge- or inn-based trip; however, the rigorousness of activities can vary substantially from one lodge to the next.

What are the outfitter's credentials?   When embarking on a wilderness trip, the quality of the outfitter means everything. No one wants lousy food, musty tents, or surly attitudes, but those concerns are merely asides to the main concern, which is safety. At least one guide on any trip should have CPR, emergency-medical, and wilderness-response training. Generally speaking, the longer an outfitter has been in operation, the better, although that's not certainly so. Make sure the outfitter has the permits and licenses required by the state, and ask about accreditation by professional organizations (for example, for mountaineers, the American Mountain Guides Association).

Can the outfitter provide a list of references?   This is a crucial one, especially since I have space here to list only a few of the many Alaska-based outfitters who have superb reputations. Any reputable outfitter can provide references of previous clients who've taken the trip you're considering—call them up and ask how things went.

What meals and accommodations are involved?   The range here is enormous, and terms can be misleading. One man's "luxurious" cabin is another man's hovel; "gourmet" is strictly a matter of interpretation. The most comfortable accommodations and the freshest food tend to be found at wilderness lodges, but don't count on it. Food for raft trips can be of a surprisingly high caliber; support rafts are capable of carrying large coolers with fresh meats, vegetables, and even beer and wine. Backpacking meals, by contrast, are usually pretty bare-bones, and don't expect any backpacking guide to haul around an ice chest or a chilled case of beer for your enjoyment over the evening campfire. Tents, incidentally, are not always tents in the strictest sense of the word. Many outfitters make use of large wood- or metal-framed tents that may include wood floors, full beds, heat, and even electricity.

What is included in the price?   Typically, package prices include almost everything except airfare to and from Alaska. "Almost" is the key word. Usually not included are tips, alcoholic beverages, gear rental (such as packs, tents, boots, and rain gear), fishing licenses, and expenses you might incur before or after the period covered by your package (such as lodging, meals, and car rentals). For example, the cost of a layover night in Anchorage between the arrival of your flight and the beginning of your wilderness trip would probably not be included. Traveling à la carte in Alaska in summer can be expensive, so be sure you know exactly what you're getting when you book.

What about children?   Because of the physical demands of wilderness travel and often because backcountry partners (such as canoe partners) must be matched by size, strength, and ability, some trip organizers set age limits. On multiday camping trips, each participant is usually expected to pull his or her own weight—in some cases, literally. Teenagers may be physically up to that responsibility, but children under 10, on any extended camping trip, probably aren't. If you really want to bring young children along, ask the outfitter about trip options.

How far in advance must I book?   Some popular trips may be fully booked as much as a year in advance. Tourism statistics show that Alaska travelers tend to plan and book their vacations several months in advance. This does not mean that you're out of luck if you start planning late in the game. However, the later you plan, the more flexible you'll have to be if the trip or lodge of first choice is full. Keep a couple of factors in mind. First, some operators offer discounts for early bookings. Second, smaller groups make for better wilderness experiences, but there are also fewer openings for last-minute planners. Requirements for deposits and prepayments vary widely from one company to the next; deposits are usually partially or completely refundable if you cancel well in advance—say, 60 days or so.

In case you want
to see the world.

At American Express, we're here to make your journey a
smooth one. So we have over 1,700 travel service locations in
over 120 countries ready to help. What else would you expect
from the world's largest travel agency?

do more.

AMERICAN
EXPRESS

Travel

http://www.americanexpress.com/travel

In case you want to be welcomed there.

We're here to see that you're always welcomed at establishments everywhere. That's why millions of people carry the American Express® Card – for peace of mind, confidence, and security, around the world or just around the corner.

do more

RECOMMENDED OUTFITTERS

The following are among the most reliable companies leading trips into the Alaskan wilderness:

Alaska Discovery. 5449 Shaune Dr., Suite 4, Juneau, AK 99801. ☎ **800/586-1911** or 907/780-6226. Fax 907/780-4220.

Based in Southeast Alaska, this company offers trips involving mostly water activities—canoeing, kayaking, and rafting—in both Southeast and the Far North. Trips tend to be of moderate difficulty.

Alaska Wilderness Journeys. P.O. Box 220204, Anchorage, AK 99522. ☎ **800/349-0064** or 907/349-2964. Fax 907/349-2964.

Originally a river-oriented outfitter, this company has broadened its scope to include backpacking and mountain biking, as well as river trips.

Alaska Wildland Adventures. P.O. Box 389, Girdwood, AK 99587. ☎ **800/334-8730** or 907/783-2928. Fax 907/783-2130.

With lodges on the Kenai Peninsula and in the Denali area, Alaska Wildland gears its program toward the softer side of adventure travel, including "safaris" specifically for seniors.

American Wilderness Experience. P.O. Box 1486, Boulder, CO 80306. ☎ **800/444-0099** or 303/444-2622. Fax 303/333-3999.

A.W.E. is an adventure-travel clearinghouse, and its catalog features selected trips from numerous outfitters.

Mountain Travel • Sobek. 620 Fairmount Ave., El Cerrito, CA 94530. ☎ **800/227-2384** or 510/527-8100. Fax 510/525-7710.

This is perhaps the granddaddy of adventure-travel companies. The company guides its own trips and also acts as an agent for other outfitters. River-running is a strong suit.

Sierra Club Outings. 730 Polk St., San Francisco, CA 94109. ☎ **415/923-5630.** Fax 415/923-0636.

In addition to its activities as an environmentalist organization, the Sierra Club oversees a large international outings program. Trips tend to be on the more strenuous side, with emphasis on wildlife viewing and naturalist activities.

Sourdough Outfitters. P.O. Box 90, Bettles, AK 99726. ☎ **907/692-5252.** Fax 907/692-5612.

Sourdough features an extensive program of moderate to strenuous trips in the Brooks Range, summer and winter. The company also provides support service for self-guided trips.

St. Elias Alpine Guides. P.O. Box 111241, Anchorage, AK 99511. ☎ and fax **907/277-6867.** This company specializes in hiking and climbing trips in Wrangell–St. Elias National Park, and also offers customized trips for individuals or groups.

WILDERNESS HAZARDS

The wilderness is not so much a dangerous place as an unfamiliar place for most people. That said, lack of familiarity can lead to bad wilderness behavior and that, in turn, *can* be dangerous. Common sense is often a reliable guide—if you're cold, for example, put on more clothing—but it can lead you astray, too. The best guideline for getting along in the wilderness, then, is to heed the advice and instructions of those in the know (like the guides on a guided trip) and use common sense when you've got nothing else to go by. Once again, you shouldn't be out on your own in Alaskan wilderness unless you have extensive outdoors experience and survival skills. You have to be ready, able, and willing to deal with the worst—and if you are, this is one of the very few places left on the planet where you can experience the exhilaration of having to deal with a land on its terms, not on yours.

There are five principal hazards to be most concerned about in the Alaskan wilds: bears, bugs, hypothermia, stream crossings, and *giardia lamblia*—known colloquially in Alaska as "beaver fever." The first three are ably addressed in the "Health" and "Safety" sections of chapter 3; I'll say a little more about the last two.

GIARDIA Generally blamed on parasites carried by dog feces, giardia is a prevalent problem in streams throughout Alaska as well as the Lower 48. The symptoms are nausea, cramps, headaches, and diarrhea—and you don't want anything to do with them. The larger the river and the nearer you are to civilization, the more apt the water is to be contaminated. Conversely, small feeder streams in remote environments may be perfectly safe to drink from. If you're on a guided trip, follow the guide's advice regarding the purity of a particular stream. But to be safe, I strongly recommend making a policy of purifying all water you plan to drink from streams; you can use iodine tablets or, better yet, a filtering system. Both are available from sporting-goods stores, and you can get reusable, simple-to-use filters today that don't cost an arm and a leg.

CROSSING STREAMS & RIVERS This can be a lot more daunting in Alaska than you'd think on the face of it. This is cold water—*really* cold water; furthermore, the silt in glacially fed streams makes the water opaque, and it can be difficult to gauge depth. And if you're hiking over tundra, a hard rain can change the character of a stream quickly—the permafrost won't absorb water, and thus a gentle creek can become a roaring river in a matter of hours. You'll want to be careful with your trip routing, picking a path that will lead you to the easiest places to cross rivers and streams. If you go out with a professional outfitter, they'll take care of this for you; but even if you're going out on your own, it's a good idea to enlist the services of an outfitter in picking your itinerary—see "Planning an Independent Wilderness Adventure," later in this chapter.

If you can't find a place to rock-hop across a stream, scout along the banks for a wide place in the stream. If you can find one, a long stick will be useful in checking depth as you wade across. I like to pack a sure-footed pair of Tevas or some such water-ignoring sandal—they serve double duty as camp shoe and river footwear. Tie your boots and socks up in your pack and wade across; putting on your dry socks and boots afterward will be a near-religious experience.

WILDERNESS REMINDER Finally, remember that the wilderness is wild—no phones, no hospital around the corner, no 911 number to call. In an emergency, help may be days away. Be prepared with extra prescription medications, extra eyeglasses, and basic first-aid equipment.

2 Traveling in the Alaskan Wilderness

What follows are recommended vacation possibilities in the Alaskan wilderness, culled from literally hundreds of trips and lodges you might want to consider. The prevailing variable to keep in mind is that almost anything can change—the dates, activities included, and particularly the prices. If you don't like what's being offered, ask about options; many outfitters are very flexible. Customization and adaptation are norms rather than exceptions, often though not always contingent on how much you're willing to spend.

Increasingly, outfitters are offering "sampler" trips for adventurers unable to make up their minds. Such samplers usually include a variety of activities, often in a variety of locales, and have become popular as intro-to-Alaska trips. They may, however, lack the wilderness intensity and reward of a more focused trip. Another trend in outfitting is customization. If you're planning a trip with a group of four or more, many outfitters (particularly smaller operators) will tailor a trip to your specific interests or needs, at little or no additional cost.

The **difficulty ratings** listed here are relative within this listing. They may not jibe with rating systems used by individual trip organizers. As a rough guideline, "easy" means pretty much anybody can do it, "moderate" means some degree of physical fitness is required, and "strenuous" means that you ought to be in good shape and should probably have at least some backcountry experience, or you're going to have a lousy time.

Traveling around in the wilderness is not cheap. If you're looking for bargain-basement deals in adventure travel, you've probably come to the wrong place in coming to Alaska. Small-plane flying to and from remote locations adds considerably to the bottom-line cost of many trips. In addition, the shortness of the Alaskan summer means that outfitters have perhaps a 3-month window of opportunity within which to ply their trade. Finally, the cost of living is generally high in Alaska. Before you rail at the prices, be comforted by the fact that few wilderness outfitters are getting rich in Alaska. They aren't in it for the money. Most do what they do because they love to do it.

SOUTHEAST

Chitistone Canyon Backpacking. St. Elias Alpine Guides, P.O. Box 111241, Anchorage, AK 99511. ☎ and fax **907/277-6867.** Approximate cost: $1,973. Dates: July–Aug. Trip length: 11 days. Group size: 2–6. Begins and ends in: Anchorage. Relative difficulty: Strenuous.

Upon being met by Bob Jacobs in McCarthy, the tiny former mining town at the confluence of the Root and Kennicott glaciers in Wrangell–St. Elias National Park, you might have good reason to be skeptical. The first impression is not impressive. Bob, head of St. Elias Alpine guides, drives an ancient tin can of a truck nicknamed Moondog, not always in full working order and not with all of its body parts firmly attached. Bob himself can come across as something of an eccentric. But he happens to be a sober-minded, preeminent alpinist who knows this neck of the Alaskan woods better than any other living being.

You'd have a hard time getting Bob to single out a favorite backpacking trip in the Wrangell–St. Elias region, given his abiding affection for just about every square inch of this exquisite wilderness. Yet stoke him with a beer or two, and he might let slip that the hike through Chitistone Canyon into the high country around Skolai Pass is about as good as backpacking gets.

This is a classic, all-in-everything trip. It begins in a canyon framed by sheer, 4,000-foot cliffs and passes by sweeping, deep-valley glaciers and waterfalls hundreds of feet high. It rises to high, tundra meadows—the grazing lands of Dall sheep—and traverses Skolai Pass before reaching the broad basin of Skolai Creek. Severe rock walls, hanging glaciers, distant peaks reaching to over 16,000 feet—all are part of the backdrop.

It's a breathtaking trek and not at all easy. This is backpacking recommended for experienced, well-conditioned backpackers. Much of the trail—if it can be called a trail—links animal tracks, making surefootedness essential. This is true alpine wilderness, where the weather can change faster than the time it takes to draw a deep breath, and where self-sufficiency instincts are the key not just to comfort but to survival. You'll have to get by on backpacker food—nutritionally adequate, culinarily forgettable—and you may find yourself quarantined in a wet tent for two days waiting for a storm to pass. Total misery is not out of the question. So why bother? The rewards—the scenery, the wildlife, the challenge, the sense of accomplishment—exceed the limits of the imagination. It's as good as backpacking gets.

Glacier Bay / Muir Inlet Sea Kayaking. Alaska Discovery, 5449 Shaune Dr., Suite 4, Juneau, AK 99801. ☎ **800/586-1911** or 907/780-6226. Fax 907/780-4220. Approximate cost: $1,890. Dates: Mid-June to Aug. Trip length: 8 days. Group size: Up to 10. Begins and ends in: Gustavus. Relative difficulty: Moderate.

Consider this syllogism: Kayaks are an essential part of Alaskan history, and Glacier Bay is one of the world's quintessential sea-kayaking regions; ergo, Glacier Bay sea kayaking has a long history. Not so—200 years ago, Glacier Bay was a mass of impassible glacial ice. It wasn't until glaciation in the area went into full retreat through the 1800s, at the astonishingly rapid rate of about half a mile a year, that the bay exposed itself as a navigable inland passage.

Glacier Bay has since become a frenzy of natural activity. With glaciers retreating at a pace unequaled in documented geological history, huge blocks of ice routinely explode into the water in a calving process the Tlingits called "white thunder." Where glaciers have receded, wildlife has flourished; as John Muir, the naturalist for whom Muir Inlet is named, said: "Out of all the cold darkness and glacial crushing and grinding comes this warm, abounding beauty and life." Whales, sea lions, bears, wolves, mountain goats, moose, eagles—it is abounding life indeed. This convolution of nature draws a sizable human audience, their access enabled by deep channels in the bay allowing cruise ships to venture far inland. Muir Inlet, however—with its strong tides and narrow entry—does not present cruise ships with easy passage. As a result, sea kayakers can have this northeastern finger of the bay pretty much to themselves.

Glacier Bay is wet country. In 1982, naturalist Harry Fielding Reid grumbled about the certainty of rain in Glacier Bay: "If the sun shines, if the stars appear, if there are clouds, or if there are none; these are all sure indications [of rain]. If the barometer falls, it will rain; if the barometer rises, it will rain; if the barometer remains steady, it will continue to rain." Don't regard this as a deterrent but simply as a likelihood to prepare for. You bring the rain gear, Alaska Discovery provides a solidly waterproof tent, and you're in business. And you never know—it might not rain. Reid might just have been having a bad day.

The kayaking itinerary, involving 60 to 70 miles in 5 days, should leave ample opportunity for beachcombing and hiking. If you're a total newcomer to paddling, you should take a guided or solo day trip before you embark on a multiday trip like this one—you won't have the option of dropping out if you don't like it. But very likely, you'll love it: The skill to propel a stable, two-person kayak can be learned within minutes, and there's no tricky water on this trip to give novices hesitation. All you'll need is an eagerness to experience the natural frenzy of Glacier Bay away from the cruise-ship crowds.

Tatshenshini River Rafting. Mountain Travel • Sobek, 6420 Fairmount Ave., El Cerrito, CA 94530. ☎ **800/227-2384** or 510/527-8100. Fax 510/525-7710. Approximate cost: $2,475. Dates: July–Aug. Trip length: 10 days. Group size: Up to 12. Begins and ends in: Haines. Relative difficulty: Moderate.

Edward Abbey, the late, great gonzo environmentalist, once described a break from rafting on the Tatshenshini thusly: "We lie in the sunshine, on the warm grass, and stare at the mountains, range after range, standing beyond the dark forest. Now and then, so remote as to be barely audible, comes the rumble of readjustments, the clash and crash of falling ice. Flowers and ice, sunlight and snow . . ."

Whitewater and icebergs, too. The river begins in southwestern Yukon Territory as a fast stream with Class IV rapids. From there it flows for more than 100 miles through glacier-draped mountains, broadening to 2 miles wide before emptying into Alsek Bay, filled with icebergs freshly calved from tidewater glaciers. It's rich country and, as such, a rich haven of wildlife, most prominently such fish-hunting raptors as eagles and ospreys.

Sobek, a modern pioneer of guided rafting trips, was the first company to take paying guests down the "Tat"—a trip that has since come to be considered a river-running classic. So classic, in fact, that increased popularity has forced the National Park Service to institute a permit system for the section of the river that runs through Glacier Bay National Park. But it has hardly become a water-borne traffic jam; the permitting assures at the very least that you won't have to share evening campsites with other river runners. Your sense of privacy should remain undefiled. Your sense of wonder should become elevated, too, on a trip that ends, in Abbey's words, where "the river blends with the bay and the bay with the sea, and the sea melts, without dividing line, into a golden sky."

ANCHORAGE & SOUTHCENTRAL ALASKA

Hatcher Pass Snowcat Skiing. Glacier Snow Cat Skiing & Tours, P.O. Box 874234, Wasilla, AK 99687. ☎ **800-373-3118.** Fax 907/373-3118. Approximate cost: $1,200. Dates: Nov–Apr. Trip length: 5 days. Group size: 12. Begins and ends in: Anchorage. Relative difficulty: Moderate to strenuous.

The shortage of ski areas in a state as mountainous and snowy as Alaska is something of a mystery. This shortage has fueled a healthy renegade attitude among Alaskan skiing enthusiasts who feel liberated to go wherever they feel like going—not necessarily where there are lifts—and whose tracks can often be spotted in outlandishly hard-to-ski places. At Thompson Pass, north of Valdez and home of the annual World Extreme Skiing Championship, self-guided heli-skiing is the current rage. Gather together your best skiing buddies, scrape up the bucks (about $25 a head) for a helicopter ride to some remote mountaintop, and bon voyage! Great stuff, but for anyone unfamiliar with the terrain and not well schooled in dealing with the deadly hazards (avalanches, crevasses) of big-mountain skiing, to go about this unguided is risk-taking on a grand scale.

Fortunately, there are safer ways to go backcountry skiing in Alaska, with guided snowcat skiing at Hatcher Pass ranking at the top of that list. Hatcher Pass is less than a 2-hour drive north of Anchorage, but it's far enough into the Interior to be only minimally affected by the moderating (that is, dampening) influences of Alaska's coastal climate. That can mean cold weather, but it can also mean wonderfully light, dry snow—nearly 500 inches' worth in an average winter. That snow covers roughly 1,500 acres and 2,000 vertical feet of skiable terrain—not eye-popping numbers, but plenty of skiing when you have to share it with only 11 other skiers in the snowcat. It's ideal for strong intermediates eager to improve their powder-skiing skills.

Don't fret too much about the cold; the snowcat is heated, and there's a warming hut where you can hole up between runs if you want to. You can also keep warm by logging 20,000 vertical feet or more in a day. The Motherlode, originally built in the 1930s when mining was active at Hatcher Pass, provides daily meals and nightly accommodations. You could spend a few dollars more to stay in fancier digs in nearby Wasilla, but the Motherlode (renovated since the mining days) has a comfortable, funky feel and a knockout view from the dining room. After 5 days of Hatcher Pass skiing, maybe then you'll be ready to take on the steeps and deep snow of Thompson Pass. Maybe.

Kenai Peninsula Rafting and Wilderness. Alaska Wildland Adventures, P.O. Box 389, Girdwood, AK 99587. ☎ **800/334-8730** or 907/783-2928. Fax 907/783-2130. Approximate cost: $1,195 (for cabins), $995 (for tents). Dates: June to mid-Sept. Trip length: 4 days. Group size: 4–10. Begins and ends in: Anchorage. Relative difficulty: Easy.

On a weekend day when the salmon are running, the Kenai River can turn into a combat-fishing zone. Fisticuffs are not out of the question as fishermen standing shoulder to shoulder attempt to assert their perceived right to occupy particular patches of fish-infested waters.

Fortunately, there are kinder, gentler ways to experience the Kenai. Start from Cooper Landing on a relaxed float by raft along the upper stretches of the Kenai River. Expect to see plenty of birds, the occasional moose, and perhaps a couple of fishermen, toe to toe, whaling at one another. From there the river picks up steam, gaining Class III force through a lower canyon before spilling into glacier-fed Skilak Lake, where the color of the water changes from aquamarine to turquoise, depending on the wind and the light of day.

Cross the lake to a small backcountry lodge, in the heart of the two-million acre Kenai Wildlife Refuge, and the sense of removal from civilization becomes quickly and dramatically complete. One Alaska Wildland Adventures employee recalls arriving one time at the unoccupied lodge to see on the front window the unmistakable imprint of two giant and muddy bear paws.

This may be considered rustic living, in that the absence of running water makes an outhouse imperative. But accommodations in outlying log cabins or wood-framed "cabin" tents are remarkably comfortable, and the food borders on gourmet. From the lodge, the main activities for the next couple of days are kayaking on the lake or hiking to tundra ridges for exceptional views of the Kenai Peninsula backcountry—or you can simply while away your time reading or card-playing in the main lodge, waiting for that bear to come banging at the window.

Prince William Sound Sailing and Sea Kayaking. Alaska Wilderness Sailing Safaris, P.O. Box 1313, Valdez, AK 99686. ☎ **907/835-5175.** Fax 907/835-5679. Approximate cost: $1,200. Dates: June–Aug. Trip length: 7 days. Begins and ends in: Anchorage. Relative difficulty: Moderate.

Prince William Sound is a name that will forever live in ecological infamy. The 1989 *Exxon Valdez* spill imprinted images on the national consciousness of oil-smothered bird carcasses, blackened beaches, and courtrooms filled with finger-pointing trial combatants. Despite the comedy of errors that the spill and subsequent cleanup efforts proved to be, Prince William Sound is well on its way to regaining its dignity as one of Alaska's great natural preserves.

You can make of this trip what you want. A base camp on tiny Growler Island, in the heart of the Sound, is the beginning and end of each day's activities. It's your choice each day as to whether to go sailing or kayaking (experience in either is not necessary as lessons are offered), and it's your call as to how devotedly you want to pursue either. Sailing trips aboard a 40-foot sloop can cover more territory, to permit viewing of the Columbia Glacier insistently pushing into the sea or (depending on the season) pods of migrating whales, sea otters, and eagles. On the other hand, kayaks—primarily stable, idiot-proof two-person inflatables—are better for exploring shorelines pocked with hidden coves and sea caves. Sedentary boat time can be relieved by short hikes through moss-floored rain forests or along alpine ridges.

The logistics of getting to and from the Growler Island camp call for a close encounter with mainstream Alaskan tourism: a tour-bus, train, and tour-boat combo (see the "Valdez" section under "Prince William Sound: Kingdom of the Orca," in chapter 8, for information on Stan Stephens Cruises). That means 2 full days devoted to coming and going. It's scenic, certainly, but you might want to expedite the process by plunking down the extra change for a round-trip flight between Anchorage and Valdez. Once in camp, the accommodations in floored, heated tents—really canvas-sided cabins—make for "camping" in the loosest, cushiest sense of the word.

Resurrection Pass Backpacking. Chugach Hiking Tours, 420 Aurora Dr., Anchorage, AK. ☎ **907/278-4453**. Fax 907/786-1771. Approximate cost: $500. Dates: June–Aug. Trip length: 6 days. Group size: 4–8. Begins and ends in: Anchorage. Relative difficulty: Moderate.

The trail over Resurrection Pass is quite possibly Alaska's most popular backpacking trip. The Chilkoot Trail in southeastern Alaska is the only real contender, and since more than half of it is actually in the Yukon, its true-Alaskan credentials are suspect. Both trails share a common history, having been cut in the late 1800s by prospectors sniffing around for rich gold deposits. The gold is gone and so are the prospectors, but the land remains relatively unscathed—clear lakes with good fishing and stark mountains that appear much more substantial than topo maps indicate. A 5,000-foot peak sounds modest until you come upon its tundra-covered flanks and sharp crags sequestering patches of summer-resistant snow.

The trek southward from Hope to Cooper Landing on the Kenai River covers 40 miles, and you are assured of seeing other backcountry travelers along the way. The trail is well formed and gradual enough to have become popular among local mountain bikers, some of whom roar over the full length of the trail in one day. There are several public-use cabins along the way to indulge those with an aversion to tent camping, further broadening the appeal of hiking the trail. Nevertheless, this is hardly a teeming thoroughfare of recreational activity, and particularly on weekdays early in the summer, the sense of wilderness isolation can be complete. You're more apt to encounter mountain bikers and horseback riders later in the summer, when trails are fully clear of snow.

This is a trip geared for people with little or no backpacking experience. "This is about learning how to backpack and learning about Alaska," says Cable Starling, proprietor of Chugach Hiking Tours. That's a learning process that begins with proper gearing and packing, includes the selection of appropriate food for the trip, and continues onto the trail, with the business of maintaining camp and preparing meals. It is learning in which, as Starling says, "everybody is an equal participant." If all of that sounds like some laborious wilderness clinic, forget about it. The hiking is fairly easy, at least by rigorous Alaskan backpacking standards. The beauty of the landscape is nonstop entertainment, and Starling himself makes for engaging backcountry company. It may be learning, but it is quite the classroom. And if you want to learn more, keep on going. A good trail, with fewer people but more bears, continues on for 30 miles from Cooper Landing, the southern terminus of the Resurrection Pass trail, to Seward.

South-Central Alaska Sampler. Mountain Travel • Sobek, 6420 Fairmount Ave., El Cerrito, CA 94530. ☎ **800/227-2384** or 510/527-8100. Fax 510/525-7710. Approximate cost: $3,575. Dates: June–Aug. Trip length: 11 days. Group size: Up to 16. Begins and ends in: Anchorage. Relative difficulty: Easy to moderate.

A sampler, by definition, is an effort to be many things to many people—which is to say, a compromise. But in a world of so many beguiling natural riches clustered within a few hours of Anchorage, a compromise may ultimately offer the most rewarding experience. Imagine, for example, devoting all your time to exploring the Kenai Peninsula and then leaving Alaska realizing you missed seeing Mt. McKinley, less than 200 miles away. It's the fear of such a missed opportunity that lends this sampler trip its appeal.

Because of their proximity to Anchorage, the Kenai and Chugach mountains feature some of the most user-friendly hiking trails in Alaska. This trip takes full advantage of that fact with day hikes in both mountain ranges, interspersed with rafting on the Kenai River and boating in Kenai Fjords National Park. Don't be misled by the proximity of metropolitan Anchorage; the spirit of wilderness within the Chugach Mountains and along the daunting glaciers of Kenai Fjords remains undefiled.

From here, it's on to Denali National Park and the stunning massif of Mt. McKinley. In 3 days of hiking in the park, you should count yourself fortunate if the peak of North America's highest mountain reveals itself. Its sheer bulk makes it a meteorological magnet for clouds and storms. You're certain, however, to spot the abundant wildlife that make this region home: caribou, moose, Dall sheep, and— if you're lucky—grizzly bears.

You needn't worry, however, about bears invading your camp or trashing your tent at night. Accommodations for this trip are in cabins, meaning you'll never be far from the comforts of a warm shower and a well-cooked meal. It's not a ruggedly pure wilderness experience; it's simply an experience in ruggedly pure wilderness.

THE INTERIOR

Iditarod Trail Dog Mushing. Lucky Husky Racing Kennel, HC 89 Box 256, Willow, AK 99688. ☎ **907/495-6470.** Fax 907/495-6471. Approximate cost: $1,995. Dates: Feb–Mar. Trip length: 5 days. Group size: 2–6. Begins and ends in: Anchorage. Relative difficulty: Strenuous.

The Iditarod is called the Last Great Race, but it has become something more than that within the cultural ethos of premillenium America. It has become symbolic of the endurance of a frontier spirit and a toughness to take on the harshest challenges the wilderness can dish out.

This trip does not try to simulate the rigors of Iditarod racing, but it does give first-time dog-sledders a feel for what the Iditarod is all about. The itinerary covers sections of both the current Iditarod trail and the original trail—the trail used by mushers in 1925 to carry antidipthereal serum from Seward to Nome.

Ruth Hirsiger—Swiss by upbringing, Alaskan by cultural adaptation—is a top-flight musher in short-distance races who still holds on to a dream of someday competing in the Iditarod. That's no small undertaking; dog food is expensive, and you've got to pay the bills somehow. To help make ends meet, Hirsiger leads dog-mushing trips covering 5 days and 100 miles through the forest and over frozen bogs and riverbeds near Willow.

No, this is not hardcore dog-sled racing. But make no mistake; the mushing is the real thing, with each trip participant in charge of his or her own six-dog team—quite a workout for both musher and dogs when covering as much as 45 miles in a day. Accommodations at night are usually in log cabins or roadhouses, but there is the occasional night when it may be necessary to bivouac on a frozen swamp with the temperature at 20°F below or colder.

Cold is a part of mushing life, and mushers have a way of appearing much bigger than they are—looming presences in bulky, fur-trimmed outerwear hiding several layers of warm clothing. Well-insulated clothing is vitally essential. However, the cold of the Alaskan Interior is more often than not a clear cold, with the sun warming the midday air and with distant mountains crisply etched against a blue sky. Within this deep-winter environment, you learn to drive your own six-dog team, which can charge along as fast as 10 miles an hour when the trail is packed and smooth. If you ever wanted to get a taste of what Iditarod racing is all about, this is your chance.

Richardson Highway Bicycling. Alaskan Bicycle Adventures, 2734 Iliamna Ave., Anchorage, AK 99517. ☎ **800/770-7242** or 907/243-2329. Fax 907/243-4985. Approximate cost: $2,295. Dates: June–Sept. Trip length: 8 days. Group size: up to 13. Begins and ends in: Anchorage. Relative difficulty: Moderate.

The Richardson Highway is Alaska's original highway, a one-time wagon trail stretching 360 miles from Fairbanks to Valdez, and it remains quite possibly its most scenic. If you like mountain views, this is your kind of highway, skirting or traversing the major mountain ranges of the state. Ride through the Alaska Range, crowned by Mount McKinley; past Wrangell–St. Elias National Park and its glaciated, 16,000-foot peaks; then through the Chugach Mountains at Thompson Pass, known for legendary snowfalls that have exceeded 5 feet in 24 hours. Unfortunately, too many Alaskan visitors figure that the only way to see it all is by tour bus or RV, often blasting through in a single day, watching this special world rush by like a rapid-fire succession of dioramas in a natural-history museum.

There is an alternative, of course. As a cyclist, you must endure the noxious presence of RVs or tour buses, which pass by in a thick stream during the July peak season, hogging highway sections where shoulders are minimal. That unpleasantness aside, this is bicycle touring according to the blueprint: smooth road, few big hills to ride over (with some notable exceptions, like Thompson Pass and the climb up into the Alaska Range), and spectacular scenery. You can pull over whenever the mood strikes, take a nap, and smell and pick the wildflowers. Daily mileages of between 50 and 75 miles might sound like a grunt, but there's a comforting catch: You can wimp out whenever your body or spirit surrenders. A support van—known as the sag wagon or broom wagon—follows along just for that purpose. You might, however, find yourself riding longer than you thought possible; the surprise, in such mountainous country, is that the greatest daily elevation gain in a day's ride is 1,800 vertical feet.

This is road-bound travel and as such is obviously not wilderness adventuring in a truly rugged, remote context. Either you appreciate the occasional conveniences of roadside civilization or you have chosen the wrong trip. Nights are spent in comfortable motels or lodges. Bikes are provided unless you want to bring your own; all you need to bring are your own clothing, legs, lungs, and eyes.

Talkeetna Mountains Backpacking. Alaska Wilderness Journeys, P.O. Box 220204, Anchorage, AK 99522. ☎ **800/349-0064** or 907/349-2964. Fax 907/349-2964. Approximate cost: $795. Dates: June–Sept. Trip length: 3 days. Group size: 4–8. Begins and ends in: Anchorage. Relative difficulty: Moderate to strenuous.

Walking a high ridgeline is, as Steve Weller of Alaska Wilderness Journeys says, "as good as it gets in Alaska." Above the treeline, you feel on a clear day as if you could see forever. That's particularly true when you can look over your shoulder with every step to see the hulking presence of the Mount McKinley massif commanding the western skies. The Talkeetnas are a humble range by big-mountain Alaska standards, being neither exceptionally high nor exceptionally rugged. They're a land between, with the more commanding Alaska Range (including McKinley) to the north and the Chugach Mountains to the south.

The ridges of the Talkeetnas are, simply, hikeable, unlike the more forbidding ridges of neighboring ranges. Sure, it might be a rough scramble at times to traverse steep, trail-less terrain, but it's do-able—nothing even close to technical mountaineering skills that might be required to hike ridges in the Alaska Range.

As wild as this country is, the trip itself isn't entirely wild; one evening's dinner is at a remote lodge (see the Caribou Lodge, under "Wilderness Lodges," later in this chapter). This means that you can get by with a fairly light pack, making the scrambling easier and reserving more energy for short after-dinner hikes—if you're a hard-core hiking junkie, that is. If 3 days sounds all too brief, you can combine this trip with others offered by Alaska Wilderness Journeys—a 3-day raft down the Tazlina River, for example.

SOUTHWEST

Wood-Tikchik Kayaking and Hiking. Alaska Wilderness Journeys, P.O. Box 220204, Anchorage, AK 99522. ☎ **800/349-0064** or 907/349-2964. Fax 907/349-2964. Approximate cost: $2,470. Dates: July–Aug. Trip length: 7 days. Group size: 4–8. Begins and ends in: Anchorage. Relative difficulty: Moderate.

It really says something about the vastness of the Alaskan wilds that a single state park, Wood-Tikchik, can be larger than the state of Delaware while remaining almost entirely anonymous. Wood-Tikchik's anonymity is no doubt due to the fact that the park is hard to get to; you've got to fly from Anchorage to Dillingham, then from Dillingham by float plane into the park. And what do you get when you get there? Large, glacially carved lakes surrounded by tundra-covered mountains and no facilities, other than a few remote fishing lodges.

Anonymity, relative difficulty of access, and an absence of user-friendly facilities enhance a spirit of wilderness in Wood-Tikchik. That's something wildlife (bears, moose, wolverines, beavers, and, unfortunately, a high concentration of insects) can appreciate. Many sportspeople who are familiar with Wood-Tikchik know the area for its fishing, reportedly some of the best Dolly Varden and trout fishing in the state. Others come simply to float on its lakes, in rafts, canoes, or kayaks, and be away from the world for a while.

This trip moves at a leisurely pace, to absorb and be absorbed by that wilderness spirit, rather than to log heroic mileages in getting from one point to the next each day. The idea is to take time to explore the shores and surrounding mountains of Nuyakuk Lake, more than 900 feet deep. Physical energy is divided more or less equally between paddling and hiking, allowing plenty of time for fishing, photography, wildlife viewing, and intense wilderness absorption. Kayaking experience isn't necessary; the first day on the lake includes lessons on maneuvering your one-person kayak proficiently enough to get by on this trip. You'll probably find yourself drifting more than paddling, anyway—quietly taking in the wild world passing by.

THE ARCTIC

Brooks Range Dog Mushing. Sourdough Outfitters, P.O. Box 90, Bettles, AK 99726. ☎ **907/692-5252.** Fax 907/692-5612. Approximate cost: $1,850. Dates: Feb–Apr. Trip length: 6 days. Group size: 3–6. Begins and ends in: Fairbanks. Relative difficulty: Strenuous.

The Brooks Range ranks as one of Alaska's wilder places in summertime, but in winter it is wilder still—less populated by sportspeople, less hospitable, more austere under the mantle of its winter beauty. It is fitting, then, that this trip leads through the Wild River valley, a 100-mile northward journey from the flatland around Bettles to the mountainous country of Wild Lake.

Dog sledding north of the Arctic Circle reaches into the soul and essence of roughing it in the Alaskan outback—the vice-grip hold of winter, the rugged countryside, the traditional form of Alaskan travel. It is neither unbearably harsh, as many non-Alaskans might imagine, nor is it easy. You must learn to dress for and cope with a climate in which –40°F temperatures are not uncommon, and you must learn to drive and manage your own dog team. The payoffs are experiencing wild Alaska at its wildest and, on clear nights, seeing displays of the northern lights that will steal your breath away. And, not least, you get to experience the thrill and satisfaction of driving and managing your own dog team.

Sourdough Outfitters does a fine job of smoothing out the rough edges. A day is spent learning the basics of dog mushing, not the least of which is familiarizing yourself with the names of all the dogs on your team. Nights are spent in preset camps along the way, where accommodations are in comfortable, wood-framed tents. Still, this is winter camping in the wilderness, where winter cold can at times make such chores as wood-gathering and unharnessing and feeding dogs more difficult than you might imagine. On the other hand, many people are unperturbed by the cold; the Sourdough folks claim that some hardy guests actually pull their sleeping bags out of the tents at night, to fall asleep watching the spectacle of the northern lights. By April, longer days and warmer weather begin returning, but the intensity of the northern lights is on the wane.

John River Canoeing. Sourdough Outfitters, P.O. Box 90, Bettles, AK 99726. ☎ **907/692-5252.** Fax 907/692-5612. Approximate cost: $1,400. Dates: June–Aug. Trip length: 6 days. Group size: 4–6. Begins and ends in: Fairbanks. Relative difficulty: Moderate to strenuous.

Bettles is a dusty, sad-sack place on the banks of the Koyukuk River, just north of the Arctic Circle. Most people come to Bettles in order to leave Bettles; it's a major take-off point for adventure travelers headed into the Brooks Range. But, inevitably, more time is spent in Bettles than ought to be spent there as small planes come and go, carrying backpackers, canoeists, fishermen, and others into and out of the wilderness. Not a moment too soon, your call to fly comes; canoes are strapped to the pontoon struts of a float plane, a week's worth of gear and food is loaded on board, and you're winging it 100 miles north, to where the Hunt Fork meets the main flow of the John River.

The contrast between this sharply etched mountain basin and drab Bettles is striking, and it's just a start. For the next 6 days, you follow the serpentine course of the John as it carves a path southward through the Brooks Range. This is wild country; in 100-plus river miles, you pass one dirt airstrip, the only sign of human intervention, and you've got to look hard to see it. In 6 days on the river, you're highly unlikely to see another human being. You're very likely to see grizzly bears, moose, and caribou—certain to see their fresh tracks on any beach where you choose to set up camp for the night.

The John is a river that takes its time. A few rapids may approach Class II status early in the summer, but later in the summer extra paddling may be required to assure forward progress through languid stretches of water. The thrill here is not in any white-water challenge but rather in the profoundly wild wilderness and the chaotic geologic beauty of the surrounding mountains. Examine stones along the shore; most are works of natural art or sculpture, and each, in its shape and striations, has a tale of geological history to tell.

There's nothing fancy about this trip. The food is simple (mostly backpacker-style entrees like macaroni and cheese), the tent accommodations are simple, the means of transport are simple. Time sneaks by, passing quietly and more quickly than you might imagine. Nearing the end of the trip, the river exits the mountains and passes by bluffs embedded with mastodon remains, where peregrine falcons soar and chatter. Within a few miles, the John comes to an end at its confluence with the Koyukuk River, a few miles downriver from Bettles—sad, dusty Bettles.

Kongakut River Rafting and Hiking. Alaska Discovery, 5449 Shaune Dr., Suite 4, Juneau, AK 99801. ☎ **800/586-1911** or 907/780-6226. Fax 907/780-4220. Approximate cost: $3,000. Dates: June–July. Trip length: 10 days. Group size: 9. Begins and ends in: Fairbanks. Relative difficulty: Moderate.

Well-seasoned Alaskan outdoorspeople have a tendency to be picky about their wilderness. Venture into a remote area and see another person, or evidence of another campsite, or even so much as another footprint, and their feeling is that true wilderness has been irreparably compromised. Indeed, many areas once all but unvisited—particularly in the Brooks Range—are beginning to see a steady, if trickling, flow of human traffic. If you really want to escape all traces of humanity, Alaska outdoor veterans say you must go deep into the heart of the Arctic National Wildlife Refuge. It is a wilderness so profound that, as one ranger describes it, "you become very aware of the sounds of birds flying, of animals moving."

Flowing north through the refuge, the Kongakut is, for the most part, a gentle river. Don't expect white-water thrills; even at their most ferocious in early summer, what pass for rapids on the Kongakut top out at Class III, relatively mellow by white-water standards. Far more compelling on this trip is simply being on the North Slope of the Brooks Range close to the summer solstice. The sun never sets, and wildlife take full advantage of it. This is the time of year when the Porcupine caribou herd, traveling in packs of up to 20,000, embark on their annual migration. Grizzly bears, Dall sheep, and foxes are also active, taking advantage of an abruptly short summer in preparing for a long winter.

Time on this trip is divided between hiking and "paddle" rafting, in which everyone chips in to propel and steer the raft forward. It is probably a good idea to be in reasonably good hiking shape, even though daily hiking groups are usually split between those out for a relatively relaxed stroll and those set on more ambitious exploration. The more fit you are for hiking, the more you will see and experience of this truly wild wilderness.

This trip involves camping, of course, but it is camping of the highest order. Campsites on flat, sand beaches with breathtaking views are an easy find along the river. Meals, because of the weight rafts can carry, may include fresh fish, meats, and vegetables. If you are a fisherman, you may find yourself in a position to make a contribution to the evening's meal; the grayling and Arctic char fishing are excellent. In an area wild enough to impress the most jaded wilderness veterans, it is safe to say that the Kongakut and its tributaries are a long way from being fished out.

3 Planning an Independent Wilderness Adventure

There's a funny thing about Alaska: The more remote the country and the more rugged the adventure, the more likely you are to encounter European travelers—English, French, German, Italians. You encounter and hear often about Europeans roaming around in faraway places: two Frenchmen bicycling the Yukon River in winter; two Italians heading off for 3 weeks on a river in the Brooks Range; an English couple cycling along the Dalton Highway from Fairbanks to Prudhoe Bay.

This doesn't necessarily mean that Europeans on the whole have greater wilderness savvy than Americans, but it probably does imply a greater willingness to rough it on personal terms, to take on the wilderness unguided. Put another way, though skill and experience are both essential to carrying off an independent wilderness trip in Alaska, proper preparation and adaptive ingenuity are probably just as important. If you aren't ready, willing, and resourceful in adapting to unpredictable wilderness conditions, you may, literally or figuratively, be up the creek without a paddle.

Probably the best way of going about an independent adventure is to enlist the services of any of a number of Alaska-based outfitters. These are outfitters in the traditional sense of the word—they provide support and gear for people heading off into remote regions. They can suggest itineraries, provide equipment, arrange flights to and from wilderness drop-off points, and assist in formulating a gear and food list. Among the companies that provide such outfitting services are **St. Elias Alpine Guides** and **Sourdough Outfitters** (see "Recommended Outfitters," above) and air-taxi services such as **Alaska Air Taxi** (☎ 907/243-3944), **K-2 Aviation** (☎ 907/733-2291), and **Rust's Flying Service** (☎ 800/544-2299 or 907/243-1595).

The services of an outfitter do not necessarily come cheaply. If you're looking for an inexpensive way to experience the Alaskan wilds on your own, backpacking in Southcentral Alaska or paddling in Southeast are probably the best ways to go. For equipment rentals, particularly backpacking and camping gear, good places to go are: **Gary King Sporting Goods,** 202 E. Northern Lights Blvd. (☎ 907/279-7454), or **REI,** 1200 W. Northern Lights Blvd. (☎ 907/272-4565), both in Anchorage; **Beaver Sports,** 2400 College Rd., Fairbanks (☎ 907/479-2494); and **Adventure Sports,** 2092 Jordan Ave., Juneau (☎ 907/789-5696). For sea-kayak rentals in Southeast, try **Outdoor Alaska,** P.O. Box 7814, Ketchikan, AK 99901 (☎ 907/225-6044). Kayak rentals must usually be reserved a month or more in advance.

Maps are available in many local sports stores, but if you know where you want to go and want to study maps before heading for Alaska, contact the **U.S. Geological Survey** (see "Preparing for the Alaskan Wilderness," earlier in this chapter). District or superintendent's offices for national parks, national forests, state parks, state forests, or wildlife refuges may also be able to provide maps and information.

A great way to go for independent travelers is to overnight in **public-use cabins,** most highly concentrated in Tongass National Forest in Southeast and in the Chugach Mountains in Southcentral Alaska. Some are road-accessible, but most are along hiking trails or remote waterways. These cabins are typically small and spare, with bunk platforms for sleeping and usually a stove and utensils for cooking. Most, however, are well maintained, and many, especially in Southeast, require reservations well in advance. Cabin-permit fees generally range between $15 and $25 per night.

You can get information on public-use cabins from the **Alaska Public Lands Information Center** (in Anchorage, ☎ 907/271-2737; see chapters 7 and 10 for Ketchikan, Fairbanks, and Tok listings) or by contacting **Alaska State Parks,** the **Bureau of Land Management, Chugach National Forest,** or **Tongass National Forest** (see "Preparing for the Alaskan Wilderness," above); a good number are also described in the regional chapters filling out the rest of this book, under the "Getting Outside" sections within a given town section.

4 Wilderness Lodges

The wilderness lodge, like other aspects of adventure travel, is an evolving concept. Not long ago, most lodges in remote locations were dedicated either to fishing or to hunting, or to both. But this is the age of eco-travel, which means lodge owners have had to adapt to a whole new breed of guest. Families, elderly people, honeymooning newlyweds—the world where virile hunters and fishermen once prowled alone is now being infiltrated by a much different sort of sportsperson.

To be sure, many hunting and fishing lodges are still in healthy operation, and at almost all lodges, fishing remains a focal activity. At the wilderness lodge of the 1990s, however, hiking, canoeing, rafting, horseback riding, and wildlife viewing fill up the day. Many lodge proprietors are still fine-tuning their activities programs in

accordance with the requests from clients; often you'll find that an activity not normally offered (a long hike, an overnight camping trip) can be arranged if you ask for
it. It may simply be that the lodge operators, still getting the hang of adventure travel,
never expected there to be an interest in a particular activity until somebody inquired
about it.

In addition, the rude, bunk-style accommodations and hardtack-basic meals often associated with hunting or fishing lodges are giving way to accommodations that
are often quite elegant and to meals of legitimately gourmet caliber. Many lodges take
great pride in the lavishness with which they can surprise guests anticipating wilderness austerity. The wilderness may be wild, but it doesn't have to be uncomfortable.

There are, obviously, a good many wilderness lodges in Alaska. (As a matter of
definition, "wilderness lodge" in this case refers here to a lodge inaccessible by road—
accessible basically only by small plane.) Most are in Interior, Southcentral, and
Southeast Alaska. (There may be more in Southwest Alaska than anywhere else,
almost all of them catering to the spectacular fishing possibilities available off the
Alaska Peninsula and Aleutians—see chapter 11, "The Bush," for detailed information.) The following is a short sampling of recommended lodges, not only to give you
a feeling for the broad range in price, accommodations, and activities, but also to
provide some idea of where they fit within the full context of wilderness/adventure
travel in Alaska. For other recommended lodges, see the "Accommodations" sections
in regional chapters in this book.

Caribou Lodge. P.O. Box 706, Talkeetna, AK 99676. ☎ **907/733-2163.** 3 cabins accommodate 6. 5-day package $700 (a sample). Open year round.

Location is everything. A lodge doesn't have to be palatial or offer a dazzling smorgasbord of activities in order to be appealing. So it is with Caribou Lodge, high on
the tundral meadows of the Talkeetna Mountains, 30 miles east of Talkeetna. This
is not a scruffy place, mind you; it just isn't anything more than it has to be. The
entire compound consists of a small main lodge, three tiny cabins, and a shared
shower and sauna. You'll get hearty meals, a clean, comfortable bed, and a roof overhead—you don't need much more when you can rise in the morning to see a setting
like this. Look to the west, and Mount McKinley rises like a ghostly presence. To the
east, at the doorstep of the lodge, lies a clear lake, mirroring the high ridges of the
Talkeetnas in the distance.

Hiking across the trail-less tundra and watching for wildlife are the activities that
consume the day. Wildflowers are most abundant earlier in the summer; August into
early September is berry season. If you want, you can broaden your horizons by combining your lodge stay with guided backpacking trips of up to 6 days. And don't rule
out a winter visit—if anything, the setting becomes more spectacular when winter
sets in. This is excellent terrain for cross-country skiing, dog mushing, snowshoeing,
or snowmobiling. What's more, the above-treeline location allows for excellent views
of the northern lights during dark winter nights.

Chelatna Lake Fishing and Rafting. 3941 Float Plane Dr., Anchorage, AK 99502. ☎ **800/
999-0785** or 907/243-7767. Cabins accommodate 16. Open June–Sept.

The people who run Chelatna Lake Lodge seem determined to demonstrate to their
guests that the wilderness need not be wild. Don't be misled by an old lodge that has
been left more or less intact, a log structure filled with antiquated sofas, a craps table,
and cases of beer. That's a sideshow relic for guests who can't relinquish the old-boy
notion that a fishing lodge must be a rough-hewn, unkempt place, where men drink
their whiskey straight-up and never shave. The rest of the Chelatna compound,

including a handsome new main lodge, is spic-and-span New Age, with plush accommodations in recently built cabins and legitimately gourmet meals at night. The old boys might gag, but Chelatna Lake Lodge, located 100 miles northwest of Anchorage, is a place a yuppie could love.

Fishing remains the lodge's raison d'être, as it was back when the old lodge was the only lodge. Each morning, guides and fishermen fly off in small planes to choice spots not far away. When the salmon are running, the fish are so ridiculously easy to catch that by lunchtime most fishermen are no longer, strictly speaking, fishermen; instead they're lolling around the beach cracking jokes and swilling beer. This is lazy man's fishing of the highest order: The guides disengage fresh catches from lures, gut and filet the fish, then prepare them on dry ice for shipping. As one recent guest commented, "You never have to touch your fish until you pull it out of your freezer back home."

But after your fill of lazy-man fishing, what's next? If you don't want to chill out at the lodge and behold the drop-dead view across the lake, rafting is a terrific alternative. The rafting program at Chelatna is still underdeveloped, primarily because most guests, men and women, come fixated on fishing. Short day trips on Lake Creek are the current offering, but Duke Bertke, the lodge proprietor, has contemplated overnight trips. If you are insistent and have enough allies among other guests to plead your case, you might talk him into arranging an excursion farther downstream. In its southward passage, the "creek"—more like a medium-sized river—gains more dramatic white-water force. It's a blast of wilderness reality that lodge guests, seeking respite from all that pampering, might appreciate.

⭐ **Riversong Lodge.** Riversong Adventures, 2463 Cottonwood St., Anchorage, AK 99508. ☎ **907/274-2710.** Fax 907/277-6256. 4-day/4-night package $1,415 (a sample). 10 guest cabins. Open year round.

Some 65 miles northwest of Anchorage, Riversong Lodge is a first-rate example of just how far the fishing-lodge concept has come from the roughing-it-in-the-wilderness days. To be sure, the reason people come here is to immerse themselves in the wilderness. But while the wilderness inspires them, it's usually the food at the lodge that ends up astonishing them—far superior to anything anyone would have a right to expect so far from civilization. Kirsten Dixon has been hailed by many restaurant critics as being the best chef anywhere in Alaska, let alone the best chef at a wilderness lodge. So good are the meals she cooks up that some guests fly in for the evening from Anchorage to do nothing but eat.

Of course, there's more to Riversong than good food. Like so many lodges, fishing (primarily for salmon) tops the activity list, but there's more than that, too. Somewhat unusual for a wilderness lodge, Riversong offers extended guided trips into the outback of Southwest Alaska. Perhaps the most intriguing of these is a 4-day trip (at $1,450 per person) into Lake Clark National Park, the great mystery among national parks in Alaska. Just across Cook Inlet from the popular Kenai Peninsula, the park is so rarely visited that even native Alaskans tend to scratch their heads in befuddlement when asked where it is.

So here's a sensible program: Take the trip into Lake Clark, where you can fish the remote Chilikidrotna River and hike in the surrounding mountains—a world you'll have almost entirely to yourself for 4 days. After that, return to the lodge, a log structure with outlying cabins sequestered in the woods, for a day or more. There are few things more satisfying than a good meal after several days in the wilderness—especially when it's a meal prepared by one of the most heralded chefs in Alaska.

✪ **Ultima Thule Lodge.** Ultima Thule Outfitters, P.O. Box 109, Chitina, AK 99566 or 1007 H St., Anchorage, AK 99501. ☎ **907/258-0636.** Fax 907/258-4642. 4 multiple-room guest cabins. 7-day package $2,800 (a sample). Open year round.

Rafting, hiking, fishing, camping, wildlife viewing, photography, horseback riding, mountaineering, backpacking, flightseeing, beachcombing, sea kayaking—that's an incomplete list of activities offered at Ultima Thule Lodge, located 100 miles west of Chitina. Why's it incomplete? Because if you come in winter, you can also go alpine skiing, ski touring, snowshoeing, ice skating, ice fishing, dog mushing, or "up-skiing." Up-skiing? Something to do with parachutes and defying the laws of physics. Don't ask—simply suffice it to say that the Ultima Thule crew has combed the planet in search of all conceivable forms of outdoor fun and games. And who knows? Bareback whale-riding or white-water water skiing may be next—the search no doubt continues. Just reading about what's possible at Ultima Thule is an exhausting exercise.

One reason that Ultima Thule can offer all that it offers is the location of the lodge, in the heart of Wrangell–St. Elias National Park. Even by big Alaskan standards, this is big country. The mountains are immense; Mount Logan, just west over the border in Canada, is said to be the world's largest mountain, in total bulk if not in height. The glaciers are long and deep, and the rivers run swift and murky with glacial silt—water that mountain people call glacial milk. Give a person a small plane and a big idea, and almost anything, as Ultima Thule seems set on proving, is possible.

If you dislike small-plane flying, Ultima Thule is not the place for you. Most activities, weather permitting, involve shuttling in and out of the surrounding mountains, landing on glaciers or gravel bars or on the beaches of the Gulf of Alaska. Unless you're planning an extended stay in the Wrangell–St. Elias backcountry—something, as you might expect, that Ultima Thule can set up for you if you want—you'll return by plane to the lodge each evening. This is a plush place as wilderness lodges go, the sleeping accommodations featuring down comforters and skylights for keeping watch on the northern lights. There's a sauna, too—probably the most welcome, muscle-relaxing feature of the lodge after 10 hours or more a day of romping around in the wilderness.

5 Further Reading

There is no shortage of books, from guides to personal narratives, on the Alaskan wilderness. An excellent source for books and maps is the **Alaska Natural History Association,** 605 W. Fourth Ave., Suite 85, Anchorage, AK 99501 (☎ **907/278-8440;** fax 907/274-8343). Books that may be helpful include *Alaska Parklands,* by Nancy Lange Simmerman (Seattle: The Mountaineers); its one- to two-page descriptions of state and national parklands in Alaska are adequate, but appendix material and nuggets of useful information on topography, climatology, edible flora, and so on make the book well worthwhile. *The Alaska River Guide,* by Karen Jettmar (Portland, Ore.: Alaska Northwest Books), is a guide for canoeing, kayaking, and rafting enthusiasts to the state's principal rivers and creeks. *The Alaska Wilderness Guide,* compiled by the editors of *The Milepost* (Bellevue, Wash.: Vernon Publications), includes brief descriptions of trails, rivers, lakes, and remote communities throughout the state. There's also an excellent directory of outfitters and wilderness lodges. *Fast and Cold: A Guide to Alaska Whitewater,* by Andrew Embick (Helena, Mont.: Falcon Press), is a large-format paperback as attractive to look at as it is informative. *Mountain Bike Alaska,* by Richard Larson (Anchorage: A T Publishing), is a good start on filling out the sparse information on mountain-biking possibilities in Alaska.

Southeast Alaska

Rich, proud people have lived in Southeast Alaska for thousands of years, fishing its salmon and hunting all through its primeval forests, where the tree trunks are up to 10 feet thick. In canoes, they explored the hundreds of misty, mossy, enchanted islands where the animals, trees, and even the ice had living spirits. (Even for a modern non-Native, it's easy to forget you don't believe in such spirits in the grand quiet of the old-growth rain forests.) And, incredibly, after all those thousands of years of exploration among the teeming, extravagant life of Southeast Alaska, the region still is being discovered—literally.

In 1987, an amateur caver looking at a map speculated that the limestone of Prince of Wales Island would be a likely place to find caves. On his vacation, he went out to look and discovered what was then the deepest vertical cave in the United States, in a place where no modern explorer had bothered to look before. In the annual explorations that have followed since, expeditions have mapped miles and miles of caverns, finding the bones of extinct animals and prehistoric people; bear dens; strange, eyeless shrimp that live nowhere else; and even underground streams that host spawning salmon. The honeycomb of caves seemed to network off in every direction from hundreds of portals. Then someone realized that the geology of many of Southeast's islands contains this same limestone and the same rainforest chemistry that helps carve the rock into caves. They're still finding dozens of new caves each year.

You're probably not planning a spelunking vacation—my point is that the mysteries of Southeast Alaska run deep below the surface. Like the fractal geometry of the endlessly folded, rocky shoreline, discoveries seem to multiply the closer you look and the more you know. On a ship, passing by a stretch of shore, you could marvel at all the little beaches you pass—but you'd surely stop watching after seeing hundreds of inviting spots pass in a day as your ship plowed on, day and night, to navigate the Inside Passage. But if you were to stop at random on any one of those particular, uninhabited beaches in a skiff or kayak, you'd find you could spend a day surveying just a few acres of rocks, the overhanging forest, and the tiny pools of water left behind by the tide. And if you gazed down into any one of those pools, you'd find a complex world all its own, with tiny predators and prey living out their own drama of life in the space of a few square feet.

So prepare to explore. Southeast Alaska is full, and what you find may be not only yours to remember, it may be yours alone.

Within Alaska, Southeast stands apart, and not only because most of it can't be reached by road. No other part of the state shares the mysterious, spirit-ridden quality of the coastal rain forest. No other area gets so much rain. (Precious few places anywhere on earth do, for that matter.) If Alaska sometimes feels like a different country from the rest of the United States, Southeast certainly feels like a different state from the rest of Alaska. Unlike the oil-based economy of most of the state, Southeast's many prosperous towns live on fishing, timber, tourism, and government. The weather, while wet, is mild—the climate is more akin to the Pacific Northwest than to the heart of Alaska. The Natives' heritage is richer—the Tlingit, Haida, and Tsimshian exploited the wealth nature gave them and amplified it by being successful traders with tribes to the south and over the mountains in today's British Columbia and Yukon Territory. In their early contact, the Tlingits even briefly defeated the Russian invaders in the Battle of Sitka, and after white dominance was established, saved many of their cultural artifacts and stories.

Along with its other riches and complexity, Southeast Alaska also has many small towns and villages—too many to include in this chapter or in a whole hefty book for that matter. They await your discovery.

1 Exploring Southeast Alaska

A unique and inviting aspect of traveling in Southeast Alaska is that no roads connect most of the communities. People are forced to get out of their speeding cars and get on boats, where they can meet their fellow travelers and see what's passing by—slowly. The islands of the region form a protected waterway called the Inside Passage, along which almost all of the region's towns are arrayed. Thanks to the **Alaska Marine Highway** ferry system, it's easy and inexpensive to travel the entire passage, hopping from town to town and spending as much time in each place as you like. And if you're short on time, air service is frequent, with jets to the major towns and commuter planes to the villages.

Why are there no roads? A tectonic plate that underlies the Pacific Ocean brought the islands of the Southeast Alaska Panhandle from far afield and squished them up against the plate that carries the land mass of Canada. Along the line of this glancing collision, large glacial mountains thrust up, and the islands themselves were stretched and torn into the fractured geography that makes the area so interesting. In short, it's just too difficult to build roads through those icy mountains and across the steep, jumbled terrain of the islands.

GETTING AROUND

BY FERRY The state-run **Alaska Marine Highway System,** P.O. Box 25535, Juneau, AK 99802-5535 (☎ **800/642-0066;** fax 907/277-4829; website http://www.dot.state.ak.us/external/amhs/home.html), founded in 1963, is a subsidized fleet of blue-hulled, ocean-going ferries whose mission is to connect the roadless coastal towns of Alaska for roughly the same kind of cost you'd pay if there were roads and you were driving. (Call for a free schedule.) There are also small state ferries in Southcentral and Southwest Alaska that don't connect to the ferry system in Southeast. The ferry system's strengths are its low cost, a convenient schedule, exceptional safety, and that it's about the most fun form of travel I can imagine—great for kids. In the summer, Forest Service guides offer interpretive talks on board. Its weaknesses are crowding during the July peak season, sometimes many-hour delays, generally

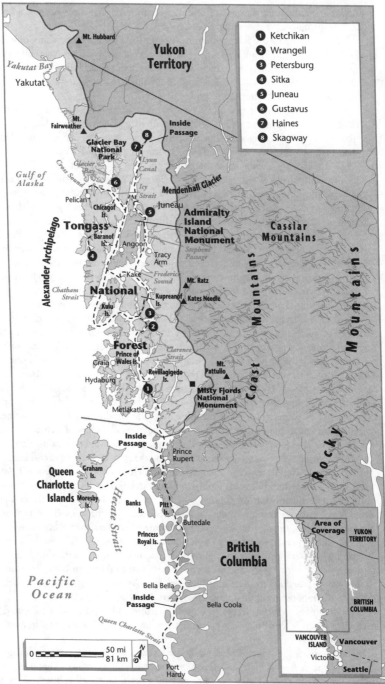

Southeast Alaska

1. Ketchikan
2. Wrangell
3. Petersburg
4. Sitka
5. Juneau
6. Gustavus
7. Haines
8. Skagway

Mt. Hubbard

Yukon Territory

Yakutat Bay
Yakutat

Mt. Fairweather

Glacier Bay National Park

Inside Passage

Glacier *Bay*

Cross Sound

Gulf of Alaska

Pelican

Chichagof Is.

Icy Strait

Lynn Canal

Mendenhall Glacier

Juneau

Tongass

Baranof Is.

Angoon

Admiralty Island National Monument

Cassiar Mountains

Chatham Strait

Tracy Arm

Stephens Passage

National

Kake

Frederick Sound

Mt. Ratz

Kates Needle

Kupreanof Is.

Kuiu Is.

Alexander Archipelago

Forest

Prince of Wales Is.

Craig

Hydaburg

Revillagigedo Is.

Clarence Strait

Mt. Pattullo

Misty Fjords National Monument

Coast Mountains

Rocky Mountains

Metlakatla

Inside Passage

Prince Rupert

Queen Charlotte Islands

Graham Is.

Moresby Is.

Hecate Strait

Banks Is.

Pitt Is.

Butedale

Princess Royal Is.

British Columbia

Pacific Ocean

Bella Bella

Inside Passage

Bella Coola

Queen Charlotte Strait

Port Hardy

0   50 mi
0   81 km

Area of Coverage

YUKON TERRITORY

BRITISH COLUMBIA

VANCOUVER ISLAND   Vancouver

Victoria

Seattle

137

lackluster food, and a shortage of cabins, which means that most people camp on deck or in chairs during overnight passages.

The main line of the ferry system runs from Prince Rupert, British Columbia, north to Haines and Skagway, a voyage of about 35 hours if you never get off to visit any of the towns in between (which would be an act of sheer lunacy, in my view). The foot-passenger, or walk-on, fare is $124 for adults, half that for children 11 and under, and free for children 2 and under.

The **B.C. Ferries** system, 1112 Fort St., Victoria, B.C., Canada V8V 4V2 (☎ 250/386-3431; fax 250/381-5452; website http://www.bcferries.bc.ca), docks right next to the Alaska ferry in Prince Rupert, so you can easily connect to wonderful places such as Vancouver Island and B.C.'s portion of the Inside Passage.

The Alaska ferry *Columbia,* the largest in the fleet at 418 feet, goes all the way south to Bellingham, Washington, taking 37 hours in a nonstop run to Ketchikan, then continuing up to Haines. The walk-on fare is $164 to Ketchikan, $240 to Haines. The Bellingham trips, running only once a week, get booked early, so even foot passengers should make reservations during the summer. Three other large ferries also work the main line, giving service roughly six times a week to Prince Rupert and points north. All four big ships stop in Ketchikan, Wrangell, Petersburg, Haines, and Skagway, providing seven departures each week in those towns. All ferries, large and small, stop in Juneau. Sitka, which lies to the west of the Inside Passage, is bypassed by some ferries, receiving port calls from a main-line ferry twice a week and from a smaller, connecting ferry, the *LeConte,* three times a week.

The two smaller ferries, the *LeConte* and *Aurora,* connect the larger towns to small towns and villages up and down the coast. These are commuter ferries, and if you have the time, taking one to the tiny towns they serve is a lot of fun. You can jump off and explore for an hour or so during port calls, or plan a longer visit to one of the quiet Bush communities, catching the next ferry or a scheduled Bush plane. The smaller boats mostly take local residents back and forth to their villages, so they're rarely crowded, and they are the definition of "off the beaten track." They have restaurants but no cabins. The risk of planning to visit towns during port calls, whether on the main line or the smaller ferries, is that if the ship falls behind its schedule, you might not be able to get off as the crew does a quick turnaround to pick up time.

While touring the region, combining flying and the ferry can save time and reduce the chances you could spend the night sleeping in a chair on board. There are, however, some runs I wouldn't miss. Going to Sitka through Peril Straits, the ferry fits through extraordinarily narrow passages where no other vessel of its size ventures; the smooth, reflective water is lovely, and you may see deer along the shore. This is where the ferries can lose time—they can go through only when the current isn't running, so if they miss the tide, they have to wait 6 hours. The Wrangell Narrows, between Petersburg and Wrangell, are also an incredible ride, day or night, as the ship accomplishes a slalom between shores that seem so close you could touch them, in water so shallow the schedules must be timed for high tide. Approaching Skagway through the towering mountains of the Lynn Canal fjord also is especially impressive.

Consider this as well: The ferries are crowded northbound in June and southbound in August. If you're flying one way, go against the flow, and you'll have the ship more to yourself.

If you're bringing a vehicle or definitely need a cabin on the ferry system during the June-through-August high season, you *must* reserve well in advance. That doesn't mean that you can't get a car on board or pick up a cabin on standby, but you'd be counting on a lot of luck. Cabins on the Bellingham run book up more than six months in advance. Obviously, fares for taking vehicles vary according to the size of the car and how far you're going; a passage from Prince Rupert to Haines for a typical 15-foot car is $273, or $568 from Bellingham. You also have to buy a ticket for each person.

An overnight, two-berth outside cabin is roughly $40 on most sailings, or $113 from Prince Rupert to Haines, $263 from Bellingham to Haines, plus the cost of your ticket—the best deal on a room with a view you're likely to find in Alaska. The cabins are small and spartan and come in two- and four-bunk configurations; staterooms come with sitting rooms attached. Most have tiny private bathrooms with showers. Try to get an outside cabin so you can watch the world go by; inside cabins can be stuffy. The staterooms don't cost that much more and provide your own private observation lounge.

Do you need a cabin? If you do a lot of layovers to see Southeast's towns, you can time most of your passages during the day, but you're likely to have to sleep on board at least once. One of the adventures of ferry travel is finding a chair to sleep in or setting up a tent on deck with everyone else. The solarium, on the top deck, is the best sleeping spot on board and the recliner lounges second best; if the ship looks crowded, grab your spot fast, but don't worry: There'll always be somewhere to lay your head. Showers are available, although there may be lines. If you're tenting, the best place is behind the solarium, where it's not too windy. On the *Columbia,* that space is small, so grab it early. And bring duct tape to secure your tent to the deck in case you don't have a sheltered spot—using exposed deck space can be like camping in an endless gale. If all that sounds too rugged, or if you have small children and no tent, reserve a cabin.

If you can, bring your own food on the ferry. Ferry food isn't positively bad, but it's quite inconsistent from one ship to the next, it's often greasy, and you can get awfully tired of it after several meals in a row. Also, during peak season, the food lines are sometimes unreasonably long. If you make a stopover or have a long port call, pick up some bagels and deli sandwiches and have a picnic.

BY AIR   Air travel is the primary link between Southeast's towns and the rest of the world. The major towns all have jet service, provided by **Alaska Airlines** (☎ 800/426-0333; website http://www.alaskaair.com), currently the region's only major airline. Juneau is Southeast Alaska's travel hub. Ketchikan and Sitka have a few flights a day while Wrangell, Petersburg, and Yakutat each have a flight going each direction daily. Some of these "milk runs" never seem to get very far off the ground on hops between small towns. On some flights, the cabin attendants never have time to unbuckle and toss bags of peanuts before the plane lands again. Haines and Skagway, which have highway connections, don't receive visits from jets, but all the towns and even the tiniest villages have scheduled prop service.

If you can possibly afford it, you'll want to take a **flightseeing trip** at some point during your trip. The poor man's way of doing this is to fly a small prop plane on a scheduled run between two of your destinations instead of taking the ferry. The plane probably won't go out of its way to show you the sights (though it can't hurt to ask), but you'll see enough to gain an appreciation for the vast richness and extreme topography of the region. The largest providers are **L.A.B. Flying Service** (☎ 800/426-0543), in the northern Panhandle; **Wings of Alaska** (☎ 907/789-0790; e-mail wings@ptialaska.net), all over Southeast; and **Taquan Air** (☎ 800/770-8800; website http://www.AlaskaOne.com/TaquanAir), in the southern Panhandle.

Like the ferries, the planes can be quite late. Each of the airports in Southeast has its own challenges caused by the steep, mountainous terrain and the water. In bad weather, even jet flights are delayed or they "overhead"—they can't land at all at the intended destination and leave their passengers somewhere else. Your only protection against these contingencies are travel insurance, a schedule that allows plenty of slack in case you're significantly delayed, and low blood pressure.

BY ROAD   Three Southeast Alaska communities are accessible by road: Haines, Skagway, and the village of Hyder, which lies on the British Columbia border east of Ketchikan and is accessible from the gravel Cassiar Highway through Canada. Haines and Skagway are each a significant detour from the Alaska Highway, but if you want to visit both on your way up, you can save more than 350 miles of driving by taking your car on the ferry the 15 water miles between the two towns. This ferry route is not as heavily booked as the routes heading between either town and Juneau, but it's a good idea to reserve ahead anyway. It's possible to take a bus or rent a car from Haines or Skagway for travel to the rest of the state at the end of a ferry journey (Haines will save you only 60 miles over Skagway); details are listed in the sections on each of those towns. If you're driving the highway in winter, you should be prepared for weather as cold as 40°F below zero. Alaska winter driving information is under "Safety" in chapter 3.

2 Outside in Southeast

One of the best ways to get into Southeast's wilderness is by staying at a remote **Forest Service Cabin.** Details about the cabins are in the text with the towns they're nearest, but here's how to reserve them for the entire Tongass National Forest, which covers the whole region. A new reservation system will use a national service called **Biospherics** (☎ **800/280-2267,** TDD/TTY 800/879-4496; fax 301/722-9802). You can reserve any cabin and some campgrounds (all campgrounds also have first-come, first-served sites) up to 180 days in advance, paying a reservation fee of $8.25 on top of the cabin fee. Cancellation fees apply. They take Visa, MasterCard, or Discover cards. You also can pay by check by mail to **USFS Reservation Center,** P.O. Box 900, Cumberland, MD 21502-0900. Cabin availability is online at website **http://www.nrrc.com**. Any Forest Service office can check for you, then hand you the phone to call Biospherics. The reservation line is open only during the day and closes at 3pm on weekends. At this writing, the system was subject to change, but you can get the latest information on cabins and access from the Forest Service offices listed in each town.

DIVING   You'll find dive shops in several towns, but Sitka and Prince of Wales Island are said to have the clearest and most biologically productive waters.

FISHING   Almost anywhere you happen to be, you can find great fishing in Southeast Alaska. The lake cabins and lodges around Ketchikan provide some of the best opportunities for remote, all-alone fly fishing. Sea charters are great all over, but you can combine them with whale watching in Gustavus, Sitka, Petersburg, and Juneau. Gustavus is known for huge halibut relatively near town. For details on runs, seasons, regulations, and licenses, contact the **Alaska Department of Fish and Game,** Division of Sport Fish, 1255 W. Eighth St. (P.O. Box 25526), Juneau, AK 99802-5526 (☎ **907/465-4180;** website http://www.state.ak.us/local/akpages/FISH.GAME/adfghome.htm).

HIKING   The **Chilkoot Trail,** near Skagway, is a 33-mile-long museum, and a challenging 3-day hike. Petersburg is a good starting point for more remote hiking, but there are trails from most towns.

SEA KAYAKING   Ketchikan, Sitka, Petersburg, Juneau, Haines, and Glacier Bay all have kayaking guides and great places to kayak. **Alaska Discovery,** listed in the Juneau section, offers extended kayak trips in various wilderness areas.

WHALE WATCHING Humpback whale feeding patterns determine where and when you can see them, and the best feeding grounds can change from year to year. In recent years, the most reliable whale watching has been near Gustavus and Petersburg, with Juneau and Sitka also good possibilities.

WINTER SPORTS Few visitors come to Southeast in the winter, as they would miss out on the boating and other watery activities. But for those who do come, it's not terribly cold, crowds are gone, and skating and Nordic skiing are available in a lot of places. Eaglecrest, in Juneau, is the region's only significant alpine skiing area.

3 Ketchikan: On the Waterfront

Had they known about it, the film noir directors of the 1950s would have chosen the Ketchikan (KETCH-e-kan) waterfront for Humphrey Bogart to sleuth. One can picture the black-and-white montage: A pelting rain drains from the brim of his hat, suspicious figures dart through saloon doors and into the lobbies of concrete-faced hotels, a forest of workboat masts fades into the midsummer twilight along a shore where the sea and land seem to merge in miles of floating docks. Along Creek Street, salmon on their way to spawn swim under houses chaotically perched on pilings beside a narrow boardwalk; inside, men are spawning, too, in the arms of legal prostitutes. Meanwhile, the faces of totem poles gaze down on the scene disapprovingly, mute holders of their own ancient secrets.

Today, the director hoping to re-create that scene would have his work cut out for him removing the T-shirt shops and bright streetfront signs that seek to draw throngs of cruise passengers in to buy plastic gew-gaws. Ketchikan was a rugged and exotic intersection of cultures built on the profits of logging Southeast's rain forest, but in just a few years, it has transformed into a tourist center, softening its rough edges while selling their charm to visitors. And the changes can only accelerate. More and bigger ships are coming, and Southeast Alaska's last major timber mill—the Louisiana Pacific–owned pulp plant in Ward's Cove, north of town—closed early in 1997 due, in part, to environmental concerns.

On summer days, the white cruise ships tower above the town like huge new buildings on the dock facing Front Street, the downtown's main drag. Each morning their gangways disgorge thousands of visitors, clogging the streets and, for a few hours, transforming the town into a teeming carnival. With only a few hours to spend, the passengers explore the closest of the twisting streets, see the museum at the Southeast Alaska Visitor Information Center, or take a tour to one of the totem pole parks. Then evening comes, the streets empty, and the cruise ships slide off quietly on the way to their next port.

That is when a sense of the old, misty, mysterious Ketchikan starts to return. Visitors with a little more time to spend, and the willingness to explore beyond the core tourist areas, can drink fully of the history and atmosphere of the place, staying in a quaint old hotel, hiking a boardwalk path through the primeval rain forest, and making unique discoveries.

There certainly is plenty to see. Ketchikan is a center of Tlingit and Haida culture, and there are two replica clan houses and totem pole parks, as well as the only museum dedicated to preserving the old, original poles from the days when the Tlingit and Haida peoples' cultural traditions were more intact. Two other museums preserve and explain the broader culture and natural history of the area. There are several art galleries that feature serious local work.

Ketchikan also makes a great jumping-off point for getting into some spectacular outdoor experiences, including Misty Fjords National Monument (see section 4, later in this chapter). As the state's fourth-largest city, Ketchikan is the transportation hub for the southern portion of Southeast Alaska. (The nickname "Gateway City" refers to its geographical location and transportation function.) Seaplanes based on docks along the waterfront are the taxis of the region, and a big interagency visitor center can get you started. Ketchikan also is one of the wettest spots on earth, with rain measured in the hundreds of inches, so any activity, outdoors or in the streets of the town, requires serious rain gear.

ESSENTIALS

GETTING THERE   By Air   Alaska Airlines (☎ **800/426-0333** or 907/225-2145; website http://www.alaskaair.com) provides Ketchikan with nonstop jet service from Seattle and with flights to the north, including Petersburg, Wrangell, Sitka, Juneau, and Anchorage. Commuter lines run float and wheeled planes from Ketchikan to the neighboring communities, as well as offering fishing packages and flightseeing. **Taquan Air** (☎ **907/770-8800** or 907/225-8800; website http://www.AlaskaOne.com/TaquanAir) has a desk at the airport as well as at 1007 Water St., on the waterfront. The airport is on a different island from the town and can be reached only by a ferry that runs each way every half hour. It leaves the airport on the hour and half hour, and leaves the Ketchikan side on quarter hours. Believe the airline when it tells you when to catch the ferry for your plane. The fare is $2.50 for adults, $1.50 ages 6 to 11, and free under 6. Returning the same day is free. The fare for cars is $5. You'll need a vehicle to get to town from the airport ferry. (See "Getting Around," below.)

By Ferry   The dock is 2¹/₂ miles north out of town. **Alaska Marine Highway** ferries (see listing under "Getting Around" at the beginning of this chapter) run 6 hours north to Wrangell and 6 hours south to Prince Rupert, B.C. The walk-on fare for Prince Rupert is $38; Wrangell is $24.

VISITOR INFORMATION   The ✪ **Southeast Alaska Visitor Information Center,** 50 Main St., Ketchikan, AK 99901 (☎ **907/228-6214**), finished in 1995 at a cost of $9.2 million, contains an extraordinary museum of the region's natural and cultural history and contemporary society. Curators have managed to tell the truth without offending either side in the community's hot debate over logging and the environment. There's also an auditorium showing a high-tech slide slow. Admission to both is $3. The center also is the best place to get guidance on your visit. The enormous concrete-and-log structure is located on the waterfront near the cruise-ship dock. An information kiosk and bookstore are located near the entrance. Downstairs is a trip-planning room, a luxurious library of outdoor material in various media, with a desk for questions. Like the interagency Alaska Public Lands Information Centers in Anchorage, Fairbanks, and Tok, the trip-planning room provides guidance for the outdoors for all areas of the state. The center is open daily 8:30am to 4:30pm May through September, Tuesday through Saturday in winter. You can reach the Forest Service **Ketchikan Ranger District** at 3031 North Tongass Ave., Ketchikan, AK 99901 (☎ **907/225-2148**).

The **Ketchikan Visitors Bureau,** 131 Front St., Ketchikan, AK 99901 (☎ **907/225-6166;** fax 907/225-4230), operates an information center on the cruise-ship dock, at Front and Mission streets; it's open 8am to 5pm daily during the summer, weekdays only in the winter, and when cruise ships are in town.

ORIENTATION   Ketchikan is on huge **Revillagigedo Island.** The downtown area with most of the attractions is quite compact and walkable, but the whole of Ketchikan is long, strung out between the Tongass Narrows and the mountains. A

Ketchikan

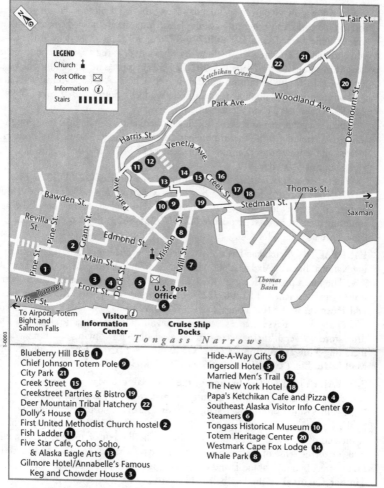

LEGEND
- Church ✝
- Post Office ✉
- Information ⓘ
- Stairs ▥▥▥▥▥▥

Blueberry Hill B&B ❶	Hide-A-Way Gifts ⑯
Chief Johnson Totem Pole ❾	Ingersoll Hotel ❺
City Park ㉑	Married Men's Trail ⑫
Creek Street ⑮	The New York Hotel ⑱
Creekstreet Partries & Bistro ⑲	Papa's Ketchikan Cafe and Pizza ❹
Deer Mountain Tribal Hatchery ㉒	Southeast Alaska Visitor Info Center ❼
Dolly's House ⑰	Steamers ❻
First United Methodist Church hostel ❷	Tongass Historical Museum ⑩
Fish Ladder ⑪	Totem Heritage Center ⑳
Five Star Cafe, Coho Soho,	Westmark Cape Fox Lodge ⑭
& Alaska Eagle Arts ⑬	Whale Park ❽
Gilmore Hotel/Annabelle's Famous	
Keg and Chowder House ❸	

waterfront road goes under various names through town, becoming North Tongass Highway as it stretches about 16 miles to the north. A tunnel divides the downtown and northwestern section of town. Saxman is 2¹⁄₂ miles to the south on the 14-mile South Tongass Highway. A good map, available at either visitor center, is a necessity, as the layout of the streets is quite confusing at first.

GETTING AROUND   A shuttle, taxi, or city bus can get you into town from the ferry terminal or the airport ferry. The **Airporter Shuttle** (☎ 907/225-5429) meets each flight and picks up at the major hotels by arrangement. The $10 fare downtown is about what you pay for a taxi but includes the airport ferry fare. The local taxis, mostly minivans, charge reasonable prices compared to some Alaska communities. Try **Yellow Taxi** (☎ 907/225-5555) or **Sourdough Cab** (☎ 907/225-5544). Taking a cab across on the airport ferry is prohibitively expensive. A **bus** operated by the Ketchikan Gateway Borough (☎ 907/225-6800) runs roughly every half hour from the airport ferry parking lot and state ferry terminal downtown from 5:30am to 9:30pm during the week and 6:40am to 7pm Saturday.

Once downtown, you can spend a day seeing the sights on foot, but to get to the totem pole parks and other interesting places, you'll need a rented car or a guided tour. **Practical Car Rental** (☎ 800/770-8778 or 907/225-8778) delivers the car to you and picks it up when you're done. Avis has a desk at the airport. Schoolteacher Lois Munch, of **Classic Tours** (☎ 907/225-3091), makes her tours fun: She wears a poodle skirt to drive visitors around in her '55 Chevy. A 2-hour tour is $43, and a 3-hour tour is $57. Longtime resident Ernie Waddell's **Sourdough Tours** (☎ 907/225-9772) also has a good reputation.

A bike is a good way to see Ketchikan, and there is a $2^1/2$-mile bike trail along the water to Saxman and the totem pole park there, described below. **The Pedalers,** located on the waterfront near the visitors center (☎ 907/723-1088), rents bikes for $8 an hour or $40 a day.

Waterfront boat cruises are available from **Alaska Cruises** (☎ 800/228-1905 or 907/225-6044) at $49 for a ride lasting 2 hours. I'd recommend taking a sea kayak and getting a closer look at the watery part of the city and the marine life of the surrounding area. **Southeast Exposure** (☎ 907/225-8829) offers a 3-hour tour, no experience necessary, for $50.

FAST FACTS   Ketchikan has a $5^1/2$% **sales tax.** Several banks have **ATMs,** including National Bank of Alaska, at 306 Main St., and Bank of America, at 2417 Tongass Ave. The **main post office** is at 3609 Tongass Ave. In **emergencies,** dial **911;** the **police** can be reached at ☎ 907/225-6631 for nonemergencies. **Ketchikan General Hospital** is at 3100 Tongass Ave. (☎ 907/225-5171). The *Ketchikan Daily News* publishes 6 days a week; some out of town papers are available at grocery and drug stores. Several **business centers** are available with copying and fax services, including **Tongass Business Center** (☎ 907/225-9015) at 607 Mission St. and **Mail Boxes Etc.** (☎ 907/247-2705) at 125 Main St.

SPECIAL EVENTS   **Celebration of the Sea,** May 1 to May 10, 1998, includes a variety of art, music, and community events; you can get a schedule from the Ketchikan Visitors Bureau. The **King Salmon Derby,** almost 50 years old and run by the Greater Ketchikan Chamber of Commerce (☎ 907/225-3184), takes place at the end of May and the beginning of June. The **Fourth of July** celebration will give you a true sense of the meaning of the holiday, with a long parade watched on Front Street by mobs of locals and cruise-ship passengers; after the parade, there's a **Timber Carnival** at the baseball field near City Park on Park Avenue and an all-afternoon loggers' competition, admission free. The **Blueberry Arts Festival,** held the second Sunday of August, has booths, music, and food, and is put on by the Ketchikan Area Arts and Humanities Council, 338 Main St. (☎ 907/225-2211). The council also organizes the **Winter Arts Faire** the first Saturday after Thanksgiving.

EXPLORING KETCHIKAN

TLINGIT, HAIDA & TSIMSHIAN CULTURAL HERITAGE   The Ketchikan area has two totem pole parks and a totem pole museum, as well as a wealth of contemporary Native art displayed all over town. Notable pieces stand at the whale park at Mission and Bawden streets and at the Westmark Cape Fox Lodge. Most of what you see in Southeast Alaska is Tlingit—the Haida and Tsimshian generally live to the south and east in British Columbia. But Ketchikan is near the boundary between the three peoples, and here their similar cultures mix.

The ✪ **Totem Heritage Center,** 601 Deermount St. (☎ 907/225-5900), near City Park, contains the largest collection of original 19th-century totem poles in existence. The poles are displayed indoors, mostly unpainted, many with the grass and moss still attached where it was when they were rescued from the elements in villages where they had been mounted up to 160 years ago. Totem poles were never meant to be maintained or repainted, instead disintegrating after about 70 years and being constantly replaced, but these were preserved to help keep the culture alive. A high ceiling and muted lighting lend to the spiritual grandeur of the art. Well-trained guides are on hand to explain what you're looking at, and there are good interpretive signs. The gift shop carries authentic Native crafts in the summer. Admission is $3 in summer, and the center is open daily from 8am to 5pm; it's free in winter and open Tuesday through Friday from 1 to 5pm.

The ✪ **Totem Bight State Historical Park** was a New Deal–era work project to save disappearing Tlingit cultural artifacts by replicating them in an authentic setting. The park, now run by the state of Alaska Division of Parks, stands out among the clan houses and outdoor totem pole collections in Southeast for having excellent interpretive signs and a printed guide that explains what you're looking at. It sits at a peaceful spot on the edge of Tongass Narrows, at the end of a short walk through the woods, 10 miles out of town on North Tongass Highway. The experience is aesthetic as well as educational, except for the logging clear-cut, ironically on Native-owned land, on the mountain right above the park. If you don't want to rent a car, a number of companies have guided tours, available through the Ketchikan Visitors Bureau. **City Tours** (☎ **800/652-8687** or 907/225-9465) offers a 2¹/₂-hour Totem Bight and rain-forest tour for $25, leaving at 10am daily.

The **Saxman Totem Pole Park** stands on a lawn above the Tlingit town of Saxman, 2¹/₂ miles south of Ketchikan on the South Tongass Highway. It has artifacts similar to those at Totem Bight park, but an added resource: Accomplished carvers are still at work here in the small building to the right of the park. The drawback of the site for independent travelers is that **Cape Fox Corp.,** the Native corporation that owns it, caters mainly to cruise-ship passengers, and no interpretive material is available other than its 2-hour tour, which includes art demonstrations, a slide show, and, during the week, dancing. The timing of the tour is different each day, depending on the ships. Admission is $30 for adults, $15 children 12 and under. Call the Saxman Village Store at ☎ **907/225-4421** for times and information.

OTHER ATTRACTIONS IN TOWN

Get the clearly presented *Ketchikan Walking Tour Map* free from the visitor center; its three routes cover everything of interest downtown. Here are the highlights:

✪ **Creek Street** was Ketchikan's red-light district until not that long ago. Now its quaint, meandering boardwalks are a tourist attraction thronged with visitors. Prostitution was semilegal in Alaska until 1952, recently enough to survive in local memories but distant enough from life today to have made Creek Street historic and to transform the women who worked there from outcasts to icons. Dolly Arthur, who started in business for herself on the creek in 1919 and died in 1975, touched both periods, and her home became a commercial museum not long after her death. **Dolly's House** is amusing, mildly racy, and a little sad. Admission is $3; it's open at least 9am to 4pm during the summer.

The street has some interesting shops and a couple of good restaurants, described below. Simply walking the creekside boardwalk, into the forest above, and over the "Married Men's Trail" is a lot of fun, especially for children. The **Cape Fox Hill–Creek Street Funicular,** a sort of diagonal elevator, runs 211 feet from the boardwalk up to the Westmark Cape Fox Lodge on top of the hill. Take it up and then enjoy the walk down through the woods. The summertime fare is $1, but if no one is around, just press the "up" button and go.

Following the creek upstream, take a look at the fish ladder at the Park Avenue bridge, then continue to the **Deer Mountain Tribal Hatchery,** 1158 Salmon Rd. (☎ **907/225-5158**), a charming little king and silver salmon hatchery where you can see the fry swimming in large tubs and even feed them and see a film. During the summer, a tour is offered for $3, 8am to 4:30pm daily. Beyond the hatchery is **City Park,** where Ketchikan Creek splits into a maze of ornamental pools and streams once used as a hatchery; my young son and I found it a magical place. The Totem Heritage Center, listed above, opens on the park.

On the downtown side of the creek, the one-room **Tongass Historical Museum,** 629 Dock St., presents the history and Native heritage of Ketchikan, along with an annually revolving exhibit. It's good for its size. Summer hours are 8am to 5pm daily, and admission is $2 (free Sunday afternoon); in winter it's open Wednesday through Sunday afternoons only. The same building houses the beautiful **Ketchikan Public Library,** with big windows that look out on the foaming rapids of Ketchikan Creek. The children's section downstairs has a play area with lots of toys; it's a great place for families to rejuvenate. It's open Monday through Wednesday from 10am to 8pm, Thursday through Saturday from 10am to 6pm, and on Sunday from 1 to 5pm.

SHOPPING   Ketchikan has become a shopping and art destination thanks to the explosion of visitors. If you want something authentically Alaskan, however, you have to be careful. For some important tips, see "Native Art—Finding the Real Thing," in chapter 3.

✪ **Soho Coho,** upstairs at 5 Creek St., is worth a visit even if you aren't a shopper. Owner Ray Troll is Alaska's leading fish-obsessed artist. His gallery shows work by Troll and other Ketchikan artists from the same school of surreal rain-forest humor. In Troll's art, subtle ironies and silly puns coexist in a solidly decorated interior world. His popular T-shirts allow people to clothe themselves in Troll's strange metaphors linking mankind and lower evolutionary forms. "Spawn Till You Die" is a classic. Troll displays his art on a website at http://www.trollart.com. The gallery, open in summer daily from 9am to 6pm, is upstairs from the Five Star Cafe, one of the best restaurants in town, and down the hall from **Parnassus Books,** a little cubbyhole with a broad and sophisticated selection of Alaskana, great for browsing. Also downstairs is **Alaska Eagle Arts,** a serious gallery featuring the bold yet traditional work of Native artist Marvin Oliver. Down the boardwalk at 18 Creek St., expert craftsmen create indigenous art and interact with visitors at **Hide-A-Way Gifts,** which carries carvings and Native crafts.

Down near the cruise-ship dock, check out **Scanlon Gallery,** at 318 Mission St., which carries Alaska contemporary art, Alaska Native art, and affordable prints and other items in various media. This is more of a traditional gallery than Soho Coho. **Finzel's Books and Gifts,** at 633 Mission St., carries local Native and contemporary art, books about Alaska, and ordinary paperbacks for your next ferry ride. **The Wood Shop,** at 632 Park, on the way to the hatchery and City Park, sells wonderful wooden toys, jewelry, and other underpriced crafts made and sold by participants in a program for the mentally ill. The **Ketchikan Arts and Humanities Council,** at 388 Main St., maintains a gallery of regional work. **KetchiCandies,** at 315 Mission St., caters to visitors and the many locals addicted to their homemade chocolates and other candies.

GETTING OUTSIDE

There's lots to do outdoors from Ketchikan, but most of it will require a boat or plane; the opportunities right on the road system are limited. See section 4 on Misty Fjords National Monument (later in this chapter) and the side trip to Prince of Wales

Island (below) for more. In any event, your first stop should be the trip-planning room at the Southeast Alaska Visitor Information Center (see address above), where a forest ranger can provide detailed information on trails, fishing, and dozens of available U.S. Forest Service cabins.

SPECIAL PLACES The U.S. Forest Service maintains more than 50 **cabins** around Ketchikan; all are remote and rustic, but at $25 a night, you can't beat the price or the settings. This is a chance to be utterly alone in the wilderness, and many of the lake cabins come with a boat for fishing and exploring. For details and descriptions of all the cabins, contact the Southeast Alaska Visitor Information Center (☎ 907/228-6214). Under a new reservation system (which could change), you can book up to 180 days in advance through the Biospherics national reservation service (listed in the "Outside in Southeast" section, above). You'll need sleeping bags, a camp stove and your own cooking outfit, a lantern, and so on. **Alaska Wilderness Outfitting,** 3859 Fairview St., Ketchikan, AK 99901 (☎ 907/225-7335), rents the gear, as well as small outboards for the skiffs, and will even take care of your grocery shopping. As the cabins are remote, it takes a plane, a boat, or a hike to get to all of them—most are accessible only by float plane. That's where the money comes in. A good rule of thumb is that a float plane charter will cost roughly $250 an hour, and you'll have to pay for the plane to get out there and back twice. **Taquan Air Service,** 1007 Water St., Ketchikan, AK 99901 (☎ 800/770-8800 or 907/225-8800; website http://www.AlaskaOne.com/TaquanAir), has round-trip charter rates for the closest cabins of $360 for a 2-passenger Cessna 185 or $600 for a 4-passenger DeHavilland Beaver. They sell a cabin planning package for $8.95 including the Forest Service maps and other information. **Promech, Air.,** 1515 Tongass Ave., Ketchikan, AK 99901 (☎ 800/860-3845 within Alaska only, or 907/225-3845), also operates these charters, among others.

Ward Lake Nature Trail. This trail circles 1.3 miles around a smooth lake among old-growth Sitka spruce large enough to put you in your place. Ward Creek has trout and salmon. To reach the trail, campground, and picnic area, travel about 8 miles out North Tongass Highway and turn right on Ward Lake Road just before the defunct pulp mill. For a slightly more challenging hike, **Perseverance Lake Trail** climbs up boardwalks with steps from the 3C's campground, 3 miles up Ward Lake Road, to another lake 2.3 miles away.

Deer Mountain Trail. This is a challenging overnight, starting only half a mile from Ketchikan, but you don't have to go all the way for dramatic views, 1 mile up the trail and at the summit, after a 2^1/2-mile, 3,000-foot climb. The trail continues to a Forest Service cabin, across another summit, through some summer snow and ice, and ends at another trailhead 10 miles away. The main trailhead is ^{1}/2 mile up Ketchikan Lakes Road. Pick up a trail guide sheet from the Forest Service at the Southeast Alaska Visitor Information Center.

BIRD WATCHING A birding guide and checklist distributed by the Forest Service and the Juneau Audubon Society lists 15 good places to go and what to look for. Pick up one at the Southeast Alaska Visitor Information Center.

✪ FISHING The **Alaska Department of Fish and Game** produces a 24-page fishing guide to Ketchikan, with details on where to find fish in both fresh and salt water, listing 17 spots accessible from the roads. You can pick up a copy at the Southeast Alaska Visitor Information Center or from the department: Contact the **ADF&G Division of Sport Fishing,** P.O. Box 25526, Juneau, AK 99802-5526 (☎ 907/465-4180; website http://www.state.ak.us/local/akpages/FISH.GAME/

adfghome.htm). For licenses and other help, the local **Fish and Game office** is at 2030 Sea Level Dr., Suite 205, Ketchikan, AK 99901 (☎ **907/225-2859**). There are plenty of charters available to get out on the water for salmon and halibut. The Ketchikan Visitors Bureau can provide you with a list. For even more remote fishing, you can fly out to meet a charter boat or fish a remote lake or stream all by yourself. See the flight services above under "Special Places." If you want to devote your time in Ketchikan to fishing, check out the fishing lodges listed below.

SEA KAYAKING   The islands, coves, and channels around Ketchikan seem infinite in complexity, creating protected waters rich with life and welcoming for exploration by kayak. Any reasonably fit adult can enjoy a kayak paddle, and your appreciation of the area's beauty will expand greatly. **Southeast Exposure,** 507 Stedman St. (P.O. Box 9143), Ketchikan, AK 99901 (☎ **907/225-8829;** fax 907/225-8849), rents kayaks and guides trips from 1 to 8 days long. A 6-hour day trip is $80 per person; an 8-day trip is $1,175 per person.

ACCOMMODATIONS
Ketchikan charges an 11.5% **bed tax.**

HOTELS
Expensive
Best Western Landing. 3434 Tongass Ave., Ketchikan, AK 99901. ☎ **907/225-5166.** Fax 907/225-6900. 45 rms, 15 suites, 15 two-bedroom apartments. TV TEL. High season, $98–$170 double, $130–$160 suites. Low season, $76–$160 double, $112–$130 suites. AE, CB, DC, DISC, MC, V.

A well-run and recently remodeled establishment with a wide variety of different types of rooms: simple hotel rooms; suites with sitting rooms, microwave ovens, refrigerators, and balconies; and full two-bedroom apartments with a TV in each room. The new wing has the best rooms. The location, right across from the ferry dock, is distant from the downtown sights, so you'll need to rent a car or use the courtesy van, which runs back and forth regularly.

The restaurant is popular with locals checking up on the day's gossip. It serves inexpensive meals in a dining room with a 1950s motif. Kids are well treated. Hours are 6am to 9pm off-season, until 10pm in summer. Drinks are available from Jeremiah's bar, upstairs, which serves more elaborate meals and has live music Wednesday through Saturday. Smoking and nonsmoking areas each have their own fireplace, and there's a deck overlooking the water across the highway.

Salmon Falls Resort. 16707 N. Tongass Hwy. (P.O. Box 5700), Ketchikan, AK 99901. ☎ **800/247-9059** (reservations) or 907/225-2752. Fax 907/225-2710. 52 rms. TEL. $139 double. Additional person in room $10 extra. AE, MC, V. Closed Sept 15–May 15.

This huge fishing lodge has its own waterfall where silvers spawn in August, as well as a dock on Clover Passage with boats for all the guests. Inclusive fishing packages start at $900 per person, double occupancy, for a 3-day stay with 2 days on the water, self-guided. With a guide, the price is $1,300 per person. The lodge is on the Tongass Highway 16¹/₂ miles north of town, so you save the cost of flying to a comparable lodge off the island. The rooms are comfortable and well decorated; the new building is best. But it's the restaurant and bar that are really amazing: a massive log octagon held up in the center by a section of the Alaska pipeline with great views from all tables, and a well-prepared menu of steak or seafood ranging from $18 to $29.

Nonfishermen will enjoy a drive out the road for dinner, even if they aren't staying here.

✪ **Westmark Cape Fox Lodge.** 800 Venetia Way, Ketchikan, AK 99901. ☎ **800/544-0970** (central reservations) or 907/225-8001. Fax 907/225-8286. Website http://www. westmarkhotels.com. 70 rms, 2 suites. TV TEL. $159 double, $199 suite. Weekend rate $99. AE, DC, DISC, MC, V.

This is the most beautiful hotel in Southeast Alaska. Owned by the Native Cape Fox Corporation and run by the Westmark chain, the hotel's understated but inspired design and masterpieces of Tlingit art lend a sense of the peace and spirit of the rain forest. All but a dozen rooms share Ketchikan's most spectacular view, looking out among huge trees over the edge of a cliff that dominates the city and waterfront. To get down the cliff merely requires stepping aboard the Creek Street funicular, which drops you in the middle of the town's most charming and popular tourist area. Even if you can't afford to stay, the elegance and view are worth a visit. Rooms have coffeemakers, clock radios, and double phone jacks, and suites are furnished with quilts and other homey features.

The restaurant and lounge share the wonderful view, and the food is consistently good, placing it among the best in the less than stellar field of Ketchikan's restaurants. Dinner entrees are in the $20 range.

Moderate

The Cedars. 1471 Tongass Ave. (P.O. Box 8331), Ketchikan, AK 99901. ☎ **907/225-1900.** Fax 907/225-8604. E-mail kthomas@ptialaska.net. 12 rms. TV TEL. $95 double; $125 studio with spa; $200 suite. Fishing packages available. AE, DC, DISC, MC, V.

The Cedars is hard against the sidewalk of a busy street, but the whole building is on pilings over the water, with a dock where float planes tie up for fishing trips. It combines being near downtown with a sense of being out of town on the water. They remodeled in 1997, and rooms that already were large became the most luxurious in town. Many have Jacuzzis, and some of the suites are palaces, with great views, kitchens, and second bedrooms up spiral staircases.

Gilmore Hotel. 326 Front St., Ketchikan, AK 99901. ☎ **800/275-9423** or 907/225-9423. Fax 907/225-7442. 36 rms, 2 suites. TV TEL. High season, $66–$98 double, $124 suite. Low season, $40–$78 double, $98 suite. Additional person in room $10 extra. AE, CB, DC, DISC, MC, V.

This 1927 concrete structure on the waterfront tries for a historic feel to match the high ceilings, dignified facade, and views over the cruise-ship dock. The front rooms are the most desirable, while some others are tiny. Nonsmoking rooms are in the minority. Services include a courtesy van and free coffee in the lobby.

Annabelle's Famous Keg and Chowder House, the hotel restaurant, serves a fine-dining steak and seafood menu and an extensive bar menu amid much brass and mahogany. The mood is festive, if the prices a bit high.

Ingersoll Hotel. 303 Mission St., Ketchikan, AK 99901. ☎ **800/478-2124** or 907/225-2124. Fax 907/247-8530. 58 rms. TV TEL. High season, $94 double. Low season, $54 double. AE, DC, DISC, MC, V.

This 1929 hotel is a slice of old Ketchikan. The rooms are on the small side, and, when I last visited, the bathrooms were ready for remodeling. But the hotel generally is well kept, and the waterside rooms have good views across the cruise-ship dock. There's free coffee in the lobby, and a courtesy van is available.

Inexpensive

✪ **New York Hotel.** 207 Stedman St., Ketchikan, AK 99901. ☎ **907/225-0246.** 8 rms. TV TEL. $79 double. AE, CB, DC, MC, V.

This funny little 1924 building, in a perfect central location just off Creek Street, contains charming, antique-furnished rooms that look out on a small boat harbor. The rooms have more attractive amenities than other hotels in town that cost much more. The tasteful restoration of the New York was a family project, and the owners still meet guests in the tiny lobby with casual small-town hospitality.

BED & BREAKFASTS

Ketchikan Reservation Service, 412 D-1 Loop Rd., Ketchikan, AK 99901 (☎ 800/ 987-5337 or fax/phone 907/247-5337; website http://www.ktn.net/krs), books more than 20 bed-and-breakfasts and outfitted apartments. I've found two truly exceptional B&Bs, which I've described below.

✪ **Blueberry Hill B&B.** 500 Upper Front St. (P.O. Box 9508), Ketchikan, AK 99901. ☎ **907/ 247-2583.** E-mail blubrry@ptialaska.net. 4 rms, 3 with bath. High season, $65–$80 double, $90 suite. Low season $60–$75 double, $85 suite. Additional person in room $15 extra. AE, MC, V.

This gracious 1917 house, once a residence for nuns, stands atop the rocky cliff that bounds the north side of the downtown waterfront, above the tunnel. It's a short drive, or 115 steps down a public stairway, to the center of the action; but up here all is peaceful, with soothing New Age music playing under the high ceiling of Elson Zimmerly and Hank Newhouse's stately living room. Each of the guest rooms is large and light, with handmade quilts and elegant furniture. The hosts try to make friends with guests and serve a full breakfast. Newhouse also operates charters on his sailboat, and Zimmerly is an accomplished fine art photographer.

✪ **Captain's Quarters Bed & Breakfast.** 325 Lund St., Ketchikan, AK 99901. ☎ **907/ 225-4912.** 3 rms. TV TEL. High season, $75 double. Low season, $65 double. Additional person in room $20 extra. AE, MC, V.

These large, quiet, immaculate rooms, with a sweeping view of the city and ocean, private telephone lines, and a self-contained, self-service breakfast room, rival the best hotel rooms in Ketchikan but cost half as much. Marv Wendeborn custom-built the B&B with his own hands, carrying the nautical theme through oak woodwork. The family interacts with guests only at their request, and the business is completely separate from their home, with its own entrance. The house perches a reasonable walk from downtown, in a mountainside neighborhood just north of the tunnel where half the streets are stairs. Children aren't allowed, and there's no smoking in the house.

A HOSTEL

First United Methodist Church. Grant and Main sts. (P.O. Box 8515), Ketchikan, AK 99901. ☎ 907/225-3319. 25 beds. $8 per person. Closed Sept–May.

Open only June through August, this church-run hostel, affiliated with Hostelling International, is just up from the tunnel in the downtown area. Free pastries and hot drinks are provided, and guests have use of the church kitchen. Bring a sleeping bag. The office is open from 7 to 9am and 6 to 11pm.

CAMPING

Two Forest Service campgrounds with a total of 29 sites are located at **Ward Lake** (see "Special Places" under "Getting Outside," above).

DINING

Ketchikan isn't a place for great dining, but there is a selection of decent places to eat. The good hotel restaurants at the Westmark Cape Fox Lodge, Gilmore Hotel, Salmon Falls Resort, and Best Western Landing (see "Accommodations," above) also should figure in your decision. If you're interested in pizza, try **Papa's Ketchikan Cafe and Pizza,** on the third floor at 316 Front St. (☎ **907/247-7272**). They deliver their fancy, Italian-style pizza free.

Creekstreet Pastries and Bistro. 127 Stedman St. ☎ **907/247-9227.** Lunch $4.50–$6.75. Dinner from $18. MC, V. Mon–Thurs 7am–7pm, Fri–Sat till 10pm, Sun 9am–4pm. BAKERY/ ECLECTIC.

A long hallway leads past the bakers and cooks, working behind glass, to a tiny, bright dining room on two levels in which each table sits next to a window on Ketchikan Creek. The specialty is rich treats from the scratch bakery, but they also serve well-prepared meals. Lunch is relatively simple and inexpensive. The dinner menu is different every night, with entrees such as duck or buffalo starting at $18. Smoking is not permitted, and there is no liquor license; they cater to families.

✪ **Five Star Cafe.** 5 Creek St. ☎ **907/247-STAR.** Lunch/dinner $3–$8. No credit cards. Daily 7:30am–6pm. VEGETARIAN/COFFEE HOUSE.

Like a place you'd find in a college town, the Five Star has good, reasonably priced sandwiches and soups in an atmosphere conducive to journal writing among the young patrons. The black-bean burrito was delicious and healthy. They're also known for coffee, serving the locally roasted "Raven's Brew," and good pastries and deserts. Ketchikan Creek flows under the building and outside windows on each side of the dining room, creating a light, soothing atmosphere. The building, which also holds two of the city's best galleries, was a brothel and dance hall at one time. Local art hung about the walls of the restaurant is for sale. (No liquor license.)

New York Cafe. 207 Stedman St. ☎ **907/225-0246.** Lunch $5–$8; dinner $15–$20. MC, V. 7am–9pm. STEAK/SEAFOOD/SANDWICHES.

The food here is good and inexpensive and the decor perfect: a wonderfully restored little room on the street and boat harbor with an old-fashioned lunch counter. Huge windows and a high ceiling pour light into a room with a black-and-white tiled floor and a lot of old woodwork. In the small dining room, however, it's hard to escape the cigarette smoke from the group of local regulars who hang out here. (No liquor license.)

Steamers. 76 Front St. ☎ **907/225-1600.** Lunch/dinner $5–$27. AE, DC, DISC, MC, V. 8am–11pm daily, opening at 11am in low season. STEAK/SEAFOOD.

On the third floor of a new building right on the dock (take the corner elevator to the top), this huge bar and grill tries for a Seattle feel, with 20 beers on tap and a long, long a la carte menu of seafood. My soup was well seasoned and the fish grilled not a moment too long. The bright dining room of light oak has towering ceilings and huge windows, with tables well separated; service was professional. They have live music and dancing every night.

KETCHIKAN IN THE EVENING

First City Players (☎ 907/225-4792) puts on a popular summer melodrama, *Fish Pirate's Daughter*, in the small Main Street Theater. Tickets are $10 per person or $30 for a family of four.

Historically, Ketchikan has been a hard-drinking town. Trap doors remain in the floors of some Creek Street buildings where bootleggers would pass booze up from boats underneath. The bars on Front Street are generally authentic waterfront places: dark gritty rooms where you can meet commercial fishermen and locals. **Annabelle's** is a more genteel, refurbished version of an old-fashioned Front Street bar. **Steamers,** at 76 Front St., is on the third floor of a new building at the south end of Front Street. They have 20 beers on tap and live music every night. Bowling, live music, and ball games on TV, as well as meals and drinks, are available at the **Roller Bay Cafe,** at 2050 Sealevel Dr. For a more refined evening and a beautiful setting, the lounge at the **Westmark Cape Fox Lodge,** at the top of the funicular on Creek Street, has an incredible view. **Jeremiah's,** at the Best Western Landing Hotel, 3434 Tongass Ave., also has live music.

A SIDE TRIP TO PRINCE OF WALES ISLAND

If you have plenty of time, the Alaska Bush is a short ferry or small plane ride from Ketchikan, ready to be explored by car. Prince of Wales Island, known locally as "POW," is 135 miles long and 45 miles wide, making it the third-largest island in the United States (after Alaska's Kodiak Island and Hawaii's Big Island), yet it is populated by only a few tiny towns and Native villages. What makes the island unique in Alaska is that it's traversed by more than 1,000 miles of gravel road network, built and maintained by the U.S. Forest Service to facilitate logging. That means you can get out on your own to beautiful places rich with fish, exploring without the expense of an airplane or boat, but rarely seeing another person. It can be a strange feeling to drive for hours without seeing a building or another car. Unfortunately, this accessibility also means that many of the beautiful places are not as beautiful as they once were, as the island is scarred by many large clear-cuts.

Fishing, in both salt and fresh water, is by far the biggest reason visitors go to the island. The Forest Service lists 32 good fishing streams and maintains some 20 cabins, mainly built for their access to remote fishing lakes and streams. Many fishing lodges operate on the island, mostly taking guests out on boats to fish salmon in the ocean, and most visitors to the island have booked inclusive packages at one of the lodges well in advance. But some people discover more of the island. Divers find clear water and a rich profusion of life in these waters; two canoe routes cross wilderness areas of the island; and few other places offer families the same opportunities for solitude and discovery along the road and trails. Plus, POW contains hundreds of barely explored caves, two of which casual visitors can safely enter, with some effort.

Before going to Prince of Wales, stop at the trip-planning room in the **Southeast Alaska Visitor Information Center** in Ketchikan (☎ **907/228-6214;** see "Visitor Information" under "Essentials," above) and pick up the Forest Service recreation guides and the $4 road guide, which is a large map showing the roads and topography and listing the cabins and facilities available around the island. Fishermen will also want to get a copy of the Alaska Department of Fish and Game's **Sport Fishing Guide** for the island, as well as other guidance they can provide at their Ketchikan Division of Sport Fish office, at 2030 Sealevel Dr., Suite 207, Ketchikan, AK 99901 (☎ **907/225-2859**). The **Prince of Wales Chamber of Commerce,** P.O. Box 497, Craig, AK 99921 (☎ **907/826-3870**), distributes listings of accommodations and businesses in the various villages.

The largest town is Craig, on the west side of the island. Here you'll find three good hotels, restaurants, a bank with an ATM, various stores, and a float plane base. Seven miles east is Klawock, a large Native village with the island's major paved landing strip, a shopping center, more restaurants and accommodations, and a rotting totem pole park built by the New Deal in the 1930s. The other towns and villages on the island are quite small and have limited services. Hollis, where the ferry lands on the east side of the island, is just a collection of houses.

You can fly to Prince of Wales on a float or wheeled plane with any of the air-taxi operators in Ketchikan. **Taquan Air Service,** 1007 Water St., Ketchikan, AK 99901 (☎ **800/770-8800** or 907/225-8800; website http://www.AlaskaOne.com/TaquanAir), has frequent flights to Craig or Klawock, as well as packages and tours of the island's highlights, including the caves. If you fly, and you're not at a lodge or on a package, you'll need to rent a car. **Wilderness Rent-a-Car,** at Log Cabin Sporting Goods in Craig (☎ **800/949-2205** or 907/826-2205), charges around $50 a day plus 30¢ a mile, which adds up fast if you plan to go far. You can also rent a car in Ketchikan and take the ferry over. The **Alaska Marine Highway** fare for a car from Ketchikan to Hollis is $41, and each passenger is $20 more (see listing under "Getting Around" at the beginning of this chapter).

FISHING   The fishing opportunities on Prince of Wales are legendary, and many of the lodges and guides are booked up many months in advance. I describe some of them below. You can also go on your own, of course, using the Forest Service cabins or camping. Several of the cabins are reached by skiffs that the Forest Service leaves tied up at the bank by the road. The cabins must be reserved, up to 180 days in advance, with **Biospherics** (☎ **800/280-2267**), listed above under "Outside in Southeast." Even without a cabin or skiff, there are dozens of good fishing spots right on the roads, listed in the Alaska Department of Fish and Game's Sport Fishing Guide (mentioned above).

CAVING   The limestone of Prince of Wales Island contains a honeycomb of miles of caves. Although wet, cold, and challenging, advanced cavers consider these to be among the world's most exciting caves, for their complexity and for the wonder of exploring areas that have never been seen by mankind. The caves originally were discovered only in 1987, and each summer a party of cavers led by the Forest Service is exploring dozens more. Two caves have been developed for the public. Forest Service guides lead visitors on 2-hour treks into **El Capitan** cave four times a day during the summer. Although the tour goes only about 600 feet into the 12,000-foot cave, it feels like you've been to the center of the earth in these incredibly complex, twisting chambers known in the business as a "spongework maze." The hike is only for the fit and starts with a climb up 350 steps to the mountainside cave opening. Visitors can wade into the grotto-like **Cavern Lake Cave** on their own. You'll need the Forest Service's road guide map mentioned above to find the caves, and it is highly advisable to contact the **Thorne Bay Ranger District,** 1312 USFS Dr., Thorne Bay, AK 99919 (☎ **907/828-3304**), before you venture on the 3-hour drive from Craig, both to get detailed directions and to be sure you can meet a tour. El Capitan Cave is blocked by a gate a couple of hundred feet in, so I strongly recommend going on the tour.

DIVING   Craig Sempert's **Craig Dive Center,** 107 Main St. (P.O. Box 796), Craig, AK 99921 (☎ **800/380-DIVE** or 907/826-3481), offers rentals and fully guided diving packages to the island. The water here is clearer and the invertebrate and marine mammal life even richer than on the Inside Passage part of Southeast Alaska. Plankton blooms can cloud things up in the summer, but winter is always clear. Sempert dives in wet and dry suits, and tailors packages to visitors' interests, diving in unexplored areas, and even in caves. He also rents out a pair of attractive apartment units by the night, for $85 double—a great place for families to stay, whether divers or not.

CANOEING A couple of lovely wilderness canoe routes cross parts of the island, on Sarkar Lake and through the Honker Divide, each with Forest Service cabins along the way. You can bring your own canoe or rent one from **Log Cabin Sporting Goods** in Craig (☎ **800/949-2205** or 907/826-2205). They charge $20 a day and also carry anything else you might need.

ACCOMMODATIONS & DINING

In addition to the rooms at Craig's Dive Shop, mentioned above, Craig has three excellent hotels: Ruth Ann's, the Haida Way Lodge, and the Sunnahae Lodge. In each case, however, most of their rooms are booked far in advance of the summer season by fishing packages. **Ruth Ann's Hotel,** P.O. Box 645, Craig, AK 99921 (☎ **907/ 826-3377**), has big, luxurious rooms in one building for $125 double, and cozy, well-appointed rooms in another for $78 double. Three-day, all-inclusive fishing packages are $1,650, roughly the going rate. No rooms are reserved for nonsmokers, and noise from a bar can be a problem in the better rooms. **Ruth Ann's Restaurant** has the fanciest dining room, overlooking the placid Craig harbor, but I have never found a restaurant on the island that served more than adequate food. **Haida Way Lodge,** P.O. Box 90, Craig, AK 99921 (☎ **800/347-4625** or 907/826-3268), is the other good hotel on the island renting nice standard rooms to people not on fishing packages. Their summer rate is $90–$100 double, but they book up by early winter for the season. The same owners operate **Sunnahae Lodge,** also in Craig (☎ **907/ 826-4000**), with comfortable, smoke-free rooms available with packages.

In Klawock, try **Fireweed Lodge,** P.O. Box 116, Klawock, AK 99925 (☎ **907/ 755-2930**), which has its own dock and a wilderness feel, but is near the airport and shopping center. **Papa's Pizza** (☎ **907/755-2244**), in the shopping center in Klawock, has some of the island's best food and free delivery.

On the northern end of the island, **McFarland's Floatel,** P.O. Box 19148, Thorne Bay, AK 99919 (☎ **888/828-3335** or 907/828-3335), lies 2 miles across the water from tiny Thorne Bay, with four large, two-bedroom cabins with bathrooms and kitchens for $180 a night. You can drive to Thorne Bay and get over on a boat, or fly in, but once there, you're mostly on your own, cooking your own meals. The proprietors charter guided fishing trips and rent skiffs for $69 a day ($75 if you're not a guest). As with all POW lodges, reserve well ahead.

One of the state's best-known luxury lodges, **Waterfall Resort,** P.O. Box 6440, Ketchikan, AK 99901 (☎ **800/544-5125** or 907/225-9461), is reached only by float plane, on the western side of the island. The cottages and rooms are in converted cannery buildings. Four-day, 3-night trips, including the ride over from Ketchikan, start at $2,665 per person.

If you don't need a hotel room, you can camp almost anywhere on the island or rent one of the Forest Service cabins. The **Eagles Nest Campground,** near the intersection of the Thorne Bay Road, has 11 well-separated sites among huge trees by the edge of Balls Lake. A ¹/₂-mile boardwalk along the edge of the lake ends at Control Creek among a grove of Sitka spruce of staggering girth and height.

4 Misty Fjords National Monument: Granite & Water

Among the vast, uninhabited islands, bottomless bays and fjords, massive trees, and inconceivably towering cliffs of the southern Alaska Panhandle are 2.3 million acres of inviolate wilderness President Jimmy Carter set aside as a national monument with a wave of his pen in 1978. It's still waiting to be discovered. Unlike Denali or Glacier Bay national parks, Misty Fjords National Monument lacks a single star attraction to which visitors can make a pilgrimage; there is no one exceptional mountain or glacier, no holy grail to seek. For that reason, and its remoteness, the monument remains relatively unvisited. But what it does offer is found few places, if anywhere else at all: seemingly endless untouched wilderness with trees and geology so extraordinary and huge they force you to admit that your own imagination is sadly puny by comparison.

The only way to get there is by boat or float plane—there's no cheap way to see the bulk of the monument, which is the size of Connecticut. The only places to stay are 13 rustic U.S. Forest Service cabins. One can get to the edge of the monument on an 18-mile trail from the little town of Hyder, which can be reached either by road from British Columbia or by a long ferry ride from Ketchikan, but that's a rare and challenging route. The most popular way to see the monument is on a tour boat from Ketchikan. It's also a good place for sea kayaking—that's how the four backcountry Forest Service rangers get around.

There are several noteworthy things to see. **New Eddystone Rock,** standing in the middle of Behm Canal, is a 237-foot-tall exclamation point of weathered rock, the remaining lava plug from an eroded volcano. **Rudyerd Bay** is like a place where the earth shattered open: The cliffs in its Punchbowl Cove rise vertically 3,150 feet from the surface of water that's 900 feet deep—topography in a league with the Grand Canyon. Waterfalls pound down out of the bay's granite. The glaciers of the northern part of the monument also are impressive, although they require a plane to visit.

But don't go to Misty Fjords to see animals. You may see harbor seals, but here the attraction is the land itself and its outrageous geology. Also, the name is accurate: It's misty. Or it could be pouring rain. This is among the rainiest spots on earth.

ESSENTIALS

GETTING THERE   By Boat   Charters are available from Ketchikan, but it's 50 miles to Rudyerd Bay, an expensive ride. A better choice is to go on one of the excellent boat excursions offered by Dale Pihlman's ✪ **Alaska Cruises,** 220 Front St. (P.O. Box 7814), Ketchikan, AK 99901 (☎ **800/228-1905** or 907/225-6044; website http://www.ptialaska.net/~akcruise). The 32-passenger boats have comfortable table seating and lots of room to get outside. Guides provide accurate, interesting, and personal commentary. The tour travels up the Behm Canal, past New Eddystone Rock, then drifts through Punchbowl Cove while you eat a hearty lunch of seafood chowder, before finally coming to a floating dock at the head of Rudyerd Bay after 6^1/$_2$ hours. There, passengers who have paid a $45 premium are picked up by a float plane and see the same terrain from the air on a 20-minute ride back to Ketchikan, a fascinating experience itself. Others take another 5 hours—and have dinner of deli sandwiches—on the return trip on the boat. The fare is $145 for the 12-hour version, $115 for children 11 and under. If you're susceptible to seasickness, try to have an alternative date to go in case of bad weather; the water is generally smooth in the fjords but more exposed on the way there.

By Kayak   Southeast Exposure, 507 Stedman St. (P.O. Box 9143), Ketchikan, AK 99901 (☎ **907/225-8829;** fax 907/225-8849), offers guided trips to the monument, starting at 4 days for $675 per person. They also have kayaks for rent for $30 to $50 a day; a 90-minute training class is mandatory, and an unguided trip deep into the fjords isn't advisable for first-timers. The Forest Service produces a good kayaker's map showing camping spots, rip tides, and dangerous waters, available for $4 from the Southeast Alaska Visitor Information Center (see "Visitor Information," below). Alaska Cruises (see "By Boat," above) drops kayakers off at Rudyerd Bay for $175, or $50 more for anywhere else along the route.

By Plane You can cover a lot more ground a lot faster this way, and flying over the cliffs, trees, and glaciers is an experience all its own. Several air-taxi operators in Ketchikan take trips; **Taquan Air Service,** 1007 Water St., Ketchikan, AK 99901 (☎ **800/770-8800** or 907/225-8800; website http://www.AlaskaOne.com/TaquanAir), for example, does a good job. Their 2-hour, $175 trip leaves at 10:30am daily and lands on a lake; 90-minute flights leave at 10:30am and 1pm daily and cost $129 per person.

On Foot Hyder is 18 miles by trail from the monument, but it's at the end of the long Portland Canal, so most of the monument is not readily accessible from there by boat. There's an opportunity to watch black and brown bears feeding from a Forest Service platform on Fish Creek, the most unregulated, developed bear viewing in the state, and the area has good birding. Hyder can be reached by the Cassiar Highway from British Columbia or by ferry once every 2 weeks from Ketchikan, a 12-hour run that costs $40.

VISITOR INFORMATION The **Southeast Alaska Visitor Information Center,** 50 Main St., Ketchikan, AK 99901 (☎ **907/228-6214**), can give you a packet about Misty Fjords in the trip-planning room downstairs. The **Ketchikan Visitors Bureau,** 131 Front St., Ketchikan, AK 99901 (☎ **907/225-6166**), can provide the names of charter operators. The monument is part of the Tongass National Forest. **Monument offices** are at 3031 Tongass Ave., Ketchikan, AK 99901 (☎ **907/225-2148**).

ACCOMMODATIONS

The only lodgings are 13 **U.S. Forest Service cabins** and several three-sided shelters. Many are little used and extremely remote.

The cabins cost $25 per night, but that's only a small part of the cost of using them. You also have to pay for a float plane to get there. I've listed the names of some of the air-taxi and gear rental operators in "Special Places" under "Getting Outside," in the Ketchikan section, earlier in this chapter. While $250 an hour for flight time may seem steep, remember that in town or at a wilderness lodge, you'd be paying for a hotel room and meals. A group of 3 could do 3 days at a Forest Service cabin for under $500.

Below are a couple of highlights. For a complete listing, contact the Forest Service at the Southeast Alaska Visitor Center or the Misty Fjords National Monument offices, listed above. For reservation information, see "Outside in Southeast," above. All the lake cabins have rowboats. **Winstanley Island Cabin** is a good destination for kayakers, and there's a chance of seeing bears. **Big Goat Lake Cabin** sits on a point on an alpine lake near a 1,700 foot waterfall; it's accessible only by plane, and because it's so beautiful, a lot of plane traffic comes by. **Ella Lake** is relatively near Ketchikan, so the cost of the trip isn't as high as some others, but it's very secluded. You can fly to it, or take a boat to the 2.3-mile traxil to the lake, then row across the lake to the cabin. Right off Rudyerd Bay, beautiful **Nooya Lake** has a three-sided shelter.

5 Wrangell: An Old-Fashioned Small Town

Wrangell just wanted to be a burly logging town, simple and conservative. Petersburg, 50 miles away up the twisting Wrangell Narrows, with its fishing fleet and government workers, was more sophisticated, and its boardwalks and clapboard houses had more charm. Wrangell was solid, blue collar, the kind of place where people stayed forever, knew each other, where the restaurants were smoky and unconcerned about cholesterol. Approaching by ship, the whole town laid itself out, simple and straightforward, on the steep side of the island that bore its name, as it had for more than 150 years. As long as there were trees to saw into lumber, the future was safe.

Then, late in 1994, the sawmill shut down. Lumber had been a mainstay of the local economy since the 1890s, and the mill was the only major employer. Now it was gone, and with it went a third of the town's payroll. People had to sell out and leave the place where they were born and raised—an insular little town from which the outside world seemed all the more intimidating.

But with that calamity in the past, Wrangell still preserves something exceptional. Here is authentic small-town America as the type once existed, unlinked from the franchises, chains, roads, and frantic worries that entangle and homogenize the country today. There's no Walmart, no serious crime, and hardly any traffic. Our family spent a jolly couple of sunny days wandering the town. (Sunny weather is not the norm.) We enjoyed playing in the two totem pole parks, and the Petroglyph Beach is a wonderful place for a family to explore and take a picnic. Wrangell has a non-threatening, small-scale feel that allows a family to wander comfortably.

For the visitor, it's an interesting formula. Wrangell sits near the wild Stikine River, has Southeast's great ocean salmon fishing, and is the jump-off for the Anan Bear Observatory. There's a day's worth of sightseeing within walking distance, and the U.S. Forest Service maintains some outdoor facilities along the island's logging roads, although not the same wealth of opportunities as found in Petersburg. Wrangell can't change its stripes—it's still a muscular town with narrow horizons—but the people are endearingly eager to please. Many are hoping tourism will be the town's new reason to exist.

Wrangell began as a fur-trading post, and the Russians built a fort in 1834. The site was valuable for its position near the mouth of the Stikine, which was a Tlingit trade route into the Canadian interior. The British leased the area from the Russians in 1840, and their flag flew until the U.S. purchase of Alaska in 1867. Over the balance of the 19th century, Wrangell experienced three gold rushes and the construction of a cannery and the sawmill. A cozy, old-fashioned feel remains in parts of town, but fires have destroyed most of the historic or interesting buildings. In 1952, the downtown area was wiped out and its boardwalk waterfront replaced by today's drab gravel fill. Those old buildings that remain, dating to the turn of the century, can be found with the help of a walking-tour map available at the visitor center or museum (see below).

ESSENTIALS

GETTING THERE   By Air   Alaska Airlines (☎ **800/426-0333;** website http:// www.alaskaair.com) serves Wrangell once daily with a jet flying 28 minutes south to Ketchikan and another 19 minutes north to Petersburg.

By Ferry   Wrangell is on the main line of the **Alaska Marine Highway System** (see listing under "Getting Around" at the beginning of this chapter), with landings six times a week in the summer. The voyage through the narrow, winding ✪ **Wrangell Narrows** north to Petersburg is one of the most beautiful and fascinating in Southeast Alaska. It's quite a navigational feat to watch as the 300-foot ships squeeze through a passage so slender and shallow the vessel's own displacement changes the water level on shore as it passes. The route, not taken by cruise ships (which approach through larger waterways), is also a source of delays, as the water in the narrows is deep enough only at high tide. The walk-on fare is $24 to Ketchikan, $18 to Petersburg.

VISITOR INFORMATION   A small visitor information center operated by the **Wrangell Chamber of Commerce,** P.O. Box 49, Wrangell, AK 99929 (☎ **800/ 367-9745** or 907/874-3901; website http://www.wrangell.com/), is located at the end of the Stikine Inn nearest the city dock, where cruise ships tie up. In addition to brochures from local businesses, it also provides tabular listings of charter-boat operators, outfitters, and other local businesses. It's open in summer, Monday through Friday from 10am to 4pm, and other hours when a cruise ship is in town. The U.S. Forest Service also has an information desk at the entry of the **Wrangell Ranger District** offices, on the hill at 525 Bennett St. (P.O. Box 51), Wrangell, AK 99929 (☎ **907/874-2323**), where you can draw on local knowledge of the logging roads and fishing holes, obtain two-page guides to each Forest Service cabin and path, and buy a detailed Wrangell Island Road Guide topographic map for $4—it shows and describes all the island's outdoor attractions.

ORIENTATION   A map is available at the visitor center. The main part of town is laid out north to south along the waterfront at the northern point of the island. **Front Street** is the main business street, leading from the small-boat harbor and **Chief Shakes Island** at the south to the city dock and the ferry dock at the north. Most of the rest of the town is along **Church Street,** which runs parallel a block higher up the hill. **Evergreen Avenue** and **Bennett Street** form a loop to the north which goes to the airport. The only road to the rest of the island, the **Zimovia Highway,** heads out of town to the south, connecting to over 100 miles of logging roads built and maintained by the Forest Service.

GETTING AROUND   For the town of Wrangell, you can go on foot. **Alaska Waters,** 241 Berger St. (P.O. Box 1978), Wrangell, AK 99929 (☎ **907/874-2378**) offers walking tours on the town's cultural history. If you're going to get out of town for a hike or overnight on the island, a car is necessary. **Practical Rent A Car** is at the airport (☎ **907/874-3975;** fax 907/874-3911), or they'll deliver to you. For a taxi, try **Porky's Cab Company** (☎ **907/874-3603**), or **Star Cab Company** (☎ **907/874-2316**).

   Rent a skiff of your own if you're comfortable running a small boat—you'll be much freer to enjoy the outdoors for fishing, wildlife viewing, or hiking. Among others, **Harbor House Rentals,** 645 Shakes St. (P.O. Box 2027), Wrangell, AK 99929 (☎ and fax **907/874-3084**), rents boats. They charge $125 to $150 a day. Get a complete list of rental companies from the visitor center.

FAST FACTS   Wrangell has a 7% **sales tax.** The National Bank of Alaska, at 105 Front St., has an **ATM.** The **post office** is at 105 Federal Way. In **emergencies,** call **911.** For nonemergency calls to the **police,** call ☎ **907/874-3304. Wrangell General Hospital,** at 310 Bennett St. (☎ **907/874-3356**), is a full-service health facility with a clinic. The local *Wrangell Sentinel* comes out every Thursday. **Stikine Drugs,** on Front Street, also carries the *Seattle Times* and *Ketchikan Daily News.* **Photocopying** services are available at the **library,** 124 Second St., and **fax** and photocopying are available at the Chamber of Commerce visitors center.

SPECIAL EVENTS   The **Garnet Festival,** the third week of April, marks the arrival of the massive shorebird migration and bald eagle congregation on the Stikine River Delta, a wonderful chance to see a tornado of wildlife in the region's largest coastal marshes. The **Wrangell Chamber of Commerce King Salmon Derby** is mid-May through mid-June. **Fourth of July** festivities start on July 1.

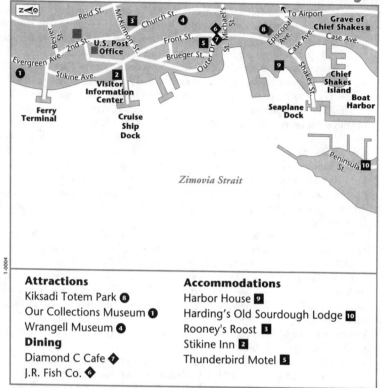

Attractions

Kiksadi Totem Park **8**

Our Collections Museum **1**

Wrangell Museum **4**

Dining

Diamond C Cafe **7**

J.R. Fish Co. **6**

Accommodations

Harbor House **9**

Harding's Old Sourdough Lodge **10**

Rooney's Roost **3**

Stikine Inn **2**

Thunderbird Motel **5**

EXPLORING WRANGELL & ENVIRONS

Wrangell's most interesting sights represent Tlingit cultural history and art. Although Sitka and Ketchikan have more and better-presented attractions along this line, Wrangell is much less visited, so there's a more relaxed, intimate feeling.

✪ **Chief Shakes Island,** a tiny island in the middle of the small-boat harbor, is the site of a Tlingit clan house and collection of totem poles constructed (like those in Ketchikan) by the Civilian Conservation Corps during the 1930s. The setting and cultural resources on the island are fascinating; the tradeoff is that the local tribal council makes little effort to show off or interpret the clan house to independent travelers. The house is open only when cruise ships are in town—then you can enter for $1.50 and hear a brief talk. If there's no cruise ship, you may find the manager of the island at the Alley Cat gift shop on Front Street (☎ and fax **907/874-3747**) and, for $15, have the clan house opened for your inspection. No matter—my son remembered much better watching a sea otter that lives near the island's footbridge feed its baby, and you can see the exterior of the clan house and the totems anytime.

Before whites arrived, Tlingits had already warred over this strategic trading location near the mouth of the Stikine River for centuries. The first Chief Shakes was a successful conqueror who enslaved his enemies, then handed down power through the female line, in the Tlingit way, for 7 generations. The clan house was moved to the present site early in the 19th century. Charlie Jones was recognized as the last of the line, Chief Shakes VII, at a potlatch in 1940, but the position had long since lost most of its status. The decline began after the Alaska purchase, in 1867. Word came of the Emancipation Proclamation, which theoretically freed a third of the residents of the coast's Tlingit villages. Chief Shakes VI sent his slaves in canoes to dry halibut; they kept paddling home to Puget Sound, never looking back.

On Front Street near the center of town, the **Kiksadi Totem Park** was built by the Sealaska regional Native corporation in the mid-1980s on the former site of a clan house. The grass is a comfortable place to sit, and the totem poles are worth a look.

The ✪ **Petroglyph Beach,** about a mile north of town, represents earlier evidence of indigenous people who may predate the Tlingit. Walk north on Evergreen Avenue and follow the signs down to the beach (don't go within an hour of high tide). The images, chipped into rocks on the beach, are of animals and geometric forms. Their purpose and the identity of their creators are lost to time. The great pleasure for a visitor is simply to search for them and wonder. It's a fine place for a family to spend an afternoon, in good weather. Don't take rubbings, however, as the experts fear that this practice is wearing away the images; try as well not to step on the markings.

Wrangell has two museums. The **Wrangell Museum** (☎ **907/874-3770**), operated by the city, is located in temporary quarters in the basement of the gymnasium at 318 Church St. It's a typical small-town hodgepodge—an ancient totem pole is displayed along with an old lawn mower—but there are some significant artifacts, such as the original houseposts of Chief Shakes' house. The staff is helpful and sells pamphlets on Wrangell history, including the excellent "Authentic History of Shakes Island and Clan" by E. L. Keithhahn, for $4. Admission to the museum is $2; in summer it's open Monday through Friday 10am to 5pm, Saturdays 1pm to 5pm, and when cruise ships are in town.

The other museum is a bit less conventional. Elva Bigelow, who admits to no more than 81 years, maintains her **Our Collections Museum** on Evergreen Avenue (☎ **907/874-3646**), on the way to the Petroglyph Beach. It's an all-inclusive gathering of her family's 60 years in Wrangell. There are old tools, outboard motors, a huge collection of dolls, bottles, a large diorama of the town assembled for the 1967 centennial celebration, old typewriters, local wildflowers, and anything else you can imagine. Mrs. Bigelow loves visitors, and her museum is open when cruise ships are in town; or you can reach her by phone, and she'll gladly show it to you. Donations are appreciated.

GETTING OUTSIDE

The **Garnet Ledge,** 7 miles across the water from Wrangell at the mouth of the Stikine River, still yields gems 130 years after its discovery. If you want to take garnets from the ledge, you'll need to take along a rock hammer—and a child: Only children have the right to take the stones since the deposit's last owner deeded the mine to the Boy Scouts and the children of Wrangell in 1962. The ledge was exploited from 1907 to 1936 by the first all-woman corporation in the nation, a group of investors from Minneapolis. Information on the history and recreational mining of the ledge is available at the Wrangell Museum and the visitor center, and you can buy garnets from the ledge from children who set up card tables at the ferry and cruise-ship docks when the ships are in, and often elsewhere, too.

Of course, you'll need a boat to get to the ledge; I recommend making a day of it on a ✪ **jet-boat tour** up the Stikine River. The ledge should be one stop, and also the Shakes Glacier and the Forest Service–owned Chief Shakes Hot Springs, where there's an indoor and an outdoor tub open for public bathing. The temperature is adjustable up to 120°F. The main feature of the trip, however, is a wild ride on the Stikine, the fastest-flowing navigable river in North America, through the

Stikine-LeConte Wilderness. If your papers are in order, you can go all the way to Telegraph, B.C. The high-powered jet boats are hot rods of the sea, capable of up to 50 m.p.h., and it's fun to zoom over the glacial water in one. Todd Harding's **Stickeen Wilderness Adventures,** P.O. Box 934, Wrangell, AK 99929 (☎ **800/ 874-2085** or 907/874-2085; website http://www.wrangell.com/business/ harding.htm), is a leading operator, charging $145 per person, with a minimum of three passengers. **Alaska Waters,** 241 Berger St. (P.O. Box 1978), Wrangell, AK 99929 (☎ **907/874-2378**), is another well-reputed operator.

At the ✪ **Anan Wildlife Observatory,** the Forest Service has set up a place to see lots of black bears and some brown bears close up as they feed on spawning pink salmon trying to make it up a waterfall in Anan Creek, on the mainland southeast of Wrangell Island. When the fish are running in July and August, more than 40 bears use the creek, sometimes walking close to the platform where people stand watching. Two Forest Service guides are on duty during the bear months, but you must take care of yourself by observing safe bear behavior (see "Safety" in chapter 3). A guided day trip from Wrangell is available from **Harbor House Rentals,** 645 Shakes St. (P.O. Box 2027), Wrangell, AK 99929 (☎ and fax **907/874-3084**), for $135. **Stikeen Wilderness Adventures,** listed in the previous paragraph, also takes groups over. A float plane also can take you the 29 miles. **Sunrise Aviation,** P.O. Box 432, Wrangell, AK 99929 (☎ **907/874-2319;** fax 907/874-2546), is a Wrangell-based operator. The walk to the observatory is half a mile on a good trail. Contact the Forest Service Wrangell Ranger Station, listed above, for details.

Several Forest Service shelters, cabins, and trails can be reached from the Wrangell Island road system, some on lakes with rowboats for public use. The **Rainbow Falls Trail,** 5 miles south of town on the Zimovia Highway, is the most popular hike, leading 0.8 miles with a 500-foot elevation gain to a picnic area. You can continue another 2.7 miles and another 1,100 feet into open alpine terrain on the **Institute Creek Trail** to the Shoemaker Overlook, where there are great views, a picnic area, and a shelter. Lake cabins and shelters on the road system are all fairly long drives on logging roads, but offer isolation and good fishing. If you're willing to charter a plane or boat, there are several Forest Service cabins with access to trophy-class fish, great wildlife viewing, or both. Contact the Forest Service Wrangell Ranger Station, listed above.

For loads of detailed fishing information, get a copy of the Alaska Department of Fish and Game's 20-page **Petersburg Wrangell Sport Fishing Guide,** ADF&G Division of Sport Fishing, P.O. Box 25526, Juneau, AK 99802-5526 (☎ **907/ 465-4180;** website http://www.state.ak.us/local/akpages/FISH.GAME/ adfghome.htm).

ACCOMMODATIONS

Besides the accommodations listed here, the **Thunderbird Motel,** 223 Front St. (P.O. Box 110), Wrangell, AK 99929 (☎ **907/874-3322**), and **Rooney's Roost Bed and Breakfast,** 206 McKinnon (P.O. Box 552), Wrangell, AK 99929 (☎ **907/ 874-2026**), also provide good, inexpensive lodgings. Get a list of other B&Bs from the visitor center. There's a $4-per-room **bed tax** on top of the 7% sales tax when you rent a room.

✪ **Harbor House.** 645 Shakes St. (P.O. Box 2027), Wrangell, AK 99929. ☎ and fax **907/ 874-3084.** 3 rms, none with bath; 2 suites. TV. $65 double; $110 suites.

Each room in this house set on pilings above the water near Chief Shakes Island has some special feature: a nautical room has queen-size bunk beds and a porthole. Besides the three smaller rooms with shared bath upstairs, there are two suites that essentially are furnished apartments with telephones and full kitchens. The upper apartment has a sleeping porch facing the water, from which you can often watch sea otters playing. The downstairs suite has two bedrooms. All guests can use a coin-op washer and dryer, a coffeemaker, a microwave oven, and a refrigerator. The Wyrick family lives downstairs and runs a delightful little coffeehouse on the porch that faces the street, and a boat charter business.

Harding's Old Sourdough Lodge. 1104 Peninsula (P.O. Box 1062), Wrangell, AK 99929. ☎ **800/874-3613** or 907/874-3613. Fax 907/874-3455. 19 rms, 14 with bath. TEL. $55 double without bath; $75 double with bath; $115–$175 suite. AE, DC, DISC, MC, V.

The energetic Bruce Harding runs his hotel almost single-handedly in the style of a fishing lodge—he rents the rooms alone or as part of fishing, hunting, or wildlife viewing packages. The attractive building with a wraparound porch is about a mile from the center of town in a waterfront area, but Harding will drive you where you want to go when he can get free. Some of the best meals in town are served here, family style—you eat what they cook—for $16 to $24 per person for dinner; nonguests can make a reservation. There's a large lounge, a sauna, a steam bath, and a wide variety of rooms, from a bunkhouse style to a massive suite with a Jacuzzi. Laundry machines are at guests' disposal.

Stikine Inn. 107 Front St. (P.O. Box 990), Wrangell, AK 99929. ☎ **888/874-388** or 907/ 874-3388. Fax 907/874-3923. 31 rms, 3 suites. TV TEL. High season, $70 double, $80 suite. Low season, $60 double, $70 suite. Additional person in room $5 extra. AE, DC, DISC, MC, V.

The town's main hotel is close to the ferry dock and stands right on the water's edge. It's a bustling place, a center of community activity. The visitor center is in the same building. Rooms are spacious, comfortable, and clean, if some are outdated. We could hear the water lapping the shore outside the window as we fell asleep. A new restaurant, the Waterfront Grill, was due to open after this writing. There's also an art gallery on the ground floor.

DINING

You don't go to Wrangell for fine dining, but you can get an adequate meal there. Other than the restaurants in the Stikine Inn and Harding's Old Sourdough Lodge (see "Accommodations," above), there is the **Diamond C Cafe,** at 215 Front St., a comfortable and somewhat less smoky coffee shop; and **J. R. Fish Co.,** across the street, a fish market with soups, sandwiches, and specials for lunch. A nonsmoking health-food restaurant was planned at this writing, which will be quite a departure for Wrangell.

6 Petersburg: Unvarnished Threshold to the Outdoors

There's a reason why Petersburg is short on tourist amenities—the residents like the town the way it is. Many look with horror on the hoards of visitors, primarily off large cruise ships, in Juneau and Ketchikan, and they're glad big ships can't get into their harbor. They prefer Petersburg to continue making its daily bread from the sea, as it has from the start, free of boutiques, jewelry shops, and summer-only businesses.

Ironically, that very lack of attractions is the town's main attraction. Petersburg is real, and the outdoor opportunities to which it provides an entryway are sublime but still little used. The humpback whales haven't grown so habituated to watchers that they hold out a flipper for tips. When you walk down Nordic Drive, the principal street, you don't see many others like yourselves—you see Norwegian fishermen in pickup trucks and blond-haired kids on bikes.

The disadvantage, of course, is a lack of good restaurants, a narrow selection of places to stay, and not much to do in town except to look at the picturesque houses and boats. That's okay if you enjoy being on the water or in the woods, but Petersburg is not the place to come for shopping or sightseeing.

Petersburg is named for its founder, Peter Buschmann, who killed himself after living here for only a few years. But that shouldn't be a reflection on the town, which is in an ideal location and has had a prosperous history since that inauspicious beginning. Today its economy, based on fishing and government work—there's a large U.S. Forest Service office here—makes for a rich, sophisticated, and stable population. In 1898, Buschmann founded a cannery on Mitkof Island facing the slender, peaceful Wrangell Narrows in what was to become Petersburg. As a proud old Son of Norway told me, Buschmann was a Norwegian and always hired Norwegians. Any Norwegian who came to him, he hired. They came from far and wide. In a short time, the cannery failed. Perhaps an excessive payroll? My suggestion was met with an icy glance and a change of subject. In any event, the Norwegians stayed, brought their families, and built a charming town, which now has about 3,400 residents.

ESSENTIALS

GETTING THERE   By Ferry   Petersburg has the most welcoming ferry terminal in the system (☎ **907/772-3855**), with a grassy lawn and a pier that's a park to watch the boats and marine animals. It's about a mile to the town center. To the north, the **Alaska Marine Highway** (see listing under "Getting Around" at the beginning of this chapter) can take you to Juneau direct, or by way of Sitka. The fare is $18 to Wrangell, $26 to Sitka, and $44 to Juneau.

By Air   Petersburg is served by **Alaska Airlines'** jets (☎ **800/426-0333**; website http://www.alaskaair.com) once north and once south each day, with the nearest stops on the puddle jumper being Sitka and Wrangell.

VISITOR INFORMATION   The Petersburg Chamber of Commerce and the U.S. Forest Service jointly operate an excellent **visitor center** at the corner of First and Fram streets (P.O. Box 649), Petersburg, AK 99833 (☎ **907/772-4636**; website http://www.petersburg.org). A ranger and a chamber representative answer questions, and in addition to the usual brochures, you can pick up a 36-page guide to the area's hiking trails and a birder's checklist by Peter J. Walsh. This also is the place to get details on Forest Service cabins you can make reservations for through the Biospherics national system described above under "Outside in Southeast." **Viking Travel**, P.O. Box 787, Petersburg, AK 99833 (☎ **800/327-2571** or 907/772-3818; fax 907/772-3940; website http://alaska-ala-carte.com), located on the waterfront near North Boat Harbor, is a good place to book tours, kayaks, whale watching, flights, fishing charters, and other activities or needs. They also sell custom Alaska tour packages.

ORIENTATION   Petersburg is on Mitkof Island, divided from the much larger Kupreanof Island by the slender channel of the Wrangell Narrows. There are three small-boat harbors—the north, south, and middle—and so many docks, boardwalks, and wooden streets that the town seems to sit on the ocean. **Nordic Drive** is the main street, running from the ferry dock through town, then becoming **Sandy Beach Road** as it rounds Hungry Point to the north. At Sandy Beach, you can circle back, past the cannery worker's tent city and the airport, which stands above the town, to **Haugen Drive,** which meets Nordic again near **Hammer Slough,** right in town. To the south, Nordic becomes the **Mitkof Highway,** which runs south to the rest of the island.

GETTING AROUND   You need some mode of transportation to really enjoy Petersburg, because the best of the place is the outdoors. The **Tides Inn Motel** and **Scandia House** (see "Accommodations," below) rent cars, but only about a dozen cars are available in town, and they get booked up well in advance. Two businesses offer **van tours** of the town and island. Judy Henderson, under the name **See Alaska Tours and Charters,** P.O. Box 1125, Petersburg, AK 99833 (☎ **907/772-4656**), offers 2- or 4-day trips in a 12-passenger van that includes beachcombing and a nature walk for $20 to $35. **Alaska Scenic Waterways,** 114 Harbor Way (P.O. Box 943), Petersburg, AK 99833 (☎ **800/ASW-1176** or phone/fax 907/772-3777), has a similar service.

   Biking is a great way to see Petersburg. You can rent a bike for $3 an hour or $20 a day, or arrange a guided tour from **Northern Bikes,** located in the lobby of the Scandia House Hotel (☎ **907/772-3978**). The hotel itself rents small boats; if you're comfortable handling a skiff, that's a good avenue to the outdoors. An 18-footer with a 40-horse outboard rents for $150 a day, gas included, $25 less for guests of the hotel.

FAST FACTS   Petersburg has a 6% **sales tax.** There are **ATMs** at the National Bank of Alaska and First Bank, both at the corner of Nordic Drive and Fram Street. The **post office** is at 12 N. Nordic Dr., at the corner of Haugen Drive. In **emergencies,** dial **911;** the **police** can be reached at ☎ **907/772-3838** for nonemergency calls. The **Petersburg Medical Center,** at Second and Fram streets (☎ **907/ 772-4291**), is a full-service hospital. The *Petersburg Pilot* comes out every Thursday. Out-of-town newspapers are available at the **Rexall Pharmacy** on Nordic Drive. There's no business center as such, but **photocopying and fax** services are available at the **library,** at the corner of Nordic and Haugen drives.

SPECIAL EVENTS   Petersburg goes wild for the **Little Norway Festival,** which celebrates the May 17, 1814, declaration of independence of Norway from Sweden. There are lots of community events planned May 14 to 17, 1998. The **King Salmon Derby** offers a $30,000 purse May 22 to 25, 1998, and the summer-long **Canned Salmon Classic** is a chance to win $2,500 for guessing how many cans of salmon will be packed in Petersburg during the season; both are run by the Petersburg Chamber of Commerce (☎ **907/772-3646**). Some say the **Fourth of July** festival is even bigger than Little Norway, but all Southeast Alaska towns have big parties on the Fourth.

EXPLORING PETERSBURG

WHAT TO SEE & DO IN TOWN   A walk around Petersburg should include the boardwalk streets of Hammer Slough. Sing Lee Alley winds past the **Sons of Norway Hall,** where a large model Viking ship used in the Little Norway Festival is often parked. Birch Street follows the slough upstream past the old houses that hang over the water. Walk down to the **waterfront** past North Boat Harbor to see the frenetic activity of the huge commercial fishing fleet in the summer. At the north end of Nordic Drive, stop at **Eagle's Roost Park,** with a grassy area to sit and a stairway that leads down to the water. The eagles like to sit in the big trees here, but in fact you can see eagles almost anytime and anywhere along the water. **Sandy Beach** is a long walk or short bike ride up Sandy Beach Road. Our family enjoyed a rare sunny afternoon relaxing there; picnic shelters are provided for the more likely rain. Around the point to the west are Native petroglyphs, although they're harder to find than those in Wrangell.

The **Clausen Memorial Museum,** at Second and Fram streets (☎ **907/ 772-3598**), focuses on Petersburg and its history. It has a living, community feel; I especially enjoyed the stories written by children of their family's history in the town. The museum is open in summer Monday through Saturday from 9:30am to 4:30pm and on Sunday from 12:30 to 4:30pm, as well as sporadically in the winter; admission is $2 for adults, free for children 11 and under.

GETTING OUTSIDE

SPECIAL PLACES There are so many great outdoor activities in Petersburg, I have listed only a few highlights. For other choices, many of which are as good as those I've written about here, or for the detailed trail and backcountry information you'll need, call or visit the U.S. Forest Service at either of two locations in Petersburg—the visitor center, listed above, or the **Petersburg Ranger District** offices at Nordic and Haugen drives (P.O. Box 1328), Petersburg, AK 99833 (☎ **907/ 772-3871**), above the Post Office. You'll also find several operators of tours oriented to natural history and nonconsumptive use of the outdoors, such as Ron Compton's **Alaska Scenic Waterways,** 114 Harbor Way (P.O. Box 943), Petersburg, AK 99833 (☎ **800/ASW-1176**). Contact Viking Travel, listed under "Visitor Information," above, for other operators.

Raven Trail & Raven's Roost Cabin. About 4 miles up a steep trail that begins behind the airport off Haugen Drive near the water tower, the Raven's Roost Forest Service Cabin sits atop a mountain with a sweeping view of the town and surrounding waters and islands. It's the sort of place that inspires artists and poets. Allow 3 hours for the climb along a boardwalk, then up a steep muddy slope, then along a ridge. Reserve the cabin with **Biospherics** (☎ **800/280-2267**), listed under "Outside in Southeast," at the start of this chapter. You'll also need sleeping bags, cooking gear, lights, and food.

✪Petersburg Creek. The lovely, grassy Petersburg Creek area can be an afternoon's family frolic among the meadows of wildflowers that meet the water, or the start to a challenging 21-mile, multiday hike into the Petersburg Creek–Duncan Salt Chuck Wilderness. You'll need a skiff or sea kayak, or get dropped off by a charter, as the creek is on Kupreanof Island, across Wrangell Narrows from town; the state maintains a dock. The creek contains four species of salmon and two species of trout. The trail is maintained by the Forest Service and has miles of boardwalks and two cabins, one at Petersburg Lake and one at East Salt Chuck, each with a boat for public use. (Reservations are required, as noted above.) Petersburg Lake has trout, and odds are good you'll see ducks, geese, loons, trumpeter swans, bald eagles, and black bears. The Kupreanof dock also provides access to the 3-mile, 3,000-foot trail that climbs Petersburg Mountain, a challenging hike that has spectacular views from the top.

On Mitkof Highway. Pick up the $4 Forest Service Mitkof Island Road Guide map at the visitor center; it shows what you'll find along the way, including king salmon fishing; swimming; ice-skating; views of swans, fish, and glaciers; and many other activities. Fourteen miles out, you come to The Dip, a declivity in the road where high school seniors have long painted their names and classes on the road, then the quarter-mile boardwalk to **Blind River Rapids,** a great place to watch and fish for king salmon in June and July and silvers in September, and to watch eagles. At 18 miles, you'll reach the **Blind Slough Recreation Area,** where locals go to swim in the amber water in the summer and skate in the winter. At 22 miles from Petersburg, you reach the **Ohmer Creek campground,** with a 1-mile trail, a floating bridge over a beaver pond, and access to king salmon in June and July and trout and some salmon in late summer.

LeConte Glacier / Stikine River Delta. The impressive tidewater glacier is also a great place to see baby seals sitting on the ice. There are plenty of operators who can take you. The going rate is about $90 per person. Steve Berry, listed under "Whale Watching," below, does a good glacier trip, too. **Alaska Scenic Waterways,** listed above, combines the glacier and the Stikine River Delta, a wildlife paradise of grass-lands, braided channels and marshes with excellent bird watching, for $175 per person. They take multiday trips to the delta in late April and early May, when the hooligan run and some 2 million birds rest there on their west coast migration and more than 1,500 bald eagles congregate. Other charter operators in Petersburg and Wrangell also go. You can get a list of all the boats from the visitor center, or book through Viking Travel (see "Visitor Information" under "Essentials," above).

✪ **WHALE WATCHING**   Most years, Frederick Sound is one of the best places in the state to see humpbacks when they're feeding in the summer. Several charter operators offer trips in small, six-passenger boats, but Steve Berry secured his position as the dean of whale watchers in the summer of 1995, when a humpback jumped right into his boat. (No one was injured, but a few people fell in the water.) He has a hydrophone on board, so you may be able to hear the whales' while waiting for them to surface. You can book his trip directly at **Sights Southeast,** P.O. Box 934, Petersburg, AK 99833 (☎ **907/772-4503**).

SEA KAYAKING   These protected waters and the variety of things to see make Petersburg an especially good place for sea kayaking. **Tongass Kayak Adventures,** P.O. Box 787, Petersburg, AK 99833 (☎ **907/772-4600;** website http://www.alaska.net/~tonkayak/), focuses on guided trips of 3 days to a week, which can get you out among the glaciers, delta, and whales, but also offers a 5-hour paddle right around the harbor and Petersburg Creek, with no experience required. It costs $55 for adults and $30 for children 11 and under.

MOUNTAIN BIKING   The largely abandoned logging roads on the island and surrounding areas that can be reached by boat provide long rides without seeing cars or other people. **Northern Bikes,** listed under "Getting Around," rents gear and can give ideas on where to go. Together with **Alaska Scenic Waterways,** listed above, they offer 3-day guided trips for $985 per person.

✪ **A COMMERCIAL FISHING TOUR**   Retired Petersburg high school principal Syd Wright runs a unique commercial fishing demonstration. Wright is a crusty and well-loved local institution, often called upon for knowledge about the area's natural history. He takes six passengers on his crude, crowded work boat, trawls for shrimp and sole, and pulls crab pots in Scow Bay, south of town, and then his wife, Vara, cooks it up with butter and garlic and a glass of wine. Wright can identify all the weird creatures that come up in the trawl. The price is $100, with a three-passenger minimum, but it's usually booked way in advance by cruise passengers on the Alaska Sightseeing Tours ship *Sheltered Seas.* Wright can be reached direct at **Chan IV Charters,** P.O. Box 624, Petersburg, AK 99833 (☎ **907/772-4859**).

SPORT FISHING   There are a number of fishing streams you can reach on the roads. The Alaska Department of Fish and Game's 20-page Petersburg Wrangell Sport Fishing Guide, ADF&G Division of Sport Fishing, P.O. Box 25526, Juneau, AK 99802-5526 (☎ **907/465-4180;** website http://www.state.ak.us/local/akpages/FISH.GAME/adfghome.htm), lists a variety of places to go, or call the local Fish and Game office at ☎ **907/772-3812.** The boat harbor has a couple of dozen licensed charter fishing boats, mostly six-passenger vessels. As elsewhere, halibut and salmon are usually the target. You can get a list of operators at the visitor center, or book through **Viking Travel** (see "Visitor Information" under "Essentials," above).

ACCOMMODATIONS

Besides the lodgings below, the **Narrows Inn,** P.O. Box 1048, Petersburg, AK 99833 (☎ **800/665-8433** or 907/772-4284), located across from the ferry dock, offers decent economy rooms, many with kitchenettes. **Nordic House Bed and Breakfast,** 806 S. Nordic Dr. (P.O. Box 573), Petersburg, AK 99833 (☎ **907/772-3620;** fax 907/772-3673; e-mail nordicbb@alaska.net), stands right over the water, with big decks and great views. The visitors center maintains a list of other B&Bs. The **tax** on rooms totals 9%.

Scandia House. 110 Nordic Dr. (P.O. Box 689), Petersburg, AK 99833. ☎ **800/722-5006** or 907/772-4281. Fax 907/772-4301. 33 rms. TV TEL. $85–$105 double, $120 double with kitchenette, $175 suite. Additional person in room $10 extra. AE, CB, DC, DISC, MC, V.

The town's historic main hotel burned recently and was rebuilt in 1995 in the same style, although no one would mistake it now for a historic structure. The brand-new rooms are large and comfortable; eight of them have kitchenettes. There's free coffee and continental breakfast, and a courtesy van is available. With its central location and community role, you'll probably find yourself here to rent a skiff, car, or bike even if you don't get a room. Book well in advance for the busy summer season.

Tides Inn Motel. 307 N. First St. (P.O. Box 1048), Petersburg, AK 99833. ☎ **800/665-8433** or 907/772-4288. Fax 907/772-4286. 48 rms. TV TEL. $85 double. Additional person in room $10 extra. AE, DC, DISC, MC, V.

This large, dark-brown hotel is comfortable and convenient. A block above Nordic Drive, it also rents cars, has free coffee in the lobby, and rents five rooms with kitchenettes at the same price as regular rooms—an excellent choice in a town short on restaurants. A new and old building face each other, so the rooms facing the narrow courtyard get little sunlight—ask for a room in the newer building, on the water side.

Water's Edge Bed and Breakfast. 705 Sandy Beach Rd. (P.O. Box 1201), Petersburg, AK 99833. ☎ **800/TO-THE-SEA** (800/868-4373) or phone/fax 907/772-3736; website http://www.alaska.net/~bbsea. 2 rms. TV TEL. High season, $90 double. Low season, $80 double. Additional person in room $10 extra. 2-night minimum stay. No credit cards.

Guests gush about teacher Kathy Bracken's hospitality at her home on the beach a mile out of town. The rooms come with use of bicycles, a canoe, and laundry facilities, and Kathy offers free pickup at the airport or ferry terminal. Children under 12 aren't allowed, and there's no smoking in the house. Kathy offers packages with her husband, Barry, a retired fisheries biologist who leads ecology tours and fishing charters on his 28-foot boat.

CAMPING

Tent City Campground. 1800 Haugen Dr. (at the intersection with Sandy Beach Rd.; P.O. Box 329), Petersburg, AK 99833. ☎ **907/772-4224** or 907/772-9864. Fax 907/772-3759. 50 wood-platform tent sites. $5 per tent site per night. Closed Oct–Apr.

The tent city was built to give the summer's cannery workers a place to stay. It's a mass of blue plastic tarps, with tent platforms connected by a boardwalk. A central pavilion has coin-op showers, sinks, phones, cooking areas, and firewood. It's a lively little community of college students and transient workers.

DINING

You won't get a memorable meal in Petersburg, but there are adequate restaurants for your sustenance. **Pellerito's Pizza,** near the ferry dock, has good Italian food for take-out. The pizza isn't as good at **Harbor Lights Pizza,** between the middle and south harbors, but they have a nice view of the water. There are two or three other good take-out and espresso places for lunch, including a cart that's usually on the waterfront near the Harbormaster's office.

Helse. 17 Sing Lee Alley. ☎ **907/772-3444.** All meals $3–$7.75. No credit cards. Mon–Fri 7:30am–5pm, Sat 10am–3pm. COFFEE HOUSE/HEALTH FOOD.

This health-food store/restaurant serves good, hearty sandwiches for lunch in a crowded, youthful setting. Each table hangs at one end from a rope, and seating is on hard stools. Excellent coffee and the best place in town for lunch.

The Homestead. 218 Nordic Dr. ☎ **907/772-3900.** Lunch $4.25–$8.50; dinner $9.75–$23. AE, MC, V. Mon–Sat 24 hours. DINER.

Your first clue that this is where the locals go is on the streetfront: There's no sign, just a window and lots of people eating inside. The Homestead—open around the clock—is for commercial fishermen coming off the boat in the middle of the night and looking for a glorious, juicy burger or deep-fried fresh halibut and a pile of greasy fries. The front room, with the lunch counter, is smoky; for clearer air, go past the kitchen to the back dining room. Kids are well treated.

7 Sitka: Rich Prize of Russian Conquest

The history that Sitka preserves is interesting not only because of the Russian buildings that record Alaska's early white settlement, but more deeply for the story of the cultural conflict of Alaska Natives—and by extension, all aboriginal peoples—with the invaders, and their resistance and ultimate accommodation to the new ways. Here, 18th-century Russian conquerors who had successfully enslaved the Aleuts to the west met their match in battle against the rich, powerful, and sophisticated Tlingit. A visit to Sitka teaches the story of that war, and also the cultural blending that occurred in the uneasy peace that followed under the influence of the Russian Orthodox church—an influence that continued after the Russians packed up and left upon the U.S. purchase of Alaska in 1867, and continues today.

Besides its historic significance, Sitka also is fun to visit. Somehow it has retained a friendly, authentic feel, despite the crush of thousands of visitors. Perhaps because cruise-ship travelers must ride boats to shore, or because Sitka is a slightly inconvenient, out-of-the-way stop on the Alaska Marine Highway's main-line ferry routes, the city's streets haven't been choked by solid rows of seasonal gift shops, as has occurred in Ketchikan, Skagway, and a large part of Juneau. It remains picturesque, facing Sitka Sound, which is dotted with islands and populated by feeding eagles. Historic photographs bear a surprising resemblance to today's city.

Beyond the town and its history, Sitka is a gateway to a large, remote portion of Southeast Alaska, in the western coastal islands. This area contains some of Tongass National Forest's least-used outdoor opportunities. The ocean halibut and salmon fishing are excellent and not overexploited. If I could visit only one Alaska town, it would probably be Sitka.

ESSENTIALS

GETTING THERE   By Ferry   Sitka sits on the west side of Baranof Island, a detour from the Inside Passage. The big, main-line ferries on the **Alaska Marine**

Sitka

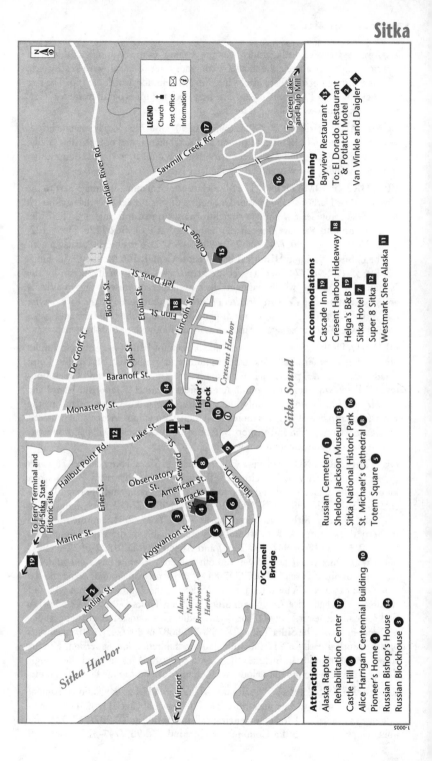

LEGEND
✝ Church
⊠ Post Office
ⓘ Information

Attractions
Alaska Raptor
Rehabilitation Center 17
Castle Hill 6
Alice Harrigan Centennial Building 10
Pioneer's Home 4
Russian Bishop's House 14
Russian Blockhouse 3
Russian Cemetery 1
Sheldon Jackson Museum 15
Sitka National Historic Park 16
St. Michael's Cathedral 5
Totem Square 5

Accommodations
Cascade Inn 19
Cresent Harbor Hideaway 18
Helga's B&B 19
Sitka Hotel 7
Super 8 Sitka 12
Westmark Shee Alaska 11

Dining
Bayview Restaurant 13
To: El Dorado Restaurant
& Potlatch Motel 2
Van Winkle and Daigler 9

169

Highway System (see listing under "Getting Around" at the beginning of this chapter) stop only twice a week; the small *LeConte* adds three connecting trips each week. The ride through narrow Peril Straits into Sitka is definitely worth the trip. The fare to either Juneau or Petersburg is $26. The ferry dock is 7 miles out of town; see "Getting Around," below, regarding transfers.

By Air   Alaska Airlines (☎ 800/426-0333 or 907/966-2266 locally; website http://www.alaskaair.com) links Sitka to Juneau and Ketchikan a total of three times daily, continuing to Seattle and Anchorage after that one stop. If you need to save time, think about flying one way and taking the ferry back.

VISITOR INFORMATION   The Alice Harrigan Centennial Building, next to the Crescent Boat Harbor at 330 Harbor Dr., houses the **visitor center,** which, although only a desk, provides refreshingly straightforward printed information. The **Sitka Convention and Visitors Bureau** can be reached at P.O. Box 1226, Dept. 122, Sitka, AK 99835 (☎ 907/747-5940; fax 907/747-3739; e-mail scvb@ptialaska.net).

The ✪ **Sitka National Historical Park Visitor Center,** 106 Metlakatla St., Sitka, AK 99835 (☎ 907/747-6281; website http://www.nps.gov/sitk/), run by the National Park Service, which maintains the most important historic sites in Sitka, is an essential stop. The ✪ *Historic Sites of Sitka* map produced by the Park Service and Sitka Historical Society is an indispensable guide to the buildings and parks around town. You can easily see Sitka's history on foot with one of these maps.

ORIENTATION   Sitka, on the west side of Baranof Island, has only a few miles of road. The **ferry terminal** is located at its north end, 7 miles out, on **Halibut Point Road;** the abandoned pulp mill is at the south end, 5 miles out **Sawmill Creek Boulevard.** The town faces Sitka Sound. Across Sitka Channel is **Japonski Island** and the **airport** (don't worry, it only looks as if your plane is going to land in the water). **Lincoln Street** contains more of the tourist attractions. A free map provided by the Sitka Convention and Visitors Bureau at the visitor center will help you navigate the initially confusing downtown streets.

GETTING AROUND   Sitka is a walker's paradise. **Sitka Tours** charges $3 to get to town from the ferry dock or airport, with buses meeting all arrivals. Bikes make a lot of sense here, too. You'll find them for rent at **S.E. Diving and Sports,** 203 Lincoln St., Sitka, AK 99835 (☎ 800/824-3483 or 907/747-3483), charging $5 an hour or $20 a day. **Sitka Cab** is available at ☎ 907/747-5001, and the ride from the ferry dock is around $15. **Rental cars** are available at the airport from **Avis** (☎ 800/331-1212 or 907/966-2404) and **Allstar** (☎ 800/722-6927 or 907/966-2552). Once you're downtown, you can walk, or the white buses and guides in red tunics of **Sitka Tours** (☎ 907/747-8443) can show you around, as they do the cruise-ship passengers. A historical tour is $25, adding the Raptor Center it's $33, and children go for half price. Or go with **Sitka Walking Tours** (☎ 907/747-5354) to find some of the lesser-known places—Jane Eidler does a great job, charging $9 for a 90-minute walk. The **Sitka Tribe** (☎ 888/270-8687 or 907/747-7290) takes tours of the historical park for $12 for adults, $6 for children; a longer version, $28 for adults, $22 for children, includes the Sheldon Jackson Museum and the Tlingit dances at the STA Community House at 200 Katlian St., next to the Pioneers' Home.

FAST FACTS   Sitka has a 5% **sales tax.** There's an **ATM** at the National Bank of Alaska, 300 Lincoln St. The **post office** is at 1207 Sawmill Creek Hwy., on the south side of town. Dial **911** for **emergencies;** call the **police** at ☎ 907/747-3245 for nonemergencies. The **Sitka Community Hospital** (☎ 907/747-3241) is at 209

Moller Dr. The *Sitka Daily Sentinel* is published weekdays. You can get a copy of *USA Today* or the *Anchorage Daily News* at the Westmark Shee Atika; the Sunday *Seattle Times* is sold at Lakeside grocery store, 705 Halibut Point Rd. **Fax** and **copying services** are available at Aurora Business Supplies, 327 Seward St. (☎ **907/747-4704**).

SPECIAL EVENTS   The **Starring Ceremony,** Jan. 7, marks Russian Orthodox Christmas with a procession through the streets and song and prayer at the doors of the faithful. The **Sitka Salmon Derby** occurs at the end of May and beginning of June, when the kings are running; contact the Convention and Visitors Bureau. The ✪ **Sitka Summer Music Festival,** P.O. Box 3333, Sitka, AK 99835 (☎ **907/747-6774**), a chamber-music series that began in 1972, is one of Alaska's most important cultural events, drawing musicians from all over the world during June. Performances and other events take place all month. Rehearsals are free. Alaska Day, October 18, commemorating the Alaska purchase, is a big deal in this former Russian and U.S. capital city; an **Alaska Day Festival** lasts 4 days leading up to the big event; the Convention and Visitors Bureau has information.

EXPLORING SITKA
SITKA'S TLINGIT & RUSSIAN HERITAGE
✪ **Sitka National Historical Park.** 106 Metlakatla St. ☎ **907/747-6281.** Free admission. Visitor center open 8am–5pm daily summer; 8am–5pm Mon–Fri winter.

In 1799, the Russian America Company, led by Alexander Baranof, landed from their base in Kodiak and established Redoubt St. Michael (today the **Old Sitka State Historic Site,** $7^1/2$ miles north of town—just a grassy picnic area with interpretive signs) and claimed the Pacific Northwest of America for Russia. The Tlingit, who were sophisticated traders and already had acquired flintlocks, attacked with knives, spears, and guns, and destroyed the redoubt in mid-June 1802, killing almost all of the Russians. Then the Natives immediately began fortifications on the site now within the national historic park, anticipating a Russian counterattack, which came in 1804. Baranof returned with an attacking force of a Russian gunship and a swarm of Aleut kayaks, which towed the becalmed vessel into position to begin the bombardment. The Tlingits withstood the siege for 6 days, then vacated their fort at night, after taking heavy losses from the shelling and from a bomb-laden canoe. The Russians founded and heavily fortified the town of New Archangel, and in 1808 it became their administrative capital. But the Tlingit name is the one that stuck: Shee Atika, since contracted to Sitka.

The historic significance of the battle site was recognized early, and President Benjamin Harrison set it aside in 1890. In 1905, a collection of totem poles from around Southeast were brought here (the originals are in storage, and replicas are on display). The historic park emphasizes, as it should, the Native perspective. In the visitor center, a display explains the history, and Alaska Native artisans from the Southeast Alaska Indian Cultural Center work in a series of windowed workshops in wood, silver, and cloth, making traditional carvings, jewelry, drums, and regalia. You can watch them work; go in and ask questions. An auditorium shows films and other programs.

I found the totem park and battle site most impressive. The totems stand tall and forbidding along a pathway through massive spruce and hemlock, where misty rain wanders down from an unseen sky somewhere above the trees. The battle site is along the trail—only a grassy area now—but among the trees and totems, with the sound of the lapping sea and raven's call, one can feel deep down what the Tlingits were fighting for. The spirits of the trees and ravens they believed in seem almost present.

And, in fact, the park and center are full of evidence of the Tlingit's living heritage. In 1996, a gathering of clans erected a major new pole in front of the center, the Indian River Tlingit History Pole, to explain their story from before the Russians' arrival, back to mankind's beginnings in North America. It took quite a bit of debate to settle the story the pole would tell. For example, the crests of the eagle and raven tribal divisions are never shown on the same pole, but they had to be to tell the whole history of the Tlingits. The obvious success of the project speaks from the beauty of the pole, a strong symbol of cultural renewal.

✪ **The Russian Bishop's House.** Lincoln and Monastery sts. No phone; call Sitka National Historical Park Visitor Center (☎ **907/747-6281;** see "Visitor Information," above). Free admission downstairs; $2 per person or $5 per family for upstairs tour. Daily 9am–1pm and 2–5pm summer; by appointment winter.

Father Ivan Veniaminov, born in 1797, translated the Bible into Tlingit and trained deacons to carry Russian Orthodoxy back to their Native villages. Unlike most of the later missionaries of other faiths, he allowed parishioners to use their own language, the key element to saving Native cultures. When the United States bought Alaska in 1867, few Russians remained, but the Russian Orthodox faith Veniaminov planted as a priest and later as Bishop Innocent remains strong in Native Alaska; there are 89 parishes, primarily in tiny Native villages. In 1977, Veniaminov was canonized as St. Innocent in the Orthodox faith.

In 1842, the Russian America Company retained Finnish shipbuilders to construct this extraordinary house for Bishop Innocent. It survived many years of neglect in part because its huge beams were fit together like a ship's. The National Park Service bought and began restoring the building in 1972, and today it makes for a fascinating visit. Downstairs is a self-guided museum; rangers take frequent tours upstairs to the bishop's quarters, which are furnished with original and period pieces. The tour concludes with a visit to a tiny chapel with many of the original icons Innocent brought from Russia.

✪ **St. Michael's Cathedral.** Lincoln and Cathedral sts. Free admission (donations requested). Mon–Sat 1:30–5:30pm, Sun for services, with longer hours in summer.

The first Orthodox cathedral in the New World stands grandly in the middle of Sitka's principal street, where it was completed in 1848 by Father Veniaminov (see above). The cathedral contains icons dating to the 17th century, including the miraculous *Sitka Madonna.* The choirmaster or another knowledgeable guide is on hand to answer questions or give talks when large groups congregate. The original building burned down in a fire that took much of Sitka's downtown in 1966, but the icons were saved, and Orthodox Christians all over the United States raised the money to rebuild it exactly as it had been, completing the task in 1976.

✪ **Sheldon Jackson Museum.** 104 College Dr. ☎ **907/747-8981.** Website http://ccl.alaska.edu/local/museum/home.html. Admission $3 for adults, free for students and children 18 and under. Mid-May to mid-Sept, daily 8am–5pm; mid-Sept to mid-May, Tues–Sat 10am–4pm.

Among the best collections of Alaska Native artifacts on display anywhere is kept here in Alaska's first concrete building, circa 1895, now a state museum run by the Alaska Department of Education on the campus of Sheldon Jackson College. Jackson, a Presbyterian missionary and major figure in Alaska history, started the collection in 1888. Although his assimilationist views today appear tragically destructive to Native cultures, Jackson also advanced Native education and economic opportunity—for example, he first imported domesticated reindeer to Alaska. This museum's small octagonal building is like a jewel box, but the overwhelming wealth is displayed in such ingenious ways that it avoids feeling cluttered. Some of the drawers in the white cabinetry open to reveal more displays. Some of the artifacts, despite their antiquity, are as fresh as if they had just been made.

OTHER ATTRACTIONS IN TOWN

The **New Archangel Dancers** (☎ **907/747-3225**) are one of the most popular attractions in the state, since most cruise-ship passengers go to the crowd-pleasing shows in the Harrigan Centennial Hall. The all-woman troupe performs male and female roles in traditional Russian dances commemorating Sitka's Russian heritage (although they're not Russian—the Russians left on the first available boat upon the sale of Alaska to the United States in 1867). Shows are geared to ship arrivals—the times are posted at the hall, or phone for information. Admission is $6. Also at the Centennial Hall is the **Isabel Miller Museum,** with exhibits on town history by the Sitka Historical Society.

The **Sitka Tribe** (☎ **888/270-8687** or 907/747-7290) sponsors performances of traditional Tlingit dance daily at the STA Community House near the Pioneers' Home. The dancers explain the dances and interact with the audience; my son was entranced. The 30-minute show is $8 for adults, $6 for children. Check at the visitor center for performance times.

Since 1980, injured eagles, hawks, owls, and other birds have been brought to the **Alaska Raptor Rehabilitation Center,** 1101 Sawmill Creek Blvd. (take the dirt road up the hill to the left after the historical park), for veterinary treatment, convalescence, and release or transfer to a zoo. The main attraction for visitors is seeing these impressive birds close up. You also get to hear a short lecture, ask questions, and learn from displays. At $10 for adults and $5 for children, the admission price is high, but think of it as a donation to the center's good works—it's a private, nonprofit organization. Year round on Sunday afternoons only, the center is open to the public for free, without guides; in the summer there are daily tours.

I highly recommend the ✪ **"Historic Sites of Sitka" walking tour,** available at either of the visitor centers; but if you just want some of the high points, don't miss these:

The brick **Pioneers' Home,** a state-run residence for retired people who helped settle Alaska, stands on a grassy park at Lincoln and Katlian, where the Russians had their barracks and parade ground. Stop to talk to one of the old-timers rocking on the porch—each has more Alaska in his or her little finger than all the tour guides you'll meet all summer. Just north on Marine Street is a replica of a **Russian Blockhouse;** across Lincoln Street to the south and up the stairs is **Castle Hill,** a site of historic significance for the ancient Tlingits, for the Russians, and for Alaskans. The American flag was first raised here in Alaska in 1867. There are historic markers and cannons. Walking east past the cathedral and Crescent Harbor, several quaint historic buildings are on the left—my favorite is **St. Peter's by-the-Sea Episcopal Church,** a lovely stone-and-timber chapel with a pipe organ, consecrated in 1899. At the east end of the harbor is a **public playground;** continue down the street to **Sheldon Jackson College** and the national historical park.

SHOPPING

There are some good shops and galleries in Sitka, mostly on Lincoln and Harbor streets. Several are across the street from St. Michael's Cathedral, on the uphill side, including **Sitka's Artist Cove Gallery** at 241 Lincoln St., and **Impressions,** right next door at 239 Lincoln St.—contemporary Alaskan prints and originals. Just down the street is a T-shirt shop with a difference: original wearable art made in Sitka—**Fairweather Prints,** at 209 Lincoln St. A couple of doors down is a good bookstore, **Old Harbor Books,** at 201 Lincoln St., a good browsing store with an excellent selection of Alaska books. **The Backdoor** espresso, behind the book store, has a relaxing art scene atmosphere for reading the newspaper or playing chess. We enjoyed an inexpensive breakfast there. The **Sitka Rose Gallery** occupies a lovely Victorian house at 419 Lincoln St., featuring sculpture, painting, and jewelry. The **Sheldon Jackson Museum Gift Shop,** 104 College Dr., has authentic Native arts and crafts from all over the state.

GETTING OUTSIDE

ON THE WATER The little islands and rocks that dot Sitka Sound are an invitation to the sea otter in all of us; you must get out on the water. Humpback whales tend to show up in large groups in the fall but are also sometimes seen in the summer. There are so many bald eagles that you're pretty well guaranteed of seeing them from shore. But the lowly sea otter is the most common and, in my experience, most amusing and endearing of marine mammals, and you'll certainly see them from a boat tour. Otters seem so friendly and happy it's hard not to anthropomorphize and envy them.

✪ **St. Lazaria Island** is a bird rookery visited by tour boats where you can expect to see puffins, murres, and rhinoceros auklets; if you stay overnight on a boat, you can be there for the return of the storm petrels, back from the sea to feed their young. As the volcanic rock drops off straight down, even big boats can come close. The public tubs at Goddard Hot Springs, 17 miles south of town, are another possible stop for charters. Many boats are available for **wildlife tours** or **saltwater fishing. Steller Wildlife & Exploring** (☎ 907/747-6157) books many of them. The Sitka Convention and Visitors Bureau also keeps a detailed list, including rates, of more than two dozen boats. Their "Sitka Through Four Seasons" booklet includes a checklist of what birds and animals you can expect to see and when.

The ✪ **Sea Otter and Wildlife Quest** operated by Allen Marine Tours (☎ 907/747-8100) does a terrific job, with well-trained naturalists to explain the wildlife you are almost certain to see—so certain to see, in fact, that they refund $40 of the $85 adult fare if you don't see an otter, whale, or bear. Children 12 and under go for $40. The 3$^{1}/_{2}$-hour cruise leaves from the Crescent Harbor dock near the Centennial Hall on Sunday, Monday, Tuesday, and Friday at 2pm during summer. You can buy tickets on board, at the Westmark Shee Atika, or from travel agents.

Barbara Bingham's 42-passenger boat is equipped with hydrophones to eavesdrop on the whales, although they often keep mum. She also takes guests for the uproarious nightly return of the storm petrels to St. Lazaria Island. Her rates—$90 for a half day, $175 for a full day, and $350 overnight—seem to be typical. Book direct through **Raven's Fire Inc.,** P.O. Box 6112, Sitka, AK 99835 (☎ 907/747-5777).

Or you could charter a guided **sailing** and wildlife trip on a wooden sailboat. Noel and Claire Johnson offer a $75 eco-sightseeing cruise on their 56-foot gaff-rigged cutter, as well as longer charters through **Southeast Alaska Ocean Adventures,** P.O. Box 6384, Sitka, AK 99835 (☎ 907/747-5011; website http://www.ptialaska.net/~jparker/saoa.htm).

Sitka's protected waters and intricate shorelines are perfect for **sea kayaking,** which is the closest thing to being a sea otter a human ever gets. Larry Edwards' **Baidarka Boats,** 201 Lincoln St., Sitka, AK 99835 (☎ 907/747-8996; e-mail 72037.

3607@compuserve.com), rents the boats and offers instruction and guided paddles for every experience level, including raw beginners. The cost of the guided trips depends on the number in your group: A half day trip is $100 for one alone, $180 for six together.

These waters tend to be clear and biologically rich, making them appealing to divers. Winter is best, when plankton isn't blooming, but good periods come in summer, too. **S.E. Diving and Sports,** 203 Lincoln St., Sitka, AK 99835 (☎ **800/ 824-3483** or 907/747-3483) is the dive shop in town.

ON & ABOVE THE SHORELINE   Humpback whales stop to feed in Sitka Sound on their way south in the winter migration. During the months of October, November, December, and March, you can watch from shore—the local government has even built a special park for the purpose. At **Whale Park,** 3½ miles south of town on Sawmill Creek Blvd., spotting scopes are mounted on platforms along a boardwalk and at the end of staircases that descend the dramatic wooded cliffs. Excellent interpretive signs, located near a surfacing concrete whale next to the parking lot, explain the whales.

Halibut Point State Recreation Area, 4.4 miles north of town on Halibut Point Road, is a great place for a picnic, ramble, and **tide pooling.** To find the best low tides, check a tide book, available all over town. To identify the little creatures you'll see, buy a plastic-covered **Mac's Field Guide** at the National Park Service visitor center at the historical park.

Fishermen should pick up the **Sitka Area Sport Fishing Guide,** which has lots of tips on places and methods in the area. You can get it from the Alaska Department of Fish and Game Division of Sport Fishing, P.O. Box 25526, Juneau, AK 99802-5526 (☎ **907/465-4180;** website http://www.state.ak.us/local/akpages/ FISH.GAME/adfghome.htm) or locally at 304 Lake St., Room 103, Sitka, AK 99835.

There are a dozen U.S. Forest Service **hiking trails** accessible from the roads around Sitka and another 20 you can get to by plane or boat. *Sitka Trails,* a handy 78-page trail guide describing them, sells for $4 at the **Sitka Ranger District,** 201 Katlian St., Suite 109, Sitka, AK 99835 (☎ **907/747-6671**). Two trailheads are walking distance from downtown. The 5½-mile **Indian River Trail** is a relaxing rain-forest walk rising gradually up the river valley to a small waterfall. Take Indian River Road off Sawmill Creek Road east of the Alaska State Troopers Academy. For a steeper mountain-climbing trail to alpine terrain and great views, the **Gavan Hill–Harbor Mountain Trail** is just past the house at 508 Baranof St., near downtown. It gains 2,500 feet over 3 miles to the peak of Gavan Hill, then continues another 3 miles along a ridge to meet Harbor Mountain Road.

At the north end of Halibut Point Road, 7½ miles from downtown, a broad boardwalk circles a grassy estuary, rich with birds and fish. The **Estuary Life Trail** and **Forest Muskeg Trail,** totaling about a mile, are beautifully developed and accessible to anyone.

U.S. FOREST SERVICE CABINS   The **Sitka Ranger District,** 201 Katlian St., Suite 109, Sitka, AK 99835 (☎ **907/747-6671**), maintains more than 20 wilderness cabins, available for $25 per night, and has a guide listing what you can find at each. (Reserve through **Biospherics,** listed in "Outside in Southeast," at the beginning of this chapter.) They're either on mountain lakes, with rowboats provided, or on the ocean, so you need either a boat or an aircraft to get to them. **Taquan Air Service** (☎ **800/770-8800;** website http://www.AlaskaOne.com/TaquanAir) can fly you out.

ACCOMMODATIONS

The **bed tax** in Sitka is 4% in addition to the 5% sales tax. Besides those hotels listed here, I can recommend the **Cascade Inn,** 2035 Halibut Point Rd., Sitka, AK 99835 (☎ **800/532-0908** or 907/747-6804), which has every amenity and waterfront balconies, but is 2.1 miles out of the downtown area. There's also the **Rockwell Lighthouse,** P.O. Box 277, Sitka, AK 99835 (☎ **907/747-3056**), which is a mock island lighthouse you can rent that was built for that purpose.

Potlatch Motel. 713 Katlian St., Sitka, AK 99835. ☎ **907/747-8611.** Fax 907/747-5810. 32 rms. TV TEL. High season, $90 double, $130–$140 suites. $8 each additional person. Low season, $60 double, $90–$100 suites. AE, MC, V.

A clean, comfortable building of reasonably priced standard motel rooms located in a business district a mile from the historic area. There's a coin-op laundry and a fish-cleaning and -freezing facility in the hotel, and free coffee in the lobby. Kitchen suites are available. The service is efficient and kid-friendly. A courtesy van will take you to the ferry dock, airport, or even downtown.

Sitka Hotel. 118 Lincoln St., Sitka, AK 99835. ☎ **907/747-3288.** Fax 907/747-8499. Website http://www.sitkahotel.com. 60 rms, 45 with bath. TV TEL. $55 double without bath, $70 double with bath. Additional person in room $7 extra. AE, MC, V.

If you choose carefully among these rooms of greatly varying size and quality, you could come up with a real bargain. Some, however, are not up to standards, none are reserved for nonsmokers, and I wouldn't recommend the 15 rooms with shared bathrooms. Common areas in the 1939 building are nicely done in heavy Victorian decor. The location is central, right among the sights, and many rooms have good views. A coin-op laundry is available.

Super 8 Sitka. 404 Sawmill Creek Blvd., Sitka, AK 99835. ☎ **907/747-8804.** 34 rms, 1 suite. TV TEL. High season, $105 double. Low season, $90 double. Additional person in room $6 extra. AE, CB, DC, DISC, MC, V.

The Super 8 is small and quiet and centrally located to walk to the sights. A coin-op laundry and a large whirlpool are in the building. The rooms also have air-conditioning—perhaps you'll be in Sitka on one of the few days each year when it's needed. Free coffee, a toast bar, and a microwave oven are in the lobby.

Westmark Shee Atika. 330 Seward St., Sitka, AK 99835-7523. ☎ **800/544-0970** (reservations) or 907/747-6241. Fax 907/747-5486. Website http://www.westmarkhotels.com. 99 rms. TV TEL. $124 mountainside double, $128 harborside double. AE, DC, DISC, MC, V.

This four-story wood structure overlooking Crescent Harbor is the community's main, upscale hotel, where events and meetings take place. In the heart of the historic district, the restaurant, lounge, and most rooms have good views. Rooms are equipped with such extras as coffeemakers and hair dryers and are very clean, if some are in need of new furniture. You can book tours and activities in the lobby. The service in the restaurant is friendly and efficient; the fine-dining menu emphasizes seafood.

BED & BREAKFASTS

The Sitka Convention and Visitors Bureau produces a chart listing the town's B&Bs, with rates and facilities. Several miles out Halibut Point Road, **Helga's B&B,** 2027 Halibut Point Rd. (P.O. Box 1885), Sitka, AK 99835 (☎ **907/745-5497**), has five large, light rooms right on the water, all with private baths and kitchenettes, for $75 a night. **The Creek's Edge Bed and Breakfast,** 109 Cascade Rd. (P.O. Box 2941), Sitka, AK 99835 (☎ **907/747-6484**), sits on a mountainside with incredible views and rooms decorated with antiques.

⊙ **Alaska Ocean View Bed and Breakfast.** 1101 Edgecumbe Dr., Sitka, AK 99835. ☎ and fax **907/747-8310.** 3 rms. TV TEL. $89 double; $129 suite. $15–$20 each additional person. AE, MC, V.

Ebullient Carol Denkinger and her husband, Bill, have a passion for making their bed-and-breakfast one you'll remember. They've thought of everything—the covered outdoor spa where you can watch the eagles, toys and games for the kids, thick robes and slippers, an open snack counter and big full breakfast, even wildflower seeds to take home. All rooms have VCRs, CD players, clocks, phones, and modem jacks. They're located on a residential street with a view of the water over a mile from the historic district. The whole place is reserved for nonsmokers.

Crescent Harbor Hideaway. 709 Lincoln St., Sitka, AK 99835. ☎ and fax **907/747-4900.** Website http://www.ptialaska.net/~bareis. 2 rms. TV. $79–$105 double. $20 each additional person. No credit cards.

This stately 1897 house, one of Sitka's oldest, stands across a quiet street from Crescent Harbor and the lovely park at the harbor's edge, with a glassed-in porch to watch the world go by. One room is a large, one-bedroom apartment with a full kitchen, the fridge stocked, and a private patio and phone line. The other nestles adorably under the eaves. Everything is clean and fresh. The operators, an artist and a skipper of eco-tours, love to tell stories of their life homesteading in Alaska's Bush. The common areas are shared with an Australian shepherd, and no smoking is permitted, even outside.

HOSTELLING & CAMPING

Hostelling International–Sitka is located at 303 Kimsham St. (P.O. Box 2645), Sitka, AK 99835 (☎ **907/747-8661**), over a mile from downtown. The 20 beds are $7 per night, no linens available. It's open June through August; office hours are 8 to 10am and 6 to 10pm.

The Forest Service **Starrigavan Campground,** at the north end of Halibut Point Road, 7^1/2 miles from town and ^{1}/2 mile from the ferry dock, is one of the loveliest in Alaska. One loop of sites branches from the Estuary Life Trail, widely separated under huge trees. The other loop is at water's edge, with some sites situated next to the ocean to make you feel like you're way out in the wilderness. The 28 sites, with pit toilets, are first-come, first-served, with an $8 fee, open May 1 through Labor Day. **RV parks** are located near the ferry dock and on Japonski Island, close to downtown.

DINING

Bayview Restaurant. 407 Lincoln St. ☎ **907/747-5440.** All meals $5.50–$18. AE, DC, DISC, MC, V. Spring–fall, Mon–Sat 6:30am–8pm, Sun 6:30am–4pm; winter, Mon–Sat 7am–7:30pm, Sun 8am–3pm. BURGERS/SANDWICHES/SEAFOOD.

Although sometimes noisy and a bit cramped, the view of the boat harbor, reasonable prices, and good, quick food make this second-story restaurant popular year round. The Russian dishes are for the tourists, but everything I've tried from the extensive menu has been well prepared and served. The clam chowder sings. Beer and wine license.

⊙ **Channel Club.** 2906 Halibut Point Rd. ☎ **907/747-9916.** Dinner $12–$37. AE, DC, MC, V. Daily 5–10pm. STEAK/SEAFOOD.

The dining room looked like a typical small-town bar and restaurant. A young guy in a baseball cap was grilling steaks against one wall, the menu was posted over the salad bar, and the service was casual to a fault. Imagine my surprise, then, to receive the best steak I've had in years and the most fascinating and delicious salads served anywhere in Alaska. In hindsight, I enjoyed having the Channel Club be a diamond in the rough. It is located several miles out Halibut Point Road, but a courtesy van will come get you. Full liquor license.

El Dorado Restaurant. 714 Katlian St. ☎ **907/747-5070.** Lunch $5–$8; dinner $9–$14. DISC, MC, V. High season, 10:30am–11pm daily; low season, 11am–10pm Tues–Sat, 11:30am–9:30pm Sun–Mon. MEXICAN.

The menu has separate lists of American/Mexican and authentic Mexican dishes. The portions are large, the prices low, and the service jolly, efficient, and pro-kid. Our Mexican dinners were excellent—subtly flavored, despite the casual, small-town, family-restaurant atmosphere. Pizza also is available. Beer and wine license.

✪ Van Winkle and Daigler. 228 Harper Dr. ☎ **907/747-3396.** Reservations recommended. Lunch $5–$9; dinner $16–$19. AE, MC, V. High season, Mon–Sat 11:30am–10pm, Sun 5–10pm; low season, Tues 11:30am–2pm, Wed–Sat 11:30am–2pm and 5pm–9pm, Sun 5pm–9pm. STEAK/SEAFOOD.

A nice balance of the casual and fine, the dining room has shelves of old books but also tablecloths. The Pacific Northwest–style cuisine concentrates on Sitka-caught seafood. Portions are huge and service quick, but the cooking is still subtle and expert. The wine list and entrees are well priced. Van Winkle and Daigler are cousins—one mans the bar, the other the kitchen. Murals out front depict them in their natural settings. Full liquor license.

8 Juneau: Forest Capital

Juneau (JUNE-oh) hustles and bustles like no other city in Alaska. The steep downtown streets echo with the mad shopping sprees of cruise-ship passengers in the summer tourist season and the whispered intrigues of the politicians during the winter legislative session. Miners, loggers, and ecotourism operators come to lobby for their share of Southeast's forest. Lunch hour arrives, and well-to-do state and federal bureaucrats burst from the office buildings to try the latest trendy restaurant or brown bag on one of the waterfront wharves, sparkling water before them and gift store malls behind. The center of town becomes an ad hoc pedestrian mall as the crush of people forces cars to creep.

My Juneau is close at hand, but very different. At a magical age as a child, I lived here with my family in a house on the side of the mountains above downtown. My Juneau is up the 99 steps that lead from the cemetery to the bottom of Pine Street—the way I walked home from school—and then to the top of residential Evergreen Avenue, where the pavement gives way to a forest trail among fiddlehead ferns and massive rain-forest spruces. That trail leads to the flume—a wooden aqueduct bringing water down from the mountains—upon which we would walk into the land of bears and salmon, the rumbling water at our feet. It's still a short walk from the rackety downtown streets to a misty forest quiet, where one can listen for the voices of trees.

Juneau is Alaska's third-largest city, with a population of almost 30,000 (Anchorage and Fairbanks are larger), but it feels like a small town that's just been stuffed with people. Splattered on the sides of Mount Juneau and Mount Roberts along Gastineau Channel, where there really isn't room for much of a town, its setting is picturesque but impractical. Further development up the mountains is hemmed in by avalanche danger; beyond is the 1,500-square-mile Juneau Icefield, an impenetrable barrier. Gold-mine tailings dumped into the Gastineau created the flat land near the water where much of the downtown area now stands. The Native village that originally stood on the waterfront is today a little pocket of mobile homes several blocks from

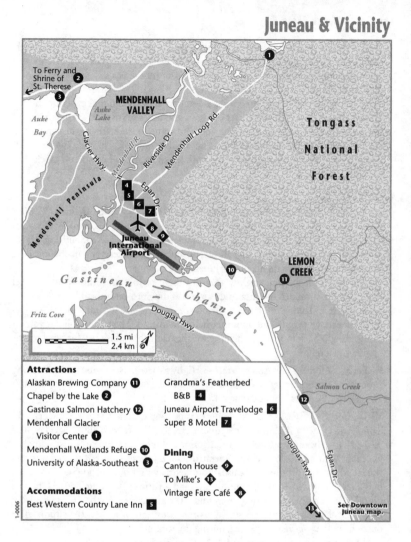

Attractions

Alaskan Brewing Company **11**
Chapel by the Lake **2**
Gastineau Salmon Hatchery **12**
Mendenhall Glacier
  Visitor Center **1**
Mendenhall Wetlands Refuge **10**
University of Alaska-Southeast **3**

Accommodations

Best Western Country Lane Inn **5**

Grandma's Featherbed
  B&B **4**
Juneau Airport Travelodge **6**
Super 8 Motel **7**

Dining

Canton House **9**
To Mike's **13**
Vintage Fare Café **8**

See Downtown
Juneau map.

1-0006

the shore. There's no road to the outside world, and the terrain forbids building one. Jets are the main way in and out, threading down through the mountains to the airport.

Gold was responsible for the location; it was found here in 1880 by Joe Juneau and Richard Harris, assisted by a Tlingit chief who told them where to look. Hardrock mining continued into the 1940s. In 1900, Congress moved the territorial capital here from Sitka, which had fallen behind in the rush of development. Alaskans have been fighting over whether or not to keep it here for many decades since, but Juneau's economy is heavily dependent on government jobs, and it has successfully fought off a number of challenges to its capital status, most recently in 1994. The closest the issue came was in the 1970s, when the voters approved moving the capital, but then balked at the cost of building a whole new city to house it—a necessity since neither Anchorage nor Fairbanks (which have their own rivalry) would support the move if it meant the other city got to have the capital nearby.

There's plenty to see in Juneau, and it's a good town to visit because the relatively sophisticated population of government workers supports good restaurants and amenities not found elsewhere in Southeast. Also, Juneau is a starting point for outdoor travel in the area, and in all of Southeast Alaska. The crush of visitors can be overwhelming when many cruise ships are in port at once, and the streets around the docks have been entirely taken over by shops and other touristy businesses. Many of these are owned by people from Outside who come to the state for the summer to sell gifts made Outside to visitors from Outside. But only a few blocks away are quiet, mountainside neighborhoods of houses with mossy roofs, and only a few blocks farther the woods and the mountains.

ESSENTIALS

GETTING THERE   By Air   Juneau is served only by **Alaska Airlines** (☎ **800/ 426-0333** or 907/789-9791 locally; website http://www.alaskaair.com), with several daily nonstop flights from Seattle and Anchorage and to the smaller Southeast Alaska towns. Most of the commuter and air-taxi operators in Southeast also maintain a desk at the airport and have flights out of Juneau.

Don't schedule anything tightly around a flight to Juneau. Although it's a travel hub, the mist-shrouded mountainside airport is tough to get into and can be a hair-raising place to land. It even has its own verb: *to overhead*. It means that when you fly to Juneau, you could end up somewhere else instead. The airline will put you on the next flight back to Juneau when the weather clears but won't pay for hotel rooms or give you a refund.

By Ferry   All main-line **Alaska Marine Highway** ferries (see listing under "Getting Around" at the beginning of this chapter) stop at the terminal in Auke Bay (☎ **907/ 465-3940**), 14 miles from downtown.

VISITOR INFORMATION   The **Davis Log Cabin Visitor Center,** 134 Third Ave. (at Seward, downtown), Juneau, AK 99801 (☎ **907/586-2201;** fax 907/ 586-6304; website http://www.juneau.com), is a replica of Juneau's first school, a log cabin with a little log belfry. Operated by the Juneau Convention and Visitors Bureau, the center distributes the usual commercial visitor information but also hands out "Free Things to See and Do in Juneau" and a **Juneau Walking Tour Map.** The center is open daily from 9am to 5pm mid-May through September, weekdays only the rest of the year. Volunteers staff a **visitor information desk** at the airport, near the door in the baggage-claim area, during the summer.

U.S. Forest Service headquarters for the 17-million-acre Tongass National Forest—encompassing the vast majority of Southeast Alaska—is in the federal building, the huge, square concrete building that dominates the skyline at Ninth Street and Glacier Avenue. The **Forest Service Visitor Information Center** is located in the Centennial Hall Convention Center, 101 Egan Dr., Juneau, AK 99801 (☎ **907/ 586-8751;** fax 907/586-7928). It maintains displays, shows films about the forest, answers questions, and distributes information about the outdoors and recreation cabins around Juneau.

Alaska Rainforest Tours, 369 S. Franklin St., Suite 200, Juneau, AK 99801 (☎ **907/463-3466;** fax 907/463-4453; e-mail artour@alaska.net), is a booking and travel-planning agency catering to travelers who want to get into the outdoors and off the beaten track. Besides crusading to save wildlife habitats, the company publishes an annual catalog of independent travel and outdoor experiences and runs the **Alaska Bed and Breakfast Association,** which books 60 B&Bs, primarily in Southeast. **Alaska Up Close,** P.O. Box 32666, Juneau, AK 99803 (☎ **907/ 789-9544;** fax 907/789-3205; website http://www.wetpage.com/upclose), is a similar independent eco-tourism catalog and booking service. Their standard itineraries, which you can customize to your own interests, are priced in a lump sum like package tours. **Last Chance Tours,** P.O. Box 22884, Juneau, AK 99802 (☎ **907/ 586-1890;** fax 907/586-9767; website http://www.alaska.net/~suparna), is a central booking agency for all kinds of local activities.

ORIENTATION   Juneau has two main parts. The city outgrew its original site downtown, and housing spread to the suburban **Mendenhall Valley,** about a dozen miles out the **Egan Expressway** or the parallel, two-lane **Glacier Highway** to the north. The glacial valley also contains the **airport, University of Alaska Southeast,** and the **Auke Bay** area. The road continues 40 miles, to a place generally called **"The End of the Road."** Across a bridge over the Gastineau Channel from downtown Juneau is the town of **Douglas,** mostly a bedroom community for Juneau. Downtown Juneau is a numbered grid of streets overlying the uneven topography like a patterned quilt over a pile of pillows. As you look at Juneau from the water, **Mount Juneau** is on the left and **Mount Roberts** on the right; Mount Roberts is a few hundred feet taller, at 3,819 feet. **Franklin Street** extends south of town 5¹/₂ miles to **Thane** and good hiking trails.

GETTING AROUND   A cab in from the airport will cost you nearly $20, but there are good alternatives. The **Island Waterways** van (☎ **907/780-4977**) meets all the planes, picks up at the major hotels, and will pick up elsewhere by arrangement, charging $8. The **Capital Transit** city bus (☎ **907/789-6901**) comes every hour at 11 minutes past the hour on weekdays only from 8:11am to 5:11pm and costs $1.25; however, your luggage has to fit under your seat or at your feet. A cab to the ferry dock costs even more than to the airport, but **Mendenhall Glacier Transport (MGT)** (☎ **907/789-5460**) meets the boats with a blue school bus, and the price of $5 from town or the airport includes the driver's commentary. Call before 8pm the night before your ferry leaves to arrange a pickup.

MGT also does a 2-hour town and Mendenhall Glacier tour for $12.50. **Capital Cab** (☎ **907/586-2772** or 907/364-3349) offers normal taxi service and does tours for $45 an hour. Also, a 90-minute mining-history tour, with gold panning, operates in the summer through **Alaska Travel Adventures** (☎ **907/789-0052**); the cost is $32 for adults and $21 for children 12 and under.

Major **car-rental companies** are based at the airport. You can get around downtown Juneau easily without a car, but if you're going to the Mendenhall Glacier or to any of the attractions out the road, renting a car for a day of your stay is a good idea. **Mountain Gears,** at 126 Front St. (☎ **907/586-4327**), rents bikes for $6 an hour or $25 a day. A full-service bike shop, they can also give you ideas for mountain biking rides.

FAST FACTS   The **sales tax** is currently 5%. There are numerous banks in Juneau with **ATMs.** The main **post office** downtown is in the federal building, 709 W. Ninth St., and in the Mendenhall Valley at 9491 Vintage Blvd., by the airport. In an **emergency,** dial ☎ **911;** for nonemergency calls to the **police,** dial ☎ **907/ 586-2780.** The **hospital (907/586-2611)** is 3 miles out the Glacier Highway. The *Juneau Empire* is published daily except Saturday; machines in the Capitol carry the *Anchorage Daily News,* and various out-of-town papers sell from boxes in the baggage area at the airport. Capital Copy, a **business center** with fax and copying services, is located at 123 S. Seward St. (☎ **907/586-9696**).

SPECIAL EVENTS   The annual **Alaska Folk Festival** (☎ **907/789-0292**) is a community-wide celebration drawing musicians, whether on the bill or not, from all over the state; it will be held April 13 to April 19 in 1998. The **Juneau Jazz and**

Classics Festival (☎ 907/364-2421), scheduled for May 15 to May 24 in 1998, includes concerts at various venues. A gathering of some 1,000 Native dancers at the Centennial Hall, scheduled for June 4 to June 6, 1998, is titled simply **Celebration** (☎ 907/463-4844). Later that month (June 26 to June 28), **Gold Rush Days** (☎ 907/463-5706) includes logging and mining events and competitions anyone can join at Riverside Park. The **52nd Annual Golden North Salmon Derby** (☎ 907/789-2399) offers cash for the biggest fish, the money raised going for scholarships (August 21 to August 23, 1998).

EXPLORING JUNEAU
DOWNTOWN

✪ **Alaska State Museum.** 395 Whittier St. ☎ **907/465-2901.** Website http://ccl.alaska.edu/local/museum/home.html. Admission $3 adults, free for students and children 18 and under. High season, Mon–Fri 9am–6pm, Sat–Sun 10am–6pm; winter, Tues–Sat 10am–4pm.

The museum contains a huge collection of Alaskan art and Alaska Native and historical artifacts, but it doesn't seem like a storehouse at all because the objects' presentation is based on their meaning, not their value. Although the museum is small, each room is full of discoveries. A clan house in the Alaska Native Gallery teaches more than the outdoor houses you see in Wrangell or Ketchikan because it contains the authentic art you'd really find there in its functional place. The ramp to the second floor wraps around the natural-history display, with an eagle screeching up in a tree, and at the top a state history gallery uses historical pieces to tell a story, not just to impress. A visit to the museum will help put the rest of what you see in Alaska in context.

The Juneau-Douglas City Museum. At the corner of Fourth and Main streets. ☎ **907/586-3572.** Admission $2 adults, free for students and children 18 and under. High season, Mon–Fri 9am–5pm, Sat–Sun 10am–5pm. Low season, Fri–Sat noon–4pm and by appointment.

This terrific little museum displays artifacts from the city's history, especially its gold-mining past, in an intelligent, meaningful way. The children's gallery lets kids play-act with real old things, like an old-fashioned desk, old clothes, and equipment. There's also a book shop where you can pick up a lot of useful information (including the historic walking-tour map and maps of the Evergreen Cemetery and the old Treadwell Mine, which I've described below). The plaza in front is where the 49-star U.S. flag was first raised in 1959—they didn't make many of those, as Hawaii was admitted as the 50th within a year.

OTHER DOWNTOWN ATTRACTIONS

At the waterfront near the cruise-ship dock, the new **Mount Roberts Tramway,** 490 South Franklin St. (**907/463-3412**), takes only 6 minutes to carry 60 passengers at a time up a 1,760-foot slope with sweeping views that used to require a day of huffing and puffing to witness. Once there, you can explore the alpine environment above tree-line on a flat nature trail and attend a performance put on by the Alaska Native owners of the tram. A restaurant serves grilled sandwiches and salads. The fare is $15.95 for adults, $9.95 for children 6 to 12.

If you need a break, the **Juneau Public Library,** atop the parking garage at the waterfront on South Franklin Street, has a big kids section and impressive views of the water and Douglas Island. Hours are Monday to Thursday 11am to 9pm and Friday to Saturday noon to 5pm.

The **Alaska State Capitol** stands on 4th Street between Main and Seward. The federal government built the nondescript brick building in 1931; it may be the least impressive state capitol in the most beautiful setting in the nation. Free tours start

Downtown Juneau

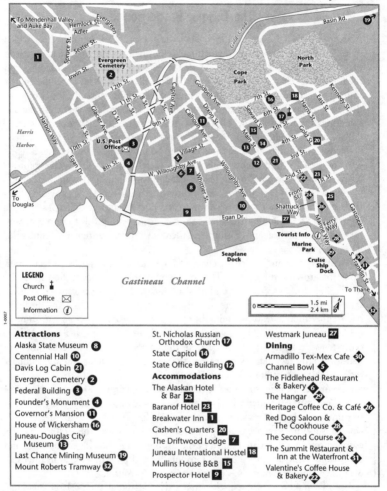

LEGEND
Church †
Post Office ✉
Information ⓘ

Gastineau Channel

0 ___ 1.5 mi / 2.4 km

Attractions
Alaska State Museum **8**
Centennial Hall **10**
Davis Log Cabin **21**
Evergreen Cemetery **2**
Federal Building **3**
Founder's Monument **4**
Governor's Mansion **11**
House of Wickersham **16**
Juneau-Douglas City Museum **13**
Last Chance Mining Museum **19**
Mount Roberts Tramway **32**

St. Nicholas Russian Orthodox Church **17**
State Capitol **14**
State Office Building **12**
Accommodations
The Alaskan Hotel & Bar **25**
Baranof Hotel **23**
Breakwater Inn **1**
Cashen's Quarters **20**
The Driftwood Lodge **7**
Juneau International Hostel **18**
Mullins House B&B **15**
Prospector Hotel **9**

Westmark Juneau **27**
Dining
Armadillo Tex-Mex Cafe **30**
Channel Bowl **5**
The Fiddlehead Restaurant & Bakery **6**
The Hangar **29**
Heritage Coffee Co. & Café **26**
Red Dog Saloon & The Cookhouse **28**
The Second Course **24**
The Summit Restaurant & Inn at the Waterfront **31**
Valentine's Coffee House & Bakery **22**

every half hour, 9am to 4:30pm during the summer; other times, pick up a self-guided tour brochure in the lobby. The legislature is in session January to mid-May. Across Fourth is the **courthouse,** with a statue of a bear in front. This bear defines Alaskan taste in art: It replaced an abstract steel sculpture called *Nimbus* that was removed by an act of the legislature, finally coming to rest in front of the state museum. The **state office building,** on the other corner, has a large atrium with great views and a 1928 movie theater pipe organ that's played on Fridays at noon. Off the lobby, the **state library** contains a history collection of newspapers and photographs, open Monday to Friday 1pm to 5pm. For a shortcut avoiding the steps over the hill to the state museum, take the elevator in the state office building.

At Fifth and Gold streets, the tiny **St. Nicholas Orthodox Church** is worth a visit. The octagonal chapel was built in 1893 by local Tlingits. Under pressure from the government to convert to Christianity, they chose the only faith that allowed them to keep their language. Father Ivan Veniaminov (see "Exploring Sitka" in section 7 of this chapter) had translated the Bible into Tlingit 50 years earlier when

The Tongass Battleground

A friend described this scene: a forest of tall, straight spruce and hemlock trees, widely spaced, the sunlight streaming down through the branches into a green, mossy glade. He stood on the soft forest floor beside the owner of the land, breathing deeply the fragrant air that seemed to cling to the trees all around him. He couldn't help smiling at such beauty, and he noticed his host was smiling broadly, too. But when the landowner opened his mouth to speak, my friend realized that this man saw something entirely different. His joy was that these trees, worth several thousand dollars apiece, would soon be logged to provide him with an ample retirement.

That scene occurred in the Prince William Sound area, but the conflict it represents is Alaska's fundamental political and social conflict—between exploiting resources and preserving them. The vast majority of Southeast is in the Tongass National Forest, a land used to many different ends—including providing for a timber harvest. Of course, cutting down trees isn't compatible with looking at them, appreciating the wildlife that relies on them, or harvesting fish from the streams they protect from heat and erosion. And there are jobs and retirement incomes tied up in those uses, too.

The heavy rain and temperate climate of Southeast Alaska create perfect conditions for growing huge trees. The main commercial species in Southeast are western hemlock, western red, and Alaska yellow cedar, and Sitka spruce, Alaska's state tree. It's a rain forest. There are tree trunks up to 10 feet across. And the forest has another unique feature—millions of acres that have never been cut, some of the last major tracts of old-growth forest in the United States. Once logged, those ecosystems are gone virtually forever, for the succession of forest development to maturity in this region takes longer than the span of a human life, and much longer than the duration of human patience.

The timber industry sustained itself for many years under 50-year contracts the federal government signed with U.S. and Japanese companies after World War II to stimulate economic growth in Japan and Alaska. They were guaranteed lots of wood at subsidized prices. Cutting was accelerated further in the 1980s by Native corporations that liquidated much of their timber assets quickly for business and tax reasons. Mills to turn the trees into lumber and pulp developed in towns all over the region, and more logs went overseas in the round.

With 17 million acres of sparsely populated land—Tongass is the largest national forest—you might think there would be enough for everyone. But in recent years,

the Russians were still in Sitka. The church still has an active Tlingit parish. Lengthy services are sung in English, Tlingit, and Slavic on Saturday evening at 6pm and on Sunday morning at 10am. A guide is on hand the rest of the week during the day to answer questions, and excellent written guides are available, too. Donations are accepted.

Holy Trinity Episcopal Church, 1 block down at Fourth and Gold, has a cozy turn-of-the-century sanctuary with a steeply pitched tin roof and interesting stained glass; it's unlocked all day. A little-known piece of church history: As an undersized acolyte at age 8, I almost smashed the stained glass in the back of the church when I lost control of the heavy crucifix and had to run down the aisle to keep up with it.

The Last Chance Mining Museum, 1001 Basin Rd. (☎ 907/586-5338), occupies old mining buildings in the valley behind Juneau along Gold Creek. The

the Forest Service concluded that the cut rates of the past were unsustainable: The trees here grow large, but they grow slow. Despite the immense area, trees were being cut faster than they could grow back. Moreover, wildlife such as bears and wolves need big blocks of intact ecosystem, not little fragments of habitat left behind by clear-cuts. And the high-value timber that the loggers want grows in river valleys and other areas that are valuable to animals and people, not the mountaintops that make up much of the National Forest.

The decisions to slow down were made in Washington, D.C. In 1990, Congress set aside more land for conservation. The U.S. Forest Service, under President Clinton, offered less wood in timber sales. Then, when the big Sitka pulp mill shut down, the federal government canceled the 50-year contract that went with it. Locals realized the timber jobs that were going weren't coming back. From 1989 to 1997, timber employment in the region dropped from 3,500 to around 2,100.

With 1994's national elections and the Republican takeover of Congress, loggers pinned their hope on Alaska's all-Republican, three-member congressional delegation. They took the chairs of the resource committees in both the House and Senate, placing them in charge of these issues for the whole country. All three are adamantly pro-development. But when the Congressmen tried to use their new muscle, it didn't bring more timber jobs to Southeast. The rest of the country had other priorities. The issue of timber supply became a sticking point in the budget stalemate between Congress and the President that shut down the government at the end of 1995. Alaska Senator Ted Stevens used the opportunity to demand more trees for Southeast Alaska's mills. Instead, Clinton agreed to a $110 million payment to help communities transition to an economy not so dependent on large-scale logging.

In 1996, Louisiana Pacific threatened that it would close its Ketchikan pulp mill unless it received a contract extension from the Forest Service to guarantee timber well into the next century. Neither the Clinton administration nor Congress would accept the deal, and the mill closed in 1997 as promised, eliminating 330 jobs.

Today, despite their powerful voice in Congress, it appears that pro-development Alaskans have lost the battle for the Tongass. Logging is unlikely ever to return at the same level as in the past. But it is doubtful that the last word has been heard. People have fought over the wealth of the forest in wars and councils since long before white explorers showed up on the scene. They probably always will.

Perseverance trailhead is nearby, as well as some of the old shafts, which are still intact. From downtown, take Gold Street to the top, then turn left, continuing up the valley to the end of Basin Road. Admission is $3, open mid-May through September 9:30am to 12:30pm and 3:30 to 6:30pm daily.

If you have time, wander the steep, mossy neighborhoods of Juneau. One good route leads from the Capitol along Fourth to Calhoun and past the white, neoclassical **Governor's Mansion,** built in 1912, then on to Gold Creek, where you can turn right to peaceful **Cope Park,** which has tennis courts. Or continue across the creek until you reach the **Evergreen Cemetery** on your left. It's an interesting place to read grave markers, especially if you have the guide from the city museum. Turning right instead of entering the cemetery, you come to the bottom of the steps that lead to the bottom of Pine Street—to get from there to the flume walk I described in the Juneau introduction, climb the stairs then turn right on Evergreen Avenue, continuing to the end. The flume connects with the Perseverance Trail, described below.

BEYOND WALKING DISTANCE & THE VALLEY

✪ **The Gastineau Salmon Hatchery,** at 2697 Channel Dr. (3 miles from downtown, turn left at the first group of buildings on Egan Drive; ☎ **907/463-4810;** website http://www.alaska.net/~dipac), was ingeniously designed to allow visitors to watch from outdoor decks the whole process of harvesting eggs and fertilizing them with milt for hatching. From mid-June to October, salmon swim up a 450-foot fish ladder, visible through a window, into a sorting mechanism, then are "unzipped" by workers who remove the eggs. Inside, large saltwater aquariums show off the area's indigenous marine life as it looks in the natural environment. In May and June, before the fish are running, the tour includes the incubation area, where the fish eggs develop in racks of trays. Without a doubt, it's the state's best hatchery tour. The tour takes 45 minutes, including time to look around on your own, and costs $2.75 for adults, $1 for children 12 and under. Regular tours operate May 15 to October 15 only, Monday through Friday from 10am to 6pm and on Saturday and Sunday from noon to 5pm; call ahead the rest of the year.

Beer lovers and aspiring capitalists will enjoy the tour of the **Alaskan Brewery and Bottling Company,** at 5429 Shaune Dr. (☎ **907/780-5866**). To get there, turn right from Egan Drive on Vanderbilt Hill Road, which becomes Glacier Highway, then right on Anka Street and right again on Shaune Drive. The brewery, now too big to be called "micro" anymore, started in 1986 when 40 friends bet $5,000 each on Geoff and Marcy Larson's idea of bringing a local gold rush–era brew back to life. It worked, and now Alaskan Amber is everywhere in Alaska and in much of the Northwest, and the brewery has won more medals at the Great American Beer Festival than any other craft brewery. The informative, free tour includes tasting of the Amber, Pale Ale, and Alaskan Frontier beers. Tours are every half hour from 11am to 5pm, Tuesday through Saturday, May to September; Thursday through Saturday the rest of the year.

At the head of Mendenhall Valley is the **Mendenhall Glacier,** the easiest glacier in Alaska to get to and one of the most visited. The Forest Service maintains a newly remodeled **visitor center** (☎ **907/586-8800**) with exhibits on glaciers, rangers who can answer questions, and a video about the glacier and the Juneau Icefield; it's open from 8:30am to 5pm, daily in summer, Saturday and Sunday from October to May. The glacier is on the opposite side of a lake from the visitor center and parking lot. A wheelchair-accessible trail leads down to the lake, or there's a covered viewing area right by the lot. In late summer, you can watch red and silver salmon spawning in **Steep Creek,** just short of the visitor center on the road.

There are several trails at the glacier, ranging from a half-mile nature trail loop to two fairly steep, 3¹/₂-mile hikes approaching each side of the glacier. At the visitor center and a booth near the parking lot, the Forest Service distributes a brochure, "Mendenhall Glacier: Carver of a Landscape," which includes a trail map. The ✪ **East Glacier Loop Trail** is a beautiful day hike leading to a waterfall near the glacier's face and parts of an abandoned rail tram and an abandoned dam on Nugget Creek; the trail has steep parts but is okay for school-age children. The **West Glacier Trail** is more challenging, leaving from 300 yards beyond the skater's cabin and campground off Montana Creek Road and following the edge of the lake and glacier, providing access to the ice itself for experienced climbers with the right equipment.

Another way to see the glacier is by raft or canoe. The Native-owned **Auk Ta Shaa Discovery,** 76 Egan Dr. (☎ **800/820-2628**), leads 3-hour raft rides down the Mendenhall River for $89 per person and 4-hour paddles in a traditional Tlingit canoe in Mendenhall Lake, in front of the glacier, for $95. Both trips emphasize Native legends associated with the scenery and wildlife.

OUT THE ROAD

On sunny summer weekends, Juneau families get in the car and drive out the road, or the Glacier Highway, as it's officially known. The views of island-stippled water from the paved two-lane highway are worth the trip, but there also are several good places to stop—besides those mentioned here, there are others for you to discover.

The **Auke Village Recreation Area** is a mile beyond the ferry dock (which is 14 miles from downtown Juneau) and is a good place for picnics and beach walks. Less than a mile farther is Forest Service campground.

The **Shrine of St. Therese,** 9 miles beyond the ferry dock, stands on a tiny island reached by a foot trail causeway. The wonderfully simple chapel of rounded stones, circled by markers of the stations of the cross, stands peaceful and mysterious amid trees, rock, water, and the cries of the raven, seeming truly of another world. The Juneau Catholic Diocese maintains a log retreat hall on the shore facing the island; be quiet when descending the gravel driveway from the highway. This is a good vantage from which to look around in the **Lynn Canal** for marine mammals or, at low tide, to go tide pooling among the rocks.

Eagle Beach, 5 miles beyond the shrine, makes a good picnic area in good weather, when you can walk among the tall beach grass or out on the sandy tidal flats and look for eagles, or go north along the beach to look for fossils in the rock outcroppings. The road turns to gravel, then comes to **Point Bridget State Park,** at mile 38 (measured from Juneau)—the trail there is discussed under "Getting Outside," below. Two miles farther, the road comes to an end, 40 miles from Juneau at pretty **Echo Cove.**

SHOPPING

Juneau, like Ketchikan and Skagway, has developed a shopping district catering primarily to the cruise ships. When the last of the 549 port calls are over late in the summer, many of the shops close their doors. If you're looking for authentic Alaskan art and crafts, be warned that counterfeiting has become widespread. For buying tips, read the "Native Art—Finding the Real Thing" section in chapter 3.

For serious galleries, check out **Portfolio Arts,** 210 Ferry Way, Suite 101, a classic gallery of Native and contemporary Alaskan art, and the **Gallery of the North,** upstairs at 406 S. Franklin St., a huge space with a mixture of artists and quality levels, and even antiquities. Rie Munñoz paints in Juneau, and her prints are represented in various galleries, including her own **Rie Munñoz Gallery,** at 2101 N. Jordan Ave. Her simple, graphic watercolors represent coastal Alaska and Native peoples in a cheerful light.

For gifts, try **Annie Kaill's** fine art and craft gallery, 244 Front St. It's a little out of the cruise-ship shopping area and gets most of its business from locals. It has a rich, full, homey feeling, with local work at various price levels. The long-established **Ad Lib,** at 231 S. Franklin St., also is reliable and oriented to real Alaskan items. **Galligaskins,** 207 and 219 S. Franklin St., features clothing with Alaska-theme designs. **Taku Smokeries,** 230 S. Franklin St., creates smoked salmon delicacies for shipment anywhere. **Hearthside** is a good little bookstore at the corner of Franklin and Front streets. The pleasingly dusty **Observatory,** at 235 Second Ave.

(☎ 907/586-9676), sells rare books, maps, and prints about Alaska. They're open Monday to Saturday noon to 5pm.

Right on the waterfront, the Native-owned **Alaska Native Artists Market** is open in summer daily from 8:30am to 8:30pm. Artists represent themselves and sometimes give demonstrations, although what you find any particular day is inconsistent.

GETTING OUTSIDE

You can rent all the equipment you'll need for outings somewhere in Juneau. Mountain Gears, listed above under "Getting Around," has mountain bikes and offers guidance on where to ride. **Gearing Up,** 369 S. Franklin, Juneau, AK 99801 (☎ 907/586-2549), rents gear by appointment, including all kinds of camping supplies, rubber boots, and rain gear.

ON LAND

BIRD WATCHING   The drive out the four-lane Egan Drive to the Mendenhall Valley crosses tidal flat bird habitat; there's a viewing platform as you near the airport. The **Juneau Audubon Society** leads Saturday birding trips during the spring migration. Tickets are $25 for adults, $5 for children; check at the visitor center for up-to-date information on when and where the walks are planned, or visit the group's website at **http://www.juneau.com/audubon**.

DIVING   The **Channel Dive Center,** 8365 Old Dairy Rd., Juneau, AK 99801 (☎ 907/790-4665; fax 907/790-4668), offers instruction, rentals, and guiding for dry-suit diving. In the fall through spring, you can dive among sea lions.

HIKING   A **trail guide** available from the Forest Service visitor center for $4 describes 29 different hiking routes in the Juneau area. **In the Miner's Footsteps,** a guide to the history behind 14 Juneau trails, is available for $3 from the Juneau-Douglas City Museum. The Juneau city **Department of Parks and Recreation** (☎ 907/586-5226) leads hikes in summer and cross-country skiing in winter on Wednesdays for adults and on Saturdays for all ages. I've also mentioned two good hikes above, under Mendenhall Glacier.

The ✪ **Perseverance Trail** climbs up the valley behind Juneau and into the mining history of the area it accesses. It can be quite crowded in summer. To reach the trailhead, go to the top of Gold Street and turn left. Follow gravel Basin Road about a mile to the end. The trail is 3 miles of easy walking on the mountainside above Gold Creek to the Perseverance Mine, at the Silverbow Basin, which operated intermittently from 1885 to 1921. Be sure to pick up the $1 historic guide to the trail at the Juneau-Douglas City Museum. Another hike right from downtown climbs **Mount Roberts**—just follow the stairway from the top of Sixth Street, a neighborhood called Star Hill. The summit is 4¹/₂ miles and 3,819 vertical feet away, but you don't have to go all the way to the top for incredible views and alpine terrain. At the 1,760-foot level, you come to the restaurant at the top of the Mount Roberts tram, mentioned above.

The **Treadwell Mine Historic Trail,** on Douglas Island, is a fascinating hour's stroll through the ruins of a massive hard rock mine complex that once employed and housed 2,000 men. Since its abandonment in 1922, big trees have grown up through the foundations, intertwining their roots with rails and machinery and adding to the site's exceptional power over the imagination. The well-written guide from the Juneau-Douglas City Museum is indispensable. This is a great hike for kids. To find the trailhead, drive over the bridge to Douglas, turn left, then continue, staying as close to the water as possible, until you reach Sandy Beach Park. Keep going the same way on foot, looking for the tall stamp mill.

Another great family outing is to the **Outer Point Trail,** a mile loop on a forest boardwalk to a beach with good tide pooling. Drive over the bridge to Douglas, then left on North Douglas Highway 11¹/₂ miles to the trailhead. Looking across the water from the beach to Auke Bay, you can sometimes see whales.

Out the road (see above) at mile 38 on the Glacier Highway, **Point Bridget State Park** is less used but easy and beautiful, and from the beach toward the end of the trail, you may see sea lions and possibly humpback whales. The flat 3¹/₂-mile trail leads through forest, meadow, marsh, and marine ecosystems. It's good for cross-country skiing, too. Pick up the free trail-guide brochure from the Forest Service visitor center in Centennial Hall.

U.S. FOREST SERVICE CABINS   Four U.S. Forest Service cabins are accessible from Juneau's road system by trails ranging from 3.3 to 5.5 miles. The **Dan Moller** cabin is located on Douglas Island right across from town. All the cabins are popular and must be reserved well in advance. Three more remote cabins require a boat or plane. Two are on **Turner Lake** in alpine terrain off Taku Inlet, each with a skiff and spectacular scenery. Get information on cabins from the Forest Service visitor center in Centennial Hall, then call **Biospherics** (☎ **800/280-2267**), listed under "Outside in Southeast," at the beginning of this chapter, to reserve up to 180 days before your visit.

ALPINE SKIING   The city-owned **Eaglecrest Ski Area** (☎ **907/586-5284**) may not be Vail, but it was good enough to train Olympic silver medalist Hillary Lindh, Juneau's favorite daughter. If the winter is snowy, the slopes on Douglas Island, 12 miles from downtown on North Douglas Highway, are the locals' favorite place. An all-day lift ticket is $25 for adults; an adult equipment package rents for $20 a day. The views are incredible.

OUT ON THE WATER

SEA KAYAKING   The protected waters around Juneau welcome sea kayaking, and the city is a popular hub for trips on the water farther afield. The area's most established eco-tourism operator is ✪ **Alaska Discovery,** 5449 Shaune Dr., Suite 4, Juneau, AK 99801 (☎ **800/586-1911** or 907/780-6226; fax 907/780-4220; website http://www.gorp.com/akdisc.htm), with trips all over Southeast and beyond. Part of the company's ethic and reason for being is to build support for protecting Southeast's wild places. A multiday trip is your chance to really know the Alaska wilderness, and there's no better way to do it than in a kayak in Southeast Alaska. Alaska Discovery has lots of trips, or they'll design one for your group. The least expensive expedition is a 2-day, 3-night trip to see whales and eagles on the far side of Douglas Island, which costs $495 per person. Other trips range up to 12 days and go some truly incredible places. If you don't have that kind of time, a 5-hour wildlife-watching **sea kayak** paddle starting from Juneau is $95 per person. If you're very short of time, **Alaska Travel Adventures** (☎ **907/789-0052**) does a 3¹/₂-hour trip, with 90 minutes on the water, for $69 per person with larger groups, mostly off the cruise ships.

Several businesses rent kayaks, including **Kayak King,** 101 Dock St., Douglas (P.O. Box 21061), Juneau, AK 99801 (☎ **907/586-8220**), and **Adventure Sports,** across from the Nugget Mall (☎ **907/789-5696**). A double rents for about $50 a day, a single for $40. Peter Wright, whose business is called **Kayak Express** (P.O. Box 210562, Auke Bay, AK 99821; ☎ **907/790-4591**), specializes in outfitting trips for experienced paddlers, setting up basecamps and drop-off.

FISHING & WHALE WATCHING   The closest I ever saw a humpback whale—within a few yards—was on the way back from king salmon fishing out of Juneau on a friend's boat. More than two dozen charter companies offer fishing from Juneau and Auke Bay; you can go to **watch whales** or fish, or both. Juneau is well protected behind layers of islands, so the water generally is very calm. The Juneau Convention and Visitors Bureau maintains a list of businesses with details on their services and prices. **Juneau Sportfishing and Sightseeing,** 2 Marine Way, Suite 230 (P.O. Box 20438), Juneau, AK 99802 (☎ **907/586-1887;** fax 907/586-9769; website http://www.alaska.net/~suparna), is one of the largest operators, with 40 six-passenger boats. They charge $195 per person for a full day of fishing, $115.50 for 4 hours, or $99 for a 3-hour whale-watching trip. Or you can drive your own boat, chartering a 32- to 110-foot vessel for fishing or cruising from **ABC Alaska Yacht Charters,** 4478 Columbia Blvd., Juneau, AK 99801 (☎ **800/780-1239** or 907/780-1239; fax 907/789-1237; website http://www.abcyacht.com). They charge $275 to $600 per day for the unskippered boat.

   Adventures Afloat, 4950 Steelhead, Juneau, AK 99801 (☎ **800/323-5628** or 907/789-0111) operates a 106-foot converted 1944 Army patrol boat with seven cabins for extended eco-tours and salmon fishing trips—they call it a lodge afloat. A 3-day, 3-night trip is $1,195 per person.

   Juneau isn't known particularly for its stream fishing, but there are a few places on the roads where you can put in a line. The **Northern Southeast Alaska and Yakutat Sport Fishing Guide,** published by the Alaska Department of Fish and Game Division of Sport Fish, 1255 W. 8th Ave (P.O. Box 3-2000) Juneau, AK 99801 (☎ **907/465-4180;** website http://www.state.ak.us/local/akpages/FISH.GAME/adfghome.htm), contains all the information you'll need. For a remote fly-in experience, contact **Alaska Fly'N'Fish Charters,** 9604 Kelly Ct., Juneau, AK 99801 (☎ **907/790-2120**). A 4-hour trip is $250 per person.

SAILING   Although Inside Passage wind can be fluky, the deck of a **sailboat** can be a great vantage point for seeing the area. **58° 22'–North Sailing Charters,** P.O. Box 32391, Juneau, AK 99803 (☎ and fax **907/789-7301;** e-mail ncharter@alaska.net), charters two 36-foot Catalinas, the only bareboat sailing charters available in Southeast.

✪ **A DAY TRIP TO TRACY ARM**   The Tracy Arm fjord, in the Tracy Arm–Fords Terror Wilderness, south of Juneau, is a popular day cruise from Juneau as a relatively inexpensive substitute for a trip to Glacier Bay. The scenery is spectacular: Sawyer Glacier and South Sawyer Glacier, at the head of the fjord, calve ice into the water, and whales and other wildlife may show up along the way, all just as it is at Glacier Bay. John Muir even visited. But unlike Glacier Bay, you can do it as a day from Juneau. Native-owned **Auk Nu Tours,** 76 Egan Dr., Juneau, AK 99801 (☎ **800/820-2628** or 907/586-8687), offers a day-long trip each morning in the summer, leaving at 9am for $99 per person. A naturalist provides commentary. Light meals and the use of binoculars are included in the price. Other large boats compete, and you can shop around. A small charter boat may cost more but gives you more control, the ability to get close to animals, and linger to watch the seals and falling ice in front of the glaciers. Many of the smaller boats book through agencies such as **Alaska Rainforest Tours** (☎ **907/463-3466**) or **Juneau Sportfishing and Sightseeing** (☎ **907/586-1887**), both listed above.

IN THE AIR

The glaciers around Juneau are rivers of ice flowing off a frozen ocean behind the mountains, the Juneau Icefield. You can fly over it in a fixed-wing plane, or land on it in a helicopter and touch the ice. Two companies offer helicopter trips: **Era Helicopters** (☎ **800/843-1947** or 907/586-2030; e-mail fltsg@era-aviation.com) and **Temsco Helicopters** (☎ **907/789-9501**). Expect to pay around $150 for an hour tour that includes 20 minutes on the glacier. Always wait for decent weather for a flightseeing trip.

The 3-hour, $169 **Taku Glacier Lodge tour,** P.O. Box 33597, Juneau, AK 99803 (☎ and fax **907/586-8258**), or **Wings of Alaska** (☎ **907/789-0790;** e-mail wings@alaska.net) includes a 50-minute float plane flightseeing experience and a salmon cookout at a 1923 wilderness lodge with a great view of a glacier. Most visitors see black bears.

ACCOMMODATIONS

Juneau's **room tax** is 12%. Hotel rooms are tight in the summer, so book ahead. The convention and visitors bureau can give you a complete list of accommodations.

EXPENSIVE

Baranof Hotel. 127 N. Franklin St., Juneau, AK 99801. ☎ **800/544-0970** or 907/586-2660. Fax 907/586-8315. Website http://www.westmarkhotels.com. 193 rms. TV TEL. High season, $152 double. Low season, $129 double. AE, DC, DISC, MC, V.

In winter, the venerable old Baranof acts like a branch of the state capitol building for conferring legislators and lobbyists; in the summer, it's like a branch of the package-tour companies. The nine-story, 1939 concrete building has the feel of a grand hotel, although some rooms are on the small side. The upper-floor rooms are modern and have great views on the water side. Phones have voice mail and modem jacks. There are many room configurations, so make sure you get what you want. Kitchenettes are available. It belongs to the Westmark chain.

The opulent, art deco **Gold Room** restaurant is Juneau's most traditional fine-dining establishment, but the food did not rise to the level of the prices when I last ate there. The hotel cafe is popular and serves good basic meals.

✪ **Grandma's Feather Bed.** 2348 Mendenhall Loop Rd., Juneau, AK 99801. ☎ **907/789-5566.** Fax 907/789-2818. TV TEL. 14 rms. $151 double. Rates include breakfast. AE, CB, DC, DISC, ER, MC, V.

Incongruously set on a busy highway near the airport, this is a ground-up re-creation of a luxurious New England country inn. Rooms have all imaginable amenities, including Jacuzzis and old-fashioned undressing screens; it's simply a building full of honeymoon suites, each an open invitation to lovemaking. Choose your room, however, as the luxurious effect is lost in the smaller rooms. There's a small restaurant in the lobby, where breakfast is served for guests and dinners are served to the public Tuesday through Saturday. There's a 24-hour courtesy car; no children, no smoking allowed.

Westmark Juneau. 51 W. Egan Dr. (P.O. Box 20929), Juneau, AK 99802. ☎ **800/544-0970** or 907/586-6900. Fax 907/463-3567. Website http://www.westmarkhotels.com. 106 rms. TV TEL. High season, $139–$159 double. Low season, $134 double. Additional person in room $15 extra. AE, DC, DISC, MC, V.

A modern hotel with large, nicely appointed rooms favored by business travelers. The rooms on the front have good views of the Gastineau Channel but cost $10 more. The atmosphere in the rooms is quiet and almost hermetic. A Mediterranean-theme restaurant, Confetti, is off the lobby. By objective measures, it's the best of the downtown hotels.

MODERATE

Breakwater Inn. 1711 Glacier Ave., Juneau, AK 99802. ☎ **800/544-2250** or 907/586-6303. Fax 907/463-4820. E-mail breakwtr@ptialaska.net. 40 rms. TV TEL. High season, $99–$109 double. Low season, $89 double. Additional person in room $10 extra. AE, DC, DISC, MC, V.

This two-story building near the small-boat harbor, long walking distance to the central downtown area, has newly remodeled standard motel rooms. The water side rooms, which cost $10 more, have balconies but also significant highway noise. On the mountain side, all 20 rooms have kitchenettes with microwave ovens. Two rooms have two double beds and a set of bunk beds and a dining table. Everything was exceptionally clean and fresh when I visited—it looked like a good bargain. There's a nautical-theme restaurant on the second floor.

Prospector Hotel. 375 Whittier St., Juneau, AK 99801-1781. ☎ **800/331-2711** or 907/586-3737. Fax 907/586-1204. 58 rms. TV TEL. High season, $100 double; $125–$135 double with kitchenette. Low season, $80–$85 double. AE, DC, DISC, MC, V.

A comfortable hotel right on the waterfront with large, standard rooms in attractive pastel colors. More than two dozen rooms have kitchenettes, and some of the more expensive ones equate to a nice furnished apartment. Those facing the channel have good views. The lower level, called first floor, is half-basement and somewhat dark. A parking garage takes care of the chronic shortage of downtown parking.

The restaurant, T.K. Maguire's, features an extensive dinner menu ranging in price from $11 to $22, with lots of fresh fish and a special prime rib. Lunch is sandwiches, salads, and fish in the $7 to $16 range.

INEXPENSIVE

The Driftwood Lodge. 435 Willoughby Ave., Juneau, AK 99801. ☎ **800/544-2239** or 907/586-2280. Fax 907/586-1034. 55 rms, 8 suites. TV TEL. High season, $78 double; $95 suite. Low season, $62 double; $87 suite. Additional person in room $7 extra. AE, DC, DISC, MC, V.

This three-story motel right downtown is popular with families, and houses legislators and aides in the winter in its apartmentlike kitchenette suites. Some rooms are out of date, and many have cinderblock walls, but others recently have been remodeled and all I saw were remarkably clean. For the price of an ordinary hotel room elsewhere, you can get a huge suite with a full kitchen here. A round-the-clock courtesy car saves guests money getting to the airport, and there's a coin-op laundry and coffee in the rooms.

Inn at the Waterfront. 455 S. Franklin, Juneau, AK 99801. ☎ **907/586-2050.** Fax 907/586-2999. 16 rms, 5 suites, 19 with bath. TEL. $86 double, $60–$72 with shared bath; $110 suite. $9 each additional person. AE, CB, DC, DISC, MC, V.

This charming little inn across from the cruise-ship dock feels like a small European hotel, with its narrow stair, oddly shaped rooms, and understated elegance. The proprietors make the most of the building's gold-rush history as a semilegal brothel, but the place is better than the typical Victorian kitsch. The Summit, one of Juneau's most sophisticated restaurants, is downstairs (and described below).

BED & BREAKFASTS

Bed-and-breakfast really is the way to go in Juneau. You'll get a better room and have more fun for less money.

There far are too many outstanding, inexpensive B&Bs to enumerate here, so I'll just list my favorites—among them these two, both with reasonable prices and convenient downtown locations: **The Mullins House,** 526 Seward St., Juneau, AK 99801 (☎ **907/586-3384**), is a wonderfully traditional homestay B&B in a historic house a block from the Capitol, with many thoughtful details. **Cashen's Quarters,** 315 Gold St., Juneau, AK 99801 (☎ **907/586-9863;** fax 907/ 586-9861; website http://www.wetpage.com/cq), has five self-contained units, all with kitchens, private entrances, private baths, televisions, phones with recorders, and many other extras. The **Alaska Bed and Breakfast Association,** 369 S. Franklin St., Suite 200, Juneau, AK 99801 (☎ **907/463-3466;** fax 907/463-4453; e-mail artour@alaska.net), books many others. You can get more names from the visitors center.

Below I've listed three of the best B&Bs I've ever seen, all of which are well out of the downtown area:

✪ **Blueberry Lodge.** 9436 N. Douglas Hwy., Juneau, AK 99801. ☎ and fax **907/463-5886.** Website http://www.wetpage.com/bluberry. 5 rms, none with bath. High season, $75–$85 double. Low season, $75 double. Rates include full breakfast. Additional person in room $10 extra. MC, V.

Staying here is like visiting a first-class wilderness lodge, except you're only 6 miles from downtown Juneau. Jay and Judy Urquhart built the spectacular log building themselves in the woods of Douglas Island, looking out on an eagle's nest and the Gastineau Channel's Mendenhall Wetlands Refuge—they keep a spotting scope in the living room and will lend you binoculars and rubber boots for an exploration by the water. The breakfast is deluxe, the rooms large, contemporary, and very clean, and the atmosphere social, with two children and two dogs resident. Its a great choice for families. You'll need to rent a car for the 10-minute drive to town.

✪ **Glacier Trail Bed & Breakfast.** 1081 Arctic Circle, Juneau, AK 99801. ☎ **907/ 789-5646.** Fax 907/789-5697. Website http://www.wetpage.com/glacier. 3 rms. TV, TEL. High season, $95–$110 double. Low season, $85–$100 double. $10 each additional person. MC, V.

You wake up to an expansive view of the Mendenhall Glacier filling a picture window in a big, quiet room decorated with infinite taste. Luke and Connie Nelson built the house with this moment in mind. Before beginning construction, they researched B&Bs all over the country, getting ideas for the soundproof rooms, microwaves, coffeemakers, and fridge in each room, and for the Jacuzzi bathtubs, free bicycles, and many other extras. They're fascinating, literate people with varied interests and life-long Alaska outdoors experience who enjoy the relationships they develop with guests. A family apartment downstairs is a perfect choice for families.

✪ **Pearson's Pond Luxury Inn and Garden Spa.** 4541 Sawa Circle, Juneau, AK 99801. ☎ **907/789-3772.** Fax 907/789-6722. Website http://www.juneau.com/pearsons.pond. 3 rms. TV TEL. High season, $139–$179 double. Low season, $79–$109 double. Additional person in room $20 extra. AE, CB, DC, MC, V.

Here's a mental game you can play: Imagine you're a slightly obsessed bed-and-breakfast host and you decide to give your guests every amenity you can possibly think of. Now go to Diane Pearson's house and count how many you missed. A private telephone line in each room? Kid's stuff—Pearson installed two lines per room so guests can make phone calls and connect to the Internet at the same time. Did you think of a private duck pond with a dock, a rowboat, and a fountain? How about stocking the pond with fish? How about VCRs, stereos, bicycles, massage, yoga, kitchenettes, a Jacuzzi, car rental, a business center, e-mail accounts, free laundry, coffee, and breakfast? There's more. To finish the game, you'll have to check in, but book far ahead. It's located in the Mendenhall Valley, 15 minutes from downtown.

A Hostel

Juneau International Hostel. 614 Harris St., Juneau, AK 99801. ☎ **907/586-9559.** 46 beds. $10 per person. Reservations essential. June–Sept.

This exceptional hostel is conveniently located in a historic white house among the downtown sights. The office is open from 7 to 9am and 5 to 11pm in the summer, 8 to 9am and 5 to 10:30pm in the winter. Kitchen and laundry facilities are available.

Camping

Forest Service campgrounds are located at Mendenhall Glacier, overlooking the lake and glacier, and at the Auke Village Recreation Area, 1.7 miles north of the ferry dock on the ocean. Both are self-registered, $8 per night.

DINING

In addition to the restaurants listed here, the **Channel Bowl,** across from the Fiddlehead, listed below, is a classic greasy spoon frequented by locals in search of a perfect breakfast. You can pick up a picnic at the deli at the **Rainbow Food** health-food grocery at the corner of Seward and Second streets. **Hot Bite,** a stand at the Auke Bay boat harbor, is a local secret, serving charcoal-broiled burgers and mind-blowing milkshakes. **Valentine's Coffee House and Bakery,** 111 Seward St., serves delicious, inexpensive soups, salads, pizza, and calzone, as well as microbrews, in an authentic, old-fashioned store front. They're open for three meals a day in summer. **Heritage Coffee Co. and Café,** 147 S. Franklin St., also serves light meals and is a good people-watching place. Near the cruise-ship dock, **The Cookhouse,** 200 Admiral Way, specializes in massive hamburgers and other big helpings, catering mainly to tourists in a pleasant dining room. In that same vein, Alaska Travel Adventures has offered its **Gold Creek Salmon Bake** for almost 30 years. It's touristy, yes, but fun, with marshmallow roasting, music, and other entertainment. The cost is $22 for adults, $15 for children. Call ☎ **907/789-0052** to arrange pickup by van.

Expensive

The Fiddlehead Restaurant and Bakery. 429 W. Willoughby Ave. ☎ **907/586-3150.** Reservations recommended for the Fireweed Room. Main courses $8.25–$22; lunch $7–$15. 15% gratuity added for parties of 6 or more. AE, MC, V. Daily 6:30am–10pm. SEAFOOD/ECLECTIC.

In 1978, the Fiddlehead was the first restaurant of its quality in the region, offering thoughtfully prepared, garden-influenced seafood in a setting of casual fine dining. It published a successful cookbook in 1991. The cuisine, tending to natural ingredients, vegetarian dishes, and occasional experimentation, is sometimes inspired and sometimes less than perfect. The upstairs Fireweed Room, open from 5 to 9pm, Thursday through Saturday, offers a more expensive and formal experience with huge picture windows and live music. Downstairs is quite reasonably priced with a cafe atmosphere amid wood and stained glass. Full liquor license.

The Hanger. 2 Marine Way. ☎ **907-586-5018.** Reservations recommended. Dinner $13–$27. AE, DISC, MC, V. 6:30am–1am, opening at 11:30am winter. STEAK/SEAFOOD.

Situated in a converted airplane hanger on a wooden pier, this bar and grill has great views and a jolly atmosphere. It can be smoky, and the food is a bit pricey for the quality, but it's a great place to drink beer, with live music, pool, and darts on a mezzanine, and 28 brews on tap.

✪ **The Summit Restaurant.** 455 S. Franklin St. ☎ **907/586-2050.** Reservations recommended. Main courses $15–$28. AE, CB, DC, DISC, MC, V. Daily 5–11pm. STEAK/SEAFOOD.

An intimate dining room with only nine tables looks over the cruise-ship dock from big windows, making the wonderfully formal service seem only the more opulent. If you're lucky enough to get one of the nine tables, you'll find the seafood and vegetables from the constantly changing, sometimes creative menu perfectly prepared. The best place in town for a romantic meal. Upstairs is the Inn at the Waterfront, listed above.

MODERATE

✪ **Douglas Cafe.** 916 Third St., Douglas (turn left after crossing the bridge from Juneau, then continue till you see the cafe on the left). ☎ **907/364-3307.** Lunch $6–$8.25. Dinner $11.25–$16.25. MC, V. Tues–Wed 11am–8pm, Thurs–Fri 11am–9pm, Sat 9am–9pm, Sun 9am–2pm. Closed Monday. ECLECTIC.

A lively, bright, casual place that surprises you with terrific and sometimes sophisticated food—dishes like marinated prawns wrapped in prosciutto and grilled. It seems like a great place for a fun weekend breakfast, and it is, but the reasonably priced dinners are among the best in town. The dining room is small and not very comfortable, but service is quick. Alaskan Amber and other craft brews are on tap.

The Second Course. 213 Front St. ☎ **907/463-5533.** Complete dinner $18–$24; buffet-style lunch $10. MC, V. Wed–Sat noon–2pm and 5–9pm. Closed for dinner in winter, except by special arrangement. ECLECTIC ASIAN.

Heidi Grimes does "New Asian Cuisine" that draws on Cantonese, Thai, Vietnamese, and other Far Eastern styles to create something completely new and different with fresh local seafood. Originally from Hong Kong, she ended up owning a restaurant because her cooking school didn't work out, but still changes the menu with constant experimentation. The storefront dining room, with white tablecloths and plastic garden furniture, is a bit odd but perfectly comfortable. Lunch is served from a buffet. No liquor license.

INEXPENSIVE

✪ **Armadillo Tex-Mex Cafe.** 431 S. Franklin St. ☎ **907/586-1880.** Lunch/dinner $6–$16. MC, V. Daily 11am–10pm. TEX-MEX.

You order lunch at a counter and choose drinks from a cooler, but this casual, infectiously cheerful place is where Alaska's best Southwestern food comes from. Locals, who swear by it, know the restaurant merely as "Tex-Mex." Chicken is a specialty, and the homemade salsa is famous, served free with a basket of chips for each diner. The tiny dining room is located near the docks. They serve wine and beer, and at this writing were planning to brew their own.

JUNEAU IN THE EVENING

The Sealaska Cultural Arts Center presents the ✪ **Naa Kahidi Theater** (☎ **907/463-4844**) in a mock clan house next to the cruise-ship dock, just south of the library and parking garage. The professionally produced story-telling and dance performances are entertaining for a wide age range and present Tlingit, Haida, and Tsimshian artifacts as they were meant to be seen. Hour-long shows are presented as frequently as four times a day during the June-to-September season; tickets are $16 for adults, $10 for children at the box office. Juneau's **Perseverance Theatre** is Alaska's largest professional theater, performing five main offerings for Juneau audiences over the winter season and occasionally touring. At this writing, they were talking about a summer show—if one materializes, it likely will be worth seeing. For information, contact the theater's office at 914 Third St., Douglas, AK 99824 (☎ **907/364-2421**). You can catch a movie at the **20th Century** (☎ **907/586-4055**), a classic old theater downtown.

A political scandal or two have put a damper on some of the infamous legislative partying that once occurred in Juneau, far away from home districts, but there still are good places to go out drinking and dancing. The **Red Dog Saloon,** at 278 S. Franklin St., is the town's most famous bar, with a sawdust-strewn floor and slightly contrived but nonetheless infectious frontier atmosphere. It's a fun place, with walls covered with lots of Alaskan memorabilia. The nightly live music doesn't entail a cover charge. **The Hanger,** listed above under "Dining," is the place for beer drinkers, with 28 brews on tap. They have a big-screen TV and live music in the evening, as well as pool and darts.

A SIDE TRIP FROM JUNEAU: ADMIRALTY ISLAND

The land mass facing the entrance to the Gastineau Channel is Admiralty Island, the vast majority of which is the protected Kootznoowoo Wilderness. Kootznoowoo, Tlingit for "fortress of bears," is said to have the highest concentration of bears on earth. Despite the town of Angoon on the western side of the island, there are more bears than people on Admiralty. The **Pack Creek Bear Viewing Area** is the most famous and sure-fire place to see bears in Southeast. The area has been managed for bear viewing since the 1930s, when hunting was outlawed. There's a platform for watching the bears up close as they feed on salmon spawning in the creek in July and August. They generally pay no attention to the people.

Only 25 miles from Juneau, **Pack Creek** is so popular that permits are allocated in a lottery for a maximum of 24 people to go during the day (from 9pm to 9am, no humans are allowed). Book early. The easiest way to go is with a tour operator who has permits. The Forest Service visitor center at the Centennial Hall can give you a list of guides, and the booking services in "Visitor Information," above, can book trips. **Alaska Discovery** (☎ **800/586-1911** or 907/780-6226; fax 907/780-4220; website http://www.gorp.com/akdisc.htm) has the most permits for canoe trips or day trips (see "Out on the Water" under "Getting Outside," above). **Alaska Fly 'N' Fish Charters,** 9604 Kelly Ct., Juneau, AK 99801 (☎ **907/790-2120**), also has permits for its 5½-hour fly-in visits, which cost $285 per person. Twelve permits per day go to the commercial operators and 12 to regular people; 8 of those 12 can be booked in advance with the Forest Service, and the other 4 are held out to be distributed 3 days before they're good, at 9am at the Forest Service visitor center at the Centennial Hall.

Admiralty Island is one of the largest virgin blocks of old-growth forest in the country, at over 900,000 acres, so there are lots of places to see bears. Protected Seymour Canal, on the east side of the island, is popular for canoeing and kayaking, and has two other sites besides Pack where bears often show up: Swan Cove and Windfall Harbor. See the "Getting Outside" section, above, on getting outfitted and out there. There are 15 Forest Service cabins on Admiralty, and the well-reputed **Thayer Lake Lodge** (P.O. Box 211614, Auke Bay, AK 99821, ☎ **907/789-5646**) is located on a wilderness inholding near Angoon. For information on the island, cabins, and an excellent $4 map, contact the Forest Service visitor center at Centennial Hall in Juneau, listed above, or **Admiralty Island National Monument,** 8461 Old Dairy Rd., Juneau, AK 99801 (☎ **907/586-8790**).

9 Glacier Bay National Park: Ice, Whales & Wilderness

Glacier Bay is a work in progress; the boat ride to its head is a chance to see creation fresh. The bay John Muir discovered in a canoe in 1879 didn't exist a century earlier. Eighteenth-century explorers had found instead a wall of ice a mile thick where the entrance to the branching, 65-mile-long fjord now opens to the sea. Receding faster than any other glacier on earth, the ice melted into the ocean and opened a spectacular and still-unfinished land. The land itself is rising 1¹/₂ inches a year as it rebounds from the weight of now-melted glaciers. As your vessel retraces Muir's path—and then probes northward in deep water where ice stood in his day—the story of this new world unravels in reverse. The trees on the shore get smaller, then disappear, then all vegetation disappears, and finally, at the head of the bay, the ice stands at the water's edge surrounded by barren rock, rounded and scored by the passage of the ice and not yet marked by the waterfalls cascading down out of the clouds above. It's often windy and cold at the head of the bay, near the glaciers. Precipitation and cold add up to glaciers. Be prepared, and try to enjoy the beauty of the mist and rain—at times the smooth, silver water, barren rock, white clouds, and ice create an ethereal study in white.

Glacier Bay, first set aside by President Calvin Coolidge in 1925, is managed by the National Park Service, which has the difficult job of protecting the wilderness while showing it to the public. This is a challenge, since this rugged land the size of Connecticut can be seen only by boat or plane, and the presence of too many boats threatens the park (plus, the whales appear to be sensitive to the noise of vessels). Since the 1970s, when in one year only a single whale returned, the park service has used a permit system to severely limit the number of ships that can enter the bay. With Alaska tourism booming, the state's powerful congressional delegation pushed for more cruise-ship permits for the bay. The Park Service agreed to an increase to take effect in 1997, and was sued by the National Parks and Conservation Association. Already, any tour boat sees several other ships on a day's journey up the bay, but how much it bothers the whales really can't be proved. As for the visitors, they seem happy: In 1996, *Consumer Reports* readers voted this the best of all the national parks to visit.

If you go, you'll either be on one of those vessels or in an aircraft. There really is no cheap way to visit Glacier Bay, but there are other places to see Alaska's glaciers that are easier and less expensive to visit. If you're in Juneau, consider a day trip to Tracy Arm instead. In Southcentral Alaska, plan a day-trip from Whittier to see the glaciers in College Fjord. The uniqueness of the glaciers of Glacier Bay lies in their size and geological activity, in their number, and in the opportunity to see them fairly close up in a remote setting. On a Glacier Bay boat ride, you'll also see wildlife— sea lions and eagles almost certainly, and possibly humpback whales. But there are other places in Southeast rich with marine wildlife, so don't feel compelled to go.

ESSENTIALS

GETTING THERE   Gustavus, described in the next section, is the gateway to Glacier Bay. Unless you're on a cruise ship, you'll fly or take a passenger ferry to Gustavus then a van to the park headquarters. The vans meet the planes and boats and cost $10 to make the 10-mile trip to the park.

The ✪ *Spirit of Adventure* tour boat is the main way for independent travelers to see the park. It is operated by park concessionaire **Glacier Bay Tours and Cruises,** 520 Pike St., Suite 1400, Seattle, WA 98101 (☎ **800/451-5952** or 206/623-2417;

fax 206/623-7809; website http://www.glacierbaytours.com), or locally, in the summer only, P.O. Box 199, Gustavus, AK 99826 (☎ **907/697-2226;** fax 907/697-2408). The fast, quiet tour boat carries up to 250 passengers in upper and lower lounges in a comfortable, table-oriented seating configuration. Bring heavy rain gear, as the windows can fog up and you'll want to spend as much time as possible outside. There's a snack bar, and a simple lunch is provided. Bring binoculars or rent them on board for $2; they're a necessity. The boat leaves Bartlett Cove at 7am for a 9-hour cruise, for $153.50. Glacier Bay Tours offers a same-day trip from Juneau, Haines, or Skagway on board **Haines Air** (☎ **907/789-2336**), but it makes for a long day—you have to board the plane at 5:30am in Juneau—and the schedule leaves no time in Glacier Bay for anything but the boat trip. The package fare from Juneau is $329.50. A better choice is to spend the night before the boat trip in Gustavus or at the lodge. The overnight lodge package is $342.50 to $411.50.

If your budget allows, there may be no better way to see Glacier Bay than on a small cruise ship on an excursion of a couple of days or more. Glacier Bay Tours and Cruises' *Wilderness Explorer* and the larger *Wilderness Adventurer* get you out into the park in a pampered outdoor experience. Leaving Juneau on trips of varying lengths, passengers hike, kayak, or boat in the bay during the day and sleep and eat in comfort on board at night. The trips range in length from 2 to 6 days and in price from $549 to $2,300.

Smaller operators based in Gustavus also do these trips. If you have a large group, you can have a boat and guide to yourself. Mike Nigro, a former backcountry ranger and 25-year resident, takes groups of four to six for $1,400 to $1,650 per day on a 42-foot yacht. **Gustavus Marine Charters** is reached at P.O. Box 81, Gustavus, AK 99826 (☎ **907/697-2233;** fax 907/697-2414).

VISITOR INFORMATION   The park service's address is **Glacier Bay National Park and Preserve,** Gustavus, AK 99826 (☎ **907/687-2230;** website http://www.nps.gov/glba/). But the concessionaire, **Glacier Bay Tours,** listed above under "Getting There," operates most of the activities in the park. The park service interprets the park mainly by placing well-prepared rangers on board all cruise and tour vessels entering the bay. The park also maintains a modest visitor center with displays on the park on the second floor of the concessionaire's lodge at Bartlett Cove. The park's offices, a free campground, a backcountry office, a few short hiking trails, a dock, and other park facilities also surround the lodge in a wooded setting.

ACTIVITIES AT THE PARK

AT BARTLETT COVE   There are two short **hiking trails,** right at the Bartlett Cove compound, for an afternoon walk. A free trail guide is available at the visitor center. A ranger leads a daily nature walk, and there are displays upstairs in the lodge. In the evening, the park service does a slide show.

OUT IN THE PARK   The great majority of people see the park on cruise ships or on one of the tour boats described above. A ✪ **sea kayak** is the outdoor way. I can only imagine what it's like to see humpback whales from a kayak. Most kayakers go to see the glaciers up the protected eastern fjords after being carried part of the way by the *Spirit of Adventure,* or stay in the Beardslee Islands, near the Bartlett Cove lodge, where there are no glaciers. The *Spirit of Adventure* beaches at several prearranged spots to put kayakers and hikers ashore. Make sure you calibrate the length of your trip to your outdoors experience—this is remote territory, and you can't just leave once you're out there. Also, everyone going into the backcountry is required to check in with the backcountry office by the lodge for orientation. **Glacier Bay Sea**

Glacier Bay National Park

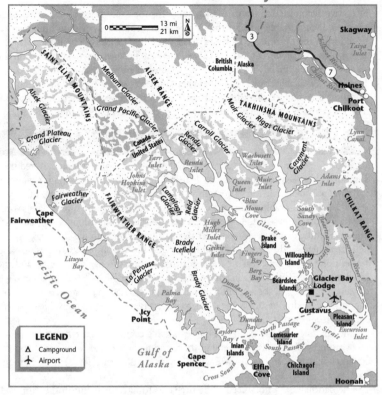

Kayaks, P.O. Box 26, Gustavus, AK 99826 (☎ **907/697-2257;** fax 907/697-3002; website http://www.he.net/~kayakak/), is the park service concessionaire, operating May 1 to September 30. They offer instruction and rentals for $50 a day, and drop-offs up the bay are $174.50 round-trip.

For guided kayak trips, **Alaska Discovery,** 5449 Shaune Dr., Suite 4, Juneau, AK 99801 (☎ **907/780-6226;** fax 907/780-4220; website http://www.gorp.com/akdisc.htm), offers trips ranging from 6 hours to 7 days. A 6-hour guided paddle around Bartlett Cove and the Beardslees is $119; a 7-day tour, $1,890.

The other way to get into the park is by **flightseeing. Frontier Air,** P.O. Box 1, Gustavus, AK 99826 (☎ **907/697-2386**), offers flights from the Bartlett Cove visitor center. Other companies offer tours from various towns, Haines being the closest, served by **L.A.B. Flying Service** (☎ **800/426-0543** or 907/766-2222). You'll see the incredible rivers of ice that flow down into the bay, and may even see wildlife. What you give up is a lingering, up-close look and the awesome sense of having all that ice and rock above you.

ACCOMMODATIONS & DINING

Glacier Bay Lodge. Bartlett Cove (P.O. Box 199), Gustavus, AK 99826. ☎ **800/451-5952** or 907/697-2226. Fax 206/623-7809 or 907/697-2408. 56 rms. TEL. $156 double. Additional person in room $9 extra. Hostel bunks $28 per person. MC, V. Closed Sept 22–May 4.

Operated by park concessionaire Glacier Bay Tours and Cruises, this is the only place to stay in the park, although Gustavus, 10 miles down the road, has some of the most attractive accommodations in Alaska, some for the same price or less. The lodge rooms are comfortable but, for the price, nothing special. They're in buildings accessed from the main lodge by boardwalks. Laundry facilities are available. The restaurant has a great view of Bartlett Cove. There are inexpensive main courses on the dinner menu, but mainly it's a fine-dining establishment with dishes in the $20 range. Breakfast is available as early as 5:45am and dinner as late as 10pm. There is no bar. For those on a budget, there are bunk rooms with six beds each for men and women. The lodge also provides showers for the free park service campground.

10 Gustavus: Country Inns & Quiet

The unincorporated town of Gustavus (gus-TAVE-us) remains an undiscovered treasure for visitors—or at least it succeeds in making itself feel that way. It's wonderfully remote, accessible for visitors only by air or a small passenger ferry, but has a selection of comfortable and even luxurious inns and lodges, and several days' worth of outdoor activities—including excellent salmon and halibut fishing, nearly sure-fire whale watching, close access to Glacier Bay National Park with the sea kayaking and activities there, and places for casual hiking and bicycle outings. Cruise ships and ferries don't come here, leaving the roads free of their throngs of shoppers and the development they bring. Miraculously, the 300 townspeople have been smart enough to value what they've got and build on it. Even the gas station is a work of art. Walking, biking, or driving down the quiet roads, everyone in a passing vehicle—every single person—waves to you.

The buildings, mostly clapboard houses and log cabins, are scattered widely across an oceanfront alluvial plain. Several of the founding homesteads were farms, and the broad clearings of sandy soil wave with hay and wildflowers. The setting is unique in Alaska.

The bad news: Visitors need to be prepared to have their fun in the rain, well bundled up. Also, the remoteness and lack of tourist development means that Gustavus is expensive. Rooms aren't cheap and neither are meals. There's only one freestanding restaurant, and it can be inconsistently open, but you can buy a meal at the lodges and inns, for a price. And the most memorable activities in the outdoors all involve charters or rentals.

ESSENTIALS

GETTING THERE   By Boat   The **Auk Nu** passenger ferry (☎ 800/820-2686 or 907/586-8687) leaves Juneau's Auke Bay harbor from 11789 Glacier Highway at 11am daily May through September. The fare is $45 one way, $85 round trip. The Auk Nu lands at the Gustavus dock at 1:15pm, goes on an afternoon whale-watching cruise, then leaves for Juneau at 5:45pm, arriving at 8pm.

By Air   Various commuter carriers serve Gustavus from the nearby towns, including **L.A.B. Flying Service** (☎ 800/426-0543 or 907/766-2222). Five daily flights from Juneau are $60 one-way.

VISITOR INFORMATION   There are no public buildings in Gustavus because there is no government: Only the informal community association and the state government hold sway. **Puffin Bed and Breakfast,** P.O. Box 3, Gustavus, AK 99826 (☎ **907/697-2260,** or 800/478-2258 in Alaska only; e-mail 73654.550@compuserve.com), has a booking agency. Generally, you'll rely on your host at the inn or B&B for information. Be certain you reserve a place to stay before showing up in Gustavus.

ORIENTATION   There are just a few roads. The main one starts at the airport and runs about 10 miles to **Bartlett Cove,** the Glacier Bay National Park base of operations. **Dock Road** branches off to the left, at the gas station, and leads to the ocean dock. Most businesses will give you a good free map, which shows everything in town, for exploring by bicycle.

GETTING AROUND   Many inns and B&Bs have courtesy vans and free bicycles. **TLC Taxi** (☎ **907/697-2239**) also will carry you and your kayak.

FAST FACTS   Gustavus isn't formally a town; it has no bank and few other businesses. Bring cash and anything you may need.

EXPLORING GUSTAVUS

Everything to do in Gustavus involves the outdoors. ✪ **Whale-watching** trips aboard the *Auk Nu* leave the town dock for Point Adolphus every day at 2pm. Icy Strait, where the vessel cruises, is the most reliable place in the state to see humpbacks in summer. They come here because a swirl of currents makes it a rich feeding ground. The fare for the 3-hour cruise is $78, and you get your money back if you don't see whales. Other, smaller operators will provide a more intimate experience on smaller boats. They'll also combine the trip with superb halibut and salmon fishing. Your inn host can make the arrangements. A boat typically charters for $200 or more per person for a full day. **Alaska Seair Adventures,** P.O. Box 299, Gustavus, AK 99826 (☎ **907/697-2215**), is a family offering their Grumman Widgeon flying boat, a 73-foot yacht, and a comfortable lodge for guided packages starting at about $2,900 for 5 days.

   Alaska Discovery, 5449 Shaune Dr., Suite 4, Juneau, AK 99801 (☎ **907/ 780-6226;** fax 907/780-4220; website http://www.gorp.com/akdisc.htm), offers a 3-day, 2-night kayaking expedition among the whales for $600 per person. They take a boat to a base camp, then kayak among the whales from there. Gustavus-based **Spirit Walker Expeditions,** P.O. Box 240, Gustavus, AK 99826 (☎ **800/ KAY-AKER** or 907/697-2266; fax 907/697-2701; website http://www.he.net/ ~kayak) leads guided 1- to 7-day trips to the whale-watching grounds and beyond. The 1-day trip is $115; 7 days, $1,850. **Sea Otter Kayak,** P.O. Box 228, Gustavus, AK 99826 (☎ **907/697-3007**) rents kayaks on Dock Road.

   ✪ **Hiking and bicycling** in Gustavus are delightful. There are few cars because they have to be hauled here on a barge, but most inns provide bikes. The roads are fun to explore, and the sandy beaches, accessed from the town dock, are a great place for a walk and a picnic. It's 14 miles from Good River Road along the shore around Point Gustavus to the Bartlett Cove national park center, 7 miles from the town dock along the beach to the airport.

ACCOMMODATIONS & DINING

There are a surprising number of good places to stay in Gustavus. I can also recommend the motel-style **Growley Bear Inn,** Dock Road (P.O. Box 246), Gustavus, AK 99826 (☎ **907/697-2730**), and **Good River Bed and Breakfast,** Good River Rd. (P.O. Box 37), Gustavus, AK 99826. (☎ and fax **907/697-2241;** website http:// thor.he.net/~river), a cozy but rustic homestay B&B back in the woods next to a creek. A new luxury inn, **Glacier Bay's Bear Track Inn,** 255 Rink Rd. (☎ and fax **907/697-3017**), was opening as this went to press.

   There isn't much of a choice for food. There's a small store, and there's a restaurant on Dock Road that isn't always open. The full-service restaurant at the Glacier Bay Lodge (see "Accommodations & Dining" in section 9, earlier in this chapter) is open all summer, and the inns that serve meals to their guests will sometimes make room for you if you call ahead.

Annie Mae Lodge. 2 Grandpa's Farm Rd. (P.O. Box 80), Gustavus, AK 99826. ☎ **907/ 697-2346.** Fax 907/697-2211. E-mail mnimaka@sprynet.com. 11 rms, 9 with bath. $80 double without bath or meals; $215 double with bath and all meals; $90 per additional person in room. AE, DC, MC, V.

The lodge of big logs, with porches that wrap around, is secluded down a dirt side road overlooking a field of wildflowers through which runs a little creek. The cozy decor is country-style, with family pictures and memorabilia on the walls and a friendly dog. The set menu emphasizes seafood. They have a courtesy car and free bicycles, but no liquor license.

Glacier Bay Country Inn. Tong Rd. (P.O. Box 5), Gustavus, AK 99826. ☎ **907/697-2288.** Fax 907/697-2289. Website http://www.glacierbayalaska.com. 6 rms, 3 cabins. $260 double. $276 cabin. Rates include all meals. Additional adult in room $75 extra; additional child under 12 $54 extra. Closed Oct–Apr.

Set on a 160-acre former agricultural homestead well back in the woods, this inn is renowned for its food and service. The quaint and quirky lodge building has lots of places to sit and watch the passing wildlife. Ponch and Sandi Marchbanks also operate Grand Pacific Charters, with three boats for fishing and whale watching, and **Whalesong Lodge** (P.O. Box 389, Gustavus, AK 99826; ☎ **907/ 697-2741**), which has a three-bedroom apartment and B&B accommodations, as well as a lodge package with meals at the Glacier Bay. Non-inn guests are welcome for dinner, too, if there's room, but must call ahead. A van to the airport, laundry, free bicycles, and car rentals are available. There is no smoking inside and no liquor license.

✪ **Gustavus Inn at Glacier Bay.** Gustavus Rd. (P.O. Box 60), Gustavus, AK 99826 (in winter, 7920 Outlook, Prairie Village, KS 66208). ☎ **800/649-5220** or 907/697-2254. Fax 907/697-2255 in summer, 913/649-5220 in winter. 9 rms, 2 suites. $270 double. Additional person in room $135 extra; children under 12 half price. AE, MC, V. Closed Sept 16– May 15.

This is the original and still the best of the Gustavus inns—although that's a fine point, as several of them are extraordinarily good. Occupying an old homestead farmhouse at the center of the community, the inn offers lovely rooms in a pastoral setting with overflowing hospitality and superb, plentiful food. The Lesh family, running the inn since 1965, has published a cookbook, and people come just to eat. The inn is unique in having a bar with beer and wine for guests. Fishing, touring, and kayaking packages are available, as is a courtesy car, free bikes, and laundry service.

A Puffin's Bed and Breakfast. Rink Creek Rd. (P.O. Box 3), Gustavus, AK 99826. ☎ **907/ 697-2260.** Fax 907/697-2258. E-mail 73654.550@compuserve.com. 3 cabins, 1 house. $85 cabin for two, $125 house for two. Additional adult in room $20 extra; additional child (up to 12 years old) in room $10 extra. MC, V.

The cabins are set among the trees, connected by paths to a central building where breakfast is served in a big room with a cathedral ceiling. The two-bedroom house with a complete kitchen and laundry facilities is a good choice for families; it does not include breakfast. The proprietors also run a full-service travel agency, offering a multitude of packages for visiting Gustavus and Glacier Bay, and have a shop selling gifts, ice cream, and Mexican food. A courtesy car, free bikes, and a coin-op laundry are available.

11   Haines: Eagles & the Unexpected

For years we always just passed through Haines on the way from the ferry up the highway. I didn't know what I was missing until I stopped and took a couple of days to really investigate. Now Haines is one of my favorite Alaska towns.

Haines is casual, happy, and slightly odd. It waits for one to find it, but once found, has wonderful charms. The mythical town of Cicely from television's "Northern Exposure" is closer to Haines than anyplace else I can think of. As I walked down a sidewalk, I saw a sign in a storefront that said to look in the big tree across the street. I looked, and there was an eagle peering back at me. At the Native cultural center, seeking an office or a ticket window or someone in charge, I wandered into a totem pole studio where a carver was completing a major commission. He gladly stopped to talk. It turned out there wasn't anyone in charge.

The Chilkat Dancers have performed here for almost 40 years, and their efforts are among the most respected and authentic in carrying on the Tlingit cultural heritage. But their membership is undefined, and their performances, while impressive, are also funny and slightly strange. Whites dance beside Natives, and rehearsals are never held; the new generation learns by being thrown into the performances, sometimes before the age of 5. Issues that are a big deal in some other towns just aren't in Haines.

Haines's chief feature, Fort William Seward, gives the town a pastoral atmosphere. The fort is a collection of grand, white clapboard buildings arranged around a 9-acre parade ground, in the middle of which stands a Tlingit clan house—out of place, yes, but wonderfully symbolic of Haines. The town is a friendly, accessible center of Tlingit culture as well as a retired outpost of seemingly pointless military activity.

And Haines has bald eagles—always plenty of bald eagles, and in the fall, a ridiculous number of bald eagles. More, in fact, than anywhere else on earth. The chance to see the birds draws people into the outdoors here. There are well-established guides for any activity you might want to pursue, all cooperating and located together. And the weather is not as rainy as elsewhere in Southeast.

ESSENTIALS

GETTING THERE & DEPARTING   By Water   The **Alaska Marine Highway System** (☎ **907/766-2111** locally, see "Getting Around" at the beginning of this chapter for a full listing) is how most people get to Haines, and the cruise on the Lynn Canal fjord from Juneau or Skagway is among the most beautiful in the Inside Passage. (The fare is $20 to Juneau and $14 to Skagway.) But there's a drawback—since this is the northern highway connection where nearly all vehicles get off or on, there often are delays. The dock is 5 miles north of town. If you're just going to Skagway, a good alternative with more sailings and sightseeing is the **Haines-Skagway Water Taxi and Scenic Cruise** (☎ **907/766-3395**). May 20 to September 15, the 80-passenger vessel offers two round-trips daily, leaving Haines at 9:30am and 4:15pm. The ride takes an hour each way and leaves from the small boat harbor downtown, near the harbor master's shack. The fare is $18 one way, $29 round-trip.

By Car   The **Haines Highway** leads 155 miles to Haines Junction, Yukon Territory, an intersection with the Alaska Highway (you must pass through Canadian customs—see the "Alaska Highway" section in chapter 10 for rules). The road runs along the Chilkat River and the bald eagle preserve, then climbs into spectacular alpine terrain. Anchorage is 775 driving miles from Haines, Fairbanks 653. One-way car rentals to Anchorage, Fairbanks, and Skagway are available from **Avis,**

at the Hotel Hälsingland (☎ **907/766-2733**) with a $300 drop-off charge plus the rental cost. You can also rent an RV one-way to Anchorage. **ABC Motorhome Rentals,** 3853 W. International Airport Rd., Anchorage, AK 99502 (☎ **800/ 421-7456** or 907/279-2000; fax 907/243-6363; website http://www.alaskan.com/ abcmotorhomes/), charges $500 plus a 1-week rental, starting around $1,400 in the high season.

By Bus   Gray Line's **Alaskon Express** bus (☎ **800/544-2206**) serves routes during the tourist season 3 days a week each to Skagway, Whitehorse, Anchorage, Fairbanks, and Beaver Creek. The fare to Anchorage is $185. The bus stops at the Hälsingland and the Captain's Choice Motel, where you can buy tickets.

By Air   Three commuter airlines come to Haines. **L.A.B. Flying Service** (☎ **800/ 426-0543** or 907/766-2222) has frequent flights, charging $65 one-way for the 30-minute trip from Juneau.

VISITOR INFORMATION   Haines's city-run **Visitor Information Center** is small but well staffed and stocked. It's open summers Monday through Friday from 8am to 5pm, Saturday 9am to 6pm, and Sunday 10am to 7pm; in winter it's open normal business hours. The center is run by the city's **Haines Convention and Visitors Bureau,** on Second Street near Willard (P.O. Box 530), Haines, AK 99827 (☎ **800/458-3579** or 907/766-2234; website http://www.haines.ak.us), which also sends out a vacation-planning packet. Near the center, **Haines Tickets, Tours, Trips and Things,** 234 2nd Ave. (P.O. Box 1309), Haines, AK 99827 (☎ **907/766-2665**), offers a central reservation service for fishing charters and other local activities.

ORIENTATION   Haines sits on the narrow Chilkat Peninsula near the north end of the Southeast Alaska Panhandle. Highways run north on either side of the peninsula; the one on the east side goes to the ferry dock, 5 miles out, and ends after 11 miles at **Chilkoot Lake.** The other is the **Haines Highway,** which leads to the Canadian border, the Alaska Highway, and rest of the world. Yukon time is an hour later than Alaska. The town has two parts: the sparsely built downtown grid and, down **Front Street** or **Second Avenue,** a short walk to the west, the **Fort William Seward area.**

GETTING AROUND   Vans and buses that meet the ferry offer free or inexpensive transfers, seeking to take you on a town tour. Hotel Hälsingland books tours, too, but your feet or a bicycle will get you around. Bikes are available from **Sockeye Cycle,** just uphill from the Port Chilkoot Dock on Portage Street in the Fort William Seward area (☎ and fax **907/766-2869**), for $6 an hour or $30 a day. **Haines Taxi** can be reached at ☎ **907/766-3138. Avis** car rental has an outlet at the Hotel Hälsingland, and **Affordable Cars** is at the Captain's Choice Motel (see "Accommodations," below).

FAST FACTS   The local **sales tax** is 5.5%. There are two **ATMs,** at the First National Bank of Anchorage, Main Street and Second Avenue, and at Howsers Supermarket, a few doors down Main. The **post office** is located at 55 Haines Hwy. In **emergencies,** dial **911.** The **police** can be reached in nonemergency situations at ☎ **907/766-2121.** The **Lynn Canal Medical Center** is on First Avenue, near the visitor center (☎ **907/766-2521**). The *Chilkat Valley News* is published weekly.

SPECIAL EVENTS   In late April in odd-numbered years, Haines hosts **Actfest,** a community theater festival drawing groups for competition from all over Alaska. In mid-May, **The Great Alaska Craftbeer and Homebrew Festival**

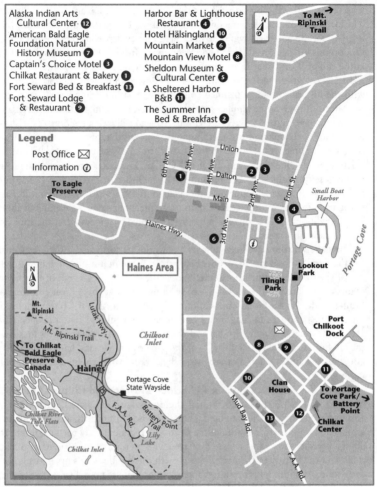

Alaska Indian Arts
Cultural Center **12**
American Bald Eagle
Foundation Natural
History Museum **7**
Captain's Choice Motel **3**
Chilkat Restaurant & Bakery **1**
Fort Seward Bed & Breakfast **13**
Fort Seward Lodge
& Restaurant **9**

Harbor Bar & Lighthouse
Restaurant **4**
Hotel Hälsingland **10**
Mountain Market **6**
Mountain View Motel **8**
Sheldon Museum &
Cultural Center **5**
A Sheltered Harbor
B&B **11**
The Summer Inn
Bed & Breakfast **2**

Legend

Post Office ⊠
Information ⓘ

(☎ **800/542-6363**) lasts 3 days. On the summer Solstice, June 21, there's a race down the Haines Highway, the **Kluane to Chilkat International Bike Relay** (☎ **907/766-2869**), with hundreds of entrants; it's quite a downhill. The Fourth of July **Independence Day** celebration is big here as elsewhere in Southeast. The biggest event of the summer is the ✪ **Southeast Alaska State Fair** and **Bald Eagle Music Festival** (☎ **907/766-2476**), held for a week in early August; it's a regional small-town get-together, with livestock, cooking, a logging show, a parade, music, and other entertainment. In early November, an **Alaska Bald Eagle Festival** (☎ **800/ 246-6268;** website http://www.haines.ak.us/eaglefest/) offers seminars and special events to mark the annual eagle congregation.

EXPLORING HAINES

ACTIVITIES IN TOWN   The main feature of Haines is ✪ **Fort William Seward,** a collection of large, white, wood-frame buildings around a sloping parade ground overlooking the magnificent Lynn Canal fjord. (Get the informative walking-tour map of the National Historic Site from the Haines Convention and Visitors Bureau.) The fort led a peaceful life, for a military installation. By the time the U.S. Army built it, in 1903, the gold rush was over, and there's no evidence it ever deterred any attack on this little peninsula at the north end of the Inside Passage. It was deactivated at the end of World War II, in which it played little part.

In 1947, a group of five veterans from the Lower 48 bought the fort as surplus, with the idea of forming a planned community. That idea didn't really work out, but one of the new white families helped spark a Chilkat Tlingit cultural renaissance that started here in the 1950s. The Heinmillers, who still own a majority of the shares in the fort, were looking for something to do with all that property when someone suggested a Tlingit tribal house on the parade grounds. The project, led by a pair of elders, took on a life of its own, and the ✪ **Chilkat Dancers** and **Alaska Indian Arts** cultural center followed. Lee Heinmiller, a member of the second generation, still manages the dance troupe his father started in 1957 as a Boy Scout project and participates in the performances with his pale, spreading paunch gleaming in abbreviated traditional Native dress. He has been adopted as a member of the tribe and given a name that accords high respect.

The dancers, who have been all over the world, perform at the **Chilkat Center for the Arts** (☎ and fax **907/766-2160**), an auditorium just off the southeast corner of the parade ground, and sometimes at the clan house. Times of the performances are geared to the arrival of cruise ships; check at the Visitor Information Center or the Alaska Indian Arts Cultural Center. Admission is $10 for adults, $5 for students, and free for children 4 and under. The cultural center is open from 1 to 5pm Monday through Friday and when cruise ships are in town, is located at the old fort hospital on the south side of the parade grounds, and has a small gallery, gift shop (see below), and a carvers' workshop where you may be able to see work in progress.

Back in the downtown area, the ✪ **Sheldon Museum and Cultural Center,** 11 Main St. (☎ **907/766-2366**; e-mail sheldmus@seaknet.alaska.edu), contains an upstairs gallery of well-presented Tlingit art and cultural artifacts; downstairs is a collection on the white history of the town. There's a uniquely personal feel to the Tlingit objects, some of which are displayed with pictures of the artisans who made them and the history of their relationship with the Sheldons. It's open in summer, daily from 1 to 5pm, plus mornings and evenings that are posted weekly; in winter, on Sunday, Monday, and Wednesday from 1 to 4pm, Tuesday, Thursday, and Friday 3 to 5pm. Admission is $3 for adults, free for children 17 and under.

An entirely unique museum is the **American Bald Eagle Foundation Natural History Museum,** at 115 Haines Hwy. (☎ **907/766-3094**), essentially a huge, hair-raising diorama of more than a hundred eagles and other animal mounts. Dave Olerud sits in a wheelchair behind the desk and will talk your ear off about the museum if you want him to—he worked on it for 18 years and was paralyzed in a fall during construction. The museum is free, but donations are requested. It's open 10am to 6pm.

SHOPPING   Haines has a few shops of interest, but you must be cautious to avoid counterfeit Native Art—see "Native Art—Finding the Real Thing" in chapter 3. **Form and Function Art Gallery,** 211 Willard St., near the visitor center, carries contemporary Chilkat carvings, prints, photography, and beadwork. Artisans often demonstrate. **The Wild Iris,** inside the Alaska Indian Arts Cultural Center, sells only prints, jewelry, and clothing made by its owners, Fred and Madeleine Shields, except for some Eskimo ivory. Fred, a former mayor, also fixes eyeglasses and is good for an entertaining conversation. **Dejon Delights,** on Portage Street, sells excellent local smoked fish and salmon caviar.

GETTING OUTSIDE

There's a lot to do in Haines—good hiking, biking, kayaking, climbing, and rafting—with a special advantage over the rest of Southeast: It's not as rainy. Also, there's a small fraternity of outdoor guides that has grown up in Haines, on Portage Street and Beach Road next to the Port Chilkoot cruise-ship dock, a kind of one-stop shop.

✪ **EAGLE VIEWING**   Haines is probably the best place on earth to see bald eagles. The **Chilkat Bald Eagle Preserve** protects 48,000 acres of river bottom along the Chilkat River. From October to January, some 3,000 eagles gather in the cottonwood trees (also known as western poplar) on a small section of the river, a phenomenon known as the Fall Congregation. (A healthy 200 to 400 are resident the rest of the year.) The eagles come for easy winter food: A very late salmon run spawns here into December in a 5-mile stretch of open water known as the Council Grounds.

During the congregation, dozens of eagles stand in each of the gnarled, leafless cottonwoods on the riverbanks, occasionally diving for a fish. The best place to see them is from the bank just off miles 18 to 21 on the Haines Highway. Don't walk on the flats, as that disturbs the eagles. The preserve is managed by Alaska State Parks, 400 Willoughby, 3rd Floor, Juneau, AK 99801, but the Haines Convention and Visitors Bureau may be a better source of information for planning a visit.

Local guides offer trips to see the eagles by raft, bicycle, or bus—mostly in the summer, when the eagles are fewer but visitors more numerous. ✪ **Chilkat Guides,** on Portage Street (on the waterfront below the fort; P.O. Box 170), Haines, AK 99827 (☎ **907/766-2491;** http://www.haines.ak.us/chilkatguides/), does a rafting trip twice a day during the summer down the Chilkat to watch the eagles. The rapids aren't threatening—there's a chance you'll be asked to get out and push—and you'll see lots of eagles. The company is run by young people who create a sense of fellowship with their clients. The 4-hour trip, with a snack, costs $75 for adults, $35 for children.

Sockeye Cycle (see "Biking," below) has guided bike tours to see eagles and Fort Seward on a 90-minute trip that costs $30, and **Alaska Tours** (☎ **907/766-2876**) takes 3-hour bus and walking tours to the preserve for $50 per person in summer.

HIKING   There are several good trails near Haines, ranging from an easy beach walk to a 10-mile, 4,000-foot climb of **Mount Ripinsky,** north of town (it starts at the top of Young Street). Get the "Haines Is for Hikers" trail guide from the visitor center. The easiest for families is the **Battery Point Trail,** which goes 2.4 miles along the beach from the end of the shore road that leads southeast from the Port Chilkoot cruise-ship dock. **Mount Riley** is south of town, with three trail routes to a 1,760-foot summit that features great views and feels much higher than it is; get the trail guide or ask directions to one of the trailheads. **Seduction Point Trail** is 7 miles long, starting at Chilkat State Park at the end of Mud Bay Road south of town and leading to the end of the Chilkat Peninsula. It's a beach walk, so check the tides; they'll give you a tide table at the visitors bureau.

BIKING   Sockeye Cycle, P.O. Box 829, Haines, AK 99827 (☎ and fax **907/ 766-2869**), leads a variety of guided trips—a couple of hours, half or full day, or even a 9-day trek. A 3-hour ride along Chilkoot Lake costs $70. Or you can go on your own for $30 a day. The area is especially conducive to biking.

SEA KAYAKING   Next door to Chilkat Guides and Sockeye Cycle on Portage Street is **Deishu Expeditions,** P.O. Box 1406, Haines, AK 99827 (☎ and fax **907/ 766-2427;** website http://www.seakayaks.com), which offers instruction, short guided trips, longer expeditions, and rentals ($35 a day for a single, plus $20 for getting dropped off somewhere). A half-day guided paddle is $70, including a snack; a full day, including lunch, is $99.

FISHING   There are several charter operators in Haines, for halibut or salmon, or guided freshwater fishing for salmon, Dolly Varden, or cutthroat trout. The Haines Convention and Visitors Bureau can help you out, and they maintain a list of operators, their specialties, and how to contact them. Or you can book through **Haines Tickets, Tours, Trips and Things,** listed under "Visitor Information," above.

FLIGHTSEEING   If you have money for one flightseeing trip in Alaska, this is a good place to choose. The Inside Passage is beautiful, and one mountain away is Glacier Bay National Park; the icefield and the glaciers spilling through to the sea are the sort of sight you never forget. **L.A.B. Flying Service,** Main Street and Fourth Avenue (P.O. Box 272), Haines, AK 99827 (☎ **800/426-0543** or 907/766-2222), offers flights from Haines starting at $105 per person.

ACCOMMODATIONS

Many towns have a lot of chainlike hotels and only one or two unique places with character. In Haines, the situation is reversed.

HOTELS

Captain's Choice Motel. Second Ave. and Dalton St. (P.O. Box 392), Haines, AK 99827. ☎ **800/247-7153** outside Alaska or 907/766-3111; 800/478-2345 in Alaska and Canada. 39 rms. TV TEL. $98–$103 double; $135 suites. AE, DC, DISC, MC, V.

These trim, red-roofed buildings house the one standard chainlike motel in town, with all the amenities that entails—objectively, probably the best hotel in town, and with a certain amount of charm. Many of the rooms have good views, and more than half are reserved for nonsmokers. Courtesy van and car rentals are available, and telephones have modem ports.

Hotel Hälsingland. Fort William Seward parade grounds (P.O. Box 1589), Haines, AK 99827. ☎ **800/542-6363** or 907/766-2000. 50 rms, 45 with bath. TV TEL. $55 double without bath, $95 double with bath. $125 suite. AE, DC, DISC, MC, V. Closed mid-Nov to Mar.

There was no need to restore this historic building—it has been operating continuously as a hotel in the same family since 1947, a year after it stopped functioning as the commanding officer's quarters at Fort William Seward. But current owner Arnie Olsson has his work cut out with redoing the rooms one by one, and some furniture looks not antique but just plain old. For my own part, the charm outweighed any shortcomings. When I stayed in a big, oddly shaped room with a nonworking fireplace and windows on the parade ground, I could almost hear the commander walking across the floor in his spurs. A courtesy van and car rental are available, and the hotel serves as a center for tours, buses, and other arrangements.

The **Commander's Room** restaurant has a wide selection of fresh seafood with views of the ocean and parade ground, and prompt service. The vegetables, served on a steam table, were limp. It's open for breakfast and dinner. The small bar has five craft brews on tap. It's a friendly, low-key place in the evening.

Mountain View Motel. Mud Bay Rd. and Second Ave. (P.O. Box 62), Haines, AK 99827. ☎ **800/478-2902** or 907/766-2900. Fax 907/766-2901. 9 rms. TV, TEL. $67 double. AE, DC, DISC, MC, V.

It doesn't look like much from the outside, but the rooms in the newer wing are an exceptional bargain for the price—large, clean, basic motel rooms. Those in the older part had worn-out furniture when I last visited. All rooms have refrigerators and coffeepots.

BED & BREAKFASTS

There are other B&Bs in Haines, but these are three of the best and most centrally located. Check the visitor center for a list of others.

✪ **Fort Seward Bed and Breakfast.** 1 Fort Seward Dr. (P.O. Box 5), Haines, AK 99827. ☎ **800/615-NORM** or 907/766-2856. Website http://www.haines.ak.us/norm/. 4 rms, 1 with bath. TV. High season, $78–$90 double; $125 suite. Low season, $70 double. Additional person in room $25 extra. Rates include full breakfast. MC, V. Closed Oct 15–Apr 7.

The fort surgeon's quarters overlook the parade grounds and the Lynn Canal with a big wraparound porch and an unspoiled historic feel. Norm Smith has lived in this house all his life and in 1981 started the B&B with his wife, Suzanne, a gifted hostess who instantly makes you feel like an old friend. The rooms have high ceilings, fireplaces, wonderful cabinetry—all kinds of authentic charm. The apartment upstairs has a full kitchen. It's a social place, with a barbecue on the porch. Smoking is not permitted, and there is a courtesy car available.

A Sheltered Harbor B&B. 57 Beach Rd. (P.O. Box 806), Haines, AK 99827. ☎ or fax **907/766-2741.** 5 rms. TV, TEL. High season, $85 double; $115 suite. Low season, $60 double; $115 suite. Rates include full breakfast. MC, V.

Upstairs from a gift shop across the street from the cruise-ship dock, these innlike rooms are a nice surprise, once you get inside. They're nicely decorated and all have private baths and entrances, more like a hotel than a typical B&B.

The Summer Inn Bed and Breakfast. 117 Second Ave. (P.O. Box 1198), Haines, AK 99827. ☎ **907/766-2970.** 5 rms, none with bath. High season, $80 double; $100 suite. Low season, $70 double; $90 suite. Rates include full breakfast. Additional person in room $10 extra. MC, V.

This lovely old clapboard house downtown has a big porch and living room. The rooms are cozy but small. The house was built by a reputed former member of Soapy Smith's gang in 1912. No smoking or drinking is allowed.

DINING

Haines doesn't have a great restaurant, but you can eat well at the Hotel Hälsingland (see "Accommodations," above), and there are lots of places for a burger or a slice of pizza. **The Lighthouse Restaurant and Bar,** at Front and Main streets (☎ **907/766-2442**), is particularly popular with one set of the locals. Another set loves the **Mountain Market,** a health-food store at Third and Mission streets that makes inexpensive sandwiches and soups in its deli—great for picnics.

Chilkat Restaurant and Bakery. Fifth Ave. off Main St. ☎ **907/766-2920.** Lunch $4–$16; dinner $6.50–$23. AE, MC, V. Summer Mon–Sat 7am–9pm, Sun 9am–9pm. Winter Mon–Thurs and Sat 7:30am–3pm, Friday 7:30am–3pm and 5–8pm. BAKERY/DINER.

This pleasant, bright family restaurant allows no smoking, in contrast to most of the other smoky places in Haines. It started out as a bakery, but now is a popular place for inexpensive breakfasts and lunches and simple steak and seafood dinners. The fish chowder had plenty of fish. This would be my first choice with kids. No liquor license.

Port Chilkoot Potlatch Salmon Bake. Fort William Seward parade grounds. ☎ **907/ 766-2000.** $22.50 per person. AE, DC, DISC, MC, V. Daily 5–8:30pm. Closed Oct–Apr. SALMON BAKE.

Salmon bakes are touristy by nature, but this long-established event is a good salmon bake. The sockeye is grilled on alder and not overcooked or ruined with overseasoning. Dining is at picnic tables, either in tents or in the clan house on the parade grounds. After you go through the line, waiters replenish your plate. One glass of beer or wine is included in the price.

12 Skagway: After the Gold Rush

It is only 100 years since white civilization came to Alaska. There were a few scattered towns in Southeast before that—Juneau, Sitka, and Wrangell, for example— but until the Klondike Gold Rush, the great mass of Alaska was populated only by Natives who had never seen a white face. Then, in a single year, the population exploded. That year, 1898, was 100 years ago. (See "The Gold Rush at 100," in chapter 10.) The people who live in Skagway, where all those people arrived for their trip to the gold fields near Dawson, expect the centennial to bring another explosion, this time of visitors. And there's every reason to believe they're right, for today Skagway gets more than 10 times as many visitors in a year as made the trip to the Klondike during the gold rush.

The tourist rush is the continuation of a 100-year-old phenomenon that's nearly as interesting as the gold rush itself. In 1896 there was a single log cabin in Skagway, in 1897 the word of the Klondike strike made it to the outside world, and in 1898 Skagway was a huge gold-rush boomtown. In 1899 the gold rush was ending, and in 1903 300 tourists arrived in a single day to do the same thing as the thousands coming for the centennial. By 1908 local businessmen had started developing their tourist attractions, moving picturesque gold-rush buildings to Broadway, the main street, to create a more unified image when visitors arrived on the steamers. By 1920 tourism had become an important part of the economy. By 1933 historic preservation efforts had started. Today, you can see history in Skagway, and you can see the history of history.

With around 800 residents and nearly half a million visitors annually, the "real" town has all but disappeared, and most of the people you'll meet are either fellow visitors or summer workers brought north to serve them. Most of the tourists are from cruise ships—it's not unusual for several to hit town in a single morning, unleashing waves of people up the wharf and into the one historic street. But there are plenty of highway and ferry travelers, too, and outdoor enthusiasts come to do the Chilkoot Trail, just as the stampeders did.

Is it worth all those visits? Skagway, spared from fire and recognized so long ago for its history, is probably the best-preserved gold-rush town in the United States. What happened here in a 2-year period was certainly extraordinary, even if the phenomenon the town celebrates is one of mass insanity based on greed, inhumanity, thuggery, prostitution, waste, and, for most, abject failure. In 1897 a group of prospectors showed up on the dock in Seattle with steamer trunks full of gold from the Yukon Territory's Klondike River, found the previous year. Even the mayor of Seattle joined the stampede. In the rush years of 1897 and 1898, Skagway or its ghost-town sibling city of Dyea were the logical places to get off the boat to head off on the trek to the gold fields near the new city of Dawson. (That fascinating town is covered in chapter 10.) Skagway instantly grew from a single homestead to a population of 15,000 to 25,000—no one knows exactly how many,

Accommodations
Gold Rush Lodge 10
Golden North Hotel/
 Gold Bar Pub & Restaurant 19
Mile Zero B&B 4
Sgt. Preston's Lodge 9
Skagway Home Hostel 16
Skagway Inn B&B/
 Lorna's Restaurant 6
Westmark Inn 18
Wind Valley Lodge 2

Attractions
Alaska Wildlife Adventure
 & Museum 15
City Hall 7
Corrington Museum
 of Alaska History 12
Eagles Hall 13
Gold Pan Theatre 5
Gold Rush Cemetery 1
Klondike Gold Rush Natioanl Park
 Visitor Center & Museum 23
Mascot Saloon 21
Mollie Walsh Park 8
Moore House 14
Arctic Brotherhood Hall/Trail
 of '98 Historical Museum 20
White Pass & Yukon Depot 24

Dining
Mabel G. Smith's 11
Pizzeria Roma II 17
Red Onion Saloon 22
Siding 21 Restaurant 3

in part because the people were flowing through so fast. But Dawson City ended up with 30,000.

While Canada was well policed by the Mounties, in Skagway there was no law—a hell on earth, as one Mounty described it. Soapy Smith, a con artist turned organized crime boss, ruled the city; the governor offered to put him officially in charge as a territorial marshal and rode with him in the 1898 Independence Day parade. Four days later, Smith was shot dead in a gunfight with Frank Reid, who led a vigilante committee upset over one of Smith's thefts. Reid died of his wounds in the shoot-out, but Smith's gang was broken. Of course, the gold rush was about to end anyway.

In 1976 the National Park Service began buying many of Skagway's best old buildings for the Klondike Gold Rush National Historic District, and now it owns about 15. Broadway is a prosperous, freshly painted 6-block strip of gold rush–era buildings, a few of which look like real businesses but turn out to be displays showing how it was back then. Other buildings restored by the park service are under lease to real businesses, and still others are just now under restoration. Visitors also can ride a gold rush–era narrow-gauge railroad into the White Pass, hike the Chilkoot Trail, or join in some other, limited outdoor activities.

ESSENTIALS

GETTING THERE   By Ferry   The **Alaska Marine Highway System** (☎ 907/
983-2941 locally, see "Getting Around" at the beginning of this chapter for a full

listing), connects Skagway with Haines and Juneau. The fare is $14 to Haines, $26 to Juneau. Or take the more convenient **Haines-Skagway Water Taxi and Scenic Cruise** excursion boat, going to Haines in summer at 10:45am and 5:30pm, for $18 one-way, $29 round-trip. In Skagway, the ticket office is at Dejon Delights, Fifth Avenue and Broadway (☎ **907/983-2083**), or you can buy them on board at the boat harbor. Haines is 15 miles away by boat but more than 350 by road.

By Car   Since 1978, ○ **Klondike Highway 2** has traced the route of the stampeders through the White Pass, a parallel route to the Chilkoot Trail, into Canada. The road runs 99 miles, then meets the Alaska Highway a dozen miles southeast of Whitehorse. The border is at the top of the pass, 14 miles from Skagway. (Information on customs is in chapter 10 in the Alaska Highway section.) This is one of the most spectacular drives anywhere in Alaska. The views are basically equivalent to the White Pass and Yukon Route railway, but a lot cheaper. Do it in clear weather, if possible, as in cloudy weather all you'll see is white-out. Car rentals are available from **Avis** (☎ **800/331-1212** or 907/983-2247), with an office at the Westmark Inn Skagway (see "Accommodations," below). Recreational vehicles are available from **ABC Motorhome Rentals** (☎ **800/421-7456** or 907/983-3222). You can rent one-way to Anchorage for the price of a rental, about $1,400 for a week, plus a $400 drop-off fee.

By Bus   Two bus lines have daily summer service to Whitehorse, where you can make connections to Anchorage or Fairbanks 3 days a week. Gray Line's **Alaskon Express** (☎ **800/544-2206**) stops at the Westmark Inn Skagway, at Third and Spring streets; the fare is $205 to Anchorage. **Alaska Direct Busline** (☎ **800/ 780-6652**) operates the same route, charging $180.

By Air   Several air taxi operators serve Skagway. **L.A.B. Flying Service** (☎ **800/ 426-0543** or 907/983-2471) has scheduled flights to Juneau for $81 one-way.

VISITOR INFORMATION   The ○ **National Park Service Visitor Center,** in the restored railroad depot at Second Avenue and Broadway (P.O. Box 517), Skagway, AK 99840 (☎ **907/983-2921;** website http://www.nps.gov/klgo), is the focal point for activities in Skagway. Rangers answer questions, give lectures, and show films, and four times a day lead an excellent guided walking tour. The building houses a small museum. Most of the park service's programs are free, but a tour of a newly restored Bernard Moore House entails a $2 fee (see below). The visitor center is open June to August, daily from 8am to 7pm, closing an hour earlier in May and September; it's closed in winter except when ferries are in town, but the park headquarters in the same building is open normal business hours, and the staff will answer questions or show the film. The **Skagway Convention and Visitors Bureau** operates a relatively modest visitor center at 333 Fifth Ave., between Broadway and State Street (P.O. Box 415), Skagway, AK 99840 (☎ **907/983-2854;** fax 907/983-3854; website http:// www.skagway.org), with listings of hotels, restaurants, and activities and an exceptionally informative ○ **Skagway Walking Tour Map** of historic sites. It's open daily from 8am to 5pm in the summer, closed weekends in the winter.

ORIENTATION   Skagway sits at the north end of the Lynn Canal fjord in a narrow mountain valley. The streets are a simple grid, with numbered streets starting at **First Avenue** at the water. The tourist attractions are on **Broadway. Klondike Highway 2** takes off up the valley to the border, 14 miles away. Yukon time is an hour later. An 8-mile gravel road branches off 2 miles up the highway to the **Dyea** historic area and the start of the **Chilkoot Trail.**

GETTING AROUND   Skagway's main sights all can be reached on foot. If you want to go to Dyea or the gold-rush graveyard, a bike is a fun way to do it. **Sockeye Cycle,** on Fifth Avenue off Broadway (☎ **907/983-2851**) rents good mountain bikes for $6 an hour and leads guided day trips (see "Getting Outside," below). No fewer than eight companies offer car, van, or bus tours of Skagway, but none goes to greater lengths for a unique experience than Steve Hites, whose ✪ **Skagway Street Car Company,** 270 Second Ave. (P.O. Box 400), Skagway, AK 99840 (☎ **907/983-2908**), uses antique touring vehicles and whose costumed guides consider their work "theater without walls." The very personal and amusing 2¹/₂-hour streetcar tour, based on a tour originally given to President Harding, is $34 for adults. Hites also offers a 90-minute van ride up the highway to the White Pass Summit for $29 and a 5-hour tour into the Yukon Territory for $69; children are charged half fare. Hites operates out of his big gift shop with an espresso counter and a theater, where he completes his tour with a slide show—in character, of course. Book the tour at least 2 weeks in advance, as they're always sold out.

FAST FACTS   Sales tax in Skagway is 4%. In **emergencies,** dial **911.** For nonemergency **police** business, call ☎ **907/983-2232;** the police station is located in city hall, at Seventh and Spring streets. The **Dahl Memorial Health Center,** a clinic, is on Eleventh Avenue between Broadway and State Street (☎ **907/983-2255**). An **ATM** is at the National Bank of Alaska, on Broadway at Sixth Avenue. The **post office** is right by it, between Sixth and Seventh avenues. **Skagway News,** on Broadway between Second and Third avenues, sells out-of-town newspapers.

SPECIAL EVENTS   The Skagway Fine Arts Council puts on a **Mini Folk Festival** in April (☎ **907/983-2276**). A race retracing the steps of the gold rush stampeders, with their same impediments, starts June 14 from Dyea. Entrants in the **Dyea to Dawson Race** will carry gold-mining gear over the Chilkoot Pass, then canoe 500 miles down the Yukon River to Dawson. Skagway's ✪ **July 4th Parade and Celebration,** organized by the city, has been a big deal since Soapy Smith led the parade in 1898. In 1998 it is billed as the official gold rush centennial celebration. In early September, the **Klondike Road Relay,** a 110-mile, overnight foot race over the pass, brings hundreds of runners in teams of 10 from all over the state (☎ **867/668-4236**).

EXPLORING SKAGWAY

WHAT TO DO & SEE   The ✪ **White Pass and Yukon Route** railway, P.O Box 435, Dept. B, Skagway, AK 99840 (☎ **800/343-7373** or 907/983-2217; website http://www.whitepassrailroad.com), a narrow-gauge line that originally ran to Whitehorse, was completed after only 2 years in 1900. It's an engineering marvel and a fun way to see spectacular, historic scenery. Tickets are expensive, however, and I wouldn't recommend going in bad weather, when the pass is socked in and all you'll see out the window are white clouds. Also, they tell you not to get out of your seat (although many people do), and children may have a hard time sitting still that long. The ride begins at a depot on Second Avenue with the spine-tingling sound of a working steam engine's whistle. The steamer pulls the train a couple of miles, then diesels take the cars, some of them originals more than 100 years old, up steep tracks that were chipped out of the side of the mountains. The summit excursion, which travels 20 miles with an elevation gain of 2,865 feet, then turns back, takes about 3 hours, and costs $78. Children are charged half price. The biggest treat for train-lovers is an 8-hour all-steam-powered round trip to Lake Bennett, where the stampeders launched their boats for the trip to Dawson City. Only a handful of departures are planned annually, and the $150 fare may change. Lunch at Lake Bennett is included. You can get all the way to Whitehorse with a train that meets a bus, for a $95 fare, one-way. These days, the line operates only as a tourist attraction and closes down for the winter at the end of September.

To see the town, take a walk with the Skagway Walking Tour Map or the National Park Service guided walking tours (see "Visitor Information" above). Also visit the **museum** at the National Park Service Visitor Center and next door. Of greatest interest is a collection of food and gear similar to the ton of supplies each prospector was required to carry over the pass in order to gain entry into Canada, a requirement that prevented famine among the stampeders, but made the job of getting to Dawson City an epic struggle for each of them. The park service also has made a museum of the **Mascot Saloon,** at Broadway and Third Avenue, complete with statues bellying up to the bar. It's open daily from 8am to 5pm. Admission to each museum is free.

The city-owned ✪ **Trail of '98 Historical Museum and Archives,** in the building with the driftwood facade on Broadway between Second and Third avenues, contains Skagway's best collection of gold-rush artifacts, including Soapy Smith's bloody tie, most of which are well explained in labels. Although cramped in the historic Arctic Brotherhood Hall, the museum contains enough to hold your interest for an hour or two. Summer hours are 9am to 5pm daily, it's closed during the noon hour on weekends, and in winter you get in by appointment only. Admission is $2 for adults, $1 for students and children. The **Alaska Wildlife Adventure and Museum,** at Fourth and Spring streets (☎ **907/983-3600**), contains an amazing collection of miscellaneous memorabilia from the long Alaska lives of Bob and Anna Groff and an immense display of their animal mounts in a room built for the purpose. Bob shows you around, and he is a museum-quality example of the solid, friendly, old-time Alaskan type. Open 8am to 6pm daily in the summer; admission is $7 for adults, $6 seniors, $4 for children. The **Corrington Museum of Alaska History** is located in Corrington's gift shop at Fifth Avenue and Broadway; admission is free, and the eclectic display is impressive and worth a stop. It's open, May 20 to September 15, from 9am to 7pm.

The park service recently completed restoration of the 1897 **Moore House,** near Fifth Avenue and Spring Street, and will lead tours there on family life during the gold rush for $2. Ten years before it happened, Captain William Moore brilliantly predicted that the gold rush would occur, and so homesteaded the land Skagway would be built on, knowing that this would be a key staging area. He built a cabin in 1887 that stands nearby. But when the rush occurred, the stampeders simply ignored his property claims and built the city on his land without offering compensation. A block east, on Sixth Avenue, is **Mollie Walsh Park,** with a good children's play area, public rest rooms, and phones. A sign tells the sad story of Skagway's first respectable woman, who chose to marry the wrong man among two suitors and was killed by him in a drunken rage. The other suitor—who'd previously killed another rival for her affections—commissioned the bust of Walsh that stands at the park. Another block east is Skagway's most beautiful building, the 1900 granite city hall and jail. Outside is a display of railroad cars, with informative historical markers.

The **Gold Rush Cemetery** is 1¹/₂ miles from town, up State Street. Used until 1908, it's small and overgrown with spruce trees, but some of the charm and mystery of the place are lost because of the number of visitors and the shiny new paint and maintenance of the wooden markers. The graves of Soapy Smith and Frank Reid are the big attractions, but don't miss the short walk up to Reid Falls. A map is available at the visitor centers. The closely spaced dates on many of the markers attest to the epidemics that swept through the stampeders.

About 9 miles north of Skagway (on a lovely drive or bike ride) is the ghost town of **Dyea,** where stampeders started the Chilkoot Trail. (See "Orientation," above, for directions.) It's a lot more ghost than town—all that remains are a few boards, broken dock pilings, and miscellaneous iron trash. But on a sunny day, the protected historical site is a perfect place for a picnic, among beach grasses, wild iris, and the occasional reminder that a city once stood here. The National Park Service leads a guided history and nature walk once a week; check at the visitor center. (See "Getting Outside," below, for other ideas on going to Dyea.)

The little-visited **Slide Cemetery,** in the woods near Dyea, is the last resting place of many of the 60 to 70 men who died in an avalanche on the Chilkoot Trail on Palm Sunday, April 3, 1898. No one knows how many are here, or exactly who died, or how authentic the wooden markers are. In 1960, when the state reopened the Chilkoot Trail, the cemetery had been completely overgrown, and the markers were replaced. But it's a ghostly place, and the sense of anonymous, hopeless hardship and death it conveys is as authentic a gold-rush souvenir as anything in Skagway.

SHOPPING   With almost 100 years of experience, Skagway knows how to do gift shops, and now has more than 50. Of course, most are closed in winter, as the town has only about 800 year-round residents. And, as always, you must be cautious about counterfeits when buying Native artwork—see "Native Art—Finding the Real Thing," in chapter 3.

Currington's, at Fifth and Broadway, is a large gift store with an entire free museum attached. **Lynch and Kennedy,** at Fourth Avenue and Broadway, is in a building owned and restored by the National Park Service and leased to the current gift store; it carries fine art, jewelry, and high-quality gifts. The **David Present Gallery,** at Third Avenue and Broadway, shows work by 50 artists and craftspeople, including Seattle-based Present's own sculpture. **Inside Passage Arts,** on Broadway between Fourth and Fifth avenues, is a gallery of Alaska Native fine art from Southeast Alaska.

GETTING OUTSIDE

SPECIAL PLACES   The National Park Service and Parks Canada jointly manage the famous **Chilkoot Pass Trail,** publishing a trail guide and offering information at their offices in Skagway and Whitehorse. Some 20,000 stampeders used the trail to get from Dyea—9 miles from Skagway—to Lake Bennett, 33-miles away, where they could launch boats bound for Dawson City. Today about 3,000 a year make the challenging hike, taking 3 to 5 days—the Chilkoot is not so much a wilderness trail as an outdoor museum. But don't underestimate it, as so many did during the gold rush. To control the numbers, **Parks Canada,** 205-300 Main St., Whitehorse, Yukon Y1A 2B5 Canada (☎ **800/661-0486;** fax 867/393-6701), allows only 50 permitted hikers a day to cross the summit. To buy the $10 permits, call with a Visa or MasterCard and the date you plan to start. If you mail the money, your reservation isn't guaranteed till it arrives. Eight of the 50 daily permits are held for walk-ins, but I wouldn't count on getting one of those. Once over the pass, you're on Lake Bennett, on the rail line 8 miles short of the road. **Chilkoot Water Charters** (☎ **867/821-3209**) picks up hikers by arrangement, and sometimes you can finish by train (inquire with the White Pass and Yukon Route, ☎ **800/343-7373,** listed above).

A **Skagway Trail Map** is available from the visitor center, listing 11 hikes around Skagway. An easy evening walk starts at the suspension footbridge at the north end of First Avenue, crossing the Skagway River to **Yakutania Point Park,** where pine trees grow from cracks in the rounded granite of the shoreline. Across the park is a shortcut taking a couple of miles off the trip to Dyea and to the **Skyline Trail and A.B. Mountain,** a strenuous climb to a 3,500-foot summit with great views. On the southern side of town, across the railroad tracks, a network of trails heads up from Spring Street between Third and Fourth avenues to a series of mountain lakes, the closest of which is **Lower Dewey Lake,** less than a mile up the trail.

There are two **U.S. Forest Service cabins** near Skagway, and official access to both is by the White Pass and Yukon Route railway. Both are on trails described in the Skagway Trail Map, mentioned above. One cabin is an old caboose parked next to the tracks 6 miles up the line at the trailhead for the 4-mile **Denver Glacier Trail.** Another cabin is 1¹/₂ miles off the track, 14 miles up on the spectacular **Lawton Glacier Trail.** You need both a $25 cabin permit (see "Outside in Southeast," at the start of this chapter, for reservations information) and a train ticket from the railroad. For details, contact the park service visitor center, or the **Juneau Ranger District,** 8465 Old Dairy Rd., Juneau, AK 99801 (☎ **907/586-8800**).

BIKING   Sockeye Cycle, on Fifth Avenue off Broadway (☎ **907/983-2851**), leads bike tours, including one that takes clients to the top of the White Pass in a van and coasts down on bikes; the 2-hour trip is $65. They also lead a tour of the quiet town-site of Dyea for $50, going over in a van. I rode to Dyea from Skagway on my own over the hilly, 9-mile coastal road, one of the loveliest and most pleasant rides I can remember.

HORSEBACK RIDING   Chilkoot Horseback Adventures leads half-day horse-back tours of Dyea and West Creek Glacier, booked through Southeast Tours at Fifth Avenue and Broadway (☎ **800/478-2990** or 907/983-2990).

FLIGHTSEEING   **Skagway, like Haines, is a good place to choose for a flightseeing trip, as Glacier Bay National Park is just to the west. **L.A.B. Flying Service, listed above under "Getting There," is one of several companies offering fixed-wing service, for $120 per person. **Temsco Helicopters** (☎ **907/983-2900**) takes 55-minute tours over the Chilkoot Trail and lands on a glacier for 25 minutes; those flights cost $149.

ACCOMMODATIONS

All the accommodations in Skagway are close walking distance to the historic district, except as noted. The **bed tax** is 8%. In addition to those listed below, you'll find good standard rooms, reasonably priced, about a mile from the sights, at **Wind Valley Lodge,** 22nd Avenue and State Street (P.O. Box 354), Skagway, AK 99840 (☎ **907/983-2236;** fax 907/983-2957). I cannot recommend the **Westmark Inn Skagway.** Although by far the largest and most expensive hotel in town, I found the rooms lacking.

Gold Rush Lodge. Sixth Ave. and Alaska St. (P.O. Box 514), Skagway, AK 99840. ☎ **907/ 983-2831.** Fax 907/983-2742. 12 rms. TV TEL. High season, $80–$90 double. Low season, $65–$75 double. Additional person in room $10 extra. MC, V.

This is a clean, comfortable motel by the airstrip 3 blocks from the historic district, with a grassy picnic area out back. The rooms are on the small side but attractively decorated. Bathrooms have shower stalls, no tubs. The hosts serve a continental break-fast and leave out coffee and a cookie jar in the lobby, writing the guests' names and hometowns on an erasable board so they can get to know each other. They offer a courtesy car. Smoking is prohibited.

Golden North Hotel. Third Ave. and Broadway (P.O. Box 343), Skagway, AK 99840. ☎ **888/222-1898** or 907/983-2294. Fax 907/983-2755. 31 rms, 28 with bath. TEL. $75–$95 double, $55 double with shared bath. Additional person in room $15 extra. AE, CB, DC, MC, V.

This big, white landmark on Broadway was built in 1898 and is Alaska's oldest operating hotel. It's a fun place to stay, and new owners promise to restore the threadbare building while keeping its campy character intact, including the placards in each room about a different gold-rush family. A courtesy car is available. At street level, the **Gold Bar Pub & Restaurant / Skagway Brewing Company** is a good spot for lunch and dinner, with a diverse American menu and tasteful, old-timey decor that makes it a good family choice, plus a raft of fine home-brewed beer that'll please the adults. (Try the Oosik Stout—mighty fine.)

✪ **Mile Zero Bed & Breakfast.** Ninth Ave. and Main St. (P.O. Box 165), Skagway, AK 99840. ☎ **907/983-3045.** Fax 907/983-3046. Website http://www.bbonline.com/ak/milezero. 5 rms. TEL. High season, $90 double, $20 each additional person. Low season, $60 double, $15 each additional person. AE, MC, V.

Howard and Judy Mallory built this building a few blocks from the historic area in 1995 to be a B&B, and they thought of everything. The large, immaculate rooms all have private bathrooms, telephone lines, and two entrances, from an internal hall and through French doors that lead to a porch. It's an exceptional place. Continental breakfast is served in a large common room, and they'll pick you up at the ferry.

Sgt. Preston's Lodge. Sixth Ave. and State St. (P.O. Box 538), Skagway, AK 99840. ☎ **907/983-2521.** Fax 907/983-3500. 30 rms. TV TEL. $75–$85 double. AE, CB, DC, DISC, MC, V.

Set in several motel-style buildings on a grassy compound, many of the rooms are large and clean, and eight of the newer rooms, reserved for nonsmokers, are huge and light with high ceilings—quite a bargain for the price. They offer a courtesy car and free coffee.

✪ **Skagway Inn Bed and Breakfast.** Seventh Ave. and Broadway (P.O. Box 500), Skagway, AK 99840. ☎ **907/983-2289.** Fax 907/983-2713. Website http://puffin.ptialaska.net./~sgyinn. 12 rms, none with bath. High season, $78–$125 double. Low season, $60–$70 double. DISC, MC, V.

Built in 1897, this cute, little Victorian inn has rooms named after prostitutes who worked in Skagway when the building was a brothel—the owners researched old police records. There are six bathrooms for the 12 guest rooms, and they're kept immaculate. Some of the rooms are frilly and quite small; the Alice Room, above the street, is larger and has a porch, but costs more. The lobby is a welcoming parlor full of books where guests visit over tea. A full breakfast is served in a windowed dining room which, at night, becomes Lorna's, Skagway's best restaurant (see below). A courtesy van is available.

HOSTEL & CAMPING

There's a free **National Park Service campground** at Dyea, with well-separated sites near the water. For recreational vehicles, there are plenty of parks in Skagway. The city maintains one at the small-boat harbor.

Skagway Home Hostel. Third Ave. near Main St. (P.O. Box 231), Skagway, AK 99840. ☎ **907/983-2131.** 2 private rms, neither with bath; 3 dorms. $15 per bunk; $40 double private room.

Frank Wasmer and Nancy Schave have really opened up their historic home to hostelers, sharing their meals, refrigerator, bathrooms, and hospitality side-by-side with guests. The atmosphere is like off-campus shared housing at college, except the house is nicer and better kept. Bunks are in separate male and female dorm rooms. To reserve, you have to send the money ahead. They don't return long-distance calls. In winter, reservations are required, as Frank and Nancy might otherwise not be there. Summer registration hours are 5:30 to 10:30pm. No pets, alcohol, or smoking.

DINING

I've already described the new restaurants at the Golden North Hotel (see "Accommodations," above). You may also enjoy lunch from **Mabel G. Smith's** (☎ 907/ 983-2609), a bakery and card and coffee shop on Fifth Avenue off Broadway, serving one generally vegetarian lunch selection daily in summer. **Pizzeria Roma II,** on Third Avenue off Broadway (☎ 907/983-3459), is a good traditional pizza place, also serving foccacia sandwiches.

✪ **Lorna's at the Skagway Inn.** Seventh Ave. and Broadway. ☎ **907/983-2289.** Dinner $17–$26. MC, V. Reservations required. May–Sept, daily 5–9pm. FRENCH.

Lorna makes it clear what she's about as soon as you walk into the Skagway Inn lobby: Her recent diplomas from Le Condon Bleu are posted by the entrance to the dining room. The deceptively simple cuisine and professional, unpretentious service lives up to the advertising. The menu changes every night but always emphasizes Alaska seafood. The intimate seven-table dining room is lovely, decorated with antiques and surrounded by windows. Beer and wine are served.

Siding 21 Restaurant. 21st Ave. and State St. ☎ **907/983-3328.** Lunch $5–$9.50; dinner $12–$15. DISC, MC, V. Daily 6am–10pm.

Built to look like an old-fashioned railway depot inside and out, this is a wonderful family restaurant. There's a complete children's menu, and the regular menu is reasonably priced. The service is friendly and quick, and the no-smoking section actually isn't smoky. It's located a mile out from the center of town, next door to the Wind Valley Lodge. No liquor license.

SKAGWAY IN THE EVENING

There are two evening tourist shows in Skagway. Incredibly, the *Days of '98 Show* has been playing since 1927 in the Fraternal Order of Eagles Hall No. 25, at Sixth Avenue and Broadway (☎ 907/983-2545). Jim Richards carries on the tradition each summer with actors imported from all over the United States. The evening shows begin at 7:30pm with mock gambling at a casino run by the actors. The performance, at 8:30pm, includes singing, can-can dancing, and the story of the shooting of Soapy Smith. Matinees are $12, and evening shows are $14; senior citizens pay $2 less, and children are charged half price.

Another vaudeville melodrama performance takes place nightly at 7:30pm during the summer at the **Gold Pan Theatre,** at Seventh Avenue and Broadway (☎ 907/983-3177). Tickets are $12 for adults, $10 for seniors, and half price for children 12 and under.

The **Red Onion Saloon,** at Second Avenue and Broadway, is an authentic-feeling old bar that often has terrific live jazz and other styles of music, but the players sometimes jump up suddenly and leave—they're cruise-ship musicians who enjoy coming here to stretch out and jam, and they can't afford to miss the boat. It was a brothel originally (what wasn't?); look in the upstairs windows. The **Frontier Bar,** at Fifth Avenue and Broadway, is more of a gritty local hangout.

Southcentral Alaska   8

As teenagers living in Anchorage, my cousin and I got a job from a family friend painting his lake cabin. He flew us out on his float plane and left us there, with paint, food, and a little beer. There was a creek that ran past the lake so full of salmon that we caught one on every cast until we got bored and started thinking of ways to make it more difficult. We cooked the salmon over a fire, then floated in a boat on the lake under the endless sunshine of a summer night, talking and diving naked into the clear, green water. We met some guys building another cabin one day, but otherwise we saw no other human beings. When the week was over, the cabin was painted—it didn't take long—and the float plane came back to get us. As we lifted off and cleared the trees, Anchorage opened in front of us, barely 10 minutes away.

This kind of fly-in fishing to a remote lake is one of the great summer experiences to be had in Alaska, and it's just a few minutes and a few hundred dollars from the busy streets of Anchorage. Southcentral Alaska is like that. You can climb an unnamed mountain and have dinner in a five-star restaurant on the same day.

The state's largest city, Anchorage—where 40% of Alaska's population resides—dominates Southcentral, a region without a clear identity of its own. Anchorage is accused crushingly of being just like a city Outside, not really part of Alaska at all, although it sits in the lap of the wild Chugach Mountains. The Kenai Peninsula is famous for the crowding on its salmon streams, not the secret and grand places it contains, easily accessible to the road system. The Copper River country and Prince William Sound have their own definition, made up of the huge and spectacular land and the few little towns it hosts. As a region, Southcentral is more of an area on a map than an interconnected way of life.

For a visitor, that's an advantage, because Southcentral Alaska's diversity contains almost everything that people come to the state to see. The glaciers are most numerous and largest here. The mountains are the most massive, if not quite the tallest. The waters of Prince William Sound and the Kenai Peninsula have the same allure as Southeast Alaska, but are more accessible by road. Caribou cross the tundra in the Copper River country just as they do in the arctic. If the area lacks history, it has art. Some people spend a lot of their time in Alaska traveling great distances to visit all parts of the state. If you have limited time—and who doesn't?—you can see a lot more staying in Southcentral.

The disadvantage, of course, is that there are more people in the way. Although the region still is more sparsely populated than most of the country, the closer you get to Anchorage, the more the human development will remind you of the outskirts of any town in the United States, with fast-food franchises, occasional traffic jams, and even crime-ridden neighborhoods with the makings of youth gangs. But if that starts to bother you, do what Anchorage residents do every weekend—head up to the Chugach Mountains, down to the Kenai Peninsula, or out on Prince William Sound.

Anchorage lies at the center of the region, near the head of Cook Inlet. South of Anchorage, two-lane highways link the three population centers of the **Kenai Peninsula. Seward,** on the eastern side of the peninsula, is the gateway to **Kenai Fjords National Park,** a spectacular, rugged area on the Gulf of Alaska side of the peninsula. The **Kenai and Soldotna area,** facing Cook Inlet on the western central Kenai Peninsula, provide access to fishing in the Kenai River. **Homer,** near the southern end of the peninsula, sits on **Kachemak Bay,** which opens into Cook Inlet. The bay is a rich natural environment and Homer a quirky community popular with artists. **Prince William Sound** is southeast of Anchorage. With more than 2,700 miles of coastline, the Sound holds a vast wealth of marine life and spectacular scenery, including many tidewater glaciers. There are three towns. **Whittier** is the Sound's closest access point to Anchorage, currently accessible only by train. **Valdez** has direct highway access. **Cordova,** tucked away on the eastern Sound, is an undiscovered gem. North along the Copper River, the **Copper River country** is a vast region of some of the world's tallest and most massive mountains. West of that area, and north of Anchorage, the **Matanuska and Susitna valleys** are both bedroom communities to Anchorage and an access route to Denali National Park.

1 Exploring Southcentral Alaska

In Southcentral, uniquely in Alaska, you have your choice of modes of transportation. The Alaska Railroad runs from Seward north to Anchorage, with a branch from Portage to Whittier on Prince William Sound, and then farther north through the Matanuska-Susitna valleys to Denali National Park and Fairbanks, in the Interior. Highways connect all the region's towns except Cordova and Whittier, but you can take your car on the train to Whittier, and the ferry connects Whittier with Valdez and Cordova. Jet airline service brings visitors into Alaska's hub airport, in Anchorage, and to Cordova. Commuter lines fan out from Anchorage to Kenai, Homer, Valdez, and other towns. Bus service also is available to many areas.

The easiest way to get around Southcentral is as residents do—**by car.** One good itinerary of 10 days to 2 weeks would be to fly to Anchorage and spend a few days taking in the sights. Then rent a car to drive down the Seward Highway, taking plenty of time to get down to Homer, perhaps with a couple of days to stop for fishing or hiking on the way in the Chugach National Forest, in Cooper Landing, or in the Kenai/Soldotna area. In Homer, plan several days, getting out on Kachemak Bay to Halibut Cove, Seldovia, or hiking and boating in Kachemak Bay State Park. Then drive back to Portage and take the car on the train through the tunnel and travel on the ferry through Prince William Sound to Valdez, seeing the glaciers and wildlife. Spend a day in Valdez, then drive up the Richardson Highway, perhaps making a 2-day side trip to historic Kennicott, in the spectacular Wrangell–St. Elias National Park, then returning on the Glenn Highway to Anchorage or continuing up to Fairbanks, if there's time.

Without a car, a possible 10-day itinerary would be to fly to Anchorage, spend a few days sightseeing there, then take the Alaska Railroad to Seward, visiting Kenai

Fjords National Park by boat, with a second day in Seward in case of bad weather or a hike or fishing. Then head back to Anchorage and fly to Cordova, taking the tour to Childs Glacier, visiting the quaint and welcoming town, and perhaps getting outdoors on a bike, a hike, a kayak, or on a fishing excursion. Then take the ferry to Valdez, spend part of a day there, and board a Stan Stephens Cruises tour boat to see Columbia Glacier and other glaciers in western Prince William Sound, either going all the way to Whittier and taking the train to Anchorage or returning to Valdez and flying back to Anchorage. If there's time left, use Anchorage as a base for a fly-in fishing trip or take a flightseeing trip on a classically restored DC-3 over Denali National Park.

I offer these plans only as a starting point. Your own exploration of the region depends, of course, on your interests and how you like to travel. You'll find that Southcentral is the easiest part of the state to get around, and travel is more flexible than in other areas. But the height of summer, from mid-June to mid-August, is heavily booked, so you can't expect to just show up and get a choice room—often, any room is hard to get. Planning extra travel days because of the weather is not as critical as in Southeast Alaska, but leave plenty of time around any boating or flightseeing excursions. Reputable tour and fishing operators simply won't go out in rough water and make you miserable. If you have a backup day, you can spend the rough-weather day on shore and try again the next day. Check on weather cancellation policies before you book any boat excursions.

2 Outside in Southcentral

Southcentral Alaska has all the outdoor opportunities found elsewhere in the state, and you can be as remote or as close to civilization as you wish. The best and most central place to get outdoor information is the Alaska Public Lands Information Center, at Fourth Avenue and F Street in Anchorage (see "Visitor Information" under "Essentials," in the "Anchorage" section, later in this chapter). Much of the region is in **Chugach National Forest**, with ranger stations in various towns listed below. To reserve Forest Service cabins and spaces in some campgrounds (all campgrounds also have first-come, first-served sites), call **Biospherics** (☎ **800/280-2267;** TDD/TTY 800/879-4496; fax 301/722-9802). You can reserve any cabin up to 180 days in advance, paying a reservation fee of $8.25 on top of the cabin fee. Cancellation fees apply. They take Visa, MasterCard, or Discover cards. You also can pay by check by mail to USFS Reservation Center, P.O. Box 900, Cumberland, MD 21502-0900. Cabin availability is online at http://www.nrrc.com. Any Forest Service office can check for you, then hand you the phone to call Biospherics. The reservation line is open only during the day and closes at 3pm on weekends. At this writing, the system was subject to change, but you can get the latest from the public lands center or the Forest Service.

FISHING   Alaska's most famous fishing stream, and the only place in the world to catch such large king salmon, is the Kenai River, accessible on the Kenai Peninsula from Kenai, Soldotna, and other towns. But there's good salmon fishing virtually anywhere you choose to go in the region—including downtown Anchorage. The most famous halibut fishing, with flat fish topping out in the 300-pound class, is from Homer, but other towns have halibut charters, too. Anchorage is a good starting point for fly-in fishing.

FLIGHTSEEING   There are flight services in all the towns for flightseeing trips. Anchorage is a good starting point with lots of choices.

HIKING & BIKING The bike trails in Anchorage let you get into the outdoors without leaving town. Chugach State Park, near Anchorage, has many good alpine trails for hiking and biking. Chugach National Forest has short and long trails, some with historic significance, and cabins along the way, on the Kenai Peninsula and in Cordova. The Matanuska Valley also has good alpine trails. Wrangell–St. Elias National Park is a vast area for wilderness trekking.

SEA KAYAKING Kachemak Bay out of Homer, Resurrection Bay out of Seward, and Prince William Sound out of Whittier, Valdez, or Cordova all present good sea-kayaking opportunities.

SKIING Anchorage is Alaska's best destination for downhill skiing, at the posh Alyeska Resort in Girdwood and at two smaller ski areas. Cross-country ski trails lace through the city and Kincaid Park, one of the nation's best Nordic skiing areas, 15 minutes from downtown.

WILDLIFE WATCHING You have a chance of seeing whales, otters, sea lions, seals, and other marine animals on cruise or charter boats out of Seward, Homer, Whittier, Valdez, and Cordova. Bears could show up anywhere, but flights out of Homer are the region's best bet if you must see one. Dall sheep are often seen on the Turnagain Arm south of Anchorage.

3 Anchorage: Alaska's Threshold

Steve McCutcheon came to Anchorage as a child in the city's first years. Anchorage started as a tent camp for workers mobilized to build the Alaska Railroad in 1915. A grid was laid out north and south of Ship Creek, and lots were sold at auction. A few houses and businesses went up to serve the federal employees who were building and later running the railroad, as McCutcheon's father did. It was a remote, sleepy railroad town, enlivened by World War II and the construction of a couple of large military bases, but never more than strictly functional. As one visitor who came in the early 1940s wrote, the entire town looked like it was built on the wrong side of the tracks.

A couple of years ago, McCutcheon looked out the picture window from his living room on a placid lake surrounded by huge, half-million-dollar houses, each with a float plane pulled up on the green front lawn, and he recalled the year people started to take Anchorage seriously. It was the year, he said, when they started thinking it would be a permanent city, not just an encampment where you went for a few years to make money before moving on—the year they started building Anchorage to last. That year was 1957. Oil was discovered on the Kenai Peninsula's Swanson River, south of here. It was around that time that McCutcheon built his own house, far out in the country with no neighbors anywhere in the area, all alone on a lake. At that time, you could homestead in the Anchorage bowl. Those who had the opportunity—my wife's family, for example—didn't do it only because it seemed improbable that flat, wet acreage way out of town would ever be worth anything.

Oil grew Anchorage like nitrogen fertilizer poured on a shooting weed. Those homesteads that went begging in the 1950s and early 1960s now have shopping malls and high-rise office buildings on them. Fortunes came fast, development was haphazard, and a lot was built that we'd all soon regret. I had the bizarre experience of coming home from college to the town I'd grown up in and getting completely lost in a large area of the city that had been nothing but moose browse the last time I'd seen it. Visitors found a city full of life, but empty of charm.

In the last 10 years, that has started to change. Anchorage is slowly outgrowing its gawky adolescence. It's still young, prosperous, and vibrant—exhausting, at times, when the summer sun refuses to set. But now it also has some excellent restaurants, a good museum and a nice little zoo, and things to do in the evening besides the tourist melodramas you'll find in every Alaska town. Some people complain that Anchorage isn't really Alaska—in Fairbanks, they call it "Los Anchorage" (and in Anchorage, Fairbanks is known as "Squarebanks")—yet the wilderness remains close by, right at the edge of town and often intertwined with it. With around a quarter million people, Anchorage is the nation's 64th-largest city, yet it still has problems in the winter with moose—they're a general pest, especially for gardeners, as they seem to consider ornamental trees and bushes a tasty delicacy. In 1997, the state even considered having an urban moose season to reduce their numbers. Bears and eagles show up in town, though less frequently, and a system of greenbelts and bike trails, the city's best feature, brings the woods into almost every neighborhood. Good downhill skiing is available, as is some of the best Nordic skiing in the United States.

Anchorage stands between the Chugach Mountains, which are protected by Chugach State Park, and the silt-laden waters of upper Cook Inlet. The site of the city is broad and flat; it's mostly built on sediment. At the water's edge, mud flats of the same material, not yet made into land, stretch far offshore when the tide is at its low point, up to 38 vertical feet below high water. There's a downtown area of about 8-by-20 blocks, near Ship Creek where it all started, but the rest of the city spreads some 5 miles east and 15 miles south along broad commercial strips and freeway frontages. Like many cities in the western United States built in the era of the car, the layout is not particularly conducive to any other form of transportation. But the city's boundaries go even farther, far beyond the reach of cars, taking in the Chugach, Turnagain Arm all the way to Portage, and even reaching over to Prince William Sound. Most of that land is there only to be explored. I can't say for sure if all the mountain peaks in the municipality have been climbed, and far from all have been named.

Most visitors use Anchorage as a hub—that's its role for Alaskans, too—spending a day or two here before heading off somewhere more remote. Yet the city has enough personality and attractions to make more time interesting. The downtown area is pleasant, but if you just walk up and down its streets of tourist-oriented shops, you'll have missed most of the city. Get out on the coastal trail, go to one of the museums, take a day trip south to Portage, and explore the Chugach Mountains.

ESSENTIALS

GETTING THERE   By Air   You'll probably get to Anchorage at the start of your trip by air, as it has by far the most flights linking Alaska to the rest of the world on many airlines. The **Anchorage International Airport** is a major hub. Flights connect the city to Asia and the Russian Far East, but Seattle has the most frequent flights, with numerous domestic carriers flying nonstop all day. Within Alaska, most flights route through Anchorage, even for communities that are much closer to each other than either is to Anchorage. **Alaska Airlines** (☎ **800/426-0333;** website http://www.alaskaair.com) is the dominant carrier for Alaska destinations, and the only jet operator to most Alaska cities. Various commuter carriers link Anchorage to rural destinations not served by jet. **Era Aviation** (☎ **800/866-8394** or 907/ 266-8394) is one of the largest for Southcentral Alaska destinations and can be booked through Alaska Airlines. For information on public transport from the airport, see "Getting Around," below.

By Car   There's only one road to the rest of the world: the Glenn Highway. The other road out of town, the Seward Highway, leads to the Kenai Peninsula. The Glenn Highway is only a significant bit of four-lane freeway, for the 30 miles

Anchorage

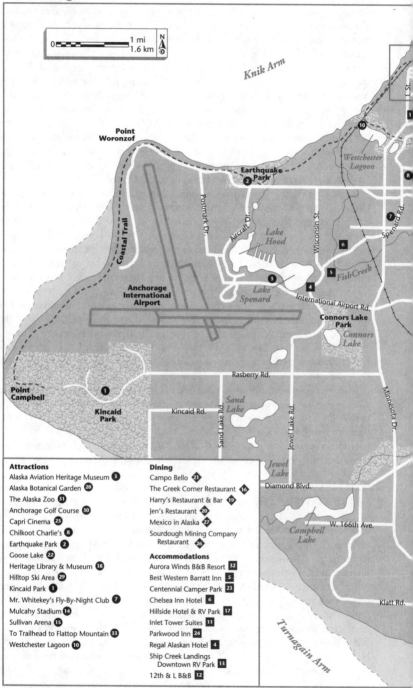

Attractions
Alaska Aviation Heritage Museum ③
Alaska Botanical Garden ㉘
The Alaska Zoo ㉛
Anchorage Golf Course ㉚
Capri Cinema ㉕
Chilkoot Charlie's ⑧
Earthquake Park ②
Goose Lake ㉒
Heritage Library & Museum ⑱
Hilltop Ski Area ㉙
Kincaid Park ①
Mr. Whitekey's Fly-By-Night Club ⑦
Mulcahy Stadium ⑭
Sullivan Arena ⑮
To Trailhead to Flattop Mountain ㉝
Westchester Lagoon ⑩

Dining
Campo Bello ㉑
The Greek Corner Restaurant ⑯
Harry's Restaurant & Bar ⑲
Jen's Restaurant ⑳
Mexico in Alaska ㉗
Sourdough Mining Company
    Restaurant ㉖

Accommodations
Aurora Winds B&B Resort ㉜
Best Western Barratt Inn ⑤
Centennial Camper Park ㉓
Chelsea Inn Hotel ⑥
Hillside Hotel & RV Park ⑰
Inlet Tower Suites ⑪
Parkwood Inn ㉔
Regal Alaskan Hotel ④
Ship Creek Landings
    Downtown RV Park ⑬
12th & L B&B ⑫

Bluff Rd.

Davis Park

Ship Creek

Glenn Hwy. ① 23

see "Downtown Anchorage" map 13

3rd Ave.

Mt. View Dr.

Turpin St.

Bragaw St.

Russian Jack Spring Park

Debarr Ave.

Muldoon Rd.

11th Ave.

12

Merrill Field

Ingra St.

Karluk St.

15th Ave. 14 15

Chester Creek Trail

Chester Creek

17

16

19 Fireweed Lane

18

22

Goose Lake

Bonnface Pkwy.

Baxter Rd.

Benson Blvd.

Northern Lights Blvd.

20 21

36th Ave.

C St.

Tudor Rd. 25

24

Lake Otis Pkwy.

Far North Bicentennial Park

28

Campbell Airstrip Rd.

26

Campbell Creek

Dowling Rd.

E. 68th Ave.

Campbell Field

Artic Blvd.

27 ①

Abbott Loop Rd.

Hillside Park

Old Seward Hwy.

New Seward Hwy.

29

Abbott Rd.

32

30 31

O'Malley Rd.

Upper O'Malley Rd.

Birch Rd.

Hillside Dr.

Johns Rd.

Huffman Rd.

Furrow Creek

Upper Huffman Rd. 33

Dearmoun Rd.

225

to the intersection with the Parks Highway. Then it continues as a two-lane road to Glennallen, Tok, and the Alaska Highway, 330 miles from Anchorage. The Parks Highway goes to Denali National Park and Fairbanks. Most major car-rental companies operate in Anchorage, at the airport or at other locations in town. A midsize car costs about $55 a day, with unlimited mileage. Book well in advance in the summer high season.

By Bus   Gray Line's **Alaskon Express** (☎ 800/544-2206 or 907/277-5581) links Anchorage to Seward, Valdez, and the Alaska Highway. The fare is about $200 to Haines. Other small vans and buses go to Seward, Homer, and Denali National Park; see the sections of each of those places for details.

By RV   A recreational vehicle is a popular way to explore the region, and you can rent one-way from the ferry in Skagway or Haines with a $400 drop-off fee. High-season rates are around $150 to $200 a day, plus the large amount of fuel you use. Major agencies include **ABC Motorhome Rentals,** 3853 W. International Airport Rd., Anchorage, AK 99502 (☎ 800/421-7456 or 907/279-2000; fax 907/243-6363; website http://www.alaskan.com/abcmotorhomes/), and **Cruise America,** 10560 Old Seward Hwy., Anchorage, AK 99515 (☎ 800/327-7799 or 907/349-0499).

By Rail   The **Alaska Railroad** (☎ 800/544-0552 or 907/265-2494) connects Anchorage to Seward to the south and to Fairbanks and Denali National Park to the north. The run to Seward, which operates only in the summer, is incredibly spectacular; the fare is $50 one-way, $80 round-trip. Heading north, you can ride the Alaska Railroad cars year-round to Fairbanks (the summer fare is $149 one-way), and in the summer to Denali in full-dome cars with Princess Tours or Holland America/Westours. For details, see chapter 9 on Denali National Park.

VISITOR INFORMATION   The **Anchorage Convention and Visitor Bureau,** 524 W. Fourth Ave., Anchorage, AK 99501-2212 (☎ 907/276-4118; fax 907/278-5559; website http://www.alaska.net/~acvb), operates five visitor information centers, distributing brochures and providing guidance for the whole state. The main location is the **Log Cabin Visitor Information Center,** downtown at Fourth Avenue and F Street (☎ 907/274-3531; fax 907/272-9564). If the cabin is crowded, go to the storefront office right behind it. The center is open daily: June to August from 7:30am to 7pm, May and September from 8am to 6pm, and October to April from 9am to 4pm; it's closed on New Year's Day, Thanksgiving, and Christmas. You'll also find a visitor center on the way into town by car, in Eagle River, at Easy Street and the Old Glenn Highway, and three at the airport—one in the baggage-claim area in the domestic terminal and two in the international terminal: in the lobby and in the transit area. A lot of information about Anchorage is on the city's website, **http://www.ci.anchorage.ak.us/**.

   The ✪ **Alaska Public Lands Information Center,** 605 W. Fourth Ave., Suite 105, Anchorage, AK 99501 (☎ 907/271-2737; website http://www.nps.gov/aplic/), in the old concrete federal building across the intersection from the log cabin at Fourth and F, has guidance for anyone planning to spend time in the outdoors, as well as displays of interest even for those who aren't. The center occupies a grand room with high ceilings in the former post office and federal courthouse. All the land agencies are represented, and there's information on the whole state. Summer hours are daily 9am to 5:30pm, winter Monday through Friday 10am to 5:30pm. Similar centers are in Ketchikan, Tok, and Fairbanks.

   The **Chugach State Park Headquarters,** in the Potter Section House on the Seward Highway at the south end of town (☎ 907/345-5014), is open normal business hours all year.

The *Anchorage Daily News* maintains a free voice-mail **Daily Newsline** (☎ 907/ 277-1500) with hundreds of recorded topics, including fishing, hiking, skiing, and snowmobiling conditions, as well as basic visitor guidance, such as the Airport Information Line, at extension 5252.

ORIENTATION   Navigating Anchorage is easy if you just remember that the mountains are to the east. Maps are available at the visitor centers or in any grocery store.

Many visitors never make it beyond the **downtown** area, the old-fashioned grid of streets at the northwest corner of town where the large hotels and the gift shops are located. Street numbers and letters work on a simple pattern. Beyond downtown, most of Anchorage is oriented to commercial strips. Three major north-south thoroughfares run from downtown, through the **midtown** commercial area, to the shopping malls and residential districts of **South Anchorage.** These are, going west to east, **Minnesota Drive,** which becomes I and L streets downtown; **C Street** and **A Street;** and the **New Seward Highway,** which is Ingra and Gambell streets downtown and heads out of town to the south. Major east-west roads in the grid are Fifth and Sixth avenues, becoming the **Glenn Highway** and leading out of town to the north; **Northern Lights Boulevard** and **Benson Boulevard** running across the city in midtown; and **Dimond Boulevard,** in South Anchorage. Some parts of Anchorage are outside the bowl defined by the Chugach Mountains. The communities of **Eagle River** and **Eklutna** are out the Glenn Highway, to the northeast. **Girdwood** and **Portage** are on the Seward Highway, to the south.

GETTING AROUND   Two **airport shuttles** charge $6 to go downtown, **Borealis Shuttle** (☎ 907/276-3600) or **Mom's Shuttle** (☎ 907/344-6667), picking up frequently at the domestic terminal. The **People Mover** city bus system (☎ 907/ 343-6543) goes to the airport roughly 10 times a day, weekdays only, and most runs you have to transfer to get downtown. Bus fare all over town is $1, but there is a free zone in the downtown core. The transit center bus depot is at Sixth Avenue and G Street. Buses generally come every half hour but are less frequent on weekends. Taxis are expensive in Anchorage because of the spread-out urban design. A ride downtown from the airport runs about $14. Try **Alaska Cab** (☎ 907/563-5353).

A bike is a great way to explore, using the network of bike trails. The **Tony Knowles Coastal Trail** comes right downtown (see "Special Places" under "Getting Outside," below). The **CycleSights** bike rental tent (☎ 907/344-1771 or 907/ 227-6109) operates in Elderberry Park, at the western end of Fifth Avenue by the water, right next to the trail. They charge $15 for a half day, $25 all day, and lead four tours a day Tuesday through Sunday. Bikes also are for rent from **Adventure Café,** at 414 K St. (☎ 907/276-8282; e-mail afjlv@uaa.alaska.edu), a couple of blocks east (they also serve espresso, vegetarian soups, and sandwiches). They charge $15 for 3 hours. **Downtown Bicycle Rental,** at Fifth Avenue and C Street, in the T-shirt shop (☎ 907/279-5293), charges $11 for 4 hours.

To visit most of Anchorage, you'll need to get beyond the downtown area. The easiest way is in a **rental car** (see "Getting There," above). The **Alaska Backpacker Shuttle** (☎ 800/266-8625 or 907/344-8775) offers rides to some trails around Anchorage, as well as to Denali National Park and Portage Glacier. The fare to either is $35 one-way.

City tours are available from at least six operators; check with the visitor center. The best downtown tour is the historic walking tour described below under "A Stroll Around Downtown Anchorage." **Anchorage City Trolley Tour** (☎ 907/ 257-5603), a bus that's been made to look like a San Francisco streetcar, takes 1-hour tours from the 4th Avenue Theater, on Fourth Avenue between F and G streets, charging only $10. They leave every hour from 8am to 7pm during the summer. **Alaska Welcomes You!** (☎ or TTY **800/349-6301** or 907/349-6301; website http://alaskan.com/vendors/welcome.html) offers 2-hour Turnagain Arm tours for $10 and 3-hour city tours for $19, as well as longer tours and travel packages. They specialize in serving people with disabilities. **Fireweed Tours** (☎ **907/333-4436**) offers a 4-hour tour three times a day for $39. **Accessible Alaska Adventures** (☎ **907/ 349-6301**) specializes in tours for people with physical, visual, or hearing disabilities.

FAST FACTS   Anchorage has no sales tax. A **bank** is never far away, and most grocery stores also have **ATMs.** There are many branches of the **post office** in town—in the downtown area, it's downstairs in the brown building at Fourth Avenue and D Street. In **emergencies,** call **911.** To reach the **Anchorage Police Department** for nonemergency problems, call ☎ **907/786-8500.** For police business outside the city, call the **Alaska State Troopers** (☎ **907/269-5511**). There are two hospitals in Anchorage serving the general public: the **Columbia Alaska Regional Hospital,** at 2801 DeBarr Rd. (☎ **907/276-1131**), and **Providence Alaska Medical Center,** at 3200 Providence Dr. (☎ **907/562-2211**). The *Anchorage Daily News* includes an extensive arts and leisure section each Friday, called "8." **Out-of-town papers** are available in street boxes or at Carrs grocery stores; downtown, Cook Inlet Book Company, at 415 W. Fifth Ave., carries many more. To connect with the local literary scene, check their website, http://www.cookinlet.com/.

SPECIAL EVENTS   The ✪ **Fur Rendezvous Winter Carnival,** February 13 to February 22, 1998 (☎ **907/277-8615**), is a huge, city-wide winter celebration, the main event of which is the **World Champion Sled Dog Race,** a 3-day sprint event of about 25 miles per heat. The ✪ **Iditarod Trail Sled Dog Race** (☎ **907/ 376-5155**) starts from Anchorage the first Saturday in March at 10am, but the teams are loaded in trucks a few miles out of town and restarted in Wasilla for the 1,000-mile run to Nome (see the section on the Matanuska and Susitna valleys, later in this chapter). The **International Ice Carving Competition** takes place that same weekend in town square, at Fifth Avenue and E Street. **Music in the Park** presents concerts Wednesday and Friday afternoons all summer in the park at Old City Hall, at Fourth and E streets. **The Anchorage Festival of Music** (☎ **907/276-2465**) presents a series of classical music concerts during June. **The Taste of Anchorage** (☎ **907/562-9911**) is a food fair in early June (June 5–7 in 1998), on the Delaney Park Strip near Ninth Avenue and I Street. **Family Kite Day** is the second Sunday in June (June 14 in 1998) at the west end of the Delaney Park Strip, near Ninth Avenue and L Street. The **Chugiak–Eagle River Bear Paw Festival** is a community celebration in July with a parade, rodeo, carnival, and other festivities. The **Great Alaska Shootout Men's Basketball Tournament** brings top-ranked college teams to the Sullivan Arena over Thanksgiving weekend (see "Spectator Sports," below). The Saturday after Thanksgiving, a **Christmas Tree Lighting** takes place in town square, with Santa usually arriving behind a team of real reindeer.

EXPLORING ANCHORAGE

I've arranged this section starting with only the sights you can visit downtown, without a car, followed by attractions that are farther afield.

DOWNTOWN MUSEUMS

✪ **Anchorage Museum of History and Art.** 121 W. Seventh Ave. ☎ 907/343-4326. Website http://www.ci.anchorage.ak.us. Admission $5 adults, $4.50 seniors 65 and older, free for children 17 and under. High season, daily 9am–6pm; low season, Tues–Sat 10am–6pm, Sun 1–5pm.

Downtown Anchorage

Accommodations
Anchorage Hotel 18
Copper Whale Inn 9
Hostelling International,
   Anchorage 26
Hotel Captain Cook 6
Oscar Gill House B&B 28
Ship Creek Hotel 23
Snowshoe Inn 27
Voyager Hotel/Corsair Restaurant 5
Attractions
Alaska Center for
   the Performing Arts 15

Alaska Experience Center 10
Anchorage Museum
   of History and Art 24
Coastal Trail Trailhead 1
Cyrano's Bookstore,
   Cafe and Playhouse 21
Fifth Avenue Mall 22
Fourth Avenue Theater 14
The Imaginarium 8
Log Cabin Visitor
   Information Center 17
Oscar Anderson House 2
Public Lands
   Information Center 12

Resolution Park 3
Saturday Market 19

Dining
Club Paris 20
Dianne's Restaurant 25
Glacier Brewhouse 7
Kumagoro/Downtown
   Deli and Cafe 16
The Marx Brothers Cafe 13
Sacks Cafe 11
Simon and Seafort's
   Saloon and Grill 4

The state's largest museum doesn't have its largest collection, but unlike the Alaska State Museum in Juneau or the University of Alaska Museum in Fairbanks, the Anchorage museum has the room and staff both to teach and to serve as a center of contemporary culture of a regional caliber. Most visitors tour the Alaska Gallery, an informative and enjoyable walk through the history and anthropology of the state. In the art galleries, you can see what's happening in art in Alaska today. The Anchorage museum also gets the best touring shows. It's the only museum in Alaska that could require more than one visit. The cafe serves some of the best lunches to be had downtown. In the summer, Native dancers perform in the auditorium daily at 12:15, 1:15, and 2:15pm.

The Imaginarium. 727 W. Fifth Ave., Suite 140. ☎ **907/276-3179.** Admission $5 adults, $4 seniors 65 and older and children 2–12. Mon–Sat 10am–6pm, Sun noon–5pm.

This is a science museum geared to children, with not many words and lots of fun learning experiences. The idea is that while they're running around having a great time, the kids may accidentally learn something; at least, the displays will excite a sense of wonder that is the start of science. There's a strong Alaska theme to many of the displays. The saltwater touch tank is like an indoor tide pool. This is one of our children's favorite places to go for a treat. Call before getting hopes up, as there was some discussion of moving the museum.

The Oscar Anderson House. 420 M St. ☎ **907/274-2336** or 907/274-3600. Admission $5 adults, $4 seniors, $1 children 5–12. Summer only, daily noon–4pm. Closed in winter.

This house museum, moved to a beautiful site in Elderberry Park over the water shows how an early Swedish butcher lived. Although far from grand, the house i quaint, surrounded by a lovely little garden. The tour provides a good explanation of Anchorage's short history. Anderson died in 1974, and the house contains many of the family's original belongings, including a working 1909 player piano around which the structure was built. If you come at Christmas, don't miss the Swedish Christmas tours, the first two weekends in December.

A STROLL AROUND DOWNTOWN ANCHORAGE

Anchorage Historic Properties, 645 W. Third Ave. (☎ **907/274-3600**), a city endowed historical preservation group, offers a ✪ **Guided Walking Tour of Historic Downtown Anchorage** June to August, Monday through Friday at 1pm. The volunteer guides are fun and knowledgeable. The 1-hour tour covers 2 miles. Meet at the lobby of old city hall, 524 W. Fourth Ave., next door to the Log Cabin Visitor Information Center. Tickets cost $5 for adults, $4 for seniors over age 65, and $1 for children. You can save $4 by buying a combination ticket with the Oscar Anderson House Museum, described above. If you can't do the guided tour, pick up their brochure at the visitor center, which tells a little about the buildings and directs you to 11 sequential historical sign kiosks.

Here are some highlights of the downtown area. I've arranged them as a walking tour, but you can also scan the text for the sights that interest you.

Start at the **Log Cabin Visitor Information Center** at Fourth Avenue and F Street. Outside is a sign that shows the distance to various cities, a popular spot for pictures. Walking east, toward the mountains, the 1936 **Old City Hall,** at Fourth Avenue and E Street, is on the right. Recently renovated, its lobby contains an interesting display on city history, including dioramas of the early streetscape.

Crossing E Street, notice on the left side of Fourth Avenue that all the buildings are modern—everything on that side from E Street east for several blocks collapsed in the 1964 earthquake. The street split in half, lengthwise, with the left side ending up a dozen feet lower than the right. That land was later reinforced with a gravel buttress by the U.S. Army Corps of Engineers and the slope below forever set aside from new construction because of the earthquake risk. This stretch of Fourth Avenue is where the **Iditarod Trail Sled Dog Race** and the **Anchorage Fur Rendezvous World Championship Sled Dog Race** start each year in March and February, respectively.

At Fourth Avenue and D Street, the **Wendler Building,** the old Club 25, is among the oldest buildings in Anchorage, but no longer the very oldest. (See the Oscar Gill House Bed and Breakfast, in "Accommodations," below, for an explanation of that conundrum.) The bronze of the dog commemorates the sled-dog races that start here. Across D Street is a mural that depicts a relief map of Alaska, with the Iditarod Trail marked.

Turn right, walking a block south on D Street to Fifth Avenue. There are several interesting little shops and restaurants on this block. The **5th Avenue Mall,** a grand, four-story shopping center, is across the street; it includes Alaska's finest upscale shopping. On the opposite side of the building—turn left on Fifth Avenue and right on C Street to Sixth Avenue—is the **Wolfsong of Alaska** (☎ **907/ 274-9653**) museum and gift shop. This nonprofit organization aims to educate and elevate the public about Alaska's most controversial mammal. Inside you'll find displays, mounts, artwork, videos, and eager volunteers. Admission is free, and it's open in summer Monday through Friday from 10am to 7pm, on Saturday from 11am to 6pm, and on Sunday from noon to 5pm. Two doors west (away from the mountains) is the free **Alaska State Troopers Museum** (☎ 907/279-5050), with lots of law enforcement insignia, equipment, and memorabilia, and a gift shop. It's open year round Monday through Friday, 10am to 4pm, Saturday noon to 4pm.

Walk west, past the mall, to Sixth Avenue and E Street, one corner of the beautifully planted **town square.** The Downtown Anchorage Association raised money for the improvements by collecting donations of $40 each for the granite bricks, with an inscription of the contributor's choosing. There are 13,344 (bet you can't find mine). The building on the north side that looks like a rolltop desk is the acclaimed **William A. Egan Civic and Convention Center.** Inside you'll find a pleasant atrium, public rest rooms, and whatever's going on in the ballrooms. On the east side of the square, the huge whale mural was painted freehand by Wyland in 1994. He painted similar whale murals in cities all along the west coast. On the west side of the square, the massive, highly decorated ✪ **Alaska Center for the Performing Arts** dominates; it's Anchorage's most controversial building, completed in 1988 at a cost of over $70 million. The lobby is usually open, and whatever your opinion of the decor, a look inside will spark a discussion. Ask at the box office about tours. Thespians believe the building is haunted by the ghost of painter Sydney Lawrence, who makes lights mysteriously vary and elevators go up and down with no one in them. An auditorium demolished to make room for the center was named for Lawrence. Check the box office also for current performances in the three theaters—this is Alaska's premier performance venue.

Cross Sixth Avenue at the light by the center's door. Continuing west, **Humpy's,** the tavern on the left side of Sixth, has a huge selection of microbrews, in case you're already thirsty, and good casual meals. The square, green office building next door is **city hall.** Turn left through the pedestrian walkway between Humpy's and city hall. A mural showing a time line of the history of Anchorage faces the parking lot. The building it is painted on is the **Exxon Valdez Oil Spill Library,** a repository of most of what's known about the 1989 spill, which houses the offices of the trustees responsible for spending $1 billion won from Exxon by the government.

Walk west, between city hall and the spill library, to G Street. The tower to the left is Arco, the company that owns much of Alaska's oil reserves. Turn right and proceed to Sixth Avenue and G. (If you're up for a longer walk, you can turn left on G Street instead and explore the Delaney Park strip and lovely South Addition residential neighborhood south of 9th Avenue.)

The **Alaska Experience Center** is on the northwest corner of Sixth Avenue and G Street, in the dome tent. A 40-minute Omnivision wraparound movie about Alaska costs $7 for adults, $4 for children. It's certainly spectacular—too much so for some people, who get motion sickness. Sit toward the center at the back. An Alaska Earthquake display that really shakes is $5 for adults and $4 for children. They're open daily from 9am to 9pm in summer, and from 11am to 6pm in winter. On the southwest corner is the transit center, for city buses. The **Decker/Morris Gallery,** one of Alaska's best, is on the northeast corner.

Walk a block north, back to Fifth Avenue. The west side of G Street between Fourth and Fifth avenues contains some of the downtown's best **off-beat businesses: Side Street Espresso,** where you can get into a lively political discussion; **Denali Wear,** which is Tracy Anna Bader's studio and shop of wearable art; **Darwin's Theory,** a friendly, old-fashioned bar with character that shows up in an Indigo Girls song; and **The Great Alaska Train Company,** a retired couple's labor of love, which sells nothing but model trains and train memorabilia. There are others, too—it's a great little block.

Going west (away from the mountains) on Fifth, **Aurora Fine Arts** is on the right. **The Imaginarium,** described above, is next, and finally **The Glacier Brewhouse,** a brew pub restaurant described below. Continuing west on Fifth Avenue and crossing H Street, the **Holy Family Cathedral,** a concrete, art deco church, is the seat of the Roman Catholic archbishop. Keep going toward the water, crossing L Street and down the hill to **Elderberry Park.** The yellow-and-brown house is the **Oscar Anderson House,** described above. There's good playground equipment here, public restrooms, and comfortable places where you can sit and watch the kids and Cook Inlet at the same time and meet other parents. This also is the easiest access point to the ✪ **Coastal Trail** (see "Special Places" under "Getting Outside," below), where it tunnels under the Alaska Railroad tracks. Even if you don't have time to go far on the trail, you may want to walk through the tunnel and see the ducks paddling around and, at low tide, the vast mud flats.

Now hike back up the hill to L Street and turn left, going north 2 blocks to **Resolution Park,** with the bronze **Captain Cook Monument.** Capt. James Cook stands on a large, wooden deck, but he's gazing out to sea—which certainly wouldn't have been the way he was facing when he discovered Cook Inlet in 1778 aboard HMS *Resolution.*

Follow Third Avenue east (back toward the mountains), then turn right again on I Street to round the front of the **Nesbett State Courthouse.** The two totem poles in the plaza, erected in 1997, represent the eagle and raven moieties of the Tlingit people, intended to symbolize the balance of justice.

Go 1 block east, then turn left again around the courthouse on H Street, continuing north across Third Avenue, then down the hill where H becomes Christensen Drive, and turn right again on Second Avenue, toward the mountains. Many of the old houses that line Second are marked, their historic significance carefully catalogued—80-year-old houses may not be "historic" where you come from, but here we have to take what we can get. If you imagine houses like this over much of downtown, you'll know what Anchorage looked like before oil.

Continue east to E Street. At Second Avenue and E, a **monument** to Alaska's 1959 admission to the Union honors President Eisenhower; you overlook the Alaska Railroad yards from here, and see part of the port of Anchorage and the neighborhood of Government Hill across the Ship Creek river bottom. This is where the tent city of Knik Anchorage, later shortened to Anchorage, was set up in 1914.

If you have the energy, there are several interesting sites down the hill in Ship Creek. (Otherwise, skip to the next paragraph.) Walking down the stairs that lead down the earthquake buttress area hillside, take a look at the old depot (an excellent brew pub is in one end of the building) and the beautifully restored steam engine on the pedestal in front. It was used on construction of the Panama Canal, then worked in the yard here as a switch engine. Continue to the creek, then follow the path east toward the mountains. Ship Creek yields good-sized salmon all summer (see "Fishing" below). The covered bridge contains the **Fairbanks Gold Company Mining Museum and Gold Works** (☎ 907/457-6058), a gold-panning tourist attraction. Gold mining occurred along Turnagain Arm, south of Anchorage, but never in this area. Farther upstream, a path crosses the creek atop a dam, where there is a plaza to watch the ducks and possibly fish. Now retrace your steps back to the Eisenhower Monument at Second Avenue and E Street.

Walk up the hill on E Street to Third Avenue. The extensively landscaped parking lot on the left becomes the ✪ **Saturday Market** every weekend in the summer, a street fair drawing hundreds of vendors and thousands of shoppers. You can buy everything from local vegetables to handmade crafts to somebody's old record collection. There are food booths and music, too.

Turn right and walk a block west (away from the mountains) on Third Avenue, then turn left on F Street. **F Street Station,** on the left, is a fun bar with an after-work crowd. Proceed to Fourth Avenue, and you're back at the Log Cabin Visitor Information Center, but don't stop. Turn right on Fourth Avenue. On the right side is the **old federal building,** a grand, white, Depression-era structure that now contains the Alaska Public Lands Information Center, with interesting displays and lots of information about the outdoors. Across the street is Anchorage's most attractive historic building, the restored ✪ **4th Avenue Theater.** It was built by Cap Lathrop, an early Alaskan business magnate, who created it as a monument to the territory and the permanence of its new society. Today it's a gift store. Don't miss going in and looking at the bas-relief murals and the blinking big dipper on the ceiling, which during many a movie over the years was more entertaining than whatever was on the screen.

SIGHTS BEYOND DOWNTOWN

Alaska Aviation Heritage Museum. 4721 Aircraft Dr. ☎ **907/248-5325.** Admission $5.75 adults, $4.50 active military and seniors over age 62, $2.75 children. High season, daily 9am–6pm; low season, Tues–Sat 10am–4pm. Take International Airport Rd. toward the airport and follow the signs to the right as you near the terminal.

Old soldiers and aviators and anyone interested in mechanical things will enjoy this collection of classic planes in hangars and a small indoor exhibit near the Lake Hood float-plane base. A highlight is the shop where they rebuild wrecked classic aircraft—you can wander in and watch the work in progress. The display of Japanese and American military artifacts, from the war for the Aleutians, has impact. Unfortunately, at this writing the museum was in financial trouble, and likely to either move or close its doors. The visitor center can give you up-to-date information.

Alaska Botanical Garden. Campbell Airstrip Rd. (off Tudor Rd.). ☎ **907/265-3165.** Free admission. Summer, daily 9am–9pm. From downtown, drive out New Seward Hwy. (Gambell St.) to Tudor Rd., exit to the east (left), turn right off Tudor onto Campbell Airstrip Rd., and park at the Benny Benson School. It's 20 minutes from downtown.

It's young and the volunteer staff still has a long way to go, but the garden already is a restful place to learn about native flora and see what else grows here while sitting on the peaceful benches and watching birds and squirrels. They've done a good job of integrating the garden into its forest setting. Kids love the paths and secluded spots. They offer storytimes and art and photography programs.

✪ **The Alaska Zoo.** 4731 O'Malley Rd. ☎ **907/346-3242.** Admission $6 adults, $5 seniors, $4 children 12–17, $3 children 3–12. Opens at 10am; closing time varies by season. Drive out the New Seward Hwy. to O'Malley Rd., then turn left and go 2 miles; it's 25 minutes from downtown, without traffic.

If you're expecting a big-city zoo, you'll be disappointed, but the Alaska Zoo has a charm all its own. Anchorage residents have developed personal relationships with the animals, many of which are named, in their campy little Eden. Gravel paths wander through the woods past bears, seals and otters, musk oxen, mountain goats, moose, caribou, waterfowl—all the animals you were supposed to see in Alaska but may have missed. (Don't get the elephants or tigers in your snapshots—they'll blow your story.)

Earthquake Park. West end of Northern Lights Blvd. Drive west on Northern Lights from Minnesota Dr. (L St. downtown), looking on the right after Lakeshore Dr.

The 1964 Good Friday earthquake was the biggest ever in North America, registering at 9.2 on the Richter Scale, killing 131 people, and flattening much of the region. Downtown Anchorage and the Turnagain residential area, near the park, suffered enormous slides that turned neighborhoods into chaotic ruins. Newly installed sculpture and excellent interpretive signs commemorate and explain the event and point out its few remaining marks on the land. This also is a good access point to the Coastal Trail.

Heritage Library and Museum. C St. and Northern Lights Blvd. ☎ **907/265-2834.** Free admission. High season, Mon–Fri noon–5pm; low season, noon–4pm.

This well-endowed little museum, in a room off the lobby of the white National Bank of Alaska building, houses a collection of paintings and Alaska Native cultural artifacts and a reference library of 2,500 volumes on Alaska-related topics.

In Eagle River & Eklutna

Eagle River, 14 miles northeast from Anchorage on the Glenn Highway, is like a whole different town, with its own business district and local concerns. Most residents commute into town or to the nearby military bases. Other than the outdoor activities in the area, described below, there's not much to do in Eagle River. The **Alaska Museum of Natural History,** at 11723 Old Glenn Hwy. (☎ **907/694-0819;** website http://www.alaska.net/~nathist), is located in the drab Parkgate Building, across from McDonald's, with the visitor information center. It's a small but cheerful volunteer effort teaching about the minerals, fossils, dinosaurs, and animals of the area—there are dioramas with mounted wild animals. Children and rock hounds should attend. Admission is $3 for adults. It's open Monday through Saturday 11am to 5pm in summer, 10am to 4pm in winter.

About 25 miles out the Glenn Highway (take the Eklutna exit, then go left over the overpass), the Native village of **Eklutna** has a fascinating old cemetery in which each grave is enclosed by a highly decorated spirit house, the size of a large doll house. The spirit houses excite the imagination in a way no ordinary marker would. The **Eklutna Tribe** (☎ **907/688-6026** or 907/696-2828) leads a 30-minute tour of the cemetery, two Russian Orthodox churches (including the **St. Nicholas Orthodox Church,** which is on the National Register of Historic Places), and a museum. It costs $3.50. Those not on a tour have to stay outside the cemetery fence. The park is open in summer only, daily from 8am to 6pm. Across the road, the 1920s **Chief Mike Alex Cabin** also is open for tours in the summer by donation. Alex, who lived 1907 to 1977, was the tribe's last traditional chief.

SHOPPING

Some interesting shops are mentioned above, in the downtown walking tour, where most galleries and gift shops are located. Before making major purchases, know what you're buying (see "Native Art—Finding the Real Thing," in chapter 3).

Many stores in Anchorage carry Native Alaskan arts and crafts. If you're going to the Bush, you'll find lower prices there but less selection. The ✪ **Oomingmak Musk Ox Producers' Co-operative,** in the house with the musk ox on the side at Sixth Avenue and H Street, sells scarves and other knitted items of qiviut (KI-vee-ute), the light, warm, silky underhair of the musk ox, which is combed out, collected, and knitted in the Bush by village women. They're expensive—some caps cost over $100—but unique and culturally significant. The **Yankee Whaler,** in the lobby of the Hotel Captain Cook, at Fifth Avenue and I Street, is a small but well-regarded shop carrying Native arts. **Alaska Native Arts and Crafts,** better known as ANAC, in the post office mall at 333 W. Fourth Ave., is the traditional and original artists' outlet for authentic Native work, in operation since 1938. **The Rusty Harpoon,** next door in the yellow Sunshine Mall, at 411 Fourth Ave., also has authentic Native items and reliable, longtime proprietors. **One People,** at 400 D St., carries folk art from all over the world, especially Native dolls, soapstone and ivory carvings, jewelry, and baskets. Farther afield, the **Alaska Fur Exchange,** at 4417 Old Seward Hwy., near Tudor Road, is a cross between an old-time wilderness trading post and a modern factory outlet. Rural residents bring in furs and crafts to sell and trade, which are displayed in great profusion and clutter. If you're in the market for pelts, go no further.

For furs in more finished condition, **David Green Master Furrier,** at 130 W. Fourth Ave., is an Anchorage institution. The **Alaska Fur Factory** is close by, at Fourth Avenue and D Street, as is the **Alaska Fur Gallery,** at 428 W. Fourth Ave., just down the block. There are others in the Anchorage Hilton Hotel and the 5th Avenue Mall. ✪ **Laura Wright Alaskan Parkys,** at 343 W. Fifth Ave., makes and sells the bright fabric coats called kuspuks really worn by Eskimos. Winter-wear parkys often have fur trim, but that isn't a requirement for beauty and authenticity.

There are lots of places to buy both mass-produced and inexpensive handmade crafts that aren't from the Bush. If you can be in town on a Saturday during the summer, be sure to visit the ✪ **Saturday Market** street fair, in the parking lot at Third Avenue and E Street, with food, music, and hundreds of miscellaneous crafts booths. You won't have any trouble finding shops on Fourth Avenue downtown. **Once in a Blue Moose** is one of our favorites, at Fourth Avenue and F Street; **Grizzly's Gifts,** at Fourth and E, and **Trapper Jacks,** at Fourth and G, are the biggest and have huge selections of gifts. The ✪ **Kobuk Coffee Company,** at Fifth Avenue and E Street, next to town square, occupies one of Anchorage's earliest commercial buildings; it's a cozy little candy, coffee, and collectibles shop. In midtown, on International Airport Road between the Old and New Seward highways, **Alaska Wild Berry Products** is a fun store to visit. There's a chocolate waterfall and a big window where you can watch the candy factory at work. The chocolate-covered berry jellies are simultaneously addictive and rich enough to make you dizzy if you eat more than a few.

Downtown has several fine art galleries. The ✪ **Decker/Morris Gallery,** at Sixth Avenue and G Street, takes its work seriously enough to maintain a permanent collection of contemporary art on display in prime gallery space. Alaska's most exciting and adventurous artists are on display here, including Duke Russell, whose seamy Anchorage street scenes, often with cartoon bubbles of words, hilariously skewer the Alaskan mystique. A block north, at Fifth and G, **Aurora Fine Arts** also is a serious gallery, carrying more pottery and prints. **Artique,** another block north at 314 G St., is Anchorage's oldest gallery and has a large selection of ceramics and sculpture as well as prints and paintings. The **International Gallery of Contemporary Art,** at 625 W. Fifth Ave., puts on sometimes challenging shows of current art. The **Stephan Fine Arts Gallery,** with a main location at 600 W. Sixth Ave. and smaller outlets in the Hotel Captain Cook and 5th Avenue Mall, is the largest in town, specializing in prints on wilderness and wildlife themes by such artists as Bev Doolittle.

GETTING OUTSIDE
SPECIAL PLACES

MUNICIPAL BIKE / FOOT / SKI TRAILS   My favorite thing about Anchorage is a ride or walk on a sunny summer afternoon on the ✪ **Tony Knowles Coastal Trail.** Leading 10 miles from the western end of Second Avenue along the shore to **Kincaid Park,** the coastal trail is a unique pathway to the natural environment from the heart of downtown Anchorage. You can join the wide, paved trail at various points; **Elderberry Park,** at the western end of Fifth Avenue, is the most popular.

Several bike-rental agencies and a bike tour operation are in close proximity—see "Getting Around" under "Essentials," above. I've ridden my bike parallel with beluga whales swimming along the trail at high tide. Toward the Kincaid Park end of the trail, I've seen moose, or had them stop me. **Westchester Lagoon** is 10 blocks south of Elderberry Park. If you're just up for a short walk, the lagoon is a great destination for a picnic or to feed the ducks. In the winter, it is groomed for ice skating, with long trails leading across the pond. On weekends hundreds of families come out to skate, talk around bonfires, and drink hot chocolate and coffee from vendors. At the lagoon, the coastal trail meets the **Lanie Fleischer Chester Creek Trail,** which runs about 4 miles through the center of town to **Goose Lake,** where you can swim in a cool, wooded pond at the end of a hot ride—still, improbably enough, in the middle of the city. The trail follows a greenbelt the whole way, so you rarely see a building, and road and railroad crossings on all the trails have bridges or tunnels, so you're never in traffic.

✪ **Kincaid Park** itself is one of the best cross-country skiing areas in the country and in the summer is a great place for mountain biking, running, or day hiking. **Little Campbell Lake** is a picturesque swimming hole. The whole place is crawling with moose. You can reach the park either along the coastal trail or by driving south from downtown on Minnesota Drive (L Street) and then west on Raspberry Road, to the very end. The park is situated on 1,400 rolling acres of birch and white spruce on a point on Cook Inlet, south and west of the airport, with about 30 miles of groomed ski trails ranging from easy to killer. Eight kilometers are lighted in winter and open until 10pm nightly. An **outdoor center** (☎ **907/343-6397**) is open Monday through Friday from 1 to 10pm and on Saturday and Sunday from 10am to 10pm. It's a warm-up house in winter and a popular venue for weddings in the summer, as the views across the inlet are spectacular. (For information on any in-town activities, call the **city's Division of Parks and Recreation,** ☎ **907/343-4474;** website http://www.ci.anchorage.ak.us/.)

THE CHUGACH MOUNTAINS   The mountains behind Anchorage are wonderfully accessible and as beautiful as areas people travel hundreds of miles from Anchorage to see. Almost the whole area is in either Chugach State Park or Chugach National Forest. There's plenty of alpine terrain to wander in, and it's possible to get off by yourself on multiday trips where you'll see few other people, and still be in cellular-phone range of Anchorage. You don't need a permit to camp, but you should get out of sight of trails. You can get ideas from the Alaska Public Lands Information Center or from the park visitor centers (see "Visitor Information" under "Essentials," above). Get a copy of the tabloid newspaper visitor guide *Ridgelines.* The best trail guide to the entire region is Helen Neinhueser and John Wolfe, Jr.'s ✪ *55 Ways to the Wilderness,* published by The Mountaineers, 1011 SW Klickitat Way, Seattle, WA 98134; it costs $12.95 and is available in any bookstore in the area.

✪ **Flattop Mountain,** right behind Anchorage, is a great family climb. It's an easy afternoon hike for fit adults, and younger children can go part way and still get to see memorable views above the treeline. From New Seward Highway, drive east on O'Malley Road, turn right on Hillside Drive and left on Upper Huffman Road, then right on the narrow, twisting Toilsome Hill Drive. The parking area at **Glen Alps,** above treeline, is a starting point for lots of winter and summer trips (in winter check on avalanche conditions with park officials). If you don't feel like climbing, you can walk or bike the broad gravel trail that leads up the valley. With the help of a copy of *55 Ways,* you can hike from here over the mountains to various alpine lakes, or over to Eagle River or to one of the trails leading down to Turnagain Arm.

You'll also find great hikes in the Chugach Mountains south of town, along the Seward Highway, described below in "A Road Trip to Turnagain Arm and Portage Glacier." North of Anchorage, on the Glenn Highway, there are trails at the head of Eagle River Road, around the park visitor center, and, from the Thunderbird Falls exit, 25 miles from Anchorage—at the latter, an easy mile-long hike leads to a crashing cataract of water. Continuing up the gravel **Eklutna Lake Road,** you come to a lovely state parks campground ($10 a night) and the beautiful glacial lake for canoeing, hiking, and mountain biking. You can make a goal of the Eklutna Glacier at the other end. (This glacial melt is where Anchorage gets much of its water.) The **Eagle River Nature Center,** at the end of Eagle River road, 12 miles up Eagle River Valley from the Glenn Highway exit, is like a public wilderness lodge, with hands-on naturalist displays about the area and guided nature walks. It's open in summer Tuesday through Saturday, 10am to 5pm. Several excellent trails in Chugach State Park start here, from strenuous, multiday trips to easy nature walks. At Arctic Valley, off an exit halfway to Eagle River, the **Alpenglow Ski Area** (☎ **907/563-2524** or 907/249-9292) is a wonderful place in the summer for alpine day hikes away from any trail, or in the winter for above-the-treeline alpine skiing close to town. On top of the mountain to the left is an abandoned Cold War–era antimissile emplacement.

HILLSIDE PARK / FAR NORTH BICENTENNIAL PARK   The 4,000-acre, largely undeveloped park on the east side of town is a unique patch of urban wilderness. Wildlife, including bears and moose, live there among the trails for dog mushing, skiing, walking, and mountain biking. The Alaska Botanical Garden is in the park, as is the **Hilltop Ski Area,** 7105 Abbott Rd. (☎ **907/346-1446**), a beginner-oriented slope where you can rent equipment and get lessons in skiing or snowboarding. Hilltop is also the venue for summer **trail riding;** guided rides are offered for $25 an hour by **Alaska Wilderness Outfitters** (☎ **907/344-2434**) all summer, daily from 10am to 10pm. To reach the Hilltop area of the park, take New Seward Highway south to Dimond Boulevard, then go east (left) until it becomes Abbott Road.

ACTIVITIES

EQUIPMENT   You can rent most anything you need for outdoor activities in Anchorage and its environs. Bike rentals are listed above, under "Getting Around." You can get advice and rent kayaks, skis, snowshoes, bear-proof containers, and mountaineering equipment at **Alaska Mountaineering and Hiking,** at 2633 Spenard Rd. (☎ **907/272-1811;** e-mail amh@alaska.net).

DOG MUSHING   In the last 20 years, sled-dog mushing has become a recreational sport as well as the utilitarian activity it once was in the Bush and the professional sport it has been for years. More and more sled-dog enthusiasts are offering a chance for visitors to drive their team, or at least ride in the basket. Of course, for real mushing, or anything remotely like it, you have to be here in the winter. **Birch Trails Sled Dog Tours,** 22719 Robinson St., Chugiak, AK 99567 (☎ and fax **907/ 688-5713**), specializes in winter trips from their bed-and-breakfast 14 miles from Anchorage. If you have the time, they'll teach you to drive the team. **Mush A Dog Team,** 17620 Birchwood Loop Rd. (☎ **907/688-1391**), offers a summer 1-hour tour with gold panning for $15 and winter trips by appointment. Take the South Birchwood exit off the Glenn Highway.

FISHING   There are salmon, stocked and natural, in some of Anchorage's streams and stocked trout in some lakes. Although the setting might not be the wilderness experience you've dreamed about, the 40-pound king you pull from the water under a highway bridge on Ship Creek may make up for it. From downtown, just walk down the hill to the railroad yard. A tackle shop rents gear in the summer. Fishing is best on a rising tide, and you'll need serious boots for the muddy banks. You can also catch stocked silver salmon in Campbell Creek and Bird Creek, in the late summer and fall. The **Alaska Department of Fish and Game** has a recorded information line on what's hot (☎ **907/267-2510**); for information on regulations or more detailed advice, call, write, or visit their office at 333 Raspberry Rd., Anchorage, AK 99518-1599 (☎ **907/267-2221**).

Serious fishermen will use Anchorage as a base, for a ✪ **fly-in fishing trip** on a remote lake or river all your own, or to go somewhere else in the state. Several companies offer fly-in trips; two of the largest and best established are **Ketchum Air Service** (☎ **800/433-9114** or 907/243-5525) and **Rust's Flying Service** (☎ **800/ 544-2299** or 907/243-1595). They can take you out guided or on your own, just for the day or to stay for a while in a cabin. You can bring your own gear, or they can provide it. You don't have to be an avid fisherman to enjoy one of these trips—there's nothing like the silence that falls as the float plane that dropped you off disappears over the horizon. Prices start around $150 per person for an unguided day trip.

If you want to be absolutely certain you're where the fish are when you're in Alaska, **Sport Fishing Alaska,** 1401 Shore Dr., Anchorage, AK 99515 (☎ **907/ 344-8674;** fax 907/349-4330; e-mail sfa@alaska.net), is an agency run by a former state fish biologist which, for a $95 fee, plans fishing vacations to Alaska. They act as a buyer's agent and, unlike a travel agent, don't take commissions from businesses they book.

FLIGHTSEEING   Small planes are the blood cells of Alaska's circulatory system, and Anchorage its heart. There are several busy airports in Anchorage, and Lake Hood is the world's busiest float-plane base. More than two dozen operators are anxious to take you on a flightseeing tour—check the visitor center for names—but the most comfortable and memorable is probably the restored DC-3 operated by ✪ **Era Aviation** (☎ **800/866-8394** or 907/266-8394). The plane re-creates the classic days of air travel—you can pretend to be Ingrid Bergman or Spencer Tracy while gazing out the oversize windows at a glacier. The daily summer flights from the South Airpark, off Raspberry Road, go to Mount McKinley for 2 hours for $185 or to Prince William Sound for 75 minutes for $130. The route is tailored to the weather and viewing opportunities. Era also offers glacier helicopter flightseeing and landings from Anchorage for $279 per person.

GOLF   There are four courses in Anchorage and two in the Matanuska Valley, north of the city. The municipal **Anchorage Golf Course** (☎ 907/522-3363), which has a good restaurant for dinner, O'Malley's on the Green, is on O'Malley Road near the zoo, uphill from the New Seward Highway.

RAFTING   There are several white-water rivers within a 90-minute drive of Anchorage. **Nova Raft and Adventure Tours,** P.O. Box 1129, Chickaloon, AK 99674 (☎ **800/746-5753** or 907/745-5753; e-mail nova@alaska.net) is a large, experienced operator offering multiday trips all over the state, and four different half-day floats in the Anchorage area, ranging from relatively easygoing Class II and III rapids on the Matanuska River to the Class IV and V white water of Six-Mile Creek, for which you may be required to prove your swimming ability before you can get in the boat. Self-paddling is an option on some trips. The half-day trips range in price from $60 to $125. The relatively calm Matanuska River float is $60 for adults, $30 for children 5 to 11. Other trips are suitable only for older children and adults. You'll need a way to get to the river and may need to bring your own lunch.

SEA KAYAKING   There essentially are no ocean sports in Anchorage proper, but two companies lead sea kayaking trips that start from here. **Coastal Kayaking and Custom Adventures Worldwide,** 414 K St., Anchorage, AK 99501 (☎ **800/ 288-3134** or 907/258-3866; website http://www.alaskan.com/kayak), leads day trips to Seward's Resurrection Bay, as well as multiday paddles to Kenai Fjords National Park, Shuyak Island State Park (near Kodiak), and Prince William Sound out of Whittier. **Alaska Sail and Trail Adventures,** 10801 Trails End Rd., Anchorage, AK 99516 (☎ and fax **907/346-1234**), takes clients sea kayaking or sailing in Prince William Sound out of Whittier. Their basic day trip is $99 plus $25 for getting you to Whittier, and they also have 3- to 7-day sailing and kayaking packages.

SKIING   Anchorage has three downhill ski areas: The **Alyeska Resort,** listed below with Girdwood, is a destination; **Alpenglow** is a good local ski area above the treeline; and **Hillside** is a good place to learn to ski. The latter two are listed above in the "Chugach Mountains" and "Hillside Park" sections. For Nordic skiing, Kincaid Park and Hillside Park, described above, are excellent. The bike trails are flat but convenient. Russian Jack Springs Park is right in town, at DeBarr and Boniface, and has a warm-up chalet.

SPECTATOR SPORTS

Anchorage has two **semipro baseball** teams—the **Anchorage Glacier Pilots** (☎ **907/274-3627**) and the **Anchorage Bucs** (☎ **907/561-2827**)—with college athletes playing short midsummer seasons. The quality may be uneven, but you may see diamonds in the rough: Tommy Seaver, Dave Winfield, Barry Bonds, and Wally Joyner all started out here. Check the *Anchorage Daily News* for game times. Mulcahy Stadium is at 16th Avenue and A Street, a long walk or a short drive from downtown. Tickets are cheap. Dress warmly for evening games. A weekend day game is warmer, but then you won't get to see baseball played at night without lights.

The **University of Alaska–Anchorage** fields an NCAA Division I **hockey** team, the Seawolves, which plays at the Sullivan Arena (see "Anchorage in the Evening," below). The men's **basketball** team hosts a major Division I preseason tournament over Thanksgiving weekend, the **Great Alaska Shootout,** and plays the regular season at the Sullivan Arena and at the University Sports Center, on campus on Providence Drive. Tickets are available from Carrs Tix (☎ **800/478-7328** or 907/ 263-2787).

ACCOMMODATIONS

Rooms can be hard to find in Anchorage in the summer. I've provided full listings for my top recommendations in each price category below, but Anchorage also has many chain and independent hotels with the same good standard rooms you'd find anywhere in the country. At the top of the quality range downtown, there's the large **Anchorage Hilton** (☎ **800/245-2527** or 907/272-7411), a luxury high-rise at the center of downtown at Third Avenue and E Street. **Anchorage Hotel** (☎ **800/ 544-0988** or 907/272-4553), a charming and historic small hotel at the same quality level, is right next door, facing E Street. The **Sheraton Anchorage** (☎ **907/ 276-8700**) is comparable to the Hilton, but a few blocks off the downtown tourist area. Also downtown, you'll find good rooms at the **Days Inn** (☎ **907/276-7226**), which has a courtesy van to the airport and many amenities; the **Holiday Inn of Anchorage** (☎ **907/279-8671**), which has a pool; the **Westmark Anchorage** (☎ **800/ 544-0970** or 907/276-7676); and the **Comfort Inn Ship Creek Anchorage** (☎ **800/228-5150** or 907/277-6887), with a tiny swimming pool, located in the railroad yard area just below downtown. Near the airport are the **Best Western Barratt**

Inn (☎ **800/221-7550** or 907/249-4909; website http://www.barrattinn.com), a sprawling property with rooms ranging from moderate to expensive; **Super 8 Motel of Anchorage** (☎ **907/276-8884**); and the **Westcoast International Inn** (☎ **907/243-2333**). The **Best Western Golden Lion,** at New Seward Highway and 36th Avenue (☎ **907/561-1522**), is located on the way into town from the south.

The **bed tax** in Anchorage is 8%.

VERY EXPENSIVE

✪ **Hotel Captain Cook.** Fourth Ave. and K St. (P.O. Box 102280), Anchorage, AK 99510-2280. ☎ **800/843-1950** or 907/276-6000. Fax 907/343-2298. 565 rms, 77 suites. TV TEL. High season, $230–$260 double; $275–$1,500 suite. Low season, $125–$155 double; $175–$1,500 suite. Additional person in room $10 extra. AE, DC, DISC, JCB, MC, V.

This is Alaska's great, grand hotel, where royalty and rock stars stay. Former Gov. Wally Hickel built the first of the three towers after the 1964 earthquake, and now the hotel fills a city block. Inside, the decor has a fully realized (maybe a little excessive) nautical theme, with art memorializing Cook's voyages and enough teak to build a square-rigger. The standard rooms are large, with great views from all sides; you don't pay more to be higher. The lobby contains 16 shops, and there's a concierge, tour desks, barbershop and beauty salon, and business center. The full-service health club in the basement has a decent-sized pool and a racquetball court. It may not be easy to book a room, however, as packages and government and corporate clients tend to fill the hotel in the summer.

Sophisticated food justifies the high prices and elaborate service at **The Crows Nest,** the city's most traditional formal restaurant on the hotel's top floor. All tables have stupendous views, and high-backed booths lend a sense of intimacy. Main courses range from $24 to $28, or a five-course fixed menu is $55 per person. **Fletcher's,** off the lobby, is an English pub serving good Italian-style pizza and sandwiches. **The Pantry** is a typical hotel cafe.

Regal Alaskan. 4800 Spenard Rd., Anchorage, AK 99517-3236. ☎ **800/544-0553** or 907/243-2300. Fax 907/243-8815. 248 rms. TV TEL. High season, $250–$265 double; $295 suite. Low season, $160–$175 double; $245 suite. AE, DC, DISC, ER, JCB, MC, V.

Among the float planes on Lake Spenard, near the airport, the large lobby suggests a big fishing and hunting lodge. But the rooms, newly remodeled in 1997, are what's really special. Decorated in a style of tasteful opulence and packed with thoughtful details, they're a delight to the eye and an invitation to relaxation. Each has a coffeemaker, fridge, hair dryer, ironing board, clock radio, and a Nintendo game on the TV. A courtesy van runs a regular schedule downtown, but for convenience you really need to rent a car if you stay in this area.

EXPENSIVE

Copper Whale Inn. 440 L St., Anchorage, AK 99501. ☎ 907/259-7999. Fax 888/WHALE-IN or 907/258-6213. E-mail cwhalein@alaska.net. 15 rms, 9 with bath. TV TEL. High season, $100 double with shared bath, $145 double with private bath. Low season, $55 with shared bath, $69 with private bath. Additional person in room $10 extra. AE, CB, DC, DISC, JCB, MC, V.

A pair of clapboard houses overlook the water and Elderberry Park right on the Coastal Trail downtown, with charming rooms of every shape and size. There's a wonderfully casual feeling to the place. The rooms in the newer building, lower on the hill, are preferable, with cherrywood furniture and high ceilings. All rooms are hooked up for TVs, phones, and voice mail, but you have to ask for the actual instrument to be connected. A limited number of bikes are available for loan, and a full breakfast is included in the price.

Ship Creek Hotel. 505 W. Second Ave., Anchorage, AK 99501. ☎ **800/844-0242** or 907/278-5050. Fax 907/276-2929. E-mail shipcrk@alaska.net. 30 suites. TV TEL. High season, $175 double. Low season, $85 double. Additional person in room $10 extra. AE, DC, DISC, JCB, MC, V.

This is a friendly little hotel of converted apartments right downtown, remodeled in 1996. The rooms are exceptionally fresh and light, and many have good water views. Each has a living room, a small bedroom, and a full kitchen. Phones have voice mail and modem ports. A free continental breakfast is served in the lobby. It's not a good choice for people with mobility problems, as all rooms require negotiating stairs.

The Voyager Hotel. 501 K St., Anchorage, AK 99501. ☎ **800/247-9070** or 907/277-9501. Fax 907/274-0333. 38 rms. TV TEL. High season, $159 double. Low season, $99 double. Additional person in room $10 extra. AE, DC, DISC, JCB, MC, V.

Thanks to an exacting proprietor, Stan Williams, The Voyager is just right. The size is small; the location central; the rooms large and light, all with kitchens; the housekeeping exceptional; the desks have modem ports and extra electrical outlets; and the hospitality is warm yet highly professional. There's nothing ostentatious or outwardly remarkable about the hotel, yet the most experienced travelers rave about it the loudest. No smoking.

MODERATE

Chelsea Inn Hotel. 3836 Spenard Rd. ☎ **907/276-5002.** Fax 907/277-7642. 34 rms, 23 with bath. TV TEL. High season, $85–$95 double shared bath, $105–$115 double private bath. Low season, $47–$57 double shared bath, $49–$59 double private bath. AE, DISC, MC, V.

These were the least expensive decent rooms I could find near the airport. (There are some real dives in the area.) Some rooms are small or have only a shower stall and no tub, and a few lack windows or are situated in the basement (they come with a $15 discount), but generally all seemed comfortable and nicely decorated. There's free coffee in the lobby and an airport shuttle.

Hillside Hotel and RV Park. 2150 Gambell St., Anchorage, AK 99503. ☎ **907/258-6006.** Fax 907/279-8972. 27 rms. TV TEL. High season, $75–$110 double. Low season, $51–$76 double. Additional person in room $5 extra. AE, DISC, MC, V.

On a busy highway with a car dealership and self-storage business, this funny little hotel is an oasis. Rooms are clean and well maintained and have features—like microwaves and refrigerators—that make them very useful, if not luxurious. A gate in the RV park leads to the Lanie Fleischer Coastal Trail, for biking or Nordic skiing. (Full hook-ups are $22.) There are coffee machines in the rooms and the lobby, and a coin-op laundry is available.

Parkwood Inn. 4455 Juneau St., Anchorage, AK 99503. ☎ **907/563-3590.** Fax 907/563-5560. 48 suites. TV TEL. High season, $99 suite for two. Low season, $59 suite for two. Additional person in room $10 extra. AE, CB, DC, DISC, MC, V.

Located in midtown, somewhat convenient to the airport but not the sights, this comfortable family hotel is a converted three-story apartment building. All rooms are suites with full kitchens. There is no elevator, and noise can be a problem. The site is in a largely industrial area, but it's completely screened by trees and nicely landscaped. Suites where smoking and pets are permitted are available; others are nonallergenic. The staff is friendly and competent. There's a coin-op laundry and free coffee in the lobby.

✪ **Snowshoe Inn.** 826 K St., Anchorage, AK 99501. ☎ **907/258-SNOW.** Fax 907/258-SHOE. 15 rms, 9 with bath. TV TEL. High season, $89 double without bath, $99–$109 double with bath. Low season, $49 double without bath, $59 double with bath. Rates include continental breakfast. Additional person in room $10 extra. AE, DISC, MC, V.

This cheerful, family-run hotel on a quiet downtown street has comfortable, light, and attractively decorated rooms with bright fabrics, all perfectly clean. The energetic Zeids seem to be constantly improving everything, and recently added refrigerators and microwaves and remodeled 10 rooms. The six rooms with shared bathrooms are in pairs, and the bathrooms are close and secure. There's no better bargain downtown. Freezer and storage space and a coin-op laundry are available. No smoking.

BED & BREAKFASTS

There are hundreds of B&Bs in Anchorage, a reaction to a hot market for rooms and high hotel prices. Bed-and-breakfasts have become pretty sophisticated, most going far beyond the old idea of just renting out the spare room. Some people are making it their livelihood, and rooms are available in every class. You can almost always get a better room for a better rate at a B&B than at a hotel, and you'll learn more about Alaska by meeting your hosts.

I've listed only three B&Bs to show the range of choices. There are so many others that smart operators are catering to their own, narrow niches: **Moosewood Bed and Breakfast** (☎ 907/345-8788; website http://www.alaska.net/~moosewd/), up in the mountains, has thought of every luxury that can be provided for vegetarians and people with disabilities; **Anna's Bed and Breakfast** (☎ 907/338-5331; e-mail annas@alaska.net) has bilingual hosts catering to German speakers. I also especially like these downtown places: **G Street House** (☎ 907/258-1717), an elegant home hosted by a wonderful family; and **Susitna Place** (☎ 907/274-3344; e-mail suplace@alaska.net), overlooking Cook Inlet from atop a bluff on a quiet side street.

There also are several booking agencies that can put you together with the right bed-and-breakfast in town or elsewhere. **Alaska Private Lodgings,** P.O. Box 200047, Anchorage, AK 99520-0047 (☎ 907/258-1717; fax 907/258-6613; website http://www.alaska.net/~apl), is the most established of the agencies. It has a downtown office at 704 W. Second Ave. The **Bed and Breakfast Association of Alaska,** Anchorage Chapter, P.O. Box 242623, Anchorage, AK 99524-2623, runs a **B&B Hotline** (☎ 907/272-5909), which puts callers directly in touch with B&Bs, and they publish a detailed B&B directory of members.

✪ **Aurora Winds B&B Resort.** 7501 Upper O'Malley Rd., Anchorage, AK 99516. ☎ **800/642-9640** or 907/346-2533. Fax 907/346-3192. E-mail awbnb@alaska.net. 5 rms. TV TEL. High season, $125–$175 double. Low season, $55–$125 double. Rates include full breakfast. Additional person in room $15 extra in high season, $10 extra in low season. AE, DC, DISC, MC, V.

The rooms in this massive house far up the hillside in South Anchorage are so grand and theatrically decorated you'll feel as if you're in a James Bond movie. The upstairs living room has a white stone fireplace (one of four) and a matching white grand piano. A downstairs rec room has a gym, pool table, sauna, and theater. Each bedroom has a sitting area, VCR, and other details such as a second phone line so you can dial up the Internet and talk at the same time. Even some of the bathrooms are showplaces: Three have Jacuzzis, and one is larger than a lot of hotel rooms, with an "environmental habitat chamber." One lovely room has windows on the deck and forest on three sides. There's a large Jacuzzi hot tub in the attractive gardens.

The Oscar Gill House Bed and Breakfast. 1344 W. 10th Ave. (P.O. Box 200047), Anchorage, AK 99520-0047. ☎ **907/258-1717** or 907/274-1344. Fax 907/258-6613. Website http://www.innsandouts.com/property/the_oscar_gill_house.htm. I3 rms, 1 with bath. TEL. High season, $85 double shared bath, $95 double private bath. Low season, $65 double. Rates include full breakfast. Additional person in room $15 extra. AE, MC, V (5% surcharge).

On the Delaney Park strip, just a few blocks from downtown, this is truly the oldest house in Anchorage—because it was built in 1913, in Knik, before Anchorage was founded, and moved here on a barge a few years later. Oscar Gill was an early civic leader. The house was to be torn down in 1982 but was moved to storage by a historic preservation group; Mark and Susan Lutz saved it in 1994, moving it to its present location and, with their own labor, restoring it authentically as a cozy, friendly bed-and-breakfast. The house is full of appropriate antiques; it's a classic B&B experience. Free laundry machines and bikes are available.

12th & L Bed and Breakfast. 1134 L St., Anchorage, AK 99501. ☎ **907/276-1225.** Fax 907/276-1224. Website http://www.customcpu.com/commercial/twelfth/default.htm. 4 rms. TV TEL. High season, $98 double; $128 suite. Low season, $53 double; $68 suite. Additional person in room $5–$10. AE, DISC, MC, V.

This light, summery B&B 6 blocks from the downtown core has attractively decorated guest rooms and common areas, with wood floors, glass bricks, and other stylish design touches. The three rooms downstairs are smallish, but everything is well thought out. The two-bedroom upstairs suite is tucked charmingly under the eaves, with skylights that open. A continental breakfast is provided, and guests use the washer and drier free. No smoking.

HOSTELS

Hostelling International, Anchorage, 700 H St., Anchorage, AK 99501 (☎ **907/276-3635;** fax 907/276-7772), is a large place right downtown. A coin-op laundry, kitchen, and baggage storage are available. The office is open daily from 8am to noon and 5pm to midnight. The unaffiliated **Spenard Hostel,** 2845 W. 42nd Ave., Anchorage, AK 99517 (☎ **907/248-5036;** website http://www.alaskalife.net/spnrdhstl/hostel.html), near the airport, has male and female dorms and semiprivate rooms. Beds are $15 summer, $12 winter. **Qupqugiaq Cafe, Inn and School,** 640 W. 36th Ave., Anchorage, AK 99503 (☎ **907/563-5633**), is a special place. The rooms, renting for $27 to $39, are like private hostel accommodations, with shared kitchens and bathrooms, but quite good for what they are. Reservations are not accepted. Downstairs, the cafe is a coffee house and community center drawing together alternative livers and idealists for music, socializing, discussion groups, and formal classes on anything from worm composting to Chinese politics.

CAMPING

Anchorage is a big city—for a real camping experience, you need to head out of town. The 28-site, $10-per-night State Parks' **Bird Creek Campground,** 25 miles south on the Seward Highway, is one of my favorites, next to Turnagain Arm. State Parks also has a 56-site campground in **Eagle River** that costs $15; take the Hiland Road exit 12 miles from Anchorage on the Glenn Highway. Forest Service campgrounds near town are listed below. Within the Anchorage bowl, there are several camper and RV parks. The municipally owned **Centennial Camper Park,** on Boundary Road at the Muldoon Road exit from the Glenn Highway (☎ **907/333-9711** or 907/343-4474), just as you enter town from the north, has 80 dry sites. There's a dump station and free showers. Camping permits are $13 a night. The **Ship Creek Landings Downtown RV Park,** in the railroad industrial area down the bluff from downtown (☎ **907/277-0877**), is the most centrally located camping area, charging $27 for full hook-ups. The **Hillside Motel and RV Park** is listed above.

DINING

Besides the sit-down restaurants listed below, there's lots of good take-out fast food in Anchorage. (Of course, all the franchise places also are represented.) The best, most original burgers are at **Arctic Roadrunner,** with locations on Arctic Boulevard at Fireweed Lane and on Old Seward Highway at International Airport Road. **The Lucky Wishbone,** at 1033 E. Fifth Ave., has the best fried chicken in town, and great, old-fashioned milkshakes—they have a drive-through, but eat in for the classic diner atmosphere, smoke free. The best deli, with legendary sandwiches, is **Atlasta Deli,** in the shopping mall at Arctic Boulevard and Tudor Road; it's really a gourmet experience, with over 100 meats and cheeses, and you can eat in. For sit-down Mexican fast food, **Taco King,** at Northern Lights Boulevard and C Street, provides the best deal—a tasty, filling meal for under $5. Anchorage is short on good Chinese food, but the **Fu-Do Chinese Restaurant,** at 2600 E. Tudor Rd. (☎ 907/ 561-6611), is better than most, and will deliver orders of $15 or more. **Omega Pizza,** 2601 Spenard Rd. (☎ 907/272-6007), has great pizza and fast delivery. The best place to pack a picnic, or get a relaxed sidewalk cafe lunch, is **New Sagaya's City Market** (☎ 907/274-6173) at the corner of 13th and I streets. It's a wonderful gourmet grocery with a cafe and Italian bakery, where we shop every night.

There are three brew pubs in downtown Anchorage. The Glacier Brewhouse is listed below. **Railway Brewing Company,** in the depot at 421 W. First Ave. (☎ 907/277-1996), has the best beer, although that's a fine point as all three are excellent. They serve good meals in a string of small dining rooms. The **Snowgoose Restaurant and Sleeping Lady Brewing Company,** 717 W. Third Ave. (☎ 907/ 277-7727), would be my choice for the best place in Anchorage to drink a beer, on the large patio overlooking the inlet, but the food and service are inconsistent.

In addition, there are coffee houses all over the city where people go for a cup of java and a pastry, and to meet people and engage in conversation. They've become the new agora of social interaction. The **Old Firehouse Cafe,** at the corner of Benson Boulevard and Spenard Road, has the young people's scene. **Cafe del Mundo,** at Fourth and K downtown and at Northern Lights and Denali in midtown, gathers an older crowd of business people, yuppies, stay-at-home parents, and anyone else looking for a comfortable meeting place. **Side Street Espresso,** on G between 4th and 5th, brings together artists, radicals, and other people who want to trade ideas. The well-intentioned should check out **Qupqugiaq,** listed above under "Hostels." And there are many others, each with its own personality—explore.

DOWNTOWN

Expensive

Club Paris. 417 W. Fifth Ave. ☎ **907/277-6332.** Reservations recommended. Main courses $14–$44; lunch $5.75–$15. AE, DISC, MC, V. Daily 11:30am–2:30pm and 5–11pm. STEAK/ SEAFOOD.

Walking from a bright spring afternoon, under a neon Eiffel Tower, into midnight darkness, past a smoke-enshrouded bar, and sitting down at a secretive booth for two, I felt as if I should lean across the table and plot a shady 1950s oil deal with my companion. And I would probably not have been the first. Smoky Club Paris will be too authentic for some, but it's the essence of old Anchorage boomtown years, when the streets were dusty and an oil man needed a class joint in which to do business. Beef, of course, is what to order, and it'll be done right. Full liquor license.

✪ **The Marx Brothers Cafe.** 627 W. Third Ave. ☎ **907/278-2133.** Reservations recommended. Main courses $17.50–$28.50. AE, DC, MC, V. Daily 6–9:30pm, closed Sunday in winter. ECLECTIC/REGIONAL.

A restaurant that began as a hobby among three friends nearly 20 years ago is still a labor of love, and has become a standard of excellence in the state. Dinner takes all night—you feel funny not ordering an appetizer—but you can spend the time watching chef Jack Amon pick herbs and vegetables for your meal from the garden behind the historic little building, one of the city's first houses. The cuisine is varied and creative, ranging from Asian to Italian, but everyone orders the Caesar salad made at the table by Van, one of the founders. The decor and style are studied casual elegance. Beer and wine license.

✪ **Simon and Seafort's Saloon and Grill.** 420 L St. ☎ **907/274-3502.** Reservations essential. Lunch/dinner $14–$35. AE, MC, V. Mon–Sat 11:15am–2:30pm and 4:30–11:00pm, Sun 2–10pm. STEAK/SEAFOOD.

Simon's, as it's known, is a jolly beef and seafood grill where voices boom off the high ceilings and brass turn-of-the-century saloon decor. On sunny summer evenings, the rooms fill with light off Cook Inlet, down below the bluff; the views are magnificent. To enjoy the ambiance cheaply, order a sandwich and soup in the well-stocked bar. In summer it is best to make reservations a couple of days in advance. Once there, I've never been disappointed by the straightforward salmon or prime rib, or anything else on the menu. The service is efficient and professional. Full liquor license.

Moderate

Glacier Brewhouse. 737 W. Fifth Ave. ☎ **907/274-BREW.** Reservations recommended for dinner. Lunch $7–$13, dinner $9–$28. AE, MC, V. High season, 11am–11pm daily; low season Mon–Sat 11am–10pm, Sun 4pm–9pm. GRILL/ITALIAN.

A tasty, eclectic, and ever-changing menu is served in a large dining room with lodge decor, where the pleasant scent of the wood-fired grill hangs in the air. They brew five hearty beers behind a glass wall. It's noisy and active, with lots of agreeable if trendy touches, such as the bread, made from spent brewery grain, that's set out on the tables with olive oil. An advantage for travelers is the wide price range—a feta cheese, spinach, and artichoke pizza is under $10.

Kumagoro. 533 W. Fourth Ave. ☎ **907/272-9905.** Main courses $11.80–$35; lunch $5.50–$18.80. AE, CB, DC, JCB, MC, V. Daily 11am–10pm. JAPANESE.

Anchorage has a lot of good, authentic Japanese restaurants, but this one, right on the main tourist street downtown, has the added advantage of convenience for travelers. The dining room is pleasantly low-key, and the sushi is good. Beer and wine license.

✪ **Sacks Cafe.** 625 W. Fifth Ave. ☎ **907/274-4022.** Reservations not accepted. Main courses $14–$21; lunch $4.75–$9.75. AE, MC, V. Sun–Thurs 11am–10pm, Fri–Sat 11am–11pm. CREATIVE/ECLECTIC.

We like to come here for a special meal because the food is creative and occasionally inspired, the atmosphere is light and arty, and the prices are reasonable. There are only a few tables, and the whole southern wall is glass—on a sunny afternoon, the patrons themselves sometimes cook. We have scientifically proven they serve the best sandwiches in Alaska, with choices such as shrimp and avocado with herb cream cheese on sourdough. In fact, we've never had less than a perfect meal. Unfortunately, although the service is professional and usually friendly, at times I've been made to feel that members of my party were not good enough for the server. Also, the inability to make reservations makes it a poor choice for large parties. An automatic gratuity is added for parties of six or more. Beer and wine license.

Inexpensive

Dianne's Restaurant. 550 W. Seventh Ave., Suite 110. ☎ **907/279-7243.** All items $4–$7.50. MC, V. Mon–Fri 7am–4pm. SOUP/SANDWICH.

Located in the base of a tall, glass office building, Dianne's has developed such a reputation for great baking, soups, sandwiches, and specials that at lunch hour, it's pretty well clogged with people in suits. The line at the cafeteria moves fast, however, and the bright, casual atmosphere is fun and full of energy. My first choice for a quick, healthy lunch downtown. No liquor license.

Downtown Deli and Cafe. 525 W. Fourth Ave. ☎ **907/276-7116.** All items $5–$12. AE, DC, MC, V. Daily 6am–9:30pm. DELI.

Tony Knowles made his Fourth Avenue sandwich restaurant the place to meet local politicians and people-in-the-know 20 years ago; when he was elected governor in 1994, President Clinton came for dinner. I didn't believe Clinton, however, when he said he enjoyed the reindeer stew—it's a gimmick. Stick with the generous sandwiches, traditional deli selections, and superior breakfasts. Some mornings the place is so overrun with tourists that service suffers, although I've never had to wait so long that it spoiled my meal. Prices are reasonable, especially for dinner, when downtown is short on inexpensive sit-down places. Kids are treated well. Beer and wine license.

BEYOND DOWNTOWN

Expensive

⊙ **Jens' Restaurant.** 701 W. 36th Ave. ☎ **907/561-5367.** Reservations recommended. Main courses $17–$25; lunch $8.50–$14.50. AE, CB, DC, DISC, MC, V. Mon 11:30am–2pm, Tues–Fri 11:30am–2pm and 6–10pm, Sat 6–10pm. Closed Jan. FRENCH.

This restaurant, in a Spenard strip mall, is an improbable playground for renowned chef Jens Hansen, who closes his doors each January to go on a gastronomic working vacation to exotic places. When he comes back, he treats the faithful to his interpretations of what he learned. Other than the traditional Danish dishes served for lunch, the menu is French influenced and new every night. Hansen presides with a booming Scandinavian accent over the cognoscenti of Anchorage, which on a random night could range from the Catholic archbishop to a group of Hell's Angels. Some nonmembers of the in-crowd have told me they don't feel they belong, and it's not a choice for kids—highchairs are not available. Beer and wine license.

Moderate

✪ **Campo Bello.** 661 W. 36th, Suite 10. ☎ **907/563-2040.** Main courses $9–$16.75; lunch $7–$10. MC, V. Lunch Mon–Fri 11:00am–2:30pm; dinner Mon–Sat 5:00–9:00pm. From downtown, take C Street to 36th Avenue and turn right. NORTHERN ITALIAN.

This quiet, little midtown restaurant has sophisticated Italian cuisine and Alaskan seafood, wonderfully hospitable service, and low prices. It stands with the best of Alaska's restaurants, but charges much less than you would pay in most comparable establishments. The cuisine doesn't try to be as trendy and far-out as some, instead creating interesting tastes mostly within the context of traditional dishes and combinations. Beer and wine license.

The Greek Corner Restaurant. 302 W. Fireweed Lane. ☎ **907/276-2820.** Main courses $11–$15; lunch $5–$9. MC, V. Mon–Thurs 11am–10pm, Fri noon–11pm, Sat 11am–11pm, Sun 4–10pm. From downtown, take C Street and turn right on Fireweed Lane. GREEK/ITALIAN.

An informal, family-operated Greek place on a busy commercial street in midtown. You're made to feel welcome, the service is quick, and the food is very reasonably priced. It's agreeably and comfortably low rent. Beer and wine license.

✪ **Mexico in Alaska.** 7305 Old Seward Hwy. ☎ **907/349-1528.** Main courses $9–$16.75; lunch $7.95. AE, MC, V. Mon–Fri 11am–10pm, Sat noon–10pm, Sun 4–9pm. From downtown, take Gambell Street south (it becomes New Seward Highway) to Dowling, then left on Old Seward Highway, looking on the left.

The down-scale building, location, and decor camouflage Alaska's best Mexican restaurant. It's the food and the service that make it so special. The food—strictly traditional, authentic cuisine of central-west Mexico—is subtle and exciting for anyone used to the heavy flavors of American-style Mexican food. The service, carried out by the family of founder Maria-Elena Ball, goes beyond friendly—they seem really interested in sharing their love of their food and culture. Regulars became so devoted, they loaned Ball large sums when her business got in trouble in the mid-1980s recession. Beer and wine license.

ANCHORAGE IN THE EVENING

THE PERFORMING ARTS   Anchorage has become an ever-more-frequent destination for major popular and classical music performers. The arts season begins in the fall and ends in the spring, but traveling performers often come through in the summer as well, and the **Anchorage Festival of Music** (☎ **907/276-2465**) presents a classical music series in June. Pick up a copy of Friday's edition of the *Anchorage Daily News* for the "8" section, which includes event listings, information on the club and arts scene, and insightful restaurant reviews.

The **Anchorage Symphony** (☎ **907/274-8668**) performs during the winter season. The **Anchorage Concert Association** (☎ **907/272-1471**) promotes a schedule of international-caliber music and other performing arts. And Anchorage has lots of community theater, opera, and limited professional theater, including the experimental, semiprofessional **Out North Theater** (☎ **907/279-8200**).

Most large events take place at one of two venues. The ✪ **Anchorage Center for the Performing Arts**, at 621 W. Sixth Ave., on town square, has three beautiful theaters ranging in size from 350 to 2,000 seats. A ticket office in the lobby is operated by **Carrs Tix** (☎ **800/478-7328** or 907/263-2787), the main ticket agency in town, which is associated with Carrs grocery stores and has outlets at each store. Popular music and other large-venue performances take place at the 8,500-seat **Sullivan Arena**, at 16th Avenue and Gambell Street (New Seward Highway). Call ☎ 907/279-2596 for a recorded listing of events.

✪ **Cyrano's Off Center Playhouse** (☎ **907/274-2599**) is a small theater at Fourth Avenue and D Street that presents more challenging, intimate work, poetry readings, comedy, and lectures. A cafe and bookstore are attached.

NIGHTCLUBS & BARS   For a fun, funny night out, nothing in town compares to ✪ **Mr. Whitekeys' Fly By Night Club,** on Spenard Road south of Northern Lights Boulevard (☎ **907/279-SPAM**). This drinking establishment seems to be an excuse for the goateed proprietor, a consummate vulgarian, to ridicule Anchorage in his crude, political, local-humor musical comedy shows, in which he costars with a fallen former Miss Anchorage. If you can laugh at dog poop, you'll love it. The summer show is at 8pm Tuesday through Saturday, with no smoking Tuesday and Thursday. Tickets are $12 to $17, and reservations are necessary well in advance. The bar has exceptional food, too.

The largest singles bar in town is **Chilkoot Charlie's,** at Spenard Road and Fireweed Lane (☎ **907/272-1010**). On the weekend the place is packed, and there are lines for the 657-person standing-room capacity. Rock, generally of the Top-40 variety, plays on various stages. The place can be claustrophobic when crowded, with low ceilings and a dark, roadhouse atmosphere. The cover is $5 on weekends, $1 or $2 during the week. The **Long Branch Saloon,** 1733 E. Dimond Boulevard, east of New Seward Highway, has country music every night and great burgers and other beef. **Humpy's,** downtown at Sixth Avenue and F Street, has 43 beers on tap, decent bar food, and live acoustic music every night. **The Wave,** 3103 Spenard Rd., is a popular gay dance club. The nonalcoholic **Gig's Music Theater,** downtown at 140 E. Fourth Ave., is one of the only venues in town for local and alternative music. To watch a game, try the **Sports Edition,** in the Anchorage Hilton Hotel at Third Avenue and E Street. If you just want to talk, check out one of the brew pubs listed under "Dining," above, or **Darwin's Theory** on G Street between Fourth and Fifth or **F Street Station,** on F between Third and Fourth.

MOVIES   There are several multiplexes in Anchorage playing all the current Hollywood output; check the *Anchorage Daily News* for listings. There's no movie theater downtown, but the **Fireweed Theater,** at New Seward Highway (Gambell Street) and Fireweed Lane, is a short cab ride away, as is the second-run **Denali,** on Spenard Road near Northern Lights Boulevard. The ✪ **Capri Cinema** (☎ 907/ 561-0064) is the only art-movie house, in a strip mall at 3425 E. Tudor Rd. (go east from New Seward Highway on Tudor, and look on the left past Lake Otis Road). The funky little place is a treat, showing foreign and avante-guard films and catering to alternative lifestyles.

✪ A ROAD TRIP TO TURNAGAIN ARM & PORTAGE GLACIER

One of the world's great drives starts in Anchorage and leads roughly 50 miles south on the Seward Highway to Portage Glacier. It's the trip, not the destination, that makes it worthwhile. The two-lane highway along Turnagain Arm, chipped from the foot of the rocky Chugach Mountains, provides a platform to see a magnificent, ever-changing, mostly untouched landscape full of wildlife. I've listed the sights in the style of a highway log, for there are interesting stops all the way along the road. It will take at least half a day, and there's plenty to do for an all-day excursion. Use your headlights for safety even in daylight and be patient if you get stuck behind a summertime line of cars—if you pass, you'll just come up behind another line ahead.

There are lots of bus tours that follow the route and visit Portage Glacier (see "Getting Around" under "Essentials," above). **Gray Line** (☎ 907/277-5581) offers a 7-hour trip that includes a stop in Girdwood and the boat ride on Portage Lake for $59, twice daily in summer.

POTTER MARSH   Heading south from Anchorage proper, the Seward Highway descends a bluff to cross a broad marsh formed by water impounded behind the tracks of the Alaska Railroad. The marsh has a boardwalk from which you can watch a huge variety of birds. Salad-green grasses grow from sparkling, pond-green water.

POTTER SECTION HOUSE   Located at the south end of Potter Marsh, the section house was an early maintenance station for the Alaska Railroad. Today it contains offices of Chugach State Park, open during normal business hours, and a small gift shop. A few old train cars and an interpretive display outside will briefly interest the kids. Just across the road is the trailhead for the **Turnagain Arm Trail.** It's a mostly level path running down the arm well above the highway, with great views breaking now and then through the trees. You can continue 9 miles south, or break off where the trails meets the McHugh Creek picnic area and trailhead, about 4 miles out.

McHUGH CREEK   Four miles south of Potter is a state park picnic area and a challenging hike with a 3,000-foot elevation gain to a mountain lake. Without climbing all the way, there are spectacular views within an hour of the road.

BELUGA POINT   When the state highway department put up scenic overlook signs on this pull-out, 1¹/₂ miles south of McHugh Creek, they weren't messing around. The terrain is simply awesome, as the highway traces the edge of Turnagain Arm, below the towering cliffs of the Chugach Mountains. If the tide and salmon runs are right, you may see beluga whales. Belugas chase the fish toward fresh water. Sometimes they overextend and strand themselves by the dozens in the receding tide, farther along, but usually aren't harmed.

WINDY POINT   Be on the lookout in this section, 4 miles south of Beluga Point, on the mountain side of the road, where Dall sheep are frequently seen picking their way along the cliffs. It's a unique spot, for the sheep get much closer to people here than is usual in the wild; apparently, they know they're safe. Windy Point is the prime spot, but you have a decent chance of seeing sheep virtually anywhere along this stretch of road. If cars are stopped, that's probably why; get well off the road and pay attention to traffic, which still will be passing at high speeds.

You may also see windsurfers in the gray, silty waters of the Arm. They're crazy. The water is a mixture of glacial run-off and near-freezing ocean water. Besides, the movement of water that creates the 38-foot tidal difference causes riverlike currents, with standing waves. At times, rushing walls of water up to 6 feet high, called bore tides, form in the arm with the incoming tide. You need perfect timing or good luck to see a bore tide.

INDIAN VALLEY   You can stop off at the Indian Gold Mine, a touristy attraction right on the road. **Turnagain House** is a good steak and seafood restaurant, open in the evening. Up the road by the restaurant is the **Indian Valley** trailhead, a gold rush–era trail that ultimately leads to the other side of the mountains. Of course, you don't have to go the whole way, and the path, while often muddy, rises to alpine terrain less steeply than other trails along the Arm. Indian Creek has trout and, late in the year, silver salmon.

BIRD CREEK   The creek is less than 2 miles beyond Indian. The **Bird Ridge Trail** comes first, a steep alpine climb with southern exposures that make it dry early in the year. An excellent state campground on the right, over the water, costs $10 per night. There also is a short trail, interpretive signs, an overlook, and a platform that makes fishing easier for people with disabilities. Salmon run late June through August.

THE FLATS   Nine miles beyond Bird Creek, the highway descends from the mountainside to the flats. At high tide, water comes right up to the highway. At low tide, the whole Arm narrows to a thin, winding channel through the mud. Since the 1964 Good Friday earthquake, the Arm has not been navigable; before the earthquake, there was never much reason to navigate it. The first to try was Capt. James Cook, in 1778, as he was searching for the Northwest Passage on his final, fatal voyage of discovery (he was killed by Hawaiians later that year). He named this branch of Cook Inlet Turnagain Arm because he had to keep turning around in its narrow confines before it petered out.

TURN-OFF TO GIRDWOOD   Seven miles after descending to the flats is the intersection with the road to Girdwood. The attractions of the town (listed below under "A Side Trip to Girdwood and Mount Alyeska") are worth a visit, but the shopping center here at the intersection is not chief among them. Stop here for a snack in the bakery, to fill your tank, and to make a potty-stop.

OLD PORTAGE   All along the flats at the head of Turnagain Arm are large marshes full of what looks like standing driftwood. These are trees killed by salt water that flowed in when the 1964 quake lowered the land as much as 10 feet. On the right, 9 miles beyond the turn-off for Girdwood and across the highway from the railroad stop where you board the train for Whittier, a few ruins of the abandoned town of Portage are still visible, more than 30 years after the great earthquake. There is good bird watching from the turn-outs, but don't think of venturing out on Turnagain Arm's tidal mud flats. They suck people up and drown them in the incoming tide. A woman died a few years ago in the arms of rescuers who were not strong enough to pull her out of the quicksand-like mud as the water covered her.

BIG GAME ALASKA   A couple of years ago, an entrepreneur fenced off 35 acres of this glacial valley to display deer, moose, bison, musk ox, and caribou—all injured or orphaned—in a more spacious setting than the Alaska Zoo, which has a greater variety of animals. Turn right about half a mile past the **Portage train station** (☎ **907/783-2025**). Visitors pick up a cassette tape and map and drive the short course looking at the animals in 3- to 5-acre enclosures. Children, who often have trouble picking out wildlife in a natural setting, may enjoy seeing the animals close up and likely won't care that the experience isn't authentic. A large log gift shop includes among its wares frozen bison burger and caribou steak. Admission is $5 for adults, $3 for children 4 to 12, with a maximum of $20 per vehicle. In summer, it's open daily from 9:30am to 7:30pm; in winter, 10am to 5pm.

PORTAGE GLACIER   The receding Portage Glacier is a rare chance to see geologic time running faster than human time. That is to say, the name attraction at this, the most popular of all Alaska attractions, has largely melted, receding out of sight of the visitor center. (The glacier you can see is Burns.) When the center was built in 1985, Portage Glacier was predicted to keep depositing icebergs into its 800-foot-deep lake until the year 2020. Instead, it withdrew from the lake in 1995. Even so, the $8 million the National Forest Service spent on the **Begich-Boggs Visitor Center** wasn't wasted, and neither is a trip to see where the glacier used to be. The center is a sort of glacier museum. If you're in Alaska any length of time, you'll likely be seeing a lot of glaciers, and this is an excellent place to learn about what you're looking at. There's also a $1 film, shown throughout the day, called *Voices of the Ice.*

The center is named after Hale Boggs, who was majority leader in the U.S. House, and Rep. Nick Begich, Democrat from Alaska. They disappeared together in a small plane in 1972 during Begich's first reelection bid. The plane was never found, but Begich, even though declared dead, was reelected anyway. Later, his opponent, Republican Don Young, won a special election. Today, Young still represents Alaska as its only congressman.

Several short trails start from the area of the center. Rangers lead nature walks on the ^{1}/$_4$-mile, paved Moraine Trail up to six times a day. Another trail leads less than a mile to Byron Glacier, in case you're interested in getting up close to some ice. Always dress warmly, as cold winds are the rule in this funnellike valley.

A **cruise boat** operated by Gray Line of Alaska (☎ **907/783-2983**), under license with the Forest Service, traverses the lake hourly to get right up to Portage Glacier, ice conditions permitting; it costs $23. If this is your only chance to see a glacier in Alaska, it's probably a good choice. If your itinerary includes Columbia, Exit, or Mendenhall Glacier, Glacier Bay National Park, or any of the other accessible glaciers, you won't be as impressed by Portage.

A restaurant and gift shop called the Portage Lodge offers basic cafeteria sandwiches and a variety of gift wares ranging from expensive jewelry and animal pelts to plastic souvenirs. There are no lodgings in Portage, but **two Forest Service campgrounds,** Black Bear ($9 fee) and Williwaw ($10), are on the road to the visitor center, with 72 sites between them. At the more developed Williwaw Campground, there's also a place to watch red salmon spawning (in mid-August—no fishing), and you have the option of reserving a site through Biospherics (see "Outside in Southcentral," at the beginning of this chapter.

A SIDE TRIP TO GIRDWOOD & MOUNT ALYESKA

The Girdwood area—actually still part of the Municipality of Anchorage—is a small town on the threshold of turning into a major resort. Originally a mining community, and more recently a weekend skiing area for Anchorage, it still has a sleepy, offbeat character. Retired hippies, ski bums, and a few old-timers live in the houses and cabins among the big spruce trees in the valley below the Mount Alyeska ski resort. They've all got their eye on the development bonanza expected to come with the discovery of skiing here as an international attraction—but so far the town is still an authentically funky community, worth an afternoon visit even in summer. In the winter, it's a destination.

The primary summer attractions are the hiking trails, the tram to the top of Mount Alyeska, and the Crow Creek Mine, described below. In winter, it's skiing. Mount Alyeska doesn't have the size or the fame of resorts in the Rockies, but it's certainly large and challenging enough—Olympian Tommy Moe trained here. Skiers used to more crowded slopes rave about the skiing here, with views of the Chugach Mountains and, between their parted, snowy, rocky peaks, Turnagain Arm.

GETTING THERE

A rental car is the most practical route to Girdwood, 37 miles south of Anchorage off the Seward Highway, but there are van shuttles and tours that could bring you. The **Alyeska Village Shuttle** (☎ **907/754-1234**) charges $28 from the Anchorage airport. Others, including the Alaska Railroad, are listed in the "Anchorage" section.

VISITOR INFORMATION

Check the "Anchorage" section. In Girdwood, **Alyeska Booking Company,** on Town Square (P.O. Box 1210), Girdwood, AK 99587 (☎ **907/783-4FUN**), takes care of booking accommodations, rafting, dog-mushing and flightseeing trips, rentals, and so on. They also have maps and give advice for hiking and outdoor activities.

EXPLORING GIRDWOOD

ALYESKA RESORT   Owned by the Japanese Seibu company, Alyeska is trying to transform itself from a local ski area to an international resort. The work is going well, but it's not there yet—and that's good for skiers who enjoy a varied, challenging mountain with a long season, low lift-ticket prices, and no crowds.

THE SKIING   Mount Alyeska, at 3,939 feet, has 786 acres of skiing, beginning from a base elevation of only 250 feet and rising 2,500 feet. The normal season is early November to April, and it's an exceptional year when there isn't plenty of snow all winter. The average snowfall is 556 inches, or 46 feet. As it's near the water, the weather is temperate. Light is more of an issue, as the days are short in midwinter. There are 75 acres of lighted skiing on 19 trails in December and on weekends through February, but the best Alaska skiing is when the days get longer and warmer in the spring. There are nine lifts, including the tram described below. An all-day lift ticket costs $38 for adults, $24 for students, and $17 for those under age 13 or over 60. Private and group instruction are available, and a basic rental package costs $20 a day for adults, $10 for age 13 and under. There are good Nordic trails as well. A **day lodge** is located at the front of the mountain, and there's a separate bar nearby. A center operated by **Challenge Alaska,** P.O. Box 110065, Anchorage, AK 99511 (☎ 907/783-2925 or 907/344-7399), allows skiers with disabilities to use the mountain without assistance, skiing down to the lift to start and back to the center at day's end. The Alyeska Prince Hotel, described below, is around the side of the mountain, where the expert North Face is served by the tram to the top.

THE TRAM At $16 per person for a 6-minute summertime ride up the mountain, the tram leaving from the Alyeska Prince Hotel isn't cheap, but I think it's worth it for anyone who otherwise might not make it to an alpine vista during an Alaska trip. (In winter, the tram is faster and comes with your lift ticket.) At 3, my son called it "the spaceship bus," and that's exactly how it feels to float smoothly from the hotel up into the mountains. At the 2,300-foot level, the tram stops at a station with an attractive but overpriced cafeteria and, in the evening, the expensive **Seven Glaciers Restaurant,** so named for its view. But most important, this is an opportunity for everyone, no matter how young, old, or infirm, to experience the pure light, limitless surroundings, and crystalline quiet of an Alaskan mountaintop. Dress very warmly.

OTHER ATTRACTIONS The **Crow Creek Mine,** on Crow Creek Road (☎ **907/278-8060** for a recorded announcement), opened in 1898 and operated until 1940. The Toohey family turned the paths and 14 small buildings into a charming tourist attraction where you can see the frontier lifestyle and watch the rabbits and ducks wandering around. A bag of dirt is provided for gold panning, guaranteed to have some gold in it, and you can dig and pan to get more if you have the patience for it, which few people do. Crow Creek Road, off the Alyeska Highway, is quite rough and muddy in the spring. Gold panning costs $5 for adults, $4 for children 11 and under. Just looking around is $3 for adults and free for children. It's open May 15 to September 15, daily from 9am to 6pm.

TRAILS There are a couple of great trails starting in Girdwood. The **Winner Creek Trail** runs 5 miles through forest from behind the Alyeska Prince Hotel to a roaring gorge where Winner Creek and Glacier Creek meet; it's muddy and snowy in the spring. The winter ski trail takes a separate route, through a series of meadows, to the same destination. The **Crow Pass Trail** rises into the mountains and passes all the way over to Eagle River, after a 26-mile hike that takes a couple of days. But you can make a long day hike of it to the pass and see the glaciers, wildflower meadows, and old mining equipment. The trailhead is up Crow Creek Road, off the Alyeska Highway.

You also can explore the area in a dog sled. **Chugach Express Dog Sled Tours** (☎ **907/783-2266**) has 30-minute to 2-hour tours ranging from $35 to $80. **Crow Creek Snowmachine Tours** (☎ **907/783-2660**) offers day tours into the snowy mountains. They'll teach beginners.

ACCOMMODATIONS

If you don't want to pay the rates charged by the Alyeska Prince Hotel, there are other good places to stay in Girdwood. Contact the **Alyeska Booking Company,** listed above under "Visitor Information," to find a bed-and-breakfast, with rates starting at $85 a night. **Alyeska Accommodations, Inc.,** on Olympic Circle (P.O. Box 1196), Girdwood, AK 99587 (☎ **907/783-2000**), offers condos, chalets, and houses ranging from $95 to $300 a night.

✪ **Alyeska Prince Hotel.** 1000 Arlberg Ave. (P.O. Box 249), Girdwood, AK 99587. ☎ **800/ 880-3880** or 907/754-1111. Fax 907/754-2290. 307 rms, 4 suites. TV TEL. Summer and Christmas, $175–$450 double; $600–$1,500 suite. Winter, $150–$290 double; $500–$1,000 suite. Additional adult in room $25 extra; children stay free in parents' room. AE, DC, DISC, JCB, MC, V.

The hotel is unique in Alaska as a large, first-class hotel in a nearly pristine mountain valley. Two of the four restaurants—a cafeteria and the gourmet Seven Glaciers Restaurant—are 2,300 feet above the lobby on Mount Alyeska, at the end of a tram ride. The Japanese cuisine particularly has developed a reputation. But check to see which of the restaurants will be open when you come, as there have been long seasonal closures since the hotel opened. The accommodations and service are as close to perfect as you're likely to find in Alaska—so perfect, in fact, as to seem inappropriately solemn at times. The standard rooms are not large but have extraordinary views and lovely cherrywood furniture, refrigerators, safes, hair dryers, and so on. The swimming pool, with a cathedral ceiling and huge windows on the mountain, has no peer in Alaska.

DINING

Chair 5. Linblad St., town square. ☎ 907/783-2500. Main courses $6.25–$19; lunch $5.25–$8.50. AE, MC, V. Daily 11am–11pm. SEAFOOD/BURGERS.

This is where Girdwood locals meet their friends and take their families for dinner. In the bar, Bob Dylan music accompanies a friendly game of pool while baseball plays on the TV, and men with ponytails and beards sip microbrews. In the restaurant, families sit at tables amid stained glass and not-quite-antique collectibles. Good, simple meals, welcoming service, and a pro-kid attitude make it work. Full liquor license.

Double Musky. Crow Creek Rd. ☎ **907/783-2822.** Main courses $16–$32. AE, CB, DC, DISC, MC, V. Tues–Thurs 5–10pm, Fri–Sun 4–10pm. Closed Nov. CAJUN.

The ski-bum-casual atmosphere and rambling, cluttered dining room among the trees match the wonderful Cajun food in a way that couldn't have been contrived—it's at once too improbable and too authentic. Service is relaxed to a fault, and food takes a long time to arrive, but when it does it's flawless. The jambalaya was hot, but not too hot to overwhelm what else was going on. A great place for steak, too. Full liquor license.

4 The Kenai Peninsula: A Microcosm of Alaska

Most of what you're looking for in Alaska you can find south of Anchorage, along a few hundred miles of blacktop. The Kenai (KEEN-eye) Peninsula, which divides Prince William Sound and Cook Inlet, is a microcosm of the state. It's got glaciers, whales, legendary sport fishing, spectacular hiking trails, interesting little fishing towns, bears, moose, high mountains—the major difference is that it's easy to get to, and that means it's not as exotic or remote as some other places where you go to find these things. People from Anchorage go to the peninsula for the weekend to fish, hike, dig clams, paddle kayaks, and so on. There's a special phrase for what happens when the red salmon are running in July on the Kenai and Russian rivers: "combat fishing." It's hard to imagine until you've actually seen fishermen standing elbow to elbow on a bank, each casting into his or her own yard-wide slice of river, and still catching plenty of fish. The peninsula also exerts a powerful magnetic force on RVs, those road-whales that one finds at the head of strings of cars on the two-lane highways. The fishing rivers, creeks, and beaches on the west side of the peninsula, and the end of the Homer Spit, become sheet-metal cities of hundreds of Winnebagos and Itascas parked side by side during the summer. Often some local entrepreneur will be selling doughnuts or newspapers door to door.

Yet you only need to be around lots of other tourists if you want to. There are towns of unspoiled charm and outdoor experiences where you can be on your own. You can paddle among the whales in a kayak in Prince William Sound; tramp over the heather in Turnagain Pass; hike, bike, or ski one of the many maintained trails in Chugach National Forest. And the peninsula has some of the state's best restaurants and most interesting lodgings.

Kenai is the largest town. It's only 10 miles from Soldotna, and together they form a unit with more than 25% of the peninsula's population of 44,000. They're also the least interesting of the peninsula's communities. Homer has wonderful art and character; Seward is smaller and quieter, but also charming and a gateway to Kenai Fjords National Park.

GETTING THERE / ORIENTATION   The Kenai Peninsula is served by a single major road, the **Seward Highway,** which carries the great majority of visitors to the peninsula in private cars. At a fork 90 miles south of Anchorage, the **Sterling Highway** heads west to Cooper Landing, Kenai and Soldotna, and Homer, 235 miles from Anchorage. The balance of the Seward Highway goes to the east side of the peninsula to the town of Seward. All the major towns also are served by frequent **commuter air service.** Seward gets rail service from the **Alaska Railroad** during the summer, and the **Alaska Marine Highway System** links Seward and Homer with outlying areas that lack roads.

VISITOR INFORMATION   Each town of significant size has a visitor information center, maps, guides, and other publications, and the peninsula as a whole also has the **Kenai Peninsula Tourism Marketing Council,** 500 N. Willow St., Kenai, AK 99611 (☎ **800/535-3624** or 907/283-3850; e-mail kptmic@alaska.net), which is eager to send you information on businesses in the area. The Kenai Peninsula Borough is the county-level government for the whole area. It levies a 2% sales tax, and individual towns add varying amounts of tax of their own.

For information on the **Chugach National Forest,** which covers the northern portion of the peninsula, contact the **Alaska Public Lands Information Center,** at 605 W. Fourth Ave., Suite 105, Anchorage, AK 99501 (☎ **907/271-2599**), or the ranger district offices in Girdwood, on Monarch Mine Road, near the Seward Highway, or in Seward, at 334 Fourth Ave. The are many great hikes on the peninsula. *55 Ways to the Wilderness,* mentioned above under "Chugach Mountains" in the "Anchorage" section, is the best trail guide to the area. *Kenai Pathways,* available from the information center for $4.95, contains guidance for 25 trails on the peninsula. The best trail map, produced on plastic by **Trails Illustrated** (see "Fast Facts: Alaska" in chapter 3), coordinates with the book.

THE SEWARD HIGHWAY   The Kenai Peninsula's main lifeline is the road down from Anchorage, a 127-mile drive to Seward on a good two-lane highway, most of it through public land without development or services. There are campgrounds and hiking trails all along this stretch of road in the Chugach National Forest (see above). The drive is more than scenic—it's really a wonderful attraction in itself, designated a National Scenic Byway. I've written in the "Anchorage" section above about the 50-mile portion along Turnagain Arm to Portage. (The mileage numbers I give here count from Anchorage, the direction most people drive the first time, but the roadside mileposts start in Seward. To correlate this log to the mileposts, subtract the distance listed from Anchorage from 127—so, for instance, a site listed as being 81 miles from Anchorage would be at milepost 46.)

Beyond the Portage Glacier turn-off, the road traverses the salt marshes to the south side of the Arm, then climbs to fresh, towering alpine terrain over 1,000-foot **Turnagain Pass.** At the pass, 59 miles from Anchorage, there's a pit toilet and a parking area providing access to summer and winter mountain recreation. This is the Chugach National Forest, and there are a couple of campgrounds on this stretch. Seventy miles from Anchorage, the Hope spur road divides off to the west, described below; then the road climbs again up a canyon before leveling out again above the treeline.

The Kenai Peninsula & Prince William Sound

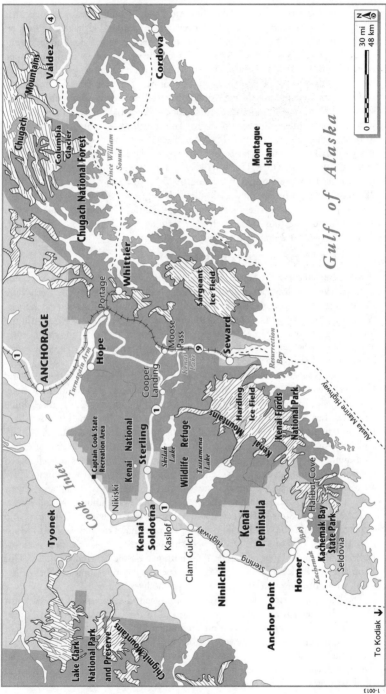

1-0013

Now come a series of alpine lakes. Summit Lake, 81 miles from Anchorage, has the spectacular Tenderfoot Creek Forest Service campground (27 sites, $9 fee), on the far side from the highway, and on the near side, **Summit Lake Lodge,** Moose Pass, AK 99631 (☎ **907/595-1520**), a wonderfully traditional log roadhouse, open every day of the year from 7am to 11pm. The food is consistently good. They take cash only. It's the only permanent habitation for many miles in either direction.

The highway continues through similar terrain before descending into the trees again and branching 90 miles from Anchorage at **Tern Lake,** where there's a bird-watching platform with interpretive signs. To the right, the Sterling Highway leads to Kenai, Soldotna, and Homer. The Seward Highway continues to the left along a string of sparking mountain lakes, and through the little community of Moose Pass, 100 miles from Anchorage. The waterwheel you see as you enter town was built just for fun. **Trail Lake Lodge,** P.O. Box 69, Moose Pass, AK 99631 (☎ **907/288-3101**), beside the lake on the left side of the highway, offers good rooms for reasonable prices and has a restaurant with a screened dining room by the water, as well as an inside dining room. The highway continues from here through the forest, descending another 23 miles to Seward.

HOPE: GHOST OF A GOLD RUSH TOWN

If you're headed down the Seward Highway to the Kenai Peninsula with a few hours to spare, a visit to Hope can make for a pleasant break. The town, on the south shore of Turnagain Arm, is at the end of a paved 17-mile spur 70 miles from Anchorage. A few white frame buildings remain from the days when Hope was a gold-mining boomtown after a strike in 1895. Many of the newer buildings in the town center are quaint, too. Salmon run in Porcupine Creek, near the main street. The year-round population is less than 200.

The gold rush–era ✪ **Resurrection Pass Trail** begins 4 miles above the town and runs over the top of the Kenai Peninsula to Cooper Landing. It's a beautiful, remote, yet well-used hike or mountain-bike ride, rising through forest, crossing the alpine pass, and then descending again to a highway trailhead, where you'll need to have transportation waiting. The 39-mile trail has nine public-use cabins, available for $25 a night, although the price is expected to go up. (See "Outside in Southcentral," at the beginning of this chapter, for reservation information.) The cabins are well spaced to cover the trail in an easy 5 days, and those on lakes have boats for fishing. They are reserved well ahead, but there are lots of good camping spots, too. The trail continues at Cooper Landing to Exit Glacier, outside of Seward, another 33 miles.

The **Hope and Sunrise Historical and Mining Museum** is a one-room log cabin displaying historic objects and photographs. It's open noon to 4pm, Friday to Monday, Memorial Day to Labor Day. Where the main street ends—the tidal meadow beyond was more of Hope before the 1964 earthquake—the **Seaview Cafe, Bar, Gift Shop and RV Park** acts as the town center. The cafe has modest meals. The bar has a wall with Polaroid photographs of everyone who lives here.

The U.S. Forest Service ✪ **Porcupine Campground** at the end of the road, just beyond the town, is one of the most beautiful in the Chugach National Forest. Twenty-four well-separated sites are on a mountainside, five with views of Turnagain Arm, and it's the trailhead for two good hikes. (The self-service fee is $9.) The level 5-mile trail to **Gull Rock** makes a good family ramble, and with some effort you can scramble down to remote beaches along the way. The **Hope Point Trail** is a stiff climb that rises 3,600 feet to expansive views.

If you need a room for the night, the best choice is the **Bear Creek Lodge,** P.O. Box 90, Hope, AK 99605 (☎ **907/782-3141**), with four pleasant cabins around a duck pond and two on a creek for $75 double. They have electric heat and wood stoves and share a bathhouse. There's an inexpensive restaurant attached.

SEWARD: GATEWAY TO RESURRECTION BAY & KENAI FJORDS NATIONAL PARK

The main reason to go to Seward has always been Resurrection Bay and the access the port provides to the great mass of Alaska. The agreeable little town started life as a place to fish and to get off the boat for Alaska, then continued as a place for Alaskans and visitors to get on boats and see the bay, Kenai Fjords National Park (described below), and the marine mammals and birds that live there. Starting in 1998, you won't even need a boat to see the wildlife: **The Alaska Sea Life Center,** a large research aquarium that's also open to the public, will begin full operation in May, displaying seals, sea lions, marine birds, and the scientists who are studying them. The huge, $50 million project, mostly funded by money won from Exxon after the *Exxon Valdez* oil spill, dominates the waterfront in downtown Seward. Combined with Seward's excellent ocean fishing, the national park, the wonderful hiking trails, and the unique and attractive town, the new center is helping make this one of Alaska's most appealing towns to visit.

In some ways, Seward is more like a town in Southeast Alaska, with its mountainside grid of streets by the ocean. The grid is lined with old wood-frame houses and newer fishermen's residences. It's the sort of place where pedestrians casually wander across the road, hardly glancing for cars, for there likely won't be any, or, if there are, they'll be ready to stop. Seward is also like Southeast in that most visitors get here on cruise ships. The dock is the beginning or end of many week-long cruises, with passengers riding buses to or from the hotels and airport in Anchorage.

Along the seashore, besides the large boat harbor that's the economic hub of the town, a beach of rounded gravel becomes a jolly city of tents and recreational vehicles at the height of summer. Late in the summer, campers can catch silver salmon out their front doors on this shoreline. Your chances are better, of course, with one of the dozens of fishing charters available in the boat harbor. Even those who don't care much about fishing will likely enjoy tagging along on a charter: You'll have a decent chance of seeing sea otters, sea lions, and even whales.

Seward's history is among the oldest in Alaska. The Russian governor Alexander Baranof stopped here in 1793, named Resurrection Bay, and built a ship, which later sank. The town was born in its modern form in 1903, when a company seeking to build a railroad north came ashore. They failed, but Seward still was an important port. Gold prospectors had begun blazing trails from here to finds on Turnagain Arm starting in 1891, and in 1907 the Army linked those trails with others all the way to Nome, finishing the Iditarod Trail. Today that route is discontinuous south of Anchorage, but you can follow it through Seward.

More relevant for current visitors and the local economy, the federal government took over the failed railroad-building effort in 1915, finishing the line to Fairbanks in 1923. Until the age of jet travel, most people coming to Alaska arrived by steamer in Seward and then traveled north by rail. The train ride to Anchorage, daily during the summer, is supremely beautiful.

ESSENTIALS

GETTING THERE   Seward can be reached by all modes of transportation.

By Car   See the Seward Highway log, above, for how to make the spectacular 127-mile drive down from Anchorage. All major car-rental agencies are represented in Anchorage.

By Bus   The **Seward Bus Line** (☎ 907/224-3608; fax 907/224-7237) makes one trip daily, year round, starting in Seward and going to Anchorage and back; the fare is $30 one way. Gray Line's **Alaskon Express** (☎ 800/544-2206), operating in summer only, instead leaves Anchorage in the morning and returns in the evening, charging $40.

By Rail   I think everyone should take the run between Anchorage and Seward on the ☻ **Alaska Railroad,** 411 W. First Ave., Anchorage, AK 99501 (☎ 800/ 544-0552 or 907/265-2494; website http://www.alaska.net/~akrr), which runs daily in summer. It's even more spectacular than the highway route, passing close by glaciers and following a ledge halfway up the narrow, vertical Placer River gorge, where it ducks into tunnels and pops out at bends in the river. The landscape looks just as it did when the first person beheld it. The train has five cars: a dining car with good deli-style food, a car with commentary, a quiet car, a dome car, and a baggage car. The railroad's young guides are well trained and provide an accurate and not overly verbose commentary. The fare for the summer-only run is $82 round-trip or $55 one-way, a fair price for a ride that I, at least, will never forget. You can stop in Girdwood or Moose Pass, too. The railroad also offers packages that include a boat tour of Kenai Fjords National Park, but I advise against trying to get down from Anchorage, do the park, and return in the same day; it's too much.

By Air   **Era Aviation** (☎ 800/866-8394) and **F.S. Air** (☎ 907/248-9595) serve Seward from Anchorage a few times a day for around $75 one-way.

By Ferry   The ferry *Tustumena,* of the **Alaska Marine Highway System** (☎ 800/ 642-0066 or 907/224-5485; website http://www.dot.state.ak.us/external/amhs/ home.html) connects Seward with Valdez (11 hours to the east) and Kodiak (13 hours to the west) roughly once a week. The adult passenger fare for Valdez is $68, Kodiak $73. Leaving from Homer cuts off 4 hours to Kodiak. The terminal is at the cruise-ship dock, on the outside of the small-boat harbor.

VISITOR INFORMATION   The **Kenai Fjords National Park Visitor Center,** at the boat harbor (P.O. Box 1727), Seward, AK 99664 (☎ 907/224-3175; fax 907/ 224-2144), open summer daily 8am to 5pm, winter Monday through Friday 8am to 5pm, is worth a stop for park information and other outdoor opportunities (see the section on the national park, below, for more specifics on the visitor center). For information on the Chugach National Forest, the **Seward Ranger District** is at Fourth Avenue and Jefferson Street (P.O. Box 390), Seward, AK 99663 (☎ 907/ 224-3374). The **Seward Chamber of Commerce,** P.O. Box 749, Seward, AK 99664 (☎ 907/224-8051), has four visitor centers. The one on the Seward Highway, as you enter town, is open year round. Summer-only centers are in a kiosk at the boat harbor, downtown in an old Alaska Railroad car at the corner of Third Avenue and Jefferson Street, and on the cruise-ship dock. A handy automated voice-mail service called **Seward Information Help Line** (☎ 907/224-2424) provides information about all kinds of local services, vacancies, and reservations and can put you through directly to the businesses described on the recordings.

ORIENTATION   The layout of Seward, strung along between mountains and bay, has a double focus. At the north end, the **Seward Highway** and **Alaska Railroad** enter near the small-boat harbor. In recent years, this has developed like any seaside tourist town, with shops, restaurants, and tourist businesses clustered along the top of the boat basin. Ten blocks to the south, old downtown Seward stands on a street grid of historic buildings and more interesting hotels. North-south avenues are numbered; cross streets are named after presidents. To the south, the dirt Lowell Point

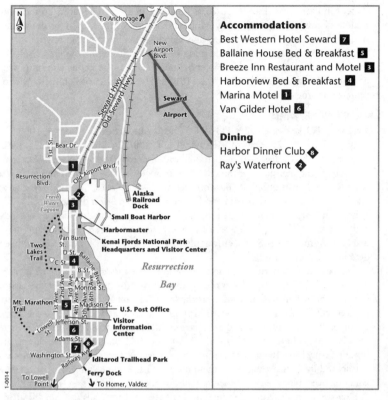

N

To Anchorage ↗

New Airport Blvd.

Seward Airport

Accommodations
Best Western Hotel Seward **7**
Ballaine House Bed & Breakfast **5**
Breeze Inn Restaurant and Motel **3**
Harborview Bed & Breakfast **4**
Marina Motel **1**
Van Gilder Hotel **6**

Dining
Harbor Dinner Club **8**
Ray's Waterfront **2**

Seward Hwy.
Old Seward Hwy.

1st. St.
Bear Dr.

Resurrection Blvd.

Old Airport Blvd.

Fresh Water Lagoon

Alaska Railroad Dock

Small Boat Harbor

Harbormaster

Van Buren St.

D St.

Ballaine Blvd.

Two Lakes Trail

C St.

B St.

Kenai Fjords National Park Headquarters and Visitor Center

Resurrection

Bay

A St.
2nd Ave.
3rd Ave.
Monroe St.
4th Ave.
5th Ave.
6th Ave.
1st Ave.

Mt. Marathon Trail

Madison St.

U.S. Post Office

Lowell St.

Jefferson St.

Visitor Information Center

Adams St.

Washington St.
Railway Ave.

Iditarod Trailhead Park

To Lowell Point ↓

Ferry Dock

↓ To Homer, Valdez

1-0014

Road runs a short distance before petering out at the trailhead to **Caines Head State Recreation Area.**

GETTING AROUND   You can easily cover downtown Seward on foot, although a little help is handy to get back and forth from the boat harbor. The **Chamber of Commerce Trolley** runs every half hour from 10am to 7pm daily in summer; it goes south along Third Avenue and north on Ballaine Street, stopping at the railroad depot, the cruise-ship dock, and the harbor visitor center. **Independent Taxi** (☎ 907/224-5000) is one of the cab companies. **Seward Shuttle Service** (☎ 907/362-3074) has a 10-passenger van. They'll take a group to Exit Glacier for $40 round-trip. If you're experienced with boats, rent a skiff for $15 an hour from **Miller's Landing,** on Lowell Point Road (P.O. Box 81), Seward, AK 99664 (☎ 907/224-5739).

FAST FACTS   The **sales tax** in Seward is 5%. There are **ATMs** at the First National Bank of Anchorage, 303 Fourth Ave., and at the National Bank of Alaska, 908 Third Ave. In **emergencies,** dial **911.** For nonemergency situations, call the **Seward Police Department** (☎ 907/224-3338) or, outside the city limits, the **Alaska State Troopers** (☎ 907/224-3346). **Providence Seward Medical Center** is at 417 First Ave. (☎ 907/224-5205). The *Seward Phoenix Log* is published each Thursday; you can usually find the Anchorage newspaper, too.

SPECIAL EVENTS   The big day of the year in Seward is the ✪ **Fourth of July,** when the whole town explodes with visitors, primarily from Anchorage. Besides the parade and many small-town festivities, the main attraction is the **Mount Marathon**

Race, run every year since it started as a bar bet in 1915. The racers go from the middle of town straight up rocky Mount Marathon to its 3,022-foot peak, then tumble down again, arriving muddy and bloody at the finish line in town. Binoculars will allow you to see the whole thing from town, including the pratfalls of the runners on their way down. The **Silver Salmon Derby** is the second and third week of August (August 8 to August 16 in 1998). The chamber of commerce visitor centers can provide information.

EXPLORING SEWARD

THINGS TO SEE & DO IN TOWN The ✪ **Alaska Sea Life Center,** 1000 Rail Way (P.O. Box 1329) Seward, AK 99664 (☎ **800/224-2525** or 907/224-3080; website http://www.alaskanet.com/sealife), promises to be the best place in Alaska to learn about the marine environment when it opens in May 1998. The center is a major research institution, so you won't see any dancing seals, but you may see real science in progress—designers intend for the scientists to be on display as well as the animals. It's the first major aquarium to completely integrate the missions of study and education. They've built a seabird colony, sea lion and seal habitat, and other displays. Admission is $12.50 for adults, $10 for children. Hours had not been determined at this writing.

The balance of Seward's attractions are of the modest, small-town variety. Explore downtown with the help of a **walking-tour map** provided by one of the visitor centers. The **Iditarod Trailhead,** near the ferry dock on Railroad Avenue, is where pioneers entered Alaska. The **Seward Museum,** at Third and Jefferson, has historical memorabilia and curiosities, and a display on the Russian ships built here in the late 18th century. Admission is $2 for adults, 50¢ for children, and it's open during the summer, daily from 10am to 5pm. The steep-roofed **St. Peter's Episcopal Church** is a delightful little chapel under the mountains at First Avenue and Adams Street. My family enjoyed using the **city library,** at Fifth Avenue and Adams Street, as a home base.

Dog-sled demonstrations and rides on a wheeled sled are available from **IditaRide Dog Sled Tours,** located on Old Exit Glacier Road, 3.7 miles out the Seward Highway (☎ **800/478-3139** or 907/224-8607).

SHOPPING Stop at the **Resurrect Art Coffee House Gallery,** at 320 Third Ave. (☎ **907/224-7161**), in an old church that's also on the walking tour. The fine art is local, and the coffeehouse is a meeting place and serves snacks. In the evening, musicians, poets, or storytellers perform. The **Bardarson Studio,** at 1317 Fourth Ave., at the boat harbor (☎ **907/224-5448**), specializes in Dot Bardarson's watercolor prints and also has a wonderful, welcoming attitude. There's a children's cave under the stairs and a husbands' recliner area with videos and reading matter upstairs. A shopping stop becomes an event. The **Resurrection Bay Galerie,** at 500 Fourth Ave. (☎ **907/224-3212;** website http://www.AlaskaOne.com/galerie), shows fine art in a lovely old house downtown. They also produce a guide to the galleries in town.

GETTING OUTSIDE

Here I've described things to do out of Seward other than the national park—which includes the fjords and Exit Glacier. See "Kenai Fjords National Park," below, for that information.

BOATING **Coastal Kayaking and Custom Adventures Worldwide** (☎ **800/288-2134** or 907/258-3866; website http://www.alaskan.com/kayak) leads sea-kayaking day trips in Resurrection Bay for $95 and longer trips into Kenai Fjords National Park. Book sailing charters on Resurrection Bay through the central agencies listed under "Fishing," below. The waters are beautiful, but it's a different experience than sailing in the Lower 48—if there's any wind, it's quite chilly.

FISHING   Seward is renowned for its saltwater silver salmon fishing, and there's a harbor full of large and small charter boats waiting to take you. There's also good halibut fishing. I prefer small boats, because you get to know the skipper better and have more of a feeling of being out there on your own. The going rate for a charter is $130 per person for salmon, or $150 for halibut, for which the boats have to go farther. There are several central charter agencies, which makes life simpler for visitors. **The Fish House,** P.O. Box 1209, Seward, AK 99664 (☎ **800/257-7760** or 907/224-3674; fax 907/224-7108), is the old, established booking agency and has a big store for supplies at the boat harbor. Another is **The Charter Option** (☎ **907/ 224-2026**).

You can fish from shore for silvers when they're running in the late summer, although your chances aren't as good as if you use a boat. The beach below the downtown area is a popular spot.

HIKING   There are several excellent hiking trails near Seward. You can get a complete list and directions at the Kenai Fjords National Park Visitor Center (see "Visitor Information," above). The **Iditarod National Historic Trail** starts as a paved path at Fourth and Railroad avenues. Through town it's a paved bike trail, then 15 miles of trail lead up through the woods starting about 2 miles out of town on Nash Road. **Seward Iditarod Trail Blazers,** P.O. Box 1923, Seward, AK 99664, can provide details and produces a trail guide brochure you can pick up at the visitors center.

The **Mount Marathon Trail** is a vigorous hike to the top of a 3,000-foot mountain. The route of the famous Mount Marathon foot race is the more strenuous choice, basically going straight up from the end of Jefferson Street; the hikers' route starts at the corner of First Avenue and Monroe Street. Either trail rises steeply to the top of the rocky pinnacle and the incredible views there. Allow all day, unless you're a racer; in that case, expect to do it in under 45 minutes.

The **Caines Head State Recreation Area** has a 7-mile coastal trail south of town. It's best done as an overnight, or with someone picking you up in a boat at the other end, as it's only accessible at low tide. The trail has some gorgeous views, rocky shores, and a good destination at the end: the World War II gun emplacement at Fort McGilvray. Three campsites are at Tonsina Point, 2 miles in, and a public-use cabin is 2 miles farther. At North Beach, 6¹/₂ miles from the trailhead, are two camping shelters, a ranger station, and trailheads to the fort, South Beach, and the 3-mile Alpine Trail. It's a great hike. The trailhead is south of town on Lowell Point Road; pull off in the lot right after the sewage plant, then cross the road through the gate and follow the dirt road a bit until it becomes the actual trail. For information and cabin permits, contact the state **Division of Parks,** 3601 C St., Suite 200, Anchorage, AK 99503 (☎ **907/269-8400;** website http://www.dnr.state.ak.us/parks/index.htm). They also produce a good trail guide you can pick up free at the Kenai Fjords National Park Visitor Center at the boat harbor.

The ✪ **Lost Lakes Trail,** with its fields of alpine wildflowers and small lakes, is among the most beautiful hikes in the area. The upper trailhead is at the 10-site **Primrose Campground,** on vast Kenai Lake, 17 miles up the highway on Primrose Road. Camping is $9. The trail rises through hemlock past a waterfall about 2 miles up (look for the spur to the right when you hear water), past an old mining cabin, and then through ever smaller trees and above treeline. A Forest Service cabin is available on a 2-mile spur about 11 miles along the 15-mile route. For detailed trail information, contact the Alaska Public Lands Information Center in Anchorage or the **Seward Ranger District,** at Fourth Avenue and Jefferson Street (P.O. Box 390), Seward, AK 99663 (☎ **907/224-3374**).

ACCOMMODATIONS

Hotels

The **room tax** in Seward is 9%.

Best Western Hotel Seward. 217 Fifth Ave., Seward, AK 99664. ☎ **800/478-4050** or 907/224-2378. Fax 907/224-3112. 38 rms. TV TEL. High season, $176–$206 double. Low season, $69–$99 double. Additional person in room $10 extra. AE, MC, V.

Energetic Brad Snowden, who also owns the neighboring New Seward Hotel and the saloon down the street, has created a hotel that's in a league of its own in Seward. The rooms are large, fresh, and attractively decorated; many have big bay windows and all have VCRs, refrigerators, and coffeemakers. The view rooms on the front go for a premium. Avoid the south-facing rooms, which look out on the back of another hotel. A two-story log cabin on a cliff over the boat harbor also is part of the hotel. With a large hot-tub spa on the magnificent deck, it's one of the most beautiful and luxurious accommodations in Alaska, renting for $324 a night.

   The New Seward Hotel operates out of a connected lobby with the Best Western. The rooms are smaller and less expensive, ranging from $58 to $96 as a double during the summer season. It has been called the "New Seward" since 1945, but some rooms have been recently remodeled with pleasant country decor.

The Breeze Inn. 1306 Seward Hwy. (P.O. Box 2147), Seward, AK 99664-2147. ☎ **907/224-5237.** Fax 907/224-7024. 86 rms. TV TEL. $115–$160 double. Additional person in room $10 extra. AE, DC, DISC, MC, V.

Located right at the boat harbor, this large, three-story, motel-style building offers good standard accommodations with the most convenient location for anyone in town for a fishing or Kenai Fjords boat trip. Twenty new rooms, at the upper end of the price range, are especially nice. A restaurant and lounge are across the parking lot.

The Marina Motel. 1603 Seward Hwy. (P.O. Box 1134), Seward, AK 99664. ☎ **907/224-5518.** Fax 907/224-5553. 18 rms. TV TEL. High season, $110–$120 double. Low season, $45–$55 double. Additional person in room $10 extra. AE, DC, DISC, MC, V.

Comfortable, convenient rooms across the Seward Highway from the boat harbor are a friendly, family-run business. Larger, lighter rooms with interior access, on the north side, rent for more, but those on the south side are perfectly adequate. All rooms have coffee machines and refrigerators.

The VanGilder Hotel. 308 Adams St. (P.O. Box 2), Seward, AK 99664. ☎ **907/224-3525.** Fax 907/224-3689. 18 rms, some with bath; 2 suites. TV. $95 double; $165 suite. Additional person in room $10 extra. AE, DC, DISC, MC, V.

A charming if creaky old place founded in 1916 and listed on the National Register of Historic Places, the VanGilder is a retirement project for Don and Deane Nelson. Some rooms have a lot of charm, but authenticity means they tend to be small and unique, so choose carefully.

Bed & Breakfasts

Seward has many excellent B&Bs; here are my favorites. (Names and addresses of others are available at the Seward Chamber of Commerce Visitor Center.)

Ballaine House Bed and Breakfast. 437 Third Ave. (P.O. Box 2051), Seward, AK 99664-2051. ☎ **907/224-2362.** 4 rms, none with bath. $72.50 double. Each additional person $15. Rates include full breakfast. No credit cards.

This 1905 house near the center of downtown is a classic bed-and-breakfast, with its wooden floors, large living room, and tall, double-hung windows. It's on the National Historic Register and the town walking tour. Marilee Koszewski has decorated with antiques and handmade quilts and provides rain coats, binoculars, and other gear for outings, and will even do laundry. She also will give back the commission on boat bookings, normally amounting to a 10% discount. Some of the rooms are small, and all bathrooms are shared. No smoking; no children under 7.

✪ **Harborview Bed and Breakfast.** 900 Third Ave. (P.O. Box 1305), Seward, AK 99664. ☎ **907/224-3217.** Fax 907/224-3218. 8 rms, 2 apts. TV TEL. High season, $85 double. Low season, $55 double. Year round, $85 apt. Rates include continental breakfast. Additional person in room $15 extra. MC, V.

Really more of an inn than a B&B—there are no shared or common rooms—Jolene and Jerry King's eight immaculate, spacious guest rooms, decorated with Alaska Native fine art and with tables for dining, are an incredible value. The nondescript building is located midway between downtown and the boat harbor. A few blocks away, the Seaview rooms are a pair of large two-bedroom apartments right on the beach, with their own front lawn and barbecue. They have full kitchens, but breakfast is not included.

Camping
A fun place to camp is the **beach** on Ballaine Avenue, which becomes a tent and RV city in the summer. The fee is $6 for tents, $8 for RVs, and showers are $2. It's operated by the city parks and recreation department (☎ **907/224-4055**). **Miller's Landing,** on Lowell Point Road south of town (P.O. Box 81), Seward, AK 99664 (☎ **907/224-5739**), offers electric hookups for $20 a night and rustic, sleeping-bag cabins starting at $40 a night, with showers and many other services, including fishing charters and equipment rentals, including boats and fishing poles. For a more remote experience, try the Primrose Campground, described above with the Lost Lakes Trail, or the Exit Glacier campground, described in the "Kenai Fjords National Park" section, below.

DINING
Besides the two steak and seafood establishments listed below, there are good casual places in Seward. **Thorne's Showcase Lodge,** 208 Fourth Ave. (☎ **907/224-3700**), makes locally famous deep-fried beer-batter halibut, served in a basket. The place is smoky, but you can get take-out. **Red's Food Wagon,** at Third and VanBuren, serves great burgers and onion rings. **The Miller's Daughter Bakery,** at the harbor at the corner of S. Harbor St. and Fourth Ave., makes wholesome sandwiches and serves soup in bowls of its hearty hearth breads.

The Harbor Dinner Club. 220 Fifth Ave. ☎ **907/224-3012.** Main courses $3–$40; lunch $5–$8.50. AE, CB, DC, DISC, MC, V. Daily 11am–2:30pm and 5–11pm. STEAK/SEAFOOD.

This old-fashioned family restaurant has been the same reliable place as long as anyone can remember. With white tablecloths and a menu that ranges from fine seafood to a $3 hamburger, you need not spend a lot of money to eat in a quiet, well-appointed dining room. The sautéed seafood special, including shrimp, halibut, and tender scallops, was fresh and not overdone. The prime rib was large and well presented. Full liquor license.

Ray's Waterfront. At the small-boat harbor. ☎ **907/224-5606.** Main courses $14–$20; lunch $6–$10. AE, DC, DISC, MC, V. 15% gratuity added for parties of six or more. Apr 2–Sept, daily 11am–11pm. Closed Oct–Apr 1. STEAK/SEAFOOD.

The lively, noisy dining room looks out from big windows across the small-boat harbor. This is where the locals will send you, and for good reason: The food is just right, and the atmosphere is fun. Salmon served on a cedar plank—done to a turn—is a specialty, or, to eat well less expensively, order the delicious fish chowder and a small Caesar salad. Don't count on speedy seating or service. Full liquor license.

KENAI FJORDS NATIONAL PARK

The park is all about remote rocks, mountains, and ice that meet the ocean, and the animals that live there. For some it's a natural cathedral, and the experience of seeing the grand and rugged terrain takes on a spiritual dimension. Anyone will find the park and its surroundings impressive. And in few places are the chances better of seeing marine mammals or adding waterfowl to a birder's list.

But most of the park is remote and difficult to get to. A large vessel, such as a tour boat operating out of Seward, is the only practical way to see the marine portion of the park—the truly exceptional part. That's not cheap or quick if you really want the full experience, and there are better destinations for people subject to seasickness. The inland portion is accessible only at Exit Glacier, near Seward, unless you're an experienced mountaineer.

The park comprises 580,000 acres on the south coast and interior land mass of the Kenai Peninsula. The shore here is exposed to the Gulf of Alaska, whose wild, recurrent storms beat mercilessly against the mountainous shore, unbuffered by any land mass against the vast expanse of the Pacific to the south. The steep topography of the shoreline, created by the collision of the tectonic plates carrying the Pacific Ocean, on one hand, and Alaska, on the other, is uninhabited, although ancient Alaska Native archeological remains suggest there were settlements at times along the deep, fingerlike fjords that penetrate the mountains.

Behind the coastal mountains, and spilling over their shoulders, is an inconceivably vast plateau of ice, the Harding Icefield. Undiscovered until this century—and there's precious little to discover other than mile after mile of featureless ice—the icefield covers an area 37 by 20 miles, the entire southern Kenai Peninsula from Resurrection Bay to Kachemak Bay. It takes days for an experienced mountaineering party to cross. Each of the park's many glaciers is a small branch of this mother ice sheet.

Kenai Fjords National Park was created in 1980, when Congress passed the Alaska National Interest Lands Act, which set aside 106 million acres—about a third of the entire state—in protected parks and wilderness. Although development-minded Alaskans howled at the time, Kenai Fjords has proven to be far more valuable as an attraction for visitors than it could have been for any potential resource exploitation.

In 1989, the park was damaged by the *Exxon Valdez* oil spill. Oil took about 10 days to arrive from Bligh Reef, in Prince William Sound, 140 miles to the northeast, and when it did, the destruction of wildlife was horrific. Many tens of thousands of birds and hundreds of sea otters perished. Although the oil quickly washed off the rocky, wave-pounded shore, some bird colonies never recovered entirely from the assault.

The damage of the spill is not perceptible to first-time visitors, however, and the tragedy has had a silver lining: Exxon Corporation's settlement with the state and federal governments, worth $1 billion, funded in part the $50-million Alaska Sea Life Center in Seward, which will allow visitors to see and learn about the marine biology of the area. It also allowed the National Park Service to buy out private holdings in the park that could otherwise have been logged or developed.

ESSENTIALS

GETTING THERE   Seward is the threshold to the park. Exit Glacier is 13 miles from the town by road; the Kenai Fjords National Park Visitor Center is at the Seward small-boat harbor; and the tour boats that visit the park leave from Seward. Many visitors try to do the park in a day, coming from Anchorage by train or road, touring the park by boat, then returning that evening. I recommend against this. To really get to the park, you need to be on an all-day boat trip—most half-day trips barely leave Resurrection Bay and hardly see the park proper. More important, a lot of the visitors I saw riding the train back to Anchorage after a 1-day marathon trip to Kenai Fjords were so tired they couldn't keep their eyes open for the extraordinary scenery passing by outside the train. A better plan is to spend a night in Seward and take in the full Kenai Fjords boat trip and Exit Glacier. See the section on Seward, above, for details on getting to and around the town.

VISITOR INFORMATION   The **Kenai Fjords National Park Visitor Center,** at the small-boat harbor (P.O. Box 1727), Seward, AK 99664 (☎ **907/224-3175;** fax 907/224-2144; website http://www.nps.gov/kefj/), is a place to ask questions and get ideas for outings. There's a fine collection of books for sale about the flora, fauna, and geology of Alaska.

SEEING THE PARK

Kenai Fjords is essentially a marine park. On a boat tour, you'll see its mountains, glaciers, and wildlife. On any of the tours, you're likely to see sea otters and sea lions, and you have a good chance of seeing humpback whales, orcas, mountain goats, and black bears. Bird watchers will see bald eagles, puffins, cormorants, murres, and various sea ducks.

Depending on the time and money you have to spend, you can choose to take a half-day trip staying generally in Resurrection Bay or a full-day trip that travels to Aialik Bay or Harris Bay, in the heart of the park. The shorter trips generally cost about $60 per person, while the longer trips are up to $115. Find out exactly where the boat is going—some tour companies call their trips Kenai Fjords tours but only scratch the edge of the park and really are Resurrection Bay tours. Resurrection Bay contains plenty of impressive scenery—its cliffs are as if chiseled from the mountains—but the fjords are even grander. Also, Holgate Glacier, in Aialik Bay, and Northwestern Glacier, in Harris Bay, at the heads of the parks' fjords, are great tidewater glaciers; Bear Glacier, at the edge of the park and visited by the half-day tours, is less impressive.

How much wildlife you see also depends on the trip you take. The half-day cruises have less of a chance of seeing whales and will see puffins and other birds in lesser numbers. The longer trips, which make it into the heart of the park proper, will see birds and animals in greater numbers and variety. If you're lucky with the weather, you may make it to the exposed Chiswell Islands, which have among the greatest bird rookeries in Alaska, supporting more than 50,000 seabirds of 18 species. The day-long trips also allow more time to linger and really see the behavior of the wildlife. Whatever your choice, binoculars will greatly enhance the trip.

An important factor in your decision is your susceptibility to seasickness. To reach the heart of the park, vessels must venture into the unprotected waters of the North Pacific. Large, rolling waves are inevitable on the passage from Resurrection Bay to the fjords themselves, although once in the fjords the water is calm. On a rough day, most boats will turn back for the comfort of the passengers and change the full-day trip into a Resurrection Bay cruise, refunding the difference in fare. Of course, they'd rather not do that, and the decision usually isn't made until the vessel is out there, probably after some of the passengers are already vomiting over the side. My advice is that if you get seasick easily, stick to the Resurrection Bay cruise, or take a boat tour in protected Prince William Sound out of Whittier or Valdez, where the water is smooth. In any event, ask about the tour company's policy on turning back.

Most important of all, try to schedule loosely, so that if the weather is bad on the day you choose for your boat trip, you can wait and go the next day. If the weather's bad, you'll be uncomfortable, and the animals and birds won't be as evident, or the boat may not go out at all. If you pay up front to hold a reservation on a boat—probably a good idea in the busiest months—find out the company's refund policy.

If you're shopping around, ask how much deck space there is outside so you can really see. What is the seating arrangement inside? How many passengers will be on board and how many crew members to answer questions? Is lunch provided, and what does it consist of?

For those with the money, time, and outdoor skills, it's possible to charter a seaplane or a boat to one of the four park service cabins, using it as a base for kayaking around in the fjords.. This is a truly remote and spectacular trip. Contact the park service visitor center for details and permits, which become available on January 1 for the entire year.

Here are some of the companies offering tours:

- **Kenai Fjords Tours / Kenai Coastal Tours,** 536 W. Third Ave., Anchorage, AK 99501 (☎ **800/478-8068** or 907/276-6249; website http://www.kenaifjords. com); 1304 Fourth Ave., Seward, AK 99664 (☎ **907/224-8068**). This is the biggest operation, with many years of experience and an excellent reputation. It offers a variety of trips, including the full-day trip to the park and half-day Resurrection Bay tours and dinner cruises, from Seward or as packages from Anchorage. Many of the trips stop at Fox Island, well out in the bay, for a salmon bake and look at the lodge there, or even an overnight. The vessels are fast and well maintained. However, they also are large and often are full of tour groups. The management has a philosophy of allowing passengers to experience the wildlife by lingering and trying to create an individual feel, but that's not so easy in such a crowd of people, all seated in rows. The refund policy is generous.

- **Mariah Charters and Tours,** 3812 Katmai Circle, Anchorage, AK 99517-1024 (☎ **800/270-1238,** 907/224-8623 in Seward, 907/243-1238 in Anchorage; website http://www.mariahtours.com). Mariah operates 22-passenger vessels to keep their tours more personal than the big boats that carry more package tour clients. This means you're less likely to find yourself in a herd of people on deck, but smaller vessels are more active in the waves, too. They specialize in the all-day trips that penetrate to the big glaciers deep in the park. Passengers bring their own lunch.

- **Major Marine Tours,** 411 W. Fourth Ave., Anchorage, AK 99501 (☎ **800/ 764-7300,** 907/224-8030 in Seward, 907/274-7300 in Anchorage; e-mail mmarine@aol.com). Making a specialty of its food, Major Marine features a dinner cruise of Resurrection Bay, but just barely enters the park proper, visiting Bear Glacier on a 4-hour trip. The menu of salmon, chicken, rice pilaf, salad, and so on, with a full bar, gets good reviews. The *Star of the Northwest,* at 115 feet, is large and stable, with lots of outside deck space. But, again, if the weather's bad, the dinner won't be such fun.

- **Alaska Renown Charters** (☎ **907/224-3806**). The lowest-cost choice, this operator runs 4¹/₂-hour and 2¹/₂-hour trips starting at $44 per person. The shorter tour of Resurrection Bay—not the park—is a good way to get out on the water and see wildlife if you're short on time or money. The longer trip makes it to Aialik Cape, enhancing your chance of seeing wildlife and part of the park. Breakfast or lunch is included. The company continues running all winter and has a package from Anchorage for $99.

EXIT GLACIER

When I visited Italy a few years ago, I got to the point that I thought I'd scream if I saw another painting of the Madonna. If your trip to Alaska is long, you may start to feel the same way about glaciers. But, although relatively small, Exit Glacier really is unique, and I enjoyed a visit even as a jaded lifelong Alaskan. (And I've probably seen even more glaciers than Madonnas.) It's possible to walk quite close to Exit Glacier, see its brittle texture, and feel the cold, dense spires of ice looming over you. The pattern of vegetation reclaiming the land that the glacier has uncovered is well explained by interpretive signs and a nature trail. At the same time, however, the area remains refreshingly primitive. The National Park Service's low-key presentation of the site makes it a casual, pleasant visit for a couple of hours; longer, if you do a hike. Kids enjoy the broad gravel trails, and as long as you don't let them go beyond the warning signs near the ice, there's not much trouble they can get into.

To get to the glacier, turn off the Seward Highway 3.7 miles north of town and follow the signs down the 9-mile road, the second half of which is gravel and can be dusty in summer. In winter, the road is closed to vehicles. Following the road along the broad bed of the wandering Resurrection River, you'll see in reverse order the succession of vegetation, from mature Sitka spruce and cottonwood trees down to smaller alders and shrubs. It takes time for nature to regrow the sterile ground left behind by a receding glacier. As you get closer, watch for a sign bearing the year 1780; more signs count upward through the years, marking the retreat of the glacier through time. If you don't want to drive, **Kenai Fjords Tours** (☎ **907/224-8068**) takes daily trips to Exit Glacier, combined with a Seward town tour. It starts at 2pm, takes $2^1/2$ hours, and costs $19. See "Getting Around," in the "Seward" section, for other options on getting there.

At the parking lot, there's a simple ranger station and pit toilets. Ranger-led nature walks start here on a sporadic schedule—check at the visitor center. Often, a spotting scope is set up to see mountain goats up in the rocky cliffs. The short trail to the glacier starts here. At the glacier, the trail splits: The steep route goes up along the side of the glacier, and the easy route runs on the flat gravel at its face. Don't go beyond the warning signs; ice can fall off and crush you. An all-day hike, 8 miles round-trip, climbs along the right side of the glacier to the Harding Icefield—the glacier gets its name for being an exit from that massive sheet. It's a challenging walk with a 3,000-foot elevation gain but is the easiest access I'm aware of to visit an icefield on foot. Because of snow, the trail doesn't open until late June or early July. The icefield itself is cold and dangerous, and there's an emergency shelter maintained by the park service. Don't trek out on the ice unless you know what you're doing. The park service sometimes guides hikes up the trail.

The **Resurrection River Trail** begins from the road just short of the last bridge to the glacier. It's a pleasant day hike, with lots of wildflowers in the fall, or the start of a long hike on the historic Resurrection Trail, leading 72 miles all the way across the Kenai Peninsula. Contact the U.S. Forest Service (see the beginning of the "Kenai Peninsula" section) for guidance and trail conditions.

A free park service tent campground is located near the glacier, at Mile 8.5 on Resurrection River Road. There's also a park service cabin a mile from the glacier, open only during the winter when the road is closed. It's accessible by ski or dog sled. Contact the park headquarters for a $30-a-day permit.

COOPER LANDING

The little roadside community of Cooper Landing, in the wooded mountain valley along Kenai Lake and the Kenai River, begins about 8 miles west of Tern Lake, where the Sterling Highway splits from the Seward Highway, and continues sporadically along the highway for about 7 miles. (The Sterling runs generally west.until Soldotna, where it heads south again.) The frothing upper Kenai River is the community's life-line. It brings the salmon each summer that draw the visitors to fill hotels, restaurants, and the date books of guides. For nonfishermen, there's not much here—a couple of operators do rafting trips, and some of the accommodations could provide a romantic mountain retreat. Cooper Landing is also the midpoint of the Resurrection Trail, described in the "Hope" and "Kenai Fjords National Park" sections. Just west of the community, the Russian River meets the Kenai, the scene, during the July red salmon season, of a mad fishing and camping frenzy. A ferry takes anglers across the river from the highway, and the Forest Service's 83-site Russian River Campground is frequently full while the sockeye are running. Sites are $11. Reserving in advance (see "Outside in Southcentral," at the beginning of this chapter) is a good idea when fish are in the river.

Cooper Landing has a post office, service stations, and small stores selling fishing gear and essentials, but it's not a center. For banking or anything else not directly related to catching a salmon, you'll have to drive to Sterling, 30 miles away to the west, or Soldotna, 44 miles away.

Each of the accommodations listed below can find you a fishing guide or tell you where to put your line in the water. **Alaska Troutfitters,** at the Alpine Inn, P.O. Box 570, Cooper Landing, AK, 99572 (☎ **907/595-1212;** fax 907/595-1593; website http://www.aktroutfitter.com), offers guided fly fishing for $165 a day. They also rent drift boats and offer rafting tours—a 2^1/2-hour trip is $35. The **Alpine Inn,** at Mile 48.2 of the Sterling Highway, in the heart of Cooper Landing, has 12 nice motel-style rooms with TVs and kitchenettes for $95 to $115 a night, double, in the high season. **Alaska Rivers Co.,** at Mile 50 (P.O. Box 827), Cooper Landing, AK 99572 (☎ **907/595-1226**), does a good job of their guided float fishing trips, charging $125 for a full day of fishing. They also offer rafting just for the scenery and rent cabins. For a rafting-oriented adventure with **Alaska Wildland Adventures** (☎ **800/ 334-8730** or 907/783-2928), see chapter 6, "Outside in Alaska." They also operate Kenai Backcountry Lodge, accessible only by boat across Skilak Lake from the town.

The most luxurious hotel on the Kenai Peninsula is up the dirt Bean Creek Road above Cooper Landing, the ✪ **Kenai Princess Lodge,** P.O. Box 676, Cooper Land-ing, AK 99572 (☎ **907/595-1425;** fax 907/595-1424). Built to service the company's cruise-ship and package-tour business, the hotel does have rooms open for independent travelers, for $179 to $189 double in the high season. When the ships stop running, but before the lodge closes in January and February, rooms rent for as little as $79. Each room is like a remote cabin, with balconies overlooking the wooded valley, wood stoves stocked with firewood, and many unique details; yet they are luxu-rious hotel rooms at a resort with exercise rooms, spas, and a fine restaurant. It would be worth a trip for nonfishermen to go just for a quiet stay. There's an attractive RV park, too.

Gwin's Lodge, at Mile 52, the west end of Cooper Landing (HC 54 Box 50), Cooper Landing, AK 99572 (☎ **907/595-1266**), is the town's old original log road-house. Standing just a mile east of the Resurrection trailhead and the Russian River

Campground, it's convenient and has loads of character. The food ranges from long-famous burgers to steaks and seafood. Cabins rent for $104 double in the high season, and full RV hook-ups are $20. There is a store, tackle shop, and booking service for fishing, rafting, and other trips.

KENAI / SOLDOTNA & STERLING

These quintessential American towns, dominated by shopping malls and fast-food franchises facing broad highways, have only a single claim to fame, but it's a pretty good claim: The largest sport-caught king salmon in the world, almost 100 pounds, came from Kenai River. The Kenai's kings run so large there's a different trophy class for the river—everywhere else in the state, the Alaska Department of Fish and Game will certify a 50-pounder as a trophy, but on the Kenai it has to be at least 75 pounds. That's because kings in the 60-pound class—enough wild muscle to fight ferociously for hours—are just too common here. Fishermen prepared to pay for a charter will be in their element on the river.

Those not interested in fishing will find no more than an afternoon's sightseeing in these towns. There are outdoor activities other than fishing, however, primarily in the lake-dotted Kenai National Wildlife Refuge, which has its headquarters in Soldotna. The refuge is crossed by two wonderful canoe trails, and there is limited hiking.

Kenai came into being with the arrival of the Russians at the mouth of the Kenai River more than 200 years ago, but came into its own only with the discovery of oil on the peninsula in 1957. Today its economy relies on oil, commercial fishing, and, to a smaller extent, tourism. Soldotna, a smaller, newer, and even less attractive town, is the borough seat, and the primary destination for sport fishermen.

ESSENTIALS

GETTING THERE   By Car   From Anchorage, the drive on the Seward and Sterling highways to Soldotna is 147 miles. Allow 3 hours, without stops: In summer, traffic will slow you down; in winter, speeds are limited by ice and the fear of hitting moose, which can be fatal for the driver as well as the moose. Most of the major car-rental companies have offices in Kenai, at the airport.

By Bus   The **Homer Stage Line,** P.O. Box 1912, Homer, AK 99603 (☎ **907/ 235-7009** or 907/399-1847) connects Anchorage, Homer, and points in between 3 days a week in the summer, less frequently in the winter. The fare from Anchorage to Soldotna is $35 one way, $60 round trip. Tickets are for sale at the Goodnight Inn on the highway (☎ **907/262-4584**).

By Air   Three commuter airlines connect Kenai to Anchorage, with several flights an hour during the day, including **Era Aviation** (☎ **800/866-8394** or 907/ 283-9091) and **Southcentral Air** (☎ **800/478-2550** or 907/283-3926).

VISITOR INFORMATION   The **Soldotna Visitor Information Center,** operated by the Soldotna Chamber of Commerce, 44790 Sterling Hwy., Soldotna, AK 99669 (☎ **907/262-9814**), is located on the south side of town; drive through the commercial strip and turn right after the Kenai River Bridge. It's open in summer, daily from 9am to 7pm; in winter, Monday through Friday from 9am to 5pm. The **Kenai Visitors and Cultural Center,** operated by the Kenai Visitor and Convention Bureau, 11471 Kenai Spur Hwy., Kenai, AK 99611 (☎ **907/283-1991**), is just past Main Street on the left. The center offers the usual visitor guidance, but also includes a free two-room museum built in honor of the 1991 bicentennial of the arrival of the Russians in the area, with natural-history displays and cultural artifacts and free films. In summer, the center is open Monday through Friday from 8am to 7pm and on Saturday and Sunday from 10am to 7pm; in winter, Monday through Friday from 8:30am to 5pm and Saturday 10am to 4pm.

The **Kenai National Wildlife Refuge Visitors Center** is up Ski Hill Road in Soldotna, P.O. Box 2139, Soldotna, AK 99669 (☎ **907/262-7021;** e-mail R7KENWR@mail.fws.gov), just south of the Kenai River Bridge, turn left, taking the dirt road uphill from the building-supply store. Besides providing outdoor information, the U.S. Fish and Wildlife Service maintains a small museum of the area's natural history where a film is shown each hour in the summer. Summer hours are daily 8:30am to 6pm; in winter, Monday through Friday from 8:30am to 4:30pm and on Saturday and Sunday from 10am to 5pm.

ORIENTATION   Sterling is 14 miles east—toward Anchorage—from Soldotna on the **Sterling Highway.** It's just a wide place in the road—incredibly wide, as a matter of fact, and no one is quite able to explain why such a small town needs such a big road. Soldotna, too, is oriented along the Sterling Highway. The **Kenai Spur Highway** is the other commercial strip, connecting Soldotna with Kenai, 10 miles west. Continuing through town, it turns north 10 miles to Nikiski, and then to the Captain Cook State Recreation Area, 25 miles from Kenai. Kenai's central business area is oriented along the Kenai Spur Highway around the **Main Street Loop** and the airport; a couple of blocks south, on the water, is the **old town** area. **Bridge Access Road** leads south across the Kenai River and the Kenai River Flats bird-viewing area. On the south side of the river, **Kalifornsky Beach Road,** also known as **K-Beach Road,** connects back to Soldotna or south along the shore.

GETTING AROUND   The area is so spread out, walking really isn't possible, and there's no public transportation. Everyone here owns a car, and you can rent one from most major agencies, located at the Kenai airport. If you plan only to fish, however, you may not need one, instead getting rides from your guide, host, or a taxi cab. There are several cab companies; try **Inlet Taxi Cab** (☎ 907/283-4711 in Kenai, 907/262-4770 in Soldotna). There are agencies offering organized tours. **Tours on the Kenai,** P.O. Box 438, Kasilof, AK 99610 (☎ **907/260-3369;** e-mail cark@alaska.net), offers a 3¹/₂-hour tour on the fishing industry and Native and Russian cultural heritage of the area; the fare is $35 for adults, $25 for age 12 and under. They also offer guided day hikes in the wildlife refuge.

FAST FACTS   The **sales tax** in Kenai and Soldotna is 5%; outside the city limits it's 2%. Kenai and Soldotna both have **banks.** In Kenai, the National Bank of Alaska is at the Kenai Spur Highway and Willow; in Soldotna, two banks are on the Sterling Highway commercial strip. In addition, **ATMs** are all over the place—in Carrs and Kmart stores, for example. In **emergencies,** call **911.** Who to call for nonemergency business with the police depends on where you are: in Kenai, the **Kenai Police Department** (☎ 907/283-7879); in Soldotna, the **Soldotna Police Department** (☎ 907/262-4455); or outside city limits, the **Alaska State Troopers** (☎ 907/262-4453). The **Central Peninsula Hospital** is in Soldotna at 250 Hospital Place (☎ 907/262-4404)—from the Sterling Highway, take Binkley Street to Vine Avenue. The *Peninsula Clarion* is published 5 days a week; out-of-town newspapers are available at Carrs grocery stores.

SPECIAL EVENTS

Kenai   The **Kenai River Festival** (☎ 907/262-5581), in early June, has food, music, crafts, and games. The **Fourth of July** celebration is a big deal in Kenai. An **Annual Juried Art Show** occurs at the Kenai Fine Arts Center, 816 Cook Ave. (☎ 907/283-7040), in September.

Soldotna   In July, Soldotna celebrates **Progress Days,** with a parade and other festival events commemorating the completion of a gas pipeline in 1960—that's the area in a nutshell.

Ninilchik   The **Kenai Peninsula State Fair** (☎ 907/567-3670), south at mile 136 on the Sterling Highway, is in mid-August, with crafts, games, agricultural exhibits, and other country attractions, but no rides.

EXPLORING KENAI & SOLDOTNA

In Kenai's old town, the **Holy Assumption Russian Orthodox Church** is the area's most significant building. The parish was founded in 1845, and the present church was built in 1895. It's a quaint, onion-domed church, brightly kept but with old icons. A donation of $1 is requested. In the tiny lobby is a fine gift shop. Several related buildings are interesting for their interlocking log construction. The buildings across the street are a re-creation of a Russian fur trading post. The bluff over the beach is nearby. When the salmon are running, you can occasionally see white beluga whales chasing them upstream from here, sometimes in great numbers. Near here, you can get down to the beach for walks.

On Centennial Park Road, behind the visitor center in Soldotna, is the free **Home-steading Soldotna Historical Society Museum,** which celebrates the 50-year-old his-tory of the town with a collection of old cabins set up as they were when pioneers lived in them; it's open in summer only, Tuesday through Sunday from 10am to 4pm.

A family looking for something to do while a parent is off fishing will do no better than the magnificent **North Peninsula Recreation Area Nikiski Pool** (☎ 907/776-8472), 10 miles north of Kenai on the Kenai Spur Road. Built with taxes on the oil property in the area, the facility occupies a large dome and has a 136-foot water slide, mushroom fountains of water, and a hot tub from which parents can watch their children play in the pool below. People travel from other towns just to swim here. Open swimming and water slide use is Tuesday through Sunday 1 to 5pm and 6 to 9pm in the summer; in the winter, they're open Friday all day and Saturday and Sunday 1 to 5pm. Admission is $3, plus another $6 to use the slide.

GETTING OUTSIDE

✪ **FISHING**   Fishing the Kenai River is the whole point of coming to the area. Check at the visitor centers for information and regulation booklets. Or contact the **Alaska Department of Fish and Game,** at 34828 Kalifornsky Beach Rd. (☎ 907/262-9368 or 907/262-2737, for a recorded fishing report; website http://www.state.ak.us/local/akpages/FISH.GAME/adfghome.htm). Licenses are for sale in virtually any sporting-goods store.

King salmon, the monsters of the river, come in two runs. The early run, which sometimes has been limited to catch and release, comes from mid-May to June. These usually are the smaller fish, in the 20- to 40-pound range. The second run comes during the month of July and has the massive fish that range up to 90 pounds. Most people fish kings from a boat, which makes them easier to catch and much easier to land. A charter averages $125 to $150 for a 6-hour, half-day trip. There are dozens of guides. Contact the visitor center in Kenai or Soldotna to get in touch with a guide; also, many hotels and lodges have their own. It's possible to rent a boat, but the river is swift and treacherous. The **Sports Den,** at 44176 Sterling Hwy. in Soldotna (☎ 907/262-7491), is one of the larger charter operators, and also rents condos, boats, and equipment for all kinds of outdoor activities.

The area really goes crazy when the reds are in the river, mid-July to early August, and the kings are still in the river. You can fish red and silver salmon from the bank, although you have better chances from a boat. Silvers come in two runs. The first run is smaller, late July to late August, and the larger run arrives in September. Of course, the fish don't punch a time clock, so to know how they're running at any particular time you have to ask around. You can catch kings and silvers on lures, but reds go mostly for flies—a lot of people fish flies on spinning gear, with little lead weights to aid in casting. Salmon eggs work well as bait on kings and silvers, but check current regulations to determine if they're legal. Trophy-size rainbow trout and Dolly Varden char also come out of the river.

There are more than two dozen public access points over the 80 miles of the Kenai River. A **guide brochure with a map** is available from the state **Division of Parks,** P.O. Box 1247, Soldotna, AK 99669-1247 (☎ 907/262-5581; website http://www.dnr.state.ak.us/parks/index.htm); you can pick up a copy at one of the visitor centers.

For fishermen interested in less competition and more of a wilderness experience, Kenai is a gateway for vast wild lands accessible by air on the west side of Cook Inlet. You can fish a stream packed with salmon all by yourself. **Alaska Adventures** (☎ 800/262-9666) and **High Adventure Air** (☎ 907/262-5237) have packages with fly-in cabins, among others.

SPECIAL PLACES   The **Kenai River Flats,** near the bridge in Kenai, are a tidal marsh populated by birds and used by migratory birds each spring and fall. State Parks has developed a viewing area near the bridge. The **Kenai National Wildlife Refuge** is dotted by lakes on flat, wet lowlands. The ✪ **Swanson River Canoe Route** and **Swan Lake Canoe Route** are beautiful multiday trips across normally placid water, usually with few people in evidence. Some 70 lakes, portage trails, and two rivers connect a 150-mile paddling network, with scores of good campsites. The refuge visitor center has a free guide map, and **Trails Illustrated** produces an excellent outdoor map of the whole area, printed on plastic (see "Fast Facts: Alaska" in chapter 3 for details). There also are several hiking trails in the refuge's uplands, and backcountry camping is permitted anywhere but close to a road or trailhead. Get guidance at the refuge visitor center.

For car camping, away from all the fishermen, the **Captain Cook State Recreation Area** is a lovely and underused seaside area on Cook Inlet, 25 miles north of Kenai on the Kenai Spur Road. There are lots of attractive sites among large birches, trails, beach walking, a canoe landing at the end of the Swanson River Canoe Route, and lake swimming. The camping fee is $10.

ACCOMMODATIONS

Rates at all hotels are on seasonal schedules with three, four, or even more levels linked to the salmon runs.

Daniels Lake Lodge Bed and Breakfast. 21 miles north of Kenai (P.O. Box 1444), Kenai, AK 99611. ☎ 800/774-5578 or 907/776-5578. Website http://puffin.ptialaska.net/~ducks/. 5 rms, 2 with bath; 2 cabins. TV. High season, $75–$105 double; $125–$180 cabins. Low season, $55–$65. MC, V. Additional person in room $15 extra.

Located on peaceful and sparsely built Daniels Lake, this lovely, relaxing place has a boat and canoe you can use for trout fishing right out the back door, among the resident ducks. The gregarious Christian hosts, with their dogs and rabbits, eagerly make friends with guests. The fanciful waterfowl-theme decor is immaculate. The Captain Cook Recreation Area, Nikiski Pool, and other attractions of the quiet, pretty area are nearby. It would be a good place to spend a few days on a honeymoon or low-key family trip. There's an outdoor Jacuzzi and a laundry, and smoking is not permitted.

Great Alaska Fish Camp. Moose River, HC1 Box 218, Sterling, AK 99672 (in winter, P.O. Box 2670, Poulsbo, WA 98370). ☎ **800/544-2261** or 907/262-4515. Fax 907/262-8797 in summer, 206/638-1582 in winter. 19 cabins. Rates from $175–$249 for day trip without lodging to $3,195 for seven-day package. Rates include all meals, guide service, and travel from Anchorage. Closed off-season.

This is a top-flight lodge, offering kayaking, bear viewing, biking, and other "ecotour" safaris as well as fishing. Guests find a bottle of wine in luxurious cabins with private bathrooms. There are as many staff as guests, and they take a video for you, providing an editing room if you want to cut the dull parts. It's located on a stretch of riverfront where the Moose River meets the Kenai, on the Sterling Highway east of Soldotna.

Kenai River Lodge. 393 Riverside Dr., Soldotna, AK 99669. ☎ **907/262-4292.** Fax 907/262-7332. E-mail Krlds@ptialaska.net. 28 rms, 1 suite. TV TEL. High season, $110 double. Low season, $60 double. $240 suite. Additional person in room $10 extra. Fishing packages available. MC, V.

Overlooking the river, next to the bridge in Soldotna, this motel has the advantages of good standard rooms (with refrigerators) and a great location for fishermen. The grassy front yard descends right to the water, with a barbecue where you can cook up your catch. They operate fishing charters from the hotel. The suite is a large apartment with a wall of windows facing the river.

Log Cabin Bed and Breakfast. 49840 Eider Rd. P.O. Box 2886, Kenai, AK 99611. ☎ and fax **907/283-3653.** 9 rms, 3 cabins. $80–$90 double. Rates include full breakfast. Additional person in room $10 extra. AE, MC, V.

Ted and Carol Titus built this huge log house specifically to be their new B&B, but with its large common room—with a cathedral ceiling and fireplace—it feels more like a luxurious wilderness lodge. Located off Kalifornsky Beach Road a little south of the bridge in Kenai, the house stands over an active beaver pond, with a deck and lots of windows to watch the beavers. The upstairs rooms, which cost $10 more, are well worth it—they're large and airy. The downstairs rooms are a half-basement. All the rooms are attractively decorated in a country style. In-room telephones are available, and there's a Jacuzzi on the porch.

Soldotna Bed and Breakfast Lodge. 399 Lovers Lane, Soldotna, AK 99669. ☎ **907/262-4779.** Fax 907/262-3201. 16 rms, none with bath, and three separate houses. TV TEL. $135–$145 double; $280–$870 complete house. Rates include full breakfast. Additional person in room $67 extra. Fishing packages available. Open in winter by special arrangement. AE, MC, V (5% surcharge).

Right on the river, right in Soldotna, yet in a wooded setting, this inn—run by the meticulous Charlotte Ischi—offers a level of elegance beyond other accommodations in Soldotna. Each room is unique, with balconies over the river or the garden, and attractive wallpaper and furnishings. There are five clean bathrooms and four separate shower rooms among the 16 bedrooms. Smoking is not permitted in the inn. The grounds slope down to the river along a sheltered boardwalk, leading to a dock where you can fish or board one of the fishing charters run by Bill Ischi's Alaska Fishing Charters.

DINING

Franchise fast-food and burger-steak-seafood places dominate in Kenai and Soldotna. **Paradisos,** at Main Street and Kenai Spur Highway in Kenai (☎ **907/283-2222**), is a good multi-ethnic family restaurant.

The Armenian Bakery / Grand Burrito. 44096 Sterling Hwy., Soldotna. ☎ **907/ 262-2228.** $6.30 buffet. No credit cards. Mon–Sat 11am–8pm; bakery closes 3pm. MEXICAN/ ARMENIAN.

> Armenian/Russian/Mexican fast food is a great example of the ethnic cuisine you find in the area—it's just about impossible to find Mexican without finding Italian, and vice versa, or other equally improbable combinations. The Armenian buffet is tasty and, I'm told, authentic—I'm not an expert. Most locals sit in the Mexican fast-food side, so I guess the Eastern European proprietors know what they're doing. They have no liquor license.

Kitchen Express and Seafood Saloon. 115 S. Willow, Kenai. ☎ **907/283-5397.** All items $6.75–$21. CB, DC, DISC, MC, V. Mon–Tues 7am–6pm, Weds–Sat 7am–9pm. Closed Sunday. SEAFOOD.

> This light, casual restaurant near the airport in Kenai has the ambience of an espresso shop, and, indeed, it has a coffee bar. But the menu, though limited, is more adventurous than most anywhere else in town, primarily revolving around shrimp, crab, and shellfish. There are lots of specials (in season) involving salmon and halibut, too. And the prices are reasonable. For meat-eaters, there are sandwiches. Beer and wine license.

✪ **Through the Seasons.** 43960 Sterling Hwy. (at intersection with Kenai Spur Hwy.), Soldotna. ☎ **907/262-5006.** Lunch $4.80–$7; dinner $15–$22. MC, V. Summer Mon–Sat 11am–3pm and 5:30–10pm, Sun 5:30–9pm; winter Tues–Thurs 11am–3pm and 5:30–9pm, Fri 11am–3pm and 5:30–9:30pm, Sat 5:30–9:30pm, closed Sun and Mon. Closed January. SEAFOOD/STEAK/PASTA.

> The small, light dining room, with a cathedral ceiling, looks out on a birch and spruce forest despite being near the intersection of two major highways. The atmosphere, with acoustic music weekend evenings, is ferny and casual. The menu is straightforward and reasonably priced and features a variety of vegetarian selections. They experiment with various cuisines, usually successfully. Without question the best meals in the area are served here. Beer and wine license.

HOMER: COSMIC HAMLET BY THE SEA

Homer's leading mystic, Brother Asaiah Bates, maintains that a confluence of metaphysical forces causes a focus of powerful creative energy on this little seaside town. It's hard to argue. Homer is full of creative people: artists, eccentrics, and those who simply contribute to a quirky community in a beautiful place. Indeed, Brother Asaiah may be the quintessential Homerite, although perhaps an extreme example, with his gray ponytail, extraordinary openness and generosity, and flowery rhetoric about "the cosmic wheel of life." Homer is full of outspoken, unusual, and even odd individualists—people who make living in the town almost an act of belief. I can say this because I'm a former Homerite myself.

The geography of Homer—physical as well as metaphysical—has gathered certain people here the way currents gather driftwood on the town's pebble beaches. Homer is at the end of the road—the nation's paved highway system comes to an abrupt conclusion at the tip of the Homer Spit, almost 5 miles out in the middle of Kachemak Bay—and believers of one kind or another have washed up here for decades. There were the "barefooters," a communal group that eschewed shoes, even in the Alaska winter—Brother Asaiah came with them in the early 1950s. There are the Russian Old Believers, who organize their strictly traditional communities around their objection to Russian Orthodox church reforms made by Peter the Great. There are the former hippies who have become successful commercial fishermen after flocking here in the late 1960s to camp as "Spit rats" on the beach. And there are even

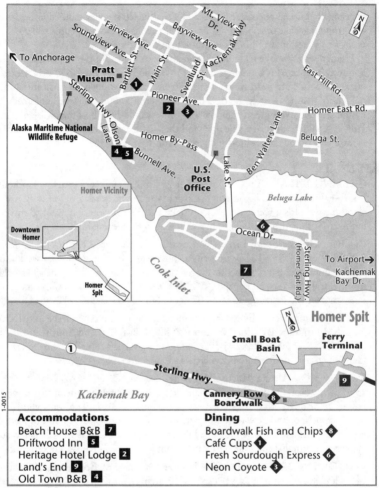

Accommodations

Beach House B&B **7**
Driftwood Inn **5**
Heritage Hotel Lodge **2**
Land's End **9**
Old Town B&B **4**

Dining

Boardwalk Fish and Chips **8**
Café Cups **1**
Fresh Sourdough Express **6**
Neon Coyote **3**

the current migrants—artists and retired people, fundamentalist preachers and New Age healers, wealthy North Slope oil workers and land-poor settlers with no visible means of support—all people who live here simply because they choose to.

The choice is understandable. Homer lies on the north side of Kachemak Bay, a branch of lower Cook Inlet of extraordinary biological productivity—the halibut fishing, especially, is exceptional. The town has a breathtaking setting on the Spit and on a wildflower-covered bench high above the bay. The outdoors, especially on the water and across the bay, contains wonderful opportunities. And the arts community has developed into an attraction of its own, drawing more artists and creating the reputation of an "arts colony." There are several exceptional galleries and the Pratt Museum, which has a national reputation.

Homer gets its name from a guy named Homer, which seems fitting since it's the sort of place where first names tend to be used. Homer Pennock came to the area around the turn of the century. Miners were exploiting the low-quality lignite common on the north side of Kachemak Bay, which means "Smoky Bay," as the seams occasionally burned and created haze. The coal-fueled steamers landed at Seldovia, a metropolis at that time but today a sleepy little village. Homer people still pick the coal that washes up on Bishop's Beach to heat their homes.

Homer began to take its modern form after two events: In the 1950s the Sterling Highway connected it to the rest of the world, and in 1964 the Good Friday earthquake sank the Spit, narrowing a much larger piece of land with a small forest into the tendril that now barely stands above the water. If not for constant reinforcement by the federal government, the Spit long since would have become an island, and Homer would hardly exist. The Spit, and the boat harbor there, are the town's vital organs; the commercial fishing and visitor industry keep it alive.

ESSENTIALS

GETTING THERE   By Car   At about 235 miles, Homer is roughly 4¹/₂ hours from Anchorage by car, if you don't stop at any of the interesting or beautiful places along the way. It's a scenic drive. If you take a rental car, you may want to drive it both ways, as the drop-off fees from Anchorage to Homer are high.

By Bus   Homer Stage Line, P.O. Box 1912, Homer, AK 99603 (☎ **907/ 235-7009** or 907/399-1847), runs to Anchorage and back three times a week during the summer, and less frequently the rest of the year. The fare is $45, or $80 roundtrip. **Central Charters,** on the Spit (☎ **800/478-7847** or 907/235-7847), sells tickets. In Anchorage the **ticket agent** is at 807 G St., Suite 250 (☎ **907/272-8644**).

By Air   Commuter airlines serve Homer's airport from Anchorage and Kenai roughly 10 times a day. **Era Aviation** (☎ **800/866-8394**) and **Southcentral Air** (☎ **907/478-2550** or 907/283-3926) are leading carriers. Small air-taxi operators use Homer as a hub for outlying villages and the outdoors.

By Ferry   The **Alaska Marine Highway System** (☎ **800/642-0066** or 907/ 235-8449; website http://www.dot.state.ak.us/external/amhs/home.html) connects Homer to Seldovia, Kodiak, and points west along the Alaska Peninsula and Aleutian Archipelago, and Seward to the east, with the *Tustumena.* The run to Kodiak takes 9¹/₂ hours and costs $48 for an adult walk-on passenger. A U.S. Fish and Wildlife Service naturalist rides the ferries to present programs and answer questions.

VISITOR INFORMATION   The **Homer Chamber of Commerce,** P.O. Box 541, Homer, AK 99603 (☎ **907/235-7740;** website http://www.xyz.net/~homer), maintains a **visitor information center** at 135 Sterling Hwy., on the right side past the intersection with Pioneer Avenue, open in summer, daily from 9am to 8pm. You can get a copy of the *Homer Tourist Guide* anywhere in town, published by the *Homer News,* which includes a map. The Alaska Division of Parks has a **ranger station,** P.O. Box 3248, Homer, AK 99603 (☎ **907/235-7024;** e-mail asphomer@xyz.net), located 4 miles from town as you approach Homer on the Sterling Highway. The **Alaska Maritime National Wildlife Refuge Visitor Center,** at 509 Sterling Hwy. (☎ **907/235-6961;** e-mail r7amnwr@mail.fws.gov), across from the intersection with Pioneer Avenue, is open in summer, daily from 9am to 6pm, with shorter hours in winter. The refuge, consisting of islands along most of the coastline of Alaska, is managed by the U.S. Fish and Wildlife Service. The visitor center has displays and films about marine natural history, and rangers lead beach and bird walks daily in the summer.

ORIENTATION   At the top of **Baycrest Hill,** coming into town on the **Sterling Highway,** you see the various parts of Homer—and the broad expanse of Cook Inlet, Augustine Volcano, and Kachemak Bay—arrayed before you in one of the most spectacular highway views anywhere. The chief feature of the town is **Homer Spit,**

jutting out several miles into the bay. The ferry dock and all marine activity are at its tip. At the base of the Spit is the airport and a narrow commercial district that lies between man-made Beluga Lake and the Spit, on **Ocean Drive.** On the near side of Beluga Lake is the downtown area. The main street is **Pioneer Avenue,** which branches off from the Sterling Highway to the left as you pass the middle school entering town. On the ocean side of the highway is the Bishop's Beach area. On the other side of town from the Sterling Highway entrance, Pioneer Avenue turns into **East End Road,** which snakes far up the bay with great views of the water. On a bench above the town, more wonderful views, broad fields of wildflowers, and miles of great walks are to be had at the top of **East Hill Road,** off East End Road, and **West Hill Road,** off the Sterling Highway.

GETTING AROUND   You can't cover the town without a vehicle—at least a bicycle, and that would only be for strong riders. Several major car-rental agencies have offices at the airport. Bicycles, skis, and snowshoes are for rent at **Homer Saw and Cycle,** at 1532 Ocean Dr. (☎ **907/235-8406**). **Trips,** the outdoors booking agency listed below, rents quality mountain bikes. There are several taxi companies in town, including **CHUX Cab** (☎ **907/235-CHUX**). **Homer Tours** (☎ **907/235-0530; website** http://www.xyz.net/~seekins/tours.htm) offers van and bus tours. A daily 4-hour tour is $40. **Day Breeze Shuttle and Tours** (☎ **907/399-1168**) offers a shuttle on the Spit and custom tours.

FAST FACTS   Homer has a **sales tax** of 5.5%; outside city limits you pay the 2% Kenai Peninsula Borough sales tax. There are banks, with **ATMs,** on Pioneer Avenue near Main Street and Sterling Highway near Heath Street. The **post office** is on the Sterling Highway at Heath Street. In **emergencies,** call **911;** for nonemergency calls within city limits, call the **Homer Police Department** (☎ **907/235-3150**); outside the city, phone the **Alaska State Troopers** (☎ **907/235-8239**). Both have offices located across Pioneer Avenue from the intersection with Lake Street. The **South Peninsula Hospital** is at the top of Bartlett Street, off Pioneer Avenue (☎ **907/ 235-8101**). Homer has two weekly newspapers: the *Homer News* and the *Homer Tribune.* You can find the Kenai and Anchorage newspapers all over town.

SPECIAL EVENTS   Homer's **Winter Carnival,** in mid-February, is a big community event, a small-town celebration with a beer-making contest, parade, and snow sculpture competition, among other highlights. In early May, the ✪ **Kachemak Bay Shorebird Festival** includes guided bird-watching hikes and boat excursions, natural history workshops, art shows and performances, activities, a wooden boat festival, and other events. It's organized by Alaska Maritime National Wildlife Refuge and the Homer Chamber of Commerce to mark the return of the annual migration in May. **Concert on the Lawn,** put on usually the second Sunday in August by KBBI radio (☎ **907/235-7721**), is a day-long outdoor music, craft, and food festival that brings together the whole town. The summer-long **Jackpot Halibut Derby,** also put on by the chamber of commerce, has a top prize that usually exceeds $15,000 for the biggest fish of the summer. Winning fish are in the 300-pound class.

EXPLORING HOMER

Homer lacks historic buildings. The attractions of the town come from its setting— the walks on the beaches and in the hilltop meadows—and from the art the setting has inspired. A widely distributed brochure lists the downtown art galleries. Here are some of the best.

✪ **Pratt Museum.** 3779 Bartlett St. (at Pioneer Ave.). ☎ **907/235-8635.** Admission $4 adults, $3 seniors over age 65, $2 children ages 13–18, $1 children 6–12. High season, daily 9am–7pm; low season, Tues–Sun noon–5pm. Closed Jan.

The Homer Society of Natural History's museum is as good as any you'll find in a town this size. The Pratt is strongest in natural history and has a saltwater aquarium in which to see the life of Kachemak Bay close up and even touch it (after you wash your hands), but the museum also has displays of local art, history, and culture. If you're wondering about all the fishing boats down in the harbor, at the Pratt you can find out about the different types of gear as well as the fish they catch. The exhibit on the *Exxon Valdez* oil spill toured nationally, to acclaim. Outside, the garden identifies local flora. Also, the volunteers will enjoy imparting local secrets about where to go, what to do, and where to eat. The Pratt also sponsors the 90-minute **Historic Harbor Tour** at 11am daily, a walk through the small-boat harbor to learn about the vessels and fishing industry. Tickets are $10 from Alaska Maritime Tours (☎ **907/235-2490**).

Commercial Galleries

✪ **Bunnell Street Gallery**. 106 W. Bunnell Ave. ☎ **907/235-2662**. Summer Mon–Sat 10am–6pm, Sun 11am–5pm; winter Mon–Sat 11am–5pm. Closed Jan and Feb.

This nonprofit, located in a perfect space in an old hardware store near Bishop's Beach at the lower end of Main Street, is one of the best in Alaska. Unlike most other Alaska galleries, which double as tourist gift shops, Bunnell was made by and for artists, and the experience is noncommercial and often challenging. You may be tempted to become a member of the nonprofit corporation that runs it, for membership comes with a one-of-a-kind plate made by one of the artists. As with all Homer art, the themes of the work tend to be fishy, and the medium and style could be anything. Don't miss the **Two Sisters Bakery** and coffee shop next door.

Ptarmigan Arts. 471 E. Pioneer Ave. ☎ **907/235-5345**. High season, Mon–Sat 10am–7pm, Sun 11am–6pm; low season Mon–Sat 10am–6pm, Sun 11am–4pm.

Often staffed by the artists themselves, Ptarmigan Arts specializes in crafts, especially ceramics and fabrics, which are the most common media in Homer and which generally are more affordable than fine art. Occasionally you can see a demonstration by one of the resident artists, and there's always a tremendous array of work in various styles.

Sea Lion Gallery. On the boardwalk on Homer Spit. ☎ **907/235-3400**. Open summer only, Mon–Sat 11am–9pm, Sun noon–8pm.

Wildlife artist Gary Lyon and his family own and staff this small gallery among the T-shirt shops on one of the boardwalks on Homer Spit. It's pleasant but a little odd to see very valuable works by Lyon and others displayed in this intimate setting. Lyon's work captures Alaska wildlife in spectacular detail, but also transforms his subjects with a distinctively dreamy vision.

✪ **Norman Lowell Studio & Gallery.** ☎ **907/235-7344**. Sterling Highway milepost 160.9 (near Anchor Point, about 12 miles out the Sterling Hwy. from Homer. Summer only, Mon–Sat 9am–7pm, Sun 1pm–5pm.

Lowell built his own huge gallery on his homestead to show his life's work. The immense oils of Alaska landscapes, which are not for sale, hang in a building that counts as one of Alaska's larger art museums. Admission is free, and Lowell or his wife Libby often host guests who walk through. Their original homestead cabin also is a museum, showing pioneer life in Alaska as it was when they originally settled here. A shop sells Lowell's paintings, which range in price from $3,000 to $30,000.

GETTING OUTSIDE

The best map of the Kachemak Bay area is produced by **Alaska Road and Recreation Maps,** P.O. Box 102459, Anchorage, AK 99510. Available all over town, it costs $3.95.

ON LAND ◐ **Tide Pooling**   Exploring Kachemak Bay's tide pools is the best way to really get to know the sea and meet the strange and wonderful animals that live in it, and it doesn't cost anything but the price of a pair of rubber boots. First, check a tide book, available for free or for a nominal price in virtually any local store, or ask a local to check one for you. You need a low tide of −2 or lower, meaning that low water will be at least 2 feet below the normal low, some 25 feet below the high. Extra-low tides expose more of the lower intertidal zone that contains the most interesting creatures. At a −5 tide, you could find octopus and other oddities. Also, the lower the tide, the more time you'll have to look. Keep track of the time: The tide will come in faster than you imagine, and you could get stranded and quickly drown in the 40°F water.

The best place to go in town is reached from Bishop's Beach Park, near the lower end of Main Street. Walk west on the beach toward the opening of the bay to Cook Inlet. It's at least a half-hour walk to the Coal Point area, where the sand and boulders end, and bedrock makes out from the shore. This is where you'll find pools of water left behind by the receding tide, all full of life. Explore patiently and gently— look at the animals and touch them, but always put them back as they were and be careful not to crush anything underfoot. Marine invertebrate identification keys and many other field guides are sold at **The Book Store** on the Sterling Highway next to Eagle Foods, and the wildlife refuge visitors center, above under "Visitor Information," is eager to help with advice. If you want to keep going, there's usually a sea otter raft offshore about 3 miles down the beach.

Hiking   There are trails on the bench above Homer as well as across the bay at Kachemak Bay State Park (see below). The **Homestead Trail** is an old wagon road used by Homer's early settlers. A trailhead is at the reservoir on Skyline Drive—drive up West Hill Road from the Sterling Highway, turn right and go till you see the water. The largely informal trail is lovely and peaceful, weaving through trees, across fields of wildflowers, and past old homestead cabins.

Driving or Mountain Biking   Several gravel roads around Homer make for exquisite drives or bike rides. East End Road goes through lovely seaside pastures, a forest, and the village of Fritz Creek, then follows the bluff line through meadows toward the head of the bay. The road eventually turns into an all-terrain-vehicle trail; don't go beyond your vehicle's ability to get out. Skyline Drive has extraordinary views of high canyons and Kachemak Bay; drive up East Hill Road just east of Homer.

ON OR ACROSS KACHEMAK BAY   It's relatively inexpensive to get out on Kachemak Bay, and boating is the whole point of Homer. Moreover, there are exquisite and remote hiking, mountain biking, and sea kayaking opportunities on the other side. I've listed some of the options here; side trips to Seldovia and Halibut Cove are listed below. You can book various across-the-bay adventures, including guided kayaking or mountain biking, with **Trips,** P.O. Box 1452, Homer, AK 99603 (☎ **907/235-0708**), an eco-tour agency next to the Harbormaster's Office on the Spit. A daily boat, the **Jakolof Ferry Service,** Red Mountain, Box RDO, Homer, AK 99603 (☎ **907/235-2376**; website http://www.xyz.net/~jakolof/home.html), runs to the south side of the bay several times a day. It's a great way to get to wilderness cabins and kayaking waters, the hiking and mountain biking roads accessible from the Jakolof Dock, Halibut Cove, Kachemak Bay State Park, and other remote points. They rent rustic cabins for $50 to $70 a night. The Jakolof Bay area offers great **mountain biking** trails where you're unlikely to see another person. The unmaintained Rocky River Road leads all the way to the outside of the peninsula. A maintained 10-mile road leads to the charming village of Seldovia, described below. **Alaska Coastal Journeys,** P.O. Box 2094, Homer, AK 99603

(☎ **907/235-2228**), offers 3- to 5-day outdoor trips across the bay led by experienced naturalist educators for $850 to $1,185 per person.

Fishing   Homer is known for ✪ **fishing for halibut,** those huge, flat bottomfish, and the harbor is full of charter boats that will take you out for the day for around $150 per person. Every day, people catch fish that are larger than they are, and halibut over 50 pounds are common. To get to where the fish are requires an early start and a long ride to fairly unprotected waters. People who get seasick easily shouldn't go, as the boat wallows on the waves during fishing. Using gear and lines that look strong enough to pick up the boat, you jig the herring bait up and down on the bottom. Halibut aren't acrobats like salmon, and fighting one can be like pulling up a sunken Buick. **Central Charters,** 4241 Homer Spit Rd., Homer, AK 99603 (☎ **800/ 478-7847** or 907/235-7847; website http://www.alaskan.com/central), is a booking agent for many operators, and also books tours, water taxis, and the *Danny J* to Halibut Cove; arranges sea kayaking trips; and even sells tickets for live theater. One good, large operator that doesn't book through Central is **Silver Fox Charters** (☎ **800/ 478-8792** or 907/235-8792).

The best **salmon fishing** is to be had in the Kenai River, 86 miles north on the Sterling Highway, or one of the other streams that drain the west side of the Kenai Peninsula to Cook Inlet, but there is some salmon fishing around Kachemak Bay. Salmon are fished with trolling gear year round, not only when they're running in the streams. **North Country Charters** (☎ **800/770-7620** or 907/235-7620) and **Dockside Tours** (☎ **800/532-8338** or 907/235-8337) run those charters, as well as excursions for halibut. Also, a lagoon on the Spit is stocked with terminal run king and silver salmon by the Alaska Department of Fish and Game. These fish have nowhere to spawn, and some fishermen scorn such "fish-in-a-barrel" angling. At the end of the run, snagging is permitted, which is something like mugging salmon. Check the fishing regulations and get a fishing license at any sporting-goods store or at the **Alaska Department of Fish and Game,** at 3298 Douglas (☎ **907/235-8191;** website http://www.state.ak.us/local/akpages/FISH.GAME/adfghome.htm). **Katch Seafoods,** on the Spit, P.O. Box 2677, Homer, AK 99603 (☎ **907/235-7953**), will process, pack, and ship your catch as ordered, and sells smoked and other fine seafood—in case you don't catch anything.

✪ **Gull Island**   Rainbow Tours' twice-a-day Gull Island trip is a tremendous value: For only $15 for an adult, the comfortable 67-foot *Rainbow Connection* takes passengers to the Gull Island bird rookery, lingering so close to the rocks it's possible to get a good view of the birds' nests with the naked eye. In season, you can see glaucus winged gulls, tufted puffins, black-legged kittiwakes, common murres, red-faced and pelagic cormorants, horned puffins, pigeon guillemots, and occasionally other species. The wildlife commentary on the boat is accurate and serious. The boat often continues on to drop off visitors at the Alaska Center for Coastal Studies in Peterson Bay, listed below, so you get to see quite a bit of the bay for the price of Gull Island alone. **Rainbow Tours** has an office on the Spit, at the Cannery Row Boardwalk (☎ **907/235-7272**). There's a snack and beer and wine bar on board.

✪ **Center for Alaska Coastal Studies**   This nonprofit foundation is dedicated to educating the public about the sea. That means the group's emphasis isn't to make money, but to interpret Kachemak Bay for visitors. You'll go for a day-long exploration of the Peterson Bay area: If the tides are right, the volunteers will take you on a fascinating guided tide pool walk; if not, you can take a nature walk. You decide what you want to do. There's also a lodge with saltwater tanks containing creatures from the intertidal zone, and those who aren't up to the hikes can have a quiet day hanging around here. **Rainbow Tours** (☎ 907/235-7272) books the trips and takes passengers at 9am daily on the *Rainbow Connection,* described above under Gull Island. At $55 per person, it's a bargain. Pack your own lunch, as none is provided.

Kachemak Bay State Park The park comprises much of the land across the water that makes all those views from Homer so spectacular. The main office is at the ranger station listed under "Visitor Information" above, and a **park ranger station** in Halibut Cove Lagoon is open in summer, where there's a dock and mooring buoys for public use. The park has about 40 miles of trails; a trail guide is available from the ranger station or the visitor centers. There are various campsites and three public-use cabins at Halibut Cove Lagoon, and more cabins and trails are being planned. Cabin permits are $50 a night and must be reserved in advance from the ranger station. Or you can go for a day trip, walk on a beach you'll have to yourself, and take a hike on one of the trails before being picked up at a prearranged time in the afternoon. Various water taxis can take you across and give you ideas on good places for beach walking, camping, sea kayaking, and hiking. **Kachemak Bay Water Taxi and Tours** (☎ 907/399-3333) charges $40 to $55 per person for that service.

McNeil River State Game Sanctuary McNeil River has the world's greatest known concentration of brown bears in June, July, and early August, when there's an easy meal to be had from the chum salmon trying to jump up a waterfall to return to spawn upriver. It's also the best place in the world to watch bears, as decades of protection and wise management have taught the bears—more than 100 at a time at the height of the run—to ignore humans standing within a few yards, even while the bears go on about their business of feeding, nursing, mating, and just being bears. It's such a valuable experience that permits to visit and tent in the campground are handed out by lottery by the **Alaska Department of Fish and Game,** 333 Raspberry Rd., Anchorage, AK 99518-1599 (☎ **907/267-2181;** http://www.state.ak.us/local/akpages/FISH.GAME/adfghome.htm). Permit applications, with a $25 fee, are taken until late March. More than 2,000 apply annually for fewer than 250 permits. There are outhouses, and water comes from a rain barrel—it's remote camping. **Kachemak Air** (☎ **907/235-8924**), listed below under "Flightseeing," can get you there and knows where else to find bears if you can't get a permit. Mike and Diane McBride, of Kachemak Bay Wilderness Lodge (see "Accommodations" section below), also operate a more comfortable lodging 8 miles north of the sanctuary.

Sea Kayaking The protected bays, tiny islands, and remote settlements on the south side of Kachemak Bay make for perfect sea kayaking. You're likely to see sea otters and may see orcas or other whales, as well as other wildlife. **The North Kayak Adventures,** P.O. Box 2319, Homer, AK 99603 (book through Trips ☎ 907/235-0708), offers day trips, even for beginners, for $140, including meals and passage across the bay. They also guide multiday trips. **Tutka Bay Boats** (☎ 907/235-7166) offers guided sea kayaking, as well as water taxis, fishing charters, and accommodations. Experienced kayakers can take a water taxi across and explore at will, camping on beaches over much of the bay. Check with the Kachemak Bay State Park rangers for guidance.

Flightseeing There are several good air-taxis in Homer, providing access to the really remote areas of the southern Kenai Peninsula and lower Cook Inlet that you can't easily reach by boat, but ✪ **Kachemak Air Service,** P.O. Box 1769, Homer, AK 99603 (☎ **907/235-8924;** website http://www.xyz.net/~decreeft/fly1929.htm), is really special. It offers spectacular scenic flights over the bay and glaciers starting at $90 per person. The personable Bill de Creeft, flying out of Homer since 1967, is experienced enough to qualify as a pioneer aviator, but he has nothing on his plane,

Hermits on the Homestead

Late in October, the snow was holding back in the clouds like a strong emotion. The ground was frozen, the swamp grasses stiff, brittle, painted with frost. This was the one time of year when, with a stout four-wheel-drive truck, you could drive in to Ben's cabin. It stood on a small rise amid his hundreds of acres of swampy ground, the only spot where trees could get out of the dampness and grow. The heavy, lovingly peeled logs of the house lay horizontally amid big birch and white spruce trees. Ben had dragged these huge tree trunks from far afield, by himself, when he started his homestead nearly 40 years earlier so he could keep living trees nearer to his house.

I'm not using his real name. Ben was a private guy. He invited us generously, offered coffee from the percolator on top of the soapstone wood stove, but it was clear that he wasn't quite sure he remembered how to talk to people—where to look, for example—and he kept mumbling and looking at my feet or the sky. He showed us around the house—the huge rocks he'd dragged in to build a foundation, the cellar where he stored his food, the collection of moose racks. Food tended to walk by each fall—he never had to go far to get his moose, and one of the biggest he shot right on the doorstep. Everything about his home was exactly the way he wanted it, the product of immense effort to make it all with his own hands. I could see plainly how he'd spent his days all these years. But I could only imagine what his nights must have been like, all alone out here—the piles of *Reader's Digest* and *National Geographic* magazines, the insistent silence.

Late in the afternoon, I finally asked Ben why he'd spent his whole adult life on this homestead, so far from other people. Why not move to town, where life is easier and there's someone to talk to? Well, he said, he did work construction in the summer for cash. But I knew that was an evasion. How, I asked, did he first end up out here, in the middle of nowhere, in a huge swamp? What made him want to be off by himself when he first came out here, so long ago? Pause—check the shoes, check the sky—well, he said, it seems there was a woman. She chose the other guy.

Years ago, *U.S. News & World Report* did an article about a homesteader on the Kenai Peninsula who was a Vietnam veteran—just one of the many mad hermits from the war who had hidden off in the Alaska woods by themselves, populating the wilderness with human time bombs. The subject of the story, a well-respected member of his little homesteading community, resented the characterization, and the magazine later paid him to settle his libel suit and printed a retraction. Everyone in the area knew the article was a bunch of baloney—Alaska homesteaders are as varied as people in the city. They aren't all crazed veterans any more than they're all victims of unrequited love, although those make the best stories. What they do have in common that's unique is a willingness to invest hard physical labor every day of their lives into the things the rest of us obtain effortlessly by turning a thermostat or a faucet handle.

Alaska's homesteaders came in waves. There were the prospectors from the gold rush who stayed. Then, after World War II, GIs with families looking for broad new opportunities came north and settled more land. The counterculture movement of the 1960s brought yet another group.

Federal homesteading laws written to open the Great Plains to agriculture in the 19th century made getting land difficult and required Alaska homesteaders to do a lot of anachronistic, absurd work—like clearing large tracts for farming that could never occur. To prove up the claim, the homesteaders had to survey the land, live on it, clear much of it, and then answer any challenges about their accomplishments at a hearing. If they passed the test, they received a patent to up to 160 acres.

The laws allowing homesteading on federal lands in Alaska were all repealed by 1986, but the state government still sometimes provides land to its citizens under laws that allow homesteading, lotteries, and sale of remote land. The parcels are very remote and smaller than the old federal homesteads, and the rules still don't make it easy—for a homestead, you have to live at least 25 months on the land in a 5-year period, for example. Many families try, with a Hollywood dream of living in the wilderness, only to give up when they learn firsthand of the hardship, privations, and cold. I know from experience that I want never again to live in a home where the heating is wood or the water is in jugs, and I've never done anything approaching building a homestead. Homesteading isn't like camping. Outdoor skills are essential, but won't help unless you also know how to repair engines below zero, build houses without power tools or proper materials, carry all your own water and firewood, and live poor, largely without an income or any of the things money can buy. You have to be willing to bathe rarely, be cold in winter and be eaten alive by mosquitoes in summer, and end up with land that isn't really worth anything.

Many successful homesteading experiences end with growing children. A couple may make it in the wilderness before having children, and young kids don't care if they can take a bath, so long as the parents don't mind being far from medical care and washing diapers by hand. But when children get to a certain age, they need to go to school and be around other children. The families often expect to go back to the homestead someday, but, somehow, they rarely do. I met a couple who worked and lived in town to educate their children; then, after they retired and the kids were through college, moved back out to their place along the railroad line north of Talkeetna. They didn't last through the winter—they'd forgotten how hard it was. Areas that were thriving little communities of neighbors in the 1950s or 1960s now are deserted, perhaps with one hermit left—like my friend Ben. Through it all, only about 160,000 acres of Alaska today—out of a total land mass of 365 million acres—shows any signs of human habitation. Less than 1% is in private ownership.

My wife's parents homesteaded in the 1950s and 1960s. They were in the post-World War II generation of families. Today the family still has some acreage, and a treasure trove of great stories—among them the tales of my late father-in-law's feats of strength and endurance, and my wife's memory of playing with dolls as a girl, and looking up to meet the eyes of a bear that had been watching her.

But my favorite is the story of Rose and her lover. They lived in the same area in northern California where Barbara's parents grew up. Everyone in town knew the story of the red-headed beauty who had an affair with an older man. Rose's parents refused to let her marry him and ruled that the couple couldn't see each other anymore. She entered a convent, and he disappeared, never to be seen in the town again. Many years later, after moving to Alaska, Barbara's parents were boating in Kachemak Bay when they got caught by bad weather on the opposite side of the bay from Homer. On their own in an open boat and looking for shelter, they found a cabin on a remote beach of an otherwise uninhabited island. They were taken in and befriended by the hermit who'd homesteaded there for years. After warming up with a cup of coffee, they got to talking about where they'd come from and how they'd ended up in Alaska. When it came time for their host to tell his story, it was about a beautiful young woman he'd loved, named Rose.

a restored 1929 Travel Air S-6000-B, one of only six remaining copies of the executive aircraft, with mahogany trim and wicker seats. De Creeft also operates a DeHavilland Otter carrying fishermen, hikers, kayakers, and those who just want to see the wilderness, as well as bear-viewing day trips on the west side of Cook Inlet.

Sailing   St. Augustine's Charters, P.O. Box 2412, Homer, AK 99603 (☎ **907/ 235-7847**) offers two daily afternoon sails on the bay for only $35, as well as wildlife cruises and Kachemak Bay State Park drop-offs.

ACCOMMODATIONS

Besides the hotels listed in detail below, you'll find good rooms at the **Baycrest View Inn,** P.O. Box 804, Homer, AK 99603, at the top of Baycrest Hill before you come into town on the Sterling Highway (☎ **907/235-8485**), with the best view you're ever likely to find at a motel, attractive little rooms, and reasonable prices. Good, inexpensive rooms in town are to be found at **Ocean Shores Motel,** 3500 Crittenden, Homer, AK 99603 (☎ **907/235-7775**). It is right behind the **Best Western Bidarka,** at 575 Sterling Hwy. (☎ **907/235-8148**), on the right as you come into town, whose rooms are the closest you'll find here to the standard American motel.

Hotels

Driftwood Inn. 135 W. Bunnell Ave., Homer, AK 99603. ☎ and fax **907/235-8019.** 20 rms, 11 with bath; 1 suite. TV. High season, $120 double. Low season, $60 double. Additional person in room $10 extra. AE, DC, DISC, MC, V.

The inn, in a historic building a block from Bishop's Beach, resembles a lodge or bed-and-breakfast with its large fireplace of rounded beach rock in the lobby, the breakfast table, where cereal and coffee are available for a nominal price, and the owner's roving dog. The rooms are quaint, but some are tiny; some have ocean views, private bathrooms, cable TV, and telephones, while others have fewer amenities. Nine bedrooms share two bathrooms. The walls are thin, so there's a no-noise policy during evening hours. The location, near the Bunnell Street Gallery and the beach, is second only to Land's End, on the Spit. There's a coin-op laundry and free coffee in the lobby, and the well-situated RV park charges $22–$25 for full hook-ups.

Heritage Hotel Lodge. 147 E. Pioneer Ave., Homer, AK 99603. ☎ **800/380-7787** or 907/ 235-7787. Fax 907/235-2804. 35 rms, 1 suite. TV TEL. High season, $60–$90 double. Low season, $50–$60 double. Additional person in room $10 extra. AE, CB, DC, DISC, JCB, MC, V.

Homer's first hotel was built in 1948 in a log building on Pioneer Avenue. Now it's considerably larger but retains an old-fashioned feel. The hallways are narrow and the rooms are not large, but they are clean, and those in the larger, new wing have all the facilities of a modern hotel. A good, low-cost choice. You're near the museum, downtown shops, and restaurants, but you'll have to drive to the Spit. There's free coffee in the lobby.

✪ **Land's End.** 4786 Homer Spit Rd., Homer, AK 99603. ☎ **907/235-0400,** 800/478-0400 in Alaska only, or 907/235-0400 or 800/478-0400 in Alaska only. Website http://www.akms.com/ landsend/. 49 rms, 12 suites. TV TEL. High season, $109–$150 double. Low season, $75–$120 double. Additional person in room $10 extra. AE, DC, DISC, MC, V.

Traditionally *the* place to stay in Homer, Land's End would be popular no matter what it was like inside because of its location at the tip of Homer Spit, the best spot in Homer and possibly the best spot in Alaska to site a hotel. It has been under constant renovation in recent years, and, although the wandering old buildings have lost some of their charm, the hotel now is quite comfortable, with decorations that range from tasteful to fanciful. There are 11 different classes of rooms, ranging from cute shiplike compartments to two-story affairs. It's near the boat harbor, and you can fish right from the beach in front of the hotel. There's free coffee.

The reasonably priced **Chart Room** restaurant makes good use of its wonderful location, looking out over the beach and bay, with a casual, relaxing atmosphere and friendly service. The deck outside has glass wind shields, making it a warm, satisfying place to sit on a sunny day. You can watch otters, eagles, and fishing boats while eating lunch. The food, although uneven from year to year in the past, currently leaves nothing to be desired—seafood simply and expertly prepared. The dinner menu provides plenty of choices of full meals from $13 to $21.

Bed & Breakfasts

Some of Alaska's best B&Bs are found here; a full list of them is available from the Homer Chamber of Commerce Visitor Center, with names and addresses. **Alaska Referral Agency** (☎ **907/235-8996;** fax 907/235-2625) books many of the B&Bs, cottages, and apartments in town. The luxurious **Victorian Heights Bed and Breakfast,** off East Hill Road (P.O. Box 2363), Homer, AK 99603 (☎ and fax **907/ 235-6357;** e-mail HGQU44A@prodigy.com), is a beautifully appointed custom-built inn overlooking Kachemak Bay from high above town. **Cranes' Crest Bed and Breakfast,** 59830 Sanford Dr., Homer, AK 99603 (☎ **907/235-2969**), 5 miles out atop the bench behind the town, has sweeping, cinematic views you can sit and watch all day.

✪ **Beach House Bed and Breakfast.** 1285 Bay Ave. (P.O. Box 2617), Homer, AK 99603. ☎ **907/235-5945.** 4 rms, 1 with bath. High season, $67–$100 double. Low season $57–$90 double. Rates include taxes. Additional person in room $25 extra. No credit cards.

This light-filled house of large rooms and decks perches over a tidal lagoon full of birds that beckons down a zigzagging staircase, yet it's hidden among trees right in town. Hosts Jack and Mary Lentfer are longtime Alaskans who know as much about wildlife and the outdoors as anyone—Jack recently retired from a long career as a marine mammal biologist and policy-maker. The huge Cormorant Room, outfitted with a Jacuzzi, spectacularly overlooks the slough and Kachemak Bay. A full breakfast is served, and smoking is not permitted.

Magic Canyon Ranch Bed and Breakfast. 40015 Waterman Rd., Homer, AK 99603. ☎ **907/235-6077.** Fax 907/235-6077. 4 rms, 2 with bath. High season, $85–$100 double. Low season, $55–$70 double. Rates include full breakfast. Additional adult in room $25 extra; additional child in room $20 extra. No credit cards.

At the top of a canyon road off East End Road, the Webb family share their charming home, 74 unspoiled acres, hot tub, tree house, and sweeping views with guests, a dog, a cat, and a herd of retired llama. The air is mountain clear and quiet between the high canyon walls—one starts to relax upon getting out of the car. They serve sherry in the evening and a full breakfast in the morning. The four rooms, some nestled cozily under the eaves, are decorated in country and Victorian style.

Old Town Bed and Breakfast. 106-D W. Bunnell, Homer, AK 99603. ☎ **907/235-7558.** 3 rms, 1 with bath. High season, $60–$70 double. Low season, 25% discount. Rates include breakfast. Additional person in room $15 extra. MC, V.

Artist and lifelong Homer resident Asia Freeman and her husband, Kurt Marquardt, casually host a bed-and-breakfast that combines the artiness of the excellent Bunnell Street Gallery downstairs (see "Exploring Homer," above) and the funky, historic feel of the old trading post/hardware store that the building used to house. The wood floors undulate with age and settling, and the tall, double-hung windows, looking out at Bishop's Beach, are slightly cockeyed. Antiques and handmade quilts complete the charming ambience. They serve a full breakfast on weekends, and during the week you get a continental breakfast at the wonderful Two Sisters Bakery, downstairs. Not a good choice for people who have trouble with stairs.

Seaside Farm. 58335 East End Rd., Homer, AK 99603. ☎ **907/235-7850.** 4 rms, 9 cabins, 12 hostel beds. $55 cabin for two; $15 per person hostel bunk; $6 campsite. Additional person in room or cabin $12 extra. No credit cards.

Take a step back in time—all the way to the 1960s. Mossy Kilcher's farm is populated by horses, sheep, geese, pigeons, and latter-day hippies, many of whom do chores in exchange for their room: $2^1/_2$ hours of work equals a night in the hostel bunks, and 90 minutes earns a campsite in the pasture above the bay. Homer's pioneering Kilcher family spawned the singer Jewel (Kilcher), whose records you likely have heard on the radio. If you can catch Mossy floating through, she'll answer any question about Homer with a breezy smile and a Swiss accent.

Wilderness Lodges

For those of us who can't afford the two luxurious options listed below, **Across the Bay Tent and Breakfast,** Red Mountain, P.O. Box RDO, Homer, AK 99603 (☎ **907/235-3633** or 907/345-2571), in the Jakolof Bay area on the road to Seldovia, rents furnished wall tents (bring a sleeping bag), serves meals, and rents sea kayaks and mountain bikes. It's a good choice for families who want to get into the wilderness.

۞ Kachemak Bay Wilderness Lodge. China Poot Bay (P.O. Box 956), Homer, AK 99603. ☎ **907/235-8910.** Fax 907/235-8911. Website http://www.xyz.net/~wildrnes/lodge.htm. 5 cabins. $400 per person per night. Rates include all meals. Mon–Fri package only. Closed Oct 15–May 1. No credit cards.

I can think of no more idyllic a way to become acquainted with Alaska's marine wilderness than at this intimate, luxurious lodge, run for more than 25 years by hospitable and generous Mike and Diane McBride—I only wish it were affordable for more people, because it's a place of unforgettable experiences. The McBrides' meals are legendary, and their four cabins manage to seem rustic while having every comfort; it's easy to pretend you're the only guest. But their site, on China Poot Bay, is what's really special—it has excellent tide pooling, kayaking, a black sand beach, and good hiking trails nearby. Experienced, environmentally conscious guide service is included for sea kayaking, hiking, and wildlife watching; outings by boat carry an extra charge.

Tutka Bay Wilderness Lodge. P.O. Box 960, Homer, AK 99603. ☎ **800/606-3909** or 907/235-3905. Fax 907/235-3909. Website http://www.alaskan.com/tutka. 4 cabins. $275–$295 per person per night. Rates include all meals. Two night minimum stay. MC, V. Closed Oct–Apr.

Trim houses connected by boardwalks overlook the smooth, green water of Tutka Bay, a narrow fjord tucked away in the forests across Kachemak Bay from Homer. The lodge offers tide pool walks, bird watching, hiking, berry picking, and other activities around the lodge, and you can pay extra for guided fishing, kayaking, and outdoor experiences that go farther afield.

DINING

Homer has inspired culinary art as good as the visual art in the galleries, and today the town is second only to Anchorage in its concentration of excellent restaurants. Besides those listed here, don't miss the **Chart Room** at Land's End, described above. For good fast food in an attractive beachfront dining room, try **Boardwalk Fish and Chips** (☎ 907/235-7749).

Anchor River Inn. Near the river on the Sterling Hwy., Anchor Point. ☎ **907/235-8531.** Main courses $7.50–$19; lunch $5.50–$9. AE, CB, DISC, MC, V. High season, daily 5am–midnight; low season, daily 7am–10pm. STEAK/SEAFOOD.

Ten miles short of Homer on the Sterling Highway, the community of Anchor Point gathers around the road and the babbling, fish-laden Anchor River. This is one of its traditional, long-established businesses, a good old-fashioned family restaurant with filling meals of beef or seafood. Full liquor license.

✪ **Café Cups.** 162 W. Pioneer Ave. ☎ **907/235-8330.** Reservations recommended. Lunch $6–$10; dinner $14–$21. MC, V. High season, daily 7am–10pm; low season, Mon–Thurs 7am–3pm, Fri–Sat 5–9pm. CREATIVE/ECLECTIC.

The facade of the yellow house on Pioneer Avenue, with its elaborate bas-relief sculpture, is truthful advertising for the arty restaurant and creative food to be found inside. The menu specializes in surprises—for example, a wide-awake steak that's encrusted with crushed coffee beans and peppercorns and topped with an espresso garlic sauce, or an appetizer of smoked salmon quesadillas. The experiments always seem to work, earning a reputation all over the state, and the prices are reasonable. Some find the bohemian atmosphere in the small dining room a bit thick; others say it's perfectly fun and relaxing. Beer and wine license.

Fresh Sourdough Express Bakery and Restaurant. 1316 Ocean Dr. ☎ **907/235-7571.** $5.50–$7.50. AE, DISC, MC, V. High season, daily 7am–10pm. Low season, daily 8am–5pm. Closed Jan–Mar.

Ebullient Donna Maltz's organic eatery is quintessential Homer, starting with its motto, "Food for people and the planet." But there's no prim New Age dogma here—Sourdough Express is fun and tasty, even as it grinds its own grain and recycles everything in sight. An inexpensive menu is served all day with items such as reindeer or halibut hoagies and various vegetarian choices, and in the evening they add fine dining seafood specials. They pack lunches for outings, too. Don't miss dessert. The aptly named "Obscene Brownie," covered with espresso and ice cream, left me in a happy daze for the rest of the afternoon.

✪ **The Homestead.** Mile 8.2, East End Rd. ☎ **907/235-8723.** Reservations recommended. Dinner $17–$24. AE, MC, V. Daily 5–10pm. STEAK/SEAFOOD.

The ambience is of an old-fashioned Alaska roadhouse, in a large log building with spare decoration and stackable metal chairs, but the food is as good as I've gotten anywhere in Alaska. After a day outdoors, it's a great, exuberant dinner house. Local paintings of marine scenes punctuate the noisy dining room. Many menu items are charbroiled, but the cuisine is far more sophisticated than the typical steak-and-seafood house, including more adventurous and creative concoctions among the simple, perfectly broiled fish and meat. Service is cordial but sometimes slow. Full liquor license.

Neon Coyote. 435 E. Pioneer Ave. ☎ **907/235-6226.** All meals $5–$9. No credit cards. Daily 11am–8:30pm. Closed Sun in winter. SOUTHWEST.

The Southwestern and nouveau Mexican cuisine, served in a bright, little dining room, is excellent and as inexpensive as fast food. It's fast, too—that's one reason locals favor it—but the black-bean burrito, only $5.50, tastes too good for that ignoble appellation. The halibut tacos sing, and the daily specials are worth trying, too. I never miss it on a trip to Homer. Beer and wine license.

HOMER IN THE EVENING

The **Pier One Theatre** (☎ **907/235-7333;** http://www.alaska.net/~wmbell/) is a strong community theater group housed in a small, corrugated-metal building on the

Spit, just short of the small-boat harbor on the left. Instead of the ubiquitous gold-rush melodrama and Robert Service readings, Pier One presents serious drama, musicals, and comedy—real art, not just schlock. They also produce dance, classical music, and youth theater events during the summer—check the *Homer News* for current listings. Performances usually play weekends only, with ticket prices around $9; they're available at **Central Charters** (☎ 907/235-7847) and various other places.

There are lots of bars in Homer. The landmark **Salty Dawg** is a small log cabin on the Spit with a lighthouse on top. It's the place to swap fish stories after a day on the water.

ONWARD FROM HOMER
○ HALIBUT COVE

A visit to the tight, roadless little community of Halibut Cove, across Kachemak Bay from Homer, is like a dream for many visitors. All the best things about a visit to the bay are here: a boat ride, the chance of seeing otters or seals, a top-notch restaurant, several galleries and open studios with some of Alaska's best fine fishy art, and even cozy, welcoming accommodations. The settlement sits on either side of a narrow, peaceful channel between a small island and the mainland; the water in between is the only road. Boardwalks connect the buildings, and stairs reach down to the water from houses perched on pilings over the shore. The pace of life runs no faster than the tide.

It's also an essentially private community. Unless you have your own boat, an excursion boat is the only way to get there. The Jakolof Bay ferry goes, but the main route is by the boat owned by the community's restaurant. Once there, you have to leave according to plan, as there's no business district and everything is privately owned. You're really a guest the whole time you're in Halibut Cove—the community is open for visitors, however they arrive, only between 1 and 9pm, unless you're staying at one of the lodges.

The classic, wooden *Danny J* (book through Central Charters at ☎ 907/235-7847—full listing above under "Fishing") leaves Homer daily in the summer at noon, brings back day trippers and takes over dinner guests at 5pm, then brings back the diners later in the evening. The noon trip includes bird watching at Gull Island. You also take the *Danny J* if you're spending the night in Halibut Cove. The noon trip is $36 for adults, and the dinner trip is $18, but you're obliged to buy a meal at the restaurant. Kids are $18 both times; seniors, $23 at noon and $14 for dinner. A steel boat, the *Storm Bird,* carries overflow passengers in summer and runs all winter as the mail boat.

On an afternoon trip, you can bring lunch or eat at the Saltry, described below, and then explore along the boardwalk that runs from the restaurant along Ismailof Island past the galleries, boat shops, and houses. There's also a barnyard where kids, who already will be in heaven, can look at rabbits, chickens, ponies, and other animals. Fine art is the community's major industry, with 16 artists in residence and three galleries, but fewer than 100 residents. The **Halibut Cove's Experience Fine Art Gallery,** P.O. Box 6468, Halibut Cove, AK 99603 (☎ 907/296-2215), is first past the farm, on pilings above the water. The airy room contains works only by Halibut Cove artists. Farther on, Diana Tillion, who, with her husband, Clem, pioneered the community, opens her **Cove Gallery** and studio to guests. Since the 1950s, she has worked almost exclusively in octopus ink, painstakingly extracted with a hypodermic needle. Alex Combs, a grand old Picasso-like figure among Alaska artists, takes visitors at his studio even though he often isn't there. The building is marked by a huge self-portrait and a sign reading, "Leave money, take pottery and paintings."

The ✪ **Saltry** restaurant, which operates in conjunction with the *Danny J*, sits on pilings in an idyllic setting, over the edge of the smooth, deep green of the cove's main watery avenue. You can sit back on the deck and sip microbrews and eat bread and sushi. Cooked seafood also is available. Prices are on the high side, but it's hard to mind. Make reservations at the same time you reserve your *Danny J* tickets.

The ✪ **Quiet Place Lodge,** P.O. Box 6474, Halibut Cove, AK 99603 (☎ **907/ 296-2212;** fax 907/235-2241), is a family-owned bed-and-breakfast perched on pilings that seem to climb up the side of the mainland across the water from the Saltry. The five cabins, linked by stairs and boardwalks, are attractively decorated with local art and look out on the cove. They share bathrooms in the main lodge, where there's also a large rec room with a piano, refrigerator, and microwave for guests. A full breakfast is served, and dinners are available 4 nights a week for $25. The hosts will carry you across to the Saltry or to kayak and skiff rentals, essential to explore the area. A trail out back connects with the Kachemak Bay State Park hiking trails. They charge $185 a night, double, and are open May 24 to September 2.

SELDOVIA

The last time we visited this town of around 300 near the tip of the Kenai Peninsula, a group of children walked up to us in the empty main street and asked, in a friendly way, what we were doing there. That's how quiet Seldovia is. But early in this century, Seldovia was a metropolis, acting as a major hub for the Cook Inlet area with steamers coming and going with fish and cargo. Unconnected to the road system, the town's decline was steady until 1964, when the Good Friday earthquake destroyed most of what was left. The entire Kenai Peninsula sank, and high tides began covering the boardwalks that comprised most of the city. When the U.S. Army Corps of Engineers came to the rescue, they replaced the boardwalks with rock and gravel and erased much of the waterfront's charm. A short section of the old boardwalk that remains runs along peaceful Seldovia Slough, where king salmon run in early summer and a sea otter is in regular residence—you can get a close look at him, if you're patient. The other roads and trails around town make for pleasant walks. Here you can see what a real Alaska fishing town is like without seeing many other tourists, wander in and out of the forest, beach walk, and maybe see wildlife—eagles certainly and maybe bears.

Essentials

GETTING THERE   The trip across Kachemak Bay to Seldovia is one of the best parts of going there. Go at least one-way on the **Rainbow Tours** (☎ 907/235-7272) boat. You have a good chance of seeing otters, seals, sea lions, puffins, and eagles, and you may see whales. The adult fare is $40, and the boat stays 2 hours in Seldovia— long enough for most people to see the town. Bring your own lunch, however, or you'll spend most of your excursion in one of Seldovia's restaurants. You can also fly on one of Homer's air-taxis. It's a cheap way to do a flightseeing trip. **Homer Air** (☎ 907/235-8591) is one good operator, charging $55 round-trip. The **Alaska Marine Highway System** ferry *Tustumena* (see "Homer," above) also visits Seldovia from Homer, but stays briefly.

FAST FACTS   Seldovia is a tiny town: There's no bank, and most businesses don't take credit cards. If you're going to stay overnight, bring lots of cash. A lot of **local information** is on the Web, at http://www.xyz.net/~seldovia/.

Things to Do

The **Otterbahn Trail,** built by students at the Susan B. English School, leads through woods, wetlands, and beach cliffs to Outer Beach, where there's a picnic shelter.

Allow a couple of hours. Seldovia is great for **mountain biking**—there are many miles of unused roads to explore. The **Jakolof Bay Express** bus, 281 Main St. (P.O. Box 26), Seldovia, AK 99663 (☎ **907/234-7479**), which stops at The Buzz coffee shop, can take you out for a ride or to Jakolof Bay, discussed above under "Outdoors." They rent mountain bikes for $3 an hour or $20 a day. **Rocky Raven's Bike Shop,** next door to the Boardwalk Hotel (P.O. Box 72), Seldovia, AK 99663 (☎ **907/234-7816**), rents and repairs bikes. The area also is good for **sea kayaking. Kayak'atak,** P.O. Box 109, Seldovia, AK 99663 (☎ **907/234-7425**), offers rentals and guided trips. Seldovia also is considerably closer to the **halibut** grounds than Homer; drop by the **harbormaster** (☎ **907/234-7886**) for a referral. There are several shops worth visiting, all on the main street. A tiny, picturesque Russian Orthodox church stands on the hill above the town. Admission is $4.50, payable to **South Shore Tours,** located at All Things Gallery on Main Street (☎ **907/ 234-8000**). They also operate a taxi and mountain bike transfer service.

Accommodations

Dancing Eagles Bed and Breakfast and Cabin Rental. On the boardwalk (P.O. Box 264), Seldovia, AK 99663 (in winter, P.O. Box 240067, Anchorage, AK 99524). ☎ **907/234-7627** in summer, 907/278-0288 in winter. Fax 907/278-0288 in winter. Website http://www.xyz.net/ ~seldovia/Accomo.html#SCRL5. 5 rms, none with bath; 1 cabin. $85 double; $125 cabin. No credit cards. Closed Oct–Apr.

The boardwalk leads to this large house, cabin, and outbuildings, themselves all nestled on rocks and pilings above the slough and connected by their own boardwalks. Judy Lethin likes to think of it as a place for healing. Guests can use the hot tub and sauna and watch the otter who lives on the water just outside. Three rooms under the eaves upstairs are cute but very small; two other rooms are larger, and the cabin is huge, with a deck, a view of the boat harbor, and its own cooking facilities.

Seldovia's Boardwalk Hotel. 243 Main St. (P.O. Box 72), Seldovia, AK 99663. ☎ **800/ 238-7862** or 907/234-7810. 13 rms. TEL. $88–$120 double. Additional person in room $20 extra. MC. V. Closed Oct–Apr.

This Seldovia institution has light, comfortable rooms with private baths and phones. Despite the name, it isn't on the boardwalk but does stand at the top of the small-boat harbor, so rooms on the water side have a great view. They offer a $119 package from Homer, which includes a boat tour over and a flightseeing trip back—quite a deal. There's a courtesy car and free coffee in the lobby.

Dining

There are three restaurants. We got happy, gregarious service and decent food at the **Kachemak Kafe.** The **Centurion Restaurant** has been lacking in the past, but is under new management and is said to have improved greatly. **The Buzz** is a great place for breakfast, with quiche and baked goods.

5 Prince William Sound: Kingdom of the Orca

Crossing Prince William Sound several years ago in a small boat, I thought I knew where I was—didn't care that much—among the tiny islands and rocks, comparing a chart to the broad, sparkling water's tussocks of bedrock and trees. Then I saw one mound, close at hand, that didn't belong. It shot forth a spray of water, and a fin appeared. A humpback. We stopped the boat for pictures until the tail flipped up high, as it does when the whale is about to sound and disappear for a while. But what was that noise behind the boat? While we'd been watching the whale, a sea lion had swum up behind us. Its light-brown shape, just below the water, was the size of a large office desk, but it moved fast, shooting toward us and then circling back in the opposite direction—as fast as the shadow of a sparrow. Finally, we started up and went on our way, a warm afternoon sun on our backs as we continued east from Whittier, into the big, wide, gentle Sound. What'll we see next?

I have a friend who has kayaked the whole Sound. He knew a place—I don't know if it's still this way—where he would camp just above a pebbled beach and wait for the moon to come out. And in the night, orcas would come, swim up on the beach, scratch their tummies on the rocks, and wriggle back into the ocean. It was their secret spot—his and the killer whales'—and they'd meet there each summer. The beach was oiled in the *Exxon Valdez* oil spill, and my friend lost the heart to kayak much after all the death he saw there and all over the Sound while trying to save birds and animals that horrible summer of 1989. But now I'm sure the oil is gone from that beach. It's time to get back out there and meet the whales.

The waters of Prince William Sound are uniquely protected and diverse. On the western side, from Whittier, there are great tidewater glaciers at the heads of long, narrow fjords. In the center of the Sound, there's an infinity of islands, remote beaches, and hidden bays—and not many people. On the east, near Cordova, the Sound gets shallower and hosts millions of migrating birds. The islands and enclosing reach of the mainland keep the seas smooth in most of the Sound. That's one reason the oil spill was so devastating: These protected waters are a rich nursery, and that oil, once landed and stuck, would not soon wash away as it did out in the rougher Gulf of Alaska.

Today the oil spill is mostly history, although an expert or subsistence gatherer likely will be able to find buried oil remaining 10 years after the spill, as the experts always predicted. Natives and longtime residents have told me that they can tell the difference in the abundance of animals compared to what was there before—government studies support that perception—but most anyone else will notice only that a mind-boggling abundance still remains.

GETTING AROUND / ORIENTATION   Most of Prince William Sound is in the Chugach National Forest. There are three major towns, each with a dramatically different character. **Valdez** is an oil town, the southern terminus of the trans-Alaska pipeline where tankers are loaded. You can drive there, on the **Richardson Highway,** and a day's boat ride will get you into the heart of the Sound. Valdez itself, however, is short on charm. **Cordova** is more attractive, a historic community on the eastern side of the Sound, with more untouched outdoor activities close at hand, but you can get there only by plane or boat. **Whittier** is a grim former military outpost, but quite a convenient gateway to the protected fjords and glaciers of the western Sound. It has frequent rail service through a mountain to the nearby **Seward Highway,** 40 miles south of Anchorage, and daily train service directly to Anchorage. One popular way to see the Sound is to take a boat from Whittier to Valdez—perhaps the state ferry, with your car on board—and then drive out of Valdez.

VALDEZ

Big events have shaped Valdez (val-DEEZ). The deep-water port, at the head of a long, dramatic fjord, first developed with the Klondike Gold Rush and the ill-fated attempt to establish an alternative route to the gold fields from here. (A centennial celebration is planned in 1998.) Later, the port and the Richardson Highway, which connected Valdez to the rest of the state, served a key role in supplying materials during World War II. On Good Friday, March 27, 1964, all of that was erased when North America's greatest recorded earthquake occurred under Miners Lake, west of town off a northern fjord of Prince William Sound, setting off an underwater landslide that caused a huge wave to sweep over the waterfront, killing 32 people. The town sank and was practically destroyed. The U.S. Army Corps of Engineers rebuilt a drab replacement in a new, safer location that slowly filled with nondescript modern buildings over the next 2 decades. A walking tour provides the locations of a few buildings that were moved to the new town site. The construction of the trans-Alaska pipeline, completed in 1977, brought a new economic boom to Valdez and enduring economic prosperity as tankers came to fill with the oil. Then, on March 24, 1989, on Good Friday 25 years after the earthquake, the tanker *Exxon Valdez,* on its way south, hit the clearly marked Bligh Reef, causing the largest and most environmentally costly oil spill ever in North America. The spill cleanup added another economic boom.

Today, Valdez is a middle American town, driven by industry but turning to the vast resources of Prince William Sound for outdoor recreation. In town you can tour the interesting history museum and pipeline terminal, and take a hike or a river float, but otherwise the city itself is short on charm or attractions for a visitor. The real reasons to come have to do with the setting—the wildlife, fishing, and sightseeing in the Sound, described above, and the spectacular drive down the Richardson Highway. Because Valdez lies at the end of a funnel of steep mountains that catch moisture off the ocean, the weather tends to be overcast and rainy. For the same reason, the area receives phenomenal snow falls, measured in the tens of feet. Although there is no developed skiing, Valdez attracts many "extreme" skiers for helicopter and snowcat skiing in the mountains behind town in late winter.

ESSENTIALS

GETTING THERE   By Car   The ✪ **Richardson Highway,** described in chapter 10, "The Alaskan Interior," is unbelievably dramatic as it crosses Thompson Pass and descends into the narrow valley where Valdez lies. Try to do the trip in daylight, in clear weather, and stop at the roadside glacier. This is the only road to Valdez. The drive from Anchorage is roughly 7 hours.

By Bus   Gray Line's **Alaskon Express** (☎ 800/544-2206) runs to Anchorage daily in the summer, taking 10 hours for the trip; the fare is $65.

By Water   The **Alaska Marine Highway System** (☎ 800/642-0066 or 907/835-4436; website http://www.dot.state.ak.us/external/amhs/home.html) calls on Valdez daily in the summer with the *Bartlett,* a ferry connecting Valdez, Whittier, and Cordova. The *Tustumena* comes from Seward roughly once a week. One time-tested way to see the Sound is to put your vehicle on the ferry in Whittier for the 6 1/2-hour run to Valdez, then drive north on the Richardson Highway. The fare is $72 for a car up to 15 feet long and $58 for a passenger. **Stan Stephens Cruises,** P.O. Box 1297, Valdez, AK 99686 (☎ 800/992-1297 or 907/835-4731; fax 907/835-3765; e-mail ssc@alaska.net) operates a daily summer cruise from Whittier to Valdez in the morning and back in the evening. The boat stops to look at the glaciers on the way and for lunch at Stephens' Growler Island camp. The one-way fare is $110.

By Air   **Era Aviation** (☎ 800/866-8394 or 907/835-2636) flies up to seven flights a day each way between Anchorage and Valdez.

VISITOR INFORMATION   The Valdez Convention and Visitors Bureau maintains a **Visitor Information Center,** at 200 Chenega Ave., off Egan Drive (P.O. Box 1603), Valdez, AK 99686 (☎ 800/770-5954 or 907/835-4636, or in winter 907/835-2984; e-mail valdezak@alaska.net). Pick up the free town map and useful "Vacation Planner." They're open in summer, daily from 8am to 8pm, and normal business hours in the winter. A booking agency, **One Call Does It All,** P.O. Box 2197,

Valdez, AK 99686 (☎ **800/242-4988** or 907/835-4988; fax 907/835-2468; e-mail onecall@alaska.net), reserves lodgings, fishing charters, activities, and tours in the area. At the airport, an **Alaska Pipeline Visitor Center** has a few displays about the line and shows a film. This is where you catch the bus tours of the pipeline's marine terminal, described below.

ORIENTATION   The layout of Valdez is a grid. The **Richardson Highway** comes in from the east, becoming **Egan Drive,** the main drag. **Meals Avenue,** which runs to the boat harbor, and **Hazelet Avenue,** which runs to the city dock and ferry dock, are the major north-south streets. The airport is several miles out Richardson Highway; farther out on the Richardson, **Dayville Road** branches off to the south, leading to the other side of Port Valdez to the Alyeska Pipeline Marine Terminal, the tanker-loading facility and tank farm directly across the water from town.

GETTING AROUND   Once you're downtown, you can walk Valdez easily. To get to the airport, taxis are available from **Valdez Yellow Cab** (☎ 907/835-2500). **Avis** (☎ **800/331-1212** or 907/835-4774) is the only major car-rental chain with a local office. **Valdez-U-Drive,** P.O. Box 1396, Valdez, AK 99686 (☎ **907/835-4402**), also rents cars at the airport. **Sentimental Journeys,** P.O. Box 2175, Valdez, AK 99686 (☎ **907/835-4988**), offers town tours in a 1937 bus.

FAST FACTS   Valdez has no sales tax. There are two banks on Egan Drive, both with **ATMs.** In **emergencies,** call **911.** For nonemergency business with the **Valdez Police Department,** call ☎ **907/835-4560.** The **Valdez Community Hospital** is located at 911 Meals Ave. (☎ **907/835-2249**). The *Valdez Vanguard* is published weekly, and the *Anchorage Daily News* is available in boxes all over town. **Fax** and **copying** services are available at Connection Solution, 121 Egan, P.O. Box 756 (☎ **907/835-4854**).

SPECIAL EVENTS   On Presidents' weekend, in February, the **Valdez Ice Climbing Festival** (☎ **907/835-2984**) is staged on the frozen waterfalls of Keystone Canyon. In early March, the **Snow Man Festival** (☎ **907/835-2330**) is a winter carnival with a food fair, ice bowling, snowman building, and a drive-in movie projected on a snow bank. In March or April, the **World Extreme Skiing Championships** (☎ **907/835-2108**) is held on the faces of mountains north of Valdez, where skiers hurl themselves down near-vertical, powder-filled chutes competing in speed and style. It's a daredevil competition. Three **fishing derbies,** for silver and pink salmon and halibut, happen each summer, in the appropriate season, with prizes totaling more than $60,000; check with the visitor center or buy a ticket at the boat-rental booth in the harbor. The ✪ **Prince William Sound Community College Theater Conference** (☎ 907/835-2678) brings famous playwrights and directors to the community for seminars and performances in August. Writers such as Arthur Miller and Edward Albee meet the public in fairly intimate settings.

EXPLORING VALDEZ

The ✪ **Valdez Museum and Historical Archive,** at 217 Egan Ave. (☎ **907/ 835-2764;** website http://www.alaska.net/~vldzmuse/index.html), contains an exceptional history display that follows the story of the area from early white exploration through the oil spill. It's a little light on Alaska Native culture, but there are other museums for that. Each gallery is well designed and some are fun, like the restored bar room. There's also a saltwater aquarium and an area with transportation relics, including shiny fire engines dating back to 1886. Admission is $3 for adults, $2.50 over age 65, and free for children under age 18. It's open in summer, daily from 8am to 5pm and 7 to 9pm; in winter, Tuesday through Saturday 9am to 5pm.

A bus tour of the **pipeline marine terminal,** where tankers carrying up to a quarter of the nation's domestic oil supply are loaded, is operated by **Valdez Tours** (☎ 907/835-2686). May through September the 2-hour ride begins several times a day from the pipeline visitor center at the airport and costs $15 for adults, $7.50 for children. You can't enter any of the buildings. The highlights are a chance to see the big ships and an impressive scenic overlook, the only point where you can get off the bus.

GETTING OUTSIDE

OUT ON THE SOUND Stan Stephens predicted and was working to prevent an accident like the *Exxon Valdez* grounding right up to the eve of the disaster, and he's still working for improved environmental safeguards for the oil companies. At the same time, he runs a large, successful business selling an environmental experience to visitors. ✪ **Stan Stephens Cruises,** P.O. Box 1297, Valdez, AK 99686 (☎ 800/992-1297 or 907/835-4731; fax 907/835-3765; e-mail ssc@alaska.net), operates several boats, so you may not be on board with Stephens himself, but his skippers are knowledgeable Alaskans. You'll see the Sound and the animals that live in it—probably seals, otters, and sea lions, and maybe whales. Trips go to Whittier and Meares Glacier, but the primary destination is the huge Columbia Glacier and Stephens's camp nearby, on Growler Island, where passengers get off and, on some trips, have a meal and can even spend the night and go boating. Prices range from $70 for a 5$\frac{1}{2}$-hour cruise to $215 for a trip that includes a night on Growler Island. Stephens's biggest drawback is that his star attraction, the Columbia, is melting too fast—it has receded more than 6 miles in recent years—and it hasn't been possible to get a vessel close or to see chunks calve off. Other tours, and some of Stephens', now more often go to the fjord glaciers such as Meares in the western Sound for those sights—which are closer to Whittier.

Jim and Nancy Lethcoe, of ✪ **Alaskan Wilderness Sailing and Kayak Safaris,** P.O. Box 1313, Valdez, AK 99686 (☎ 907/835-5175), wrote the standard cruising guide to the Sound and have helped lead the fight to protect it. Their naturalist-guided **sailing, sea kayaking,** and **hiking** trips use Stephens's Growler Island camp as a base. Prices are $50 for a half day, $90 for a day, or $100 per person per night to stay on the island, plus the fare to get there, which is $94 from Valdez, $110 from Whittier, round-trip. **Raven Charters,** Slip C-25, Valdez Boat Harbor (P.O. Box 2581), Valdez, AK 99686 (☎ 907/835-5863), is a family who live on their 50-foot boat and take clients **sailing** and exploring the Sound. The wind tends to be light and changeable, but a sailboat makes a comfortable base for discovering interesting, isolated places. All-inclusive prices start at $650 per night for up to four passengers. They also rent their staterooms as a bed-and-breakfast while in port for $55–$65 a night.

Anadyr Adventures, at 203 N. Harbor Dr. (☎ 800/TO-KAYAK or 907/835-2814; website http://www.alaska.net/~anadyr/anadyr.index.html), by the boat harbor, offers 3-hour kayak tours out of Valdez itself for $55, or day trips to Shoup or Columbia Glacier for $95 plus a share of the cost of getting there, which could be as much again. They also lead multiday trips and rent kayaks. For a truly remote self-guided trip to the unvisited southwest Sound, take your kayak on the ferry *Tustumena's* weekly trip from Valdez to Seward (see "Getting There," above) for the whistle stop in the village of Chenega Bay. The ferry stops there only when a passenger has a reservation.

Remote cabins in the Sound are available from **Port Fidalgo Adventures,** P.O. Box 904, Valdez, AK 99686 (☎ 907/835-5807), including the floatplane trip from Valdez and a skiff for you to use once you arrive. Most U.S. Forest Service cabins are closer to Whittier or Cordova.

Fishing for salmon and halibut are popular in Valdez. You can fish from shore, in season, off Dayville Road on Allison Point on the far side of the port from Valdez. Salmon here are returning to the Solomon Gulch Hatchery and are primarily pinks in July and silvers in August. There are lots of fishing charters available in the boat harbor. Halibut charters cost around $150 per person, as they have to go a long way. Half-day salmon charters are around $80, right in Port Valdez. The Vacation Planner from the visitor center lists operators. **Popeye Charters** (☎ **907/835-2659**) is reliable, and **Lil' Fox Charters** (☎ **907/835-4696**) also is a longtime operator. The **One Call Does It All** booking agency (listed under "Visitor Information," above) books charters. If you're up to running your own boat, they're for rent on the docks from **Valdez Harbor Boat and Tackle Rentals** (☎ **907/835-5002**); a 16-foot boat costs $125 a day, plus fuel. **Ketchum Air Service,** with desks at the airport and boat harbor (☎ **800/825-9114** or 907/835-3789), offers fly-in fishing starting at $199 per person.

BIRD WATCHING & BEACHCOMBING   Between the airport and downtown Valdez, the Duck Flats, a tidal marsh met by a salmon spawning stream, lies along the Richardson Highway. It's a productive bird and marine habitat, busy with activity at spring and fall migrations, and a good place for bird watching or picnicking all summer at one of the two viewing areas. The National Forest Service, which has a ranger station nearby, has set up a salmon-viewing station where you can watch fish do the deed in shallow, clear water. A bird checklist is distributed by the visitor center.

HIKING   A pleasant forest and shore walk to **Dock Point,** with interpretive signs, borders the opposite side of the Duck Flats from the road, starting at the east side of the boat harbor, at the end of North Harbor Drive. It's a peaceful, natural walk close to town. **Mineral Creek Road,** behind town, leads up a canyon to a stamp mill and historic mining site.

RAFTING   **Keystone Raft and Kayak Adventures,** P.O. Box 1486, Valdez, AK 99686 (☎ **800/328-8460** or 907/835-2606; website http://www.alaskawhitewater. com), takes five trips a day 4¹/₂ miles down the amazing Keystone Canyon, a virtual corridor of rock with a floor of frothing water, past the crashing tumult of the 900-foot Bridal Veil Falls. It costs only $30 per person. The company also has numerous longer trips, ranging from a day to 10 days, on many of the region's rivers.

FLIGHTSEEING   There are plenty of fixed-wing operators at the airport, but I love the extra thrill of helicopters. **Era Helicopters** (☎ **800/843-1947** or 907/835-2595) has an office and helipad downtown, near the ferry dock at Hazelet and Fidalgo. A 1-hour, $168 trip overflies Columbia Glacier and lands in front of Shoup Glacier.

ACCOMMODATIONS

Valdez charges a 6% **bed tax.** In addition to the hotels listed below, you'll find standard motel rooms at the **Totem Inn,** on the Richardson Highway as it enters town (P.O. Box 648) Valdez, AK 99686 (☎ **907/835-4443;** fax 907/835-5751).

Hotels

Keystone Hotel. 401 W. Egan Dr. (P.O. Box 2148), Valdez, AK 99686. ☎ **907/835-3851.** Fax 907/835-5322. 107 rms. TV TEL. $95 double. Rates include continental breakfast. Additional person in room $10 extra. AE, MC, V.

This building, made of modular units, was built by Exxon to serve as their offices for the oil spill cleanup operation but wasn't completed until late summer of 1989, so the company occupied it for only about a month. In 1994, after standing vacant, a new owner remodeled it into a hotel, with small rooms that mostly have two twin beds or one double bed—they were clean and pleasant when I visited. A coin-op laundry is available.

Village Inn. 100 Meals Ave. (P.O. Box 365), Valdez, AK 99686. ☎ **907/835-4445.** Fax 907/835-2437. 79 rms. TV TEL. High season, $129 double. Low season, $85 double. Additional person in room $10 extra. AE, MC, V.

There are good standard rooms, a cut above the Keystone or Totem, such as you'd find in a midscale chain. The less-desirable 300-level rooms are in a half-basement, where there's also a fitness center. Free coffee, laundry, and a sauna are available. The **Sugarloaf Saloon and Restaurant** across the parking lot serves seafood, pasta, and Mexican food in an attractively decorated dining room with booths.

Westmark Valdez. 100 Fidalgo Dr. (P.O. Box 468), Valdez, AK 99686. ☎ **800/544-0970** (reservations) or 907/835-4391. Fax 907/835-2308. 97 rms. TV TEL. High season, $149 double. Low season, $110 double. Additional person in room $15 extra. AE, DC, DISC, MC, V.

This is the only Valdez hotel on the water. There's a pleasant grassy area with tables where you can watch the boats come in the entrance to the small-boat harbor, and the office for Stan Stephens Cruises is just outside on a dock. The rooms don't all have views, however, and the quality is inconsistent. Those that have been recently remodeled are top-notch; others are dark and out of date—if possible, take a look before you check in. Call ahead and ask for the "highway rate," which may save you a lot of money. The hotel maintains a tour desk, gift shop, and fuel dock.

The **Captain's Table Restaurant** serves main courses ranging from $12 to $17 in a lovely dining room overlooking the harbor.

Bed & Breakfasts

Valdez has many bed-and-breakfasts, several quite good. A binder with descriptions is available for inspection at the visitor center, and there's a list in the vacation planner they hand out. Here are two good choices in town.

✪ **Cliff House Bed and Breakfast.** Off Hazelet Ave. near the city dock (P.O. Box 1995), Valdez, AK 99686. ☎ **907/835-5244.** E-mail Cliffhse@alaska.net. 3 rms. $125–$135 double. Rates include continental breakfast. MC, V. Closed in winter.

Owen Meals, who gave his family's land for the new Valdez town site, built this architecturally brilliant house—it's modern, yet fits perfectly into a priceless natural setting on its own 6-acre hill right at the waterfront in the center of Valdez. The family that now owns it lends binoculars to guests so they can watch the animals and ships in the water below—you could spend the day that way. Rooms are elegantly decorated with lots of perfect little touches and have private baths, although only one is attached. Two have TVs. The Cliff Room is something to write home about. Book well ahead. No smoking.

Head Hunters Inn. 328 Egan Dr. (P.O. Box 847), Valdez, AK 99686. ☎ **907/835-2900.** 5 rms, 1 with bath. TV. $70–$84 double. Additional person in room $15 extra. MC, V.

The bizarre name is owing to the beauty salon that hostess Ida Rhines runs downstairs—if no one answers at the B&B, inquire there. Once upstairs, you'll find surprisingly comfortable accommodations right on the main street. Four rooms share two bathrooms, all very clean when I visited. Rhines serves a full breakfast. Children and smoking are not allowed.

Camping

Valdez is a popular RV destination, and there are lots of places to camp. Camping at the **Allison Point** fishing area (☎ **907/835-2282**) is $10 a night. The State Park's

Blueberry Lake Campground, on the Richardson Highway before you get into town, has 15 tent sites and 63 RV spaces, without hook-ups; it costs $10. Right on the boat harbor downtown, the **Bear Paw Camper Park,** P.O. Box 93, Valdez, AK 99686 (☎ **907/835-2530**), has full facilities and a tour desk. Full hookups are $20.

DINING

There isn't a top-flight restaurant in Valdez, but there are some good places to eat. You'll find good fast-food fish at the **Alaska Halibut House,** at Fairbanks and Meals Avenue; it's open all day, and a tasty and filling halibut basket is only $6.25. For an espresso or latte, healthy sandwiches and good seafood specials, **Cafe Valdez,** on the ground floor of an office building at 310 Egan Dr., is a great lunch spot. The restaurant at the **Totem Inn,** on the Richardson Highway as it comes into town, is a local hangout, with meatloaf-and-mashed-potatoes kinds of meals, a TV that is always on, and coffee cups that are never empty. They show a movie about the 1964 earthquake daily at 4:30pm.

Mike's Palace Ristorante. 201 N. Harbor Dr. ☎ **907/835-2365.** Main courses $7–$17; lunch $4–$7. MC, V. Daily 11am–11pm. PIZZA/STEAK/SEAFOOD.

This is a good, family pizza restaurant, a place where Valdez residents come for a casual evening out. The calzone is good, service skilled, and everything consistent. Mike's has a place in history: Capt. Joseph Hazelwood was waiting for a take-out pizza here when he slipped next door to the Club Bar for his last drink before getting on the fateful voyage of the *Exxon Valdez* that hit Bligh Reef. Beer and wine license.

Oscar's. 143 N. Harbor Dr. ☎ **907/835-4700.** Dinner $7.50–$15.25. Lunch $5.50–$8.75. MC, V. Daily 4:30am–1am. BURGERS/STEAK/SEAFOOD.

This large, light cafe on the waterfront is abuzz with fishermen and outdoors people eating at all hours to take advantage of the endless summer days. The service is friendly and quick, and the food is good, solid diner fare. An outdoor covered deck is pleasant on warm days, with a bar serving craft brews, including Alaskan beers.

The Pipeline Club. 112 Egan Dr. ☎ **907/835-4332.** Main courses $7.50–$23.75. AE, DISC, MC, V. Open dinner only.

This is a traditional beef-and-seafood house with excellent steaks, perhaps the most formal meal to be had in Valdez. The dark decor and low lighting create an eternal midnight to which my eyes never adjusted. The lounge is where Capt. Joe Hazelwood got loaded on vodka tonics before taking command of the *Exxon Valdez*. Full liquor license.

CORDOVA

The first time I ever went to Cordova, we arrived at the Mudhole Smith Airport in a small plane and happened upon an old guy with a pickup truck who offered to let us ride in back with some boards the 10 miles to town. The highway led out onto a broad, wetland plain—the largest contiguous wetland in the western hemisphere, as it happens. Our guide's voice, studded with profanity, boomed through the back window as he told us proudly about the diversity of the wildlife to be found out there. Then, absolutely bursting with enthusiasm, he leaned on the horn and bellowed, "Look at them f--king swans!" We looked; trumpeters paddling in the marsh looked back. He would have invited them along to the bar, too, if he'd known how.

Every time I've been to Cordova since, I've been taken under the wings of new friends. Although they usually don't express themselves the same way that first gentleman did, they are just as enthusiastic to show off the amazing natural riches of their little kingdom. Tourists are still something of a novelty here, for Cordova not only is off the beaten track, it's not on the track at all—there's no road to the rest of the world. Boosters call their town "Alaska's Hidden Treasure." Forgotten treasure would be more like it, for Cordova isn't difficult to get to, and once there, the charm and attractions of the place are self-evident.

It's possible to feel a bit like an anthropologist discovering a tribe lost to time, for Cordova has the qualities small towns are supposed to have had but lost long ago in America, if they ever did have them. Walking down First Street, you pass an old-fashioned independent grocery store, the fishermen's union hall, and Steen's gift shop, in the same family since 1909—not chains or franchises. People leave their keys in the car and their doors unlocked at night. When a friend of mine bought one of the quaint, moss-roofed, hillside houses a few years ago, he didn't receive a key—the simple reason was that the front door didn't have a lock.

Yet Cordova also possesses a surprising level of sophistication. The commercial fishermen who power the economy like good food and an interesting place to live. They keep the bars lively at night when the salmon are running. Some are politically involved and well connected, battling the oil industry to protect Prince William Sound before the 1989 oil spill and then, after the disaster (which hurt Cordova worst of all), pushing for the money won from Exxon to be spent on the Sound's environment. They want Cordova to stay the way it is—with no road. Another faction in town, the merchants and tourism workers, want a road. The debate is hot, and a few years ago a mayoral election between pro- and antiroad candidates was decided by a single vote.

This controversy has been going on for 50 or 60 years. The town's heyday was in 1911, when the Copper River and Northwestern Railroad opened, carrying copper ore down from the mine at Kennicott; it hit a low when the mine closed in 1938. Since then, boosters have been trying to get a road built on the old rail line, north along the Copper River to Chitina. They've only made it about 50 miles out of town so far, despite an effort a few years ago by former Gov. Wally Hickel to send maverick maintenance crews out to punch the road through by stealth. From Cordova, the long-established portion of the Copper River Highway provides access to the best bird watching and, in my judgment, the most impressive glacier in Alaska, as well as trails and magnificent vistas and areas to see wildlife. In town, the small-boat harbor is a doorway to Prince William Sound. And the town itself has to be experienced, at least for an afternoon.

ESSENTIALS

GETTING THERE   By Air   Alaska Airlines (☎ **800/426-0333** or 907/424-7151; website http://www.alaskaair.com), flies one jet daily each direction, from Anchorage to the west and Yakutat, Juneau, and Seattle to the southeast, with two more flights to Anchorage operated by **Era Aviation** (☎ **800/866-8394**).

By Water   Cordova is served a few times a week from Valdez by the ferry *Bartlett* of the **Alaska Marine Highway System** (☎ **800/642-0066** or 907/424-7333; website http://www.dot.state.ak.us/external/amhs/home.html). The passenger fare for the 5$^{1}/_{2}$-hour run from Valdez is $30, an inexpensive way to see a lot of Prince William Sound.

VISITOR INFORMATION   The well-informed **visitor information person** is also the director of the museum and library, and her office is in the same building, at 622 First St. (P.O. Box 391), Cordova, AK 99574 (☎ **907/424-6665**). Summer hours are Monday through Saturday 10am to 6pm, Sunday 2 to 4pm; winter Tuesday through Friday 1 to 5pm. The **Cordova Chamber of Commerce,** P.O. Box 99,

Cordova, AK 99574 (☎ **907/424-7260**), in the back of the fishermen's union hall on First Street, near Council, is open Monday through Friday from 8am to 4pm; they have visitor information and a 60-minute recorded walking tour that you can listen to as it guides you around town. The **Cordova Ranger District** of the Chugach National Forest, upstairs in the old white courthouse at Second Street and Browning (P.O. Box 280), Cordova, AK 99574 (☎ **907/424-7661**), has displays and handouts about the area's natural history, as well as rangers who will sit down and help you figure out what you want to do.

ORIENTATION   Cordova is nestled among mountains on the east side of Prince William Sound between Orca Inlet and Eyak Lake. The airport is about 10 miles out the **Copper River Highway,** on the massive Copper River Delta. The highway enters the forest along Eyak Lake and finally turns into **First Street**—which is also known as **Main Street** as it passes through the center of town. One block down, **Railroad Avenue** runs along the small-boat harbor. Continuing through town on First Street, you come to the **ferry dock** and the canneries. A good, free map is widely available.

GETTING AROUND   To get in from the airport, take the **Airport Shuttle** that meets all planes (☎ **907/424-5356** or 907-253-RIDE), $9 one-way or $15 round-trip. **Taxis** are usually available as well from Wild Hare Cab (☎ **907/424-3939**). Becky Chapek, who owns the local tour company, meets the ferry and will take you where you need to go for nothing. You can easily walk around downtown Cordova, but that's not where the most interesting sights are. To get out of the Copper River Highway, you'll need a car, bus (described below), or, if you're vigorous, a bike. **Cars** are for rent from the Reluctant Fisherman Hotel (listed below) or **Imperial Car Rentals** (☎ **907/424-5982**), at the airport. The going rate is $55 a day, without mileage charges. Bikes, kayaks, skiffs, and fishing and camping gear are for rent from **Cordova Coastal Outfitters,** at the boat harbor below the fishermen's memorial (P.O. Box 1834) Cordova, AK 99574 (☎ **800/357-5145** or 907/424-7424; e-mail coastal@ptialaska.net).

FAST FACTS   Cordova's **sales tax** is 6%. Two banks on First Street have **ATMs.** The **post office** is located at Railroad Avenue and Council. In **emergencies,** call the police at **911;** for nonemergency police calls, dial ☎ **907/424-6100.** The **Cordova Community Hospital** is on Chase Street (☎ **907/424-8000**), off the Copper River Highway near the slough. The *Cordova Times* is published weekly. You can find the *Anchorage Daily News* at various stores around town.

SPECIAL EVENTS   The **Cordova Ice Worm Festival** is a winter carnival the first full weekend in February; the big iceworm or, to be precise, ice centipede, marches in a parade. The 5-day ✪ **Copper River Delta Shorebird Festival** (☎ **907/424-7260**) revolves around the coming of dizzying swarms of shorebirds—estimates range from 5 to 22 million—that use the delta and beaches near the town as a migratory stopover in early May. It's an opportunity to see immense waves of birds. The whole community gets involved to host bird watchers and put on a full schedule of educational and outdoor activities. There's a **king salmon derby** in late June and a **silver salmon derby** in late August.

EXPLORING CORDOVA

Save some time to wander around town, possibly with the help of the historic-walking-tour booklet produced by the historic society or with the recorded walking tour from the chamber of commerce. Cordova is full of wonderful little discoveries to make on your own.

The **Cordova Historical Museum,** at 622 First St., is a well-presented one-room display with some valuable artifacts reflecting Cordova's eventful past. The three-seat kayak and other artifacts of Prince William Sound Native peoples are of particular interest. Cordova is the home of the last few Eyak, a Native people whose language now has only one speaker left. The museum is open summer Monday through Saturday 10am to 6pm, Sunday 2 to 4pm; winter Tuesday through Friday 1 to 5pm, Saturday 2 to 4pm. Admission is $1, free under age 18.

GETTING OUTSIDE

THE COPPER RIVER DELTA The delta seems to go on forever, a vast patchwork of marsh, pond, a few trees, and the huge, implacable, gray river itself. A well-maintained gravel road leads across it, all in Chugach National Forest. The Forest Service rents public-use cabins (for reservation information, see "Outside in Southcentral," at the beginning of this chapter), and maintains pull-offs for bird-watching platforms and interpretive signs. The road itself is the old bed of the Copper River and Northwestern Railroad. It leads 50 miles to the Million Dollar Bridge. Built by Michael Heney, a magician of a 19th-century railroad builder who also constructed the White Pass and Yukon Route in Skagway, the 200-mile Copper River line was an engineering triumph. The bridge over the Copper River went up in a race against time between two surging glaciers in 30-foot-deep, fast-flowing glacial water, in winter. The bridge stood 56 years, until the 1964 earthquake knocked down one end of one of the spans, augering it into the riverbed. But you can still drive across on a jerry-rigged ramp and go a few miles farther on unmaintained road.

The best attraction, however, is just this side of the bridge: ❂ **Childs Glacier.** This is the most amazing glacier I've ever seen, and no one seems to know about it outside Cordova. It comes right down to the quarter-mile-wide river, where the flowing water cuts it off like a knife, eroding the base and bringing down huge chunks of ice. At the Forest Service viewing and picnic area across the river, salmon have been found high up in the trees and boulders in odd places. Why? When a big piece of ice falls off the glacier, it can create a wave large enough to flood the picnic area and uproot trees, not to mention hurling a few fish around. Several years ago, such a wave injured some visitors it pulled into the river, and now the Forest Service warns that anyone who can't run fast should stay in the observation tower. You can hear the glacier clicking and cracking and, with luck and patience, see it put on a spectacular show.

Driving a rented car to the bridge and glacier and stopping for the birds and wildlife on the way is a good day's activity. Pick up the road guide from the Forest Service Cordova Ranger Station. Don't miss **Alaganik Slough,** where there's a 1,000-foot boardwalk for watching wildlife. The ranger station also can provide you with a trail guide of hikes on the delta, and a wildlife-viewing guide. The animals you may see along the way include black and brown bears, moose, and mountain goats. The entire world population of dusky Canada geese nests on the delta, and you're sure to see eagles and trumpeter swans. Aside from Alaganik Slough, one of the best bird-watching areas is between the airport and town.

Copper River and Northwest Tours, P.O. Box 1564, Cordova, AK 99574 (☎ **907/424-5356**), takes trips on Monday, Wednesday, Thursday, and Saturday during the summer. On Wednesday it's timed to the arrival and departure of the ferry, so you can do the whole thing as a day trip from Valdez. Operated by the irrepressible Becky Chapek and her husband, Bill Myers, whose father cut ties on the Copper River line, the tours make numerous stops, spend an hour at the glacier for an excellent lunch prepared by Becky, and include a recorded narrative that's been checked for accuracy by the Forest Service and the historical society. The 6-hour trip costs $35. They also drop off hikers and bikers along the road.

I think **biking** the highway would be a great adventure. There's a Forest Service cabin about halfway along, at Mile 22, and several other cabins on trails that branch from the road. Of course, you don't have to ride all the way to see lots of birds and wildlife. The only drawback is that the delta can be terribly windy, which makes for hard riding. Bikes are for rent from Cordova Coastal Outfitters for $20 for 24 hours, and they also provide a drop-off service.

Fishing on the delta and in the lakes and streams around Cordova includes all species of Pacific salmon, as well as Dolly Varden and cutthroat trout. The Cordova Ranger Station can offer guidance and regulation booklets, and the **Alaska Department of Fish and Game** (☎ 907/424-3212) has a Cordova office as well.

OUT ON THE SOUND The waters of Prince William Sound around Cordova, although lacking the tidewater glaciers found in the western Sound, are calm, little used, and rich in marine life.

Dave Janka operates the classic, wooden ✪ *Auklet,* P.O. Box 498, Cordova, AK 99574 (☎ **907/424-3428;** e-mail auklet@ptialaska.net), a 58-foot former Fish and Wildlife Service patrol boat, to carry researchers and visitors into the Sound from Cordova, Valdez, and Whittier. He doesn't enjoy fishing and doesn't believe in hunting, so this is a wildlife and scenery experience. Within a few hours of Cordova, Janka knows where to find otters, sea lions, seals, and sometimes killer whales—and he'll know the whales you're looking at and the history of the pod. Half days are $75 per person, and full days $115, including meals. Longer charters are available, but the accommodations on board are nautical, not luxurious. He also drops off kayakers. **Discovery Voyages Alaska,** P.O. Box 1500, Cordova, AK 99574 (☎ **800/324-7602** or 907/424-7602), offers multiday excursions all over the sound starting from Whittier or Cordova aboard the comfortable *Discovery.* They offer set itineraries of various lengths, with a 6-day, 5-night trip at $1,940 per person.

Several vessels are available for fishing charters, and each offers the strong possibility of seeing wildlife. **Cordova Fishing Charters** (☎ 907/424-5467) charges $150 per person for a full-day trip. **Orca Bay Charters** (☎ 800/881-7948 or 907/ 424-5777) guides fishing and hunting, and has a "floating cabin" for rent.

Cordova is a good starting point for a sea-kayak trip, although Whittier, which is easier to get to and closer to Forest Service cabins, is more popular. **Cordova Coastal Outfitters** (see "Getting Around, above) offers kayak rentals and guided day and overnight trips.

IN THE AIR Cordova is all by itself, with untouched wilderness in all directions. An airplane or helicopter can get you out there for fishing, hunting, or just communing with nature. There are several Forest Service cabins in spectacular settings, accessible only by air. Flightseeing is available, but the most inexpensive way to do it, or to get deep into the Sound, is to take a mail plane to one of the villages or fish hatcheries. **Cordova Air** (☎ 907/424-3289) is the largest operator. **Fishing and Flying** (☎ 907/424-3324), located at the airport, is a friendly operation and has remote cabins for rent; John Tucker, of **Wilderness Helicopters,** can be reached at the same number, for even-harder-to-reach spots.

HIKING AROUND CORDOVA The Cordova Ranger Station can provide you with a trail-guide booklet with lots of ideas and maps. One of the best hikes is the **Power Creek Trail.** Take Power Creek Road along the north side of Eyak Lake to the end, 7 miles from town. The creek has spawning red salmon in July and attracts a lot of bears; watch, but don't get out of your car if you come upon one. The trail follows the creek through dramatic scenery 4.2 miles to a Forest Service cabin with a great view. Strong hikers can continue to Crater Lake, which is connected by a trail back to Eyak Lake, 1¹/₂ miles from town.

ACCOMMODATIONS

There are more establishments than those listed here (including several B&Bs), though these are the best. You can get a list of the others from either visitor center.

✪ **The Northern Lights Inn.** 500 Third St. (P.O. Box 1564), Cordova, AK 99547. ☎ **907/424-5356.** 5 rms. TV TEL. $50–$65 double. Additional adult in room $5 extra; children stay free in parents' room. AE, DISC, MC, V.

These large, lovely rooms, with private bathrooms, antiques, and views, are an almost unreal value. They're upstairs in Becky Chapek and Bill Myers's historic 1906 house, a couple of blocks above the main street. Each room has been lovingly renovated, three with kitchenettes. There are VCRs, a coin-op laundry, and a freezer that's available for fish. The family also operates the well-run tour business in town.

Prince William Motel. Second St. and Council (P.O. Box 908), Cordova, AK 99574. ☎ **907/424-3201.** Fax 907/424-2260. 16 rms. TV TEL. $75–$95 double. Additional adult in room $10 extra; children 11 and under stay free in parents' room. AE, MC, V.

A fishing family renovated this old building into a clean, comfortable, modern motel. The lower rooms look out onto an airshaft, but that may be to your liking if you're trying to get to sleep when it's still light out. All rooms have coffee machines and six have kitchenettes with microwave ovens. There's a coin-op laundry, a barbecue, and a freezer for fish.

✪ **The Reluctant Fisherman.** 401 Railroad Ave. (P.O. Box 150), Cordova, AK 99574. ☎ **907/424-3272.** Fax 907/424-7465. 50 rms. TV TEL. High season, $125 double. Low season, $95 double. Additional person in room $10 extra. AE, CB, DC, DISC, JCB, MC, V.

Margy Johnson presides at Cordova's main hotel with limitless energy. She and her husband, Dick Borer, have created one of the best waterfront lodgings in Alaska, overlooking the small-boat harbor. The decor in the lobby, lounge, and restaurant capture the town's railroad and copper-mining history, with rich wood and pressed-copper ceilings. The rooms are comfortable and modern, and those on the water side have views. There's a gift shop and travel agency in the hotel; car rental and VCRs are available.

The ✪ **restaurant** serves the town's best dinners. Main courses of fish, steaks, and pasta range from $15 to $30. A deck overlooks the harbor. Order the Copper River king salmon in season—the river produces exceptionally rich, oil-filled fish.

DINING

Other than the restaurants listed here, try the **Reluctant Fisherman,** described above, and the **Baja Taco** (☎ **907/424-5599**), a bus at the boat harbor with a covered dining area elevated on a small tower. The proprietor, who lives in Baja in the winter, specializes in salmon tacos. There also are a couple of other decent restaurants on First Street.

Ambrosia. First St. ☎ **907/424-7175.** Main courses $5.75–$18.75; lunch $5.75–$9.75. MC, V. High season, daily 11am–11pm; low season, daily noon–9pm. GREEK/ITALIAN.

This is a comfortable Greek and Italian family restaurant with an extensive menu and pizza. The food is reliable and the portions large—as a friend said, if you order the carbonara, plan to share it, unless you just got off a week on a seiner. Beer and wine license.

Cookhouse Cafe. 1 Cannery Row. ☎ **907/424-5926.** All items $4–$9. MC, V. Daily 7am–3pm. Closed in winter. DINER.

A former cannery cookhouse on a dock with a working cannery—to find it, go out toward the ferry dock—this clean, bright cafe with bench seating has a very agreeable feeling. The food, including fresh seafood, isn't fancy, but it's well prepared and inexpensive. No liquor license and no smoking.

✪ **Killer Whale Cafe.** In Orca Book and Sound, First St. and Council. ☎ **907/424-7733.** All items $6.50–$8.50. No credit cards. Mon–Fri 7am–4pm, Sat 8am–4pm.

If not for the healthy sandwiches, salads, and soups, this cafe would still be a must for the atmosphere and the regulars—young fishermen, New Age practitioners, and other eco-people—found here drinking the excellent coffee. The bookstore belongs to oil-spill hero Kelly Weaverling, who became the only member of the Green Party to hold elective office in the United States when he was Cordova's mayor a few years ago. (He later lost to Margy Johnson, of the Reluctant Fisherman, by one vote.) The bookstore has a comfortable, arty feel, and the restaurant seating is in a pair of lofts looking down on the shelves. No liquor license.

WHITTIER

Whittier is a portal on Prince William Sound, close to Anchorage. It's also one of the oddest places in America. Out of a population of less than 300, the great majority of the townspeople live in a single 14-story concrete building. (The balance live in one other building.) The Begich Towers, as the dominant structure is called, was built during World War II, when Whittier's strategic location on the Alaska Railroad and at the head of a deep Prince William Sound fjord made it a key port in the defense of Alaska. Today, with its barren gravel ground and ramshackle warehouses and boat sheds, the town maintains a stark military-industrial character. As one young town ambassador told me once on a visit, "You're thinking, 'Thank God I don't live here,' right?" The official boosters look more on the bright side: A brochure points out that having everyone live in one building saves on snow removal in a town that gets an average of 21 feet per winter.

If all this sounds negative, it needn't be for a visitor traveling to the glaciers, beauty, and rich marine environment of Prince William Sound. Indeed, Whittier is a funny little stop along the way. For now, there is no road, but there is a rail link. A 30-minute **Alaska Railroad** (☎ **800/544-0552** or 907/265-2494 year round, 907/265-2313 in summer) train runs through two mountains to the Seward Highway several times a day, stopping near the abandoned town of Portage. For visitors, the train ride in funny if ill-maintained old double-decked cars is well worth the trip, and you can drive your car on flat cars to connect with the ferry in Whittier. The passenger fare is $18 round-trip for adults, half for children, $72 round-trip for a car. A nicely appointed daily train with a dining car makes a **round-trip from Anchorage** in the summer an excellent choice if you are going out on a boat (see below), although the 6-hour stay in Whittier is too long otherwise. The round-trip fare is $49. Pending an environmental lawsuit, the state plans to pave the railway tunnels, but won't finish until the year 2000. The **Alaska Marine Highway System** ferry *Bartlett* (☎ **800/642-0066;** website http://www.dot.state.ak.us/external/amhs/home.html) makes a 6¹⁄₂-hour run to Valdez several times a week, where you can drive north on the beautiful Richardson Highway. The fare is $72 for a car up to 15 feet long and $58 for a passenger.

The **Greater Whittier Chamber of Commerce,** P.O. Box 607, Whittier, AK 99693 (☎ **907/344-3340**), maintains a **visitor center** in an old railroad car near the

boat harbor, where you can get a free cup of coffee to warm up from the rain, and maps, brochures, and guidance on finding a fishing charter or other ways out on the water.

For lunch, try **Hobo Bay Trading Company,** at the boat harbor, with good burgers and fried fish and a children's menu. Seating is only on stools. If you need lodgings, you'll find adequate rooms with cinderblock walls above the store at the **Anchor Inn** (☎ 907/472-2354). They have private baths, TVs, and phones, and book fishing charters. **June's Whittier Bed and Breakfast,** P.O. Box 715, Whittier, AK 99693 (☎ **907/472-2396**), has rooms and vacation apartments with full kitchens and ocean views in Begich Towers. Ken and June Miller maintain an office on the waterfront, where they also book fishing and sightseeing charters on their double-ended steel boat, the *Bread and Butter.* A full-day trip is $140.

GETTING OUT ON THE SOUND   Whittier is the entrance to western Prince William Sound, the area with its most protected waters, up long, deep fjords, and among tiny islands and passages. You're likely to see marine mammals and eagles. Glaciers lurk at the heads of many of the fjords, dumping ice in the water for the tour boats that cruise from Whittier.

Tour Boats   Several companies compete for your business for day-trip tours to the Sound's western glaciers, mostly based in downtown Anchorage. Besides the incredible scenery, the water is calm and seasickness virtually unknown—for the queasy, it's a much better choice than Kenai Fjords National Park. Each operator times departures to coordinate with the daily Alaska Railroad train from Anchorage, which is $49 round-trip. **Phillips' Cruises and Tours,** 519 W. Fourth Ave. in Anchorage (☎ **800/544-0529** or 907/276-8023), offers a 26-glacier cruise on a three-deck tour boat for $119, with lunch included. **Major Marine Tours,** with its office at 411 W. Fourth Ave. in Anchorage (☎ **800/764-7300** or 907/274-7300; e-mail mmarine@aol.com), operates a smaller vessel, specializing in a 6-hour dinner cruise that passes 10 glaciers for $99. **Stan Stephens Cruises,** P.O. Box 1297, Valdez, AK 99686 (☎ **800/992-1297** or 907/835-4731; fax 907/835-3765; e-mail ssc@alaska.net), runs a tour boat from Whittier to Valdez daily, stopping off for a visit at Stephens' Growler Island camp. An inclusive rail/boat/bus/plane package making the circle back to Anchorage in one day costs $200.

If you have more time to spend, several operators offer cruises of a few days and longer. Two small operators with intimate eco-tour vessels are listed in the Cordova section. **Alaska Sightseeing / Cruise West,** Fourth and Battery Building, Seattle, WA 98121 (☎ **800/888-9378**), which also has a downtown Anchorage office, provides 2- and 3-night cruises on the 54-passenger *Spirit of Discovery.*

Fishing Charters   Better than a dozen charter fishing boats operate out of Whittier. It's the closest saltwater fishing to Anchorage. You can get a list from the visitor center or book through **Anchor Services Unlimited** (☎ 907/472-2354).

Sea Kayaking   Whittier is a popular starting point for kayak trips to the beautiful and protected western Prince William Sound. Several businesses offer guided trips. **Prince William Sound Kayak Center,** P.O. Box 233008, Anchorage, AK 99523-3008 (☎ **907/472-2452** in summer or 907/276-7235 year round), offers guided 2-hour trips, starting at $65 for a single person or $50 each for a couple, and escorted trips of 2 to 4 days. The 2-day trip is $140 per person. For experienced paddlers, they also rent kayaks for unguided trips out of Whittier for $40 a day for a single, $60 double. Two other companies based in Anchorage that offer guided sea kayaking from Whittier are listed under "Sea Kayaking" in the "Anchorage" section.

For longer trips, most people charter a boat to drop them off among the islands beyond the long, deep fjord in which Whittier is located. There are six Forest Service cabins in the idyllic area popular with kayakers, off Port Wells. Unfortunately, they're so popular they often are reserved the maximum 180 days in advance (for reservation information, see "Outside in Southcentral," at the beginning of this chapter). The Forest Service or Alaska Public Lands Information Center in Anchorage can tell you where to find campsites, too.

6 The Copper River Valley & Wrangell– St. Elias National Park

Looking at a relief map of Alaska, you'd think the portion drained by the Copper River so overweighted with mountains as to topple the whole state into the Pacific. The Alaska Range, in the center of the state, has the tallest mountain, but this Gulf of Alaska region, straddling the Alaska-Yukon border, has more mass—the second- and fourth-tallest mountains in North America—Logan and St. Elias—and 9 of the tallest 16 in the United States. Four mountain ranges intersect, creating a mad jumble of terrain covering tens of millions of acres, a trackless chaos of unnamed, unconquered peaks. The Copper River and its raging tributaries slice through it all, swallowing the gray melt of innumerable glaciers that flow from the largest icefield in North America. Everything here is largest, most rugged, most remote; words quickly fall short of the measure. But where words fail, commerce gives a little help: These mountains are so numerous and remote that one guide service makes a business of taking visitors to mountains and valleys that no one has ever explored before.

The dominant landowner in this forbidding region is Wrangell–St. Elias National Park. Over 13 million acres in area, it's the largest national park in the United States, about 25% larger in area than the entire country of Switzerland. The protected land continues across the border in Canada, in Kluane National Park, which is similarly massive. Driving 180 miles from Valdez to Slana on the Richardson and Glenn highways, you keep the Copper River and its tributaries, and the park boundary, on your right almost all the way. The other half of the Copper River country is to the left. There are a few tiny towns along the way, and tiny villages off in the Bush, but precious few people for all that land. The region isn't a destination for visitors looking for a standard hotel room at night or structured activities during the day, although most will enjoy the views on the drive through. But for travelers interested in outdoor exploration, this untouched land is waiting.

WRANGELL–ST. ELIAS NATIONAL PARK

The park has two rough gravel roads that allow access to see the mountains from a car. On the south side, the old Kennecott Copper mine has big, abandoned buildings to walk around (the name of the company is spelled differently from the place, Kennicott, where it was founded because of an early misspelling). But for those who don't want to put on a pair of hiking boots or get in a raft, the park holds few other attractions. After all, wilderness is the whole point.

APPROACHES TO THE PARK   Park headquarters is just north of Copper Center, on the old Richardson Highway (☎ **907/822-5235;** website http:// www.nps.gov/wrst). It's open Memorial Day to Labor Day, daily from 8am to 6pm; in winter, during normal business hours. You can write for information at P.O. Box 439, Copper Center, AK 99573.

The **Slana Ranger Station** (☎ 907/822-5238) is in Slana, on the Nabesna Road near the intersection with the Glenn Highway's Tok Cut-Off, 65 miles from Tok and 74 miles from Glennallen. The Nabesna Road goes 46 miles into the park. Like the Denali Park Road, it's an avenue to see wilderness and wildlife, on mountain taiga, but here you can take your own car. The road can be rough, and there are a couple of river crossings that may be impassable at high water; however, you should be able to make it at least to Mile 29. Pick up a copy of the road guide from the ranger station or the Alaska Public Lands Information Center in Tok (see chapter 10). In this northern portion of the park, at the divide between the Tanana and Copper River drainages, the terrain isn't as fierce as elsewhere in the park. Hiking on the taiga is muddy, but not as technical as in the steep mountains to the south. You can camp anywhere you want on park lands, but wilderness hiking in the park is only for proficient outdoors people who know what to bring, how to handle stream crossings and emergencies, and generally how to take care of themselves far from any other person.

The **Chitina Ranger Station** (☎ 907/823-2205) is at the most popular gateway to the park, the old mining town of Chitina (CHIT-na), 33 miles down the paved Edgerton Highway, which starts about 17 miles south of Copper Center on the Richardson Highway. Like almost all visitor services in the area, it is closed in winter. Chitina, a town of around 50 people, has a post office and some services, the noted **Spirit Mountain Artworks** gallery, and a bridge over the Copper River. When the reds are running, they're so numerous Alaska residents are allowed to fish for them by ladling them out of the water with long-handled dip nets.

The northern end of the unfinished and abandoned Copper River Highway runs south from here—the former road bed of the Copper River and Northwestern Railroad, with its tunnels still intact almost 60 years after the rails were removed. You can drive south along the river to fish if you have four-wheel-drive and are an intrepid driver. It's a great mountain-biking route.

A more popular but very rough, narrow road continues 60 miles to the east to McCarthy, also on the remains of the Copper River line, where a footbridge connects to the great Kennecott Mine historic site, described below. Check with the ranger station for road conditions and a copy of the McCarthy Road Guide. With the condition of the road, plan 3 hours and bring a full-sized spare tire, as flats are common from the protruding railroad spikes. It's best to plan to spend the night if you want time to see the sights.

To save your car the beating, **Backcountry Connection,** P.O. Box 243, Glennallen, AK 99588 (☎ 907/822-5292 or 800/478-5292 within Alaska), runs a van from Glennallen and Chitina to McCarthy daily in summer except Sunday, leaving at 7am and 8:30am, respectively, arriving in McCarthy at 11:45am, and returning at 4pm. The fare is $75 round-trip from Chitina, $90 from Glennallen, $10 more if you return on a different day. Whether you drive or take the van to McCarthy, you'll have to walk the last bit, across a new foot bridge over the Kennicott River. Another alternative is to fly from Glennallen, Chitina, or any of the other larger towns in the region, avoiding the road.

The **Yakutat Ranger Station** (☎ 907/784-3295) is the park's back door. This is the most rugged and undeveloped approach to the park, although some people have started using the area for sea kayaking. The peaks rising from the Pacific near here are the largest coastal mountains in the world, with a vertical rise greater than the Himalayas.

THINGS TO SEE & PLACES TO STAY IN MCCARTHY & KENNICOTT The destination is the ghost-town communities of **McCarthy** (not quite a ghost town—there are a few dozen residents left) and **Kennicott.** McCarthy was a rough little frontier town and now is a charming, unspoiled little historic community. The **McCarthy Lodge,** P.O. Box MXY, McCarthy, AK 99588 (☎ **907/554-4402**), has rooms with shared bathrooms, a restaurant, and a saloon, and there's a small museum and an art gallery in town. Kennicott, 5 miles away, uphill, by foot or shuttle from McCarthy, was a genteel company town for the rich copper mine that operated there from 1910 until its abrupt closure in 1938. When the ax fell, the residents just locked the doors and left, so there's more to see than you might expect. Some of the 40 buildings, including a 14-story mill, were stabilized with a grant from the park service and have remained largely intact. They're privately owned, but people generally wander around to take a look at will. You cannot go into the buildings without a guide from **St. Elias Alpine Guides,** P.O. Box 111241, Anchorage, AK 99511 (☎ **907/277-6867**), which leads daily summer tours for $25 per person.

There are two good places to stay in the area. **Kennicott Glacier Lodge,** P.O. Box 103940, Anchorage, AK 99510 (☎ **800/582-5128;** 907/554-4477 in season only), stands among the ghost-town buildings and was built in much the same style, with red walls, white trim, and a metal roof. It is open May 15 to September 15. The well-prepared meals are served family style, at long tables. Rooms are small, but the views from those in front make up for it—and for the fact that 25 rooms share three bathrooms. A tour of the ghost town comes with the room. Including meals, rooms are $240 double, $70 per additional person; without meals, a double room is $174. **Historic Kennecott Bed and Breakfast,** McCarthy #4 P.O. Box MXY, Glennallen, AK 99588 (☎ **907/544-4469**), in a restored mine building, has two rooms with shared baths for $100 double.

GETTING OUTSIDE IN THE PARK   Rafting   A popular activity in the park, river trips are offered by some 15 guide services, including **Alaska Wildland Adventures** (see chapter 6, "Outside in Alaska"), and **Keystone Raft and Kayak Adventures** (see "Valdez" under "The Kenai Peninsula"). Based in McCarthy during the summer, **Copper Oar Adventures,** P.O. Box MXY McCarthy, Glennallen, AK 99588 (☎ **800/523-4453;** e-mail howmoz@aol.com), has day trips and expeditions. A Nizina Canyon float takes all day; lunch and a bush plane flightseeing ride back are included in the $195 price. A Kennicott River run takes only an hour or two and costs $45.

Hiking   Hiking guides also are plentiful, but there are few trails. A couple of good day hikes start from McCarthy or the mine, but mostly the park is trackless wilderness. **St. Elias Alpine Guides,** P.O. Box 111241, Anchorage, AK 99511 (☎ **907/277-6867,** or 907/554-4445 summer only), is a company based in McCarthy during the summer that offers day hikes, mountain biking, rafting, backpacking trips, and alpine ascents, but specializes in guiding extended trips to unexplored territory. Bob Jacobs, president of the company, stopped guiding on Mount McKinley years ago because of the crowds. He claims never to have seen another party in more than 20 years of guiding expeditions in Wrangell–St. Elias, and has led more than 30 parties of customers up previously unclimbed peaks. Half-day glacier walks start at $55 per person, and a 4-day backpacking trip is $775. Rafting starts at $195, and mountain biking at $80; they also rents bikes for $35 a day.

Hiking on your own in a wilderness largely without trails is a whole new kind of experience for experienced backpackers and outdoors people who are used to more crowded parts of the planet. You feel like an explorer rather than a follower. If you're not prepared to select your own route—a task only for those already experienced in trackless, backcountry traveling—use a trip synopsis provided by the National Park Service. More than a dozen are available, cataloged on a Trip Synopsis List you can get from the headquarters. This is only for those who know how to take care of themselves in the woods, cross rivers, and deal with wilderness emergencies.

ALONG THE WESTERN PERIMETER OF THE PARK

The people of the Copper River Country, as the area is known, live on homesteads and tiny settlements, and in a couple of towns near the regional hub of **Glennallen,** at the intersection of the Glenn and Richardson highways. The volunteer-run **Copper River Visitor Center** is in a log cabin right at the intersection, P.O. Box 469, Glennallen, AK 99588 (☎ **907/822-5555**); in summer it's open daily from 8am to 7pm. Glennallen has a bank with an ATM, a post office, a medical center, and government offices.

The best accommodations in the area are at the **Caribou Hotel,** at Mile 187 of the Glenn Highway, P.O. Box 329, Glennallen, AK 99588 (☎ **907/822-3302**). The rooms are the equal of a good chain. A double is $109 in the summer. They also have economy rooms in a surplused camp for pipeline workers that was moved to this site. The hotel's **Caribou Restaurant** is inexpensive and good for comfort food—meatloaf, roast beef, pork chops. There are a couple of good fast-food places in town, too.

Most of the land in the area west of the national park is managed by the **Bureau of Land Management Glennallen District,** with a log cabin office in town on the north side of the Glenn Highway, P.O. Box 147, Glennallen, AK 99588 (☎ **907/822-3217;** website http://wwwndo.ak.blm.gov/), open Monday through Friday 8am to 4pm, Saturday noon to 4pm. Information also is available from the public land information centers in Anchorage, Fairbanks, and Tok. This huge area, about the size of a midsized eastern U.S. state, has outdoor recreation more accessible than the park. There are several large alpine lakes, two National Wild Rivers, many hiking trails, and five campgrounds, all accessible on the Richardson, Glenn, and Denali highways. Guides are available for **rafting** and **fishing** in the rivers. Check at the visitor center or BLM office for referrals. The salmon are not as desirable this far inland as they are near the coast, as they've begun turning red, softened, and lost oil content with their spawning changes.

Fourteen miles south of Glennallen, **Copper Center** is a tiny Athabascan community on the old Richardson Highway. A historic roadhouse, the **Copper Center Lodge,** Drawer J, Copper Center, AK 99573 (☎ **907/822-3245**), is worthy of an overnight stop, if it's time for a rest on your drive. Rooms with shared bathrooms in the big old log building rent for $80 a night. The history of the lodge goes back to the bizarre gold-rush origins of Copper Center and Valdez, when about 4,000 stampeders to the Klondike tried a virtually impossible all-American route from Valdez over the glaciers of the Wrangell–St. Elias region. Few made it, and hundreds who died are buried in Copper Center. The original lodge was built on the leavings. The existing building dates to 1932.

7 The Matanuska & Susitna Valleys

For most visitors, the Mat-Su Valley, as the area is known, will be a place to pass through on the way somewhere else—along the Glenn Highway to Valdez or the Alaska Highway, or up the Parks Highway to Denali National Park from Anchorage. When I wrote those words in the last edition of this guidebook (and a few others about the unattractiveness of most of the area's development), local tourism authorities got so upset the flap was covered in the area's newspapers. At the next annual meeting of the Mat-Su Convention and Visitor Bureau, at which I spoke, boosters insistently reminded me of the Valley's good qualities: the sweeping beauty of the Hatcher Pass area, the Matanuska and Knik glaciers, the Iditarod Sled Dog Race, the river running and fishing. The area does have some lovely spots and fun outdoor opportunities, as well as proud residents, but for anyone with limited vacation time, the highlights here comprise not a destination but a day trip from Anchorage or a stop on the way to the state's major attractions.

The Matanuska Valley developed from the Great Depression until the 1970s as a farming area. The New Deal relocated colonists from other parts of the country to settle the prime growing land. But as transportation links improved both within the state and Outside, farming in Alaska lost in competition to shipping goods in from Seattle. Farms became subdivisions, housing a population overflow from booming Anchorage, only an hour's drive south on the Glenn Highway. With its adamantly antigovernment philosophy preventing any community planning, Mat-Su's rush of development produced the worst kind of suburban sprawl of highway-fronting shopping malls and gravel lots.

A few farmers still thrive in the Valley, growing vegetables that command a premium in Anchorage grocery stores, and some of the back roads still yield postcard vistas of frontier farms amid snowy peaks. The community museums and attractions are worth stopping for. There are some great hiking trails, and the historic mine and alpine terrain of Hatcher Pass should not be missed.

The entire area is enormous. The county-level government, the Matanuska-Susitna Borough, covers an area about as large as West Virginia, vaguely defined by the drainages of the Matanuska and Susitna rivers. Most of the people live in the section near Anchorage, in and around the towns of Palmer and Wasilla. In 1996, the Big Lake area, west of Wasilla, was swept by the most costly forest fire in Alaska history, which destroyed more than 400 buildings and seared 35,000 acres of land. For the casual visitor, however, fire's ravages are no more than a curiosity and will not affect a visit to the area.

Palmer is a traditional small town, built by the Depression-era colonists, and the borough seat. One side of the quiet main street, Colony Way, is lined with little storefront businesses; the other is an open vista of the mountains. About 10 miles west, **Wasilla** was created mostly by a building boom of the 1970s and 1980s. The town exists primarily as a string of shopping centers along the Parks Highway, and you have to really look to find its center. The area is dotted with lakes surrounded by houses, where people water-ski and fish in the summer and snowmobile and run sled dogs in the winter. **Hatcher Pass** is in the Talkeetna Mountains on the north side of the Matanuska Valley. The Talkeetnas aren't as tall as other ranges, but they have the striking, rugged beauty of cracked rock. A historic mining site nestles up in the pass, and it's a terrific place for summer hikes and winter recreation, including Nordic skiing and snowmobiling. **Talkeetna,** at the northern end of the Susitna Valley, is covered in chapter 9, on Denali National Park.

ESSENTIALS

GETTING THERE / GETTING AROUND   You can't get around the broadly spread Valley without a car. The Glenn Highway passes through Palmer, 40 miles north of Anchorage, on the way to Glennallen and the Alaska Highway. The Parks Highway meets the Glenn south of Palmer and passes through Wasilla on the way to Denali National Park and Fairbanks.

VISITOR INFORMATION   The **Mat-Su Visitors Center,** mile 35.5 Parks Hwy., HC 01, Palmer, AK 99645 (☎ **907/746-5000**), is located on the right side of the Parks Highway just after the intersection with the Glenn Highway, as you enter the area from the south. It's open in summer, daily from 8:30am to 6:30pm, fewer hours in winter. The **Palmer Visitor Center,** at 723 S. Valley Way in the center of town (☎ **907/745-2880**), has a small museum on the 1935 colony project that developed the Valley. It's open in summer, daily from 8am to 6pm, winter Monday through Friday 9am to 4pm.

ORIENTATION If you plan to explore the valley, buy a map. The best is the widely available $3.95 map produced by **Alaska Road and Recreation Maps,** P.O. Box 102459, Anchorage, AK 99510. The **Parks Highway** divides from the **Glenn Highway** about 7 miles south of Palmer on the Glenn and 7 miles east of Wasilla on the Parks. Turn left at the junction for Wasilla, Denali National Park, and Fairbanks. Go straight for Palmer, Glennallen, and the rest of the world. If you're in either Palmer or Wasilla and want to get to the other, the **Palmer-Wasilla Highway** is the direct route. The Butte area, south of Palmer, is on the **Old Glenn Highway,** which runs from Palmer to an exit on the Glenn just south of the Knik River. **Knik River Road** runs up the river from the Old Glenn.

FAST FACTS The city of Palmer levies a 3% **sales tax,** and Wasilla 2%. You'll find several **banks** on the Parks Highway in Wasilla and on Bailey Street or S. Colony Way in Palmer; they have **ATMs,** as do most large shopping centers and grocery stores. In **emergencies,** call **911.** For nonemergency business with the police, call the **Palmer Police Department** (☎ **907/745-4811**), the **Wasilla Police Department** (☎ **907/373-9077**), or, outside either town, the **Alaska State Troopers** (☎ **907/ 745-2131**). The **Valley Hospital** is at 515 Dahlia Ave. in Palmer (☎ **907/ 746-8600**). **West Valley Medical Campus** is at 950 E. Bogard Rd. in Wasilla (☎ **907/352-2800**). The *Frontiersman* newspaper is published twice weekly, and the *Anchorage Daily News* is widely available.

SPECIAL EVENTS The **Iditarod Restart,** on the first Sunday in March, enlivens Wasilla at the end of a long winter. The Iditarod Trail Sled Dog Race starts officially in Anchorage the day before, but then the dogs are loaded in trucks and carried to Wasilla, where the trail becomes continuous to Nome. The restart is the real beginning of the race, and the area makes the most of it. The ✪ **Alaska State Fair,** the 11 days leading to Labor Day, is the biggest event of the year for the Valley, and one of the biggest for Anchorage; it's a typical fair, except for the huge vegetables. The good soil and long days in the Valley grow cabbages the size of bean-bag chairs. A mere beach-ball-size cabbage wouldn't even make it into competition.

EXPLORING THE ROADS OF MAT-SU

A trip to ✪ **Independence Mine State Historical Park,** in Hatcher Pass, combines one of the area's most beautiful drives, access to great hiking and Nordic skiing, and interesting old buildings to look at. If you're headed north to Denali National Park or Fairbanks, the rough, winding gravel road through Hatcher Pass to Willow makes a glorious alpine detour around the least attractive part of your drive. Past the mine and skiing area, the road is open only in summer and is not suitable for large RVs. Just after the Parks Highway branches from the Glenn, turn right on the Trunk Road and keep going north on Fishhook Road. From the Glenn near Palmer, take Fishhook just north of town. The state **historic site** (☎ **907/745-2827** or 907/ 745-3975) is the remains of a hard rock gold mine operation that closed down in 1943. Some buildings have been restored, including an assay office that's a museum and the manager's house that's a welcoming visitor center, while other structures sag and lean as picturesque ruins. A $3 guided tour enters more buildings 1:30pm and 3:30pm weekdays, plus 4:30pm weekends, or you can wander with the help of an excellent walking-tour map. The visitor center is open 11am to 7pm daily in the summer and may be open winter weekends. The high Talkeetna Mountains valley the site occupies is idyllic for a summer ramble in the heather or for Nordic or Telemark skiing in winter. Ski passes are $3 per vehicle. There are four hiking trails and two mountain-biking routes in the area—ask at the visitor center. One great hike is the 8-mile Gold Mint Trail, which starts across the road from the Motherlode Lodge on Fishhook Road.

The **Musk Ox Farm,** two miles north of Palmer on the Glenn Highway and left on Archie Road, P.O. Box 587, Palmer, AK 99645 (☎ **907/745-4151**), raises the beasts for research and breeding, and offers tours 10am to 6pm daily in the summer season for $7 for adults, $6 seniors, and $5 ages 6 to 12. The family-operated **Reindeer Farm,** in the Butte area (☎ **907/745-4000**), raises reindeer for pets and puts them in harness each Christmas. The tour teaches all about reindeer and gives you an opportunity to feed them. Take the Old Glenn Highway to the intersection with Bodenburg Butte Road and Plumley Road, going toward the butte less than a mile. They're open 10am to 6pm daily in the summer. Admission is $5 for adults, $4 for seniors, and $3 for children 2 to 12. Across the road is a great short hike to the top of the butte.

The **Dorothy G. Page Museum,** at 323 Main St. in Wasilla (☎ **907/373-9071**), preserves the early history of the area in a collection of pioneer buildings, including the recently restored Teeland's General Store. Volunteers are often on hand to tell stories about the Valley's past, including some real area pioneers who lived and made this recent history. Several buildings are open for tours daily from 9am to 6pm in the summer, and the small museum is open daily from 8am to 5pm in the winter as well. Admission is $3 for adults, $2 for seniors, and free for children 17 and under.

The **Museum of Alaska Transportation and Industry,** off the Parks Highway at Mile 47, west of Wasilla, P.O. Box 870646, Wasilla, AK 99687 (☎ **907/ 376-1211;** website http://www.alaska.net/~rmorris/mati1.htm), is a paradise for gearheads and tinkerers. The volunteers have gathered every conceivable machine and conveyance—13 fire trucks, for example—and fixed up to running order as many as they can. An indoor museum displays their finished masterpieces, while the 15 acres outside are crammed with future projects and many railroad cars and aircraft, all grist for memories and imagination. It's open summer 9am to 6pm daily, winter Tuesday through Saturday 9am to 5pm. Admission is $5 for adults, $4 for students and seniors.

GETTING OUTSIDE

The Alaska Public Lands Information Center, described in the Anchorage section, is the best place for advice on the outdoors. **Rafting** in the Mat-Su is described under "Getting Outside" in the Anchorage section, earlier in this chapter. The best **hikes, skiing,** and **snowmobiling** are at Hatcher Pass, described above. For a challenging climb, go up 6,398-foot Pioneer Peak to the ridge below the top, with stupendous views, a 7- to 10-hour trip. The trailhead is on Knik River Road, off Old Glenn Highway. The Mat-Su area has many road-accessible salmon **fishing** streams and stocked lakes, as well as plenty of campgrounds to get close to the fishing. Call the **Alaska Department of Fish and Game** (☎ **907/745-5016,** or 907/745-0678 for recorded information) for current fishing information. **Knik Glacier Adventures,** 7.5 miles up Knik River Road, HC02, P.O. Box 7726, Palmer, AK 99645 (☎ **907/ 746-5133**), runs twice-daily **air boat** tours up the river to the glacier, often seeing bear, moose, Dall sheep, and eagles, and always taking a glacier walk. The 4-hour trip is $60 for adults, half price for children 12 and under. They also rent three rustic cabins and lead llama treks. Trail riding is popular in the countryside of Mat-Su.

Rafter T Ranch, P.O. Box 1563, Palmer, AK 99645 (☎ **907/745-8768**), offers guided rides of half an hour to a full day for $20 to $225, and unguided rides for slightly more. The Valley is a center of **sled-dog mushing,** both for racing and recreational dog driving. Raymie Reddington, of **Reddington Sled Dog Tours,** at mile 12.5 Knik–Goose Bay Road, HC 30, Box 5420, Wasilla, AK 99654 (☎ **907/376-6730**), son of Joe Reddington, father of the Iditarod race, offers trips up the Iditarod Trail, ranging from half an hour to several days, and will teach you to mush as well. The 30-minute ride is $35. Short summer rides are available, too.

ACCOMMODATIONS

If you're headed down the Glenn Highway, there are two good remote lodges near the **Matanuska Glacier,** an hour from Palmer. The historic **Sheep Mountain Lodge,** Mile 113.5, Glenn Hwy., HC 03, Box 8490, Palmer, AK 99645 (☎ **907/745-5121;** fax 907/745-5120), has 10 attractive cabins with private baths for $95 double, as well as a hostel. Hiking trails and the Matanuska Glacier are nearby. **Majestic Valley Wilderness Lodge,** at Mile 114.9, Glenn Hwy., HC03, Box 8514, Palmer, AK 99645 (☎ **907/746-2930;** fax 907/746-2931), offers basic rooms with private baths and all meals included for $90 per night, $120 with guiding to the great wildlife viewing opportunities. It's a good wintertime base for Nordic skiing.

There are two good lodges at **Hatcher Pass,** as well. **Hatcher Pass Lodge,** P.O. Box 763, Palmer, AK 99645 (☎ **907/745-5897;** fax 907/745-1200), has nine lovely A-frame cabins with chemical toilets right in the treeless bowl of the 3,000-foot alpine pass, renting for $115 double. Running water and showers are available in the fun, funky little restaurant. It's a great family place where, in the winter, you can ski out the front door on up to 20 kilometers of Nordic trails. **The Motherlode Lodge,** Mile 14, Fishhook Rd., P.O. Box 3021, Palmer, AK 99645 (☎ and fax **907/746-1464**), on the road to the pass, has good basic rooms with private baths for $65 double. There's a cafe, bar, and a restaurant with surprisingly sophisticated fine dining in a grand room. It's a good base for snowmobiling or hiking trips.

Below I've listed the best hotels in **Palmer** and **Wasilla.** Bed-and-breakfasts are a good choice in the Valley, too. **Alaskan Agate Bed and Breakfast Inn,** 4725 Begich Circle, Wasilla, AK 99654 (☎ **800/770-2290** or 907/373-2290; fax 907/376-2294; website http://www.akcache.com/alaskanagate), has big, comfortable apartments with full kitchens for $95 double, and attractive rooms with private baths for $75 double. Some 30 other B&Bs book through **Bed and Breakfast Association of Alaska, Mat-Su Chapter,** P.O. Box 873507, Wasilla, AK 99687 (☎ **800/401-7444** or 907/376-4461).

The Mat-Su borough charges a 5% **bed tax,** which is added to the 3% sales tax in Palmer and 2% in Wasilla within their city limits.

Best Western Lake Lucille Inn. 1300 W. Lucille Dr., Wasilla, AK 99654. ☎ **800/528-1234** (reservations) or 907/373-1776. Fax 907/376-6199. 54 rms, 4 suites. TV TEL. High season, $95–$125 double; $175–$185 suite. Low season, $75–$85 double; $125–$145 suite. Additional person in room $10 extra. AE, DC, DISC, MC, V.

This well-run, attractive lakeside hotel right in Wasilla has the best standard hotel rooms in the Valley. They're large and well appointed, and those facing the lake, which command a $10 premium, have balconies and a grand, peaceful view. Various kinds of boats can be rented for play on Lake Lucille, and flightseeing trips take off right from the dock below the lawn. There's a Jacuzzi, sauna, workout room, self-service laundry, small playground, and free coffee in the lobby. The **restaurant** is one of the best in the area, with a light, quiet dining room looking out on the water.

It's open for three meals a day, with the beef and seafood dinner menu ranging from $14 to $33.

✪ **Colony Inn.** 325 E. Elmwood, Palmer, AK 99645. ☎ **907/745-3330.** Fax 907/746-3330. 11 rms, 1 suite. TV TEL. $75 double; $100 suite. Additional person in room $5 extra. AE, DC, DISC, MC, V.

This perfect country inn occupies a lovingly restored teacher's dormitory from the New Deal Colony Project, right in the middle of Palmer. The rooms feel fresh and new, yet at the same time wonderfully old-fashioned—they have rockers and comforters, but also Jacuzzi bathtubs and big TVs. A large sitting room and a dining room downstairs are decorated with historic photographs that help tell the building's story, and excellent meals are served there for lunch and dinner during the summer. A coin-op laundry is available. This is one of the best places to stay in Southcentral Alaska, and an incredible bargain. Guests check in at the Valley Hotel, at 606 S. Alaska St., where you'll find basic rooms for very low rates.

DINING

The best restaurants in the Valley are at the Best Western Lake Lucille, the Colony Inn, the Motherlode Lodge, and Hatcher Pass Lodge, described above. In Palmer, don't miss **Vagabond Blues,** 642 S. Alaska (☎ **907/745-2233**), a great little coffee house with hearty soups and breads, and jazz, blues, poetry readings, and other performances on weekend nights. **Limani's Bar and Grill,** 800 Evergreen Ave. in Palmer (☎ **907/746-6000**), offers good, inexpensive lunches and evening meals in a fine-dining atmosphere. The extensive dinner menu of steak, seafood, and pasta is very reasonably priced.

9

Denali National Park: Wilderness by Bus

Denali (den-AL-ee) National Park contains Mount McKinley, at 20,320 feet the tallest mountain in North America, but you don't need to go to the park to see the mountain, and most people don't see it even when they do go. And Denali encompasses a broad expanse of alpine tundra and taiga populated by bears, wolves, Dall sheep, caribou, moose, eagles, fox, beavers, and small mammals, but that's typical of much of Interior and Arctic Alaska. And in and around the park, opportunities exist for river rafting, flightseeing, hiking, and tourist activities—but again, you don't have to go to the park for that.

What makes Denali National Park a unique place to visit is the human management of the wilderness—in Denali, anyone, even for modest expense, can get into a pristine natural environment and see wildlife in its natural state. A single National Park Service decision makes that possible: The only road through the park is closed to the public. This means that to get into the park, you must ride a crowded bus over a dusty gravel road hour after hour, but it also means that the animals are still there to watch, and their behavior remains essentially normal. From the window of the bus, you're likely to see grizzly bears doing what they would be doing even if you weren't there. It may be the only $20 safari in the world.

What's even more unique is that you can get off the bus pretty much whenever you want to and walk away from the road across the tundra, out of sight of the road, and be alone in a primeval wilderness utterly undisturbed by human development. Most anywhere else, it costs a lot of money or requires a lot of muscle and outdoor skill to get to places where you can do that. Unfortunately, most Denali visitors never take advantage of the opportunity. Being alone under God's big sky makes many people nervous, perhaps because most of us never have been really away from other people, much less apart from anything people have made. But that's the essence of Alaska—learning, deep down, how big creation is and how small are you, one more mammal on the tundra under the broad sky. Uniquely at Denali, you can be there, and then, when you're ready to return to civilization, you can just walk to the road and catch the next bus—they come every half hour.

It's little wonder that Denali is so popular when it offers such a valuable experience at such a low cost—or at least it wouldn't be a wonder if that were why it is so popular. As it happens, mass

Denali National Park

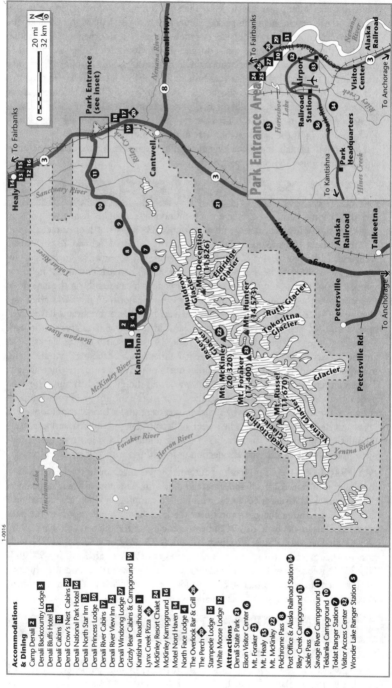

Accommodations & Dining

Camp Denali 2
Denali Backcountry Lodge 3
Denali Bluffs Hotel 31
Denali Cabins 18
Denali Crow's Nest Cabins 29
Denali National Park Hotel 36
Denali North Star Inn 13
Denali Princess Lodge 30
Denali River Cabins 17
Denali River View Inn 25
Denali Windsong Lodge 27
Grizzly Bear Cabins & Campground 19
Kantishna Roadhouse 1
Lynx Creek Pizza 26
McKinley Resort Chalet 24
McKinley Kampground 16
Motel Nord Haven 14
North Face Lodge 4
The Overlook Bar & Grill 28
The Perch 20
Stampede Lodge 15
White Moose Lodge 12

Attractions

Denali State Park 21
Eilson Visitor Center 6
Mt. Foraker 23
Mt. Healy 35
Mt. McKinley 22
Polchrome Pass 8
Post Office & Alaska Railroad Station 34
Riley Creek Campground 33
Sable Pass 9
Savage River Campground 11
Teklanika Campground 10
Tokat Ranger Station 7
Visitor Access Center 32
Wonder Lake Ranger Station 5

1-0016

marketing may be the real reason. More than half a million visitors go annually during a 3-month season, many on package tours that rush them through so quickly the park becomes more a picture outside a window rather than an experience. Denali has become a thing people feel they must do, and seeing Mount McKinley is a thing they must do when they visit Denali. Since the mountain is usually shrouded in clouds, the chance that they'll succeed in that mission is probably less than one in three. So why spend so much money to stay at the ticky-tacky roadside development at the park's entrance and then to ride on a bus over a bumpy road for most of a day? A friend swears she overheard a tourist ask, as she boarded the train leaving Denali, "Why did they put the park way out here in the boondocks?"

Do come to Denali, but come long enough to do something, to learn something, and, in some sense, to become part of the place.

1 Orientation

Denali National Park and Preserve is a 6-million-acre, roughly triangular polygon about the size of Massachusetts, with an entrance 230 miles north of Anchorage and 120 miles south of Fairbanks on the paved **George Parks Highway** or the **Alaska Railroad.** Although Mount McKinley is visible from as far away as Anchorage, you can't see it at all from the area of the park entrance. The **park entrance,** site of the railroad depot and all services accessible by private vehicle, stands on the far side of the park from the mountain, in a wooded area. A mile north on the Parks Highway, along a cliff-sided canyon of the **Nenana River,** hotels and restaurants have developed a kind of seasonal town on private land in the immediate area of the park entrance. Other services are at **Carlo Creek,** 14 miles south on the Parks, or at another gathering of roadside development 7 miles south of the park entrance, and in the year-round town of **Healy,** 10 miles north of the park entrance. Increasingly, **Talkeetna** has become an alternative gateway, even though it's 150 miles from the park entrance by car, as it is physically closer to the mountain. From the park entrance, a road accessible only by shuttle bus (except under special conditions—see "Fees and Regulations" under "The Essential Details," later in this chapter) leads west 90 miles through the park, past a series of campgrounds and a visitor center, and ending at the **Kantishna district,** a collection of inholdings with wilderness lodges.

FAST FACTS   There is no **bank** or automatic-teller machine in the Denali area— the closest is in Fairbanks, 120 miles away to the north. The **post office** is located near the park hotel. **Convenience stores,** with limited camping supplies, are located near the park hotel and at the gas station near the large hotels a mile north of the park entrance. Outside the park, dial **911** in **emergencies;** within the park, phone ☎ **907/ 683-9100.** The **Alaska State Troopers** (☎ **907/683-2232** or 907/768-2202) handle nonemergency calls from Cantwell, 28 miles south. A **health clinic** (☎ **907/ 683-2211**) is located in Healy, 10 miles north of the park entrance, open 24 hours a day for emergencies, or normal office hours for nonemergencies; you'll also reach them in emergencies by dialing 911. National newspapers are available at the Park Hotel.

2 Planning a Visit to the Park

CHOOSING AN ITINERARY

I have always enjoyed traveling without an itinerary, so you can believe me when I say that you *must* plan a trip to Denali National Park and reserve all accommodations, campsites, and trips into the park well in advance—for mid-July peak travel, make reservations by May. The park hotel is sometimes booked up by December for midsummer. Travelers who just show up at the visitor center without any reservations often have to spend at least a day—and probably two—outside the park before they can get a seat on a shuttle bus, a campground site, or a backcountry permit. It's quite a letdown to arrive at the park for a wilderness experience and have to spend the first few hours standing in line at the always-crowded visitor center trying to buy a bus ticket for 2 days later. Since it can be difficult to know before you've been there exactly what you want to do, I've tried to help by preparing some sample plans for visitors with different budgets and degrees of "roughing it."

PAMPERED EXPLORERS   Arrive by train at the park, checking into accommodations either at the park, a mile north, or in Healy—shuttles and courtesy vans will get you around. Attend a ranger talk, the *Cabin Nite* dinner-theater show, or go on a short nature walk around the park hotel in the evening. Get to bed early, and the next morning take a shuttle bus before 7am into the park, riding to the Eielson Visitor Center to see the terrain and animals, and possibly to get a view of the mountain, arriving there in late morning. Now ride part way back toward the entrance before getting off the bus at a place of your choosing for a walk and to eat the bag lunch you've brought along with you (pack all trash out, of course), or take one of the park service guided walks. After enjoying the wilderness for a few hours, head back on the bus, finishing a long day back at the hotel. Next day try a rafting ride, flightseeing trip, or other activity near the entrance to the park before reboarding the train.

FAMILY CAMPING & EXPLORING   Arrive at the park entrance by car with your camping gear and food for a couple of nights. Camp that evening at the Riley Creek campground near the visitor center and enjoy the evening ranger program or the lecture at the park hotel, or take one of the short hikes near the park entrance. Next day, catch a shuttle bus or camper bus into the park to one of the campgrounds there—either set up camp early at the eastern end of the park and then ride west for sightseeing, or ride the bus all the way to the Wonder Lake campground. Hike around the campground or take the bus to one of the broad vistas of alpine tundra and explore. Next day, take the bus ride through the park to see the wildlife, hike the backcountry, then head back to the campground for another night, or out. Your final evening, spend the night at a hotel in Healy for a shower and a rest. Add a day outside the park, if you want, for rafting or horseback riding.

OUTDOOR ADVENTURE   Arrive by train, bus, or car with your backpack, camping gear, and food for at least several days' hiking. Go immediately to the visitor center to orient yourself to the backcountry-permit process, buying the information you need for your trek (see "Hiking the Backcountry" under "Out in the Park," later in this chapter) and choose the unit area that looks most promising. Backcountry permits cannot be reserved in advance, only in person for the next day, and they go fast. If you're lucky, permits will be left for the day after you arrive; more likely, you'll need to camp at the Morino Backpacker's Campground, 1.9 miles on the park road from the highway, and arrive at the visitor center by the 7am opening to get your permit for the following day. Now you've got another day to wait; if you've reserved a shuttle-bus seat, you can get a preview of the park and see some wildlife, or outside the park, go on a rafting trip. The next morning, you can start your backcountry hike, taking the camper bus to your unit, then traveling for up to 2 weeks in a huge area of wilderness reserved almost exclusively for your use.

WILDERNESS LODGES   For those who can afford it, this may be the best way to see Denali. The lodge will fly you out—or, if it's in Kantishna, drive you through the park—and you'll immediately be away from the crowds in remote territory. The lodges all have activities and guides to get you out into the wilderness. If you're not staying in Kantishna, you may want to schedule a day to ride the shuttle bus into the park to see the mountain and wildlife anyway, with an evening in a hotel near the park or in Healy.

THE TALKEETNA OPTION   Drive only as far as Talkeetna, about 110 miles north of Anchorage, and board a flightseeing plane from there to the park, perhaps landing on a glacier on Mount McKinley itself. You'll stand a better chance of seeing the mountain than anyone else, since the weather tends to be better on the south side and you won't have to go on a certain, prearranged day when the weather may be poor. You'll also save yourself hours of driving to the park and the bus ride into the park. But you'll miss the wildlife-viewing opportunities that can be had only on the ground in the park. See the Talkeetna section at the end of this chapter.

CLIMBING MOUNT MCKINLEY   McKinley, because of its altitude and weather, is among the world's most challenging climbs. Every year experienced climbers die—most years, several. If you're looking here for advice, you're certainly not up to an unguided climb. A guided climb is a challenging and expensive month-long endeavor for experienced climbers in excellent condition. Climbs generally start with a flight from Talkeetna to a Kahiltna Glacier base camp. You must preregister at least 60 days before your departure with the park service's **Talkeetna Ranger Station,** P.O. Box 588, Talkeetna, AK 99676 (☎ **907/733-2231**). It also can provide names of qualified guides. There's a $150-per-climber fee to help cover the cost of administering the mountaineering program.

WHEN TO GO: CROWDS OR SNOW

Crowding is relative. Once you're out in the park, Denali is never crowded. A transportation bottleneck—the shuttle system—protects the park from over-use. What makes the busy season difficult is getting through that bottleneck from the crowded park entrance into the wilderness. For that, planning to avoid the busy season may help.

The park is populated by people beginning in mid-May, when there still is some snow; the humans migrate south again in mid- to late September, when winter is closing in. In the off-season, only a few dozen residents remain—caretakers who watch over the hotels and other buildings and sled-dog-driving rangers who patrol the backcountry. During the visitor season, you can improve your chances of getting away from others of your species by avoiding the peak month of July. The season really gets into high gear in mid-June and starts to wind down in mid-August, providing a month of relative quiet and often reduced prices at the beginning of the season and another at the end.

May is iffy at Denali, but fall is a wonderful time to go. The weather gets nippy at night, and there can be surprise snowfalls, but rain is less likely, and the trees and tundra turn wonderful colors. By early September, visitors are so few that the park no longer takes telephone reservations. By mid-September, private cars can drive on the park road for 4 days—the park service holds a lottery to determine who will get that treat.

Another way to avoid the crowds is to book a stay in a wilderness lodge. Three lodges in Kantishna, listed below, have the right to carry clients to their businesses over the park road in buses and vans. Outside the park, several other lodges fly in clients. Either way, you bypass the bottleneck at the park entrance.

Finally, remember that there are other beautiful places that are relatively unexploited by visitors. You're not obliged to go to Denali to see alpine terrain or to have a chance of seeing bears or caribou. The Denali Highway, leading 135 miles east through the Alaska Range from Cantwell, 30 miles south of the park entrance, is in some ways more spectacular than the park road (see chapter 10). Wrangell–St. Elias National Park, the nation's largest park, is barely used. The Richardson Highway and Steese Highway cross areas of broad, Arctic tundra with limitless vistas similar to those found in the park. The vast Arctic contains many more remote and inspiring vistas, if you can afford a flight to the North or a drive up the Dalton Highway, through the Brooks Range.

3 The Essential Details

RESERVATIONS & VISITOR INFORMATION

Most of the Park Service's dealings with the public are handled by ARA's **Denali Park Resorts,** P.O. Box 87, Denali Park, AK 99755, or 241 W. Ship Creek Ave., Anchorage, AK 99501 (☎ **800/622-7275** or 907/272-7275; fax 907/264-4684). ARA also operates the buses and handles reservations for seats, for sites at the park service campgrounds (except the self-serve Morino Backpackers campground), and for the only hotel within the park, as well as reserving rooms in its two other hotels outside the park and booking rafting trips and a dinner-theater show. **Destinations in Travel,** P.O. Box 76, Denali National Park, AK 99755 (☎ **800/354-6020** or 907/683-1422), takes care of reservations for independent travel at Denali as well as arranging park and outdoor-oriented trips all over the state.

The **park visitor center,** to the right less than a mile from the Parks Highway intersection, is the place to pick up bus tickets and campground permits from a desk staffed by ARA employees. There's usually a long line for walk-in purchase, but a will-call desk speeds things up if you have reservations. Rangers roving the center and at an information desk can answer questions before you waste a lot of time in line; they also provide rudimentary information on local businesses other than ARA. The **National Park Service,** P.O. Box 9, Denali Park, AK 99755 (☎ **907/683-2294;** website http://www.nps.gov/dena/), provides a free map and a newsprint park guide, *Denali Alpenglow.* Get a copy in advance, if you can, and get questions answered at the interagency **Alaska Public Lands Information Center** (☎ **907/271-2737** in Anchorage or 907/456-0527 in Fairbanks). The visitor center also has an auditorium showing a slide show and a bookstore with maps and publications. There's a neat little area for kids. Rangers staff a backcountry permit desk (see below).

If you have limited time, plan your visit around your bus and campground reservations, making them well in advance. Hotel reservations, while also tight, are easier to get and less important to the purpose of your visit. Space loosens up considerably in the early and late season (see "When to Go: Crowds or Snow" under "Planning a Visit to the Park," earlier in this chapter).

Here's the system for reservations: Forty percent of the available shuttle-bus seats and campsites (except at Morino, Sanctuary River, and Igloo Creek campgrounds) are available for reservation by fax or mail starting December 1 the preceding year, and by phone daily between 7am and 5pm Alaska time, starting sometime in February. Some years, this number has been perpetually busy. Fax requests, which can be sent 24 hours a day until 2 days before the reservation, may be your best shot. The website has a fax form, or make your own, including the dates, times, and campgrounds you want, alternative dates, names, and ages of the people in your party, entrance fees (see below), $4 reservation fee, and a Visa, MasterCard, American Express, or Discover card number, with expiration. You don't have to figure out the total. You can pay by check as well if reserving by mail. A confirmation is sent by mail or fax within 2 days. Beginning 2 days in advance, the remaining 60% of the shuttle and campground spots are available in person only, at the visitor center, and are quickly booked up. When you get to the front of the line, if there's still a night available 2 days hence, you can book that night and book up to 14 continuous nights afterward at that campground or any other. (A backcountry permit qualifies to keep the 14 days continuous, but 14 days of camping or backcountry time is all you can have all year, total.) Sometimes less desirable shuttle times, with departures later in the day, remain available even until the day of departure. The doors of the visitor center open at 7am, and in the peak season the line is already in place when they do, forming as early as 6am.

Under this system, if you arrive without reservations, you must get to the visitor center early and take what you can get. Even then, you may have to wait 2 days before staying at a park campground or riding the bus. That means spending your time outside the park in private accommodations. The park service has worked on improving the process, but still it's basically a rationing system to allocate a scarcity of seats and sites. Those who make reservations get first dibs, and the rest are weeded out according to their level of their desire through the frustration and delays of the system.

GETTING THERE

BY RAIL   The most popular way to get to Denali National Park is by train. The **Alaska Railroad,** P.O. Box 107500, Anchorage, AK 99510-7500 (☎ **800/544-0552** or 907/265-2494; website http://www.alaska.net/~akrr), which pioneered tourism to the park before the George Parks Highway was built in 1972, has daily service in the summer from Anchorage and Fairbanks. Trains leave both cities at 8:15am, arriving at the park from Anchorage at 3:45pm and from Fairbanks at noon, crossing and going on to the opposite city for arrival at 8:15pm in each. The fare from Anchorage to Denali is $99 one-way. The full train runs only from mid-May to mid-September, with slightly lower fares in May and September than during the summer. During the winter, the Alaska Railroad runs a single passenger car from Anchorage to Fairbanks and back once a week. If you're here, ride it one-way—it's a truly spectacular, truly Alaskan experience.

The advantages of taking the train to Denali are that it's a historic, unspoiled route through beautiful countryside; there's a good chance of seeing moose and caribou; it's fun and relaxing; there's commentary along the way; and the food on any of the three sets of cars is good. There are disadvantages, too. The train is more expensive. You can rent a car for 4 days and drive up for the same price as two one-way tickets on the train. It's slow, adding 3 hours to a trip from Anchorage to the park, and when it's late, it can be very late. And, once you arrive, you have to rely on shuttles and courtesy vans to get around outside the park—not a big drawback, since shuttles are frequent.

The Alaska Railroad's locomotives also pull two sets of cars with full domes owned by **Princess Cruises and Tours,** 2815 Second Ave., Suite 400, Seattle, WA 98121-1299 (☎ **800/835-8907**), and **Holland America–Westours / Gray Line of Alaska,** 300 Elliot Ave. West, Seattle, WA 98119 (☎ **907/277-5581**). Each provides separate, distinct service and operates independently, as described below. You can't walk from one kind of car to another. Fares are $129 on the Princess cars, and $125 on the Holland America–Westours cars; lodging packages are available.

The Princess and Holland America–Westours cars cater primarily to their cruise-ship and package customers but do sell tickets to independent travelers. They offer a luxurious but controlled experience wherein each passenger has his or her own dome-car seat on a unique, beautifully appointed railroad car. You're expected to stay in your assigned seat and eat during a scheduled dining seating, and you may have to ride backward or sideways in cars designed with tables and living room–style furniture, and spend almost 8 hours sitting across a table from strangers whom you may or may not like. The Alaska Railroad cars are traditional railroad cars, with seats facing forward, and you can sit anywhere you want, move between cars and stand in the breezeway between cars, and eat when you want to. The food is not the luxurious fare the cruise lines strive for, but it's still quite good, served in an old-fashioned dining car with table cloths and flowers. A couple of dozen dome-car seats are available, with a 20-minute limit on staying in them—not the dome-to-yourself arrangement of the cruise-line cars. Well-trained guides provide intermittent commentary and answer questions in each car. Children will enjoy the Alaska Railroad cars more; adults can judge for themselves which approach is more appealing.

Between the two cruise-line car offerings, Princess's Midnight Sun Express Ultra Dome Rail Cars appeared clearly preferable to me. The decor was fresher and better maintained than in the Holland America–Westours cars, there was more headroom in the upstairs dome area, and rear platforms allowed passengers to get out of their seats and enjoy the fresh air. However, my personal preference would be for the Alaska Railroad cars. Even if you can't sit in a dome the whole way, the windows still are large and clean, and I think half the fun of riding on a train is moving around and meeting a variety of people.

BY CAR   Renting a car and driving from Anchorage will prove cheaper than taking the train for most parties. The drive is about $4^1/2$ hours from Anchorage, $2^1/2$ from Fairbanks, on good two-lane highway. Many of the views along the Parks Highway are equal to the views on the train, but large stretches, especially in the Matanuska and Susitna valleys, near Anchorage, have been spoiled by ugly roadside development—which you don't see on the train. A long but spectacular detour around the mess leads through Hatcher Pass on a mountainous gravel road open only in the summer. See the "Matanuska and Susitna Valleys" section in chapter 8. Further north from Anchorage, the Parks Highway passes through Denali State Park. If the weather's clear, you can see Mount McKinley from the pull-outs here. The state park also contains several campgrounds and hiking trails and a veterans memorial.

BY BUS   Several van and bus services inexpensively connect Anchorage and Fairbanks to Denali. Most will carry bikes and other gear for an additional fee. **Alaska Direct Busline** (☎ **800/770-6652** or 907/277-6652) charges $45 from Anchorage to Denali and $25 from Fairbanks to the park. The **Alaska Backpacker Shuttle** (☎ **800/266-8625** or 907/344-8775) carries passengers from Anchorage in a van that leaves from the hostel at 700 H St., downtown. The fare is $35 one-way, $60 round-trip. **Fireweed Express** (☎ **888/505-8267** or 907/452-0521) offers van service starting from Fairbanks for $25 one-way, $40 round-trip, picking up at the visitor center, among other places.

BY AIR   Flightseeing trips to Denali from Anchorage are listed in chapter 8. You also can charter to Denali from Anchorage or Fairbanks, although it's liable to be costly.

GETTING AROUND

If you drive to the park, you'll still need to take the **shuttle bus,** described below, to get into its heart. If you take the train or bus, you'll find that virtually all accommodations have arrangements to get you around, although this becomes less convenient as you get farther from the park entrance. If your hotel doesn't have a courtesy van of its own, there usually is a scheduled shuttle. **ARA** operates a bus that carries guests from its Denali Park Resorts hotels, a mile north and 7 miles south of the park, to the park entrance. You can use the bus even if you're not staying at an ARA hotel—have the desk at your hotel call for a pickup. You can also get around on a rented **bike.** See "Out in the Park," below.

FEES & REGULATIONS

ENTRANCE FEES   The park service charges an entrance fee to come into Denali National Park, but there is no gate, and no one collects the fee or asks for a ticket or receipt to show you've paid it. When you book a campground site or a bus ride, the fee is automatically added to your bill. Individual fees are $5, $10 for families, and they're good for 7 days. Annual passes are available but are unlikely to be worthwhile unless you're planning more than three visits, each separated by more than a week. U.S. residents 62 or older can obtain a lifetime family pass to all the national parks with a 50% discount on camping, called a Golden Age Passport, for $10. This is a very good deal. U.S. residents with disabilities can get such a pass free, called a Golden Access Passport. For people who fall in neither of these categories, the Golden Eagle Pass costs $50 and is good for a year. It will yield savings if you soon plan to visit a lot of parks outside Alaska. You can buy any of the passes at any park, or call or write the Denali National Park addresses listed above under "Reservations & Visitor Information."

WHO CAN DRIVE THE PARK ROAD   Lodges in Kantishna can use the park road to bring in customers, but everyone else is under strict controls. You can drive past Mile 14 on the park road only under certain circumstances: (1) You have a 3-day camping permit at Teklanika Campground (you must remain parked at the campground for the entire three days); (2) you are a credentialed professional photographer or researcher with a special permit; or (3) it is the last few days in September, and you have won a permit in a lottery that allows 1,600 cars free passage on the road. After the 4 days of permit driving are over, the road is open to anyone as far as Mile 30 until the snow flies; then it's maintained only as far as the headquarters, 3 miles from the entrance.

CAMPING PERMITS & FEES   Each park service campground has different fees, regulations, and access limitations. All sites must be reserved, except the Morino Backpacker campground, which has a self-registration system and is only for people without vehicles. The Sanctuary and Igloo campgrounds can be reserved only in person, and sites may not be available when you arrive, so it's wise to at least start your stay with reservations at another campground. There's a one-time reservation fee of $4 per campground in addition to the campground permit fees. Canceling or changing camping reservations carries a fee of $6 per site and is possible only up to 2 days before the reservation. When you make your reservation, you'll receive a confirmation in the mail or by fax. Take that document to the visitor center to pick up your camping permit. The visitor center is open 7am to 8pm. If you won't make it by 8pm, you must call ☎ **907/683-1266** to avoid losing your site. Fees and regulations for individual campgrounds are in the "Denali Campground Facts" table, below. Descriptions are in the "Out in the Park" section, below. Reservation procedures are given above. To get beyond the 14-mile checkpoint, you need to ride on the camper bus or go by bicycle. The camper bus fare is $15.

BUS FARES   Riding a bus over a bumpy gravel road is an integral part of the Denali experience. If that starts to bother you, just remember that most of what's attractive about the park wouldn't be there if free access by private vehicles were allowed—instead, it would just be a busy rural highway. For details on the trip, see "On (and Off) the Bus," later in this chapter. For fares and other details, see the "Denali Park Road Bus Facts" chart, later in this chapter.

Denali Campground Facts

Campground	Fee	No. of Sites	Access & Special Rules
Riley Creek	$12 per night	100 sites	Near park entrance. Private vehicle or free front-country bus.
Morino Backpacker	$6 per night	60 sites	Near park hotel. Free front-country bus. No parking or vehicle camping. Maximum 2 people per site. No reservations.
Savage River	$12 per night	33 sites	13 miles from park entrance. Private vehicle access or $15 camper bus.
Savage Group	$40 per night	3 sites	Group sites at Savage River. No discount for Golden Age or Golden Access passes.
Sanctuary River	$6 per night	7 sites	23 miles from park entrance. Tent camping only. Store food in lockers. Stove only, no fires. Reservations in person only. Access by $15 camper bus.
Teklanika River	$12 per night	53 sites	29 miles from park entrance. Minimum 3-night stay for vehicles. Access for private vehicles with camping permit or by $15 camper bus.
Igloo Creek	$6 per night	7 sites	34 miles from park entrance. Tent camping only. Store food in lockers. Stove only, no fires. Reservations in person only. Access by $15 camper bus.
Wonder Lake	$12 per night	28 sites	85 miles from park entrance. Tent camping only. Maximum four people per site. Store food in lockers. Stove only, no fires. Access by $15 camper bus.

BACKCOUNTRY PERMITS   The permit system for staying overnight in the undeveloped backcountry is onerous enough to weed out those who aren't serious about a wilderness experience. For details on choosing your route and information for your trek, see "Hiking the Backcountry" under "Out in the Park," later in this chapter.

Permits are free but can be obtained only 24 hours in advance and only in person at the backcountry desk in the visitor center. Since the unit areas book up quickly during the summer season, you may have to wait outside the park before you can start your hike. Camping at the Morino Backpacker campground during the wait is a good, inexpensive choice that doesn't require advance reservations.

The park is divided into 43 backcountry units, 29 of which are accessible from the park road. For your first night, you have to stay in one of these 29, as it isn't practical in 1 day to get into the park and hike across a roadside unit to camp in a unit that's off the road. Each unit generally has only a few permits available. You can reserve up to 14 days in the backcountry during the summer, planning a route from one unit to another and getting all the permits at the start. Because of this regulation, you may find the units you're most interested in already booked, even if you're first in line on the first morning they become available. Have second and third choices ready.

Before venturing into the backcountry, everyone is required to watch an orientation film called the *Backcountry Simulator*. The park service will provide bear-resistant food containers in which you are required to carry all your food. Guns are not permitted in the park; a pepper spray for self-defense is a good idea and proper camping etiquette essential to avoid attracting bears.

4 On (and Off) the Bus

Your visit to Denali will likely revolve around your ride on the shuttle bus into the park to see the wildlife and get out for a walk in the wilderness. Some planning will make it a more comfortable ride.

You can buy shuttle tickets to the Toklat (TOE-klat) River, 53 miles into the park; the Eielson (AISLE-son) Visitor Center at 66 miles; Wonder Lake at 85 miles; or Kantishna, at about 95 miles. Of course, you have to go both ways unless you have a campground reservation, a backcountry permit, or accommodations in Kantishna—which means that you're in for a long drive. If you don't get off the bus along the way, the round-trip takes 6½ hours to Toklat, 8 hours to Eielson, and 11 hours to Wonder Lake. The park service shuttles don't make one-day round-trips to Kantishna. In choosing your destination, you need to balance your stamina, your desire to save time for a day hike, and your desire to see wildlife. In the early morning, people often see moose and black bear in the first part of the road. In the summer, brown bear are seen most in the higher country, beyond Toklat, which also is the best area for caribou, but in the fall berry season, the grizzlies show up all along the drive. The best views of McKinley show up after mile 61, also beyond Toklat. The mountain is most likely to be visible in the morning, as clouds often pile up during the day. Going beyond Eielson to Wonder Lake provides more amazing views, including a land-covered glacier and many classic images of Mount McKinley. In general, however, I think Eielson is the best destination for most people, offering both the chance to see the mountain and some wildlife while leaving some time to get out and walk.

ARA also operates narrated bus tours, booked mostly with package visitors. The **Natural History Tour** provides just a taste of the park, going 17 miles down the park road. The **Wildlife Tour** goes to Toklat when the mountain is hidden by clouds, and 8 miles farther, to Highway Pass, when it is visible. Food is provided, but you can't get off the bus along the way, and the route skips the beautiful grizzly and caribou habitat towards the Eielson Visitor Center. The **Kantishna Roadhouse** (listed below under "Wilderness Lodges") offers a 190-mile, 1-day marathon with lunch and a dog sled and gold panning program at the halfway mark, at the lodge. It's well done, with commentary, but you can't get off the bus along the way, and the return trip may be too rushed to stop for all wildlife sightings.

Reserve your shuttle ticket for as early as you can stand to get up in the morning. This strategy will give you more time for day hikes and enhance your chances of seeing the mountain and wildlife. Many animals are more active in the morning, especially on hot days. The first bus leaves the visitor center at 5am, the next at 6am, and then every half hour until the 2:30pm bus, which gets back at 10:30pm. By taking an early bus, you can get off along the way for a hike, then walk back to the road and get the next bus that comes along with a spare seat. If you were to take the 5am bus, you'd have 9½ hours of slack time before you'd have to catch the last bus heading east. (To be on the safe side, don't push it to the very last bus.) The sun won't set until after 11pm May to July, so there'll be plenty of light. If you need to get back to the park entrance at a certain hour, leave yourself plenty of time, because after getting off your eastbound bus, you can't reserve seats going back the other way, and you may have to wait for a bus with room to take you.

Here's the hard part for families: Young children will go nuts on an 8-hour bus ride, and often can't pick out the wildlife—this isn't a zoo, and most animals blend into their surroundings. Older children also have a hard time keeping their patience on these trips, as do many adults. The only solution is to get off the bus and turn

Denali Park Road Bus Facts

Bus	Purpose	Route	Frequency	Fare
ARA courtesy shuttle	Links hotels to park entrance	Hotels 1 mile north and 7 miles south and within park	Continuous loop	Free
Front-country shuttle	Links facilities within park entrance area Park Hotel	Visitor Center, Riley Creek Campground, trail depot,	Continuous loop	Free
Camper shuttle	Access to campgrounds beyond the park entrance	From the visitor center to Wonder Lake Campground, 85 miles into the park	Several times a day	$15 adults, $7.50 children 13–16, free children 12 and under
Backcountry shuttle (or just "the shuttle")	General access to the park and wildlife viewing; limited commentary, depending on the driver; no food service	From the visitor center as far as Kantishna, 95 miles away through the park	Every 30 minutes to Eielson Visitor Center, every hour to Wonder Lake, less frequently to Kantishna	$20 to Eielson, $26 to Wonder Lake, $30 to Kantishna; children 13–16 half price, children 12 and under free
Wildlife Tour	Seven-hour guided bus tour with lunch provided; passengers may not get off en route	From the visitor center to the Toklat River or Highway Pass, 53 to 61 miles into the park	Twice daily	$58, half price for children
Natural History Tour	Three-hour guided bus tour at the edge of the park	From the visitor center 17 miles into the park	Three times daily	$34, half price for children
Kantishna Roadhouse bus	All-day bus tour to a lodge in Kantishna, operated separately from the park or concessionaire	From the park entrance 95 miles to Kantishna	Once a day	$99

your trip into a romp in the heather. When you've had a chance to revive, catch the next bus. Besides, just because you buy a ticket to Eielson doesn't mean that you have to go that far. If your child normally needs a car seat, you must bring it along on the bus, or borrow one from the park service.

Shuttle-bus tickets can be canceled only with 2 days' advance notice, and then at a cost of $6 each. The weather is unpredictable that far in advance. If it's rainy, your chances of seeing wildlife are reduced and your chance of seeing Mount McKinley nil. Don't lose hope, however, as the park is large and the weather can be different at the other end of your long drive; besides, there's nothing you can do about it. Dry, overcast weather is best for wildlife watching.

Before you leave for the visitor center to get on your shuttle bus, you need a packed lunch and plenty of water; you should be wearing sturdy walking shoes and layers of warm and cooler clothing with rain gear packed; you should have binoculars or a spotting scope at the ready; and you should have insect repellent handy. You may also want a copy of Kim Heacox's worthwhile booklet **"Denali Road Guide,"** available for $5 at the visitor center bookstore, published by the Alaska Natural History Association, 401 W. First Ave., Anchorage, AK 99501 (☎ **907/274-8440**). It provides a milepost commentary you can follow as you ride. The same firm publishes guides to Denali birds, mammals, geology, and trails. Most shuttle-bus drivers do a good job of providing commentary, too. If you'll be doing any extensive day hiking, you may also want to bring a detailed topographic map printed on waterproof plastic (available for $8.99 from the visitor center) and a compass; if you're just going to walk a short distance off the road, you won't need such preparations. There are no reserved seats on the bus. The left side has the best views on the way out.

Shuttle-bus etiquette is to yell out when you see wildlife. The driver will stop, and everyone will rush to your side of the bus. After you've had a look, give someone else a chance to look out your window or to get a picture. Try to be quiet and don't stick anything out of the bus, as that can scare away the animals. Of course, you have to stay on the bus when animals are present. Most buses will see grizzly bears, caribou, Dall sheep, and moose, and occasionally wolves, but, as one driver said, the animals aren't union workers, and it's possible that you won't see any at all.

Here are some of the highlights along the road (check the visitor center or the park service information handouts to confirm times of the guided walks):

Mile 9   In clear weather, this is the closest spot to the park entrance with a view of Mount McKinley. This section also is a likely place to see moose.

Mile 14   The end of the paved road at the Savage River Bridge. This generally is as far as private vehicles can go. A park service checkpoint stops anyone who doesn't have a proper permit. A good picnic spot.

Mile 17   The Park Service discourages hiking here due to damage to the ground cover, but Primrose Ridge is an attractive spot for a walk. The portable toilets are as far as the Natural History Tour bus goes.

Mile 30   A large rest stop overlooking the Teklanika River has flush toilets, the last until the Eielson Visitor Center. The Teklanika, like many other rivers on Alaska's glacier-carved terrain, is a braided river—a relatively small stream wandering in a massive gravel stream bed. It's thought that the riverbed was created by water from fast-melting glaciers at the end of the last ice age.

Mile 33   Craggy Igloo Mountain is a likely place to see Dall sheep. Without binoculars, they'll just look like white dots. Heathery, open terrain suitable for an outing.

Mile 37.5   Tattler Creek, a good place for a steep day hike to see sheep and maybe bears.

Mile 38–43   Sable Pass, a critical habitat area for bears, is closed to people. A half-eaten sign helps explain why. Bears show up here mostly in the fall. This is the start of the road's broad alpine vistas.

Mile 46   The top of 5-mile-wide Polychrome Pass, the most scenic point on the ride. Caribou sometimes pass in a great valley framed by mountains of colored rock—the look the size of ants from the mountainside rest stop. Another toilet break.

Mile 53   The Toklat River, another braided river, is a flat plain of gravel with easy walking. The river bottom is habitat for bears, caribou, and wolves. A ranger leads a hike here of up to 2 hours, the Toklat Trek—check the visitor center for times.

Mile 58   Highway Pass, the highest point on the road. In good weather, dramatic views of Mount McKinley start here. The alpine tundra to the Eielson Visitor Center is inviting for walking.

Mile 64   Thorofare Pass, where the road becomes narrow and winding, is a good area to look for bear and caribou. Bus drivers know best where the animals are on any particular day; they exchange information among themselves.

Mile 66   The Eielson Visitor Center, the end of most bus trips, has flush toilets, a covered picnic area, and a small area of displays where rangers answer questions. Among the displays is one explaining why you probably can't see the mountain from this best of vantage points, just 33 miles from its summit. Mount McKinley creates its own weather and is visible about a third of the time in the summer. Starting late in June, a ranger-guided tundra walk occurs daily at 1:30pm, lasting no more than an hour. If you leave the bus here for a hike, you can get a ride back later by signing up on the standby list kept by a ranger.

Mile 68.5   The incredibly rugged terrain to the north is the earth and vegetation covering Muldrow Glacier. The road comes within a mile of its face, then continues through wet, rolling terrain past beaver ponds, and finally descends into a small spruce patch near Mile 82.

Mile 86   Wonder Lake campground, the closest road point to Mount McKinley, 27 miles away. Some buses continue another half hour to Kantishna.

5 Out in the Park

ACTIVITIES   The park service offers several guided hikes out in the park, beyond the 14-mile checkpoint. The daily **Discovery Hike** lasts 4 hours and goes somewhere different every day. You need to wear hiking shoes or boots and bring food, water, and rain gear. A special bus carrying the hikers leaves the visitor center at 8am, starting in mid-June. Reserve a place in advance. The **Toklat Trek** is an irregularly scheduled ranger-led walk in the Toklat River stream bed. The **Tundra Walk,** at 1:30pm daily starting in late June, is a short guided stroll from the Eielson Visitor Center, at Mile 66 on the park road. Check in at the visitor center for late word on all the hikes before heading out on a long bus trip. **Fishing** in the park is nothing special. There are grayling in some of the clear streams, but most of the water in the park is too thick with glacial silt to serve as fish habitat.

CAMPGROUNDS   The park has eight campgrounds. Recreational vehicles can find a place, as can tent campers who want to be away from people out in the wilderness. I've listed the fees and regulations for each campground in the table

First to the Top

On September 27, 1906, renowned world explorer Dr. Frederick Cook announced to the world by telegraph that he had reached the summit of Mount McKinley after a lightning-fast climb, covering 85 miles and 19,000 vertical feet in 13 days with one other man, a blacksmith, at his side. On his return to New York, Cook was lionized as a conquering explorer and published a book of his summit diary and photographs. Even today, the Frederick Cook Society meets regularly to memorialize and celebrate the deed.

They spend even more effort trying to convince the rest of the world that it wasn't just a huge hoax.

In 1909, Cook again made history, announcing that he had beat Robert Peary to the North Pole. Both returned to civilization from their competing treks at about the same time. Again Cook was the toast of the world. Then his Eskimo companions mentioned that he'd never been out of sight of land, and his story began to fall apart. After being paid by Peary to come forward, Cook's McKinley companion also recanted. (It turns out Peary probably also faked his pole discovery.) A year later, Cook's famous summit photograph was re-created on a peak 19 miles away and 15,000 feet lower than the real summit.

In 1910, four prospectors from Fairbanks took a more Alaskan approach to the task. Without fanfare, they marched up the mountain carrying a large wooden pole they could plant on top to prove they'd made it. But on arriving at the top, they realized that they'd climbed the slightly shorter north peak. Weather closed in, so they set up the pole there and descended. Then, when they got back to Fairbanks, no one could see the pole, and they were accused of trying to pull off another hoax. In 1913, Episcopal missionary Hudson Stuck was the first to reach the real summit—and reported he saw the pole on the other peak.

Since then, some 18,000 climbers have attempted McKinley, around 10,000 have made the summit, and more than five dozen climbers have died trying. Hundreds more try every year, flying to the Kahiltna Glacier from Talkeetna and then taking about a month to reach the top and get back down. Altitude and weather are the primary killers and deterrents to those who don't reach the summit.

No one has managed to re-create the feat Frederick Cook claimed to his death to have accomplished. But the 150 members of the Frederick Cook Society, based in New York, fight on to clear his name and establish Cook as the first to the Pole and the top of North America's tallest mountain. And they continue to gather evidence to discredit Peary, charging that Cook's difficulties were caused by a conspiracy of Peary supporters. As recently as 1994, the society funded an expedition to retrace part of Cook's route and validate his photographs and diaries.

Ninety years after Cook's telegram, the world isn't listening anymore.

(I am indebted to Dermot Cole's article on Cook in the April 1995 issue of *Alaska* magazine.)

"Denali Campground Facts" under "The Essential Details," earlier in this chapter. Here I aim to give you a feel for what each is like so you can choose which you'd prefer. For private campgrounds see "Accommodations," later in this chapter.

To get to campgrounds beyond Mile 14 on the park road, you have to take the $15 camper bus (unless you're staying 3 days or more at Teklanika). If it seems expensive, consider this: The ticket is a free pass to travel all over the park, which would cost as much as $11 more if bought for the shuttle.

Riley Creek   This is the traditional family campground in the woods right at the entrance to the park. With 100 sites, paved roads, flush toilets, and a sewage dump station, it's far from wilderness; but it is readily accessible, easy to get a permit, and young children won't care if it's not exactly the back country. For more ambitious campers, Riley Creek is a good stop for your first night in the park, when you need time to get your bearings before heading to a more remote area. The front-country shuttle bus stops in the parking lot, where there's a single pay phone. Riley Creek is a roaring tributary of the Nenana, running just below the campground; the best sites back onto the creek. Riley is the only campground open all year, although the water is off in the winter.

Morino Backpacker   Set aside for walk-in campers, Morino is especially attractive for backcountry travelers waiting for their permits. It is essentially just a wooded area about a mile from the visitor center where backpackers can put up their tents and use portable outhouses. Sites are designated by stakes and are self-registered. There is no parking area.

Savage River   Just a mile short of the park road checkpoint beyond which vehicles cannot go, Savage River is both easily accessible and relatively remote, 13 miles from the park entrance. It's the best choice for car or RV campers who want to get away from the park entrance but don't have 3 days to spend camping at Teklanika. There are 33 sites. The bathrooms have flush toilets. Savage Group is the nearby group camping area. The taiga (sparsely wooded tundra) is good for exploring, and there's a decent chance of seeing moose and possibly black bear.

Sanctuary River   This small, primitive campground with seven tent sites is 9 miles beyond the road checkpoint. There are chemical toilets. The campground is in the woods near a ranger station.

Teklanika River   At Mile 29 on the park road, this is the only campground for car or RV camping beyond the checkpoint. There is no RV dump station. You can drive in if you agree not to move your vehicle for at least 3 days. You'll also need a special $20 shuttle pass, good for the duration of your stay, which allows free exploration of the park. With 53 sites, it's a large campground, but the sites are adequately separated by trees. It has flush toilets.

Igloo Creek   The last campground for 52 miles, Igloo Creek is a primitive tent camp with seven sites near a ranger station. It's the closest campground to the open terrain of alpine tundra.

Wonder Lake   The 28 tent-camping sites at this campground near the end of the park road are in high demand, next to placid Wonder Lake and with spectacular views of Mount McKinley. Despite the remote location, it has flush toilets, and a ranger station is only 2 miles away. Winter stays late at this end of the park, and the campground doesn't open until sometime in June.

HIKING THE BACKCOUNTRY   Trekking the backcountry on a multiday backpacking journey is challenging and rugged, but also the most authentic way to see the park and understand its meaning. Only people with strong outdoor skills who are in good physical condition should attempt a strenuous backcountry overnight, however, as there are no trails or other people to guide you. For this reason, I haven't included a list of needed gear and supplies.

You must be flexible about where you're going and be prepared for any kind of terrain, because you can't choose the backcountry unit you will explore until arriving at the backcountry desk at the visitor center and finding out what's available. This information, and a map of the units, is posted on a board behind the desk. Groups of four or more may have a hard time finding a place to hike, but there's almost always *somewhere* to go. A couple of rangers are there to help you through the process. (For details on how to get a permit, see "Fees & Regulations" under "The Essential Details," earlier in this chapter.)

At the visitor center bookstore, buy the $8.99 **Denali National Park and Preserve topographical map,** published by Trails Illustrated, P.O. Box 4357, Evergreen, CO 80437-4357 (☎ **800/962-1643** or 303/670-3457; fax 303/670-3644; website http://www.colorado.com/trails). Printed on plastic, it includes the boundaries of the 43 backcountry units and much other valuable information. Also, you'll want to consult **Backcountry Companion,** by Jon Nierenberg, a book selling for $8.95 that describes each of the units. Published by the Alaska Natural History Association, 401 W. First Ave., Anchorage, AK 99501 (☎ **907/274-8440**), it's for sale at the visitor center, or you can look at a well-thumbed copy kept at the backcountry desk.

The alpine units are most popular. That's where you get broad views and can cross heathery valleys walking in any direction. But to go far, you'll also have to be ready to climb over some rugged, rocky terrain, and the tundra itself is deceptively difficult walking—it's soft and hides ankle-turning holes. The wooded units are least popular, since bushwhacking through overgrown land is anything but fun. The best routes for making time here and anywhere in the Alaska Bush are along the braided river valleys and stream beds. You need to be ready for a lot of stream crossings.

You can reserve permits only 1 day in advance, but you can reserve permits for continuation of your trip for up to 14 days at the same time. Units that aren't contiguous to the park road are more likely to be available, because you can't expect to make it that far on the first night of a hike. Because of the way the system is set up, the first night of a trip is the hard one to get; after that, each night gets progressively easier. You'll have to take the camper bus to get to your backcountry unit.

Before you decide to go to Denali, however, you may want to broaden your thinking—if you're up to a cross-country hike without a trail, there are tens of millions of acres in Alaska available for backpacking that don't require a permit. Check with the Alaska Public Lands Information Center in Anchorage or Fairbanks for ideas about road-accessible alpine wilderness in Gates of the Arctic National Park, on the Denali Highway; in Wrangell–St. Elias National Park; and elsewhere.

BIKING   A bicycle provides special freedom in the park. Bicyclists can ride past the checkpoint where cars have to turn back, at Mile 14 on the park road. Park campgrounds have bike stands, and you can take a bike on the shuttle or camper bus. The longest stretch on the park road between campgrounds is 52 miles. On the downside, the buses kick up a lot of dust, and bikes may not go off-road. Pick up a copy of the bicycle rules from the backcountry desk before you start. **Denali Mountain Bike,** P.O. Box 448, Denali National Park, AK 99755 (☎ **907/683-2453** summer, 907/457-2453 winter), rents bikes, including helmets and gear, for $25 a day. They also lead extended guided trips on the Denali and Elliott highways and are the only bike-repair shop in 130 miles (Fairbanks is the next closest).

6 Things to Do at the Park Entrance & Environs

RANGER PROGRAMS & ACTIVITIES   The park service offers lectures, guided hikes, and a sled-dog demonstration at the park entrance to keep you entertained and interpret the park while you wait for a bus or permit. Pick up a copy of the park newspaper, *Denali Alpenglow,* at the visitor center for current offerings and times.

✪ **Sled-Dog Demonstration**   In the winter, rangers patrol the park by sled dog, as they have for decades. In the summer, to keep the dogs active and amuse the tourists, they run a sled on wheels around the kennel, and a ranger gives a talk two to three times a day. Although there's no substitute for seeing dogs run on snow, this is as close as you'll get in the summer. It was the highlight of my 3-year-old's trip to Denali. A free bus leaves the visitor center for each show, at the kennels near the headquarters at Mile 3.4 on the park road. Or you can join a guided 2-mile hike at the visitor center, which heads up the Rock Creek Trail to arrive at the kennels for each sled-dog show.

Hotel & Visitor Center Programs   Rangers offer a talk and film at 1:30pm daily, and a lecture, possibly with slides, at 8pm, in the auditorium at the park hotel. There are ranger talks at the visitor center auditorium at 11am, 1:30pm, and 8pm.

Guided Hikes   Various ranger-guided nature walks take off around the park entrance every day, the longest of which is 3 miles. Check the *Alpenglow* or the visitor center for daily offerings.

CAMPGROUND PROGRAMS   The Riley Creek, Savage River, Teklanika, and Wonder Lake campgrounds have ranger programs almost nightly.

TRAILS   The park service is making a concerted effort to discourage the making of trails in the tundra or taiga of the park proper, but there are six easy, well-maintained trails around the park entrance area, the longest of which is the **Mount Healy Overlook,** a 5-mile round-trip. The others are strolls of 2 miles or less. A trail guide of sorts is printed in the *Denali Alpenglow* park newspaper, handed out by the park service; "The Nature of Denali," available at the visitor center, is a natural-history guide to the trails.

FLIGHTSEEING   Getting a good, close look at Mount McKinley itself is best accomplished by air. Frequently, when you can't see McKinley from the ground, you can see it from above the clouds. It's an impressive mountain, standing huge and white far above most of the surrounding terrain. The best flights take at least 90 minutes and circle McKinley. **Denali Air** (☎ 907/683-2261) has an office in the Nenana Canyon and flight operations at mile 229.5 of the Parks Highway. An hour-long flight going within a mile of the mountain costs $150. **Denali Wings** (☎ 907/683-2245), operating out of Healy, has similar rates, and is half price for kids 14 and under with an adult. **Era Helicopters** (☎ 800/843-1947 or 907/683-2574; e-mail fltsg@era-aviation.com) has hourly flights for $179, including van pickup from the hotels. The drawback of a helicopter is you can't get near wildlife because the aircraft is so noisy. They also offer guided hiking with a helicopter drop-off outside the park boundaries for $265. See the end of this chapter for flightseeing from Talkeetna.

✪ **RAFTING & BOATING**   Floating the swift, glacial water of the Nenana River Canyon as it passes the park entrance has become a major activity at the park because it's convenient and fun. The entire trip is outside the park. Several companies compete for your business, most offering a choice of slow, Class II water, suitable for children as young as age 5, or a white-water trip with numerous Class III and IV rapids, with minimum ages around 12. Each trip takes 2 to 2½ hours and costs around $50, or floating through both costs around $70 and takes twice as long. Most of the companies fit you out with rain gear for the white-water trips, but you get soaked to the skin anyway; afterward, you'll need a shower, as the glacial silt sticks to your skin and hair.

The **Denali Outdoor Center** (☎ 907/683-1925) supplies dry suits to whitewater passengers, so they remain warm and dry, and offer runs where clients help paddle. Their office is on the right across from the McKinley Chalet Hotel as you head north on the Parks Highway through the business area nearest the park. The cooperative of five guides also offers inflatable kayak schools and tours. **Denali Park Resorts** (☎ **800/276-7234**), the park concessionaire, also does a fine job (but no dry suits), and allows children as young as age 5 on the slow-water version of its raft trips with a half-off discount to kids 11 and under.

HORSEBACK RIDING   There is no riding in the park itself, but several opportunities in similar terrain outside its boundaries. **Beaver Lake Trail Rides**, P.O. Box 107, Denali National Park, AK, 99755 (☎ **800/893-6828** or 907/683-1699), offers rides in groups of up to six in the Healy Valley. Trips range from 1 hour for $60 to 4 hours for $125, leaving several times a day. **Wolf Point Ranch,** P.O. Box 127, Cantwell, AK 99729 (☎ and fax **907/768-2620**), offers 4- and 6-day pack trips for $910 or $1,350 per person, respectively.

7 Accommodations

Patterns of land ownership and the furious pace of development around Denali have led to a hodge-podge of roadside hotels, cabins, lodges, campgrounds, and restaurants in pockets arrayed along more than 20 miles of the Parks Highway. There are rooms of good quality in each of the pockets, but the going rates vary widely. The most expensive rooms, and the first booked, are in the immediate area of the park entrance. Next are the hotels south of the park. Both these areas are entirely seasonal. The best deals are in Healy, 10 miles north of the park, where you can find a room for $50 less than a comparable room near the park entrance. Of course, if you don't have a car, it's most convenient to stay in or near the park. The other choices are to stay in Talkeetna, the back door to the park, described below; at a lodge in the Kantishna inholding within the park; or at a remote wilderness lodge. I've listed each of the choices separately. Despite their high prices, rooms can be hard to find in the high season, and it's wise to book well ahead. If you don't mind gambling, however, you can often get great last-minute deals from hotels that have had large cancellations from their package tour clients.

The local **bed tax** is 7%.

NEAR THE PARK

This area, sometimes known as Denali or Nenana Canyon, extends about a mile north of the park entrance on the Parks Highway, including the park hotel, which is 1 ¹/₂ miles within the park. Two huge hotels that primarily serve package tour passengers dominate the area, the **Denali Princess Lodge,** Mile 238.5, Parks Hwy. (P.O. Box 110), Denali National Park, AK 997555 (☎ **800/426-0050;** fax 206/443-1979), and the **McKinley Resorts Chalets,** Mile 238.5, Parks Hwy. (mailing address: 241 W. Ship Creek Ave., Anchorage, AK 99501 (☎ **800/276-7234** or 907/276-7234; fax 907/258-3668). If they have a cancellation, you may be able to get attractive rooms at one of these places at the last minute for a fraction of their astronomical rack rates. The McKinley Resorts Chalets also is a good place to book activities.

Since most readers are independent travelers, I've concentrated instead on smaller lodgings that cater to individual bookings. In addition to those I've listed, you'll find good rooms at **Sourdough Cabins,** Mile 238.5 Parks Hwy. (P.O. Box 118), Denali, AK 99755 (☎ **907/683-2773**), which has comfortable little cabins in the woods below the highway in the $120–$130 range; and at **Denali River View Inn,** Mile 238.4 Parks Hwy. (P.O. Box 49), Denali National Park, AK 99755 (☎ **907/683-2663;** fax 907/683-7433), with 12 good standard rooms for $134 double. All of the hotels in this area are open only during the tourist season, roughly May 15 to September 15.

Denali Bluffs Hotel. Mile 238.4 Parks Hwy. (P.O. Box 72460, Fairbanks, AK 99707). ☎ **907/683-7000.** Fax 907/683-7500. 112 rms. TV TEL. High season, $179 double. Low season, $126 double. $10 each additional person. AE, DISC, JCB, MC, V.

A series of buildings, brand new in 1996, look down from the mountainside above the highway. Most of the light, tastefully decorated rooms have balconies, two double beds, coffeemakers, and small refrigerators, and those on the upper floor have vaulted ceilings. A courtesy van will take you anywhere in the area, and a coin-op laundry is available.

♻ **Denali Crow's Nest Cabins.** Mile 238.5, Parks Hwy. (P.O. Box 70), Denali National Park, AK 99755. ☎ **907/683-2723.** Fax 907/683-2323. 39 cabins. High season, $139 cabin for two. Low season, $89. Additional person in cabin $10 extra. MC, V.

Perched in five tiers on the side of a mountain above the Nenana Canyon area, looking down on Horseshoe Lake and the other (big) hotels, the cabins are large and comfortable, especially those on the 100 and 200 level. A log cabin and the warmth of the Crofoot family create more of an appropriate, Alaskan feeling than the modern, standard rooms that have filled the canyon. You spend a lot of time climbing stairs, however, and despite the great views and the price, the cabins are simple, not luxurious. They book tours and offer a courtesy van, free coffee, and an outdoor Jacuzzi. The restaurant, **The Overlook,** is recommended separately under "Dining," later in this chapter.

Denali National Park Hotel. Mile 1.5, Denali National Park Rd. (P.O. Box 87), Denali Park, AK 99755. (For reservations, contact Denali Park Resorts, 241 W. Ship Creek Ave., Anchorage, AK 99501; ☎ **800/276-7234.**) 100 rms. High season, $147 double. Low season, $109 double. Additional person in room $10 extra. AE, DISC, MC, V.

The only hotel within the park burned down in 1972; this "temporary" structure, cobbled together from old railroad cars and modular housing units, has served ever since, gaining an oddly historic feel of its own. The park hotel is a center of park activities, with hiking trails out the back door, and has more character than the other big hotels, but it needs remodeling, and the rooms have no views. There's a courtesy shuttle, coffee in the rooms, and a tour desk.

The attractive **dining room** serves large portions. The lounge, in a pair of railroad cars, has a good, campy feel. Smoking is permitted in only one of the two rail cars it occupies, a fair arrangement for both sides of that debate. For fast food, the snack bar is quite adequate and probably the best place for take-out in the area. The gift shop has reasonable prices, regulated by the park service.

Denali Windsong Lodge. Mile 238.6, Parks Highway (P.O. Box 31) Denali Park, AK 99755. ☎ **800/208-0200** or 907/683-1240. (Winter P.O. Box 2210011, Anchorage, AK 99522.) Website http://www.alaskalodges.com. 48 rms. TV. High season, $149 double. Low season, $99–$129 double. Additional person in room $10 extra. AE, DISC, MC, V.

Two-story, wooden buildings sit in a quiet area back in the trees behind the Princess Lodge near an appealing little campground. The proximity to the big lodge means a variety of restaurants are within easy walking distance. The good standard rooms, with exterior entries, have two double beds, satellite TV, coffeemakers, and views from the top of a bluff. A free shuttle is provided to the train station.

IN HEALY

Healy is 10 miles north of the park entrance, but a world away. It's a year-round community with an economy based primarily on a large coal mine and only secondarily on the park. There are a number of hotels and bed-and-breakfasts with rooms that cost from $20 to $90 less than those near the park. They say the water tastes better, too.

Besides my two favorites listed below, you'll find hundreds of small, serviceable rooms with twin beds at a converted pipeline camp, the **Denali North Star Inn,** Mile 248.5, Parks Hwy. (P.O. Box 240), Healy, AK 99743 (☎ **800/684-1560** or 907/ 683-1560; fax 907/683-4026), for $110 double. Across the highway, the **Stampede Lodge,** Mile 248.8, Parks Hwy. (P.O. Box 380), Healy, AK 99743 (☎ **907/ 683-2242;** fax 907/683-2243), has attractively decorated rooms, on the small side, in a renovated 1946 railroad building. They charge $90 double, in the summer. There's a reasonably priced restaurant inside serving three meals a day.

✪ **Motel Nord Haven.** Mile 249.5, Parks Hwy. (P.O. Box 458), Healy, AK 99743. ☎ **907/ 683-4500,** or 800/683-4501 in Alaska only. 24 rms. TV TEL. High season, $108–$117 double. Winter, $70 double. AE, MC, V.

This fresh, new little hotel has large, immaculate rooms with one or two queen-size beds. They're equal to the best standard rooms in the Denali Park area and a lot less expensive. Bill and Patsy Nordmark offer free newspapers, coffee, tea, and hot chocolate, and a sitting room with a collection of Alaskan books. The rooms have interior entrances, and some have kitchenettes. All have been nonsmoking since construction. Up to four people can stay in the rooms with two beds for the price of a double.

White Moose Lodge. Mile 248, Parks Hwy. (P.O. Box 68), Healy, AK 99743. ☎ **800/ 481-1232** or 907/683-1233. 9 rms. TV. $85 double. Rates include coffee, tea, and pastry breakfast. Additional adult in room $10 extra, additional child $5 extra. AE, DC, DISC, MC, V. Closed Oct to mid-May.

This old, low-slung building among stunted black spruce contains an unlikely find—comfortable, cheerfully decorated rooms with flower boxes, plus a hospitable host, former wildlife photographer and New Zealander Kirsty Knittel. It's a good value for a basic room.

SOUTH OF THE PARK

There are several groups of accommodations south of the park. I've listed just a few. You may also want to try **McKinley Creekside Cabins,** 13 miles south at Mile 224, Parks Hwy. (P.O. Box 89), Denali National Park, AK 99755 (☎ **907/683-2277;** fax 907/683-1558), which has cabins with private or shared baths starting at $99 double, including a hot breakfast.

Denali Cabins. Mile 229, Parks Hwy. (P.O. Box 229), Denali National Park, AK 99755. ☎ **907/ 683-2643.** Fax 907/683-2595. (In winter, 200 W. 34th Ave., Suite 362, Anchorage, AK 99503; ☎ **907/258-0134;** fax 907/243-2062.) 41 rms, 2 suites. High season, $124 cabin for two; $159 suite. Additional person in room $10 extra. Low season, $84 cabin for up to four people. MC, V. Closed mid-Sept to mid-May.

These roomy cedar cabins, arranged around a grassy compound with a pair of hot tubs, are a good choice for families. The kids may well find someone their own age to play with on the boardwalks or lawns. Also, with a cabin you don't have to worry as much about noise. There's a scheduled courtesy van and free coffee.

Denali River Cabins. Mile 231, Parks Hwy. (mailing address: P.O. Box 81250, Fairbanks, AK 99708). ☎ **800/230-7275** or 907/683-2500. Fax 907/456-5212. Website http:// www.denalirivercabins.com. High season, $140–$150 cabin for two. Low season, $95–$105 cabin for two. Additional person in room $10 extra. MC, V.

These cedar cabins along boardwalks above the Nenana River feel fresh and luxurious. The sauna has a picture window on the river, there's a Jacuzzi, free coffee and newspapers, a van to the train station, and bicycle rentals. They'll even throw a wine and cheese party with advance notice. But the cabins have shower stalls, not tubs, and for the rate you may be expecting something more. The 17 cabins on the river, with decks over the water, are $10 more.

✪ **The Perch.** Mile 224, Parks Hwy. (P.O. Box 53) Denali National Park, AK 99755. ☎ and fax **907/683-2523.** 11 cabins, 4 with bath. $65–$95 cabin for two. Additional person in cabin $10 extra. AE, MC, V. Closed Sept 15–May 16.

In the trees along rushing Carlo Creek, 13 miles south of the park entrance, a variety of cabins range from duplexes with large, modern rooms with private baths to adorable little A-frames with lofts that share a bath house. There's a sense of privacy and of being out in the woods along the wooden walkways. It's an exceptional value. Atop a steep hill, the **restaurant and bar,** one of my favorites in the area, provides reason for the name. It's a friendly, light place with solid meals of fish, beef, and bread ranging in price from $14 to $40. In summer they're open for three meals a day, in winter only on weekends.

PRIVATE CAMPGROUNDS

McKinley Kampground, Mile 248.5, Parks Highway (P.O. Box 340) Healy, AK 99743 (☎ **907/683-2379,** or 800/478-2562 in Alaska), is the best private campground in the Denali area. The campsites are surrounded by birch trees. There's a coin-op laundry and other facilities. Basic tent sites are $16.75 to $19.25, $27.50 for full hookups. **Denali Grizzly Bear Cabins and Campground,** Mile 231, Parks Highway (P.O. Box 7) Denali National Park, AK 99755-9998 (☎ **907/683-2696**), has some wooded campsites and some in a gravel lot, for $16. Cabins are for rent, too, starting at $21.50 for a small tent cabin. Cabins with their own bathrooms are $92.

WILDERNESS LODGES

For those who can afford it, there's no better way to be in the wilderness without giving up civilized comforts than to book a few days at a wilderness lodge. The first three establishments I've listed are in the Kantishna district, an area of park inholdings near McKinley, reached by bus or van 95 miles over the park road. Once there, you can explore the park using a special pass for shuttle rides starting in Kantishna, which costs $15.

✪ **Camp Denali / North Face Lodge.** Kantishna District (P.O. Box 67), Denali National Park, AK 99755. ☎ **907/683-2290** or 907/683-1568. 17 cabins, none with bath (Camp Denali); 15 rms with bath (North Face Lodge). $315 per person per night, double occupancy, all inclusive. Minimum stay 3 nights in cabins, 2 nights in rooms. No credit cards. Closed early Sept to early June.

Uniquely at this pioneering eco-tourism establishment, you can wake to the white monolith of Mount McKinley filling your window. Also uniquely, the naturalist guides here have the right to use the park road free of the shuttle system for hikes, biking, lake canoeing, bird watching, photography sessions, and other outdoor learning activities. During some sessions, nationally reputed academics and other experts lead the program. All arrivals and departures are on fixed session dates and start with a picnic on the park road on the way out. The lovely Camp Denali cabins each have their own outhouse and share a central bath house and wonderful shared lodge rooms—it would be my first choice for anyone who can stand not having their own flush toilet. North Face Lodge has traditional rooms with private baths. A conservation ethic pervades the operation, from the homegrown vegetables to the proprietors' efforts to preserve the natural values of private land in the park.

Denali Backcountry Lodge. Kantishna District (P.O. Box 189), Denali National Park, AK 99755. ☎ **800/841-0692** or 907/683-2594. Fax 907/783-1308. E-mail denalibl@alaska.net.

(In winter: P.O. Box 810, Girdwood, AK 99587; ☎ 907/783-1342.) 30 cabins. $285 per person per night, double occupancy, all inclusive. MC, V.

Thirty comfortable, modern cedar cabins sit in rows on a deck next to babbling Moose Creek and a two-story lodge building. Guests can sit in a screened porch away from the mosquitoes and watch the day go by, or join a choice of guided hikes, natural history programs, or other activities around the lodge each day. To go out into the park, you're on your own, either on a lodge mountain bike or the shuttle, although the ride in from the entrance is treated as a safari. Stay at least 2 nights. It's run by Alaska Wildland Adventures, which offers a variety of well-regarded ecotourism packages all over the state.

Kantishna Roadhouse. Kantishna District, Denali National Park (mailing address: P.O. Box 81670, Fairbanks, AK 99708). ☎ **800/942-7420** or 907/683-1475. Fax 907/683-1449. 28 rms. $550 double, all inclusive. AE, DISC, MC, V.

This well-kept property of many buildings along Moose Creek in the old Kantishna Mining District trades on both the mining history and outdoor opportunities of the area. Some rooms are large and luxurious, while others are in smaller single cabins with lofts. The log central lodge has an attractive lobby with people coming and going—it's got more of a hotel feel and might be more attractive to an older, less active set than the other lodges in the Kantishna District. Daily activities include guided hikes, wagon rides, biking, and gold panning, and there's an excellent sled-dog demonstration that coincides with a $99 day trip that comes out for the bus ride and lunch only.

Denali Wilderness Lodge. Wood River (mailing address: P.O. Box 50, Denali National Park, AK 99755). ☎ **800/541-9779** year round or 907/683-1287. Fax 907/479-4410. Website http://www.AlaskaOne.com/dwlodge. (In winter: P.O. Box 71784, Fairbanks, AK 99707; ☎ 907/479-4000.) 23 rms and cabins. $290 per person per night, double occupancy, all inclusive. AE, DISC, MC, V.

The extraordinary log buildings were built by the late big-game guide Lynn Castle along the Wood River, and his amazing collection of mounted exotic animals from all over the world is in a sort of museum room. They don't kill the animals anymore: Now they're more valuable to look at alive, and the lodge has become an eco-establishment, flying guests in for as little as a half day for flightseeing, horseback riding, hiking, and talks by naturalists and the like. But stay at least a couple of days to really experience the place. The 25-horse stable is the unique centerpiece, and this is the best place for riders. The cabins, while not luxurious, are quite comfortable and have private bathrooms. The food is terrific. The location is distant from Mount McKinley, in a remote valley 30 miles east of the park entrance.

8 Dining

The large hotels all have fine dining and casual restaurants. The restaurants at the **Denali Princess Lodge** have beautiful dining rooms with great views. The **Chalet Center Cafe** at the McKinley Resorts Chalets is one of my favorites for an inexpensive meal. It's a cafeteria serving good sandwiches and healthy dishes, in a large, light room. See **The Perch,** listed above under "Accommodations," for another good choice.

Lynx Creek Pizza. Mile 238.6, Parks Hwy. ☎ **907/683-2547.** All items $3.25–$22.95. AE, DISC, MC, V. Daily 11am–11:30pm. Closed late Sept to early May. PIZZERIA.

This ARA-managed pizza restaurant is a center of activity for the less-well-heeled visitors to Denali, as its only place to get a slice and a cheap beer. The food isn't anything special, and there often are lines to order, but the dining room is a low-key, relatively non-touristy place to meet young people.

◯ **The Overlook Bar and Grill.** Mile 238.5, Parks Hwy., up the hill above the Denali Canyon area. ☎ **907/683-2641.** Lunch main courses $9–$15; dinner $9–$25. MC, V. 11am–11pm. Closed mid-Sept to mid-May. BURGERS/STEAK/SEAFOOD.

This fun, noisy place has the feeling of a classic bar and grill. The dining room, with woodsy lodge decor, looks out on a spectacular view of the Nenana Canyon. The salmon and filet mignon were well seasoned and done to a turn, and the service was friendly and jocular. The lunch menu prices seemed a bit high. A huge variety of craft beers is available, with nine on tap. Full liquor license.

9 Denali in the Evening

The main evening event is the concessionaire's **Cabin Nite Dinner Theater,** at the McKinley Resorts Chalets (☎ 800/276-7234), a professionally produced musical revue about a gold rush–era woman who ran a roadhouse in Kantishna. You can buy the $35 tickets, half price under age 11, virtually anywhere in the area. The actors, singing throughout the evening, stay in character to serve big platters of food to diners sitting at long tables, doing a good job of building a rowdy, happy atmosphere for adults and kids. You go for the show, not the all-you-can-eat salmon and ribs—they try to make up for the quality with quantity. Princess Cruises and Tours puts on a similar evening show, **Mt. McK's Roadhouse Review,** in a big wall tent at the Denali Princess Lodge. The food is basically the same, too. Tickets are for sale at the hotel's tour desk (☎ 800/426-0500) for $35, or $14 for the show without the meal. The **Northern Lights Theater and Gift Shop,** across the Parks Highway from the McKinley Resorts Chalets (☎ 907/683-4000), shows the *Northern Lights Photosymphony,* a music-accompanied slide show on a 34-foot-wide screen. Admission is $6.50. It's also a good gift shop, with a mixture of the usual T-shirts and higher-quality gifts.

10 Talkeetna: Back Door to Denali

Talkeetna, a historic and funky little town with a sense of humor but not much happening, slept soundly from its decline around World War I until just a few years ago. Now there are paved streets (both of them), a new National Park Service building of stone, a new railroad depot, and a large new luxury hotel north of town. It seems that while Talkeetna slumbered in a time capsule, an explosion of visitors was happening at Denali National Park. Now, not entirely voluntarily, Talkeetna finds itself enveloped in that boom.

As a threshold to the park, Talkeetna has significant pros and cons that you must take into account. On the positive side, it's closer to Anchorage; the development is much more interesting and authentic than at the park entrance; there's lots to do in the outdoors and great views of the mountain, less frequently obscured by clouds. On the negative side, a big minus: You can't get into the park from here. That means you miss the dramatic scenery, easy backcountry access, and unique wildlife viewing of the park road.

The town itself dates from the gold rush, and there are many charming log and clapboard buildings. You can spend several hours looking at two small museums and meeting people in the 2-block main street, then go out on the Talkeetna or Susitna river for rafting, a jet boat ride, or fishing, or take a flightseeing trip to the national park.

GETTING THERE   By Car   Talkeetna lies on a 13-mile spur road that branches from the Parks Highway 99 miles north of Anchorage and 138 miles south of the park entrance.

By Train   The Alaska Railroad serves Talkeetna daily on its runs to Denali National Park during the summer, and weekly in the winter. See the listing earlier in this chapter.

By Van   The **Talkeetna Shuttle Service,** P.O. Box 468, Talkeetna, AK 99676 (☎ **907/733-2222** or 907/355-1725), runs back and forth to Anchorage, for $40 to $90 per person, depending on the size of your group.

VISITOR INFORMATION   The commercially operated **Denali/Talkeetna Visitor Center** is at the intersection of the Parks Highway and Talkeetna Spur Road (☎ **907/733-2688** summer, 907/733-2499 winter), open in summer, daily from 8am to 7:30pm; in winter, Monday through Friday from 9am to 4pm. A new $1.5 million **Talkeetna Ranger Station,** P.O. Box 588, Talkeetna, AK 99676 (☎ **907/ 733-2231**), primarily serves people who aim to climb Mount McKinley, but will answer other's questions, too.

ORIENTATION   This town of 600 doesn't take long to figure out. Just drive the spur road till you hit the historic area on Main Street, then explore on foot. Turn right across the railroad tracks as you get into town for the **Talkeetna State Airport,** campground, and boat launch, and some businesses.

GETTING AROUND   You can walk everywhere in Talkeetna, but there are good **mountain biking** routes, too. **CGS Bicycles,** on Main Street (P.O. Box 431), Talkeetna, AK 99676 (☎ **907/733-1279**), rents mountain bikes or $18 a day and leads trail tours starting at $20 per person.

FAST FACTS   A 2% **sales tax** applies. At this writing, there is **no bank** or **ATM,** the nearest being in Wasilla, an hour south on the Parks Highway. In **emergencies** dial **911.** The **Alaska State Troopers** (☎ **907/733-2256**), at mile 97.8 on the Parks Highway, are just south of the intersection with the spur road, next to the **Denali Medical Center,** (☎ **907/733-1833**), which has a 24-hour emergency room.

SPECIAL EVENTS   The **Talkeetna Moose Dropping Festival,** over a weekend in mid-July, is a community fair to raise money for the Talkeetna Historical Society (☎ **907/733-2487**). The main event doesn't involve dropping moose, as an aggrieved animal lover once complained, but dropping moose droppings.

IN TOWN

Talkeetna is famous for its laid-back atmosphere and outdoors, not for activities, but there are two small museums. The **Talkeetna Historical Society Museum,** on the Village Airstrip a half block south of Main Street (☎ **907/733-2487**), contains artifacts and displays on the local mining history, including photographs and biographies of individual characters. It's also a good place to get community information, open daily in summer, 10am to 6pm. The **Museum of Northern Adventure** is a wax museum of Alaska scenes and memorabilia, on the east end of Main Street (☎ **907/ 733-3999**). It's funny and corny, and great for children. Admission is $2.50 for adults, $1.50 for children.

GETTING OUTSIDE

The only way you'll get into the park from Talkeetna is by ✪ **flightseeing** with one of the glacier pilots who supports McKinley climbs, which typically begin with a flight from here to Kahiltna Glacier. **K2 Aviation,** a renowned McKinley expedition operator with a main office at Talkeetna State Airport (P.O. Box 545-B), Talkeetna, AK 99676 (☎ **800/764-2291** or 907/733-2291; website http://www.alaska.net/ ~flyk2), also has a booking office on the Parks Highway. They offer a flightseeing tour that circles the mountain and shows it off from every angle, and even lands on a glacier on the mountain itself (possible from November to mid-July). Depending on the length of the tour, prices range from $85 to $175 per person; add $40 to land on a glacier. **Doug Geeting Aviation,** at the state airport (P.O. Box 42), Talkeetna, AK 99676 (☎ **800/770-2366** or 907/733-2366; website http://www.alaska.net/ ~airtours/), is another well-regarded mountain flying operation, with a flight that lands on two different glaciers, and even an acrobatic flight in a two-seat biplane. Prices range from $65 to $250 per person.

Talkeetna is at the confluence of the wild Talkeetna and Susitna rivers. **Mahay's Riverboat Service,** P.O. Box 705, Talkeetna, AK 99676 (☎ **907/733-2223**), is a top guide, with 5-hour jet-boat charters for $115 per person, operating from a dock near the public boat launch on the Talkeetna River. Owner Steve Mahay is legendary, the only person ever to shoot Devil's Canyon in a jet boat. Besides **fishing**, Mahay offers **river tours** ranging from 20 minutes to 5 hours, concentrating on sightseeing and natural history; prices start at $19.95 per person. For a quieter look at the river, **Talkeetna River Guides,** on Main Street (P.O. Box 563), Talkeetna, AK 99676 (☎ **800/353-2677** or 907/733-2677; website http://www.alaska.net/~trg/ trg_dir/), offers a 2-hour wildlife **river rafting** tour on the Talkeetna three times a day for $39 adults, $15 children. They also offer guided fishing.

ACCOMMODATIONS & DINING

The beautiful new **Mt. McKinley Princess Lodge,** Mile 133.1, Parks Hwy., Denali State Park, AK 99755 (☎ **800/426-0500** or 907/733-2900; fax 907/733-2904), finished in 1997 by the Princess cruise line, capitalizes on a striking view of the mountain, only 42 miles away as the crow flies. The hotel isn't really near anything, 100 miles south of the park entrance and about 45 road miles from Talkeetna, but the operator puts on a full set of activities. Standard rooms are $175 a night in the high season. They're open mid-May to mid-September.

In Talkeetna itself, the choices are more modest but perfectly adequate. **Swiss-Alaska Inn,** near the boat launch (P.O. Box 565), Talkeetna, AK 99676 (☎ **907/ 733-2424**), is a friendly family business with good, reasonably priced meals, specializing in German dishes, and large, attractive rooms in the newer of its buildings, which rent for $100 a night. The **Talkeetna Motel,** at the west end of Main Street (P.O. Box 115) Talkeetna, AK 99676 (☎ **907/733-2323**), has clean, basic rooms for $80 double. There are other lodgings and several B&Bs available for booking through the visitor center. **Latitude 62,** on the right as you come into town (☎ **907/ 733-2262**), serves good food in a roadhouse vein. A couple of fun little places on Main Street serve lunch.

10 The Alaskan Interior

A warm summer evening in a campground; a slight breeze rustling the leaves of ghostly paper birches, barely keeping the mosquitoes at bay; the sounds of children playing; a perpetual sunset rolling slowly along the northern horizon—this is Interior Alaska. You know it's time to gather up the kids, separate them according to who belongs to whom, and put them to bed; it's 11 o'clock, for heaven's sake. But it's too difficult to feel that matters, or to alter the pace of a sun-baked day that never ends, meandering on like the broad, silty rivers and empty two-lane highways. Down by the boat landing, some college kids are getting ready to start on a float in the morning. An old, white-bearded prospector wanders out of the bar and, offering his flask to the strangers, tries out a joke while swatting the bugs. "There's not a single mosquito in Alaska," he declares. Waits out for the loud, jocular objections. Then adds, "They're all married with big, big families." Easy laughter; then they talk about outboard motors, road work, why so many rabbits live along a certain stretch of highway. Eventually, you have to go to bed, leave the world to its pointless turning as the sun rotates back around to the east. You know it'll all be there tomorrow, just the same—the same slow-flowing rivers, the same long highways, the same vast space that can never be filled.

Interior Alaska is so large—it basically includes everything that's not on the coasts or in the Arctic—you can spend a week of hard driving and not explore it all. Or you could spend all summer floating the rivers and still have years of floating left to do before you'd seen all the riverbanks. It's something like what one imagines the great mass of America's Midwest once was, perhaps a century and a half ago, when the great flatlands had been explored but not completely civilized and Huckleberry Finn could float downriver into a wilderness of adventures. As it happens, I have a friend who grew up on a homestead in the Interior and ran away from home at age 15 in that exact same fashion, floating hundreds of miles on a handmade raft, past the little river villages, cargo barges, and fishermen. During an Interior summer, nature combines its immensity with a rare sense of gentleness, patiently awaiting the next thunderstorm.

Winter is another matter. Without the regulating influence of the ocean—the same reason summers are hot—winter temperatures can often drop to –30°F or –40°F, and during exceptional cold snaps, much lower. Now the earth is wobbling over in the other direction, away from the sun. The long, black nights sometimes make Fairbanks, the region's dominant city, feel more like an outpost on a barren planet, far off in outer space. That's when the northern lights come, spewing swirls of color across the entire dome of the sky and crackling with electricity. Neighbors get on the phone to wake each other and, rising from bed to put on their warmest parkas and insulated boots, stand in the street, gazing straight up. Visitors lucky enough to come at such times may be watching from a steaming hot-spring tub. During the short days, they can bundle up and watch sled-dog racing or race across the wilderness themselves on snowmobiles.

Besides Fairbanks, the Alaska Interior is without any settlements large enough to be called cities. Instead, it's defined by roads, both paved and gravel, which are strands of civilization through sparsely settled, swampy land. Before the roads, development occurred only on the rivers, which still serve as thoroughfares for the Athabascan villages of the region. In the summer, villagers travel by boat. In the winter, the frozen rivers become highways for snowmobiles and sled-dog teams. White homesteaders and gold miners live back in the woods, too, but except in alpine terrain much of the land is impossible to hike when not frozen. Fairbanks itself is an entertaining, modern city worthy of visiting for several days, but it still maintains the Interior spirit.

1 Exploring the Interior

More than anywhere else in Alaska, having your own car in the Interior provides the freedom to find the out-of-the-way places that give the region its character. Bus service connects Fairbanks with the Alaska Highway, including the ferry terminus at Haines or Skagway, and trains run between Fairbanks and Anchorage. But that will show you only the larger, tourist-oriented destinations. If you have the time and money, you may enjoy driving one of the remote gravel highways, or just poking along on the paved highways between the larger towns, ready to stop and investigate the roadhouses and meet the people who live out in the middle of nowhere. You'll find them friendly and, often, downright odd—"colorful," to use the polite term. I saw my all-time favorite roadside sign driving the Alaska Highway, years ago. Spray-painted on plywood, it said: SALE—EEL SKINS—ANVILS—BAIT. I've always wished I'd stopped in to window-shop and meet the man or woman who came up with that business plan.

The down-side of driving your own car is that you have to cover a lot of ground, with much dull driving through brushy forest with no horizon visible. Furthermore, the paved sections often have frost heaves—back-breaking dips and bumps caused by cycles of freeze and thaw—and the gravel roads are dusty and tiring and threaten your windshield or headlights with flying rocks. Also, bringing a private car from the Lower 48 adds a week to each end of your trip.

A good alternative is to fly or take the train to Fairbanks, then rent a car for an exploration. Renting a car one-way is a good way to go, too, if you can stand the drop-off fee. One itinerary that makes sense is to rent a car in Fairbanks, explore eastward to Dawson City, drop the car in Skagway or Haines, and then board the ferry south before flying out from Juneau, Sitka, or Ketchikan; I'd allow a good 10 days for such a plan, and expect a drop-off fee of around $300. An especially fun way to go is in an RV. They're everywhere on these highways, so services are well developed. See the "Fairbanks" section for rental details.

Vernon Publications' *The Milepost,* a highway guide to Alaska and northwestern Canada, has long been considered the indispensable handbook for Alaska drivers. It has mile-by-mile descriptions of all the major roads and is available for sale everywhere along the Alaska Highway. Most of the book, however, is taken up by advertisements which are included in the text as listings, so don't expect objective descriptions.

INTERIOR'S MAJOR HIGHWAYS

At the **Alaska Public Lands Information Center** in Tok, the first major visitor center on the U.S. side of the border on the Alaska Highway, the first question most visitors ask is: "Do you have a road map?" Then: "No, I mean a map that shows *all* the roads." The answer: "That's all the roads there are—welcome to Alaska." Paved two-lane highways make a triangle, connecting Tok, Fairbanks, and Anchorage, with links to the Kenai Peninsula and Valdez. Otherwise, there are a few gravel highways reaching out a little way into the Bush, and that's it.

The few roads Alaska does have are long and scenic. They have route numbers, but everyone knows them by names. Elsewhere in this chapter and in the chapters on Southcentral and Denali National Park, you'll find local details on all the roads. To help you decide your route, I've written descriptions for the major and scenic Interior highways here.

ALASKA HIGHWAY (Route 2 from the border to Delta Junction): Running nearly 1,400 miles from Dawson Creek, British Columbia, to Delta Junction, Alaska, a couple of hours east of Fairbanks on the Richardson Highway, this World War II road is paved, but that doesn't mean it's always smooth. Like other northern highways, it's subject to bone-jarring frost heaves and spring potholes. The prettiest part is on the Canadian side, in the Kluane Lake area.

PARKS HIGHWAY (Route 3): The George Parks Highway, opened in 1972, is a straight line from Anchorage to Fairbanks, 358 miles north, providing access to Denali National Park. There are some vistas of Mount McKinley from south of the park, and beautiful treeless terrain just south and north of the park, but the Parks Highway is mostly just a transportation route, less scenic than the Richardson or Glenn highways.

GLENN HIGHWAY (Route 1 from Anchorage to Tok): This is the road you'd take if you were coming from the Alaska Highway on your way to Southcentral Alaska, including Prince William Sound, Anchorage, and the Kenai Peninsula. It connects Tok to Anchorage, 330 miles southwest. (The section between Glennallen and Tok is sometimes called the "Tok Cut-Off.") The northern section, from Tok to Glennallen, borders Wrangell–St. Elias National Park, with broad tundra and taiga broken by high, craggy peaks. Glennallen to Anchorage is even more spectacular, as the road passes through high alpine terrain and then close by the Matanuska Glacier and along a deep valley carved by the glacier's river.

✪ RICHARDSON HIGHWAY (Route 4 from Valdez to Delta Junction, Route 2 from Delta Junction to Fairbanks): The state's first highway, leading 364 miles from tidewater in Valdez to Fairbanks, has lost much of its traffic to the Parks Highway, which saves over 90 miles between Anchorage and Fairbanks, and the Glenn Highway, which saves about 120 miles from Glennallen to Tok. But it's still the most beautiful paved drive in the Interior. From the south, the road begins with the heart-stopping drive through steep Thompson Pass, just out of Valdez, then passes the huge, distant peaks of southern Wrangell–St. Elias National Park. North of Glennallen, the road climbs into the Alaska Range for a series of broad vistas comparable to Denali National Park, but with the addition that the road snakes along the shores of a series of long, alpine lakes. Finally, it descends again to the forested area around Delta Junction and meets the Alaska Highway before arriving in Fairbanks.

✪ DENALI HIGHWAY (Route 8): I simply couldn't believe my eyes when I first drove this 133-mile gravel road. It connects the midpoints of the Parks and

Richardson highways, crossing stunningly grand alpine vistas, and provides access to a rich network of trails and mountain lakes and a good chance to see caribou, bear, moose, and waterfowl. It's popular with mountain bikers, canoers, trout fishermen, and hunters. There are three **Bureau of Land Management** campgrounds, and you can camp anywhere you want outside a campground. Pick up the road guide and Tangle Lakes National Register District guide from an Alaska Public Lands Information Center in Fairbanks, Anchorage, or Tok, or directly from the **Bureau of Land Management Glennallen District Office,** P.O. Box 147, Glennallen, AK 99588 (☎ **907/822-3217**).

THE YUKON RIVER: You can't drive it, but that doesn't mean the Yukon isn't a highway. It's by far the broadest, smoothest, and longest in the state. The Yukon is navigable over most of its 2,300 miles, including all 1,900 miles in Alaska. It starts in British Columbia, leads through Yukon Territory, then crosses the Interior to its mouth, across Norton Sound from Nome. Tugs, barges, skiffs, canoes, and rafts traverse the river in the summer, snowmobiles and dog sleds in the winter. You can reach the river on the Dalton Highway 140 miles north of Fairbanks, on the Steese Highway in Circle, on the Taylor Highway in Eagle, or on the Top of the World Highway in Dawson City, Yukon Territory, and float between any of those towns—108 miles from Dawson City to Eagle, 158 miles from Eagle to Circle, and 300 miles from Circle to the Dalton Highway. Large-scale river tours run from Dawson City to Eagle, and smaller operations on the Dalton out of Fairbanks and in Circle.

2 Outside in the Alaskan Interior

The Interior is so vast, there are plenty of ways to get away from other people and see wildlife—primarily caribou, moose, bears, wolves, foxes, and a wide variety of birds.

RIVER FLOATING   Floating any of the thousands of miles of the Interior's rivers opens great swaths of wilderness. Beginners will want to take a guided trip before venturing on their own. (See the lists of operators in chapter 3 or 6.) For Yukon River day trips, see the sections on Dawson City or the Dalton Highway. To plan your own trip, get Karen Jettmar's *The Alaska River Guide,* published by Alaska Northwest Books, P.O. Box 10306, Portland, OR 97210 (☎ **800/452-3032**), which includes details for floats on 78 rivers across the state. Also, check with the **Alaska Public Lands Information Center** in Fairbanks, Tok, or Anchorage for guidance on setting up your trip. Among the most accessible and historic rivers in the region are the Yukon, Fortymile, Chena, and Chatanika (see the sections on Dawson City, Eagle, Chena Hot Springs Road, and the Steese Highway, respectively).

HIKING   There are fewer trails here than in Southcentral Alaska, but you'll find good trail hikes off the Steese Highway or Chena Hot Springs Road. If you don't need a trail, the Brooks Range beckons off the Dalton Highway. Again, the **Alaska Public Lands Information Center** can provide essential guidance before you head out. The virtues of Interior hiking are the remoteness, the animals you'll see, and the low treeline, which provides millions of acres of upland tundra. On the down-side, much of the region is miserable swamp, and the mosquitoes are voracious.

MOUNTAIN BIKING   Many hiking trails also are open to mountain bikes. In addition, the Denali Highway, described above, is a popular road route. See "Small & Specialty Tours" in chapter 3, and the Denali National Park sections for businesses leading guided rides.

3 Fairbanks: Alaska Heartland

If the story of Fairbanks's founding had happened anywhere else, no one would admit it, for the city's father was a swindler, and its undignified birth contained an element of chance not usually admitted in polite society. As the popular story goes (and the historians' version is fairly close), it seems that in 1901, E. T. Barnette had it in mind to get rich by starting a gold-mining boom town like the others that had sprouted from Dawson City to Nome as the stampeders of '98 sloshed back and forth across the territory from one gold find to the next. He booked passage on a riverboat going up the Tanana with his supplies to build the town, having made an understanding with the captain that, should the vessel get stuck, he would lighten the load by getting off with the materials on the nearest bank. Unfortunately, the captain got lost. Thinking he was heading up a slough on the Tanana, he got sidetracked into the relatively small Chena River. That was where the boat got stuck and where Barnette got left, and that was where he founded Fairbanks.

An Italian prospector named Felix Pedro found gold on the Tanana, and Barnette dispatched his cook off to Dawson City to spread the word. The cook's story showed up in a newspaper that winter, and a stampede of hundreds of miners ensued, heading toward Fairbanks in weather as cold as 50° below zero. Barnette's town was a success, but the cook nearly got lynched when the stampeders found out how far he'd exaggerated the truth. Then much more gold was found, and half the population of Dawson City came down the Yukon to Fairbanks. Barnette had made it big. He cemented the town's future with a little political favor to the powerful Judge James Wickersham—he named the settlement for Wickersham's ally in Congress, Sen. Charles Fairbanks of Indiana, who later became vice president. In return, Wickersham moved the federal courthouse to Fairbanks from Eagle, establishing it as the hub of the region. Barnette didn't get to enjoy his laurels, however, as he was run out of town for bank fraud.

Fairbanks is Alaska's second-largest city now, with a population of about 38,000, but it has never learned to put on airs. It sprawls, broad and flat, along big highways and the Chena, a friendly, easy-going town, but one where people still take gold and their independence seriously. There's another gold rush going on, north of the city, and plenty of prospectors are still searching the hills. There are strange political movements, such as the secessionist Alaskan Independence Party. Fairbanks is an adamant, loopy, affable place; it doesn't seem to mind being a little bizarre or residing far from the center of things. And that makes it an intensely Alaskan city, for those are the qualities Alaskans most cherish in their myth of themselves.

As a visitor, Fairbanks could strike you a couple of ways, depending on what you expect and what you like. Fairbanks could come across as a provincial outpost, a touristy cross between Kansas and Siberia, and you could wonder why you went out of your way. Or you could relax and take Fairbanks on its own terms, a fun, unpretentious town, full of activities and surprises, that never lost its sense of being on the frontier. There's plenty to do in Fairbanks, much of it at least a little corny. It's a terrific destination for families—my son would still be there if it were up to him. And there are good opportunities for hiking and mountain biking, and great opportunities for canoeing and slow river float trips.

ESSENTIALS

GETTING THERE   By Car or RV   Fairbanks is a transportation hub. The Richardson Highway heads east 98 miles to Delta Junction, the end-point of the Alaska Highway, then south to Glennallen and Valdez. The Parks Highway heads

Greater Fairbanks

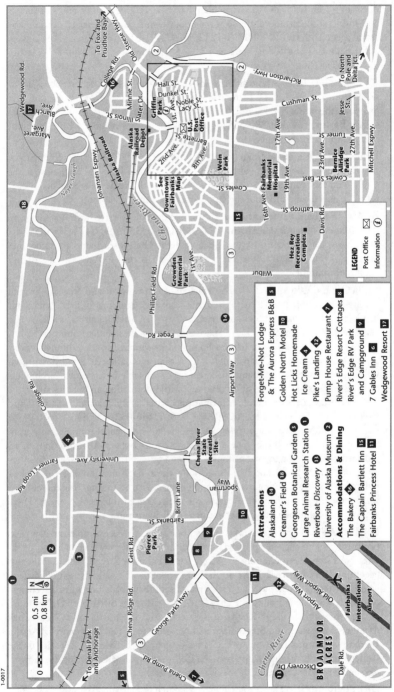

Attractions
- Alaskaland 14
- Creamer's Field 18
- Georgeson Botanical Garden 3
- Large Animal Research Station 1
- Riverboat Discovery 13
- University of Alaska Museum 2

Accommodations & Dining
- The Bakery 16
- The Captain Bartlett Inn 15
- Fairbanks Princess Hotel 11
- Forget-Me-Not Lodge & The Aurora Express B&B 5
- Golden North Motel 10
- Hot Licks Homemade Ice Cream 4
- Pike's Landing 12
- Pump House Restaurant 7
- River's Edge Resort Cottages 8
- River's Edge RV Park and Campground 9
- 7 Gables Inn 6
- Wedgewood Resort 17

LEGEND
- ⊠ Post Office
- ⓘ Information

0   0.5 mi
0   0.8 km

N

1-0017

345

due south from Fairbanks to Denali National Park, 120 miles away, and Anchorage, 358 miles south. Exploring the region on your own requires a car. There are many rental agencies. **Avis** (☎ 800/331-1212 or 907/471-3101) is located at the airport; **Affordable Car and RV Rentals** is at 3101 S. Cushman St. (☎ **800/471-3101** or 907/452-7341).

By Bus   Gray Line's **Alaskon Express** (☎ **907/456-7741**) offers service 3 days a week from the Westmark Fairbanks down the Alaska Highway to Haines and Skagway (the fare is $180 and $205, respectively), with stops along the way. **Alaska Direct Busline** (☎ **800/780-6652**) goes direct to Anchorage on the Parks Highway 3 days a week, for $65 one-way.

By Rail   The **Alaska Railroad** (☎ **800/544-0552** or 907/456-4155; website http://www.alaska.net/~akrr/) links Fairbanks to Denali National Park and Anchorage to the south, with tour commentary. The fare is $53 to Denali and $149 to Anchorage, one-way. A detailed description of the services available are in chapter 9.

By Air   **Fairbanks International Airport** has direct jet service from Anchorage on four airlines, with **Alaska Airlines** (☎ **800/426-0333** or 907/474-9175; website http://www.alaskaair.com) having the most flights. Round-trip fares are sometimes as low as $100. The airport is a hub with various carriers to Alaska's Interior and Arctic communities.

VISITOR INFORMATION   The **Fairbanks Convention and Visitors Bureau** maintains a comprehensive visitor center in a large log building on the Chena River by Golden Heart Plaza, at 550 First Ave. (at Cushman Street), Fairbanks, AK 99701 (☎ **800/327-5774** or 907/456-5774; website http://www.polarnet.com/users/fcvb/), open in summer, daily from 8am to 8pm, and in winter, Monday through Friday from 8am to 5pm. Get maps, including a road map and the good downtown walking-tour map. It also maintains a registry of available hotel rooms and binders covering dozens of local bed-and-breakfasts, with information and photographs.

The ✪ **Alaska Public Lands Information Center,** at 250 Cushman St. (at Third Avenue), Suite 1A, Fairbanks, AK 99701 (☎ **907/456-0527;** TDD 907/456-0532; fax 907/456-0514; website http://www.nps.gov/aplic), open in summer daily from 9am to 6pm, and in winter Tuesday through Saturday from 10am to 6pm, is an indispensable stop for anyone planning to spend time in the outdoors, and an interesting one even if you're not. Besides providing detailed information on all of Alaska's public lands and answering questions and giving advice on outings, the center has a small museum about the state's regions and the gear needed to explore them. There are daily films and naturalist programs in a small auditorium.

ORIENTATION   The old downtown section of Fairbanks is simple and compact, comprising a grid aligned along the slow, muddy **Chena River.** The main thoroughfares are **First Avenue,** along the river, and **Cushman Street,** which crosses it, becoming **Illinois Street** to the north. But development largely has left downtown behind, with businesses moving out to major suburban roads that form a rectangle of strip development around the city—the east-west strips of **Airport Drive,** south of the river, and **College Road,** to the north, and the north-south **University Avenue,** to the west, and **Steese Expressway,** to the east. The **University of Alaska Fairbanks campus** lies west of Fairbanks proper, on **University Avenue,** in the **College** area, but the distinction between College and Fairbanks has lost meaning as development now continuously melds the two areas.

GETTING AROUND   It's possible to see much of Fairbanks without a car, staying in the downtown area and making excursions by bus, but the city is designed around the car, and that's the easiest way to get around. Rental agencies are listed above. Good road maps are available free at the visitor center. A cab downtown from the airport is about $12 with **Yellow Cab** (☎ **907/455-5555**). The city is too spread out to use taxis much.

To see the widely scattered attractions without a car, try the popular **G.O. Shuttle Service** (☎ **800/478-3847** or 907/474-3847; website http://www.akpub.com/akttt/goshu.html), a unique bus, van, and car system geared to independent travelers. Besides guided tours of various attractions, which cost $25, the company offers on-call shuttle service to the airport, train depot, and major attractions for flat fares of $5 or $15, round-trip, depending on the distance. The lowest-cost option is the Fairbanks North Star Borough's three-route **MACS bus system,** linking the University, downtown, North Pole, and shopping areas, and some hotels. The fare is $1.50, or an all-day pass is $3. Service is every 30 minutes, at best, and virtually nonexistent on weekends. Pick up timetables at the visitor center. All buses connect at the transit park downtown, at Fifth Avenue and Cushman Street. **Bicycles** are for rent from **Great Land Sports,** at 261 College Road (☎ **907/479-8438**). They'll bring the bike to you.

FAST FACTS   There is no sales tax. Fairbanks has numerous banks with **ATMs** in the downtown area and along the commercial strips; you can also find ATMs in many grocery stores. In **emergencies,** dial **911.** For nonemergency police business, call the **Alaska State Troopers** (☎ **907/452-2114**) or the **Fairbanks Police Department** (☎ **907/459-6500**). **Fairbanks Memorial Hospital** is at 1650 Cowles St. (☎ **907/452-8181**). You can phone for a **recorded weather forecast** (☎ **907/452-3553**). The *Fairbanks Daily News-Miner* is published daily and contains arts and community-activity listings. The *Anchorage Daily News* and *USA Today* are widely available in machines, and you can find other out-of-town papers at grocery and book stores all over town. For **business services,** a Kinkos Copy Center is at 418 Third Ave. (☎ **907/456-7348**).

SPECIAL EVENTS   A recording of current local happenings can be reached at ☎ **907/456-INFO.** In early February, the **Yukon Quest International Sled Dog Race** (☎ **907/452-7954**) starts or finishes in Fairbanks (Fairbanks has the start in even-numbered years; Whitehorse, Yukon Territory, in odd-numbered years). The challenge of the 1,000-mile race is equal to the Iditarod. In late February, in Nenana, the **Nenana Ice Classic** (☎ **907/832-5446**) starts with a weekend celebration; the classic is a sweepstakes on who can guess closest to the exact date and time the ice will go out on the Tanana River (see "A Stop in Nenana," below). In the middle of March, a spectacular ✪ **Ice Art Competition** (☎ **907/452-8250**) brings carvers from all over the world to sculpt immense clear chunks cut from Fairbanks lakes. In late March, the **North American Sled Dog Championships** (☎ **907/479-8166**), a sprint with two 20-mile heats and one 30-mile heat, begins and ends downtown. **June 20 or 21,** around the summer solstice, the local **semipro baseball** team, the Fairbanks Goldpanners (☎ **907/451-0095**), plays a game under the midnight sun without lights, beginning at 10:30pm. **Golden Days,** over 2 weeks in mid-July, includes crafts fairs and a parade (☎ **907/456-8848**). The ✪ **Fairbanks Summer Arts Festival,** on the University of Alaska Fairbanks campus (P.O. Box 80845), Fairbanks, AK 99708 (☎ **907/474-8869**), is July 24 to August 9, 1998; besides offerings for the public in music, dance, theater, opera, ice skating, and the visual arts, there are opportunities for instruction for all levels, without the requirement for audition tapes. The **Tanana Valley Fair** (☎ **907/452-3750**), in early August, shows off the area's agricultural production, arts and crafts, and entertainment, and includes a carnival and rodeo. In early November, the **Athabascan Fiddling Festival** (☎ 907/ 452-1825) draws together musicians and dancers from the Interior region for performances and workshops. The **Top of the World Classic,** late in November, brings NCAA Division I basketball teams to the University for a weekend tournament (☎ **907/474-6830**).

EXPLORING FAIRBANKS

DOWNTOWN   If you want to explore the few sites downtown, pick up the walking-tour map available at the visitor center. Among the highlights is the **Golden Heart Park,** a waterfront plaza with a fountain and a bronze of a Native family, where community events often occur. The town's most interesting building is the Roman Catholic **Church of the Immaculate Conception,** across the river on Cushman Street. The white clapboard structure, built in 1904, has ornate gold-rush decoration inside, rare for its authenticity, including a pressed-tin ceiling and stained-glass windows—an appealing if incongruous mix of gold-rush and sacred decor. At First Avenue near Kellum Street, east from the visitor center, **St. Mathew's Episcopal Church** is a cute old log church with a working rope-pull bell. It was founded by missionary and explorer Hudson Stuck in 1904. The original church burned; the present structure dates from 1948. At Second Avenue and Lacey Street, the **Fairbanks Ice Museum** aims to show summer visitors what winter is like. A stunning high-tech slide show explains the annual Ice Art Festival, and a large, windowed freezer contains ice carvings. Admission is $6, open 10am to 9pm daily in summer. At 410 Cushman Street, the former city hall is becoming **The Fairbanks Community Museum** (☎ 907/452-8671), a volunteer operation showing old newspapers, memorabilia, and other items that no doubt have been installed since this writing. Hours are Wednesday through Saturday noon to 4pm, but are not always observed.

✪ ALASKALAND, AIRPORT WAY & PEGER ROAD   Built for the Alaska purchase centennial in 1967, Alaskaland is the boiled-down essence of Fairbanks. It's called a theme park, but don't expect Disneyland or anything like it. Instead, Alaskaland is a city park with a theme. It's relaxing and low-key, entrancing for young children and interesting for adults—you have to give in to the charm of the place. Admission to the park is free, and the tours and activities are generally inexpensive. It's open Memorial Day to Labor Day, daily from 11am to 9pm. Depending on the pace you like to keep and the age level of your group, you could spend a couple of hours to a whole day.

The SS *Nenana* is the park's centerpiece. Commissioned by the federally owned Alaska Railroad in 1933, it was the largest sternwheeler built west of the Mississippi, plying the Yukon and Tanana rivers until 1957. In 1967 the *Nenana* came to Alaskaland, but was unmaintained and had nearly collapsed from rot by 1982. It was about to be burned when a major community restoration effort began to save the ship. Today the *Nenana* is fully restored, and you can walk through for $2. On the bottom deck are detailed historical dioramas of each riverside town the *Nenana* served.

Most of Fairbanks's history has been moved to Alaskaland. A village of log cabins contains shops and restaurants, each marked with its original location and place in Fairbanks's history. **Judge Wickersham's house** is kept as a museum, decorated appropriate to the period of the town's founding. President Warren Harding's rail car, from which he stepped to drive the golden spike on the Alaska Railroad, sits near the park entrance. An exceptional **Pioneer Air Museum** is housed in a geodesic dome toward the back of the park. Besides the aircraft, there are displays and artifacts of the crashes of Will Rogers and Wiley Post and of Carl "Ben" Eielson, a key figure

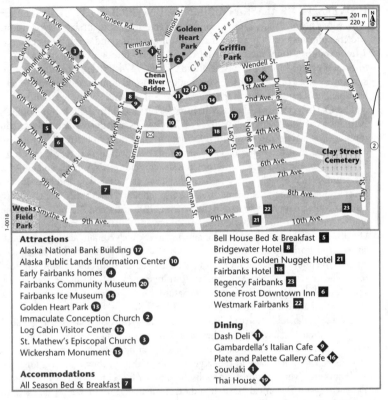

Attractions
Alaska National Bank Building **17**
Alaska Public Lands Information Center **10**
Early Fairbanks homes **4**
Fairbanks Community Museum **20**
Fairbanks Ice Museum **14**
Golden Heart Park **13**
Immaculate Conception Church **2**
Log Cabin Visitor Center **12**
St. Mathew's Episcopal Church **3**
Wickersham Monument **15**

Accommodations
All Season Bed & Breakfast **7**

Bell House Bed & Breakfast **5**
Bridgewater Hotel **8**
Fairbanks Golden Nugget Hotel **21**
Fairbanks Hotel **18**
Regency Fairbanks **23**
Stone Frost Downtown Inn **6**
Westmark Fairbanks **22**

Dining
Dash Deli **11**
Gambardella's Italian Cafe **9**
Plate and Palette Gallery Cafe **16**
Souvlaki **1**
Thai House **19**

in Alaska aviation, after whom a major air force base near Fairbanks is named. A large, round building that looks like a birthday cake standing at the center of the park is a **civic center,** where summer theater is often in session, and **art shows** are mounted in the first floor and third floor. The **Pioneer Museum** contains early Fairbanks relics; a 45-minute narrated show of paintings tells the story of the gold rush six times daily; admission is $2 for adults, 50¢ for children 10 and over, and free for children 9 and under.

If you have children, you certainly won't escape Alaskaland without a ride on the **little train** that circles the park twice, with a tour guide pointing out the sights; rides cost $2 for adults, $1 for children, free under age 4. Kids also will enjoy the large **playground,** with equipment for toddlers and older children, where lots of local families come to play, and the miniature golf course. The only carnival ride is a nice old **merry-go-round.** There's a boat landing and a mining display with a mechanical waterfall.

Tour groups generally come to Alaskaland in the evening for the **Alaska Salmon Bake,** at the mining display (☎ **907/452-7274**), and the **Golden Heart Revue,** at the Palace Theater (☎ **907/456-5960;** e-mail intrasea@polarnet.com), open mid-May to mid-September. The salmon bake brings guests from the hotels and campgrounds in courtesy buses 5 to 9pm daily. The all-you-can-eat halibut, ribs, or brown-sugar salmon costs $18.95, or you can get a steak for the same price. Beer and wine are available. June 15 to August 15, lunch is served from noon to 2pm for $8.95. The revue, nightly at 8:15pm, covers the amusing story of the founding of Fairbanks with comedy and song in a nightclub setting; admission is $12 for adults.

UNIVERSITY OF ALASKA FAIRBANKS, UNIVERSITY AVENUE The state university's historic main campus contains several interesting attractions for visitors, and the administration makes a real point of attracting and serving tourists. Free 2-hour **walking tours** meet at the museum Monday through Friday at 10am, June to August except July 4 and 5. Call ahead (☎ **907/474-7581**) to confirm the time and any weather cancellations. If you don't want to take the time for a full tour, at least pick up a campus map at the museum so you can find your way around.

The ✪ **University of Alaska Museum,** 907 Yukon Drive (P.O. Box 756960), Fairbanks, AK 99775-6960 (☎ **907/474-7505;** website http://www.uaf.alaska.edu/museum), is a rich, interdisciplinary museum explaining the natural history and culture of each of the state's regions. In fact, its only weakness is that it tries to do so much in too small a space, and sometimes seems cluttered. A display on emission spectrums is side-by-side with a stuffed lynx, a woven root basket, and a broad-view aurora camera. The presentation is serious and scholarly. Don't miss the temporary exhibits, which have been superb in the past, and daily shows on Alaska Native games and on the aurora—UAF's scientists lead the world in study of the phenomenon. Downstairs are the nine museum labs and archives, which contain among the world's largest repositories of northern region artifacts and biological samples (these aren't open to the public, though, unless you've made special arrangements with the curators). The museum is open daily 9am to 7pm June to August, closing at 5pm in May and September, and opening at noon on Saturday and Sunday in the winter. Admission is $5 for adults, ages 13 to 18 $3, free 12 and under.

The **Large Animal Research Station,** on Yankovich Road (☎ **907/474-7207**), is a farm where the university studies captive musk ox and caribou (it's more commonly known as the musk ox farm). Walking along the fence, you can see the animals behaving naturally in the large pastures, although they may be a long way off. Tours are given five times a week in the summer for $5 for adults; call for times. The **Georgeson Botanical Garden** and experimental farm, on West Tanana Drive (☎ **907/474-1959**), will be of interest to serious gardeners. Plots are laid out to compare seeds and cultivation techniques, each with an explanatory monograph you can take. Children will enjoy looking at the pigs and cows in the barns. It's open Monday through Friday from 7am to 8pm; free guided tours are at 2pm on Friday.

COMMERCIAL TOURIST ATTRACTIONS The ✪ **Riverboat** *Discovery,* 1975 Discovery Dr., Fairbanks, AK 99709 (☎ **907/479-6673;** website http://www2.polarnet.com/~discovry), belongs to the pioneering Binkley family; they've been in the riverboat business since the Klondike gold rush, and family members still run the boat. The *Discovery* is a real sternwheeler, a 156-foot steel vessel carrying 700 passengers on as many as three trips a day—there's nothing intimate or spontaneous about the 3½-hour ride. What's amazing is that with so many people on board so often, the Binkleys still provide a fun, educational experience for the bargain price of $36.95 for adults and $25.95 for children. After loading at a landing with shops off Dale Road, near the airport, the boat cruises down the Chena and up the Tanana past demonstrations on shore—among others, a bush plane taking off and landing, fish cutting at a Native fish camp, and a musher's dog yard (in recent years, five-time Iditarod champion Susan Butcher's yard, and she'd often show off the dogs herself). Finally, the vessel pulls up at the bank for a tour of a mock Athabascan village. Sailings are 8:45am and 2pm, with a less crowded evening sailing sometimes added.

The Binkleys also own the **El Dorado Mine,** off the Elliot Highway, 9 miles north of town (☎ **907/479-7613**), a working gold mine with a train that carries visitors through a tour (including a tunnel in the permafrost) and ends with gold panning—

my son ended up with enough gold to fill a plastic locket and couldn't think about anything else for a week. The whole thing takes 2 hours, happens twice daily, and costs $24.95 for adults and $19.95 for children. The hosts of the tour are Dexter and Lynette Clark; they're real miners, perfect examples of the type—Lynette has even been involved in the Alaskan Independence Party.

Gold Dredge Number 8, 1755 Old Steese Hwy., Fairbanks, AK 99712 (☎ **907/ 457-8888**), is a 1928 machine—similar to dredges in Dawson City and Nome—that will fascinate anyone interested in mechanical things. Standing five decks tall on a barge, it would float in a pond it created, creeping across the terrain by digging at the front and dumping the spoils at the back. In between, the machine would digest the gravel and separate out the gold. The many sterile areas you see in this area were created by these earth-eaters, for nothing grows on their tailings for decades after. After a 2-hour tour, you can pan for gold in the pay dirt yourself. Admission is $19; it's open May 31 to September 15, daily from 9am to 6pm; the last tour starts at 4pm. To get there, go north on the Steese Expressway from town, turn left on Goldstream Road, and again on the Old Steese Highway.

The town of **North Pole,** 13 miles east of Fairbanks on the Richardson Highway, is a bedroom community to Fairbanks—but if your group is like mine was, with young fans of Santa Claus in the car, you can't be within 13 miles of the North Pole without dropping in on him. You'll find Santa hanging out at a huge gift shop and RV park just off the highway as you enter North Pole. It's called, appropriately, **Santa Claus House,** 101 St. Nicholas Dr., North Pole, AK 99705 (☎ **907/488-2200**), and is open daily in the summer, closed January and February. (The **Santa Land RV Park** is under different ownership; ☎ **907/488-9123.**) There are some reindeer in a pen, a tiny train young children can ride, and, of course, an opportunity to have your picture taken sitting in Santa's lap, year round.

SHOPPING   Fairbanks has a few good shops downtown. ✪ **Arctic Travelers Gift Shop,** at 201 Cushman St., specializes in Native crafts, carrying both valuable art and affordable but authentically Alaskan gifts. The staff is friendly and knowledgeable, and the store has a long and excellent reputation. The **Yukon Quest Trading Company,** at 522 Second Ave., supports the incredible 1,000-mile sled-dog race between Whitehorse and Fairbanks; you'll find race memorabilia and a little museum. **Site 250,** at Courthouse Square Suite 2A, 250 Cushman St., Fairbanks, AK 99701 (☎ **907/ 452-6169**), is a great little fine art gallery, without the usual tourist junk, in the art deco federal building above the public lands center. Near the airport, at 4630 Old Airport Rd., the **Great Alaskan Bowl Company** (☎ **907/474-9663**) makes and sells bowls of native birch. The factory is open for tours, whether you buy or not, to see raw logs made into smooth bowls. **Santa's Smokehouse,** 2400 Davis Rd. (☎ **907/ 456-3885**), sells delicious smoked salmon in gift packs to take home, and processes fish and game for sportsmen (take Peger Road south from Airport Road).

GETTING OUTSIDE

In this section, I've described the outdoor opportunities local to Fairbanks, but some other choices are barely farther afield: Make sure to look at the sections on Chena Hot Springs Road and the Steese Highway, later in this chapter.

SPECIAL PLACES   ✪ **Creamers's Field**   At 1300 College Road, right in Fairbanks, this migratory waterfowl refuge is a 1,800-acre former dairy homestead that was saved from development in 1966 by a community fund drive. The pastures are a prime stopover point for Canada geese, pintails, and golden plovers in the spring and fall. Sandhill cranes, shovelers, and mallards show up all summer. The **Alaska**

Department of Fish and Game (☎ 907/459-7307) manages the refuge, including a small visitor center with bird and history displays, open Tuesday through Friday from 10am to 5pm and on Saturday from 10am to 3pm. I especially enjoyed the well-interpreted boreal forest nature walk; borrow a guide booklet from a stand at the trailhead when the visitor center is closed. There are other trails, too. Guided walks take place four times a week.

✪ **Chena Lakes Recreation Area**   This is a wonderful and unique place for a family camping trip. A birch-rimmed lake created for a flood control project has been developed by the local government to provide lots of recreational possibilities: flat walking and bike trails; a swimming beach; fishing; a place to rent canoes, sailboats, and paddle boats; a guided 2$\frac{1}{2}$-mile nature trail; a playground; big lawns; and the terrific campground, with 80 camping sites, from pull-throughs for RVs to tent sites on a little island you can reach only by boat. In the winter, it's a popular cross-country skiing area. Drive 17 miles east of Fairbanks on the Richardson Highway and turn left on Laurance Road as you leave North Pole.

CANOEING   There are lots of places for day trips. The Chena River is slow and meandering as it flows through Fairbanks, and you have your pick of restaurants on the bank. Or you could go up Chena Hot Springs Road or to the Chatanika River, on the Steese Highway (see those sections later in this chapter). The Alaska Public Lands Information Center can provide guidance and a list of companies that rent equipment. **7 Bridges Boats and Bikes** rents canoes, kayaks, and rafts for $35 per day, and provides the essential service of dropping you off at the river and picking you up at your destination for $1.25 per mile out of town, with a $10 minimum. They're located near the Cushman Street Bridge and at the 7 Gables Inn, 4312 Birch Lane (P.O. Box 80488), Fairbanks, AK 99708 (☎ 907/479-0751; fax 907/479-2229; website http://www.alaska.net/~gables7).

BIKING   7 Bridges, above, rents bicycles: street bikes are $10 a day; mountain bikes, $15. Also see "Getting Around," above. There are a lot of good mountain-bike rides to be had around Fairbanks, including the cross-country ski trails at the university or the trails at the Birch Hill Recreation Area, a few miles north of town on the Steese Expressway.

FISHING   Salmon fishing isn't as good as nearer the coast, where the fish are brighter, but kings and silvers are found in Fairbanks streams. You can also fish for pike, grayling, burbot, whitefish, and various kinds of trout. You can even fish right in the Chena as it flows through town; the visitor center provides a brochure on where to fish and buy a license. The **Alaska Department of Fish and Game** is at 1300 College Rd., Fairbanks, AK 99701 (☎ 907/459-7207; website http://www.state.ak.us/local/akpages/FISH.GAME/adfghome.htm). Guided trips by boat or plane will get you out into the country, where you may see wildlife, too. Check at the visitor center for current operators; going prices seem to be $250 for a boat for half a day, $450 for a full day. Lake flyouts start at $250 for two people.

GOLF   They may not be what you're used to at home, but Fairbanks does have a couple of golf courses, and here you can play all night under the midnight sun. The **Fairbanks Golf & Country Club** is at 1735 Farmers Loop Rd. (☎ 907/479-6555).

WINTER RECREATION   Winters in Fairbanks can be awfully cold, but that just means you have to bundle up more (or at least that's what the locals claim). Cross-country skiing, snowmobiling, and sled-dog mushing are the main participatory sports. Many local mushers offer rides; get a referral from the visitor center, or from the brochure produced by **Mushing Magazine,** 3647 Main St. (P.O. Box 149),

Ester, AK 99725 (website http://www.polarnet.com/users/mushing). There are Nordic trails at the university, and **7 Bridges Boats and Bikes,** listed above under "Canoeing," also rents snowmobiles, skis, and other winter gear. There's also a minor ski area, **Moose Mountain,** 100 Moose Mountain Rd. (P.O. Box 84198), Fairbanks, AK 99708 (☎ **907/479-8362**).

ACCOMMODATIONS

Fairbanks is a popular destination in the peak summer season, and a good hotel room can be hard to find on short notice. Several establishments book up with tour groups a year ahead, then have last-minute cancellations available for independent travelers. The **Bridgewater Hotel,** 723 First Ave., Fairbanks, AK 99701 (☎ **907/452-6661;** fax 907/452-6126; website http://www.mosquitonet.com/~fountain), falls in this category, with good rooms right downtown. You'll also find good downtown rooms at the **Fairbanks Golden Nugget Hotel,** 900 Noble St., Fairbanks, AK 99701 (☎ **907/452-5141;** fax 907/452-5458). The new **Comfort Inn Chena River,** 1908 Chena Landings Loop, Fairbanks, AK 99701 (☎ **800/201-9199** or 907/479-8080) has a small pool and a lovely wooded site near the river. The local **bed tax** is 8%.

EXPENSIVE

Captain Bartlett Inn. 1411 Airport Way, Fairbanks, AK 99701. ☎ **907/452-1888.** Fax 907/452-7674. 196 rms, 2 suites. TV TEL. High season, $140 double. Low season, $95 double. $175 suite. Additional person in room $10 extra. AE, CB, DC, DISC, JCB, MC, V.

Although it faces busy Airport Way, the Captain Bartlett succeeds in feeling like a rural Alaska roadhouse, from the log exterior and plantings to the historic photographs in the halls and the room decor—it makes you want to have fun. The rooms are comfortable if small for the price. Those on the first floor are in a half-basement without air-conditioning, and most of the rooms have no tub, just a shower stall. You'll find a courtesy car, coffee in the rooms, and a business center available.

Slough Foot Sue's restaurant has hearty meals for reasonable prices. The menu has sandwiches and a salad bar for lunch, beef and seafood for dinner. Patrons at the restaurant or bar can sit on a deck over the parking lot. The **Dog Sled Saloon** deserves its fun reputation. You're expected to throw peanut shells on the floor, and you can barbecue your own burger or steak on the deck from 8 to 10pm. A 24-ounce draft costs only $2.75, and there's no cover for live music that starts at 5pm.

Fairbanks Princess Hotel. 4477 Pikes Landing Rd., Fairbanks, AK 99709. ☎ **800/426-0500** or 907/455-4477. Fax 907/455-4476. 198 rms, 2 suites. TV TEL. High season, $189–$220 double. Low season, $110–$150 double. $285–$500 suite. Additional person in room $10 extra. AE, MC, V.

This well-thought-out gray clapboard structure in a wooded area on the banks of the Chena, near the airport, was built to serve Princess cruise line passengers. The rooms, while not large, are elegant in shades of tan, and many look out on the river. The lobby is attractive, and the bar and Edgewater Restaurant have a large deck. The dinner menu is short, with entree prices in the $20 to $25 range, but the food is consistently good. Additional facilities include a courtesy car, health club, steam room, business center, and tour desk.

✪ **River's Edge Resort Cottages.** 4200 Boat St. (mailing address: 3165 Riverview) Fairbanks, AK 99709. ☎ **800/770-3343** or 907/474-0286. Fax 907/479-9113. E-mail landersn@polarnet.com. TV TEL. 48 cottages. June–Aug $139 double. May and Sept $119 double. $10 each additional person. MC, V. Closed Oct–Apr.

These trim little cottages, new in 1997, stand in a grassy compound next to the Chena River. Inside, each is an excellent standard hotel room, with high ceilings and two queen beds. Outside, they're like a little village, where guests can sit on the patio, watch the river go by, and socialize. The owners got the idea for the place from their RV park next door, when they noticed how their guests enjoyed visiting together. It's perfect for families, as the outdoor areas are safe for playing, and noise inside won't bother the neighbors. Take Sportsman Way off Airport Way to Boat Street.

○ **Wedgewood Resort.** 212 Wedgewood Dr., Fairbanks, AK 99701. ☎ **907/452-1442.** Fax 907/451-8184. Website http://www.mosquitonet.com/~fountain. 157 rms, 283 apartments. A/C TV TEL. High season, $180 double, $150 apartment for two. Low season, $105 apartment for two. Additional person in apartment $10 extra. AE, DC, DISC, MC, V.

Off College Road near the Creamer's Field Refuge, this huge, well-kept hotel sprawls across a grassy complex in eight large buildings. Seven are converted three-story apartment buildings, without elevators but with large living rooms, separate dining areas and full kitchens, air conditioners, and balconies, all recently updated with new decor. There couldn't be a better place for a family or businessperson to stay—the only difference from home is that someone else cleans up after you. Another 157 rooms, new in 1996, are large, thoughtfully designed, and beautifully appointed. There are two restaurants, one with pleasant outdoor tables; a scheduled courtesy van to the sights; newspapers; coin-op laundries,; a tour desk; and a nightly slide show and lecture about Alaska. Many of the facilities are not available in the winter.

Westmark Fairbanks. 813 Noble St., Fairbanks, AK 99701. ☎ **800/544-0970** (reservations) or 907/456-7722. Fax 907/451-7478. Website http://www.westmarkhotels.com. 225 rms, 13 suites. TV TEL. High season, $125–189 double. Low season, $95–$129 double. Additional person in room $15 extra. AE, DC, DISC, MC, V.

Taking up a full block downtown, the Westmark Fairbanks—not to be confused with the seasonal and somewhat less expensive Westmark Inn on South Cushman Street— fulfills the role of the city's grand, central hotel. It's made up of a hodge-podge of different buildings and room configurations surrounding a central courtyard—you get a map when you check in. The rooms are typical of any upscale chain, the suites quite luxurious. Facilities include a courtesy van, tour desk, informal restaurant, lounge, and gift shop.

INEXPENSIVE

○ **Fairbanks Hotel.** 517 Third Ave., Fairbanks, AK 99701. ☎ **888/329-4685** or 907/ 456-6411. Fax 907/456-1792. Website http://www.alaska.net/~fbxhotl. 35 rms, 11 with bath. TEL. High season, $65–$89 double. Low season, $55–$70. AE, MC, V.

Four women transformed a notorious flop house into a charming art deco–style historic hotel, in the core of downtown. Although small, the rooms are light and attractively decorated, including brass beds and other period touches. Everything was clean and bright when I visited. The place should be popular, as a decent room in this price range is hard to find in Fairbanks, much less in the downtown area. For now it's still undiscovered, and a bargain.

Golden North Motel. 4888 Old Airport Way, Fairbanks, AK 99701. ☎ **800/447-1910** in the U.S., 800/478-1910 in Canada, or 907/479-6201. 41 rms, 21 suites. TV TEL. $69 double; $99 suite. AE, DISC, MC, V.

The Baer family, owners since 1971, keep the rooms in this two-story motel clean and up-to-date, making it a good bargain favored by Alaskans in town from the Bush to shop or just visiting Fairbanks by car. The rooms are small, but the reasonably priced suites are a good choice for families. They have fans, but no air conditioners. The location is near the airport. They provide a courtesy van to the airport or railroad station and free continental breakfast and coffee in the office.

BED & BREAKFASTS

Nearly 100 bed & breakfasts have sprouted like fireweed in Fairbanks, perhaps because the hotels are so tightly booked, and good rooms for low prices are rare. B&Bs range from simple homes to luxurious accommodations, and in general are a better value and more memorable experience than a hotel. The **Bed and Breakfast Reservation Service,** P.O. Box 71131, Fairbanks, AK 99707 (☎ **800/770-8165** or 907/479-8165; fax 907/474-8448; website http://www.alaska.net/~bnbres), represents more than 30 B&Bs in Fairbanks, and many more south to Homer. You can also get detailed information at the visitor center. Here are some good B&Bs I didn't have room to describe individually: **Stone Frost Downtown Inn,** 851 Sixth Ave., Fairbanks, AK 99701 (☎ **907/457-5337;** fax 907/457-3761), and **Bell House Bed and Breakfast,** 909 Sixth Ave., Fairbanks, AK 99701 (☎ **907/452-3278**), have inexpensive rooms in a nice old neighborhood downtown. **7 Gables Inn,** 4312 Birch Lane (P.O. Box 80488), Fairbanks, AK 99708 (☎ **907/479-0751;** fax 907/479-2229; website http://www.alaska.net/~gables7), has rooms with Jacuzzis and VCRs in a subdivision near the university, and rents canoes and other outdoor gear, with discounts for guest. **A Cloudberry Lookout Bed and Breakfast,** south of town off Goldhill Road (P.O. Box 84511), Fairbanks, AK 99708 (☎ **907/479-7334**), has rooms with great views arrayed off a four-story spiral staircase in a wooded setting. **A Taste of Alaska Lodge,** 5.3 Mile Chena Hot Springs Road (mailing address: 551 Eberhardt Rd., Fairbanks, AK 99712; ☎ **907/488-7855;** fax 907/488-3772), has lovely country-decorated rooms in a log building out of town.

✪ **All Seasons Inn.** 763 Seventh Ave., Fairbanks, AK 99701. ☎ **888/451-6649** or 907/451-6649. Fax 907/474-8448. Website http://www.alaska.net/~bnbres. 8 rms. TV TEL. High season, $99 double. Low season, $65 double. Rates include full breakfast. Additional person in room $20 extra. AE, CB, DC, DISC, MC, V.

This charming and comfortable country inn shows up improbably on a pleasant residential street a couple of blocks from the downtown core. Renovated in 1996, the design and decoration are inspired and detailed and the housekeeping perfect. You'll be comfortable enough in your room, but if you want to socialize, there's a series of large, elegant common rooms that include a wet bar with hot drinks and a sun porch with books and games. Complimentary newspapers come with the full breakfast. It's quite a value.

✪ **Forget-Me-Not Lodge and the Aurora Express Bed and Breakfast.** 1540 Chena Ridge Rd. (P.O. Box 80128), Fairbanks, AK 99708. ☎ **907/474-0949.** Fax 907/474-8173. 9 rms, 7 with bath. High season, $85–$135 double. Low season, $75–$110 double. Rates include full breakfast. MC, V.

Susan Wilson's late grandmother appeared to her in a dream and told her there would be a train on a bank below her house, on the family's 15 acres, high in the hills south of Fairbanks. So Wilson went out and got a train—a collection that includes a pair of 1956 Pullman sleepers—and her husband, Mike, hauled the cars from the Alaska Railroad up onto the mountain and installed them below the house, right in the spot indicated. One sleeper, in its original form, is rented to groups of up to seven for $135 to $300 a night, while another has been remodeled into four fancy rooms, each with a theme related to Fairbanks history, renting for $115 a night. Then there's the caboose, dedicated to Grandma—simply incredible. As I write this, they're remodeling a locomotive. The three rooms in the house are perfectly sumptuous, including a large room with a Jacuzzi and a great view (it and the caboose are each $135). Only the rooms in the house are open in the winter.

A Hostel & Camping

There are a lot of RV parks in Fairbanks with full service and then some. Pick up a list at the visitor center. Among the best is **River's Edge RV Park and Campground,** at a wooded riverside bend of the Chena at 4140 Boat St., off Airport Way and Sportsman Way (☎ **800/770-3343** or 907/474-0286), with lots of services, including free shuttles and organized tours. Full hook-ups are $25 and tent camping $15.50. The **Chena River State Recreation Site** (not to be confused with the recreation "area" of the same name described in the next section of this chapter), where University Avenue crosses the river, has riverside sites surrounded by birch with self-service fees of $15 for RVs, $10 for tents. See "Special Places" under "Getting Outside," above, and the section on Chena Hot Springs Road for other wonderful public campgrounds out of town.

The Fairbanks visitor guide lists five hostels, although none is affiliated with Hostelling International–American Youth Hostels. **Grandma Shirley's Hostel,** 510 Dunbar St., Fairbanks, AK 99701 (☎ **907/451-9816**), offers a bed with linens, towels, soap, cooking facilities, and free bicycles for $15 a night. The hostel is in a subdivision east of the Steese Expressway, 1 1/2 miles from the railroad station.

DINING

For a quick lunch or take-out downtown, try the fun **Dash Deli,** at the corner of First Ave. and Cushman St. They make good panini sandwiches. Just across the river, tasty, inexpensive Greek meals are served at **Souvlaki,** 112 N. Turner St. (☎ **907/ 452-5393**); they also have a booth at Alaskaland. For a family pizza, try the popular **Pizza Bella** on Airport Way. **Hot Licks Homemade Ice Cream,** on College Road near University Avenue, has the best cones and sundaes in town. Across the street, a trailer often is parked, dispensing baked goods that make the locals rave.

DOWNTOWN

✪ **Gambardella'a Italian Cafe.** 706 Second Ave. ☎ **907/456-3417.** Main courses $9.50–$17; lunch $6–$10. 15% gratuity added for parties of five or more, or for split checks. AE, MC, V. Mon–Sat 11am–10pm, Sun 5–10pm. SOUTHERN ITALIAN.

The quality of the southern Italian cuisine—the lasagna particularly—is a cut above everything else in Fairbanks, the prices are low and the service efficient. You can eat in an attractive dining room on white tablecloths, but on a sunny day nothing could be more pleasant than to dine on the patio among the hanging flowers. Beer and wine license.

✪ **Plate and Palette Gallery Cafe.** 310 First Ave. ☎ **907/451-9294.** Dinner $7.50–$16.50. Lunch $4–$8. MC, V. Mon–Sat 11am–3pm, 5–9pm; Sun 9:30am–2pm. ECLECTIC/VEGETARIAN.

Patrons sometimes wander the small dining room while awaiting their orders, looking at the art hanging in this restaurant that's also a serious gallery. The food is frequently artful, too. Ambitious and interesting combinations of tastes draw on many cultures. An "artichoke panache" turns out to be a delicious cheesy quiche, served with soup and bread for a filling lunch under $7. Thanks to the art, the atmosphere is at once low-key and stimulating, especially in cozy little chambers off the main room, each containing a table or two and the diverse artwork of this college town. Take your kids if you can trust them not to break anything, as children are exceptionally well treated—even the PB&J is special, with a choice of jelly. They serve beer and wine.

Thai House. 526 Fifth Ave. ☎ **907/452-6123.** Lunch $3.50–$8; dinner $7–$12. MC, V. Mon–Sat 11am–4pm and 5–10pm. THAI.

In a small storefront in the downtown area, this is a simple, family-run restaurant with authentic Thai cuisine that has made it a favorite in Fairbanks. Beer and wine license.

WITHIN DRIVING DISTANCE

The Bakery. 69 College Rd. ☎ **907/456-8600.** Lunch $6–$7.50; dinner $7–$14. No credit cards. Mon–Sat 6am–9pm, Sun 7am–4pm. DINER.

There are an infinite number of old-fashioned coffee shops in Fairbanks—the kind of place where a truck driver or gold miner can find a big, hearty meal, a motherly waitress, and a bottomless cup of coffee. This is the best of the lot—which is really saying something. The sourdough pancakes are mind-expanding, the service friendly, the prices low, and the quality of baked goods testified to by the number of police cars always in the parking lot. Our children enjoyed it, and it's nice taking them to a low-key place where they can relax. No liquor license.

Pike's Landing. 4438 Airport Way. ☎ **907/479-7113.** Main courses $20–$55; lunch $6.50–$13.50. AE, DC, DISC, MC, V. Daily 11:30am–2:30pm and 5–11pm. STEAK/SEAFOOD.

The large dining room overlooking the Chena River near the airport divides its fine-dining menu between the "surf and turf" and the "gourmet corner," which includes the veal, duck, and more sophisticated cuisine. It's all well prepared, with huge servings and occasional flashes of brilliance. For an inexpensive meal, the bar serves food on the deck over the river, a pleasant choice on a sunny day. Full liquor license.

The Pump House Restaurant and Saloon. 1.3 Mile Chena Pump Rd. ☎ **907/479-8452.** Main courses $13–$24. AE, MC, V. Daily 11am–10:30pm. STEAK/SEAFOOD.

The historic, rambling building on the Chena River is beautifully decorated and landscaped with authentic gold-rush relics. Sitting on the deck, you can watch the riverboat paddle by or a group in canoes stop for beer and appetizers. Lunch comes from an excellent $10 buffet. The dinner menu is reasonably priced, with all the usual steak and fish house items. The dining rooms are large, but we found service quick.

○ Two Rivers Lodge / Tuscan Gardens. 4968 Chena Hot Springs Rd. ☎ **907/488-6815.** Main courses $11.50–$27. AE, DISC, MC, V. Mon–Sat 5–10pm, Sun noon–10pm. STEAK/SEAFOOD/NORTHERN ITALIAN.

Inside the log lodge building, chef Tony Marsico brings interesting touches to a steak and seafood menu—such as his wonderful soups, about which he's published a cookbook. Service is quick and efficient. The dining room is dark and can be hot; nonsmokers get to sit in the solarium, but there may not be room for all. Outside, on a deck over the duck pond, a whole separate restaurant serves meals from a brick Tuscan oven in the open air. Start there for appetizers, or eat a whole inexpensive Tuscan meal under the evening sun. There are full bars at both spots. It's worth the 25-minute drive from Fairbanks for a special meal.

FAIRBANKS IN THE EVENING

Fairbanks has a lot of tourist-oriented evening activities, as well as entertainment also attended by locals. Call the 24-hour event recording of what's playing currently, or check the *Fairbanks Daily News-Miner*. The best of the summer arts scene is at the **○ Fairbanks Summer Arts Festival** (☎ **907/474-8869;** see "Special Events" under "Essentials," above). There also are **movie theaters**—a large multiplex is located on Airport Way. The evening show at the **Palace Theater** is discussed with Alaskaland (see "Exploring Fairbanks," above).

The **Ester Gold Camp,** P.O. Box 109, Ester, AK 99725 (☎ **907/479-2500;** fax 907/474-1780), is an 11-building historic site, an old mining town that's been turned into an evening tourist attraction. The main event is a gold-rush theme show at the

Malemute Saloon, with singing and Robert Service poetry, nightly at 9pm; admission is $12. A "photosymphony" slide show about the aurora takes place every summer evening at 6:45 and 7:45. There's also a restaurant that serves a buffet and has mess-hall seating for $14.95 for adults, $6.95 for big kids, and $3.95 for little kids. If you have crab, it's $21.95 for adults. The gift shop is open in the evening, and there are simple, inexpensive rooms in the old gold-mine bunkhouse. A free bus is available from Fairbanks.

The **Howling Dog Saloon,** north of town in Fox (☎ **907/457-8780**), claims to be the "farthest north rock 'n' roll club in the world." That's questionable, but the bar does have quite a reputation for a good time. The music is classic rock and blues; a selection of 13 craft brews is on tap at $4 each, while regular American beer is $2.75; and there's no cover charge. There are volleyball nets and the like outside. The saloon usually closes for a few months in midwinter.

A STOP IN NENANA

Although there's little to justify a special trip, you might spend a pleasant hour or so wandering the deserted streets of Nenana, a little riverside town an hour's drive south of Fairbanks, as you travel the Parks Highway to Denali National Park or Anchorage. The town has a unique memory, keeping alive a sleepy, riverbank lifestyle Samuel Clemens might have found familiar. The Tanana River docks still serve barges pushed by river tugboats, carrying the winter's fuel and supplies to villages across the region. The Alaska Railroad still rumbles through, although it made its last stop at the depot in 1983, passing the spot where President Warren G. Harding drove the golden spike marking the line's completion on July 15, 1923. (The first president to visit Alaska, Harding died soon after the trip, supposedly from eating some bad Alaska shellfish—but we don't believe that, now *do* we?)

A log cabin **visitor center** stands at the intersection of the highway and A Street, the main business street. At the other end of A Street, by the river, the **old railroad depot** has been made, with little meddling, into a summer-only museum and gift shop. A block down Front Street, along the river, **St. Mark's Episcopal Church** is the town's most historic and loveliest building; its 1905 log-cabin construction remains unspoiled, even though it's still in use. The church predates most of the town, which was built as a railroad camp. On the left of Front Street, you can see the **barge docks.**

Nenana's claim to fame these days is the **Nenana Ice Classic** (☎ **907/832-5446**), a traditional statewide gambling event in which contestants try to predict the exact date and time of the ice break-up on the Tanana. The pot builds to over $100,000 by spring, but it's generally shared among several winners who pick the same time. The town kicks off the classic each February with a celebration that includes dancing and dog-mushing races and the raising of the "four-legged tripod," a black-and-white log marker whose movement with the ice indicates that spring has arrived and that someone, somewhere, has won a lot of money.

There are accommodations in Nenana, but not much reason to stay. A couple of diners serve basic burgers and fries. There are a couple of shops, a library, clinic, and school, and RV park as well.

4 Chena Hot Springs Road

The 57-mile paved road east from Fairbanks is an avenue to an enjoyable day trip or a destination for up to a week's outdoor activities and hot-spring swimming. The road travels through the Chena River State Recreation Area, with spectacular hikes and float trips and well-maintained riverside campgrounds, and leads to the Chena

Hot Springs, where there's a year-round resort perfect for soaking in hot mineral springs and for use as a base for summer or winter wilderness day trips. The resort is open to people who want to rent one of the comfortable rooms or to campers and day trippers, and it's equally as popular in the winter as in the summer (the slow seasons are spring and fall). Japanese visitors especially make the pilgrimage in winter to see the northern lights, but Americans are discovering it as well. Of all the roads radiating from Fairbanks, this short highway will be most rewarding to most outdoors people, as well as providing some of the best remote lodgings accessible on the Interior road system.

The paved road leads through a forest of birch, spruce, and cottonwood, first passing an area of scattered roadside development and then following the Chena River through the state recreation area. It's a pleasant drive, around 1¹/₄ hours from Fairbanks, but not particularly scenic. On a sunny summer weekend, the people of Fairbanks migrate to the riverside and the hiking trails; on a sunny winter weekend, they take to the hills on snowmobiles, cross-country skis, or dog sleds.

A pair of prospectors, the Swan brothers, discovered the hot springs in 1905, having heard that a U.S. Geological Survey crew had seen steam in a valley on the upper Chena. Thomas Swan suffered from rheumatism; incredibly, he and his brother poled up the Chena River from Fairbanks, found the hot springs, built a cabin and rock-floored pool, and spent the summer soaking. He was cured! More visitors followed, drawn by stories that whole groups of cripples were able to dance all night after soaking in the pools—by 1915 a resort was in operation, drawing worn-out miners and gold-rush stampeders and many others as well. The resort has been in constant use ever since—you can rent one of the original cabins, if you want to rough it.

ESSENTIALS

GETTING THERE   The Chena Hot Springs Road meets the Steese Expressway about 10 miles north of downtown Fairbanks. You can rent a car in Fairbanks. The resort offers rides—$55 per person with a minimum of two.

VISITOR INFORMATION   For outdoors information, check the Fairbanks **Alaska Public Lands Information Center,** 250 Cushman St. (at Third Avenue), Suite 1A, Fairbanks, AK 99701 (☎ 907/456-0527; TDD 907/456-0532; fax 907/456-0514; website http://www.nps.gov/aplic). The **Alaska Division of Parks,** 3700 Airport Way, Fairbanks, AK 99709 (☎ 907/451-2695; website http://www.dnr.state.ak.us/parks/index.htm), manages the area and produces trail, river, and road guides, which are available at trail head kiosks or from the public lands center. The **Chena Hot Springs Resort** owns and operates the springs; they are discussed below.

STOPS ALONG THE ROAD

There isn't much to see along the road. **Tacks General Store,** at Mile 23.5 (P.O. Box 16004), Two Rivers, AK 99716 (☎ 907/488-3242), is an old-fashioned country store, greenhouse, post office, and lunch counter—the friendly center of the rural community. The dining atmosphere is like a picnic, and people make a special trip from Fairbanks for the pies. The **Two Rivers Lodge,** a fine-dining establishment and bar, and **A Taste of Alaska Lodge,** a bed and breakfast, are listed in "Dining" and "Accommodations" in the Fairbanks section.

CHENA RIVER STATE RECREATION AREA

HIKING   The best trail hikes in the Fairbanks area are in the Chena Hot Springs State Recreation Area. The **Angel Rocks Trail** is an easy 3¹/₂-mile loop to a group of granite outcroppings, with alpine views. The trailhead is well marked, at Mile 48.9 of the road. The 15-mile loop of the ✪ **Granite Tors Trail,** starting at Mile 39 of the road, is a bit more challenging, rising through forest to rolling alpine terrain, but the towering tors more than reward the effort. Like surrealist experiments in perspective, these monolithic granite sentinels stand at random spots on the broad Plain of Monuments, at first confounding the eye's attempts to gauge their distance and size. They were created when upwelling rock solidified in cracks in the surrounding earth, which then eroded away into the alpine plain. For a longer backpacking trip, the **Chena Dome Trail** makes a 29-mile loop, beginning at Mile 50.5 and ending at Mile 49. Along the way, the upper and lower Angel Creek cabins can be reserved for $25 from State Parks at the address listed above.

RIVER FLOATING   The Chena is an often-lazy Class I river as it flows through much of the recreation area and into Fairbanks. The faster-flowing, clearer water is found higher upstream, farther along the road. It's possible to float for days, all the way down to Fairbanks, but the road crosses the river four times and there are lots of access points, so you can tailor a trip to the amount of time you have. Get the State Parks river guide to choose your put-in. 7 **Bridges Boats and Bikes,** 4312 Birch Lane (P.O. Box 80488), Fairbanks, AK 99708 (☎ **907/479-0751;** fax 907/479-2229; website http://www.alaska.net/~gables7), rents canoes for $35 per day, and will drop you off and pick you up for $1.25 per mile out of town.

FISHING   Several of the ponds are stocked with trout, which you can keep; signs along the road mark access points. You can catch-and-release for arctic grayling in the Chena, depending on the current regulations and bait restrictions. Check with the **Alaska Department of Fish and Game,** 1300 College Rd., Fairbanks, AK 99701 (☎ **907/459-7207**).

THE HOT SPRINGS

Our family enjoyed a relaxing outing here centered around swimming and exploring. The hot springs bubble up in fenced pools at 165°F, hot enough to heat the buildings, or to cook you. There's an indoor swimming pool with lots of windows kept at a comfortable swimming temperature. It's not large and is occasionally crowded. Various hot tubs and spas allow you to soak at your chosen temperature, inside or outside. The facility is open daily 9am to midnight; kids are kept out from 10pm to midnight. The locker room is clean and modern. Swim passes come with your room; for campers or day trippers, a day pass is $8 for adults, $6 for children and senior citizens. At 7pm, the prices drop by $2.

ACCOMMODATIONS

✪ **The Chena Hot Springs Resort.** Mile 56.5, Chena Hot Springs Rd. (P.O. Box 73440), Fairbanks, AK 99707. ☎ **907/452-7867.** Fax 907/456-3122. 46 rms, 1 suite, 10 cabins. High season, $75–$115 double. Low season (spring and fall), $65–$70 double. Additional person in room $10 extra. Packages available. AE, CB, DC, DISC, JCB, MC, V.

The resort—scattered buildings around a nicely renovated log lodge—is well managed to create as many ways to get into nature as possible. Everything from sleigh rides and horseback riding to swimming and ice skating happen every day in their appropriate season. Other activities include bicycling, rafting, fishing, gold panning, Nordic skiing, guided nature walks, and snowmobiling. The 440-acre resort has its own trails, in addition to the excellent trails in the state recreation area. But it's not the sort of place that pushes you out to get involved; the atmosphere is so relaxed that nobody notices if you do nothing at all. Although there's no alpine skiing, the resort is the one place that has most fully developed Alaska's other winter assets. You could come here for a winter vacation, knowing that it would be snowy and you'd see the northern lights and have something to do every day. There's an indoor pool, hot tubs, and a launderette.

The rooms range from the crude, original cabins built by the prospectors who discovered the area (which rent for $40, in summer only) to large standard rooms with private balconies. None of the rooms are grand or luxurious, but all are a good value for the price and location. All lack televisions and phones—you'll be out of touch here. The larger cabins ($110 for up to six people) are simple but adequate for a family or group looking for inexpensive lodgings; the chemical toilets are essentially a bucket with a toilet seat, emptied once a day. The lodge building contains the restaurant and bar. We got good food and service there.

CAMPING AT THE HOT SPRINGS

The resort has an RV parking area with electric hookups and two campgrounds. A tent campground wraps itself around the bends in a creek. There are chemical toilets. Dry camping is $10; with electricity, $12; and a free dump station is available.

CAMPING ALONG THE ROAD

Two beautiful campgrounds with water and pit toilets on the road by the Chena are managed by the state Division of Parks, and cost $8 per night. The **Rosehip Campground,** at Mile 27, has 38 sites, well separated by spruce and birch, with 6 suitable for RVs. Some sites are right on the river, and some are reserved for more private tent camping, back in the woods. The **Granite Tors Campground** is near the trailhead at Mile 39; it has 23 sites, 7 suitable for RVs.

CABINS

There are four public-use cabins in the recreation area, available for a permit fee of $25 to $35; contact the Alaska Public Lands Information Center or state Division of Parks. The **North Fork Cabin** is a quarter-mile off the road at Mile 47.7. The others are all at least 7 miles into the countryside. The trails can be muddy, and the country is remote, so be prepared.

5 The Steese Highway

The Steese Highway leads from Fairbanks 162 miles northeast to Circle, a village on the Yukon River about 50 miles south of the Arctic Circle (they were mistaken about the town's exact location when they named it—oh well). The historic gold-rush route parallels the Davidson Ditch, a huge aqueduct and pipe that carried water to the mining operations near Fairbanks. Small-time miners and prospectors still scratch the hills. They bring their gold into the bar in Central, where they can get a shower and the current metal price is posted on the wall. Circle Hot Springs is out here, too, with a big, hot outdoor pool. There are a couple of good hikes from the road, and it provides many access points to river floats. The clear, Class I water of the Chatanika River is perfect for family day trips or relaxed expeditions of a week or more. And the road meets two National Wild and Scenic Rivers: Beaver Creek, for trips of a week or more over easy Class I water, and Birch Creek, for more experienced paddlers. Get *The Alaska River Guide,* mentioned at the beginning of this chapter, for detailed guidance.

The Steese is paved only for the first 40 miles, and you can drive only so fast on these rural gravel roads without bouncing into the ditch or getting your windshield broken by rocks kicked up by a speeding truck. Consequently, you'll spend much of your day in the car going out the highway—driving both ways in one day would be absurd. On the other hand, the overnight accommodations to be had on the high-way are below many people's standards, and if you're not interested in a hike or float trip, there isn't that much to do. Circle Hot Springs is the main attraction—more on that below. If you go, above all take mosquito repellent.

ESSENTIALS

GETTING THERE   The Steese begins as a four-lane expressway in Fairbanks. You can rent a car there.

VISITOR INFORMATION   The **Alaska Public Lands Information Center,** at 250 Cushman St. (at Third Avenue), Suite 1A, Fairbanks, AK 99701 (☎ **907/456-0527;** TDD 907/456-0532; fax 907/456-0514; website http://www.nps.gov/aplic), can provide information on the outdoors, as can the federal **Bureau of Land Management (BLM),** 1150 University Ave., Fairbanks, AK 99709 (☎ **800/437-7021** or 907/474-2200; website ttp://wwwndo.ak.blm.gov/). The **Fairbanks Convention and Visitors Bureau,** 550 First Ave. (at Cushman Street, by Golden Heart Plaza), Fairbanks, AK 99701 (☎ **800/327-5774** or 907/456-5774; website http://www.polarnet.com/users/fcvb/), is the best place to check for other travel information. For **road conditions,** call the state hot line (☎ **907/456-7623**).

A HIGHWAY LOG

11 miles   The Steese and Elliot highways split, the Steese heading east into hilly, wooded land. The big piles of gravel and the machinery you may see in the trees are the many-years-old remains of the environmentally destructive form of mining prac-ticed in this region, which requires the excavation and sorting of large amounts of gravel.

28 miles   Chatanika, an old gold-mining settlement, has a couple of roadhouses where you can stop for a burger, a beer, and, if necessary, a room or place to park your RV. The **Chatanika Gold Camp,** 5550 Old Steese Hwy., Fairbanks, AK 99712 (☎ **907/389-2414**), is authentically unrestored, with corrugated metal walls and roof and simple rooms with a bathroom at the end of the hall for $55 to $70 as a double. The cafe is in a nice old dining room. Beyond Chatanika, there's little more in the way of any kind of services from here to Central.

30 miles   The University of Alaska's **Poker Flat Research Range** (☎ **907/474-7558**) is marked by a small rocket by the road. This is where the Geophysical Institute launches rockets to study the aurora and other high-altitude phenomena. Tours, $5 for adults, are scheduled most Fridays in the summer at 1:30pm. Call to confirm before making the drive.

39 miles   The inviting state parks' **Upper Chatanika River Campground** sits on the river below a bridge on the highway, with 35 sites, pit toilets, and a hand pump for water. Camping is $8. There are grayling in the river, and it's a good spot to start or end a Chatanika float trip. State Parks produces a brochure covering the 12-hour float to the Elliot Highway, available from the Alaska Public Lands Information Cen-ter. The road is paved for another 5 miles, slowly rising along the Chatanika with some good views.

57 miles   The old **Davidson Ditch** water pipeline is along here—it's not much to look at, just a big rusted pipe. It carried water to mining operations nearer Fairbanks. The Nome Creek Road provides access to the **White Mountains National Recre-ation Area,** a 1-million-acre area managed by the BLM with some summer hiking trails, lots of rafting opportunities, more than 200 miles of winter trails with cabins, and extensive recreational gold mining. The new 19-site **Ophir Creek Campground**

is 12 miles west on Nome Creek Road, a put-in for a long float of Nome Creek and Beaver Creek. The self-service camping fee is $6. At the other end of the road, 4 miles east, is a similar 13-site campground at the trailhead for the upper Nome Creek Valley.

60 miles   The 12-site BLM campground at **Cripple Creek** has a $^1/_2$-mile nature trail and put-in for Chatanika River floats. This is the last public campground on the highway. The fee is $6.

86 miles   Twelvemile Summit—The drive becomes really spectacular from here to just short of Central, as it climbs over rounded, wind-blown, tundra-clothed mountaintops. There's a parking lot for interpretive signs and the lower end of the BLM's 28-mile **Pinnell Mountain Trail,** a challenging 3-day hike over this amazing terrain. (The upper trailhead is at Eagle Summit.) There are two emergency shelters on the way to protect from the ferocious weather that can sweep the mountains. Get the free BLM trail guide from one of the agencies listed above. Over the next 20 miles, the scars you see in the land are gold mines.

94 miles   The **Upper Birch Creek** wayside is the put-in point for a challenging 126-mile wild river float trip. The take-out is at highway mile 140.

107 miles   Eagle Summit, at 3,624 feet, is the highest place on the highway, and the best place to be on June 21 each year—the summer solstice. Although still a degree of latitude below the Arctic Circle, the sun never sets here on the longest day because of the elevation and atmospheric refraction. People come out from Fairbanks and make a celebration of it. The midnight sun is visible for about 3 days before and after the solstice, too, assuming the sky is clear. The BLM has installed a toilet and a viewing deck on a 750-foot loop trail.

CENTRAL

After descending from the mountains and entering a forest of spruce that continues to the Yukon, the road at Mile 128 suddenly reaches a stretch of pavement and is surrounded by the spectral white trunks of paper birches—like a breath of fresh air after hours bouncing over gravel. You're in the friendly little gold-mining town of Central. We were made to feel like we were the first tourists ever to come this far. From Central you can turn right for the 8-mile drive to Circle Hot Springs, or continue straight on the Steese for a featureless 34-mile drive to Circle.

The big annual event is the **miners picnic** in August. The town's main attraction is the **Circle District Museum** (☎ **907/520-1893**), which concentrates on the gold mining that has sustained the area since 1893. It's surprisingly good for a town of this size. Admission is $1 for adults, 50¢ for children; it's open Memorial Day to Labor Day, daily from noon to 5pm.

There are two restaurants, both with acceptable rural diner food, but the **Central Motor Inn,** P.O. Box 24, Central, AK 99730 (☎ **907/520-5228;** fax 907/ 520-5230), is a bit more ambitious in its cuisine, and the dining room is lighter and less dominated by the bar. They serve daily from 7am to 11pm all year. The six rooms with TVs and private baths rent for $60 as a double (they accept Discover, MasterCard, and Visa). A shower is $3, and there's a coin-op laundry. The other establishment, **Crabb Corner,** P.O. Box 30109, Central, AK 99730 (☎ **907/ 520-5599**), at the corner of Circle Hot Springs Road and the Steese, has good, inexpensive food and a tiny grocery and liquor store, bar, and gas station and a pleasant campground among the birches, for $7 a night.

Don't miss taking the 8-mile side trip to Circle Hot Springs, turning right from the Steese in Central. The **Circle Hot Springs Resort,** Mile 8, Circle Hot Springs Rd. (P.O. Box 254), Central, AK 99730 (☎ **907/520-5113;** fax 907/520-5442), is worth a stop to swim in the large outdoor pool, which is fed directly by the hot springs. In wintertime, Fairbanksans like to come out here for snowmobiling and to swim outdoors in subzero weather, toasty warm in the water while their hair freezes. The creaky old lodge building has 24 rooms with shared baths, and they rent cabins with or without water. The camping area is suitable for RVs and has electric hook-ups. The place is rustic to a fault, but many people love the old-fashioned charm, history, and home-style meals

CIRCLE

Another 34 miles past Central along the winding gravel road is a collection of log buildings and fewer than 100 people—mostly Athabascans—at the town of Circle. The Yukon flows by, broad and flat like a big field of water; it looks as if you could walk right across it, but the gray water is moving swiftly westward. As broad as it is, you can see only the nearest channel from Circle. The boat launch has a sign with facts about the river. Boaters can put in here bound for the town of Fort Yukon or the Dalton Highway to the west; the Dalton Highway bridge is 300 miles downstream. Or you can use Circle as a take-out after coming down from Eagle, 550 miles away by road but only about 158 miles and 5 days to a week over the water. **Yukon River View Motel** (☎ 907/773-8439) offers boat tours.

You can camp free on a little patch of grass by the boat launch. The **Yukon Trading Post** (☎ 907/773-1217), open year round, has a cafe, store, bar, liquor store, and tire-repair shop. The **H.C. Company Store** (☎ 907/773-1222) has gas, groceries, and so on.

6 The Dalton Highway

Although it was built to service the trans-Alaska pipeline, one of humankind's largest private construction projects, the glory of the 414-mile Dalton Highway is the wilderness it passes through. Running straight through Interior Alaska to the Arctic coast, the Dalton crosses all kinds of scenic terrain, including forested, rounded hills, the rugged peaks of the Brooks Range, and the treeless plains of the North Slope. This is still some of the most remote and untouched land on the globe. To the west of the highway, Gates of the Arctic National Park protects 8.4 million acres of the Brooks Range. West of the park, lands managed by the National Park Service continue, in the Noatak National Preserve, headquartered in Kotzebue, and beyond, to the ocean. This immense wilderness receives only a few thousand visitors a year.

Wildlife shows up all along the road, from grizzly bears to sport fish to songbirds. The road passes through Alaska's history of mineral extraction, too—there's the gold rush–era town of Wiseman and the current oil industry complex at Prudhoe Bay. Also, the Dalton provides Fairbanks's closest access to the Yukon River. But surely the reason most people drive all the way on the newly opened Dalton is because of where it goes, and not what's there. It goes to the very end of the earth, as far north as you can drive. It's quite a rough trip to nowhere, but a dramatic one if you have the time and endurance.

The Dalton is known to most Alaskans as the Haul Road—it was built to haul supplies to the Prudhoe Bay oilfield and the northern half of the 800-mile pipeline—but its real namesake is James Dalton, an oil engineer who helped explore the North Slope fields. Coldfoot is the northernmost truck stop in the United States. Just 15 miles up the road from Coldfoot, Wiseman now is home to about 25 people year round. A glimpse of the past can be found at the Wiseman Trading Company, which offers a museum and tours of Wiseman. That's it for human settlement until you reach the modern industrial complex at Prudhoe Bay, where you must join a shuttle or tour to see the Arctic Ocean or the oilfield.

ESSENTIALS

GETTING THERE   You can drive the highway yourself, staying in the few motels along the way or in a tent or motor home. The highway starts north of Fairbanks at Mile 73 of the Elliot Highway—take the Steese Highway north from town till it becomes the Elliot. The gravel-and-dirt Dalton has a reputation for being notoriously bad, but now much of it is kept in good condition. Still, it's dusty, with soft shoulders, and flat tires are common. For **road conditions,** call the state hot line (☎ **907/ 456-7623**).

This is a remote trip, and you must take some precautions. Services are as far apart as 240 miles. Drive with your headlights on at all times. Bring at least one spare tire, extra gasoline, car tools, and spare parts. A Citizen's Band radio is a good idea in case of an emergency. Insect repellent is an absolute necessity. Truck traffic is dominant, and there are some steep grades, a few on corners, where truckers must go fast to keep their momentum. Slow down or even stop to allow trucks to pass you either way, and be careful on bridges, as some are not wide enough for two vehicles to pass safely. Also, get well off the road for views or pictures—don't just stop in the middle as some people do.

For those who want to let someone else do the driving, several companies offer a variety of packages, including flights to or from Deadhorse, or flying both ways. See the "Prudhoe Bay" section in chapter 11 for details.

VISITOR INFORMATION   Fairbanks's **Alaska Public Lands Information Center,** at 250 Cushman St. (at Third Avenue), Suite 1A, Fairbanks, AK 99701 (☎ **907/ 456-0527;** TDD 907/456-0532; fax 907/456-0514; website http://www.nps.gov/ aplic), is the best source of information on the Dalton Highway. Rangers there have driven the road themselves. Much of the road runs through land managed by the federal **Bureau of Land Management,** 1150 University Ave., Fairbanks, AK 99709 (☎ **800/437-7021** or 907/474-2200; website http://wwwndo.ak.blm.gov/). For information specific to Gates of the Arctic National Park, contact the **Park Headquarters,** at 201 First Ave. (P.O. Box 74680), Fairbanks, AK 99707-4680 (☎ **907/ 456-0281;** website http://www.nps.gov/gaar/). For travel information, try the **Fairbanks Convention and Visitors Bureau Visitor Center,** 550 First Ave., Fairbanks, AK 99701 (☎ **907/456-5774;** website http://www.polarnet.com/users/ fcvb/). Along the highway, there are two **visitor information centers** shared by land management agencies, one just north of the Yukon River bridge, which has no phone, and one in Coldfoot (☎ **907/678-5209** in summer).

ON THE ROAD

The bridge over the Yukon River at Mile 56 is the only crossing in Alaska, and many people drive the Dalton just to get to the Arctic Circle at Mile 115, where you'll find a colorful sign for pictures. A number of places along the highway have incredible views, including Finger Rock at Mile 98; Gobbler's Knob at Mile 132, which offers the first view of the Brooks Range; and Atigun Pass at Mile 245, where the road crosses the Brooks Range, winding through impossibly rugged country. The pass is the highest point on the Alaska road system, and you may find summer snow. All along the highway are opportunities for animal watching and bird watching. Animals that you might see include rabbits, foxes, wolves, moose, Dall sheep, bears, and caribou. Sit still if you want to see the skittish caribou, as they may wander closer to an unmoving vehicle.

The **Wiseman Trading Co.,** a museum and general store at Mile 188, offers a glimpse of the area's mining past. Ask for information in Coldfoot. The 4-foot-wide **trans-Alaska pipeline,** which has fed the United States up to 25% of its domestically produced oil, parallels the road all the way to Prudhoe Bay. Finished in 1977, the pipeline climbs over mountain ranges and goes under and over rivers. The final stop on the road is a fence; on the other side is the **Prudhoe Bay complex,** where the pipeline originates, and access to the Arctic Ocean, a few miles away. The only way through the gate is with a tour operator. Longer tours of the area include a trip to the ocean and some oilfield operations, but a $20 shuttle to the water is available from the Eskimo-owned **Tour Arctic** (☎ **907/659-2368** in summer or 907/659-2840 in winter). See the Prudhoe Bay section in chapter 11 for details.

OUT OF THE CAR

Some of the world's most remote wilderness was opened up by the Dalton Highway. Experienced outdoors people can go it alone, but some package outdoor tours are available.

BOATING   River tours from the Dalton Highway bridge to a traditional Native fish camp on the Yukon River are offered by **Yukon River Tours** (☎ **907/452-7162;** fax 907/452-5063). The 90-minute trips run three times a day from June 1 to September 1 and cost $30 for adults, $15 under 12. You can buy a ticket at the bridge. An overnight option is available, in wall tents and with your own sleeping bag and food. The bridge also is a take-out for floats down the Yukon River.

HIKING   The road has no established hiking trails, but most of the area is open to hikers who are willing to pick their own route. Open country can be found in the alpine Brooks Range, north of the Chandalar Shelf at Mile 237, and on North Slope tundra. Forests make cross-country traveling more difficult south of the shelf. A popular destination is the Gates of the Arctic National Park and Refuge, to the west of the road, but consider going east. The country is more open, and major rivers lie between the road and the park. Hikers who want to hike in the park without crossing the rivers can leave the road in the Wiseman area, where a short part of the road runs on the west riverbank. Topographical maps and advice on the Brooks Range area along the highway are available at the sources listed under "Visitor Information," above. Remember, this is remote wilderness; be prepared and tell someone where you're going and when you'll be back.

FISHING   The Dalton is not a top fishing area, but there are fish in streams and lakes along the highway. Many of the streams have grayling, but you'll want to hike farther than a quarter mile from the road to increase your chances. A good bet is the Jim River area between Mile 135 and 144, where the river follows the road, and fishing pressure is more spread out. Many of the lakes along the road have grayling, and the deeper ones have lake trout and Arctic char. Salmon fishing is closed along the road. For more detailed information, pick up the pamphlet "Sport Fishing Along the Dalton Highway" published by the **Alaska Department of Fish and Game,** available from the Alaska Public Lands Information Center or from Fish and Game, 1300 College Rd., Fairbanks, AK 99701 (☎ **907/459-7207**).

HIGHWAY SERVICE

You won't find anything luxurious, or even similar to standard chains, as you drive the Dalton among the three places offering services along the 414 miles.

Yukon Ventures Alaska, at Mile 56, just past the Yukon River Bridge (P.O. Box 60947, Fairbanks, AK 99706; ☎ **907/655-9001**), has a motel, a restaurant, a gift shop, fuel, and tire repair. The motel, a former pipeline construction camp, is clean and comfortable, and the food is basic trucker fare.

The truckstop in Coldfoot, run by **Sourdough Fuel,** at Mile 175 (P.O. Box 9041), Coldfoot, AK 99701 (☎ **907/678-5201**), offers a variety of services including lodging, a 24-hour restaurant, fuel, minor repairs, towing, RV hookup, laundry, a post office, and a gift shop. As at the Yukon, the inn is made of surplus construction worker housing—not fancy, but the rooms are clean and have private bathrooms. The park service has a small campground.

After Coldfoot, the next service area is at **Deadhorse,** at the end of the road 240 miles north, with three hotels, fuel, restaurants, a post office, vehicle maintenance, a general store, and an airport. See the Prudhoe Bay section in chapter 11.

CAMPING

The Bureau of Land Management has several camping sites along the road, mostly just gravel pads left over from construction days. They are at:

- **Mile 60:** artesian well and outhouses.
- **Mile 98, Finger Mountain:** nice views, outhouse, and wheelchair-accessible trail with interpretive signs.
- **Mile 115, Arctic Circle:** outhouses and picnic tables, an interpretive display, and undeveloped campground.
- **Mile 136, Prospect Creek:** no conveniences.
- **Mile 180, Marion Creek:** 27 campsites, a well, and outhouses; the fee is $6.
- **Mile 275, Galbraith Lake:** outhouse.

7 The Alaska Highway

The 200 miles of the Alaska Highway from the border with Canada to the terminus, in Delta Junction, is pretty boring driving—hours of stunted black spruce and brush, either living or burned out. It's a relief when you hit the first major town, Tok (rhymes with Coke), 100 miles along. Don't get your hopes up. This is the only place where I've ever walked into a visitor center and asked what there is to do in town, only to have the host hold up her fingers in the shape of a goose egg and say, "Nothing." Another 100 miles (I hope you brought plenty of cassette tapes), and you've made it to Delta Junction. There's a little more to do here, but it's still not a destination. Another 100 miles, and you're in Fairbanks.

Remember to set your watch back an hour when crossing the border east to west—it's an hour later in Yukon Territory. Also, if you make significant purchases or rent rooms in Canada, you may be able to get a refund on the 7% Goods and Services Tax. See the section on Dawson City, below, for details.

CUSTOMS   Canada is another country, with different laws. Here are a few possible trouble areas in crossing the border: **Firearms** other than hunting rifles or shotguns may cause you problems crossing into Canada; U.S. citizens don't need a visa but may need **proof of citizenship,** and a driver's license doesn't always cut it, although a passport or birth certificate will, or a driver's license in combination with some other identification; **children** with their parents may need a birth certificate, and children or teens under 18 unaccompanied by parents may need a letter from a parent or guardian; products you buy made of **ivory, fur, or other wildlife** should be sent home ahead just to be on the safe side, as they could cause a problem going either way on the border; there are rules concerning **animals,** as well. If in doubt, call **Canadian customs** in Whitehorse (☎ **867/667-3943**).

EAST OF TOK

The first 60 miles after entering the U.S., the road borders the Tetlin National Wildlife Refuge. A **visitor center** 7 miles past the border, at Mile 1,229, overlooks rolling hills and lakes. It is open 7am to 7pm. The U.S. Fish and Wildlife Service also has two small campgrounds over the next 20 miles.

TOK

Originally called Tokyo Camp, a construction station on the highway, the name was shortened to Tok when it became politically incorrect after Pearl Harbor. Since then, Tok's role in the world hasn't expanded much beyond being a stop on the road. With its location at the intersection of the Alaska Highway and the Glenn Highway to Glennallen—the short way to Anchorage and Prince William Sound—the town has built an economy of gas stations, gift stores, cafes, and hotels to serve highway travelers.

ESSENTIALS

GETTING THERE   You're surely passing through Tok with your own set of wheels. If you get stuck for some reason, the Gray Line **Alaskon Express** (☎ 800/544-2206 or 907/883-2291) stops most days during the summer at the Westmark Inn.

VISITOR INFORMATION   There are two large, interesting visitor centers to serve highway travelers arriving at this entry to Alaska; both are located in a large log building at the highway intersection that forms the town's locus. The ✪ **Alaska Public Lands Information Center,** P.O. Box 359, Tok, AK 99780 (☎ 907/883-5667; website http://www.nps.gov/aplic), open daily from 8am to 8pm in summer and from 8am to 4:30pm in winter, has displays on the public lands and ecology of the area that provide a good introduction to the state, as well as staff to answer questions. The **Tok Chamber of Commerce Visitors Center,** P.O. Box 389, Tok, AK 99780 (☎ 907/883-5887), provides commercial information on Tok and anywhere else you may be bound on the highway.

ORIENTATION   The businesses all are along a couple of miles of the **Alaska Highway** and **Glenn Highway,** but there is a residential district for a couple of blocks north of the intersection.

FAST FACTS   There is no sales tax—there is no local government, for that matter. An **ATM** is to be found at the bank in Frontier Foods, near the center of town, and at the Texaco station across the road from Fast Eddy's restaurant. The **Alaska State Troopers** (☎ 907/883-5111) police the region; they maintain an office near the intersection of the Alaska Highway and Glenn Highway; in **emergencies,** phone **911.** The **public health clinic** (☎ 907/883-4101) is located at the State Troopers Building. The *Anchorage Daily News* and *Fairbanks Daily News-Miner* are often available.

THINGS TO DO & SEE

Mukluk Land, under the big fiberglass mukluk 3 miles west of town (☎ 907/883-2571), is a homemade theme park that may amuse young children or even adults in a certain frame of mind; admission is $5 for adults, $4 senior citizens, $2 children and teens, and it's open June to August, daily from 1 to 9pm. Gold panning is an extra $5. The **Burnt Paw Gift Shop** has a free sled-dog demonstration on wheels June to August, Monday through Saturday at 7:30pm.

ACCOMMODATIONS
Standard Hotels & Motels

The motels are numerous and generally quite competitive in Tok. Shop around, if you want to take the time. There also are many bed-and-breakfasts—check at the visitor center.

Snowshoe Motel & Fine Arts and Gifts. Across the highway from the information center (P.O. Box 559), Tok, AK 99789. ☎ **800/478-4511,** in Alaska, Yukon, and part of B.C. or 907/883-4511. 24 rms. TV TEL. High season, $68 double. Low season, $48–$58 double. Rates include continental breakfast in summer. Additional person in room $5 extra. MC, V.

The 10 newer nonsmoking rooms near the front are a great bargain. Each is divided into two sections by the bathroom, providing two separate bedrooms—great for families. The furnishings are clean and modern, and the outside walkways are decorated with flowers.

Westmark Tok. Intersection of Alaska Hwy. and Glenn Hwy. (P.O. Box 130), Tok, AK 99780-0130. ☎ **800/544-0970** (reservations) or 907/883-5174. Fax 907/883-5178. Website http://www.westmarkhotels.com. 72 rms. TV TEL. $119 double. AE, DC, DISC, MC, V. Closed Sept 15–May 15.

The central hotel in town is closed in the winter, as its clientele is primarily the package-tour bus trade. It's made up of several buildings connected by boardwalks. The older rooms are narrow, without enough room at the foot of the bed for the TV, but comfortable and up to date. The new section has larger, higher-priced rooms. Ask for the "highway rate," $79 to $89 for a double. There's a "factory outlet" gift store in the lobby which sells remainders from Westmark's other shops for lower prices. A greenhouse grows huge vegetables. The restaurant has light-wood decor and serves three meals a day. Dinners are in the $14 to $20 range.

Young's Motel. Behind Fast Eddy's Restaurant on the Alaska Hwy. (P.O. Box 482), Tok, AK 99780. ☎ **907/883-4411.** Fax 907/883-5023. 43 rms. TV TEL. High season, $68 double. Low season, $55 double. Additional person in room $5 extra. AE, MC, V.

Good standard motel rooms occupy three one-story structures on the parking lot behind Fast Eddy's restaurant, where you check in. Eighteen newer, smoke free rooms are the pick of the litter, but all are acceptable.

A Hostel & Camping

The **Tok International Youth Hostel,** P.O. Box 532, Tok, AK 99780 (☎ **907/883-3745**), is made up of wall tents a mile off the Alaska Highway, 8 miles west of town on Pringle Drive. There are 10 beds for $10 apiece, and no showers. It's closed September 15 to May 15.

Don't fail to get the free state highway and campground map from the public lands center, which includes all the public campgrounds in Alaska. The 43-site **Tok River Campground** just east of town, managed by the state Division of Parks, lies along the river bottom below an Alaska Highway bridge. But if you're not ready to stop for the night, there are others along the highway which you can find on the map. There are lots of competitive RV parks in Tok. One that has wooded sites suitable for tent camping, too, is the **Sourdough Campground,** 1 1/2 miles south of town on the Glenn Highway (P.O. Box 47, Tok, Alaska 99780; ☎ **907/883-5543**).

DINING

The restaurants in Tok are all of the roadside diner variety, with roughly similar prices and long hours. All are located close together on the right as you come into town from the east on the Alaska Highway. Other than the Westmark, mentioned above, the best is **Fast Eddy's** (☎ 907/883-4411). The dining room, in dark wood and brass, is in a different league than the other diners; the service is quick and professional, and the food quite good. The **Gateway Salmon Bake** has an attractive picnic setup by the road and a dining room, and the food is good; it's a casual experience for families. Like all salmon bakes, it's touristy, but so what? You're in Tok, after all.

FROM TOK TO DELTA JUNCTION

There's not much to look at, but you may be curious about the Bison Range as you pass the sign. In the late 1970s and early 1980s, the state tried to start a massive barley-growing project in Delta Junction, selling would-be farmers tens of thousands of acres to clear so Alaska could become the barley basket of the Pacific. Among other problems, introduced bison kept trampling the crops, so the state built another hay farm to lure the bison away from the barley farms. Meanwhile, the majority of the barley farms went bust. The landowners came out nicely, however, since they soon began receiving federal payments not to plant crops that far exceeded anything they ever made from barley. The bison are sitting pretty, too, with their own 3,000-acre farm. Who says government doesn't work? In summer, there's slim chance of seeing a bison from the road.

DELTA JUNCTION

This intersection with the Richardson Highway, which runs from Valdez to Fairbanks, is the official end of the Alaska Highway. It's an earnest little roadside town set in a broad plain between the Delta and Tanana rivers. People make their living from farming, tourism, work at a trans-Alaska pipeline pump station south of town, and the military—although nearby Fort Greely will close in 2001. West of town is a historic roadhouse museum, and there are several good campgrounds and lake recreation. You can spend an enjoyable half day here as a break in your travels.

ESSENTIALS

A helpful **visitor center** run by the Delta Chamber of Commerce, P.O. Box 987, Delta Junction, AK 99737 (☎ 907/895-5068), stands at the intersection of the Alaska and Richardson highways, in the middle of town. You can buy a certificate saying you drove the Alaska Highway. The historic **Sullivan Roadhouse** has been installed next door. At this writing, there were plans to open it as a museum on the area's early days.

Delta has no taxes of any kind. The **National Bank of Alaska** has a branch right at the center of town, on the Richardson Highway, with an **ATM.** The **post office** is on the east side of the Richardson, 2 blocks north of the visitor center. In **emergencies,** phone **911;** for nonemergencies, call the **Alaska State Troopers** (☎ 907/895-4800). The **Family Medical Center** is at Mile 267.2 on the Richardson Highway, 2 miles north of the visitors center (☎ 907/895-4879 or 907/895-5100).

THINGS TO DO & SEE

The **Buffalo Wallow square dance festival** occurs over Memorial Day weekend at the school. There's a **Buffalo Barbecue** for the Fourth of July. The biggest event of the year is the annual **Deltana Fair,** held for a weekend in late July or early August; it's a community celebration, with a parade, outhouse race, livestock, carnival, and games.

Trans-Alaska pipeline **Pump Station 9,** 7 miles south of town on the Richardson Highway (☎ 907/869-3270), has free, 1-hour technical tours six times a day during the summer; it's the only one of the 12 pump stations open for tours.

Powered by jet engines, the pump stations keep the thick, viscous oil moving the 800 miles from Prudhoe Bay to Valdez. Call ahead to make sure the tours are still operating. Children and cameras are not allowed, and you must wear a hard-hat and goggles. **Rika's Roadhouse and Landing,** 10 miles northwest of town on the Richardson Highway (☎ **907/895-4201**), makes a pleasant stop on your drive. The state historical park preserves a log 1917 building and its lovely grounds, at the confluence of the Delta and Tanana rivers. The furnishings and museum pieces may be younger than some of the visitors, but the site as a whole, with its gorgeous vegetable garden and domestic fowl, does a good job of conveying what Alaska pioneer life was like. The roadhouse and a restaurant serving soups, salads, and sandwiches are open daily 9am to 5pm, the grounds and museum 8am to 8pm, May 15 to September 15. An impressive suspension bridge carries the trans-Alaska pipeline over the Tanana River, and boaters use the shoreline as a landing.

Alaska State Parks also maintains five campgrounds on the rivers and lakes in and around Delta Junction, with some limited fishing. The **Quartz Lake State Recreation Area,** 11 miles northwest of town on the Richardson and down a 3-mile turn-off, has an 80-site campground on the shallow lake; the fee is $8 a night,

The **Delta River National Wild and Scenic River** is a popular float of up to 3-days for experienced canoe or raft paddlers, or an easy 18 miles on just the lower portion near town. The long version starts at Tangle Lakes, on the Denali Highway. Contact the public lands center in Tok or Fairbanks for guidance, or get a copy of the *Alaska River Guide* mentioned at the beginning of this chapter.

ACCOMMODATIONS

In addition to the two somewhat idiosyncratic places listed here, you'll find inexpensive basic rooms at **Alaska 7 Motel,** 3548 Richardson Hwy. (P.O. Box 1115), Delta Junction, AK 99737 (☎ **907/895-4848**). To park an RV, or if you're tent camping and need a shower, **Smith's Green Acres RV Park and Campground,** 1¹/₂ miles north on the Richardson from the visitor center (☎ **907/895-4369**), is a well-developed establishment.

Bed and Breakfast at the Home of Alys. 2303 Alys Ave., Delta Junction, AK 99737. ☎ **907/895-4128.** 2 rms. TV. $75 double, $15 each additional person. No credit cards.

As the name says, these rooms are fully part of Henry and Alys Brewis's home, but that's good, because you wouldn't want to come to Delta Junction without meeting this fascinating couple, hearing their stories of a lifetime pioneer homesteading in Alaska, and being treated like a member of their family. Henry's parents both came to Alaska in the Klondike gold rush. The comfortable rooms look out on a yard with a greenhouse and impressive gardens, where moose often wander through. Take Brewis road off the Richardson Highway just north of town.

Kelly's Country Inn. Intersection of Richardson and Alaska hwys. (P.O. Box 849), Delta Junction, AK 99737. ☎ **907/895-4667.** 21 rms. TV TEL. $80 double. AE, MC, V. Additional person in room $5 extra.

The low-slung gray buildings with rose trim contain unique, charming rooms. Some have floral designs, others arched wooden ceilings, and there are lots of other unexpected touches. The proprietor is Chaddie Kelly, who has been here forever. All rooms have refrigerators and free coffee, and most have microwave ovens.

DINING

There are several restaurants near the intersection that defines the town. These two each accept MasterCard and Visa: The **White Raven** is a smoky but clean hangout for locals, with reasonable prices for roadside cafe food and an evening menu that includes a welcome break from the constant diet of beef generally found on the highway; **Pizza Bella** has a beer and wine license and reasonably priced pizza pies.

8 Dawson City: Gold-Rush Destination

Driving east from Tok toward Dawson City, by the third hour bouncing over gravel road, orange midnight twilight falls to the north and a huge moon rises to the east, lighting the silhouettes of rounded mountains that stand all around in countless, receding layers, all quiet, all empty. The border to Canada is closed for the night; camping by the road, no vehicles pass in the alpine silence. Next morning, passing through Customs, you go on for an hour and a half more over the Top of the World Highway, no sign of humankind within the distant horizon other than the thread of gravel you're following. Turn another corner, and there it is—down below, a grid of city streets on the edge of the Yukon and Klondike rivers: Dawson City, once the second-largest city on the West Coast of North America, is still way out in the middle of nowhere 100 years later.

Suddenly the radio's working again, bringing in an urbane situation comedy originating in Toronto. At the gravel river landing, a free car-ferry pulls up. A moment later, on the other side, there are people all over broad, straight streets, looking at well-kept old buildings. Inside a museumlike visitor center, guides dressed in period costumes are providing tourists with directions and selling them tickets to shows. Looking back at the hill across the river, at the wilderness so close at hand yet so separate, it's suddenly possible to understand the incongruity and shock of the gold rush. One hundred years ago, the world suddenly went mad and rushed to this riverbank beyond the edge of civilization and created a sophisticated city. One day it was a quiet riverbank, unknown except by the indigenous people; the next day, a city. It arrived as suddenly as it arrives in your windshield driving east on the highway.

Dawson City was the destination for some 100,000 stampeders hoping to strike it rich on the Klondike River in 1898, about 30,000 of whom actually made it here. Mining for gold and other minerals continues today, but the town's main focus is on the visitors who come to see a well-preserved gold-rush boom town. Parks Canada does a good job of keeping up the buildings that make up part of the Klondike National Historic Sites and providing activities that bring history alive; you can spend 2 full days here, if you're interested in the period the town celebrates. Dawson City sometimes feels like one big museum, and it doesn't suffer from the commercialism that pervades Skagway, the other major gold-rush town in the region. Gambling in a small casino happens every night during the summer, but from mid-September to mid-May, the town essentially shuts down, as the extreme weather of the region drives tourists and miners away.

For those who get their fill of gold-rush history quickly, the long drive may not be justified, although there are some mountain-biking and river-floating opportunities. Floating the Yukon down to Eagle is a popular trip, and other, more remote water is available to explore in the area, too.

ESSENTIALS

GETTING THERE   The main way visitors come to Dawson City is by making a long detour from the Alaska Highway. The paved Klondike Highway, also known as Yukon Highway 2, splits from the Alaska Highway a few miles west of Whitehorse, heading 327 miles north over scenic, fairly smooth road to Dawson City. For guidance on that part of the trip, get the excellent "Canada's Yukon Official Vacation

Dawson City

LEGEND
⊠ Post Office
ⓘ Information

Dawson City Area

Attractions
Bear Creek Historic Mining Camp ③
Commissioner's Residence ⑰
Dawson City Museum ⑱
Diamond Tooth Gertie's ⑧
Gold Dredge # 4 ④
Jack London Cabin ⑲
Palace Grand Theatre ⑤
Robert Service Cabin ⑳
St. Paul's Anglican Church ⑯
Accommodations & Dining
The Bunkhouse ⑪
Dawson City River Hostel ②
Eldorado Hotel ⑩
5th Ave. Bed & Breakfast ⑮

Goldrush Campgrounds RV Park ⑦
Klondike Kate's Restaurant ⑥
Melinda's ⑬
Triple J Hotel ⑨
Westmark Inn ⑫
White Ram Manor B&B ⑭
Yukon River Campground ①

Guide" from **Tourism Yukon,** P.O. Box 2703, Whitehorse, Yukon, Canada Y1A 2C6 (☎ **867/667-5340;** fax 867/667-3546; website http://www.touryukon.com/). The gravel Top of the World Highway heads west from Dawson City, crossing the border before connecting with the Taylor Highway, which leads north to Eagle and south to rejoin the Alaska Highway, 175 miles after Dawson City. The 502 miles for the detour compare to 375 miles if you stay on the pavement of the Alaska Highway. You do miss the spectacular vistas on Kluane Lake. Below, you'll find a description of the Top of the World and Taylor highways and Eagle. The border is open 5am to 10pm Alaska time, and the road closes in winter.

If you don't want to drive, many package tours include Dawson City. The best is probably Gray Line of Alaska's tours (see "Package Tour or Do-It-Yourself" in chapter 3). **Air North** (☎ **867/993-5110;** fax 867/668-6224) flies round-trip Dawson City to Fairbanks on Tuesday, Thursday, and Sunday.

VISITOR INFORMATION The **Parks Canada Visitor Reception Centre,** at King and Front streets (P.O. Box 390), Dawson City, YT, Canada Y0B 1G0 (☎ 867/993-7228), is open daily from 8am to 8pm during the visitor season. A mix of information center, museum, and theater of historic films, it's an indispensable stop. The hosts are knowledgeable and provide free maps and guides, as well as selling tickets to all the Klondike National Historic Sites tours, events, and shows. If you plan to do all or most of the gold field attractions, an events pass for $10 Canadian is a good deal. Generally, the prices for attractions are low, especially when you consider that Canadian dollars are worth about 30% less than U.S. dollars.

ORIENTATION   The town lies on a flat piece of land below a bluff on the bank of the Yukon River where it's joined by the Klondike River. **Front Street** runs along the river dike; behind it, a simple grid counts up to **Eighth Avenue** before the town runs out of room against the bluff. The whole thing is easily walkable. A few attractions are located out the **Klondike Highway,** which connects to Front Street on the south of the town. **Bonanza Creek Road** splits off to the right just after you leave town.

GETTING AROUND   You probably got to Dawson City in a car or RV. If not, cars are for rent from **Budget** (☎ 867/993-5644) or **Norcan Rentals** (☎ 867/ 993-6465). Dropping off in Whitehorse is around $100. **Gold City Tours** (☎ 867/ 993-5175), on Front Street across from the riverboat *Keno,* offers a 3¹/₂-hour tour that includes Gold Dredge No. 4 and gold panning every afternoon in the summer for $33. They also have an airport limousine. **Bikes** are a fun way to get to the outlying sights for strong riders and are available for rent at the **Dawson City River Hostel,** listed below.

The free **George Black Ferry** crosses the Yukon 24 hours a day from a landing at the north end of Front Street, providing a connection to the Top of the World Highway, a provincial campground, and the hostel.

FAST FACTS   *Note:* All the prices in this section are listed in Canadian dollars, unless I've stated otherwise.

Dawson City is on Pacific time, 1 hour later than Alaska. You'll pay the 7% **Goods and Services Tax (GST)** for almost everything, but if you're not a Canadian, you can apply to get up to $500 of it back at a Duty Free Shop or from Visitor Rebate Program, Revenue Canada, Summerside Tax Centre, Summerside, PE, C1N 6C6 Canada (☎ 800/668-4748 in Canada; 902/432-5608 outside Canada). Pick up a booklet containing the rules and an application from the visitor center. The rebate counts only if you spent more than $200, and only on taxes paid for goods and accommodations, not food, services, rentals, transportation, fuel, and the like. There is one **bank** in town, the Canadian Imperial Bank of Commerce, at Second Avenue and Queen Street; it has an **ATM.** The next closest bank is 330 miles southeast in Whitehorse or 175 miles southwest in Tok. The **post office** is on Fifth Avenue near Princess Street, and a historic post office, with limited services, is at Third Avenue and King Street. In **emergencies,** call the **Royal Canadian Mounted Police,** on Front Street near Turner (☎ 867/993-5555), or the **ambulance** (☎ 867/ 993-4444). A **nursing station** is located at Sixth and Mission streets. Dawson City once had eight **newspapers,** but today the *Klondike Sun* is published only bimonthly; other newspapers are available at Maximillian's, at Front and Queen streets. The CBC also provides **news,** at 560 AM, and a visitor radio station broadcasts on 96.1 FM.

SPECIAL EVENTS   The social event of the year in Dawson City is the **Commissioner's Grande Ball,** in early June. The **Yukon Gold Panning Championships** and **Canada Day Celebrations** are on July 1.

EXPLORING DAWSON CITY

GOLD RUSH ATTRACTIONS   Parks Canada leads a ✪ **town walking tour** from the Visitor Reception Centre daily for $5. The guides are well trained and can open historic buildings you won't get to look inside otherwise. They also lend a 90-minute cassette tape version with headphones. Or you can use one of the maps they distribute to make up your own walking tour; there are interesting buildings almost anywhere you wander. Here are some of the highlights. On Front Street, just south of the visitor centre, the newly restored steamer *Keno* sits on timbers. The free **Dawson As They Saw It** display of historic photographs is at Third Avenue and Princess Street.

Across the intersection, the **Bigg's Blacksmith Shop** is next to a gold rush–era building that is slowly sinking into the permafrost. At Front and Church streets, 2 blocks south, **St. Paul's Anglican Church** is a charming, creaky 1902 structure on the riverfront. Next door, the **Commissioner's Residence,** an impressive mansion with a wraparound porch, standing amid beautifully planted grounds, has been restored with mostly original furnishings. A tour goes through daily at 4pm for $5. In back of the house, you'll find a log building that was part of the 1897 **Fort Herchmer,** and later a jail.

The ✪ **Dawson City Museum,** on Fifth Avenue between Church and Turner streets (P.O. Box 303, Dawson City, Yukon, Y0B 1G0; ☎ 867/993-5291), is the best-presented gold-rush museum I've seen. The fascinating, tin-roofed federalist building housed the Territorial Government starting from 1901, and upstairs one of the galleries still doubles as an impressive courtroom. The galleries downstairs display gold-rush artifacts in a way that makes them seem immediate and alive. Guides dressed in costume lead tours further expanding on the teaching power of the objects and excellent placards. The clutter common to this kind of museum is confined to the "visible storage" gallery upstairs, where a rich collection is housed inside glass-fronted cabinets. A cafe serves soup, muffins, coffee, and tea, and there's a gift shop. Admission is $3.50; the museum is open Victoria Day to Labour Day, daily from 10am to 6pm. Next door is a free display of 19th-century locomotives from the short-lived Klondike Mine Line Railway, which ran 32 miles up Bonanza Creek.

The **Jack London Cabin,** at Eighth Avenue and Grant Street along the foot of the bluff, is a replica with some logs from the original cabin where London probably spent his winter in the Klondike. (The rest of the logs are in a replica in Oakland, California, where London also lived.) A small museum with a guide who gives lectures is at the site. London found a gold mine of material for his classic adventure stories, but little gold, when he stampeded north.

Poet **Robert Service** spent more time at his cabin, at Eighth Avenue and Hansen Street, just down the road. Service wrote his ballads about the North while working as a bank clerk in Dawson City, reciting them for free drinks in the bars. Today you can hear them in tourist shows all over Alaska, but Tom Byrne is the granddaddy of Service readers. He's been reciting the poems from a rocking chair on the pleasant, grassy slope in front of the cabin since 1979, never canceling an outdoor show because of inclement weather. He has the right touch. Admission is $6 for adults, $3 for children; recitals are at 10am and 3pm.

After the initial gold rush, the Rothschilds and Guggenheims financed large-scale industrial gold mining here. The remains of that amazing technical effort are preserved outside of town. **Gold Dredge No. 4,** 8 miles down Bonanza Creek Road south of town, is maintained by Parks Canada to show how these incredible earth-eating machines worked their way across the landscape, sifting gold out of the gravel; similar dredges are in Fairbanks and Nome. Hour-long tours, which circle the outside of the machine but don't go inside, take place hourly from 9am to 5pm and cost $5. Another 7 miles up the road, the site of the original Klondike strike is marked. Parks Canada also manages the ✪ **Bear Creek Historic Mining Camp,** 7 miles up the Klondike Highway. The camp was headquarters for the company that owned the gold diggings. It's been kept as if the workers just left, including warehouses and workshops full of odd and interesting mechanical relics. The highlight is the gold room, where the gold was melted into bricks. At the end, you can watch a documentary film about the mining made before the operation shut down in 1966. The 1-hour tour takes place five times a day from 9am to 4:30pm and costs $5.

The Gold Rush at 100

The biggest event in Alaska history happened 100 years ago: the 1898 Klondike Gold Rush. If you're coming to Alaska, you'll be hearing a lot about it. Here's some of the context for the barrage of anecdotes you can expect.

Gold prospectors had been combing the Alaska Territory for decades. On the Fortymile River, just west of the Canadian border along the Yukon River, gold had been found in 1886, and hardy searchers were looking for more 10 years later when word came that white prospector George Carmack and his Native partners, Tagish Charlie and Skookum Jim, had struck gold on the Klondike River, a tributary to the Yukon in Canada. Within 48 hours, the Fortymile Country was empty.

Miners dug gravel from the creek that winter. When they washed it in the spring, it yielded big hunks of solid gold. They were instant millionaires in a time when a million dollars meant something, but the import of their find was far greater: U.S. currency was on a gold standard at that time, and the scarcity of gold had caused a deflationary vice on the economy that in 1893 brought a banking collapse and unemployment of 18%. When, in 1897, a steamer arrived in Seattle bearing the men from the Klondike with their trunks and gunny sacks of gold, it brought salvation for the national economy and caused 100,000 people to set out for Alaska.

As late as 1880, Alaska had fewer than 500 white residents; about 30,000 came all the way to Dawson City, mostly in 1898. Few of that number struck it rich, but those who built the towns and businesses to serve them did—there were suddenly saloons and brothels, dress shops and photo studios. Promoters sold a credulous public newly laid-out towns on the routes to the gold fields. The White Pass above Skagway and the Chilkoot Pass above Dyea were the busiest. Gold seekers arrived by steamer from Seattle, then ferried their goods over the passes to Lake Bennett— the Canadian authorities wisely required each to bring a ton of supplies, a rule that undoubtedly prevented famine. Next they built boats, crossed the lake, and floated down the Yukon River to Dawson City, a 500-mile journey from the sea.

By the time most arrived, the gold claims had all been staked, and big companies were taking over. Ever larger and more sophisticated machinery dug the Klondike claims and washed the gravel until the 1960s, and gold mining remains an important part of the economy to this day, but the prospectors looking to strike it rich quickly moved on. Their wild chase for gold founded Alaska's first towns, many of which disappeared as soon as the frenzy cooled. The gold sands of Nome came in 1899, Fairbanks in 1902, Iditarod in 1908—and it's not over. Small-time prospectors are still looking, and sometimes someone does make a significant new strike. A 1987 find north of Fairbanks has been developed at a cost of $400 million. Gold mining is hotter now than at any time in the last 100 years.

But there's a much bigger and safer business in mining the tourist trade. The rush of visitors each summer dwarfs the numbers who came in 1898, and, in the true spirit of the event whose centennial they celebrate, the gold rush towns of Skagway, Dawson City, Fairbanks, and Nome know there's more money to be made from people than from gold.

(I am indebted to Stan Jones, of the *Anchorage Daily News,* for his writing on the economic conditions that led to the gold rush. On the Internet, see http://Gold-Rush.org, for centennial events and information.)

ON THE RIVER   Dawson City is the largest town on the Yukon River after Whitehorse, and the most developed access point near Alaska. There are other good floating rivers in the region, too. The Yukon, flowing 5 to 10 miles per hour, is a slow-paced westward-flowing highway. Two companies offer tour-boat rides, and three self-guided canoe or raft floats.

The *Yukon Lou*, with a log cabin office and dock on Front Street (P.O. Box 859), Dawson City, YT, Canada Y0B 1G0 (☎ **867/993-5482**), takes 90-minute tours on a sternwheeler to Pleasure Island each afternoon, where passengers get off for a sled-dog exhibition, mining display, and other activities; it costs $20 for adults. The boat also takes an evening dinner cruise to the island for barbecued salmon; it's $40 for adults, $20 for children. Gray Line Yukon operates the *Yukon Queen* (☎ **867/ 993-5599**), which runs daily from late May to early September 108 miles down-river to Eagle. The modern 49-passenger boat leaves at 8:30am for a 4-hour, narrated ride to Eagle; once there, you can eat at the cafe and visit the museum. It returns the same day, going upstream in 5 hours and serving a dinner of beef stew before arriving at 8pm back in Dawson City. Most passengers are on Holland America–Westours packages, but you can book a place if space is available. It's $81 U.S. one-way, $133 round-trip; or you can fly back. The office is across Front Street from the Visitor Reception Centre.

One popular trip is to float 3 or 4 days in a canoe or raft to Eagle and come back on the *Yukon Queen;* there also are other more remote floats in the area, or you can keep floating down the Yukon to Circle, or even farther. The **Dawson Trading Post,** P.O. Box 889, Dawson City, YT, Canada Y0B 1G0 (☎ **867/993-5316**), rents canoes and camping gear, and operates a shuttle that can drop you off on the more remote Stewart or Klondike River for $25 an hour plus gas (they charge both ways). Or you can float down to Eagle. Canoes rent for $30 a day or $150 a week. Two companies offering one-way floats to Eagle are listed in the "Eagle" section, below.

ACCOMMODATIONS

Hotels have been burning down in Dawson City for 100 years, yet still all the wooden buildings I saw lack sprinklers.

STANDARD ACCOMMODATIONS

The Bunkhouse. Front and Princess sts. (Bag 4040), Dawson City, YT, Canada Y0B 1G0. ☎ **867/993-6164.** Fax 867/993-6051. 31 rms, 5 with bath. $50 double without bath, $80–$95 double with bath. Additional person in room $5 extra. MC, V.

This is a unique place—it looks like a riverboat from the outside, and is fresh and trim, but it's intended for a budget traveler. The rooms, all no-smoking with exterior entries, have varnished wooden floors and attractive fabrics. The beds are really bunks—no bed springs. Those that share bathrooms are quite small; the bathrooms are clean, but women may feel funny about the showers, which are in booths that enter into a shared room. The rooms with private bathrooms have telephones and TVs and are delightful.

El Dorado Hotel. Princess St. and Third Ave. (P.O. Box 338), Dawson City, YT, Canada Y0B 1G0. ☎ **867/993-5451.** Fax 867/993-5256. 53 rms, 4 suites. TV TEL. $121 double; $150 suite. Additional person in room $9 extra. AE, DC, DISC, ER, JCB, MC, V.

Locals come to this year-round hotel daily to check the price of gold, posted in the lobby. The rooms are large and clean, and many have new beds, carpeting, and curtains, although some furniture and fixtures remained a bit out of date when I visited. There's a choice of lighter motel-style rooms in a newer building and larger rooms in a large old wood structure. All rooms have fans and coffee pots, and a courtesy car, coin-op laundry, and kitchenettes are available. The attractive but smoky **Bonanza Dining Room** has an extensive and varied menu, with entrees ranging from $17 to $23. There's a bar on the other side of the lobby.

Triple J Hotel. Fifth Ave. and Queen St. (P.O. Box 359), Dawson City, YT, Canada Y0B 1G0. ☎ **867/993-5323.** Fax 867/993-5030. 47 rms, 20 cabins. TV TEL. High season, $95–$117 double or cabins for two. Low season, $65–$75 double. Additional person in room $10 extra. AE, MC, V. Closed Nov–Apr.

This rambling set of structures has three different kinds of rooms: large hotel rooms in the old, wooden main building; smallish rooms in the low-slung motel building; and cabins with kitchenettes and little porches, some of which were about to receive a needed remodel when I visited. Some of the rooms are excellent, others nothing to brag about but still clean and serviceable. All rooms have fans and coffeemakers, and the hotel also provides a courtesy car and a coin-op laundry. The **restaurant** has a menu with a broad range of prices and varied cuisine, and they hold a popular barbecue on the deck of the lounge.

○ **Westmark Inn Dawson.** Fifth Ave. and Harper St. (P.O. Box 420), Dawson City, YT, Canada Y0B 1G0. ☎ **800/544-0970** (reservations) or 867/993-5542. Fax 867/993-5623. Website http://www.westmarkhotels.com. 120 rms, 9 suites. TV TEL. $159 double. AE, CB, DC, ER, MC, V. Closed Sept 15–May 15.

The modern, well-run Westmark is the best hotel in town, especially the newer Jack London and Robert Service wings, where wide, well-lit hallways lead to large rooms with crisp gold rush–theme decorative touches. The older rooms are good, too, but are smaller and have older decor. All rooms have fans and clocks, and there's a coin-op laundry. Ask for the "highway rate." A patio in the grassy courtyard is the site of a daily barbecue. **Belinda's Restaurant,** with light-wood decor and well-spaced tables, is open daily from 6am to 10pm; there's also a lounge.

BED & BREAKFASTS

There are several good B&Bs in Dawson City. The **5th Avenue Bed and Breakfast,** on Fifth Avenue next door to the museum (P.O. Box 722), Dawson City, YT, Canada Y0B 1G0 (☎ **867/993-5941**), has seven rooms—basic, but fresh and well done. Three have their own bathrooms, and there are two kitchens for guests to use. The bright-pink **White Ram Manor,** at Seventh Avenue and Harper Street (P.O. Box 302), Dawson City, YT, Canada Y0B 1G0 (☎ **867/993-5772**), has 10 generally small rooms with TVs, all but one with shared baths, but the great feature is the large deck with a hot tub, barbecue, and picnic table, and the hospitable hostess, Gail Hendley.

A HOSTEL & CAMPING

Dieter Reinmuth operates the **Dawson City River Hostel,** P.O. Box 32, Dawson City, YT, Canada Y0B 1G0 (☎ **867/993-6823**), across the Yukon from Dawson City on the free ferry. Bunks in cabins, private rooms, and camping are available, as well as a sweatlodge and cold showers. He also rents bicycles and canoes. The wooded provincial **Yukon River Campground,** just down the road, has 98 sites; the fee is $8. The **Goldrush Campground RV Park,** at Fifth Avenue and York Street (☎ **867/993-5247**), is a conveniently located lot right downtown.

DINING

I've described restaurants at the Westmark, El Dorado, and Triple J hotels, above, and the *Yukon Lou* Pleasure Island Restaurant dinner cruise. The best place I found was **Melinda's,** at 842 Fifth Ave. (☎ **867/993-6800**), across from the Westmark. Primarily a dinner place, they specialize in Greek and Italian cuisine and also serve pizza. Reservations are recommended. **Klondike Kate's Restaurant,** in a historic building at Third Avenue and King Street (☎ **867/993-6527**), offers decent food for low prices, with a fully licensed bar. The patio is pleasant.

DAWSON CITY IN THE EVENING

Some of Dawson City's most famous and fun activities are in the evening. **Diamond Tooth Gertie's,** at Fourth Avenue and Queen Street (☎ **867/993-5575**), operated by the Klondike Visitors Association, is a gambling hall and bar, with tame cabaret singing and can-can dancing floor shows. It's a fun place to go with a group. The shows, each different, are at 8:30 and 10:30pm and 12:30am Tuesday through Sunday. It's open daily from 7pm to 2am, and admission is $4.75 for all evening, with only those at least 19 years old admitted.

The *Gaslight Follies* is a 2-hour vaudeville show on 8pm Wednesday through Monday in the **Palace Grand Theatre,** a historic building at Second Avenue and King Street that has been renovated by Parks Canada. Tickets—$15 to $17 for adults, $6 for children—are on sale at the box office from 3pm. Parks Canada also leads tours through the theater at 11am daily; it costs $5 at the Visitors Reception Centre.

9 Eagle and the Top of the World & Taylor Highways

The tiny town of Eagle got lost in an eddy in the stream of history sometime before World War I, where it still awaits discovery by the outside world. The town was founded in 1898 as a subtle fraud, when a group of prospectors staked out the land then cleverly created a buzz in Dawson City, just upriver across the border, of gold to be found there. The federal government followed the rush, and Judge James Wickersham chose Eagle for a new courthouse to try to bring law to the wild country in 1900. But when gold really was found in Fairbanks, the attention of prospectors and of Wickersham moved on, leaving Eagle slowly to decline to a ghost town of only nine residents by 1953. But that's where the really exceptional part of the story begins. The few remaining people recognized the value of the history that had been left behind—Wickersham's papers were still in his desk where he'd left them—and formed the historical society that today is the main activity for the town's 140 residents. Visitors can tour the courthouse, customs house, and five museums, and use Eagle for the start or end of a history-drenched Yukon River float. You'll also see the places John McPhee wrote about in his classic *Coming Into The Country*.

The reason Eagle is still so interesting is that it's still isolated, 173 dusty miles from Tok or 144 from Dawson City. It's a major side trip from the route between the two cities, which are 187 road miles apart, adding at least a day to your trip.

The **Taylor Highway** runs 160 miles north from the Alaska Highway just east of Tok to Eagle, 4 or 5 hours over a rough gravel road that's open only in summer. There are no services or signs of human development on the way except at the town of Chicken, barely a wide spot in the road 66 miles north, with gas, a couple of shops, a bar, and a cafe, but no phone. The drive does have impressive views in spots. There are two campgrounds, at mile 49 and mile 82, maintained by the **Bureau of Land Management,** Tok Field Office, P.O. Box 309, Tok, AK 99780 (☎ **907/ 883-5121**). The fee for each is $6. The BLM also is responsible for the **Fortymile National Wild and Scenic River,** a system with several floats of various lengths and levels of difficulty. The BLM or the public land information center in Tok can provide a river guide brochure and advice, or get *The Alaska River Guide,* mentioned at the beginning of this chapter. The BLM also produces a Taylor Highway road guide that's worth picking up.

The **Top of the World Highway** begins at mile 96 of the Taylor and heads 79 miles east to Dawson City. If you choose to go to Eagle, this is where you turn to the north for the last 66 miles of rough, windy driving through lovely canyons and forest. The Canadian part of the gravel highway is better maintained and stunningly beautiful on a clear day. You drive over the tops of mountains, treeless alpine vistas spreading far to the horizon. Just short of the border, 13 miles from the junction, there's a small roadhouse at a place called Boundary, the only habitation on the way. Information on crossing the border is in the Dawson City section, above.

Don't plan on making 60 miles an hour on any of these roads. In the Canadian section, most of the road is fairly broad and smooth, but speeds over 45 or so contribute to losing control or losing a headlight or windshield to a rock from a passing vehicle. On the U.S. side, the road is poorly maintained in places, and you sometimes have to go quite slowly.

Eagle has the historic sites and the Yukon River. The **Eagle City Historical Society,** P.O. Box 23, Eagle, AK 99738 (☎ 907/547-2325), offers town tours Memorial Day to Labor Day, daily at 9am; the 3-hour tour costs $5. Or for the admission plus $10 more for a group, they'll do the tour any time you like, winter or summer. The guides are local people, brimming with pride and knowledge about the area. Find them at the courthouse at Second and Berry streets. In addition to the tour, a great little museum downstairs is open around the middle of the day. The tour takes you through various historic buildings loaded with the original materials left behind after the gold rush, including five buildings in the army's 1899 Fort Egbert, where General Billy Mitchell had his first major assignment, in 1901 (before he was a general), to build a telegraph line to Valdez. You'll also notice the monument to Norwegian explorer Roald Amundsen, who stopped off in Eagle in 1905 during his journey through the Northwest Passage—400 miles away by dogsled—to use the telegraph.

The headquarters of the Yukon–Charley Rivers National Preserve is across the airstrip on the west side of town. The preserve starts a few miles downstream on the Yukon and extends almost to Circle. The National Park Service **visitor center,** P.O. Box 167, Eagle, AK 99738 (☎ 907/547-2233; website http://www.nps.gov/yuch/), is a good place to get information on floating the river and to register your journey. It's open Memorial Day to September, daily from 8am to 5pm, and normal business hours year round. They also can provide lots of information on the natural history of the area and historic sites downstream.

You can start or finish a **river float** in Eagle. From Dawson City to Eagle is 108 miles and takes 3 or 4 days, and from Eagle to Circle is 158 miles and 5 to 7 days. Mike Seger's **Eagle Canoe Rentals,** P.O. Box 4, Eagle, AK 99738 (☎ 907/547-2203 in Eagle or 867/993-6823 in Dawson City), allows you to drop off the canoe at the end of your float, and also rents rafts. The Dawson City office is located at the Dawson City River Hostel on the west side of the river next to the free ferry landing. The price, including return of the canoe, is $110 for up to 4 days to Eagle, $160 up to 5 days to Circle, and additional days are $20. **Elmore Enterprises,** P.O. Box 145, Eagle, AK 99738 (☎ 907/547-2355), rents canoes and rafts, offers guided trips and shuttle services, books flights, and operates a store, and fax.

The **Eagle Trading Company,** P.O. Box 36, Eagle, AK 99738 (☎ 907/547-2220; fax 907/547-2202), is the main business in town, with a grocery store, gas station, public showers, restaurant, and motel. Their Riverside Cafe is exceptionally good for the Bush, with tasty, inexpensive food and a dining room overlooking the river. The nine motel rooms also are surprisingly good, with TVs and phones, tubs with showers, two queen beds in each, and a rate of only $60 double.

A BLM campground is located in the woods above Fort Egbert.

The Bush 11

The Bush is most of Alaska. On a map of the state, the portion with roads and cities is really just a smallish corner. Yet most visitors—and, indeed, most Alaskans—never make it beyond that relatively populated corner. It's not uncommon for children to grow to adulthood in Anchorage, Fairbanks, or Southeast Alaska without ever traveling to the Arctic, the Aleutians, or the vast wetlands of western Alaska. The reason they don't is the same simple reason most tourists don't go to Bush Alaska—getting to the Bush is expensive, and there's not much there in the way of human activity once you arrive. Bush Alaska is one of the planet's last barely inhabited areas, where indigenous people still interact with the environment in their traditional way, and new places still remain to be explored by self-reliant outdoors people.

Although there are few people, the hospitality of those you meet in the Bush is special and warming. In Bush Alaska, it's not uncommon to be befriended and taken under wing by total strangers for no other reason than that you've taken the trouble to come to their community and are, therefore, an honored guest. Even in the larger towns, people look you in the eye and smile as you pass in the street, and if you have a questioning look on your face, they'll stop to help. Living in a small place where people know each other and have to work together against the elements makes for a tight, friendly community.

The cultural traditions of Alaska's Native people go beyond simple hospitality. Theirs is a culture based more on cooperative than competitive impulses, where honesty, respect, and consensus carry greater weight than in white society. Cooperation also requires slowing down, listening, not taking the lead—people from our fast-paced culture can leave a village after a visit wondering why no one spoke to them, not realizing that they never shut up long enough to give anyone a chance. (For more on the culture of Alaska's Native peoples, see chapter 2.)

The Native people of the Bush also have terrible problems trying to live in two worlds. There's too much alcohol and too many drugs in the Bush, too much TV, but not enough of an economic base to provide for safe drinking water or plumbing in many villages. Even in some of the relatively prosperous village hubs described in this chapter, visitors will glimpse a kind of rural poverty they may not have seen before—where prices are extremely high, and steady jobs interfere with traditional hunting and food gathering.

The world the Native people survive in is extreme in every respect—the weather, the land, even the geography. There's a special feeling to walking along the Arctic Ocean, the virtual edge of the earth, on a beach that lies between flat, wet tundra and an ocean that's usually ice. The quantity and accessibility of wildlife are extreme, too, as are the solitude and uniqueness of what you can do. Unfortunately, the prices also are extreme. With few exceptions, getting to a Bush hub from Anchorage costs at least as much as getting to Anchorage from Seattle. And once you're in the hub, you're not done. Getting into the outdoors can cost as much again. Most families and young people can't afford to make a Bush sojourn, instead satisfying their curiosity about the state's unpopulated areas on Alaska's rural highways. Most who can afford the trip usually make the most of their time and money with brief prearranged tours or trips directly to wilderness lodges. Only a few explorers head for the Bush unguided, although there are some good places to go that way—Nome, Kodiak, and Unalaska among them.

Covering the Bush also is a challenge for the writer of a book like this one. There are more than 200 Alaska villages, many lodges, camps, and guides, and a vast, undefined territory to describe. All that information would fill a larger book than this one but would be of little use to the great majority of readers. I've taken the approach, instead, of providing sections on a few Bush hubs that are most accessible and popular with visitors, that have modern facilities, and can be used as gateways to much more of the state for those who want to step out beyond the fringe of civilization. For more exhaustive information on even small Native villages, I recommend *The Alaska Wilderness Guide,* published by Vernon Publications, 3000 Northup Way, Suite 200, Bellevue, WA 98009-9643 (☎ **800/726-4707** or 206/827-9900). The core of that book is a directory of even the tiniest villages, with the basic facts on what you'll find there.

If you find yourself in a town such as Nome, Kotzebue, Barrow, or Kodiak—a hub for outlying Native villages—there's a simple and relatively inexpensive way to get out and see how village people live. Mail and scheduled passenger planes—typically small, single-engine craft—make daily rounds of the villages from each hub. Without the difficulty, expense, and dubious interest of going for a longer trip to a village, you can fly out on one of these planes for a quick day trip, walk around and meet people, then fly back to the hub city on the next one to come through. *One warning:* Don't make such an excursion in lowering weather, as you could get weathered in at a remote village. A journalist friend of mine was weathered in for more than 2 weeks on one occasion. You'll find the air-taxi operators—true bush pilots—friendly, informal, and most willing to oblige you in working out your Bush adventure. To find out where to go, just walk into the office and tell them what you're interested in seeing and how much time and money you want to spend. It's also an inexpensive way to go flightseeing.

1 Exploring the Bush

Alaska's Bush is better defined by what it's like there than where it is. For the purposes of this book, following the most convenient and common conception, the Bush is everything beyond the road system—everything north or west of Fairbanks. But there also are Bush villages in the Interior, in Southcentral, and in Southeast Alaska. There are even Bush villages you can drive to. After a while, you'll know a Bush community when you see one—it's a place where the wilderness is closer than civilization, where people still live off the land and age-old traditions survive, and where you have to make a particular effort to get in or out.

THE REGIONS

There are at least five commonly accepted regions in the Bush, which group easily into three:

THE ARCTIC   The Arctic Circle is the official boundary of the Arctic. The line, at 66° 33' north latitude, is the southern limit of true midnight sun—south of it, at sea level, the sun rises and sets, at least a little, every day of the year. But in Alaska, people think of the Arctic as beginning at the Brooks Range, which is a bit north of the circle, including Barrow and Prudhoe Bay. The Northwest Alaska region, which includes Kotzebue and, slightly south of the Arctic Circle, Nome, also is Arctic in climate, culture, and topography. The biggest geographic feature in Alaska's Arctic is the broad North Slope, the plain of swampy tundra that stretches from the Arctic Ocean to the northern side of the Brooks Range. It's a swampy desert, with little rain or snowfall, frozen solid all but a couple of months a year.

WESTERN ALASKA   This is the land of the massive, wet Yukon-Kuskokwim Delta and the fish-rich waters of Bristol Bay. The Y-K Delta, as it's known, was never really exploited by white explorers, and the Yup'ik people who live there have maintained some of the most culturally traditional villages—in a few, Yup'ik is still the dominant language. Bethel is the main hub city of the delta, but holds little attraction for visitors. Bristol Bay is known for massive salmon runs, and avid fishermen may be interested in its wilderness lodges, using Dillingham as a hub.

SOUTHWEST ALASKA   Stretching from the Aleutians—really a region of their own—to the Alaska Peninsula, Kodiak Island, and the southern part of the mountainous west side of Cook Inlet, this is a maritime region, like Southeast, but far more remote. The hub of the wet, windy Aleutians is Unalaska and its port of Dutch Harbor. Katmai National Park and the adjoining wild lands are the main attraction of the Alaska Peninsula, although there also are fishing lodges on the salmon-rich rivers and on the lakes to the north, including areas in Lake Clark National Park and Iliamna Lake. (The McNeil River Bear Sanctuary is included in the Homer listing in chapter 8, as that's its main access point.) The lakes and west side of Cook Inlet are accessed primarily by Kenai, Homer, and Anchorage flight services for fishermen and hunters. Kodiak is hardly a Bush community, but fits better in this chapter than anywhere else.

GETTING AROUND

With a few exceptions for strongly motivated travelers, who can take the ferry to Kodiak and Unalaska or drive to Prudhoe Bay, getting to each town in this chapter will require flying. **Alaska Airlines** (☎ 800/426-0333; website http://www.alaskaair.com) jets fly to all the towns described. Other, smaller operators serve each town as well. Throughout the chapter, I've listed the plane fare to various communities from Anchorage, based on flying coach and getting a significant discount for advance purchase and some restrictions. Full Y-class fares are more. With the way airfares fluctuate, it would be unwise to use these numbers as anything more than rough guides for preliminary planning. To get the current best fare, use a travel agent.

Kodiak, which barely fits a chapter on the Bush, is the easiest to get to of the communities in the chapter, but it still requires either a 10-hour ferry ride from Homer or a $250 to $300 round-trip plane ticket from Anchorage. It's more similar to Southeast Alaska than to the other Bush towns listed. Unalaska, in the Aleutian Islands, is an interesting place to go way off the beaten path while staying in great comfort, but is short on the Native culture you may be looking for. A visit requires a $700 to $800 round-trip plane ticket. **Kotzebue and Barrow** are the most purely Native of the communities in the chapter. **Nome** has the advantages of Arctic surroundings easily accessible on gravel roads, but is more of a gold-rush town than a Native village. **Prudhoe Bay,** at the end of the Dalton Highway, is an industrial complex without a significant identity of its own. Fares range from $350 to $600 for these communities. Buying an Alaska Airlines package tour saves a lot of money to Nome, Kotzebue, or Barrow.

2 Outside in the Bush

The number of opportunities for outdoor solitude in the Bush are limitless. I've provided some ideas for the more popular destinations, and you can find more in chapter 6.

BIRD WATCHING   In the Alaska Bush, serious birders can easily add to their lists birds they have scant chance of seeing anywhere else in the world. Nome, with its long gravel roads, may be the best destination for unguided trips. Unalaska is a good choice for sea birds you won't see elsewhere. Kotzebue, Barrow, the Pribilof Islands, and Saint Lawrence Island all receive visits from avid birders in the summer, too.

FISHING   Kodiak Island, the Alaska Peninsula, Bristol Bay, and the Lake Clark area have among the best salmon and trout fishing to be found anywhere. I've even heard the complaint that it's too easy—at times there's not enough time waiting for a bite, and fishermen's arms get too tired fighting one big salmon after another. Poor things! Access is expensive, and that's why the fishing is so good—you need to fly in to a camp or wilderness lodge. The biggest halibut anywhere are caught off Unalaska.

HIKING   The green hills and mountains of the Aleutians are stunningly beautiful for walks across smooth heather, free of bears or many bugs. Kodiak has some good trails. Katmai National Park is a destination for dramatic backcountry hikes.

RAFTING & KAYAKING   The Noatak River and other rivers draining west from the Brooks Range are increasingly popular routes for remote float trips through massive areas of national park and conservation lands. Guided trips are available, or you can fly out of Kotzebue for an unguided trip. Less ambitious trips are guided from Nome. Kodiak provides sea kayakers with access to pristine, protected ocean waters.

WILDLIFE VIEWING   I'm still boring my friends with the tale of the musk ox I saw from one of the roads out of Nome. I don't know of a better place to see unusual wildlife without getting out of a car or off a bike than these remote roads across the tundra. Katmai National Park has incredible bear viewing, as does Kodiak, where you also can see marine mammals in abundance.

3 Kodiak: Bears, Fish & History

The habitat that makes Kodiak Island a perfect place for bears also makes it perfect for people. Runs of salmon clog unpopulated bays and innumerable, unfished rivers; the rounded green mountains seem to beg for someone to cross them; the gravel beaches and protected rocky inlets are free of people, but full of promise. But, in this respect, bears are smarter than people. Brown bears own the island, growing to prodigious size and abundant numbers, but Kodiak is as yet undiscovered by human visitors. That's a part of the wonder of the place. I'll never forget flying over the luxuriant verdure of Kodiak's mountains and the narrow string of glassy Raspberry Strait on a rare sunny day, seeing no sign of human presence in the most beautiful landscape I had ever beheld. That's something the bears will never experience, despite their superior collective intelligence.

The streets of the town of Kodiak are a discovery, too. Narrow and twisting over hills with little discernible order, they were the original stomping grounds of Lord Alexander Baranof, the first Russian ruler of Alaska, who arrived here more than 200 years ago—and before Baranof, of the Koniag, the first people who lived off the incomparable riches of the island, and who today recover their past in a fascinating little research museum. The Russian heritage includes the oldest Russian building in North America. It was nearly lost in the 1964 Good Friday earthquake, which destroyed most of the town (explaining the general lack of old buildings) and brought a 30-foot wave that washed to the building's doorstep. A marker near the police station on Mill Bay Road shows the wave's incredible high-water point.

The town still looks to the sea. Along with the Coast Guard base, fishing makes Kodiak prosperous, creating a friendly, energetic, unpolished community. Kodiak is separate from the rest of Alaska, living its own salmon-centered life without often thinking of what's going on in Anchorage or anywhere else. It's off the beaten path because it doesn't really need anything the path provides.

For the visitor, Kodiak is an undiscovered gem. When I took my family there on the ferry recently, our 3-day visit just scratched the surface of the charming, vibrant town and the easily accessible wild places. In the middle of the summer, other tourists were barely in evidence.

There are several Native villages on the island—a flight to one of them and back on a clear day is a wonderful, low-cost way to see remote areas of the island and to get a taste of how Alaska Natives live. Ranches on the road system around town offer riding and lodging. You can fly out to see the famous bears on a day trip, or stay at one of several wilderness lodges for wildlife watching, fishing, sea kayaking, and hunting, and even an archeological dig you can participate in.

ESSENTIALS

GETTING THERE   By Air   It's a 1-hour flight from Anchorage to Kodiak on **Alaska Airlines** (☎ **800/426-0333;** http://www.alaskaair.com). A round-trip ticket costs around $250 to $300, or their 1-night package is $399 per person, double occupancy, or $450 for two nights.

By Ferry   The ferry *Tustumena,* of the **Alaska Marine Highway System** (☎ **800/642-0066** or 907/486-3800; http://www.dot.state.ak.us/external/amhs/home.html), serves Kodiak from Homer and Seward. If you have the time for the 10-hour run from Homer—the closest port with a road—this boat ride is truly memorable. The vessel leaves land behind and threads through the strange Barren Islands. The ocean can be quite rough, and when it is, lots of passengers get seasick. A cabin is a good idea for an overnight run. The U.S. Fish and Wildlife Service staffs the trips with a naturalist. The adult passenger fare is $48. The Kodiak terminal is in the same building as the visitor center.

VISITOR INFORMATION   The **Kodiak Island Convention and Visitors Bureau** is at 100 Marine Way, Kodiak, AK 99615 (☎ **907/486-4782;** fax 907/486-6545; website http://www.kodiak.org/kodiak), near the ferry dock. It's open in summer, Monday 8am to 10pm, Tuesday through Friday 8am to 5pm, Saturday 9am to 5pm, and Sunday 1pm to 9pm; in winter, Monday through Friday 8am to 5pm, closed for lunch hour. The **Kodiak National Wildlife Refuge Visitors Center,** 4 miles south of town, near the airport on Buskin River Road (☎ **907/487-2600**), is headquarters for a refuge that covers most of the island, home of the famous Kodiak brown bear. There are remote public-use cabins all over the refuge, reachable by chartered plane. Permits are $20, available by phone or lottery 3 months in advance. The center has interesting displays and is a good place to stop for outdoors information. It's open May through September, Monday through Friday from 8am to 4:30pm and June through August, Monday through Saturday 10am to 4:30pm; in winter, Monday through Friday from noon to 4:30pm. **Custom Tours of Alaska,** in the lobby of the Kodiak Inn (P.O. Box 985, Kodiak, AK 99615; ☎ and fax **907/486-4997**), books activities and excursions.

ORIENTATION   The Kodiak Archipelago contains Kodiak, Shuyak, and Afognak islands, and many other, smaller islands. Kodiak is the nation's second largest island, after Hawaii's big island. The city of Kodiak is on a narrow point on the northeast side of Kodiak Island, surrounded by tiny islands. There are seven Native villages on other parts of the island. The airport and Coast Guard base are several miles southwest of town on **Rezanof Drive,** which runs through town and comes out on the other side. The center of Kodiak is a hopeless tangle of steep, narrow streets—you need the excellent map given away by the visitor center. The ferry dock is on **Marine Way,** and most of the in-town sights are right nearby. Several gravel roads, totaling 87 miles, make wonderful exploring from Kodiak to deserted shorelines, gorgeous views, pastures, recreation areas, and salmon streams. The visitors guide contains a mile-by-mile guide to each drive.

GETTING AROUND   You can walk the downtown area, where the main historic sites are, but to get in from the airport, you'll need a ride. The **Airporter Shuttle** (☎ 907/486-7583) costs $5; call for pickup. A **cab,** from Ace Mecca (☎ 907/486-3211), runs around $13 from the airport. Several companies rent cars, including **Avis** (☎ 800/478-2847 or 907/487-2264) and **Budget** (☎ 800/527-0700 or 907/487-2220), which has offices at the airport or downtown. **Island Terrific Tours,** P.O. Box 3001, Kodiak, AK 99615 (☎ and fax **907/486-4777**), will pick you up at the airport by arrangement and show you around for $75.

FAST FACTS   The **sales tax** is 6% in the city limits of Kodiak. There are several banks downtown with **ATMs,** including Key Bank on the mall at the waterfront and National Bank of Alaska at Mission and Marine. The **post office** is near Lower Mill Bay Road and Hemlock Street. In **emergencies,** call **911.** For nonemergency police business, call the **Kodiak Police Department** (☎ 907/486-8000). The **Kodiak Island Hospital** is at 1915 E. Rezanof Dr. (☎ **907/486-3281**). The *Kodiak Daily Mirror* is published weekdays. The *Anchorage Daily News* is widely available, too. **Business services** are available at Mail Boxes Etc., at 202 Center St., Suite 315 (☎ **907/486-8780**).

SPECIAL EVENTS   **Russian Orthodox Christmas,** coming about 2 weeks after the Western celebration, includes the Starring Ceremony, in which a choir follows a star in the evening to sing at the homes of church members. The late-March **Pillar Mountain Golf Classic** (☎ **907/486-4782**) is played on a one-hole par-70 course that climbs 1,400 feet from tee to flag; dogs, guns, chain saws, and two-way radios are strictly prohibited. The **Kodiak Crab Festival,** on Memorial Day weekend, includes a carnival and survival suit races, and also the solemn blessing of the fleet and memorial service to lost fishermen. In early September, the **Kodiak State Fair and Rodeo** has all kinds of small-town contests. The **Harbor Stars,** in mid-December, is a fleet parade of vessels decorated for Christmas.

EXPLORING KODIAK

A walking tour in the front of the local visitors guide will show you what's available in town. The **Fishermen's Memorial,** near the harbormaster's office at the head of the St. Paul Harbor, has a soberingly long list of Kodiak fishermen who have lost their lives at sea. The warship set in concrete on Mission Way is the **Kodiak Star,** the last World War II Liberty Ship built, which was brought here as a fish processor after the 1964 earthquake destroyed the canneries, and is still in use.

The ✪ **Baranov Museum,** at 101 Marine Way (☎ **907/486-5920**), is the oldest Russian building of only four standing in North America, built in 1808 by Alexander Baranof as a magazine and strong-house for valuable sea otter pelts. It stands in a grassy park overlooking the water across from the ferry dock. Inside is a little museum rich with Russian and early Native artifacts. The guides know a lot of history and show 30 educational albums on various topics. The gift store is exceptional, selling antique Russian items and authentic Native crafts. The museum is open in summer, Monday through Friday from 10am to 4pm and on Saturday and Sunday from noon to 4pm; in winter, it's open 10am to 3pm every day but Thursday and Sunday. Admission is $2, free for children 12 and under.

The Native-funded and -governed ✪ **Alutiiq Museum,** at 215 Mission Rd., Suite 101, Kodiak, AK 99615 (☎ **907/486-7004;** fax 907/486-7048), seeks to document and restore the Koniag Alutiiq people's culture, which the Russians virtually wiped out in the 18th century. The museum manages its own archeological digs (see "Getting Outside," below) and repatriates Native remains and artifacts, which researchers removed by the thousands in the 1930s. The message of the well-presented exhibits in the one-room gallery is subtle but strong—for example, beautiful Native art displayed next to a picture of three Alutiiq people who were put on display like objects at the 1904 World's Fair in St. Louis. It's interesting for children, too. Summer hours are Monday to Saturday 10am to 4pm, Sunday noon to 4pm; closed Sunday and Monday in winter. Admission is $2 for adults.

Across the street, at Kashevarof and Mission, the **Holy Resurrection Russian Orthodox Church** was founded in 1794, although the present building dates only to 1945, when it was rebuilt after a fire. Half-hour Native dance performances take place June through August daily at 3:30pm at the **Kodiak Tribal Council Barabara,** at 713 Rezanof Dr. (☎ **907/486-4449**). Admission is $15.

GETTING OUTSIDE

ARCHEOLOGY The **Afognak Native Corporation,** 214 W. Rezanof Dr. (P.O. Box 1277), Kodiak, AK 99615 (☎ **800/770-6014** or 907/486-6014; fax 907/486-2514), offers visitors a chance to help in scientific excavations of Koniag sites on Afognak Island aimed at putting back together their cultural heritage. **Dig Afognak** visitors are instructed in the natural history of the beautiful area as well as archeology, but they're also expected to work, digging and working in a remote lab. Accommodations are in heated tents, and food is often seafood caught in nets at the beach. A 6-day session is $1,650.

BROWN BEAR VIEWING To see Kodiak's famous bear, you need to get out on a plane or boat. The quickest way is on one of the air services making a business of finding bear, landing on the water, and watching from the safety of the plane's floats. When the salmon aren't running, many flights cross over to the east coast of the Alaska Peninsula to watch bears digging clams from the tidal flats. **Uyak Air Service** (☎ **800/303-3407** or 907/486-3407) offers bear flights and will give your money back if you don't see them—a safe bet for them. The **Karluk Lake Brown Bear Sanctuary,** owned by one of the Native corporations and operated by **Kodiak Wilderness Tours,** 1873 Shell Simmons Dr., Juneau, AK 99801 (☎ **800/556-8101** or 907/789-7818; fax 907/789-4228; website http://www.ptialaska.net/~bears/), is a camp on a lake island near a river where bears congregate for the salmon run. Guests watch from a platform. They charge $799 for the shortest, overnight stay in bunk-house accommodations, airfare from Kodiak included. Reserve well ahead.

TWO RECREATION AREAS   North on Rezanof Drive a couple of miles, the ✪ **Fort Abercrombie State Historic Park** encompasses World War II ruins set on coastal cliffs amid huge trees. Paths lead to the beaches and good tide pool walking, a swimming lake, and lots of other discoveries. The gun emplacements, bunkers, and other concrete buildings defended against the Japanese, who had attacked the outer Aleutians and were expected to come this way. A wonderful 14-site campground sits atop the cliffs in among the trees and ruins. Camping is $10 a night. The **Division of State Parks,** Kodiak District Office, S.R. Box 3800, Kodiak, AK 99615 (☎ 907/486-6339; fax 907/486-3320; e-mail kodsp@ptialaska.net), maintains an office here where you can pick up a walking tour brochure or, during the summer, join the Saturday night interpretive program or a guided tide pool walk, scheduled to coincide with the tides. Or investigate the tide pools on your own, picking up an identification guide at the Shire Bookstore, 104 Center Ave. (☎ 907/486-5001), or the Fish and Wildlife Service visitor center. The **Buskin River State Recreation Site,** 4 miles south of town off Rezanof Drive near the Fish and Wildlife Service visitor center, has 17 sites, a hiking trail, and access to fishing.

FISHING   The roads leading from Kodiak offer access to terrific salmon and trout fishing. Some kind of salmon, somewhere, are available all summer. You can get a guide, including where to fish and the names and addresses of guides for remote fishing, from the visitor center or the **Alaska Department of Fish and Game,** at 211 Mission Rd., Kodiak, AK 99615 (☎ 907/486-1880; http://www.state.ak.us/local/akpages/FISH.GAME/adfghome.htm), where they'll also explain regulations and sell you a license. To fish the remote areas, you'll need to charter a plane to a remote public-use cabin or go to a wilderness lodge. Several boats are available for ocean salmon and halibut fishing. Check with the visitors center.

HIKING/BIRD WATCHING   There aren't a lot of trails on Kodiak, but there are some good day hikes. Pick up a copy of the *Kodiak Hiking Guide* at the visitor center for a variety of mountain climbs and day hikes from the road system. They'll also have the field-trip program of the **Kodiak Audubon Society,** with guided hikes and bird watching trips; or write to the society at P.O. Box 1756, Kodiak, AK 99615.

HORSEBACK RIDING   The fields of grass and wildflowers that cover much of the island are idyllic grounds for riding. **Kodiak Cattle Co.,** P.O. Box 1608, Kodiak, AK 99615 (☎ 907/486-3705), is one of several offering rides.

SEA KAYAKING   The Kodiak Archipelago, with its many folded, rocky shorelines and abundant marine life, is a perfect place for sea kayaking. Tom Watson does a professional job with **Wavetamer Kayaking,** P.O. Box 228, Kodiak, AK 99615 (☎ 907/486-2604; e-mail wavtamer@ptialaska.net). Fun introductory paddles start from the boat harbor, round Near Island to a bird rookery, then traverse shallow channels teeming with invertebrate life. The 2-hour trip costs $40. A 4¹/₂-hour paddle, with a stop for a snack and beachcombing, is $85, for people who have kayaked before.

   If you're already an experienced kayaker, **Shuyak Island State Park,** 54 miles north of Kodiak, is the place to go. The park is a honeycomb of islands and narrow passages in virgin Sitka spruce coastal forest. State Parks (see address under "Two Recreation Areas," above) maintains four public-use cabins, which rent for $50 a night in the summer, and distributes a free kayaking guide with route descriptions. Wavetamer Kayaking, above, rents double kayaks for use in the park.

ACCOMMODATIONS

Besides the hotels listed below, you'll find good budget rooms at **Russian Heritage Inn,** 119 Yukon, Kodiak, AK 99615 (☎ 907/486-5657; fax 907/486-4634). Below I've listed five places in town, but there also are 20 or more wilderness lodges on and around Kodiak Island. You can get a list from the visitor center. One of the best-established is **Afognak Wilderness Lodge,** P.O. Box 1, Seal Bay, Kodiak, AK 99697-FR (☎ **800/478-6442;** fax 907/486-2217). A lodge is an opportunity to spend extended time in the wilderness in comfort, watching wildlife, fishing, or hunting.

The **room tax** inside the Kodiak city limits totals 11%.

Buskin River Inn. 1395 Airport Way, Kodiak, AK 99615. ☎ **800/544-2202** or 907/487-2700. 44 rms, 6 suites. TV TEL. $89–$125 double. Additional person in room $15 extra. AE, DISC, MC, V.

This quiet, well-kept hotel with standard rooms is near the airport, not the downtown sights, so it's a good choice if you're heading into the wilderness or have a rented car. Rooms on one side look out on the parking lot. It's near the wildlife refuge visitor center, a hiking trail, and the nine-hole golf course at the Coast Guard base. The Buskin makes a specialty of booking activities and offering package discounts for outdoor explorations of the island. The rooms all have refrigerators, clocks, and hair dryers, and they'll pick you up at the airport. The **Eagle's Nest Restaurant** has reliable food from a complete beef and seafood menu, and a pleasant setting.

Kodiak Bed and Breakfast. 308 Cope St., Kodiak, AK 99615. ☎ **907/486-5367.** Fax 907/ 486-6567. E-mail monroe@ptialaska.net. 2 rms, neither with bath. $82 double. AE, MC, V.

Hospitable, active Mary Monroe runs this is comfortable, homey place with a big, friendly dog. There is a porch to eat breakfast on sunny mornings, overlooking the harbor. Fish is often on the menu. The location is convenient, right downtown, and the entry for the bedrooms and shared sitting room downstairs doesn't require you to walk through Monroe's living quarters.

Kodiak Inn. 236 W. Rezanof Dr., Kodiak, AK 99615. ☎ **888/563-4254** or 907/486-5712. Fax 907/486-3430. 81 rms. TV TEL. High season, $129–$139 double. Low season, $99 double. AE, DC, DISC, MC, V.

This is the best hotel in downtown Kodiak, with attractive, up-to-date rooms perched on the hill overlooking the boat harbor, right in the center of things. Rooms in the wooden building vary in size and view, although all are acceptable and have coffeemakers. There's a tour desk in the pleasant lobby. The **Chart Room** restaurant, specializing in seafood and with a great view of the water, is a good choice for a nice dinner out, with entrees in the $15 to $20 range.

Shelikof Lodge. 211 Thorsheim Ave., Kodiak, AK 99615. ☎ **907/486-4141** or 907/ 486-4116. 38 rms. TV TEL. $65 double. Additional person in room $5 extra. AE, CB, DC, DISC, MC, V.

This economy choice right in town has large standard rooms that were recently remodeled. It's a very good deal. There's an inexpensive, windowless restaurant with a fish tank and a lounge. They offer free coffee in the lobby.

Wintels Bed and Breakfast. 1723 Mission Rd. (P.O. Box 2812), Kodiak, AK 99615. ☎ and fax **907/486-6935.** 3 rms, one with private bath. $70–$90 double, $35 each additional person. No credit cards.

Long walking distance from downtown, this house stands with the ocean on one side and a lake on the other, so all rooms have water views. The family of longtime residents can tell you a lot about Alaska and show off their mounted sea ducks and furs. The rooms are attractive, the breakfasts large, and there's a sauna and a Jacuzzi surrounded by potted plants.

DINING

Besides the hotel restaurants listed above at the Kodiak Inn and Buskin River Inn, try these. **El Chicano,** at 104 Center St. (☎ 907/486-3424), is a good Mexican family restaurant, with friendly service and reasonable prices. **Beryl's** is a great little sandwich and breakfast shop on a pedestrian way at 202 Center St. (☎ 907/486-3323). It started out as a candy and ice cream place, but now serves meals all day until 6pm. **Harborside Coffee and Goods,** at 216 Shelikof St. (☎ 907/486-5862), on the south side of the boat harbor, is a comfortable coffee house with bagels and light sandwiches, popular with commercial fishermen and young people. **Henry's Great Alaskan Restaurant,** at 512 Marine Way (☎ 907/486-3313), on the waterfront mall, is a popular bar and grill.

4 Katmai National Park: Natural Ferocity

Most of the land of the Alaska Peninsula, pointing out to the Aleutian Archipelago, is in one federally protected status or another, centering on Katmai National Park, which was originally set aside in 1918. Katmai (CAT-my) lies just west of Kodiak Island, across the storm-infested Shelikof Strait. Bears and salmon are the main attractions today: Brooks Camp, with a campground and lodge within Katmai, is probably the most comfortable place for foolproof bear viewing in Alaska. Here, in July and September only, you can sit back on a deck and watch 900-pound brown bears walk by, going about their business of devouring the spawning salmon that contribute to their awesome size. Staying the night will require you to reserve a place in the 16-space campground the previous winter (see below) or stay in the pricey lodge. You can go for a day trip, too, if you can afford round-trip airfare of around $500.

Katmai originally exploded into world consciousness in 1912, with the most destructive volcanic eruption to shake the earth in 3,400 years. When Katmai's Novarupta blew, it released 10 times more energy than Mount St. Helens's eruption of 1980 and displaced twice as much matter as 1883's Krakatoa. People could clearly hear it in Juneau; acid rain melted fabric in Vancouver, British Columbia; and the skies darkened over most of the northern hemisphere. All life was wiped out in a 40-square-mile area and buried as deep as 700 feet. But so remote was the area, then still unnamed, that not a single human being was killed. The Valley of Ten Thousand Smokes, the vast wasteland created by the blast, belched steam for decades after. Today it's dormant, but still a barren moonscape, making a fascinating day tour or hiking trip.

ESSENTIALS

GETTING THERE   The most common way to get to Katmai is through the village of King Salmon, which lies just west of the park, and then by air-taxi to Brooks Camp. The park concessionaire, **Katmailand, Inc.,** with offices at 4550 Aircraft Dr., Anchorage, AK 99502 (☎ 800/544-0551 or 907/243-5448; fax 907/243-0649), offers round-trip airfare packages of $460—a good deal. **Alaska Airlines** (☎ 800/426-0333) is one of several operators serving King Salmon from Anchorage daily. Various air-taxis operating float planes make the link to Brooks Camp. **Katmai Air** is the operator owned by the Katmailand concessionaire. More and more visitors are exploring the supremely rugged wilderness on the east side of the park from the beaches along Shelikof Strait. Air taxi operators make drops-offs and do bear-viewing day trips from King Salmon, Homer, or Kodiak, and boats out of Kodiak go across for extended expeditions.

VISITOR INFORMATION   The **park headquarters** is in King Salmon, P.O. Box 7, King Salmon, AK 99613 (☎ **907/246-3305;** website http://www.nps.gov/ katm/). There's also a visitor center at the airport in King Salmon and at Brooks Camp. In Anchorage, you can get information, including the excellent 40-page *Bear Facts* guide, at the Alaska Public Lands Information Center, at Fourth Avenue and F Street (☎ **907/271-2737;** see the complete listing in chapter 8). To reserve a **campground** site, call **Destinet** (☎ **800/365-2267** or 619/452-8787). The 16 sites become available January 15, and dates during the bear season go quickly. The camping fee is $10 per person per night, and there is a $10 park admission fee.

GETTING AROUND   Once at Brooks Camp, there's a bus that carries visitors to the Valley of Ten Thousand Smokes, 23 miles by gravel road from the camp. The park concessionaire, **Katmailand,** charges $62 per person, round-trip, for the all-day excursion, plus $7 more for lunch. One-way transfers for hikers are $37.

FAST FACTS   This is a remote area, but King Salmon does have **banking** services. In **emergencies,** call **911** outside the park (☎ **907/246-3305** within the park). For nonemergency police matters, call the **police** in King Salmon (☎ **907/246-4222**) or the **Alaska State Troopers** (☎ **907/246-3346**). The **Camai Clinic,** in Naknek (☎ **907/246-6155**), is open during normal business hours, and the number goes to emergency dispatchers after hours.

EXPLORING KATMAI

The time to go to Katmai is when the bears are congregated near the Brooks River to catch salmon, during July and September, and maybe the last week of June or the first week of August. This is when you're assured of seeing bears from the elevated platforms near the Brooks River falls, half a mile from Brooks Camp, even on a day trip. Other times in the summer, you could easily miss the bears altogether.

   Brooks Camp, with the park service campground, visitor center, and lodge, is located where the Brooks River flows into Naknek Lake. Unfortunately, when the area was first developed for fishing in the 1950s, the camp was placed on top of a valuable archeological site. The archeology is one of the attractions today, but the park service wants to move to a more suitable location in the future. The most comfortable way to stay in the camp is at the **Brooks Lodge,** operated by Katmailand (see address under "Getting There," above). The lodge has 16 units, with private bathrooms with shower stalls. To save money, book the lodge rooms as packages with air travel. The least expensive, 1-night visit is $582 per person, double occupancy, meals not included; 3 nights is $896. A double room without airfare is $294. The place books up a full year ahead; reservations open January of the year before the visit. Three buffet-style meals are served daily for guests and visitors who aren't staying in the lodge. Breakfast is $10; lunch, $12; and dinner, $22. For food, they take plastic at the lodge—American Express, MasterCard, and Visa. There's also a small store at Brooks Camp, the park service visitor center, and the 16-site campground. See "Visitor Information" for info on campground reservations, which should be made 6 months in advance. The rangers require special precautions to keep bears away from campers.

   Backcountry hiking in Katmai crosses a wilderness without trails and is only for experienced outdoors people. The most popular routes are on the desolate Valley of Ten Thousand Smokes, which provides awesome views but sometimes is swept by blinding sand storms. Be prepared for mosquitoes. The park service asks hikers to obtain a voluntary permit for backcountry travel. There also are several lodges on inholdings along the park's huge lakes, and you can fly in for fishing or kayaking in rarely visited remote areas of the park. The park service has a list of dozens of fishing, hiking, and air guides.

5 Dutch Harbor / Unalaska: Aleutian Boom Town

After a lifetime of hearing how desolate the Aleutians (uh-LOO-shuns) were, I felt a bit as though I was leaving the edge of the earth the first time I traveled to Unalaska (oon-ah-LAS-ka). Shortly after I arrived, a storm started slinging huge raindrops horizontally through the air so hard that they stung as they splattered on my face. People went on about their business as if nothing special was happening—stormy weather constantly batters these rocks that pop up from the empty North Pacific. My expectations seemed justified.

But the next day, the storm cleared like a curtain opening on a rich operatic scene—simultaneously opening the curtain of my dark expectations. Unalaska may lack trees, but it's not a barren rock—the island is covered with heather and wildflowers. Rounded mountains that invite wandering exploration rise from the ocean like the backs of huge beasts. For sightseeing, it has only a few hours of attractions, but for outdoor exploring, bird watching, and halibut fishing, few places come close.

With the protected port of Dutch Harbor so far out in a ferocious ocean habitat rich in crab and bottomfish, Unalaska has grown in 2 decades from a tiny, forgotten Native village to the nation's largest fishing port. The pattern of growth followed the form of the early gold rushes. There was a wild, lawless time in the 1970s when crab fishermen got rich quick and partied like Old West cowboys. Then the overfished crab stocks crashed, only to be replaced, starting in the mid-1980s, by an even bigger boom, when waters within 200 miles of the U.S. shore were rid of foreign vessels and American bottomfishing took off. Big factory ships began unloading here, and huge fish plants were built on ground chipped from the rock. Today that expansion has reached a more steady state, and more women and families are coming to town—another part of the gold-rush pattern. But domestication isn't done yet. It's hard to build on the Aleutians' volcanic bedrock, and housing and public services still lag far behind the boom. Most of the population lives in bunk houses and flies back to Seattle when the processing plants close for the season. Unalaska may be the best current example of the American cultural phenomenon of the frontier boomtown.

Ironically, Unalaska is Alaska's oldest town as well as its newest city. The value of a good port out in the middle of the ocean was recognized from the beginning by the Aleuts. In 1759, the Russians began trading here, and fought a war with the Aleuts from 1763 to 1766, the outcome of which was slavery for the Aleut hunters and the massacre of their people. The Russians built a permanent settlement here in 1792, their first in Alaska. Unalaska also was a key refueling stop for steamers carrying gold-rush stampeders to Nome a century ago, which brought an epidemic that killed a third of the indigenous population. In 1940, Dutch Harbor—the seaport on Amaknak Island associated with the town and island of Unalaska—was taken over by the U.S. Navy to defend against Japanese attack. That attack came— in June 1942, Japanese planes bombed Unalaska, killing 43. The Aleut people were removed from the islands for the duration of the war and interned in inadequate housing in Southeast Alaska, where many died of disease. The military pulled out in 1947, but the remains of their defenses are interesting to explore. Today, thanks to a 1971 act of Congress settling Native claims, the Aleut-owned Ounalashka Corporation owns most of the island. Despite all the history, however, the old Russian Orthodox church and military ruins are all there is to see.

ESSENTIALS

GETTING THERE   By Air   Several operators fly to Dutch Harbor from Anchorage, including **Alaska Airlines** (☎ **800/426-0333;** http://www.alaskaair.com). You're likely to pay $700 to $750 round-trip. An air/hotel package makes sense and saves money—see the Grand Aleutian Hotel, described under "Accommodations," below.

By Ferry   The **Alaska Marine Highway System** ferry *Tustumena* (☎ **800/642-0066**) runs once a month from Homer, leaving Tuesday night and arriving in Unalaska, after stopping in Kodiak and the villages along the way, on Saturday morning. The passenger fare is $242, and an outside cabin, with facilities, is $328. I don't know anyone who has actually done this, but it must be an adventure. Of course, unless you want to spend only 3 hours early on a Saturday morning in Unalaska and then make the long return trip, you'll need to fly back.

VISITOR INFORMATION   The **Unalaska–Port of Dutch Harbor Convention and Visitors Bureau,** P.O. Box 545, Unalaska, AK 99685 (☎ **907/581-2612**), operates the Henry Swanson Visitor Center, on West Broadway between Second and Third, with information, maps, and gifts. Swanson, a late fox farmer, fisherman, and community leader, lived in the building.

ORIENTATION   The main historic part of the town is a tiny street grid on a narrow peninsula facing Iliuliuk Bay. The **Bridge to the Other Side** (that's the official name) leads to Amaknak Island, the site of the airport, big hotels, and the fishing industrial area of Dutch Harbor. Traveling down the road in the other direction leads a little way up into the mountains, a starting point for walks.

GETTING AROUND   Van taxis are the main way of getting around town for the hordes of fishermen. One company is **Blue Check Taxi** (☎ **907/581-2186**). You can rent a car, truck, or forklift from **North Port Rentals** (☎ **907/581-3880**) or a couple of other companies. The Grand Aleutian Hotel (see "Accommodations," below) and the city department of Parks, Culture, and Recreation (☎ **907/581-1297**) rent **bicycles,** which, in good weather, are a nice way to get around an island with only a few miles of roads. **Aleut Tours** (☎ **907/581-6001**) offers town tours in the summer, including all the major sights, with a Native guide driving the van. It lasts 2 to 3 hours, with pickup wherever you are, and costs $40.

FAST FACTS   The **sales tax** in Unalaska and Dutch Harbor is 3%. Key Bank has a branch near the Alaska Commercial Store, at the UniSea plant in Dutch Harbor, with an **ATM.** In an **emergency,** call **911;** in nonemergencies, call the **Unalaska Department of Public Safety,** just above the bridge on the Unalaska side (☎ **907/581-1233**). **Iliuliuk Family and Health Services** (☎ **907/581-1202**) offers complete clinic services. The *Dutch Harbor Fisherman* is published weekly, and the *Anchorage Daily News* is available at the airport and a few places around town.

EXPLORING UNALASKA TOWNSITE

Unalaska's main sight is the **Holy Ascension Cathedral.** Completed in 1896 on the site of churches that had stood since 1808, the white, onion-domed church contains 697 icons, artifacts, and artworks—a significant collection that has been continuously in use by the Aleut congregation. The congregation was founded by Fr. Ivan Veniaminov, who translated the Gospel into Aleut and has been canonized as St. Innocent. The building was not well maintained, and the buffeting of rugged weather and history left it in peril. Today the church is undergoing a $1.3 million

The Aleutians: The Quiet After War

In 1995, the navy deactivated the secret naval base at Adak, in the outer Aleutian Islands, leaving only a few caretakers. Few civilians had ever seen the base, which had been hurriedly built more than 50 years before to fight back a Japanese invasion. With its closing, the book closed on a bizarre and bitter tale with few parallels in American history. The battle for the Aleutians was costly, point-less, and miserable, bringing ruin and disease to the Aleuts and death to thousands of Japanese and American soldiers. What began as a diversion became a ferocious fight for honor with little strategic meaning. When the fighting was done, it turned out that no one even wanted the land enough to stay. With the 50th anniversary of the war, Japanese and American soldiers met on the deserted islands they'd fought for and dedicated a monument. Then they left again—leaving behind the site of death and struggle to the fog, whipping wind, and migrating geese.

The Japanese attacked the islands of Kiska and Attu at the start of the Pacific war to divert the main core of the American navy away from what became the Battle of Midway. But the Americans had intercepted and decoded Japanese transmis-sions, and weren't fooled. Meanwhile, the Japanese had sent 24 ships, including two aircraft carriers, on a fool's errand to bomb the new American naval base at Dutch Harbor/Unalaska and occupy islands in the western Aleutians. Those ships could have tipped the balance at Midway, among the most important battles of the war. Instead, the Japanese met stiff antiaircraft fire in 2 days of bombing at Dutch Harbor, and although 43 Americans were killed, the defensive function of the base was not greatly impaired.

The Japanese then took Kiska and Attu, meeting no resistance from 10 Ameri-cans staffing a weather station, or from a small Aleut village whose few inhabitants were all—even the children—sent to a prison camp in Japan to mine clay for the duration of the war. About half the prisoners survived to return to Alaska.

The Americans had their own plan to remove the Aleuts, but the idea of depopu-lating all the islands had been turned down. Now, with the Japanese attack, it was swiftly put into effect. All the Aleuts were rounded up and put on ships. As they pulled away from their ancestral islands, they could see the glow of huge fires destroying their villages. The U.S. military had torched the villages to deny the modest assets of the islands to the Japanese, should they advance farther. With little thought given to their living conditions, the Aleuts were interned in abandoned summer camps and similarly inadequate facilities in Southeast Alaska. Shunned by the local communities and without the basic neces-sities of life, many died of cold and disease. The U.S. Fish and Wildlife Service took Aleut hunters to hunt furs as virtual slaves, much as the Russians had done 200 years before.

The Japanese and American military fared not much better on their new real estate. Although the Aleutians quickly became irrelevant to the rest of the war, significant resources were committed to a largely futile air and sea battle in the fog and endless storms. Flying at all was difficult and extremely dangerous, and finding the enemy in the fog over vast distances close to impossible. The Americans couldn't spare a land invasion force at first, and had to rely on bomb-ing Kiska and Attu to punish the Japanese and try to deter a further advance up the chain. To that end, they built the base at Adak, among others, so shorter-range fighter escorts could accompany the bombers. Construction in the spongy tundra was difficult in any case, made more so by the length of supply lines.

The Japanese high command never had any intention of advancing up the chain, but also saw no reason to abandon their new Kiska air base when it was causing the Americans to exert such effort—even if it had no strategic value to either side. The Japanese concentrated on fortifying Kiska, which became a honeycomb of underground bunkers and heavy antiaircraft guns and withstood constant bombing raids from the Americans.

Finally, on May 11, 1943, almost a year after the Japanese took the islands, Americans landed on Attu, and a brutal 18-day battle for the rugged island began. The Japanese were massively outnumbered but heavily dug in. Finally, with only 800 soldiers left from an original force of 2,600, the Japanese mounted a banzai attack. Only 28 were taken prisoner—the rest were killed in battle or committed suicide. The Americans lost 549 killed, 1,148 wounded, and 2,132 injured by severe cold, disease, accident, mental breakdown, or other causes. In the end, it was the second most costly island battle in the Pacific, after Iwo Jima.

The battle for Kiska was less dramatic. The Japanese withdrew under cover of fog. After a massive bombardment of the empty island and the rallying of heavy reinforcements, the Americans landed to find that no one was there. Still, 105 American soldiers died in the landing in accidents and fire from their own forces.

After the Aleutian battle was over, American forces in Alaska declined drastically, but never went away altogether. Before the war, the absurd little Fort William Seward, in Haines, had been the totality of Alaska's defenses, with a couple of hundred men armed with Springfield rifles and no reliable means of transportation. Afterward there were large bases in several areas of the state. Military spending became the biggest economic boom the territory had ever seen, connecting it by a new road to the Lower 48 and bringing precious year-round jobs. A new wave of postwar settlers, many former GIs looking for a new, open field of opportunity, brought a population boom. The advent of the Cold War, and Alaska's prime strategic location in defense against the Soviet Union, brought ever-greater increases in military spending in Alaska. To this day, the military is one of the largest sectors of the Alaska economy, and the state has been relatively unscathed in base closures except for remote outposts like Adak.

The end of the war was more bitter for the Aleuts. Everything they had in their villages had been destroyed. Many who had survived the terrible period of internment never returned to the islands where their villages had once stood, and some of the villages never revived. "When I came back to Atka after World War II, my buddy said, 'Why are you going back to the Aleutians? They say even the sea gulls are leaving there,'" villager Dan Prokopeuff has been quoted as saying. "I told him I was going because it's peaceful and quiet."

Today Atka is the westernmost village remaining in the Aleutians. On Kiska there are only ruins of the Japanese fortifications. As for Adak and the assets the U.S. military left behind, it's being taken over by Aleut Corp., the regional Native corporation, which hopes to redevelop it as a town.

restoration that will take a number of years. The site and cemetery outside are very picturesque.

There are several **World War II military ruins** around town, including some that are still in use—like a submarine dry dock that today fixes fishing boats. The activity at the port is interesting to see, too, if only for the size of the vessels and harvest and the incredible investment in buildings and equipment.

GETTING OUTSIDE

The attractive thing about Unalaska is that, while it provides hiking, ocean fishing, and remote bird watching for species you can't see elsewhere, you still can stay in complete comfort in a luxurious hotel. The island is out in the middle of nowhere, but it has an active, big-money economy, and that makes a difference in comfort and convenience for visitors.

You exploit this port far out in the ocean by using it for access to **fishing** and **bird watching.** Of course, you can do both at once, with sea lions and other marine mammals thrown in. Several rare bird species nest in the area, and Asian birds occasionally drop in as accidentals. The whiskered auklet and red-legged kittiwake are among the birds commonly found around Unalaska that don't show up anywhere else. There also are rookeries with many species of birds, and you generally see lots of marine mammals, too. You can fly out for salmon fishing from black sand beaches, but Unalaska has become more famous for having the largest halibut caught in the state. In 1995, a local sport fisherman caught a 395-pound halibut from an 18-foot skiff within a half mile of town; to kill the behemoth he had to beach it and beat it over the head with a rock.

The island's green heather and rounded mountains of wildflowers are inviting for **hiking.** You can walk pretty much in any direction, looking at the abandoned World War II defenses, or making a goal of a beach or one of the small peaks around the town, or, for the ambitious, even the top of an active volcano, Mount Makushin. There are no bears and not many bugs, but there is great berry picking and beachcombing. The weather can be a threat, however, and fox holes can trip you up. As always in remote outdoor areas, you must be well dressed, know how to take care of yourself, and leave word of where you're going and when you'll be back. Most of the island belongs to the **Ounalashka Corp.,** P.O. Box 149, Unalaska, AK 99685 (☎ **907/581-1276**), the Native village corporation. Get a permit to hike, bike, or camp on their land from their office on Margarets Bay, near the Grand Aleutian Hotel, open Monday through Friday from 8am to 5pm.

There are several charter and guide operators. The Grand Aleutian Hotel (see "Accommodations," below) offers packages and halibut and salmon fishing, fly-in fishing and flightseeing, and guided kayaking and mountain biking. For other operators charging around $150 per person for a day trip, contact the visitors center. For flightseeing and day trips or overnight fly-in fishing, try **Volcano Bay Adventures,** P.O. Box 432, Unalaska, AK 99685 (☎ **907/581-3414**). **PenAir** (☎ **800/448-4226**) offers flight services in the area, including trips to outlying villages.

ACCOMMODATIONS & DINING

There are several other accommodations besides the two I've listed here, both of which belong to the huge UniSea fishing company. A list is available from the visitor center.

✪ **Grand Aleutian Hotel.** 498 Salmon Way (P.O. Box 921169), Dutch Harbor, AK 99692. ☎ **800/891-1194** or 907/581-3844. 100 rms, 6 suites. TV TEL. $150 double. $195–$225 suite. Additional person in room $15 extra. Packages available. AE, DC, DISC, JCB, MC, V.

It's almost unreal to arrive in this big, luxurious hotel in a hard-driving Alaska Bush community. The Grand Aleutian is among the best hotels in Alaska, to say nothing of the Bush. For the same room in Anchorage, you'd pay considerably more. They have a courtesy van and bike rentals; the rooms are well designed and comfortable; the lobby grand, with a huge stone fireplace; and there's a piano bar. As you walk outside into a driving gale, it's like teleporting from a big city hotel back to an exposed rock out in the North Pacific. Why build such a big hotel in such a remote place? I don't know, but I've heard it called the "Grand Illusion." The ✪ **Chart Room** restaurant is first-rate, with sophisticated treatments of local seafood in the $20 to $30 range. The **Margaret Bay Cafe** is nice too, if pricey.

The Japanese-owned UniSea fish-processing company that built the hotel has developed a full scope of tour packages to keep it busy, and booking one of those packages, including airfare, should save money over traveling independently. A basic 2-night package starts at about $1,000 per person, double occupancy. Birding packages range up to $1,253 per person, for 3 nights, a boat trip, and birding on the islands by bike or truck. They also have guided salmon and halibut fishing, hiking, mountain biking, and flightseeing.

UniSea Inn. At the small-boat harbor (P.O. Box 921169), Dutch Harbor, AK 99692. ☎ **800/ 891-1194** or 907/581-1325. 44 rms. TV TEL. $100 double. Additional person in room $15 extra. AE, DC, DISC, JCB, MC, V.

Overlooking the harbor, in the midst of the surging UniSea processing operation, the UniSea Inn is a less expensive alternative to the Grand Aleutian. More fishermen stay here than tourists, but it's adequate if you just want a room. The sports bar in the same building can be noisy, so try to get a room that's not next to it.

A SIDE TRIP TO THE PRIBILOFS

The Pribilof Islands of St. Paul and St. George sit out in the middle of the Bering Sea, due north of Unalaska, teeming with marine mammals and sea birds. Some 600,000 fur seals meet at the breeding rookeries in the summer, and 2 million birds of more than 200 species use the rocks. Bird watchers go for one of the most exotic and productive wildlife-viewing opportunities in Alaska from May to August. Indeed, the National Audubon Society's *Field Guide to North American Birds* calls it "perhaps the most spectacular seabird colony in the world." However, the islands are extremely remote and the accommodations rustic and poorly developed. The only place to eat, for example, is a cafeteria at a fish processing plant. **Reeve Aleutian Airways** (☎ **800/544-2248**) arranges packages from Anchorage to St. Paul ranging from $799 to $1,549.

6 Nome: Arctic Frontier Town

The accidents of history deposited the streets and buildings of this lusty little town on the shore of Norton Sound, just south of the Arctic Circle in Northwest Alaska, and gave it qualities that make Nome an exceptionally attractive place for a visitor to go. For once, the local boosters' motto—in this case, THERE'S NO PLACE LIKE NOME—is entirely accurate. For Nome, although itself nothing special to look at, combines a sense of history; a hospitable, somewhat silly attitude; and an exceptional location on the water in front of a tundra wilderness that's crossed by 250 miles of road. Those roads are the truly unique thing, for Nome is the only place in Arctic Alaska where a visitor can drive or bike deep into the open country, coming across musk ox, reindeer, rarely seen birds, Native villages, undeveloped hot springs, and even an abandoned 1881 elevated train from New York City. Elsewhere, you're obliged to fly from rural hubs to get so far into the Bush, a more expensive and ambitious undertaking for casual explorers.

The accidents of history have been rather frequent in Nome—history has been downright sloppy. Start with the name. It's essentially a clerical error, caused by a British naval officer who, in 1850, was presumably in a creative dry spell when he wrote "? Name" on a diagram rather than name the cape he was sailing past. A mapmaker interpreted that as "Cape Nome." The original gold rush of 1898 was caused by prospectors in the usual way, but a much larger 1899 population explosion happened after one of the '98 stampeders, left behind by an injury in a camp on the beach, panned the sand outside the tent—and found that it was full of gold dust. By 1900, a fourth of Alaska's white population was in Nome, sifting the sand. Small-time operators and tourists are still at it, and major gold mining rumbles on just outside town. A floating gold dredge of the kind that makes major historic sites in Fairbanks and Dawson City sits idle on the edge of town. In Nome, it stopped operation only a couple of years ago. Historic structures are few, however, as fires and storms have destroyed the town several times since the gold rush.

Nome has a particular, broad sense of humor. It shows up in the *Nome Nugget* newspaper and in silly traditions like the Labor Day bathtub race, pack ice golf tournament, and the Memorial Day polar bear swim. The population is half white and half Native, and the town is run largely by the white group. Some see Nome as a tolerant mixing place of different peoples, while the town strikes others as a bit colonial. Booze is outlawed in Kotzebue, the Native-dominated city to the north, but in Nome there is still a sloppy, gold rush–style saloon scene. That sort of thing is prettier as historic kitsch than when it shows up in the form of a staggering Front Street drunk.

But you can ignore that, instead taking advantage of the great bargains to be had on Inupiat art and crafts. And, most important, you can use one of the pleasant little inns or bed-and-breakfasts as a base to get into the countryside that beckons, down one of the gravel roads. Bird watchers find the roads especially useful, and Nome is popular with birders.

ESSENTIALS

GETTING THERE   You can get to Nome only by air. **Alaska Airlines** (☎ 800/426-0333) flies a 90-minute jet flight either direct from Anchorage or with a brief hop from Kotzebue. The fare from Anchorage is likely to be in the range of $380 to $480, round-trip. Many visitors come on a package sold by **Alaska Airlines Vacations** (☎ 800/468-2248), which is $474 per person, double occupancy, but there's no need to be on a package in Nome. **Yute Air** (☎ 888/359-9883) serves Nome with 19-passenger aircraft.

VISITOR INFORMATION   The **Nome Convention and Visitors Bureau,** at Front and Hunter streets (P.O. Box 240), Nome, AK 99762 (☎ 907/443-5535; website http://www.alaska.net/~nome), is exceptionally well run, providing maps and detailed information for diverse interests, and screening videos for those interested. It's open mid-May to mid-September daily from 9am to 9pm, to 6:30pm the rest of the year. The headquarters of the **Bering Land Bridge National Preserve,** on Front Street (P.O. Box 220), Nome, AK 99762 (☎ 907/443-2522), is a good source of outdoors information, especially on the rarely visited 2.3-million-acre national park unit, which covers much of the Seward Peninsula north of the Nome road system.

ORIENTATION   The town is a mostly unpaved grid along the ocean. **Front Street** follows the sea wall, **First Avenue** is a block back, and so on. A harbor is at the north end of town, and the gold-bearing beach is to the south. The airport is east of town. Three roads branch out from Nome. I've described them below, under "Getting Outside."

GETTING AROUND   Within the grid of town streets, you can walk most places. But you need a taxi, such as one from **Nome Cab** (☎ 907/443-3030), to get in from the airport. All taxis operate according to a standard price schedule you can get from the visitor center. A ride to town from the airport is $5. To get out on the roads, you need to take a tour or rent a car. Several local car rental agencies operate in town; the visitor center maintains a list, with rates. **Stampede Rent-A-Car** (☎ 907/443-3838) charges $75 a day for a van or Ford Bronco, $125 for a camper. Bikes are for rent and guided day trips are available from **Bering C Bikes** (☎ 907/443-4994), about which there is more information below under "Getting Outside."

Two companies offer organized tours. ✪ **Nome Discovery Tours** (☎ 907/443-2814) has the asset of talented professional actor Richard Beneville as the van driver and tour guide. He'll pick you up and drive you anywhere in the area, sharing his quirky enthusiasm and extensive knowledge of the surroundings. The highlight is the wildlife and scenery on the roads out of town. Half days are $45 per person, full days $80. **Nome Tour and Marketing,** at the Nugget Inn, at Front and Bering streets (☎ 907/443-2651), is a more traditional tour, with a dog-sled demonstration and gold panning, lasting 3 1/2 hours. It goes twice a day, with times depending on flights into town, and costs $25 per person. The tour runs in summer only.

FAST FACTS   The **sales tax** is 4%. The **post office** and National Bank of Alaska have branches at Front Street and Federal Way. The bank has an **ATM.** In **emergencies,** dial **911;** for nonemergency business with the **police,** call ☎ 907/443-5262. The **Norton Sound Regional Hospital** is at Fifth Avenue and Bering Street (☎ 907/443-3311). The *Nome Nugget* and the *Bering Sea Record* are published weekly; the *Anchorage Daily News* is available at the airport.

SPECIAL EVENTS   The **Gold Rush Classic Snowmachine Race** (☎ 907/563-4414), in mid-February, covers the Iditarod Trail—twice. Nome is the halfway point. The biggest event of the year is the ✪ **Iditarod Trail Sled Dog Race** (☎ 907/376-5155), a marathon of more than 1,000 miles that ends in Nome in mid- to late March. The sled-dog racers and world media descend on the town for a few days of a madness, with lots of community events planned. Other dog-sled races continue into April. The **Bering Sea Ice Golf Classic** (☎ 907/443-5278), in mid-March, showcases Nome's well-developed sense of humor—six holes are set up on the sea ice. The pressure ridges constitute a bad lie. Various similar silly events take place all year—you can get a list from the visitor center. The **Polar Bear Swim** occurs in the Bering Sea on Memorial Day, ice permitting. The **Midnight Sun Festival** (☎ 907/443-5535) celebrates the June 21 summer solstice, when Nome gets more than 22 hours of direct sunlight, with a parade, beauty pageant, softball tournament, bank holdup, and similar events.

EXPLORING NOME
THINGS TO SEE & DO IN TOWN

Most of Nome's original buildings were wiped out by fires or by storms off Norton Sound that tore across the beach and washed away major portions of the business district. A sea wall, completed in 1951, now protects the town. An interesting **Historical Walking Tour,** produced by the Alaska Historical Commission, is available from the visitor center; it takes less than an hour. Below the library, at Front Street and Lanes Way, the small **Carrie M. McLaine Memorial Museum** exhibits items found on the beach and some Native artifacts. Of greatest interest are copies of the *Nome Nugget* dating from the gold rush—the price, 50¢, is still the same today, indicating just how inflated the local economy was in 1899. The museum is free and open year round Tuesday through Friday from 10am to 5pm, Saturday noon to 5pm.

In good weather, a pleasant walk is to be had southeast of town, along the **beach.** Small-time miners are camped there, but the gold-bearing sand extends for miles more of solitary walking. You can buy a gold pan in town and try your luck, but the sand has been sifted for nearly 100 years, so don't expect to gather any significant amount of gold. On the other side of town, there's an impressive abandoned gold dredge of the kind that crept across the tundra, creating its own pond to float in as it went. It operated until quite recently. The **cemetery,** with white, wooden crosses on top of a little hill just out of town, also is worth a look.

SHOPPING

If you're in the market for walrus ivory carvings and other Inupiat art and crafts, you'll find low prices and an extraordinary selection in Nome. Jim West trades money for drinks for Native art from visiting villagers at his shop in front of the historic **Board of Trade Saloon** on Front Street, and consequently he has a legendary collection. The **Arctic Trading Post** is more of a traditional gift shop and also has a good ivory collection, and try **Sitnasuak Ivory Shop,** also on Front Street. **Chukotka-Alaska, Inc.,** on West First Avenue, is an importer of art and other goods from the Russian Far East, and is really worth a look.

GETTING OUTSIDE

ON THE ROADS   The modest attractions downtown would hardly justify a trip to Nome, but the city's surroundings do. The roads provide unique access to a large stretch of the Seward Peninsula, and unlike other Arctic Bush areas, where you need to have someone take you where you want to go, all you have to do in Nome is rent a car, camper, or bike and go. The only way to get a vehicle to Nome is to ship it in on a barge during the few ice-free months, and there aren't many people for all that land, so if you rent a car, you'll have a huge expanse of spectacular territory to yourself, with wildlife-viewing opportunities as good as anywhere in the state. Most of the land is managed by the **Bureau of Land Management** (BLM) P.O. Box 925, Nome, AK 99762 (☎ **907/443-2177;** website http://wwwndo.ak.blm.gov/), which produces a free "Kigluaik Mountains Recreation Opportunities" map. The **Alaska Department of Transportation** (☎ **907/443-3444**) can provide current information on road conditions. You have a good chance to see moose, reindeer, owls, foxes, bears, and musk ox anywhere you drive, but check in with the visitor center or the **Alaska Department of Fish and Game,** at Front and Steadman streets, for where you're most likely to see animals. They can also give you guidance on fishing along the roads and a "Nome Roadside Fishing Guide."

Car rental agencies are listed above under "Getting Around." Or if you don't want to drive yourself, you can go with Richard Beneville's **Nome Discovery Tours** (see "Getting Around" under "Essentials," above). Beneville knows where the wildlife is likely to be found, and the history and natural history of the area. For **mountain bike** enthusiasts, the roads of Nome are a unique and wonderful ride—where else can you bike past musk oxen and reindeer? **Bering C Bikes** (☎ **907/443-4994** summer, 907/ 642-4161 winter) rents and repairs bikes and provides guided day trips and van-supported multiday camping expeditions—it's the same family that runs Inua Expeditions (see "On the Water," below).

Bird watchers will find a rich hunting ground out on the roads and use many new pages of their bird books. A bird list is available at the visitor center, and they can tell you where to look—each of the three roads has different habitat. The best times to visit for birding are right around Memorial Day, and from July to mid-August. Lana and Richard Harris were Nome's leading birders when I last visited, and the only local members of the American Birding Association. They maintain a **birders' hot line** on their home phone recorder (☎ **907/443-5528**) and don't mind talking with visiting bird watchers, but please don't call before 6am or after 10pm, Alaska time. There's a chance to see Siberian birds, and you can count on bluethroats, yellow wagtails, wheatears, Arctic warblers, and Aleutian and Arctic terns. Nome is the only place to see a bristle-thighed curlew without chartering a plane. You don't need a guide, although guided trips are available (check with the visitor center). As Lana put it, "If you haven't found a yellow wagtail, you haven't left the bar yet."

None of the three roads radiating from Nome has services of any kind—just small Native villages, a few dwellings, and some reindeer herders—so you must be prepared and bring what you need with you, including insect repellent. The visitor center provides a good road guide. Here are some highlights:

The **Nome-Council road** heads 72 miles to the east, about half of that on the shoreline. It turns inland at the ghost town of Solomon, an old mining town with an abandoned railroad train, known as the Last Train to Nowhere. The engines were originally used on the New York City elevated trains in 1881, then were shipped to Nome in 1903 to serve the miners along this line to Nome. This is a great scenic spot for bird watching, and fishing is good in the Solomon River, all along the road. Council, near the end of the road, has a couple of dozen families in the summer; you have to get a boat ride across a river just short of the village.

The **Nome-Taylor road,** also known as the Kougarok road, runs north of town into the Kigluaik Mountains, 85 miles from Nome, petering out and becoming impassable. Lovely Salmon Lake, with a campground, is 38 miles out. A few miles farther, a road to the left leads to the Pilgrim Hot Springs, near the ruins of a Catholic church and orphanage. The two hot tubs are 100° to 125°F. Check with the visitor center before going, as the hot springs are privately owned and the open invitation may have changed since this writing.

The **Nome-Teller road** leads 73 miles to the village of Teller, which has about 200 residents, a gift shop, and a store. It's an opportunity to see an authentic Arctic Native village.

ON THE WATER The **Inua Expedition Company of Nome,** P.O. Box 65, Brevig Mission, AK 99785 (☎ **907/443-4994** in summer, 907/642-4161 in winter), is the summer job of Keith and Annie Olanna Conger, who in the winter teach school in the tiny village of Brevig Mission. Keith, a biologist, leads the kayaking tours and teaches about the ecology of the land they paddle through. His $100 trips float down the Snake and Nome rivers for half a day; long, full-day trips float down the beautiful Pilgrim River to the Hot Springs, then drive back to town after a soak, for $165, or overnight for $215. They also do 8-day trips in the Imuruk Basin.

IN THE AIR Nome is a hub for Bush plane operators. Flightseeing charters are available, or you can just fly one of the mail-run routes out to the villages, spending a couple of hours touring for only $120. You can also fly 150 miles over to Russia, above the route where the first Americans arrived, up to 30,000 years ago. **Bering Air,** P.O. Box 1650, Nome, AK 99762 (☎ **907/443-5464**), offers various flightseeing options. Bering Air and the other air-taxis in town can also take you to **Saint Lawrence Island,** an even better bird watching destination than Nome, with many Siberian birds, and a community where the Eskimo subsistence culture survives in the traditional way. The village of Savoonga has two small lodges with cooking facilities. For local information, contact the Saint Lawrence Economic Development Corp., P.O. Box 169, Savoonga, AK 99769 (☎ **907/984-6613**). **Gray Line of Alaska** (☎ **800/628-2449**) also offers tours.

IN WINTER   Visitors come to Nome in winter mostly for the Iditarod, perhaps volunteering to help with the race (call the race offices, listed above under "Special Events"). If you do come when there's snow on the ground, you should take a **dog sled ride. Flat Dog Kennel,** P.O. Box 1103, Nome, AK 99762 (☎ **907/443-2958**), owned by the racing Burmeister family, offers rides for $50 per person and will arrange longer rides.

ACCOMMODATIONS

The **room tax** in Nome totals 8%. There are two main hotels in town, neither of which is particularly good. The **Nugget Inn,** on Front Street at Bering Street (P.O. Box 430), Nome, AK 99762 (☎ **907/443-2323;** fax 907/443-5966), is the main tourist hotel, where package visitors go, but the smallish rooms are no more than adequate. I cannot recommend the Polaris Hotel at all. You'll do better at any of the other establishments listed. Apartments are for rent by the day in various buildings as well. Check with the visitor center.

June's Bed and Breakfast. 231 E. Fourth Ave. (P.O. Box 489), Nome, AK 99762. ☎ **907/443-5984.** 3 rms, none with bath. $75 double. Rates include breakfast and airport pickup. No credit cards.

June Wardle runs this traditional little B&B, proudly declaring, "I really am a gold digger's daughter." Her sourdough pancake starter came over the Chilkoot Trail in 1898. The rooms are cozy, not commodious, but June's gregarious hospitality makes it special. Each has one of her handmade quilts.

Ponderosa Inn. Third Ave. and Spokane St. (P.O. Box 125), Nome, AK 99762. ☎ **907/443-5737.** Fax 907/443-4149. 10 rms, 1 suite. TV. $75–$95 double; $125 suite. Additional person in room $15 extra. AE, DC, MC, V.

Hidden in a pair of houses a few blocks back from the main drag, this inn has the best hotel rooms in town; those in the new section are light and spacious, and all have coffeemakers and refrigerators. The more expensive rooms have kitchens, and the suite is a large, two-bedroom apartment. Some rooms have only shower stalls, not tubs. Four have telephones. There's a coin-op laundry, free coffee, and shared kitchen facilities. Book ahead, as experienced business travelers keep it full year round.

Trails End. 49 E. First Ave. (P.O. Box 1834), Nome, AK 99762. ☎ and fax **907/443-5746,** or 800/443-4043 in Alaska. 2 apartments. TV TEL. $85 double. Additional person in room $15 extra. MC, V.

These attractive apartments are stocked with soft drinks and some food in a full kitchen. The upstairs unit has one bedroom, the downstairs unit two. The building is new, standing a block off the main drag. It's quite a deal.

DINING

There's not a selection of great places to dine, but you can find an adequate family meal at various establishments, all along Front Street, and all but Pizza Napoli accept Visa and MasterCard. The **Polar Cub Cafe** (☎ 907/443-5191) and **Fat Freddy's Restaurant** (☎ 907/443-5899) are traditional, burger-and-fries diners overlooking the water. **Nachos Restaurant** (☎ 907/443-5503) is an American-style Mexican place that I've been told is good. There are two Italian restaurants, **Pizza Napoli** (☎ 907/443-5300) and **Milano's Pizzeria** (☎ 907/443-2924), serving about what you'd expect for a small-town family pizzeria.

   Fort Davis Roadhouse, on the beach about a mile east of town (☎ 907/443-2660), is more of an experience. With open views of the tundra and water, the large dining room with linen tablecloths is quite pleasant. A lounge upstairs has an even better view. The menu is mainly beef and seafood, or a $25 buffet—prime rib on Saturday or seafood on Friday. In summer, they're open 6 to 11pm Tuesday through Saturday; in winter, call.

7 Kotzebue: Big Village

Although its 4,000 residents make Kotzebue (KOTZ-eh-biew) a good-sized town, with a bank, a hospital, and a couple of grocery stores, I've heard it called a village instead. A "village," in Alaskan parlance, is a remote Native settlement in the Bush, generally with fewer than a few hundred residents, where people live relatively close to the traditional lifestyle of their indigenous ancestors. Kotzebue is a support hub for the villages of the Northwest Arctic, with jet service and a booming cash economy, but it's populated and run by the Inupiat, fish-drying racks and old dog sleds are scattered along the streets, and Native culture is thriving. It does feel like a village.

For visitors, this characteristic makes Kotzebue unique because you can see real Eskimo culture without leaving the comforts of Western society behind. Or if you don't mind giving up some of those comforts, you can get even closer to the Inupiat way of life. For adventurous outdoors people, Kotzebue offers access to huge areas of remote public land through which you can float on a raft or canoe.

It's important to realize from the outset, however, that outside of organized activities for tourists, there's nothing to do in Kotzebue. As I was told, "You have to shoot something or burn a lot of gas to have any fun around here." Kotzebue is not set up for independent travelers except those of the most intrepid ilk, and they will most likely use the town as a way to get into the remote public lands. Nome offers more for the independent traveler interested in something in between an organized tour and a wilderness expedition.

The dominant business in town is the NANA Corp., a regional Native corporation representing the roughly 7,000 Inupiat who live in a Northwest Arctic region the size of Indiana. NANA, which stands for Northwest Arctic Native Association, has successful operations in institutional catering and oil drilling, and is half owner of the Red Dog zinc mine that employs its members and supplies much of the world's supply of the mineral. It also owns the main hotel and tourist businesses in Kotzebue.

ESSENTIALS

GETTING THERE   The only way there is by air, and it's not cheap. Alaska Airlines (☎ **800/426-0333;** website http://www.alaskaair.com) has several daily jets from Anchorage and Fairbanks in the summer. You'll pay in the range of $320 to $400 from Anchorage. They also fly from Kotzebue to Nome. Once in Kotzebue, there are many air-taxis and commuter lines to the outlying villages (more on that below). The cheapest and most convenient way to go to Kotzebue is to take a package offered by **Tour Arctic** and **Alaska Airlines Vacations,** described under "Exploring Kotzebue," below.

VISITOR INFORMATION   There is no town visitor center. The National Park Service staffs the **Kotzebue Public Lands Information Center** at Second Avenue and Lake Street (P.O. Box 1029), Kotzebue, AK 99752 (☎ **907/442-3890** or 907/ 442-3760; fax 907/442-8316), providing information and displays on the immense area of protected land in the region. Employees will answer questions about the town as well. It's open May 21 to September 18, daily from 8am to 5pm, only sporadically the rest of the year; but the local headquarters of the park service, Fish and Wildlife Service, and Bureau of Land Management are open during normal business hours all year.

ORIENTATION   Kotzebue is 26 miles north of the Arctic Circle on the Chukchi Sea. The town, about a mile by 2 miles in size, sits on a low spit of land extending into the shallow Kotzebue Sound. The gravel streets are on a warped grid radiating from **Shore Avenue,** also known as **Front Street,** which runs along the water. Roads extend only a few miles out of town.

GETTING AROUND   You can walk pretty much everywhere you need to go. The main hotel is a 10-minute walk from the airport, but there are taxis available from **Polar Cab** (☎ 907/442-2233) and **Cab Company** (☎ 907/442-3555). If you're on the Tour Arctic package, buses will pick you up at the plane and deliver you and your luggage to the hotel.

FAST FACTS   The sale of **alcohol** is illegal in Kotzebue, but possession for personal use is permitted. Kotzebue has a National Bank of Alaska branch with an **ATM** at the corner of Lagoon Street and Second Avenue. The **post office** is at Shore Avenue and Tundra Way. In **emergencies,** dial **911.** For nonemergencies, contact the **Kotzebue Police Department** (☎ 907/442-3351) or the **Alaska State Troopers** (☎ 907/442-3222). A **hospital** with a 24-hour emergency room is located at Fifth Avenue and Mission Street (☎ 907/442-3321).

SPECIAL EVENTS   The **Fourth of July** is something special in Kotzebue. Besides the Independence Day celebration, it's as early as you can count on all the snow being gone.

EXPLORING KOTZEBUE

There is only one activity in town, and it's part of an organized tour. **Tour Arctic** (☎ 907/442-3301) hosts around 10,000 visitors annually in its cultural and natural-history program, the centerpiece of which is the ✪ **NANA Museum of the Arctic.** For most people, the packages, also sold through **Alaska Airlines Vacations** (☎ 800/468-2248), are the best deal and the best way to get to the Arctic and learn about Native culture. The tour, owned and operated by the Inupiat, teaches a lot about their culture and relationship with the land in 5 hours while keeping customers comfortable and insulated from the harshness of the Arctic. A show at the museum includes children dancing, a blanket toss, and a serious, high-tech slide show about the struggle to save Inupiat culture. The tour also includes a talk and demonstration in a tent about the clothing and survival techniques of the Eskimos. There's also a brief opportunity to walk on the tundra. Independent travelers in town for outdoor activities can attend the hour-long museum program only for $20; shows are timed to match the arrival of flights, at 3 and 6pm.

Day-trip packages are $349 from Anchorage—less than a full-fare ticket. The same tour with a night at NANA's Nullagvik Hotel is $469, based on double occupancy. A 2-night trip that includes a tour of Nome is $543. Adding an excursion to the village of Kiana and a lengthy flightseeing trip over the Northwest Arctic region requires another night and an additional $265.

GETTING OUTSIDE

NEAR KOTZEBUE   Some rugged and curious travelers may want something a bit less pampered and scripted than the Tour Arctic program. **Arctic Circle Educational Adventures,** P.O. Box 814, Kotzebue, AK 99752 (in winter: 200 W. 34th Ave., Suite 903, Anchorage, AK 99503; ☎ 907/442-3509 in summer, 907/276-0976 in winter; fax 907/274-3738 in winter; website http://www.alaska.net/~akhal/fishcamp/lavcamp1.htm), offers a chance to stay at a camp similar to the fish camps where Native people spend the summer gathering food for the winter—and participate in setnet fishing, fish cutting, food gathering, and other traditional subsistence activities, as well as hiking, town tours, and bird watching. The camp on the beach 4 miles south of town is extremely rustic, and only for people who don't mind using an outhouse or sleeping in a plywood cabin. Elder Hostel groups sometimes come for a week. Rates are $150 for the tour activities plus $95 for lodgings and meals. The season is mid-June to late August.

You can get an idea of what Native villages look like and see the **Kobuk Valley National Park,** including the Great Kobuk Sand Dunes, a desertlike area of shifting 100-foot dunes, from the air by buying a round-trip seat on one of the scheduled bush planes that serve the area. **Cape Smythe Air** (☎ **907/442-3020**) charges $152 for its loop that includes Shungnak and Kobuk and overflies the dunes (make sure to tell the pilot what you want to see). For $88 you can fly a shorter, northern loop to Noatak and Kivalina, over the **Cape Krusenstern National Monument.**

INTO THE BUSH   There are several remote rivers near Kotzebue with easy self-guided floating for experienced outdoors people. This is a rare chance to get deep into the Arctic. The great Noatak River originates in the Brooks Range and passes through the impressive scenery of the Noatak National Preserve. The Selawik, Squirrel, and Kobuk rivers all have long sections of easy water. **Alaska Discovery,** listed in the Juneau section of chapter 7, **Nova Raft and Adventure Tours,** listed in the Anchorage section of chapter 8, and **Equinox Wilderness Expeditions,** listed in the "Tips for Travelers with Special Needs" section of chapter 3, all do trips in the area. Expect to pay $2,500 to $3,000 per person, including air travel. Most river running in the region is self guided. *The Alaska River Guide,* by Karen Jettmar, director of Equinox, published by Alaska Northwest Books (☎ **800/452-3032**), provides detailed guidance. Obviously, you should be experienced in the outdoors and in floating before heading out for a multiday trip in the Arctic. And plan ahead, arranging details with the park service and your pilot well in advance. Most visitors bring all their gear from Anchorage, but Buck Maxxon, of **Arctic Air Guides Flying Service,** P.O. Box 94, Kotzebue, AK 99752 (☎ **907/442-3030**), rents rafts and canoes for $35 a day. An experienced bush pilot, he also will fly you out; how much you pay depends on where you go, but charter rates are typically $250 an hour. You can minimize your costs by putting in or taking out at villages along the river and using scheduled air services.

Lorry and Nellie Schuerch, of the village of Kiana, will take you up the Kobuk River in an enclosed, high-powered jet boat. You can visit the dunes and likely see a lot of birds and wildlife. The day trip is $300 per person. Their **Kobuk River Jets,** P.O. Box 89, Kiana, AK 99749 (☎ **907/475-2149**), also offers fishing charters for sheefish and other species, and they own the Kiana Lodge, where rooms with private bathrooms are $175 per person, with all meals.

ACCOMMODATIONS

Bayside Inn and Restaurant. 303 Shore Ave. (P.O. Box 870), Kotzebue, AK 99752. ☎ **907/442-3600,** 800/478-6169 Alaska only. 12 rms. TV TEL. High season, $95 double. Low season, $80. MC, V.

If you want to save on your room over the Nullagvik, two doors down, these white-walled rooms with shower stalls in the bathrooms likely will suffice. They have a coin-op laundry. The restaurant downstairs is popular with locals and a little cheaper than the other hotel restaurant, but also not as good.

Nullagvik Hotel. Shore Ave. and Tundra Way (P.O. Box 336), Kotzebue, AK 99752. ☎ **907/442-3331.** Fax 907/442-3340. 73 rms. TV TEL. $125 double. Additional person in room $10 extra. AE, DC, MC, V.

The NANA-owned hotel is thoughtfully designed and comfortably furnished. The rooms are large and up-to-date, have tables and chairs and two queen-size beds, and have windows that angle out from the building so that all get at least some ocean view. It can be startling to see Eskimo women in kuspuks cleaning in the halls.

The **restaurant** is clean and nicely decorated, and has a good view and excellent service—a combination found nowhere else in Kotzebue. Reindeer steak and Arctic salmon are on the menu for the tourists. Locals are more likely to order the less expensive sandwiches and beef.

DINING

Other than the two hotel restaurants described above, the only place I'd recommend is **Mario's Pizza and Deli,** 606 Bison St. (☎ 907/442-2666). I was told that the sushi was good in this Japanese-Chinese-pizza-burger take-out place, but I couldn't believe that was possible, in Kotzebue, in this grubby little dining room, so I ordered barbecued pork instead. After a really excellent, spicy meal, I could only imagine how good the sushi might have been. The price range is $5.25 to $12, and they don't take credit cards.

8 Barrow: Way North

The main reason visitors go to Barrow is its latitude. The Inupiat town is the northernmost settlement on the North American continent, above the 71st parallel. Here half-liquid land comes to an arbitrary point at the tip at the north of Alaska. The tundra around Barrow is dotted with lakes divided by tendrils of swampy tundra no more substantial than the edges of fine lace. On this haven for migratory waterfowl, the flat, wet land and the ocean seem to merge. Indeed, for all but a few months, it's all a flat, frozen plain, ocean and land. For more than 2 months in the winter, the sun never rises. In the summer, it doesn't set, and the ice recedes from the shore only for the months of the brief summer. Such extreme geography is a strong attractor—people want to stand in such a place, perhaps dip a toe in the Arctic Ocean.

And then what do you do next? If you're on a package trip, you can see an Eskimo blanket toss and dancing, look at whale bones and maybe buy Native crafts, and see a few other manifestations of traditional Inupiat life amid a modern, oil-enriched town. There are mounds where ancient Eskimo houses stood, the site of archeological digs. Then you can get back on the plane and return to Fairbanks or Anchorage because there isn't much else to do in Barrow.

The village of 4,000 is culturally unique. It's ancient, and still a center of whaling from open boats and a summer festival celebrating a successful hunt and distribution of the meat to the community. But Barrow also is the seat of the North Slope Borough, a county government encompassing a larger area than the state of Nebraska, in which lies North America's largest oil field. The borough has everything money can buy for a local government, yet the people of the villages still must contend with crushing ice, snooping polar bears, and utter isolation.

ESSENTIALS

GETTING THERE   **Alaska Airlines** (☎ 800/426-0333; website http:// www.alaskaair.com) flies to Barrow daily from Anchorage and Fairbanks, and offers one-day and overnight tour packages, described below. The packages are a good deal, competitive with round-trip tickets alone from Anchorage in the area of $425 to $525. Book them through **Alaska Airlines Vacations** (☎ 800/468-2248).

VISITOR INFORMATION   A chamber of commerce **visitor center,** at Momegana and Ahkovak street, near the airport, operates in the summer only, with a guide to talk to but little else. The **North Slope Borough Public Information Division,** P.O. Box 69, Barrow, AK 99723 (☎ **907/852-0215**), produces a listing of tourism-related businesses in the area.

ORIENTATION   Facing on the Chukchi Sea, Barrow has two sections, lying on each side of Isatkoak Lagoon. **Browerville,** primarily a residential area, is to the east, and **Barrow,** containing the offices and businesses, is to the west. The northern tip of Alaska, **Point Barrow,** is north of the town on a spit. Tour buses advertise visits to the "farthest north point navigable by bus," but the absolute end is farther out, beyond the road. All-terrain vehicles are for rent in town, if you're going to be compulsive about it.

GETTING AROUND   The airport is walking distance to much of the town. **Polar Taxi** (☎ 907/852-2227) provides cab service. There are a couple of car-rental agencies, but not much of anywhere to drive. Buses come every 20 minutes on three routes, and the fare is 50¢. Jim Vordestrasse (☎ **907/852-6166**) does bicycle rentals and tours. Check with the visitor center for other current outdoor tours. The main tour business in town is **Tundra Tours,** P.O. Box 189, Barrow, AK 99723 (☎ **800/882-8478** or 907/852-3900), which, with the Top of the World Hotel, is owned by the Arctic Slope Regional Corp., a Native corporation covering the region. Their tour is described below and is the same one sold through Alaska Airlines Vacations.

FAST FACTS   Thanks to all that oil, there is no sales or bed tax in Barrow. There is a **bank** at Agvik and Kiogak streets. An **ATM** is located at the Stuaqpaq Alaska Commercial general store. In **emergencies,** call **911** (or ☎ **907/852-6111**). The **hospital** is on Agvik Street (☎ **907/852-4611**).

SPECIAL EVENTS   If the traditional bowhead whaling season has been a success, the **Nalukataq festival** in late June celebrates the event. The length of the celebration depends on the number of whales landed. Captains who land the behemoths from their open boats are held in high honor. If you're very lucky, as I was recently, you'll be there when a whale is landed, pulled up on the town beach, and butchered by the community.

EXPLORING BARROW

For most people, it makes most sense to visit Barrow on a package because the Native cultural demonstrations are staged for the tours and there are few attractions. Birders and outdoors people, however, may enjoy coming just to see an alien landscape and see rarely encountered birds. Also consider Kotzebue and Nome for those activities.

The Native-owned **Tundra Tours** (see listing under "Getting Around," above) does a competent job of presenting the town to visitors who arrive with little idea of what to expect. The tour, in a small bus, drives around the town to show off the modest sights, including the school, an Eskimo boat, the cemetery, a stop for a dip of toes in the Arctic Ocean at the farthest-north point, and so on. The part that interested me most was driving one of the short roads out of town to find snowy owls and Arctic fox. The owls stand still out on the flat tundra like bowling pins. After lunch, there's a blanket toss and a Native drumming and dance performance, and a chance to buy gifts from local craftspeople. If you're choosing which town to visit, the Barrow tour has the advantage of the farthest north point, but lacks the depth and thought of the Kotzebue tour.

The 1-day tour is $388 from Fairbanks, $558 from Anchorage. Adding an overnight stay at the Top of the World Hotel and some time to walk around on your own, the package is $432 per person, double occupancy, from Fairbanks; $602 from Anchorage. Book the tour through Alaska Airlines Vacations or with Tundra Tours at the numbers listed above. Tundra Tours offers winter tours, too, from mid-September to mid-May, with many of the same elements except the cultural program and, during the darker part of the year, a chance to see the northern lights.

With more time, visit the Borough Hall to see the small museum and crafts for sale there, and get some extra time out on the tundra, walking on your own or going with an outdoor tour operator.

ACCOMMODATIONS & DINING

The **Top of the World Hotel,** at 1200 Agvik St. (P.O. Box 189), Barrow, AK 99723 (☎ 907/852-3900; fax 907/852-6752), is the main accommodation in town. It's a well-kept-up establishment with 50 standard rooms you'd be happy to find anywhere in the U.S., although not for this price: $179 double if you book separately from the tour. The **Barrow Airport Inn,** 1815 Momegana St. (P.O. Box 933), Barrow, AK 99723 (☎ 907/852-2525; fax 907/852-2316), has 14 attractive rooms, nine with kitchenettes. They charge $135 double, $10 each additional person, with a $10 discount if you don't pay with plastic.

There are several decent restaurants in Barrow. Adjoining the Top of the World Hotel, **Pepe's North of the Border,** at 1204 Agvik St. (☎ 907/852-8200), is a good and elaborately decorated family restaurant serving American-style Mexican food. The tours leave here for lunch, and host Fran Tate hands out souvenirs. **Arctic Pizza,** at 125 Apayauk St. (☎ 907/852-4222), is a regular pizzeria downstairs and a white-table-cloth Italian and steak/seafood place upstairs, with a gorgeous view of the Arctic Ocean. **Teriyaki House,** 1906 Takpuk St. (P.O. Box 907), Barrow, AK (☎ 907/852-2276), serves Japanese, Chinese, and Korean food in a quiet, light dining room in a barn-shaped building near the airport. Of the three, it's the only one that doesn't take credit cards.

9 Prudhoe Bay: Arctic Industry

Touring an oil field may not be your idea of what to do on vacation, but the Prudhoe (PREW-dough) Bay complex is no ordinary oil field. It's a historic and strategic site of great importance and a great technological achievement. It was built the way you'd have to build an oil field on the moon, with massively complex machinery able to operate in winters that are always dark and very, very cold. But in some ways, it might be simpler to build on the moon—here, the industry has to coexist with a fragile habitat for migrating caribou and waterfowl, on wet, fragile tundra that permanently shows any mark made by vehicles. It's quite an accomplishment.

You must sign up for a tour to get into the oil complex—everything is behind chain-link fences and security checkpoints. The town of **Deadhorse,** which serves the oil facility, barely deserves to be called a town, and certainly isn't anything you'd travel to see: It's simply a rectangular gravel pad with modular housing units that act as lodgings and other businesses. From the air, it looks like part of the apron for the landing strip. If you want to go, fly up from Fairbanks or Anchorage for the day and take the tour from Deadhorse. There's no need to spend the night if you fly, as the tour takes 6 hours and there's nothing else to do and nowhere else to go. Or if you drive up on the Dalton Highway, you can engage a tour in Deadhorse, or just get a lift to the water, through the oil complex. See chapter 10, on the Interior, for information on driving the Dalton. **Alaska Airlines** (☎ 800/426-0333) flies frequently to Prudhoe Bay. A round-trip ticket costs $600 to $750 from Anchorage. You can save money on a bus/air package, described below.

Once at Prudhoe, by whatever means, the Native-owned **NANA Development Corp.,** P.O. Box 340112, Prudhoe Bay, AK 99734 (☎ **907/659-2368** in summer, 907/659-2840 in winter), provides visitor services, including a hotel, cafeteria, showers for RV passengers and campers, fuel and vehicle repairs, and tours and a shuttle service to the Arctic Ocean. Their 96-room hotel, the **Arctic Caribou Inn,** has accommodations starting at $100. It's near the airport in Deadhorse and serves as the starting point for the tours. The restaurant has a buffet for three meals a day. Access to the oil complex is provided by NANA's well-run **Tour Arctic.** A 4-hour tour—which includes a pump station, views of the pipeline, oil rigs, a visitor center, a video, and a stop at the shore of the Arctic Ocean—costs $50. The 1-hour round-trip just to the ocean allows time to walk on the beach, but doesn't tour the oil field. It costs $20, and is mainly intended for those hearty travelers who drive to the northernmost point on the U.S. road system and want to make it all the way to the water before turning back.

Princess Tours (☎ **800/835-8907** or 907/279-7711 in Anchorage) and **Gray Line of Alaska** (☎ **800/478-6388** or 907/277-5581 in Anchorage) both operate summer trips from Fairbanks that fly one-way and drive the other over the Dalton Highway in buses. Princess charges about $600 per person, double occupancy, for a 3-day/2-night trip from Fairbanks that returns to Anchorage. Gray Line charges $715 for a similar itinerary leaving each Monday, but brings you back to Fairbanks, where you started. Both trips can be arranged as an add-on to a longer tour or with a cruise. **Northern Alaska Tour Company,** P.O. Box 82991, Fairbanks, AK 99708 (☎ **907/474-8600;** e-mail natc@alaska.net), offers van passage up the Dalton Highway, a Prudhoe tour, an optional visit to Barrow, and a flight back to Fairbanks. The Prudhoe trip is about $600, and the Barrow option adds $289.

Index

414 Index

FROMMER'S COMPLETE TRAVEL GUIDES

(Comprehensive guides to destinations around the world, with selections in all price ranges—from deluxe to budget)

Acapulco, Ixtapa & Zihuatenejo
Alaska
Amsterdam
Arizona
Atlanta
Australia
Austria
Bahamas
Barcelona, Madrid & Seville
Belgium, Holland & Luxembourg
Bermuda
Boston
Budapest & the Best of Hungary
California
Canada
Cancún, Cozumel & the Yucatán
Cape Cod, Nantucket & Martha's Vineyard
Caribbean
Caribbean Cruises & Ports of Call
Caribbean Ports of Call
Carolinas & Georgia
Chicago
Colorado
Costa Rica
Denver, Boulder & Colorado Springs
England
Europe
Florida
France
Germany
Greece
Hawaii
Hong Kong
Honolulu, Waikiki & Oahu
Ireland
Israel
Italy
Jamaica & Barbados
Japan
Las Vegas
London
Los Angeles
Maryland & Delaware
Maui
Mexico
Miami & the Keys
Montana & Wyoming
Montréal & Québec City
Munich & the Bavarian Alps
Nashville & Memphis
Nepal
New England
New Mexico
New Orleans
New York City
Northern New England
Nova Scotia, New Brunswick
    & Prince Edward Island
Paris
Philadelphia & the Amish Country
Portugal
Prague & the Best of the Czech Republic
Provence & the Riviera
Puerto Rico
Rome
San Antonio & Austin
San Diego
San Francisco
Santa Fe, Taos & Albuquerque
Scandinavia
Scotland
Seattle & Portland
South Pacific
Spain
Switzerland
Thailand
Tokyo
Toronto
Tuscany & Umbria
U.S.A.
Utah
Vancouver & Victoria
Vienna & the Danube Valley
Virgin Islands
Virginia
Walt Disney World & Orlando
Washington, D.C.
Washington & Oregon

FROMMER'S DOLLAR-A-DAY BUDGET GUIDES
(The ultimate guides to low-cost travel)

Australia from $50 a Day	Ireland from $45 a Day
Berlin from $50 a Day	Israel from $45 a Day
California from $60 a Day	Italy from $50 a Day
Caribbean from $60 a Day	London from $60 a Day
Costa Rica & Belize from $35 a Day	Mexico from $35 a Day
England from $60 a Day	New York from $75 a Day
Europe from $50 a Day	New Zealand from $50 a Day
Florida from $50 a Day	Paris from $70 a Day
Greece from $50 a Day	San Francisco from $60 a Day
Hawaii from $60 a Day	Washington, D.C., from $50 a Day
India from $40 a Day	

FROMMER'S PORTABLE GUIDES
(Pocket-size guides for travelers who want everything in a nutshell)

Charleston & Savannah	Puerto Vallarta, Manzanillo & Guadalajara
Dublin	San Francisco
Las Vegas	Venice
Maine Coast	Washington, D.C.
New Orleans	

FROMMER'S IRREVERENT GUIDES
(Wickedly honest guides for sophisticated travelers)

Amsterdam	Miami	Santa Fe
Chicago	New Orleans	U.S. Virgin Islands
London	Paris	Walt Disney World
Manhattan	San Francisco	Washington, D.C.

FROMMER'S AMERICA ON WHEELS
(Everything you need for a successful road trip, including full-color road maps and ratings for every hotel)

California & Nevada	Northwest & Great Plains
Florida	South-Central States & Texas
Great Lakes States & Midwest	Southeast
Mid-Atlantic	Southwest
New England & New York	

FROMMER'S BY NIGHT GUIDES
(The series for those who know that life begins after dark)

Amsterdam	Madrid & Barcelona	Paris
Chicago	Manhattan	Prague
Las Vegas	Miami	San Francisco
London	New Orleans	Washington, D.C.
Los Angeles		

WHEREVER YOU TRAVEL, *H*ELP IS NEVER FAR AWAY.

From planning your trip to providing travel assistance along the way, American Express® Travel Service Offices are always there to help you do more.

Alaska

American Express Travel Service
5011 Jewell Lake Road
Anchorage
907/266-6600

American Express Travel Service
Anchorage
907/274-5588

American Express Travel Service
11409 Business Blvd., #4
Eagle River
907/694-2169

American Express Travel Service
400 Cushman Street
Fairbanks
907/452-7636

American Express Travel Service
8745 Glacier Hwy., #328
Juneau
907/789-0999

American Express Travel Service
202 Center Street
Kodiak
907/486-6084

American Express Travel Service
Old Federal Building
Nome
907/443-2211

do more AMERICAN EXPRESS®

Travel

http://www.americanexpress.com/travel

American Express Travel Service Offices are found in central locations throughout Alaska.